The American People in the
Great Depression

The Oxford History of the United States

C. Vann Woodward, *General Editor*

Volume III

ROBERT MIDDLEKAUFF

THE GLORIOUS CAUSE

The American Revolution, 1763–1789

Volume VI

JAMES MCPHERSON

BATTLE CRY OF FREEDOM

The Civil War Era

Volume IX

DAVID M. KENNEDY

FREEDOM FROM FEAR

The American People in Depression and War, 1929–1945

Volume X

JAMES T. PATTERSON

GRAND EXPECTATIONS

The United States, 1945–1974

The American People in the Great Depression

Freedom from Fear
Part One

DAVID M. KENNEDY

OXFORD
UNIVERSITY PRESS

OXFORD
UNIVERSITY PRESS

Oxford   New York
Auckland   Bangkok   Buenos Aires   Cape Town
Chennai   Dar es Salaam   Delhi   Hong Kong   Istanbul   Karachi
Kolkata   Kuala Lumpur   Madrid   Melbourne   Mexico City   Mumbai
Nairobi   São Paulo   Shanghai   Taipei   Tokyo   Toronto

Copyright © 1999 by David M. Kennedy

First published in one volume by Oxford University Press, Inc., 1999
198 Madison Avenue, New York, New York 10016
www.oup.com
First issued as a one-volume Oxford University Press paperback, 2001
First issued as a two-volume Oxford University Press paperback, 2004

Oxford is a registered trademark of Oxford University Press

Library of Congress Cataloging-in-Publication Data
Kennedy, David M.
Freedom from fear / David M. Kennedy.
p. cm. — (The Oxford history of the United States ; v. 9)
Originally published as one vol. in 1999.
Includes bibliographical references and index.
Contents: Pt. 1. The American people in the Great Depression—
Pt. 2. The American people in World War II.
ISBN 0-19-516892-5 (pt. 1, pbk.) — ISBN 0-19-516893-3 (pt. 2, pbk.)
1. United States—History—1919-1933.
2. United States—History—1933-1945.
3. Depressions—1929—United States.
4. New Deal, 1933-1939.
5. World War, 1939-1945—United States.
I. Title.
II. Series.

E173.O94 vol. 9
[E801]
973 s—dc22
[973.91]   2003058491

1 2 3 4 5 6 7 8 9 10

Printed in the United States of America
on acid-free paper

This book is for Ben, Bess, and Tom
qui laetificant vitam meam.

Contents

Illustrations appear following page   232

Preface

The Great War of 1914–1918 raised the curtain on an extraordinarily painful, lengthy, and consequential chapter in American history, indeed in the history of the world. That chapter would not conclude until a second and even greater war ended more than a generation later, in 1945. Few episodes in American history — the Revolutionary and Civil War eras alone excepted — have witnessed as much turmoil or left such a lasting imprint on the national character.

This book relates the first installment of that colossally rich and compelling story. It tells the dark and disturbing tale of the Great Depression of the 1930s, including its wrenching human impact as well as the fumbling efforts to understand and overcome it on the part of citizens and policy-makers alike. It seeks to make sense out of the tangled record of President Franklin D. Roosevelt's struggle to cope with the Depression crisis, a set of measures, some successful, some silly, known to history as the New Deal. And it documents the American people's groping effort to comprehend the gathering global catastrophe that became the Second World War, and to decide on their relation to it. Part Two of this history tells the story of America during the war itself.

The United States participated only marginally, and late in the day, in what would eventually be known as the First World War. But even that relatively modest departure from the nation's historic tradition of isolating itself from European affairs was sufficiently costly and so disillusioning that Americans turned their country decidedly inward in the

1920s. The armed forces deployed during the war were swiftly demo-
bilized and the nation's war machinery thoroughly dismantled. The
United States Senate refused to ratify the Treaty of Versailles and thereby
declined membership in the nascent League of Nations, even though
the League had been the brainchild of America's wartime president,
Woodrow Wilson. In 1922 the Congress passed one of the highest tariffs
in American history, effectively closing the American market to foreign
vendors. It sealed off that market even more tightly when it passed the
notorious Smoot-Hawley Tariff eight years later. The United States government insisted throughout the postwar decade that the Europeans
must repay in their entirety the loans extended to them by the U.S.
Treasury during the war—a short-sighted, penny-pinching, Scrooge-like
policy that added heavy additional ballast to an international financial
system already staggering under the economic burdens imposed by the
war. And in 1924 the republic for the first time in its history imposed a
strict limit on the number of immigrants who could annually enter the
country, slamming the door shut against millions of souls who wanted
to claim the American dream—or the American refuge—as their own,
including (though Americans could not yet know it) would-be fugitives
from Nazi Germany in the disastrous decade that followed. Militarily,
diplomatically, commercially, financially, even morally, Americans thus
turned their backs on the outside world and plunged headlong into the
intoxicating diversions of the slap-happy, high-stepping, go-get-'em, get-
rich-quick Jazz Decade.

The prosperity of the 1920s in America was real enough, but it was
not nearly so pervasive as legend has portrayed. Few black Americans
drank from the wells of its affluence. Neither did many of the millions
of immigrants who had swarmed into the nation's teeming industrial
cities in the preceding decades and remained culturally isolated and
economically precarious in gritty ethnic ghettoes. Most blacks still lived
in the South, the country's most agricultural and therefore most backward region. Well before the Great Depression of the 1930s smote the
land, a severe economic crisis beset the farm belt almost as soon as the
Great War concluded. It did not entirely lift until the next world war,
more than twenty years later. The sorely afflicted countryside was still
home to nearly half of all Americans in the 1920s. Prosperity seemed
perpetually to pass them by. Virtually none of them enjoyed such common amenities of urban life as electricity and indoor plumbing. Yet the
mood of the country, impervious to news of accumulating international
dangers and buoyed by wildly ascending stock prices as well as the con-

genital optimism that is every American's birthright, remained remarkably upbeat.

In the fateful autumn of 1929, the bubble burst. The Great Crash in
October sent stock prices plummeting. Banks failed. Business collapsed.
Millions—nobody knew how many, so primitive were the government's
fact-finding organs—went unemployed. Herbert Hoover, elected just
months earlier amid lavish testimonials to his peerless competence, integrity, and can-do talents, saw his presidency shattered and his reputation forever shredded because of his inability to tame the depression
demon—though, again contrary to legend, he toiled valiantly to get the
upper hand.

By 1932, some 13 million Americans were unemployed, one out of
every four able and willing workers in the country. Given the demog-
raphy of the labor force and prevailing cultural norms that kept most
women—and almost all married women—out of the wage-paying economy, every fourth household in America had no breadwinner, no
income, no hope. Many Americans believed they were witnessing not
just a massive market downturn but the collapse of an historic economic, political, and social order, of the entire American way of life. Yet
curiously, as many observers noted, most Americans remained inexplicably docile, even passive, in the face of this unprecedented calamity.

Into this scene of accelerating social disintegration and spiritual paralysis arrived Franklin D. Roosevelt, elected to the presidency in 1932
on a platform that promised "a new deal for the American people." He
was destined to hold office for more than a dozen years, thrice reelected, a record matched by no previous incumbent and forbidden to
all future presidents by the passage of the Twenty-second Amendment
to the Constitution in 1951. FDR was then and has remained ever since
a surpassingly enigmatic figure. His personality perplexed his contemporaries and has challenged his biographers for more than half a century.
His long-serving Secretary of Labor, Frances Perkins, called him "the
most complicated human being I ever knew," and the pages that follow
offer abundant confirmation of the complexities and contradictions of
his make-up. Yet I argue that for all the opacity of his innermost character, he clearly brought with him to the presidency, and bequeathed
to the American people, one simple and supremely important belief:
that American life could be made more secure.

Roosevelt, like Hoover before him, never did find a remedy for the
Great Depression. It hung heavily over the land for the entire period
covered in the pages that follow, through virtually all of Hoover's

presidency, through Roosevelt's first two terms, down to 1940 and even beyond. Before World War II came along and revolutionized all political and economic formulas, none of FDR's exertions managed to wrestle the unemployment rate below 14 percent. For the decade of the 1930s as a whole, it averaged 17 percent. Some critics in fact blame the economy's inability to recover on Roosevelt's own allegedly anti-business policies—a vexed and arcane topic which I try to elucidate.

Yet while Hoover's failure to restore the economy led to his political ruin, Roosevelt seized upon the stubbornly persisting economic crisis as a matchless political opportunity. FDR used the occasion of the Great Depression to break the untamed bronco of let-er-rip, buccaneering, laissez-faire capitalism that had gone unbridled for more than a century before the 1930s. The New Deal invented new governmental institutions like the Federal Deposit Insurance Corporation, the Securities and Exchange Commission, and the National Labor Relations Board to bring stability to the historically shaky banks, the wild and wooly stock exchanges, and the often violently tumultuous world of labor relations. New Dealers found artful ways to make mortgage lending more secure, unleashing the money and the energy that built the suburbs of the Sunbelt after World War II. Probably most famously, they erected a comprehensive system of unemployment and old-age insurance to protect laid-off workers and the elderly against what FDR called "the hazards and vicissitudes of life." Achieving security was ever the core value and always the dominant motif of the New Deal's many initiatives. Americans have lived ever after in a world rendered more predictable, less volatile, safer—and for those reasons more prosperous and probably also more just—than they would have enjoyed, or endured, without FDR's achievements.

The drama of the New Deal is the central theme of this volume, a drama populated with colorful characters like Huey Pierce Long, the swashbuckling populist from Louisiana; Father Charles Coughlin, the charismatic "radio priest" who first embraced, and then excoriated, Roosevelt's New Deal; Harry Hopkins, the emaciated, chain-smoking former social worker who became FDR's most trusted confidant; Harold Ickes, the incorruptible and curmudgeonly Secretary of the Interior who presided over the New Deal's enormous public works programs; and Eleanor Roosevelt, the most prominent First Lady up to her time and a formidable public figure in her own right as well. I seek to explain the historical context in which the New Deal brought the modern American regulatory and welfare state came into being and to illuminate the peculiarly American values it reflected and methods it employed, including its crotchets, limitations, and failures as well as its successes.

The American People in the Great Depression also argues that the world the American people tried to exclude after the First World War could not, in the final analysis, be kept at bay. Adolf Hitler and Franklin Roosevelt came to power within weeks of one another. Hitler was installed as German Chancellor on January 30, 1933. Roosevelt was inaugurated as President of the United States just thirty-three days later, on March 4. The entire history of Roosevelt's presidency unfolded under the shadow of Hitler's chancellorship. All of the drama of the famed "Hundred Days" in 1933, of the great social and economic reforms of 1934 and 1935, of the battle over the composition of the Supreme Court in 1937, and of course FDR's struggle against isolationism, and the attendant agony of uncertainty about Europe's fate, and Asia's, and America's relation to the gathering maelstrom of war — all played out against the menacing backdrop of Hitler's dictatorship, the rising threat of Naziism, and the opportunistic belligerency of Japanese militarists. The challenges of the Great Depression and the accomplishments and shortcomings of the New Deal, and of FDR, cannot be understood outside of that framework. In that sense what follows is not simply the story of the American people in a moment pregnant with danger and opportunity; theirs is but part of a larger story of people in every part of the globe who were swept up in the enormous calamities of the Great Depression and, ultimately, World War II.

Acknowledgments

In writing this book I have drawn on a rich body of scholarship and imposed on the kindness of a great many colleagues, friends, and kin. I want to say a special word of appreciation for the pioneering work on the New Deal era by a remarkable generation of scholars, including John Morton Blum, James MacGregor Burns, Kenneth S. Davis, Frank Freidel, William E. Leuchtenburg, and Arthur M. Schlesinger Jr. Though I sometimes disagree with their emphases and evaluations, they laid the foundation on which all subsequent study of that period has built, including my own. I also learned much about World War II from the veterans with whom I traveled to battlefields in Italy, the Solomon Islands, and Normandy. For their service to their country, and for their generosity to me, I thank them.

Several research assistants have given me invaluable help: Leslie Berlin, Elizabeth Kopelman Borgwardt, Mark Brilliant, Kyle Graham, Tom Jackson, Sean Malloy, John McGreevy, and Jonathan Schoenwald. Their contributions and the comments of participants in Stanford's faculty–graduate student American History Workshop have greatly improved this book.

Stanford University granted me two research leaves, one spent at the Center for Advanced Study in the Behavioral Sciences, the other at the Stanford Humanities Center, both partly financed by the National Endowment for the Humanities, which greatly facilitated my research and writing. The Harmsworth Family, the Faculty of Modern History, and the Provost and Fellows of Queen's College, Oxford, provided material support and stimulating collegiality during a year I spent as the Harmsworth Professor of American History at Oxford University. A seminar I co-taught there with John Rowett of Brasenose College proved particularly helpful in shaping my thinking about the New Deal.

I am especially indebted to Jack Beatty of the *Atlantic Monthly*, James T. Patterson of Brown University, and James J. Sheehan of Stanford University, each of whom read the entire manuscript, rescued me from innumerable errors and infelicities, and challenged me to think harder and write more clearly. Co-teaching a course on World War II with my Stanford colleague Jim Sheehan has contributed substantially to my work on this project, not least because of his example of deeply thoughtful scholarship and inspired teaching. I also want to thank others who acceded to my requests to comment on various parts of the manuscript: Barton J. Bernstein, Lizabeth Cohen, Paul David, Peter Duus, James Kloppenberg, Karen Sawislak, and Gavin Wright. Henry Archer rescued me from countless mistakes.

Sheldon Meyer at Oxford University Press first asked me to undertake this book, and his wisdom and counsel, not to mention patience, cheer, and good company, have sustained me over the years of work on it, as have the invariably thoughtful commentaries of the general editor of the Oxford History of the United States, C. Vann Woodward. Joellyn Ausanka, India Cooper, and Susan Day provided the excellent editorial support for which Oxford Press is justly renowned.

My wife, Judy, read the entire manuscript, endured life as a writer's widow, and provided unflagging support. Our three children, Ben, Bess, and Tom, grew up with this book, and to them I lovingly dedicate it, with the hope that this history may prove useful to their voyage, and their generation's, into the future.

Stanford, California   David M. Kennedy
July 4, 1998

Editor's Introduction

The brief period from 1929 to 1945 is unique in American history for its complexities of change and violence of contrasts. People who lived through the years of the Great Depression, the New Deal, and the Second World War — only half the years normally assigned to one generation — experienced more bewildering changes than had several generations of their predecessors. These changes included a transition from economic and social paralysis to unprecedented outbursts of national energy, the emergence from wretched years of poverty to unparalleled levels of prosperity, and the repudiation of a century-and-a-half of isolation as America entered World War II.

Events of this magnitude and global significance make extraordinary demands upon the historian. Fortunately, David M. Kennedy is richly endowed with the talents and skills required by his challenging task — plus gifts as a writer. He is not the kind of historian who dwells upon abstract "forces." His emphasis is upon *people* — not only leaders but followers and opponents as well as victims and beneficiaries. Readers of *Freedom from Fear* will encounter vivid portraits not only of American statesmen and commanders, but of their foreign counterparts as well. Their decisions, errors, blunders, and such measures of luck as shaped the course of history are given due attention, but not to the neglect of the people who suffered or endured the results.

It is the people who suffered in the Great Depression who receive David Kennedy's primary attention, and more of them did suffer, and more deeply, and longer, than has been generally assumed. Southern white sharecroppers, for example, averaged an annual cash income of $350, black sharecroppers $294. At wages of $1 a day miners subsisted on a diet suggesting that of domestic animals. Emaciated children who never tasted milk wandered the streets, some shoeless in winter, too poorly clad to go to school. Milch cows dried up for lack of feed, and starving horses dropped in their harnesses. More surprising than the people's despair was their prevailing submissiveness. Their creed of individualism may account for much of this: If success and prosperity were due to merit and striving, failure and poverty must be due to the lack of them. Much more common than rebellion among Americans of those years was a sense of shame and a loss of self-respect. Year after year of depression went by with little or no sign of the recovery promised by politicians.

Franklin D. Roosevelt and his New Deal have been both credited with recovery from the depression and blamed for the failure of recovery. David Kennedy refuses to settle for either simplification. He traces the complex interplay between continuing economic stagnation and Roosevelt's remarkable programs of social and economic reform, new ones almost every year until 1938. Granting the inconsistencies, contradictions, and failures of the New Deal, Kennedy nevertheless summarizes its "leitmotif" in a single word: security. Its programs extended security not only to vulnerable individuals, races, and classes but to capitalists and consumers, bankers and homeowners, workers and employers, as much security and freedom from fear as democratic government might provide. FDR set out, he once declared, "to make a country in which no one is left out." Without resort to revolution or abandonment of the Constitution, the New Deal constructed an institutional framework for such a society as its main heritage. What it did *not* do was to end the Great Depression and restore prosperity. That proved in the end to be the incidental and ironic work of a terrible war.

It was a war—really two wars—that the will of the people as expressed repeatedly by congressional majorities wanted no part in. As for the quarrelsome Europeans, let them settle their differences themselves this time, as American intervention had failed to do in the previous war. And as for the Japanese, let the vast Pacific Ocean serve as our shield. Appeals and threats from both sides of the globe seemed only to increase the zeal of American isolationists and the stubborn resistance to intervention. What military preparation the country made (and it started virtually from scratch) must be limited to the protection of national rights and property. Increasingly, however, the survival of Britain, and then of the Soviet Union, came to be seen as crucial to America's own survival. After years of agonizing neutrality, war eventually came to America with the Japanese attack on Pearl Harbor.

In the half of his book that deals with the war, its coming and its conduct, Kennedy exhibits remarkable talents in discussing diplomacy, especially relations with Churchill and Stalin. He also shows unusual skills in analyzing and depicting modern warfare in two hemispheres, including naval war and air combat. Readers are not spared accounts of the most gruesome and brutal atrocities, especially in the savage Pacific War. Without neglecting any essentials of military history, including the greatest naval battle ever fought and the development and use of the most powerful weapon ever made, *Freedom from Fear* also gives us a superb account of what the war did to the hundreds of millions of noncombatants on the homefront. Their lives were as much revolutionized as the lives of those in uniform. Women replaced or joined men in the work force; blacks gained jobs and skills; southerners moved north, easterners moved west. The whole population was profoundly shaken up and the American way of life deeply changed.

This volume of the Oxford series covers an incomparable period of American history, a period of extraordinary challenges and demands upon the historian, demands that David Kennedy has met surpassingly well.

C. Vann Woodward

Abbreviated Titles Used in Citations

C&R   Warren F. Kimball, ed., *Churchill and Roosevelt: The Complete Correspondence*, 3 vols. (Princeton: Princeton University Press, 1984)

Cantril   Hadley Cantril, ed., *Public Opinion, 1935–1946* (Princeton: Princeton University Press, 1951)

Dallek   Robert Dallek, *Franklin D. Roosevelt and American Foreign Policy, 1932–1945* (New York: Oxford University Press, 1979)

Davis   Kenneth S. Davis, *FDR*, 4 vols. (New York: Random House, 1985–93)

FRUS   *Foreign Relations of the United States* (Washington: USGPO, various years)

HSUS   *Historical Statistics of the United States*, 2 vols. (Washington: USGPO, 1975)

Ickes Diary   Harold L. Ickes, *The Secret Diary of Harold L. Ickes*, 3 vols. (New York: Simon and Schuster, 1953–54)

L&G, *Challenge*   William L. Langer and S. Everett Gleason, *The Challenge to Isolation, 1937–1940* (New York: Harper and Brothers, 1952)

L&G, *Undeclared*   William L. Langer and S. Everett Gleason, *The Undeclared War, 1940–1941* (New York: Harper and Brothers, 1953)

Leuchtenburg   William E. Leuchtenburg, *Franklin D. Roosevelt and the New Deal* (New York: Harper and Row, 1963)

Morgenthau Diary   John Morton Blum, *Roosevelt and Morgenthau* (Boston: Houghton Mifflin, 1972)

PPA   *The Public Papers and Addresses of Franklin D. Roosevelt,* 13 vols. (New York: Random House and Harper and Brothers, 1938–50)

Schlesinger   Arthur M. Schlesinger Jr., *The Age of Roosevelt,* 3 vols. (Boston: Houghton Mifflin, 1956–60)

Stimson Diary   Diary of Henry L. Stimson, microfilm, Green Library, Stanford University (original in Sterling Library, Yale University)

*The American People in the
Great Depression*

Prologue: November 11, 1918

...and a knell rang in the ears of the victors, even in their hour of triumph.

— Winston Churchill, 1927

The Great War ended on November 11, 1918. It had lasted 1,563 days, claimed the lives of some ten million soldiers, wounded twenty million others, and devoured more than $300 billion of the world's treasure. It destroyed empires and dethroned dynasties — the Hohenzollerns in Germany, the Hapsburgs in Austria, the Romanovs in Russia. In the war's final hours, new regimes were aborning in Vienna, Warsaw, Budapest, Prague, and Dublin, while revolutionaries huzzahed through the streets of Berlin and Petersburg.

A strange stillness settled over the fighting fronts, a grim herald of two decades of tense armistice in the twentieth century's Thirty-Year War.

News of the war's end reached Lance Corporal Adolf Hitler in a military hospital in the town of Pasewalk, near Stettin in Pomerania. A twice-decorated message runner with the Sixteenth Bavarian Reserve Infantry Regiment, Hitler had huddled through the night of October 13 on a hillside in Flanders while the British rained gas grenades on the German trenches. Through the darkness the gas hissed from the canisters toward the German lines. By morning Hitler's eyes were "red-hot coals," and he was blind. Clutching his last report of the war, he groped his way to the rear and was put aboard a train for the east.[1]

Now, four weeks later, on November 10, a sobbing hospital chaplain informed Hitler and his recuperating comrades that a revolution had dethroned the kaiser. The civilian leaders of the new German republic

1. Adolf Hitler, *Mein Kampf* (New York: Stackpole Sons, 1939), 200–201.

1

had sued for peace, even while the German army was still intact in the field. For the good soldier Hitler this was "the greatest infamy of this century." Still half blind, he stumbled back to his cot, buried his head in his pillow, and wept. "So it had all been in vain," he grieved. "In vain all the sacrifices and starvation, in vain the hunger and thirst often of months without end . . . in vain the death of two millions." Revolution and surrender, Hitler concluded, were the work of depraved Marxist and Jewish criminals. Their infamy must be avenged. Tossing on his cot, he conjured legions of his slain comrades arising from their graves to restore the Fatherland. His destiny would be to lead them. "The flush of indignation and shame burned in my cheek," he wrote, and "in the next few days I became conscious of my own fate. . . . I resolved to become a politician."[2]

While Hitler's mind spun with ghoulish fantasies in Pomerania, Winston Churchill, minister of munitions in Britain's War Cabinet, stood musing at the window of his makeshift office in the Hotel Metropole in London. He stared up Northumberland Avenue toward Trafalagar Square, awaiting the first chime of Big Ben at 11:00 A.M., Greenwich Mean Time, which would signal the war's official conclusion. "Our country had emerged from the ordeal alive and safe," he reflected, "its vast possessions intact . . . its institutions unshaken." How different was the fate of Germany, "shivered suddenly into a thousand individually disintegrating fragments. . . . Such a spectacle appalls mankind; and a knell rang in the ears of the victors, even in their hour of triumph."

And then at last, "suddenly the first stroke of the chime." Through the pane Churchill spotted the slight figure of a lone girl dart from a hotel doorway into the street. As all the bells of London began to clash, the pavement around her filled with shouting, screaming, triumphant Britons. The scene was exhilarating, but Churchill remained pensive. "Safety, freedom, peace, home, the dear one back at the fireside—all after fifty-two months of gaunt distortion. After fifty-two months of making burdens grievous to be borne and binding them on men's backs, at last, all at once, suddenly and everywhere the burdens were cast down. At least," Churchill brooded, "so for the moment it seemed."[3]

Nearly two thousand miles to the east, Josef Stalin, people's commissar for nationalities, also brooded. He scanned the patchy news reports

2. Hitler, *Mein Kampf*, 203.
3. Winston Churchill, *The World Crisis, 1916–1918* (New York: Charles Scribner's Sons, 1927), 2:273–75.

from the west for confirming proof that the war's chaotic end signaled the predicted death of capitalism in the collapsing belligerent countries. Awaiting the moment of world revolution, he meantime fought savagely to protect the revolution in Russia, imperiled in its very infancy by civil war and foreign intervention. Commissar Stalin's special assignment was the defense of the southern front, centered on the Volga River city of Tsaritsyn—later Stalingrad, still later Volgograd—gateway to the Caucasus and its precious supplies of grain. There he dealt with suspected counterrevolutionaries in the summer and fall of 1918 with the calculating terror that was to become his hallmark. On a large black barge anchored in midriver, he nightly ordered the shooting of dozens of prisoners, whose bodies were then tossed into the current. "Death solves all problems," Stalin said. "No man, no problem." Returning to Moscow in November, he gloated at the execution of Roman Malinovsky, the informer who had betrayed him to the czar's Ohkrana in 1913, resulting in Stalin's banishment to Siberia. There, alone and embittered for four years, he had plotted his way to power and retribution.[4]

Franklin Delano Roosevelt spent those same four years savoring a measure of power as assistant secretary of the navy, in Washington, D.C. On the morning of November 11, 1918, Roosevelt awoke in Washington to a riotous din of honking automobile horns, pealing bells, piping whistles, and shouting people. "The feeling of relief and thankfulness," his wife, Eleanor, remembered, "was beyond description."[5]

Yet for Franklin Roosevelt the end of the war also came as something of a disappointment. Impetuous, romantic, ambitious, he had been compelled to serve out the war bound to his desk as a civilian administrator. His magical political name, his familial Rooseveltian vigor, his handsome, youthful presence, his apparent ubiquity, his volleys of crisply phrased memos had all earned him a reputation as one of the most able and charismatic of Washington's wartime personalities. But it was not enough. Like his kinetic cousin Theodore, he longed for the fray, yearned to emulate his legendary "Uncle Ted," who had resigned the

4. H. Montgomery Hyde, *Stalin: The History of a Dictator* (New York: Farrar, Straus and Giroux, 1971), 156–64. A somewhat less lurid, but not inconsistent, account of Stalin's role in Tsaritsyn is given in Robert C. Tucker, *Stalin as Revolutionary, 1879–1929* (New York: Norton, 1973), 190ff. See also Dmitri Volkogonov, *Stalin: Triumph and Tragedy* (London: Weidenfeld and Nicolson, 1991), 40; and Robert Conquest, *Stalin: Breaker of Nations* (New York: Viking, 1991), 79.

5. Eleanor Roosevelt, *This Is My Story* (New York: Garden City, 1939), 272.

very position that Franklin now held to take up arms in the Spanish-American War.

Neither Franklin Roosevelt nor the world had yet absorbed the dreadful lessons of the Great War, and in his martial yearnings the youthful assistant secretary had something in common with both Hitler and Churchill. Hitler, the sulking and penurious Viennese art student, had abandoned his native Austria and fled to Munich to join the German army in 1914. In his military regiment he found the warmth of comradeship that had eluded him in the aching vacuity of his civilian life. The outbreak of war, he wrote, "seemed like deliverance from the angry feelings of my youth."[6] Churchill owed both his manhood and his fame to his soldierly exploits in India and in the Boer War. In 1914, while a cabinet minister, he had dashed across the Channel to take personal charge of the defense of Antwerp. Having "tasted blood," Prime Minister Herbert Asquith wryly noted, Churchill was "beginning like a tiger to raven for more and begs that . . . he may be . . . put in some kind of military command." He soon got his wish. In January 1916, a middle-aged man accustomed to brandy and silks, Lieutenant Colonel Churchill led an infantry battalion of the Sixth Royal Scots Fusiliers up to their rough billets in the front near Ypres — facing the Germans across the same hellish landscape into which Adolf Hitler's Sixteenth Bavarian Reserve Infantry Regiment was repeatedly sent.[7]

Roosevelt knew no such satisfactions. Late on the night of October 31, 1918, he called at the White House to ask President Woodrow Wilson for a naval commission. "Too late," Wilson replied; he had already received the first armistice proposals from the newly forming German government, and the war would be over very soon.[8]

Roosevelt had to content himself with an official inspection trip to the front in the summer of 1918. It was this journey that underlay the claim he made nearly twenty years later: "I have known war." On July 31 a British destroyer put him ashore at Dunkirk, not forty miles from the spot where Hitler was to be gassed some ten weeks afterward. Impatient and reckless, Roosevelt plunged about the battlefields and courted such danger as he could find. In Belleau Wood, where Amer-

6. Hitler, *Mein Kampf*, 163.

7. William Manchester, *The Last Lion: Winston Spencer Churchill: Visions of Glory, 1874–1932* (Boston: Little, Brown, 1983), 477–651.

8. Frank Freidel, *Franklin D. Roosevelt: The Apprenticeship* (Boston: Little, Brown, 1952), 370. See also Davis 1:548 and Geoffrey C. Ward, *A First-Class Temperament* (New York: Harper and Row, 1989), 417.

ican troops had helped to stop the final German advance just weeks earlier, he threaded his way around water-filled shell holes and past countless rude graves, marked only by whittled wooden crosses or bayoneted rifles stuck in the earth. At Mareuil en Dole he jerked the lanyards to fire artillery shells at a German rail junction some twelve miles distant. At Verdun he donned helmet and gas mask and clambered underground into the fetid labyrinth of Fort Douamont. He heard the muffled thudding of German artillery shells bursting on the earthworks above. On August 7, after a whirlwind battleground tour of less than a week, Roosevelt departed the front. In September he returned to the haven of the United States, where he remained at the time of the armistice on November 11. Like the vast majority of his countrymen, he had not truly known war. "He was fascinated rather than repelled," a biographer concludes, "thrilled by the patriotism and heroism of the American Allied troops, and oppressed by a sense of guilt and deprivation because he was not sharing their vicissitudes."[9]

FOUR MEN IN NOVEMBER 1918: Each of them molded by the Great War, each fated to lead a nation, each nation destined to be convulsed by the war's aftermath and eventual resumption. All four men coveted power, and all would hugely possess it. The two victors had already drunk at the well of power and now thirsted for even greater drafts. Stalin struggled to close his hand over power amidst the chaos of revolution. Hitler lusted for power sufficient to avenge his nation's humiliating defeat. The wheel of time would eventually carry all four of these men into one of history's darkest circles. Indeed, history had already thrown them into sometimes eery proximity, physical as well as metaphorical.[10] Churchill and Roosevelt had both passed within a day's march of the trenches where Lance Corporal Hitler scurried with his

---

9. Freidel, *Apprenticeship*, 358–61. As Freidel observes elsewhere, at this stage of his life the young Roosevelt was "impatient and far from reflective." In 1936, an older and more seasoned Roosevelt would famously recollect his time at the front by observing that "I have seen war. . . . I have seen blood running from the wounded. I have seen men coughing out their gassed lungs. . . . I have seen the agony of mothers and wives. I hate war." (Freidel, 287, 356); *PPA* (1937), 289.

10. Each of these men, too, would know his own kind of imprisonment. Stalin had already chewed the salt bread of exile in the frozen reaches of Siberia. Hitler, arrested after the failed Beer Hall Putsch in Munich in 1923, was to spend nine months in the Fortress of Landsberg, dictating *Mein Kampf* (My Struggle) to Rudolph Hess. Churchill was to feel the oppressive confinement, for him, of being

dispatches. All three, like moths to the flame, felt drawn by the thrilling allure of soldiering and battle. The Briton and the American actually met at a dinner at Gray's Inn in London on July 9, 1918, though neither made much impression on the other at the time.[11]

Stalin, born in the Caucasus on the frontier between Europe and Asia, dreamt of a new Red empire that would arise from the ashes of the Romanovs' Russia and spread far beyond its old imperial boundaries—just as Hitler, born on the frontier that separated Germany from Austria, nursed his febrile dream of fusing all the Germanic peoples of the toppling Hohenzollern and Hapsburg regimes into a vast, new, racially pure Teutonic *Reich*. The clash of those dreams would one day be the world's nightmare.

BUT IN NOVEMBER 1918, the fighting momentarily ended, humankind could still for a fleeting season dream the dreams of hope. Much of that hope was invested in the person of the American president, Woodrow Wilson. "What a place the President held in the hearts and hopes of the world!" when he boarded the *George Washington* for the Paris Peace Conference on December 4, 1918, exclaimed the British economist John Maynard Keynes. Buoyant and eager, Roosevelt followed his chief to Paris aboard the same ship a month later. But there, hovering on the periphery of the peace negotiations, he witnessed the remorseless demolition of the liberal settlement that Wilson had championed.

It was the young Keynes who most famously chronicled the hope-smothering defects of the treaty that was signed on June 28, 1919, in the Hall of Mirrors at the Palace of Versailles. Wilson had envisioned a liberal peace, a peace without victory, a peace that would magnanimously restore Germany to its rightful place in an open world of free trade and democracy. In that world commerce would be unshackled from political constraint, politics would be based on the principle of self-determination, and order would be maintained by a new international body, the League of Nations. But what emerged from the ordeal of the Paris peace negotiations was a document that mocked those ideals.

---

deprived of political office in 1922 and 1923, when he began to write *The World Crisis*, his history of the Great War. Roosevelt would be partly imprisoned in his immobile body after suffering an attack of poliomyelitis in 1921.

11. Roosevelt failed to record the meeting in his detailed diary, and Churchill apparently forgot the episode entirely. Freidel, *Apprenticeship*, 354.

The Versailles Treaty, Keynes wrote in his embittered and astute tract of 1919, *The Economic Consequences of the Peace*, contained three lethal flaws. It transferred important coal, iron, and steel properties from Germany to France and prohibited their utilization by German industry. "Thus the Treaty strikes at organization," Keynes declared, "and by the destruction of organization impairs yet further the reduced wealth of the whole community." The treaty further stripped Germany of her overseas colonies, foreign investments, and merchant marine and restricted her control of her own waterways and tariffs. Most economically punishing of all, the victorious powers then imposed on this drastically weakened Germany a colossal bill for some $33 billion in reparations payments. Adding insult to injury, the treaty's Article 231—the notorious "guilt clause"—forced the Germans to acknowledge sole responsibility for the outbreak of the war.[12]

The treaty, Keynes concluded, insanely perpetuated in peacetime the economic disruptions of the war itself. To the military catastrophe of the fighting was now added the economic burden of a vengeful peace. Germany, struggling to become a republic, bore most of the fearful tonnage. But all nations, victors and vanquished alike, were bowed beneath its crushing ballast in the interwar decades.

Keynes was not the only observer to sense mortal liabilities in the legacy from Versailles. A young statesman who had come to Paris from a distant corner of the planet, twenty-seven-year-old Prince Fumimaro Konoye of Japan, also found grounds for complaint. Konoye warned his countrymen in a celebrated article to "reject the Anglo-American–centered peace." Why should Japan, he asked, accept a settlement that refused to acknowledge the principle of racial equality? That refused to honor Japan's rightful claims in China? That perpetuated in the name of high idealism a world order that relegated small, resource-poor Japan to second-class status? Like Germany, Konoye argued, Japan had "no resort but to destroy the status quo for the sake of self-preservation." Two decades later, Premier Konoye would link Japan's fate to that of Nazi Germany and Fascist Italy in the Tripartite Pact—an aggressive bid to destroy the status quo in Europe and Asia alike, not merely for the sake of self-preservation but for the sake of imperial expansion.[13]

12. John Maynard Keynes, *The Economic Consequences of the Peace* (New York: Harcourt, Brace and Howe, 1920), 100–101, 152.

13. Yoshitake Oka, *Konoe Fumimaro: A Political Biography* (Tokyo: University of Tokyo Press, 1983), 13.

The Versailles Treaty thus sowed the wind that would eventually lash the world with gale fury. Woodrow Wilson's adviser, Colonel Edward House, reflected as he watched the German representatives scratch their signatures on the parchment in the Hall of Mirrors that "it was not unlike what was done in olden times, when the conqueror dragged the conquered at his chariot wheels." The Berlin *Vorwarts* urged its readers: "Do not lose hope. The resurrection day comes."[14]

Adolf Hitler aimed to be the agent of that resurrection. Returning to Munich in 1919, he plunged into the furtive, turbulent world of political organizing among the discontented army veterans who shared his resentment of their army's betrayal by civilian leaders in 1918. By 1920 he had helped to organize the National-sozialistische Deutsche Arbeiterpartei—the Nazi Party, with its distinctive *Hakenkreuz*, or swastika, symbol. By 1921 he was its undisputed leader, and its brown-shirted toughs, the Sturmabteilungen (SA), stood ready to enforce his will. He played like a virtuoso the swelling chords of German resentment, and the Nazis advanced as Germany's democratic experiment retreated. The Weimar Republic, saddled from birth with the ignominy of defeat and the harsh economic and psychological weight of the Versailles settlement, staggered and reeled through the 1920s. When it defaulted on reparations payments in 1922, France occupied the Ruhr, Germany's industrial heartland, touching off a fantastic spiral of hyperinflation that rendered the German *Mark* virtually worthless. Hitler seized the occasion to attempt a coup in Munich—the failed "Beer Hall Putsch" that earned him a jail sentence in the fortress at Landsberg. Released in late 1924, he again focused his demonic energy on building the Nazi Party, including now an elite personal bodyguard, the black-shirted Schutz Staffeln (SS). By 1928 the party claimed more than a hundred thousand members and polled 810,000 votes in the Reichstag elections.[15]

Then came the world economic crisis that began in 1929, and with it Hitler's great opportunity. As German unemployment mounted to three million persons in 1930, Nazi Party membership doubled. When Germans went to the polls in September 1930, the Nazi vote vaulted to 6.4 million. Hitler now commanded the second-largest party in the Reichstag, with 107 seats. Two years later the Nazis won an additional

14. Both remarks quoted in Thomas A. Bailey, *Woodrow Wilson and the Lost Peace* (New York: Macmillan, 1944), 302–30.

15. The account of Hitler's rise to power is drawn from Alan Bullock, *Hitler: A Study in Tyranny* (New York: Harper and Row, 1962) and from Joachim Fest, *Hitler* (New York: Harcourt Brace Jovanovich, 1974).

113 seats, and Hitler demanded that he be given the chancellorship. On January 30, 1933, he got it. Five weeks later, Franklin D. Roosevelt was inaugurated as president of the United States.

Time takes strange turnings. As former lance corporal Hitler and former assistant secretary Roosevelt now stepped to the center stage of history, another figure whom the Great War had summoned to that stage prepared to leave it: Herbert Hoover, the great humanitarian who had organized food relief for occupied Belgium in 1914 and fed much of the world in the tumultuous months that followed the armistice. He was "the only man," said John Maynard Keynes, "who emerged from the ordeal of Paris with an enhanced reputation." Keynes believed that if Hoover's realism, his "knowledge, magnanimity, and disinterestedness," had found wider play in the councils of Paris, the world would have had "the Good Peace."[16]

But there would be no good peace, only a precarious truce followed by a decade of depression and then an even greater war. When the global economic hurricane of the 1930s stripped power from Hoover and conferred it on Hitler and Roosevelt, Hoover knew the source of the storm: "[T]he primary cause of the Great Depression," reads the first sentence of his *Memoirs*, "was the war of 1914–1918."[17]

16. Keynes, *Economic Consequences of the Peace*, 247.
17. Herbert Hoover, *The Memoirs of Herbert Hoover: The Great Depression, 1929–1941* (New York: Macmillan, 1952), 2.

1

The American People
on the Eve of the Great Depression

We in America today are nearer to the final triumph over poverty than ever before in the history of any land.

— Herbert Hoover, August 11, 1928

Like an earthquake, the stock market crash of October 1929 cracked startlingly across the United States, the herald of a crisis that was to shake the American way of life to its foundations. The events of the ensuing decade opened a fissure across the landscape of American history no less gaping than that opened by the volley on Lexington Common in April 1775 or by the bombardment of Sumter on another April four score and six years later.

The ratcheting ticker machines in the autumn of 1929 did not merely record avalanching stock prices. In time they came also to symbolize the end of an era. The roaring industrial expansion that had boomed since the Civil War hushed to a near standstill for half a generation. The tumult of crisis and reform in the ten depression years massively enlarged and forever transformed the scanty Jeffersonian government over which Herbert Hoover had been elected to preside in 1928. And even before the battle against the Great Depression was won, the American people had to shoulder arms in another even more fearsome struggle that wreathed the planet in destruction and revolutionized America's global role.

None of this impending drama could have been foreseen by the tweedy group of social scientists who gathered at the White House for dinner with President Hoover on the warm, early autumn evening of September 26, 1929. The Crash, still four weeks away, was unimagined and almost unimaginable. Nearly three decades of barely punctuated economic growth, capped by seven years of unprecedented prosperity, gave to the mood in the room, as in the entire country, an air of masterful confidence in the future. The president personified the national temper. Attired as always in starched high collar and immaculate business suit, he greeted his guests with stiff, double-breasted dignity. He exuded the laconic assurance of a highly successful executive. He was arguably the most respected man in America, a man, said the novelist Sherwood Anderson, who had "never known failure."[1] A wave of popular acclamation had lifted him to the White House just six months earlier, after a famously distinguished career as a mining engineer, international businessman, relief and food administrator in the Great War of 1914–18, and exceptionally influential secretary of commerce in the Republican administrations of Warren G. Harding and Calvin Coolidge.

Hoover was no mossback conservative in the Harding-Coolidge mold, and the men gathered in the White House dining room knew it. "[T]he time when the employer could ride roughshod over his labor is disappearing with the doctrine of 'laissez-faire' on which it is founded," he had written as early as 1909.[2] Long sympathetic to the progressive wing of his party, Hoover as secretary of commerce had not only supported the cause of labor but also urged closer business-government cooperation, established government control over the new technology of radio, and proposed a multibillion-dollar federal public works fund as a tool to offset downswings in the business cycle. As president, he meant to be no passive custodian. He dreamt the progressive generation's dream of actively managing social change through informed, though scrupulously limited, government action. "A new era and new forces have come into our economic life and our setting among nations of the world," he said in accepting the Republican presidential nomination in 1928. "These forces demand of us constant study and effort if prosperity, peace, and contentment shall be maintained."[3]

Organizing that study was the dinner meeting's agenda. The little assemblage around the president's dining table symbolized, in a sense, the core progressive faith in knowledge as the servant of power. Hoover intended to possess knowledge, and with it to rule responsibly. After

1. Joan Hoff Wilson, *Herbert Hoover: Forgotten Progressive* (Boston: Little, Brown, 1975), 121.
2. Herbert Hoover, *Principles of Mining* (New York: McGraw-Hill, 1909), 167–68.
3. Herbert Hoover, *The Memoirs of Herbert Hoover: The Cabinet and the Presidency, 1920–1933* (New York: Macmillan, 1952), 195.

methodically interrogating each of his guests over the coffee cups as the table was cleared, Hoover explained his ambitious project. He meant to recruit the best brains in the country, he said, to compile a body of data and analysis about American society that would be more comprehensive, more searching, and more useful than anything ever before attempted. Their findings, he went on, would serve as "a basis for the formulation of large national policies looking to the next phase in the nation's development."[4]

The following month's upheavals in the financial markets, and their aftershocks, rendered ironic Hoover's confident anticipation of "the next phase in the nation's development." Underscoring the irony, Hoover eventually disowned the study he so confidently commissioned on that Indian summer evening. In the four years between its conception and its publication—the four years of Herbert Hoover's presidency—the world changed forever. Among the casualties of that violent mutation was Hoover's research project and the hope of an orderly command of the future that it represented—not to mention his own reputation. A massive dreadnought of scholarship, its pages barnacled with footnotes, it was launched at last in 1933 onto a Sargasso Sea of presidential and public indifference.

Useless to Hoover in 1933, the scholars' work has nevertheless provided historians ever since with an incomparably rich source of information about the pre-Depression period. Entitled *Recent Social Trends*, it ran to some fifteen hundred pages densely packed with data about all aspects of American life. It ranged from an inventory of mineral resources to analyses of crime and punishment, the arts, health and medical practice, the status of women, blacks, and ethnic minorities, the changing characteristics of the labor force, the impact of new technologies on productivity and leisure, and the roles of federal, state, and local governments. From its turgid prose and endless tables emerged a vivid portrait of a people in the throes of sweeping social, economic, and political change, even before they were engulfed by the still more wrenching changes of the Depression era.

President Hoover's charge to the assembled scholars at that hopeful supper registered his commitment to what Walter Lippmann in 1914

4. President's Research Committee on Social Trends, *Recent Social Trends in the United States* (Westport, Conn.: Greenwood, 1970), 1: xi; French Strother, memorandum of June 26, 1934, E. H. Hunt Collection, box 23, "Memoranda," Hoover Institution Archives, Stanford, Calif. See also Barry Karl, "Presidential Planning and Social Science Research: Mr. Hoover's Experts," *Perspectives in American History* 3:347–409.

had called mastery, not drift, in the nation's affairs and to government as the instrument of that mastery.[5] Hoover's dinner-table speech to the social scientists also accurately reflected their shared sense — indeed the sense of most Americans in pre-Crash 1929 — that they dwelt in a land and time of special promise. "A new era," Hoover called it, one that was witnessing breathtaking transformations in traditional ways of life and that demanded commensurate transformations in the institutions and techniques of government.

This sense of living through a novel historical moment pervaded commentaries on American society in the 1920s. Even the sober academic authors of *Recent Social Trends* marveled at the social and economic forces that "have hurried us dizzily away from the days of the frontier into a whirl of modernisms which almost passes belief."[6] The same sense of astonishment suffused the pages of the decade's most famous sociological inquiry, Robert and Helen Merrell Lynd's *Middletown*, drawn from an exhaustive examination of Muncie, Indiana, in 1925. Measuring from the baseline of 1890, the Lynds found dramatic alterations in every conceivable aspect of the Middletowners' lives. "[W]e today," they concluded, "are probably living in one of the eras of greatest rapidity of change in the history of human institutions."[7]

The list of changes in the generation since the close of the nineteenth century seemed endlessly amazing. *Recent Social Trends* began with a brief recital of some of the "epoch-making events" that had filled the first third of the twentieth century: the Great War, mass immigration, race riots, rapid urbanization, the rise of giant industrial combines like U.S. Steel, Ford, and General Motors, new technologies like electrical power, automobiles, radios, and motion pictures, novel social experiments like Prohibition, daring campaigns for birth control, a new frankness about sex, women's suffrage, the advent of mass-market advertising and consumer financing. "These," the researchers declared, "are but a few of the many happenings which have marked one of the most eventful periods of our history."[8]

THE SHEER SCALE of America in the 1920s was impressive, and its variety was downright astonishing. The nation's population had nearly

5. Walter Lippmann, *Drift and Mastery* (New York: Mitchell Kennerley, 1914).
6. *Recent Social Trends* 1:xii.
7. Robert S. Lynd and Helen Merrell Lynd, *Middletown: A Study in Modern American Culture* (New York: Harcourt, Brace and World, 1929), 5.
8. *Recent Social Trends* 1:xi.

doubled since 1890, when it had numbered just sixty-three million souls. At least a third of the increase was due to a huge surge of immigrants. Most of them had journeyed to America from the religiously and culturally exotic regions of southern and eastern Europe. Through the great hall in the immigrant receiving center on New York's Ellis Island, opened in 1892, streamed in the next three decades almost four million Italian Catholics; half a million Orthodox Greeks; half a million Catholic Hungarians; nearly a million and a half Catholic Poles; more than two million Jews, largely from Russian-controlled Poland, Ukraine, and Lithuania; half a million Slovaks, mostly Catholic; millions of other eastern Slavs from Byelorussia, Ruthenia, and Russia, mostly Orthodox; more millions of southern Slavs, a mix of Catholic, Orthodox, Muslim, and Jew, from Rumania, Croatia, Serbia, Bulgaria, and Montenegro. The waves of arrivals after the turn of the century were so enormous that of the 123 million Americans recorded in the census of 1930, one in ten was foreign born, and an additional 20 percent had at least one parent born abroad.[9]

Immigrants settled in all regions, though only scantily in the South and heavily in the sprawling industrial zone of the Northeast. To an overwhelming degree they were drawn not to the land but to the factories and tenements of the big cities. They turned urban America into a kind of polyglot archipelago in the predominantly Anglo-Protestant American sea. Almost a third of Chicago's 2.7 million residents in the 1920s were foreign born; more than a million were Catholic, and another 125,000 were Jews. New Yorkers spoke some thirty-seven different languages, and only one in six worshiped in a Protestant church.[10]

Everywhere immigrant communities banded together in ethnic enclaves, where they strove, not always consistently, both to preserve their old-world cultural patrimony and to become American. They were strangers in a strange land, awkwardly suspended between the world they had left behind and a world where they were not yet fully at home. They naturally looked to one another for reassurance and strength. The Jewish ghettoes and Little Italys and Little Polands that took root in American cities became worlds unto themselves. Immigrants read newspapers and listened to radio broadcasts in their native languages. They

9. Thomas J. Archdeacon, *Becoming American: An Ethnic History* (New York: Free Press, 1983), 112–42.

10. Harvey Green, *The Uncertainty of Everyday Life* (New York: HarperCollins, 1992), 5.

shopped at stores, patronized banks, and dealt with insurance companies that catered exclusively to their particular ethnic group. They chanted their prayers in synagogues or, if they were Catholic, often in "national" churches where sermons were preached in the old-world tongue. They educated their children in parish schools and buried their dead with the help of ethnic funeral societies. They joined fraternal organizations to keep alive the old traditions and paid their dues to mutual aid societies that would help when hard times came.

Times were often hard. Huddled on the margins of American life, immigrants made do with what work they could find, typically low-skill jobs in heavy industry, the garment trades, or construction. Isolated by language, religion, livelihood, and neighborhood, they had precious little ability to speak to one another and scant political voice in the larger society. So precarious were their lives that many of them gave up altogether and went back home. Nearly a third of the Poles, Slovaks, and Croatians returned to Europe; almost half the Italians; more than half the Greeks, Russians, Rumanians, and Bulgarians.[11] Old-stock Americans continued to think of the foreigners who remained in their midst as alien and threatening. Many immigrants wondered if the fabled promise of American life was a vagrant and perhaps impossible dream.

The flood of newcomers, vividly different from earlier migrants in faiths, tongues, and habits, aroused powerful anxieties about the capacity of American society to accommodate them. Some of that anxiety found virulent expression in a revived Ku Klux Klan, reborn in all its Reconstruction-era paraphernalia at Stone Mountain, Georgia, in 1915. Klan nightriders now rode cars, not horses, and they directed their venom as much at immigrant Jews and Catholics as at blacks. But the new Klan no less than the old represented a peculiarly American response to cultural upheaval. By the early 1920s the Klan claimed some five million members, and for a time it dominated the politics of Indiana and Oregon. The nativist sentiment that the Klan helped to nurture found statutory expression in 1924, when Congress choked the immigrant stream to a trickle, closing the era of virtually unlimited entry to the United States. The ethnic neighborhoods that had mushroomed in the preceding generation would grow no more through further inflows from abroad. America's many ethnic communities now began to stabilize. Millions of immigrants awaited the day when they might become American at last.

11. Archdeacon, *Becoming American*, 118–19, 139.

From peasant plots in the basins of the Volga and Vistula, from rough pastures high in the Carpathians and Apennines, as well as from the cotton South and the midwestern corn belt, new Americans as well as old flowed to the throbbing industrial centers in the northeastern quadrant of the United States. The region of settlement defined as the "frontier" had officially closed in 1890. By 1920, for the first time in the nation's history, a majority of Americans were city dwellers. In the following decade, some six million more American farmers quit the land and moved to the city.

Yet the urbanization of early twentieth-century America can be exaggerated. More than one in five working Americans still toiled on the land in the 1920s. Forty-four percent of the population was still counted as rural in 1930. Well over half the states of the Union remained preponderantly rural in population, economy, political representation, and ways of life.

In many respects, those country ways of life remained untouched by modernity. The fifty million Americans who dwelt in what F. Scott Fitzgerald called "that vast obscurity beyond the city" still moved between birth and death to the ancient rhythms of sun and season. More than forty-five million of them had no indoor plumbing in 1930, and almost none had electricity. They relieved themselves in chamber pots and outdoor latrines, cooked and heated with wood stoves, and lit their smoky houses with oil lamps. In the roadless Ozark mountains, future Arkansas governor Orval Faubus's mother could not do the family laundry until she had first boiled the guts of a freshly butchered hog to make lye soap. In the isolated Texas Hill Country, future president Lyndon Johnson's mother grew stoop-shouldered lugging buckets of water from well to kitchen. As it had for most of mankind for all of human memory, sunset routinely settled a cloak of darkness and silence over that immense domain where the fields of the republic rolled on under the night. Another Texas Hill Country woman remembered from her girlhood the scary after-dark trips to the outhouse: "I had a horrible choice of either sitting in the dark and not knowing what was crawling on me or bringing a lantern and attracting moths, mosquitoes, nighthawks and bats."[12]

The widening gap between country and city life had helped to fuel the Populist agitation of the late nineteenth century and had prompted

12. Robert A. Caro, *The Years of Lyndon Johnson: The Path to Power* (New York: Knopf, 1982), 513.

Theodore Roosevelt to appoint a Commission on Country Life in 1908. By the 1920s a stubborn agricultural depression, the product of war and technological change, badly exacerbated the problems of the country-side. When the guns of August 1914 announced the outbreak of fighting in Europe, American farmers had scrambled to supply the world's disrupted markets with foodstuffs. They put marginal lands under the plow, and they increased yields from all acreage with more intensive cultivation, aided especially by the advent of the gasoline-engine tractor. The number of motorized farm vehicles quintupled in the war years, to some eighty-five thousand. With the return of peace this trend accelerated. By the end of the 1920s nearly a million farmers chugged along their furrows mounted atop self-propelled tractors. And as tractor-power substituted for horse- and mule-power, some nine million work animals were destroyed, releasing an additional thirty million acres of pastureland for the planting of wheat or cotton or for the grazing of dairy animals.[13]

After the armistice of November 1918, however, world agricultural production returned to its familiar prewar patterns. American farmers found themselves with huge surpluses on their hands. Prices plummeted. Cotton slumped from a wartime high of thirty-five cents per pound to sixteen cents in 1920. Corn sank from $1.50 per bushel to fifty-two cents. Wool slid from nearly sixty cents per pound to less than twenty cents. Although prices improved somewhat after 1921, they did not fully recover until war resumed in 1939. Farmers suffocated under their own mountainous surpluses and under the weight of the debts they had assumed to expand and to mechanize. Foreclosures increased, and more and more freeholders became tenants. The depopulation of the countryside proceeded ever more rapidly.

Congress tried repeatedly to find a remedy for the ills of farmers in the 1920s. As the agricultural depression persisted through the decade, the federal government assumed regulatory control over commodity markets and eventually established a modestly funded federal agency to provide financing for agricultural cooperatives. Congress twice passed, and President Coolidge twice vetoed, the McNary-Haugen Bill. It proposed that the federal government should become the buyer of last resort of surplus farm products, which it should then dispose of—or "dump"—in overseas markets.

Herbert Hoover needed no comprehensive study to know that the farm issue was urgent. Virtually his first act as president, even before he

---

13. *HSUS*, 469; *Recent Social Trends* 1:105.

commissioned his wide-ranging examination of recent social trends, was to convene a special congressional session to resolve the farm crisis. It produced the Agricultural Marketing Act of 1929, which created several government-sponsored "stabilization corporations" authorized to buy surpluses and hold them off the market in order to maintain price levels. But as the agricultural depression of the 1920s merged with the general depression of the 1930s, the corporations quickly exhausted both their storage capacity and their funds. The misery of rural America knew no relief. As the decade of the Great Depression opened, the already reeling farmers would be its hardest-hit victims.

THE SOUTH IN THE 1920s was the nation's most rural region. Not a single southern state met the superintendent of the census's modest definition of "urban" in 1920 — having a majority of its population in cities of twenty-five hundred or more souls. From the Potomac to the Gulf the land looked little different than it had at the end of Reconstruction in the 1870s. Inhabiting a region of scarce capital and abundant labor, southerners planted and picked their traditional crops of cotton, tobacco, rice, or sugarcane with mules and muscle, just as their ancestors had done for generations. And like their forebears, they bled not only against the blade of chronic agricultural depression but also against the uniquely American thorn of race.[14]

The Great War had drawn some half a million blacks out of the rural South and into the factories of the North. With the throttling of immigration in 1924, northern industry needed to find new sources of fresh labor. Southern blacks (as well as some half a million Mexicans, who were exempted from the new immigration quotas) seized the opportunity. By the end of the 1920s another million African-Americans had left the old slave states to take up employment in the Northeast and upper Midwest (only about a hundred thousand blacks dwelt west of the Rockies). There they found jobs in metalworking shops, automobile factories, and packing houses. The political implications of this migration were vividly illustrated in 1928 when Chicago alderman Oscar De Priest, a Republican loyal to the party of the Great Emancipator, became the first black elected to Congress since Reconstruction and the first ever from a northern district.

Yet as late as 1930 more than four out of five American blacks still

14. Jack Temple Kirby, *Rural Worlds Lost: The American South, 1920–1960* (Baton Rouge: Louisiana State University Press, 1987), 49.

lived in the South. There they tortuously made their daily way through what the historian C. Vann Woodward has called an "anthropological museum of Southern folkways," which history knows as the Jim Crow system. Despite its antiquated and grotesquely burdensome character, that system was deeply entrenched in southern life. Indeed, as Woodward notes, it "reached its perfection in the 1930s."[15]

Jim Crow meant, above all, that blacks could not vote. They had been almost universally disfranchised throughout the South in the post-Reconstruction decades. In the eleven states of the former Confederacy, fewer than 5 percent of eligible African-Americans were registered to vote as late as 1940.[16] Jim Crow also meant social and economic segregation. Blacks sat in separate waiting rooms in railroad and bus stations, drank from separate drinking fountains, worshiped in separate churches, and attended strictly segregated and abysmally inferior schools. The South's few industrial jobs were largely barred to them. Southern blacks thus constituted an extreme case of rural poverty in a region that was itself a special case of economic backwardness and isolation from modern life. Hoover's social scientists discovered that infant mortality rates for blacks were nearly double those for whites in 1930 (10 percent and 6 percent respectively) and that blacks had an average life expectancy fifteen years shorter than whites (forty-five years compared with sixty). African-Americans in the South were bound as fast to the land by debt, ignorance, and intimidation as they had been by slavery itself. As for the white folk of the South, declared the eminent southern historian Ulrich B. Phillips in 1928, they shared "a common resolve indomitably maintained—that it shall be and remain a white man's country."[17]

To AMERICANS who were white and lived in the city, blacks were nearly invisible and the complaints of the farmers seemed a distant annoyance, the mewlings of laughably untutored hayseeds as modernity passed them by. Urban sophisticates snickered with approval when H. L. Mencken lampooned the South as the "Sahara of the Bozart." They nodded knowingly when Sinclair Lewis, in books like *Main Street* (1920) and *Babbitt* (1922), satirized the same midwestern small towns

15. C. Vann Woodward, *Thinking Back: The Perils of Writing History* (Baton Rouge: Louisiana State University Press, 1986), 87.

16. Nancy J. Weiss, *Farewell to the Party of Lincoln: Black Politics in the Age of FDR* (Princeton: Princeton University Press, 1983), 21.

17. *Recent Social Trends* 1:584; Ulrich B. Phillips, "The Central Theme of Southern History," *American Historical Review* 34 (1928):31.

from which many of them had fled to the metropolis. They clucked appreciatively when Lewis unmasked the tawdry hypocrisy of rural America's fundamentalist faiths in *Elmer Gantry* (1927). They smirked at the biblical literalism of the "yokels" who swarmed out of the east Tennessee hills in 1925 to gape at the trial of John T. Scopes, indicted for violating Tennessee law by teaching Darwinian evolution to high school students. They smiled with satisfaction when street-smart Chicago attorney Clarence Darrow humiliated rural America's historic paladin, William Jennings Bryan, in the course of that trial.

Bryan's mortification symbolized for many the eclipse of rural fundamentalism and the triumphant ascendancy of the metropolis as the fount and arbiter of modern American values. New national magazines, like *Time*, first published in 1923, Mencken's *American Mercury* in 1924, and the *New Yorker*, whose first issue appeared in 1925, catered to the "caviar sophisticates" and testified to the new cultural power of the great urban centers. Urban America was confident that the city—like Darrow's and Carl Sandburg's Chicago, "stormy, husky, brawling . . . proud to be Hog Butcher, Tool Maker, Stacker of Wheat, Player with Railroads and Freight Handler to the Nation"—was the big-shouldered master to whom rural America must pay tribute.

But to thoughtful observers and policymakers the contrast between country and city life was a matter for neither laughter nor poetry. They worried obsessively about "balance" between rural and urban America, which *Recent Social Trends* called "the central problem" of the economy. Politicians sought interminably for ways to solve it.[18]

The economic disparities between the agricultural and industrial sectors were gaping. Both areas of the economy had grown since the turn of the century, but the urban-based manufacturing sector had expanded far more robustly. While American farmers brought about 50 percent more product to market in 1930 than they had in 1900, manufacturing output had doubled and redoubled again over the same period, to four times its earlier level. Factory workers had achieved remarkable productivity improvements of nearly 50 percent, thanks largely to more efficient means of industrial organization and to the revolutionary introduction of electrically driven machinery on the shop floor. Fully 70 percent of American industry was powered by electricity in 1929, much of it from generating plants fueled by oil from newly developed fields in Texas, Oklahoma, and California. By 1925 a completely assembled Model T

---

18. *Recent Social Trends* 1:xxxi.

Ford rolled off the continuously moving assembly line at Henry Ford's Highland Park plant every ten seconds. Just a dozen years earlier it had taken fourteen hours to put together a single car.[19]

Shrinking export markets, along with the dampening of American population growth after the closure of immigration, spelled stable or even declining demand for American agricultural products. Yet the capacity of Americans to buy ever more industrial goods seemed limitless, as the automobile revolution vividly illustrated. Essentially a cottage industry when the century opened, automobile manufacturing accounted for 10 percent of the nation's income two decades later and employed some four million workers. The motorcar in 1900 had been the plaything of the rich, who purchased some four thousand vehicles. By 1929 ordinary Americans were driving more than twenty-six million motor vehicles, one for every five people in the country. They bought nearly five million vehicles in that year alone, and they paid far less for them than they had a generation earlier.

In a stunning demonstration of the fruitful marriage of innovative technologies to mass markets, the effective price of an automobile fell steeply from the century's opening onward. A car that cost the average worker the equivalent of nearly two years' wages before the First World War could be purchased for about three months' earnings by the late 1920s. This low-price, high-volume marketing strategy was among the miracles of mass production — or "Fordism," as it was sometimes called in honor of its most famous pioneer. Largely an American invention, the technique of mass-producing standardized products was in a sense an American inevitability, as, in its time, would be the revolution in consumer electronics: a means to tap the economic potential of a democratic society whose wealth was nearly as widely diffused as its formal political power.

Yet even this fabulously successful strategy had limits. Mass production made mass consumption a necessity. But as Hoover's investigators discovered, the increasing wealth of the 1920s flowed disproportionately to the owners of capital. Workers' incomes were rising, but not at a rate that kept pace with the nation's growing industrial output. Without broadly distributed purchasing power, the engines of mass production would have no outlet and would eventually fall idle. The automobile industry, where Fordism had begun, was among the first to sense the

19. William E. Leuchtenburg, *The Perils of Prosperity* (Chicago: University of Chicago Press, 1958), 179.

force of this logic. A spokesman for General Motors Corporation acknowledged in 1926 that

> while the industry has been subject to an unusually rapid rate of ex-
> pansion in the past, the volume has now reached such large propor-
> tions that it seems altogether unlikely that tremendous annual in-
> creases will continue. The expectation is rather for a healthy growth,
> in line with the increase in population and wealth of the country, and
> the development of the export market.[20]

Here was among the first recognitions that even a youthful industry
like automobile manufacturing might rapidly grow to "maturity." The
carmakers had apparently saturated available domestic markets. The introduction of consumer credit, or "installment buying," pioneered at
General Motors in 1919 with the creation of the General Motors Acceptance Corporation, constituted one attempt to stretch those markets
still further by relieving buyers of the need to pay full cash for cars at
the moment of sale. The explosive growth of advertising, an infant industry before the 1920s, provided further sign of the fear that the limits
of "natural" demand were being reached. General Motors alone annually spent some $20 million on advertising in the 1920s in an effort
to nurture consumer desires that transcended consumer needs. Together, credit and advertising sustained automobile sales for a time, but
without new foreign outlets or a significant redistribution of domestic
purchasing power—especially to the impoverished rural half of the
country—the boundaries of consumer demand were apparently being
approached.

Yet in the pulsing industrial cities, virtually all Americans dramatically
improved their standards of living over the course of the post–World
War I decade. While farmers' living standards eroded through the 1920s,
real wages for industrial workers rose by nearly 25 percent. By 1928
average per capita income among nonagricultural employees had
reached four times the average level of farmers' incomes. For urban
workers, prosperity was wondrous and real. They had more money than
ever before, and they enjoyed an amazing variety of new products on
which to spend it: not only automobiles but also canned foods, washing
machines, refrigerators, synthetic fabrics, telephones, motion pictures

20. Albert Bradley, "Setting Up a Forecasting Program," *Annual Convention Series*,
American Management Association, no. 41 (March 1926), quoted in Alfred D.
Chandler Jr., *Giant Enterprise: Ford, General Motors, and the Automobile Industry*
(New York: Harcourt, Brace and World, 1964), 132.

(with sound after 1927), and—along with the automobile the most revolutionary of the new technologies—radios. In the unelectrified countryside, of course, many of these modern conveniences were nowhere to be found.

THE AUTHORS OF *Recent Social Trends* found that thirty-eight million male and ten million female workers produced and distributed this abundance of goods in 1930. Agricultural laborers had constituted the largest category of employment as recently as 1910, but by 1920 the number of workers in manufacturing and mechanical industries eclipsed the number in farming. The workweek of the typical nonfarm employee had shortened since the turn of the century, but the regimen of virtually continuous labor long familiar on the farm had been imported onto the factory floor in the earliest days of industrialization and had only slowly relaxed. Not until 1923 did United States Steel Corporation grudgingly abandon the twelve-hour day, its grinding human damage made worse by the periodic "turnover" of the night and day gangs, when the men were required to stand a continuous twenty-four-hour shift. Most industrial workers in 1930 put in forty-eight hours a week. The two-day "weekend" was not yet a fixture of American life, and paid vacations for workers were almost unknown. "Retirement," too, was still an elusive fantasy for the average American worker, whose days of toil extended virtually to the end of the life cycle.[21]

The very forces that increased productivity and benefited consumers also carried some implications that deeply troubled Hoover's experts. The most serious issue, they explained, stemmed from "the widespread introduction of machinery [which] is having the general effect of replacing skilled with semi-skilled and unskilled labor and is thus reducing the status of the trained and skilled worker, if, in fact, it is not tending to eliminate him entirely from many industries." Machine power presented a paradox. It offered employment to large numbers of the unskilled, which was why millions of European peasants and American farmers migrated to the cities in search of industrial jobs and the chance for a better life. At the same time, it commodified labor and volatilized it, robbing workers of craft pride and, most important, of job security. What was more, the longer-term effect of increased mechanization might be the disappearance of some jobs altogether. The irregularity of employment patterns in the technologically innovative mass-production industries was especially worrisome. Somewhat surprisingly, given the

21. *Recent Social Trends* 2:829, 1:277.

decade's reputation, the annual rate of unemployment in those sectors exceeded 10 percent at the height of "Coolidge prosperity" from 1923 to 1928. Few features of the emerging industrial economy were more potentially troublesome.[22]

The Lynds' study of Muncie detailed the complex personal and social implications of those employment patterns. The principal factor that distinguished the "working class" from the "business class," they found, was insecurity of employment with its consequent disturbance in the rhythms of life. The business class, they noted, "are virtually never subject to interruptions of this kind," while among the working class "the 'shut-down' or 'lay-off' is a recurrent phenomenon." Indeed, they suggested that interruption in employment, even more than occupational category or income, was the chief defining characteristic for membership in the social group they called "working class." Those members of the community who enjoyed a measure of job security were not, virtually by definition, "the workers." They had careers, not jobs. Their very conception of time was different, as were their life chances. They planned with confidence for their futures and for their children's futures. They took annual vacations. They aspired to a better way of life. They also built and sustained the elaborate network of organizations—the Rotary Club, the PTA, the Chamber of Commerce, the Women's Club, and, not least, the political parties—that bound the community together and gave it organic life. From much of that activity the workers were excluded, less by active discrimination than by the simple but cruel forces of circumstance.[23]

Workers without job security lived in what the Lynds called "a world in which neither present nor future appears to hold . . . much prospect" of job advancement or social mobility. They worked feverishly when times were good, when the mills were roaring and the forges hot, in order to lay something away against the inevitable moment when times would turn bad, when the factory gates would swing shut and the furnaces be banked. The unpredictable perturbations in their lives constantly disrupted relations among family members and left little oppor-

22. Reliable government statistics on unemployment were not compiled in the 1920s. *Recent Social Trends* 2:806–8 cites Paul Douglas' estimates that unemployment ran at about 9 percent from 1923 to 1926. Considerably higher estimates, ranging from 10 percent to 13 percent between 1924 and 1929, are cited in Irving Bernstein, *The Lean Years: A History of the American Worker, 1920–1933* (Boston: Houghton Mifflin, 1960), 59.

23. Lynd and Lynd, *Middletown*, 55–56.

tunity for social or civic involvement, or even for trade union organization. This precarious, disconnected, socially thin, pervasively insecure way of life was the lot of millions of Americans in the 1920s. They had a periodic taste of prosperity but precious little power over their conditions of work or the trajectories of their lives.[24]

Few employers, no state, and surely not the federal government provided any form of insurance to cushion the blows of unemployment. As late as 1929 the American Federation of Labor (AFL) remained in agreement with employers in adamantly opposing government unemployment insurance, already an established practice in many European countries. Samuel Gompers, the AFL's longtime leader who died in 1924, had repeatedly denounced unemployment insurance as a "socialist" idea and therefore inadmissable in the United States. His successors perpetuated that philosophy right down to the eve of the Great Depression. The rigidity of the AFL's leadership, combined with the hostility of most employers and the general prosperity of the decade, remorselessly thinned the ranks of organized labor. Trade union membership steadily declined from its wartime high of some five million to less than three and a half million by 1929.

The AFL itself deserved some of the blame for this shrinkage. Embittered by a long history of government interventions on the side of management, Gompers preached the philosophy of "voluntarism." In his view, labor should shun government assistance and depend only on its own resources to wring concessions from employers. Unfortunately, those resources were painfully meager. Their value, in fact, was diminishing, as unskilled workers relentlessly displaced the skilled craftsmen whose craft-based guilds composed the AFL. Unskilled laborers were heavily concentrated in the behemoth mass-production industries like steel and automobiles that increasingly dominated the American economy. The health of the union movement depended on organizing them according to the principles of "industrial unionism," which gathered all the workers in an industry into a single union. But that strategy clashed headlong with the elitist and exclusionary organizational doctrines of the AFL, which grouped workers according to skills—as machinists, carpenters, or sheet-metal workers, for example.

Fancying themselves as labor's aristocracy, craft unionists ignored the problems of their unskilled co-workers. Ethnic rivalries exacerbated the troubles in the house of labor. Skilled workers tended to be old-stock,

24. Lynd and Lynd, *Middletown*, 80.

native-born white Americans, while the unskilled were mostly recent urban immigrants from the hinterlands of Europe and rural America. The AFL, in thus insulating itself from the men and women who were fast becoming the majority of industrial workers, handed management a potent antilabor weapon. Management knew how to use it. U.S. Steel cynically exploited the ethnic divisions that were the bane of American unionism when the AFL in 1919 hesitantly abandoned its traditionally elitist attitudes and led a strike to organize an industrial union in steel. The corporation sent agents into the steel districts around Chicago and Pittsburgh to spawn animosity between native and immigrant workers. They excited the strikers' darkest anxieties by recruiting some thirty thousand southern blacks, hungry to possess previously forbidden jobs, to cross the picket lines. On these rocks of racial and ethnic distrust, the great steel strike of 1919 foundered miserably. Following its catastrophic failure, the American Federation of Labor retreated to its historic exclusiveness and largely left unskilled workers to fend for themselves.

Manipulating ethnic and racial fears was only one among the several tools that management used to suppress workers' organizations. The most fearsome of those tools was the "yellow-dog" contract, which bound individual workers, as a condition of employment, never to join a union. Employers also relied upon friendly judges to issue injunctions prohibiting strikes, picketing, the payment of strike benefits, and even communication between organizers and workers. "[T]he marriage of the labor injunction with the yellow-dog contract," says labor historian Irving Bernstein, "was a peril to the survival of trade unionism in the United States. The Supreme Court had officiated at the wedding in 1917 in the case of *Hitchman Coal & Coke Co. v. Mitchell.*" The Hitchman doctrine made yellow-dog contracts enforceable at law. In effect, it rendered illegal almost any effort to organize a union without the employer's consent. Employers seized on this legal instrument with a vengeance in the 1920s. Fully half of the labor injunctions recorded in the half century after 1880 were issued in that single decade. This judicial animosity spawned frustration and outrage among workers. "The growing bitterness of organized labor toward the federal courts," declared conservative Pennsylvania senator George Wharton Pepper in 1924, threatened "revolutionary" results. Congress at last provided some relief in the Norris–La Guardia Anti-Injunction Act of 1932, which forbade federal courts from issuing injunctions to enforce yellow-dog contracts. But even as he signed the bill, Herbert Hoover instructed his attorney general to declare that its provisions "are of such a controversial nature that they . . . can only be set at rest by judicial decision." Pepper's warning about labor's restiveness thus resounded loudly into the Depression decade. In 1937 it would shake the very pillars of the Supreme Court.[25]

The organized labor movement was also being killed by kindness. The precepts of "welfare capitalism" found increasing favor with personnel managers who adopted the industrial management techniques promulgated earlier in the century by Frederick Winslow Taylor. Some corporations, typically large and antiunion, sought simultaneously to win the loyalty of their workers and to defang union organizers. They set up "company unions" and offered stock bonuses and profit-sharing plans, as well as life insurance, recreational facilities, and even old-age pensions. It was among the precepts of welfare capitalism, however, that control of all these programs remained tightly in the hands of their corporate sponsor, who could modify or terminate them at will. When the Crash came, the transient generosity of employers was starkly revealed as a shabby substitute for the genuine power of collective bargaining that only an independent union could wield—or for the entitled benefits that only the federal government could confer.

THE TEN MILLION WOMEN who worked for wages in 1929 were concentrated in a small handful of occupations including teaching, clerical work, domestic service, and the garment trades. As the service sector of the economy had expanded, so had women's presence in the labor force. Women made up about 18 percent of all workers in 1900 and 22 percent in 1930, when about one of every four women was gainfully employed. The typical woman worker was single and under the age of twenty-five. Once she married, as almost every woman did, typically before the age of twenty-two, she was unlikely to work again for wages, particularly while she had children at home. Only one mother in ten worked outside the household, and the numbers of older women workers, with or without children, were few. Even in this late phase of the industrial era, the traditional division of family labor that the industrial revolution had introduced a century earlier—a husband working for wages outside the home, and a wife working without wages within it— still held powerful sway in American culture.[26]

25. Bernstein, *Lean Years*, 196, 201, 414. For the full text of the *Hitchman* decision, see 245 U.S. 229 (1917).
26. *Recent Social Trends* 1:277. See also Alice Kessler-Harris, *Out to Work: A History of Wage-Earning Women in the United States* (New York: Oxford University Press, 1982), esp. chap. 8.

Yet traditional definitions of the family, and of women's place within it, were weakening. Married women might remain a distinct minority of all women workers, but their numbers were increasing at a rate nearly triple the rate of growth in female employment as a whole. Here, well before the century's midpoint, the dynamic changes in women's employment patterns that would transform the very fabric of family life by the century's end were already visible, however faintly.[27]

Other evidences of changes in women's status were more immediately apparent. The legendary "flapper" made her debut in the postwar decade, signaling with studied theatrical flourishes a new ethos of feminine freedom and sexual parity. The Nineteenth Amendment, enacted just in time for the 1920 presidential election, gave women at least formal political equality. The Equal Rights Amendment, first proposed by Alice Paul of the National Women's Party in 1923, sought to guarantee full social and economic participation to women. An organized movement for the promotion of birth control, founded by Margaret Sanger in 1921 as the American Birth Control League, heralded a growing feminine focus on reproductive control and erotic liberation. Countless women, especially if they were urban, white, and affluent, now used the new technologies of spermicidal jelly and the Mensinga-type diaphragm, both first manufactured in quantity in the United States in the 1920s, to limit the size of their families. This development worried the authors of *Recent Social Trends*, who feared that the old-stock, white, urban middle class would be demographically swamped by the proliferation of the rural and immigrant poor, as well as blacks.

Many of these developments unsettled the guardians of traditional values, but others they found pleasing. The exploitation of child labor, a practice that had outraged critics from Charles Dickens in Victorian England to Jane Addams in early twentieth-century America, had slowly receded as rising wages enabled a single wage-earner to support a family. While almost one in five ten- to-fifteen-year-olds was employed in 1890, fewer than one in twenty was in 1930, though the Supreme Court repeatedly struck down federal efforts to legislate a total ban on child labor.[28]

27. *Recent Social Trends* 1:666. See also Kessler-Harris, *Out to Work*, 229.
28. *Recent Social Trends* 1:271ff. The Keating-Owen Child Labor Act of 1916 had been invalidated by the Supreme Court in 1918 in the case of *Hammer v. Dagenhart* (247 U.S. 251), on the grounds that the act illegitimately relied on the commerce power to regulate local labor conditions. Four years later the Court threw out a second child labor act on similar grounds, in *Bailey v. Drexel Furniture* (259 U.S. (20).

Fewer children working meant more children in school. The authors of *Recent Social Trends* saw grounds for celebration in their finding that in the 1920s, for the first time, a near majority of high school–age students remained in school—constituting an eightfold increase in high school enrollments since 1900. This, they concluded, was "evidence of the most successful single effort which government in the United States has ever put forth."[29]

THE EDUCATIONAL SUCCESSES of the decade were as costly as they were dramatic. Virtually all of that cost was borne by the states, as were most of the expenditures for improved roads on which to drive all those new automobiles. As a consequence, the indebtedness of the states increased sharply in the 1920s, in many cases rising to formal ceilings defined by legislation or to practical ceilings imposed by the credit markets. State and local taxes also rose steeply, far outpacing the rate of growth of personal income. By 1929 government at all levels collected in taxes a share of the national income twice as large as in 1914. Americans were devoting a growing share of their wealth not just to private consumption but to collective purposes—and many of them resented it. Though the 15 percent of the value of gross national product that went to taxes in 1929 looked puny by later standards, it represented a historically unprecedented tax bite and was beginning to provoke a political backlash. The rising cry for "balanced budgets" and for restraints on government spending arose not only from the musty vaults of fiscal orthodoxy but at least as loudly from the throats of citizens whose tax bills had doubled in little more than a decade.[30]

The federal government had also vastly increased its tax levies, though most of that new revenue went not to pay for new social infrastructure like education and roads but to service the debt incurred while fighting the World War. To a later generation the debt created by the war might seem trifling, but to contemporaries it was enormous—some $24 billion, or ten times the indebtedness generated by the Civil War. Interest payments on the national debt rose from an insignificant level of about $25 million annually before 1914 to the largest single government

---

These cases symbolized the social and economic conservatism on the Court that so outraged reformers from Theodore Roosevelt to Franklin Roosevelt, whose frustration finally erupted in the notorious "Court-packing" proposal of 1937 (see Chapter 11).

29. *Recent Social Trends* 1:xlvii.
30. *Recent Social Trends* 2:1333–39.

expenditure in the 1920s: nearly a billion dollars a year, or a third of the federal budget.

Together with expenditures for veterans' benefits, another obligation that mushroomed because of the war, interest payments composed more than half the federal budget through the postwar decade. Expenses for a modest army of some 139,000 men and a navy of about 96,000 sailors accounted for virtually all the remainder. Beyond these items, all of them related to national security, the federal government spent and did little. Calvin Coolidge thus spoke with small exaggeration when he said: "If the Federal Government should go out of existence, the common run of people would not detect the difference in the affairs of their daily life for a considerable length of time." So negligible was the role of the federal government in their lives that a majority of citizens did not even bother to vote in presidential elections. For the first time since the emergence of mass-based democratic politics in the age of Andrew Jackson, electoral participation rates fell below 50 percent in the election of 1920; they sank still further in 1924. Some observers attributed this precipitous drop-off to the recent enfranchisement of women, who were largely unfamiliar with the ballot and perhaps justifiably indifferent to a national political apparatus that was in turn indifferent to their particular political interests. Others pointed to the apparent political apathy of immigrants, many of whom had not yet made a permanent commitment to remaining in the United States. But women and immigrants may have only been special cases of a general unconcern in American culture for the federal government, which remained a distant, dim, and motionless body in the political firmament.[31]

Since the election of William McKinley in 1896, with the singular interruption of Woodrow Wilson's presidency from 1913 to 1921, the federal government had been securely in the hands of the Republican Party. Grover Cleveland, president from 1885 to 1889 and again from 1893 to 1897, was the only other Democrat besides Wilson to have occupied the White House since before the Civil War. For generations after Appomattox, the Democrats had retained much of the character of a purely regional party, with the "solid South" their only sure electoral base. They struggled to win presidential elections, with only fitful success, by adding to this core of support what votes they could muster from immigrant communities in northeastern cities like Boston and New York. Occasionally, too, they could count on support in the "But-

31. Coolidge quoted in Schlesinger 1:57.

ternut" regions of the Illinois-Indiana-Ohio tier of states populated largely by white migrants from the Old South and still very much southern in temperament and political preference.

Democrats, strong in the cotton region, generally agreed on a low-tariff policy but on little else. Hard-money "Bourbon" Democrats in the Grover Cleveland mold clashed with inflationists whose perennial champion was William Jennings Bryan, "Boy Orator of the Platte," the "Great Commoner" whose affected rusticity symbolized the economic and cultural gulf that separated Main Street from Wall Street. Self-made men like James Michael Curley of Boston or Al Smith and Robert Wagner of New York, champions of labor who had scrambled up out of immigrant ghettoes like Roxbury or Hell's Kitchen, sat uneasily in party councils with cotton-South barons like Mississippi's Senator Pat Harrison or rural Texans like John Nance Garner, men who saw in cheap, nonunion labor their region's major economic resource. Cerebral reformers like Harvard law professor Felix Frankfurter barely coexisted in the same party with antic populist demagogues like Louisiana's Huey Long. Cultural differences, too, cleaved the party along the lines that separated Catholics and Jews from old-stock Protestants, divided anti-Prohibition "wets" from fundamentalist "drys," and distanced urban immigrants from rural Klansmen. These conflicting forces had locked in such irreconcilable conflict at the Democrats' presidential nominating convention of 1924 in New York that only after 103 ballots did the weary and sweltering delegates settle on a compromise ticket. It had corporation lawyer John W. Davis at its head and Nebraska governor Charles W. Bryan, brother of the Great Commoner, in the vice-presidential slot. Davis's crushing defeat by Calvin Coolidge seemed to confirm the suspicions of many pundits that the roiling, fractionated mob known as the Democratic Party could never be fashioned into a coherent instrument of governance. "I don't belong to an organized political party," quipped America's favorite humorist, Will Rogers. "I'm a Democrat."

Hoover's decisive victory over Al Smith in 1928 clinched the point. Smith was not merely defeated. He was humiliated, the victim of an electoral mortification that may have contributed to his later political transmutation from working-class hero to embittered foe of the New Deal. Following a campaign notoriously marred by religious bigotry against the Catholic Smith, Hoover swept to one of the most decisive victories in the history of American presidential elections. He even cracked the solid South, winning five former Confederate states. Smith took Massachusetts, Rhode Island, and the tier of six "black belt" states—South Carolina, Georgia, Alabama, Mississippi, Arkansas, and Louisiana—that held to their traditional Democratic allegiance. That was all. The remainder of the country thunderously rejected a candidate who was not only Catholic but a "wet" foe of Prohibition as well as a rasping symbol of the urban, immigrant culture that America was still not ready to recognize as its own. Democrats took what comfort they could from the fact that Smith cobbled together a majority of votes in the dozen biggest cities—foreshadowing the urban-based coalition that the New Deal would fully forge in the next decade.[32]

The Republican Party, then as always, was more economically and ethnically homogenous than the Democratic Party, but it too, in the manner of mass-based, "catch-all" American parties, contained its own conflicting elements. Under Theodore Roosevelt's leadership in the century's first decade, the Republicans had bid for a brief season to recapture their birthright claim to be the party of reform. But TR had shepherded his progressive followers out of the Republican fold and into the third-party "Bull Moose" schism of 1912. He thereby ensured the election of Wilson and contributed as well to the consolidation of conservative rule in the GOP. Some former Bull Moosers, like Chicago reformer and future New Deal secretary of the interior Harold Ickes, became Democrats in all but name; others, like Nebraska's Senator George Norris, were relegated to an impotent minority in party councils during the triumphal conservative ascendancy of the 1920s.

The progressives of Theodore Roosevelt's day were a varied lot, and some of their disagreements would reverberate, often loudly, right through the New Deal. But they shared a commitment, as Walter Lippmann had said, to substitute mastery for drift, or, as Hoover might have put it, social planning for laissez-faire: a commitment, in short, to use government as an agency of human welfare. Progressives of all persuasions believed that government must somehow superintend the phenomenal economic and social power that modern industrialism was concen-

32. Samuel Lubell, *The Future of American Politics* (New York: Harper and Row, 1952), first made the argument that "before the Roosevelt Revolution there was an Al Smith Revolution," one that began the process of gathering into a durable electoral majority the urban ethnic voters who sustained the New Deal and the Democratic Party well into the post–World War II period. That view has been sharply challenged by Allan J. Lichtman, *Prejudice and the Old Politics* (Chapel Hill: University of North Carolina Press, 1979), which concludes that Smith's urban majorities were paper thin and that it was not, therefore, the events of the 1920s but the catastrophe of the Depression that truly realigned American political behavior.

trating into fewer and fewer hands. No longer could the public interest simply be assumed to flow naturally from the competition of myriad private interests. Active governmental guidance was required.

The conservative Republicans who recaptured the Congress in 1918 and the White House in 1920 had small use for any form of government activism. The Republican administrations of the 1920s abandoned or reversed many progressive policies and eviscerated most others. Harding's attorney general, Harry M. Daugherty, extinguished a railroad workers' strike in 1922 by successfully petitioning a federal judge for the most stifling antilabor injunction ever issued. In the same year, Congress reverted to traditional Republican protectionism, as the Fordney-McCumber Tariff raised import duties to the forbidding levels that obtained before the World War. Coolidge appointed to the chairmanship of the Federal Trade Commission in 1925 a man who believed the commission was "an instrument of oppression and disturbance and injury," a statement that only slightly exaggerated conservative opinion about all regulatory agencies. Both the Harding and Coolidge administrations resisted progressive proposals for federal development of hydroelectric generating stations on the Tennessee River, notably at Muscle Shoals, Alabama. And Harding's minions displayed their rapacious regard for the nation's environmental endowment in the Teapot Dome and Elk Hills scandals, when they tried to lease the U.S. Navy's oil reserves in Wyoming and California to private interests with which they were associated.[33]

No one better represented the hoary precepts of laissez-faire that were now reenshrined in policy than the unfortunate Harding's phlegmatic successor, Calvin Coolidge. "Mr. Coolidge was a real conservative, probably the equal of Benjamin Harrison," said Herbert Hoover, who was frequently at odds with his chief. "He was a fundamentalist in religion, in the economic and social order, and in fishing," added Hoover, who had a fly fisherman's disdain for Coolidge's artless reliance on worms. Famously mum, Coolidge occasionally emitted pithy slogans that summarized conservative Republican orthodoxy. "The chief business of the American people is business," he legendarily pronounced in 1925. He declared only somewhat more expansively on another occasion that "the man who builds a factory builds a temple; the man who works there worships there."[34]

33. William E. Humphrey quoted in Schlesinger 1:65.
34. Hoover, *Memoirs: The Cabinet and the Presidency*, 56; Coolidge quoted in Schlesinger 1:57.

Coolidge's epigrams faithfully reflected the principles of frugality and laissez-faire that informed federal policies in the 1920s. The few, frail organs of the positive state spawned by the prewar progressives withered from inanition. Coolidge personally quashed Herbert Hoover's ambitious plans for federally financed river-control projects, especially in the parched West, because he deemed them too expensive. On similar grounds, he vetoed proposals for farm relief and for accelerated "bonus" payments to veterans of the World War. He resisted all efforts to restructure the $10 billion in Allied war debts owed to the U.S. Treasury. ("They hired the money, didn't they?" he declared in another pellet of policy summary.) Content with "Coolidge prosperity," he napped peacefully and often. He played pranks on the White House servants. He stayed silent. ("If you don't say anything, you won't be called on to repeat it," he reportedly said.) He believed, Hoover later recounted, that nine out of ten troubles "will run into the ditch before they reach you" and could therefore be safely ignored. "The trouble with this philosophy," Hoover commented, "was that when the tenth trouble reached him he was wholly unprepared, and it had by that time acquired such momentum that it spelled disaster. The outstanding instance was the rising boom and orgy of mad speculation which began in 1927, in respect to which he rejected or sidestepped all our anxious urgings and warnings to take action." For his part, Coolidge said of Hoover in 1928: "That man has offered me unsolicited advice for six years, all of it bad."[35]

Fortune smiled on the recumbent Coolidge until he made his somnambulatory exit from the White House in early 1929. (A wit allegedly greeted the news that Coolidge was dead in 1933 by asking: "How can you tell?") "In the domestic field there is tranquility and contentment," he serenely informed the Congress in his last State of the Union message on December 4, 1928. The country should "regard the present with satisfaction and anticipate the future with optimism."[36]

PROSPERITY LASTED long enough for Coolidge to sound plausible in 1928. But deep down in the bowels of the economy, small but fateful contractions had already set in. The agonies of agriculture had long been apparent. Now other sectors began to feel similar pain. Automobile manufacturing slowed its prodigious rate of growth as early as

35. Hoover, *Memoirs: The Cabinet and the Presidency*, 56; Wilson, *Herbert Hoover*, 122.
36. Quoted in John Kenneth Galbraith, *The Great Crash* (Boston: Houghton Mifflin, 1955), 6.

1925. Residential construction turned down in the same year. A boom in Florida real estate drowned in a devastating hurricane in September 1926. Bank clearings in Miami sank from over a billion dollars in 1925 to $143 million in 1928, a chilling adumbration of the financial clotting that would soon choke the entire banking system. Business inventories began to pile up in 1928, nearly quadrupling in value to some $2 billion by midsummer of 1929.[37]

Most ominous of all was what Hoover bluntly labeled the "orgy of mad speculation" that beset the stock market beginning in 1927. Theory has it that the bond and equity markets reflect and even anticipate the underlying realities of making and marketing goods and services, but by 1928 the American stock markets had slipped the bonds of surly reality. They catapulted into a phantasmagorical realm where the laws of rational economic behavior went unpromulgated and prices had no discernible relation to values. While business activity steadily subsided, stock prices levitated giddily. By the end of 1928, John Kenneth Galbraith later wrote, "the market began to rise, not by slow, steady steps, but by great vaulting leaps." Radio Corporation's stock, symbolic of the promise of new technologies that helped to feed the speculative frenzy, gyrated upward in ten- and twenty-point jumps. By the summer of 1929, Frederick Lewis Allen recorded, even as unsold inventories accumulated in warehouses, stock prices "soared . . . into the blue and cloudless empyrean."[38]

Money to fuel the skyrocketing stock market flowed from countless spigots. It flowed so copiously, according to Galbraith, that "it seemed as though Wall Street were by way of devouring all the money of the entire world." Some of the money flowed directly from the pocketbooks of individual investors, though their resources were generally meager and their numbers surprisingly few. More money poured from big corporations. Their healthy profits in the 1920s endowed them with lavish cash reserves, a good share of which they began to divert from productive investment in plant and machinery to stock market speculation. Still more money came from the banking system. It, too, was flush with funds that found fewer and fewer traditional outlets. By 1929 commercial bankers were in the unusual position of loaning more money for stock market and real estate investments than for commercial ventures. The Federal Reserve Board flooded the banks with more liquidity in 1927 by

37. Frederick Lewis Allen, *Only Yesterday* (New York: Harper and Brothers, 1931), 282.
38. Galbraith, *Great Crash*, 17; Allen, *Only Yesterday*, 309.

lowering its rediscount rate to 3.5 percent and undertaking heavy purchases of government securities.[39]

This easy-money policy was due largely to the influence of Benjamin Strong, the stern and influential governor of the New York Federal Reserve Bank. Strong's policy was meant to support the imprudent decision Chancellor of the Exchequer Winston Churchill had made in 1925 to return Britain to the prewar gold standard at the old exchange rate of $4.86 to the pound. That unrealistically high rate crimped British exports, boomed imports, and threatened to drain the Bank of England of its gold reserves. Strong reasoned, not incorrectly, that lower interest rates and cheaper money in America would stanch the hemorrhage of gold from London to New York, thus stabilizing an international financial system that was still precariously recovering from the strains of the World War. The same policies, of course, facilitated vast speculative borrowing in the United States. It was that disastrous consequence that prompted Herbert Hoover's contemptuous description of Strong as "a mental annex to Europe"—a remark that also hinted at Hoover's conception of where the blame for the ensuing depression should be laid.

Significantly, much of the money lent by banks for stock purchases went not directly into stocks but into brokers' call loans. Call loans enabled purchasers to buy stocks on margin, leveraging a cash payment (sometimes as little as 10 percent, but more typically 45 or 50 percent, of the stock's price) with a loan secured by the value of the stock purchased. The lender could theoretically "call" for repayment if the stock price dropped by an amount equal to its collateral value. Though some of the larger brokerage houses shunned the call-loan device, most made profligate use of it. The practice became so popular that brokers at the height of the boom could charge prodigious interest rates on their stock-secured loans to customers. Thanks to the Federal Reserve System's low rediscount rate, member banks could and did borrow federal funds at 3.5 percent and relend them in the call market for 10 percent and more. When the demand for call loans overwhelmed even the abundantly liquid resources of the banking system, corporations stepped in. They accounted for roughly half the call-loan monies in 1929. Standard Oil

---

39. Galbraith, *Great Crash*, 73. The composition of banks' loan portfolios had changed significantly in the 1920s. In 1913 commercial banks placed 53 percent of their loans in commercial ventures, 33 percent in securities, and 14 percent in real estate. By 1929 those figures were respectively 45, 38, and 17 percent. Susan Estabrook Kennedy, *The Banking Crisis of 1933* (Lexington: University Press of Kentucky, 1973), 13.

of New Jersey was then loaning some $69 million a day; Electric Bond and Share, over $100 million.[40]

All of this extravagantly available credit did not in itself cause the boom, just as fuel alone does not make a fire. Combustion in the financial world, no less than in the physical, requires not only fuel but also oxygen and ignition. No observer has succeeded in pinpointing the spark that set off the roaring conflagration that swept and eventually consumed the securities markets in 1928 and 1929. Clearly, however, its sustaining oxygen was a matter not only of recondite market mechanisms and traders' technicalities but also of simple atmospherics — specifically, the mood of speculative expectation that hung feverishly in the air and induced fantasies of effortless wealth that surpassed the dreams of avarice.

Much blame has been leveled at a feckless Federal Reserve System for failing to tighten credit as the speculative fires spread, but while it is arguable that the easy-money policies of 1927 helped to kindle the blaze, the fact is that by late 1928 it had probably burned beyond controlling by orthodox financial measures. The Federal Reserve Board justifiably hesitated to raise its rediscount rate for fear of penalizing nonspeculative business borrowers. When it did impose a 6 percent rediscount rate in the late summer of 1929, call loans were commanding interest of close to 20 percent — a spread that the Fed could not have bridged without catastrophic damage to legitimate borrowers. Similarly, the board had early exhausted its already meager ability to soak up funds through open-market sales of government securities. By the end of 1928, the system's inventory of such securities barely exceeded $200 million — a pittance compared to the nearly $8 billion in call loans then outstanding. By ordinary measures, in fact, credit was tight after 1928. Mere money was not at the root of the evil soon to befall Wall Street; men were — men, and women, whose lust for the fast buck had loosed all restraints of financial prudence or even common sense.

The first rumbles of distress were heard in September 1929, when stock prices broke unexpectedly, though they swiftly recovered. Then on Wednesday, October 23, came an avalanche of liquidation. A huge volume of more than six million shares changed hands, wiping out some $4 billion in paper values. Confusion spread as the telegraphic ticker that flashed transactions to traders across the country fell nearly two hours behind.

40. Galbraith, *Great Crash*, 36.

In this atmosphere of anxiety and uncertainty, the market opened on "Black Thursday," October 24, with a landslide of sell orders. A record-shattering 12,894,650 shares were traded. By noon, losses had reached some $9 billion. The ticker ran four hours late. Yet when it clacked off the day's last transaction at 7:08 in the evening, it appeared that a small recovery in prices had contained the session's losses to about a third of the previous day's.

If Thursday was black, what could be said of the following Tuesday, October 29, when 16,410,000 shares were bought and sold—a record that stood for thirty-nine years? "Black Tuesday" pulled down a cloak of gloom over Wall Street. Traders abandoned all hope that the frightful shake-out could somehow be averted. For two more ghastly weeks stock prices continued to plummet freely down the same celestial voids through which they had recently and so wondrously ascended. The stark truth was now revealed that leverage worked two ways. The multiplication of values that buying on margin made possible in a rising market worked with impartial and fearful symmetry when values were on the way down. Slippage of even a few points in a stock's price compelled margin loans to be called. The borrower then had to put up more cash or accept forced sale of the security. Millions of such sales occurring simultaneously blew the floor out from under many stocks. The mercilessly downward slide went on for three weeks after Black Tuesday. By mid-November some $26 billion, roughly a third of the value of stocks recorded in September, had evaporated.[41]

Much mythology surrounds these dramatic events in the autumn of 1929. Perhaps the most imperishable misconception portrays the Crash as the cause of the Great Depression that persisted through the decade of the 1930s. This scenario owes its durability, no doubt, to its intuitive plausibility and to its convenient fit with the canons of narrative, which require historical accounts to have recognizable beginnings, middles, and ends and to explain events in terms of identifiable origins, development, and resolution. These conventions are comforting; they render understandable and thus tolerable even the most terrifying human experiences. The storyteller and the shaman sometimes feed the same psychic needs.

---

41. Colorful accounts of the stock market crash of 1929 can be found in Allen's *Only Yesterday* and Galbraith's *Great Crash*. Somewhat more reliable are Robert Sobel's *The Great Bull Market: Wall Street in the 1920s* (New York: Norton, 1968) and *Panic on Wall Street* (New York: Macmillan, 1968).

The disagreeable truth, however, is that the most responsible students of the events of 1929 have been unable to demonstrate an appreciable cause-and-effect linkage between the Crash and the Depression. None assigns to the stock market collapse exclusive responsibility for what followed; most deny it primacy among the many and tangled causes of the decade-long economic slump; some assert that it played virtually no role whatsoever. One authority states flatly and summarily that "no causal relationship between the events of late October 1929 and the Great Depression has ever been shown through the use of empirical evidence."[42]

Certainly contemporaries took this view of the matter in the immediate aftermath of the Crash, as 1929 gave way to 1930. They could scarcely do otherwise, since in point of fact there was as yet no evident depression, "Great" or otherwise, to be explained. Some writers later made much sport of Herbert Hoover for pronouncing on October 25, 1929, that "the fundamental business of the country, that is, production and distribution of commodities, is on a sound and prosperous basis."[43] Yet in retrospect that statement appears reasonably and responsibly accurate. To be sure, a business slowdown was detectable by midsummer 1929, but as yet there was little reason to consider it anything more than a normal dip in the business cycle.

What was clearly abnormal was the explosive near doubling of stock prices since 1928. Hoover had long warned against speculative excesses and could now credibly regard the Crash as the long-predicted correction, one that would at last purge the economic system of unhealthy toxins. In this view he had abundant company, much of it distinguished. John Maynard Keynes opined from England that Black Thursday had been a healthy development that would redirect funds from speculative to productive uses. The respected *New York Times* financial writer Alexander Dana Noyes called the Crash "a reaction from an orgy of reckless speculation" and echoed Hoover's appraisal by adding that "no such excesses had been practiced by trade and industry." The American

---

42. Sobel, *Great Bull Market*, 147. Other recent scholars are not quite this categorical but substantially share Sobel's conclusion. See, for example, Peter Temin, *Did Monetary Forces Cause the Great Depression?* (New York: Norton, 1976), esp. 69–83; and Michael A. Bernstein, *The Great Depression: Delayed Recovery and Economic Change in America, 1929–1939* (Cambridge: Cambridge University Press, 1987), esp. 4–7.

43. Notably Schlesinger in *The Crisis of the Old Order* (Schlesinger 1) and Galbraith in *The Great Crash*.

Economic Association in December 1929 predicted recovery by June 1930. Early in 1930 the *New York Times* obliquely indicated contemporary assessment of the significance of the Crash when it declared that the most important news story of 1929 had been Admiral Byrd's expedition to the South Pole.[44]

The behavior of the financial markets themselves confirmed these sentiments in the weeks following the Crash. By April 1930 stock prices had regained some 20 percent of their losses of the previous autumn. The *New York Times* average of industrial stocks then stood about where it had at the beginning of 1929, which was approximately double the level of 1926. Unlike previous panics on Wall Street, this one had thus far seen the failure of no major company or bank. As the last moments of 1929 slipped away, the great crash could be plausibly understood as an outsized but probably freakish event. For many individual stockholders, the Crash had assuredly constituted a calamity, but the calamity was not a depression. Not yet.

Another of the fables that has endured from that turbulent autumn — thanks largely to the immense popularity of Frederick Lewis Allen's nostalgic essay of 1931, *Only Yesterday* — portrays legions of slap-happy small stockholders, drunk with the dreams of the delirious decade, suddenly wiped out by the Crash and cast en masse into the gloom of depression.[45] This familiar picture, too, is grossly distorted. Allen probably relied on an estimate by the New York Stock Exchange in 1929 that some twenty million Americans owned stocks. That figure was later shown to be wildly exaggerated. The chief actuary of the Treasury De-

44. Sobel, *Great Bull Market*, 136–37, 145–46; David Burner, *Herbert Hoover: A Public Life* (New York: Knopf, 1979), 250. Noyes, it is true, prudently added: "We do not yet know whether this present episode is or is not an old-time 'major crisis.'"

45. Galbraith cites Allen's description of a chauffeur, a window cleaner, a valet, a nurse, and a cattleman who all played the market. Even so august an authority as Paul Samuelson, citing Allen, declares: "In the United States during the fabulous stock-market boom of the 'roaring twenties,' housewives, Pullman porters, college students between classes — all bought and sold stocks." See Galbraith, *Great Crash*, 82, and Paul Samuelson, *Economics: An Introductory Analysis*, 5th ed. (New York: McGraw-Hill, 1961), 143–44. Peter Temin also blames Allen in part for giving powerful impetus to the myth of the Crash as the principal cause of the Depression: "The stock-market crash was for [Allen] the dividing point between unbounded optimism and equally uncontainable pessimism. . . . In Allen's mind . . . the stock-market crash became the symbol of the vast discrepancy between the 1920s and the 1930s. . . . [But] the symbol and the reality must be carefully distinguished." Temin, *Did Monetary Forces*, 75–76.

partment calculated that only about three million Americans — less than 2.5 percent of the population — owned securities in 1928, and brokerage firms reported a substantially lower number of 1,548,707 customers in 1929.[46]

So, legend to the contrary, the average American — a description that in this case encompasses at least 97.5 percent of the population — owned no stock in 1929. Even indirect ownership of stock must have been minimal, in this age before the creation of pension funds gave millions of workers a financial stake in capitalism. Accordingly, the Crash in itself had little direct or immediate economic effect on the typical American. The Depression, however, would be another story.

AS 1930 OPENED, the investigators compiling *Recent Social Trends* were just beginning their researches. Taking their presidential mission seriously, they were much interested in that typical American.[47] His age, they determined, was twenty-six. (He would have been a male, this hypothetically abstracted individual, as men continued to outnumber women in the United States until 1950, when the effects of declining immigration, heavily male, and rising maternal survival rates made women for the first time a numerical majority in the American population.) He had been born during the first term of Theodore Roosevelt's presidency, in the midst of the progressive reform ferment. His birth occurred about the time that Japan launched a surprise attack on the Russian fleet at Port Arthur, China — an attack that led to war, Russian defeat, and the first Russian revolution (in 1905) and that heralded Japan's ambition to play the great-power game.

About a million immigrants — virtually none of them Japanese, thanks to a distasteful "gentlemen's agreement" by which the Japanese government grudgingly agreed to limit its export of people — entered the United States in every year of his early childhood. He had reached the age of ten when World War I broke out in 1914, and he had just become a teenager — a term, indeed a concept, not yet in wide use — when President Woodrow Wilson took the United States into the war. By the time the fighting ended, in 1918, he had left the eighth grade and completed his formal schooling. (He would have completed it some three years earlier if he had been black.)

46. Sobel, *Great Bull Market*, 73–74; Galbraith, *Great Crash*, 83.
47. The discussion that follows is mainly based on *Recent Social Trends*, passim, and on *HSUS*. It takes as its point of departure for defining the life cycle of the "typical" American of 1930 the datum that the median age in that year was 26.5.

He was too young to have seen battle, but he soon concluded that the whole business of sending American troops to Europe was a useless, colossal blunder and an inexcusable departure from the venerable American doctrine of isolation. The spectacle of wretched Europeans going bankrupt in Germany, knuckling under to a fascist dictator in Italy, welcoming Bolsheviks — Bolsheviks! — in Russia, and then, to top it off, refusing to pay their war debts to the United States confirmed the wisdom of traditional isolationism, so far as he was concerned.

Raised in the country without flush toilets or electric lighting, as the 1920s opened he moved to the city, to an apartment miraculously plumbed and wired. In the streets he encountered the abundant and exotic offspring of all those immigrants who had arrived when he was a baby. Together they entered the new era when their country was transiting, bumpily, without blueprints or forethought, from an agricultural to an industrial economy, from values of simple rural frugality to values of flamboyant urban consumerism, and, however much the idea was resisted, from provincial isolationism to inevitable international involvement.

Jobs were plentiful for the moment and paid good wages. With hard work he was making a little more than a hundred dollars a month. He had been laid off several times in the preceding years but had built a small cushion of savings at his bank to tide him over when unemployment hit again, as he knew it must. The stock market had just crashed, but it seemed to be recovering, and in any case he owned no stocks — for that matter, neither did anybody he knew. Evenings he "radioed." Weekends he went to the movies, better now that they had sound. Sometimes he broke the law and lifted a glass. On his one day a week off, he took a drive in the car that he was buying on the installment plan.

He was living better than his parents had ever dreamed of living. He was young and vigorous; times were good, and the future promised to be still better. He had just cast his first presidential vote, in 1928, for Herbert Hoover, the most competent man in America, maybe in the world. In that same year he married a girl three years younger than he. She gave up her job to have their first baby. They started to think of buying a house, perhaps in one of the new suburbs. Life was just beginning.

And their world was about to come apart.

2

Panic

You know, the only trouble with capitalism is capitalists; they're too damn greedy.

— Herbert Hoover to Mark Sullivan

When Herbert Hoover was inaugurated on March 4, 1929, wrote journalist Anne O'Hare McCormick, "[w]e were in a mood for magic. . . . [T]he whole country was a vast, expectant gallery, its eyes focused on Washington. We had summoned a great engineer to solve our problems for us; now we sat back comfortably and confidently to watch the problems being solved. The modern technical mind was for the first time at the head of a government. . . . Almost with the air of giving genius its chance, we waited for the performance to begin."[1] The wait was not long, as Hoover promptly summoned Congress into special session to deal with the stubborn depression in agriculture.

Convening on April 15, the representatives quickly learned that the new president would not tolerate any revival of McNary-Haugen proposals for export subsidies. Instead, Hoover demanded "the creation of a great instrumentality clothed with sufficient authority and resources to . . . transfer the agricultural question from the field of politics into the realm of economics."[2] Awed by Hoover's aura of command, Congress swiftly obliged. "The President is so immensely popular over the country," said one senator, "that the Republicans here are on their knees and the Democrats have their hats off."[3] On June 15 the president signed

1. Anne O'Hare McCormick, "A Year of the Hoover Method," *New York Times*, March 2, 1930, sec. 5, 1.
2. Quoted in Harris Gaylord Warren, *Herbert Hoover and the Great Depression* (New York: Oxford University Press, 1959), 169.
3. South Dakota Republican senator Peter Norbeck to G. J. Moen, April 20, 1929, quoted in Jordan A. Schwarz, *The Interregnum of Despair: Hoover, Congress, and the Depression* (Urbana: University of Illinois Press, 1970), 6.

the Agricultural Marketing Act, creating the Federal Farm Board, with capital of $500 million, to promote agricultural cooperatives and stabilization corporations. The cooperatives were to sustain orderly markets in various commodities—cotton, wool, and pecans, for example—by facilitating voluntary agreements among producers. If the co-ops failed to bring order to their respective markets, the stabilization corporations would stand ready to buy unmanageable surpluses. When the members of the Farm Board gathered at the White House on July 15, a triumphant Hoover rightly informed them that they had been invested with "responsibility, authority and resources such as have never before been conferred by our government in assistance to any industry."[4]

The great performance seemed well begun, and not without a touch of magic. In just sixty days the Great Engineer had wrung from Congress a bold remedy for the agricultural depression that had persisted for nearly a decade. What was more, the remedy bore the unmistakable signs of Hoover's own distinctive political genius. It embodied the principle of government-stimulated voluntary cooperation that lay at the heart of his social thought, even while it provided for direct government intervention in the private economy if voluntarism proved inadequate.

To a degree uncommon among presidents, Hoover was a reflective man of scholarly bent, even something of a political philosopher. Ironically, the very care with which he had crafted his guiding principles, and the firmness of his commitment to them, would in time count among his major liabilities as a leader. So would his habits of solitude, formed early in life and reinforced by cruel experience.

Hoover had been born into a Quaker family in West Branch, Iowa, in 1874. His father died when Herbert was six; his mother, just over three years later. The shy orphan child was shunted among Quaker relatives and friends, first in Iowa, and then all the way to Newberg, Oregon, where at the age of fifteen he was sent to live with an uncle who was a schoolmaster and a stern disciplinarian. All his life he bore the imprint of his rural, Quaker origins. He dressed plainly, spoke simply, faced the world with a serenely impassive demeanor, and listened gravely to the voice of his conscience. The early loss of his parents and his upbringing among near strangers forged the growing boy's natural

---

4. By the time the Farm Board was fully functional, the deepening global depression had so dampened agricultural prices that even the unprecedented sums appropriated in June 1929 were woefully insufficient to stem the downward slide. The board went out of existence in 1933, after having lost some $371 million in the futile effort to prop up prices. Schwarz, *Interregnum of Despair*, 172, 176.

aloofness into the mature man's studiously glacial reserve. By the time he arrived in Oregon, Hoover had already established his reputation as a withdrawn but conscientious loner, "the quietest, the most efficient, and the most industrious boy" she had ever met, said an Oregon acquaintance.[5]

After graduating with a degree in geology in Stanford University's "pioneer class" in 1895, Hoover worked briefly as a day laborer in the nearly spent Sierra mining fields. Then in 1897 he accepted a job with Bewick, Moreing, a London-based international mining concern that sent the intense young engineer to Australia to scout for gold. He soon found it and quickly thereafter helped to develop new technologies for more efficiently extracting gold from ore. His employers were well pleased. When Hoover returned from an another assignment to China in 1900 with the deed to a vast new coalfield, Bewick, Moreing made him a partner. For the next fourteen years Hoover traveled the world, developing and supervising mining operations in Australia, Asia, Africa, and Latin America. In 1909 he published *Principles of Mining*, a manual for engineers and managers that advocated collective bargaining, the eight-hour day, and serious attention to mine safety. The book became a standard text in mining schools and helped spread Hoover's reputation as an unusually progressive, enlightened businessman. In 1914, at the age of forty, having amassed a fortune estimated at some $4 million, he retired from active business. His Quaker conscience prodded him toward good works. So did his wife, Lou Henry Hoover, a fellow Stanford geology graduate he had married in 1899. She was a formidable woman who was his lifelong shield against the intrusive world, the organizer of punctiliously correct dinner parties at which Hoover took refuge behind a mask of decorum and formality.

When the Great War broke out, Hoover volunteered to organize international relief efforts for Belgium, then suffering under German occupation. His success at "feeding the starving Belgians" earned him an international reputation as a great humanitarian. Hoover returned to the United States in 1917 to serve as food administrator in Woodrow Wilson's wartime government. At war's end he accompanied Wilson to Paris as the president's personal adviser and as economic director of the Supreme Economic Council, chairman of the Inter-Allied Food Council, and chairman of the European Coal Council. As much as any one man

---

5. Joan Hoff Wilson, *Herbert Hoover: Forgotten Progressive* (Boston: Little, Brown, 1975), 10.

could, he got the credit for reorganizing the war-shattered European economy. He caused mines to be reopened, rivers to be cleared, bridges and roads rebuilt, food and medicine delivered. By the time the signatories penned their names on the treaty at Versailles, Hoover was a celebrated figure, an object of admiration tinged with awe. The reforming jurist Louis Brandeis thought him "the biggest figure injected into Washington life by the war." Hoover's "high public spirit, extraordinary intelligence, knowledge, sympathy, youth, and a rare perception of what is really worth-while for the country," enthused Brandeis, "would, with his organizing ability and power of inspiring loyalty, do wonderful things in the presidency." Assistant Secretary of the Navy Franklin D. Roosevelt proclaimed Hoover "certainly a wonder and I wish we could make him President of the United States. There could not be a better one."[6] Hoover's party affiliation was unknown at the war's end, and progressives of both parties courted him. But before long he declared himself a Republican, campaigned for Warren G. Harding, and was rewarded with appointment as secretary of commerce, a post he held for eight years.

Hoover's many years overseas had bred in him an acute interest in his own country's distinguishing cultural traits, and in 1922 he gathered his thoughts on this subject into a little book, *American Individualism*. A reviewer in the *New York Times* placed it "among the few great formulations of American political theory."[7] That praise may have been exaggerated—the product, perhaps, of the reader's wonder that a modern secretary of commerce could even hold his own in the intellectual precincts of Hamilton, Madison, and Jay—but *American Individualism* was by any measure an unusually thoughtful reflection on the American condition. It also provided an instructive guide to the ideas that informed Hoover's behavior as president.

"Individualism" was, after all, a concept that had been invented to describe a social development considered unique to American society. Alexis de Tocqueville had first given the term currency a century earlier in *Democracy in America*, in which he declared that "individualism is of democratic origin." It was different from mere selfishness, and in many ways more dangerous because more isolating. Selfishness, said Tocqueville, "leads a man to connect everything with himself, and to prefer himself to everything in the world," but individualism was still

6. Schlesinger 1:80–82.
7. Quoted in Wilson, *Herbert Hoover*, 55.

more pernicious, because it "disposes each member of the community to sever himself from the mass of his fellows, and to draw apart."[8]

Hoover argued, in effect, that Tocqueville had it all wrong; that *American* individualism was in its essence neither selfish nor solipsistic. Rather, it embraced regard for others and attachment to the community as a whole. In Hoover's lexicon, the word that captured the essence of American individualism was *service*. "The ideal of service," Hoover wrote in *American Individualism*, was a "great spiritual force poured out by our people as never before in the history of the world." It was a uniquely American ideal, and one that happily rendered unnecessary in America the repugnant growth of formal state power that afflicted other nations.[9]

Hoover revived, in a sense, the vision of a spontaneously mutualistic society inhabited by virtuous, public-spirited citizens that had inspired the republican theorists of the American Revolutionary era. No doubt his thinking was also influenced by his Quaker upbringing, with its gentle but firm emphasis on the values of consensus and reciprocity. From whatever source, Hoover gave voice to an individualism that was not simply the "rugged" and solitary sort that caricaturists somewhat unfairly put into his mouth (though he did in fact utter the phrase). His ideal individualism was, rather, communal and cooperative, arising from a faith in the better self of each citizen. The chief role of government was to articulate and orchestrate the aspirations of these better selves and to provide the information as well as the means for them to come together. Government might indeed step in where voluntarism had manifestly failed, but only after a fair trial. It was decidedly not the government's role arbitrarily and peremptorily to substitute coercive bureaucracy for voluntary cooperation. That way lay tyranny and the corruption of America's unique political soul.

Hoover could believe without difficulty that this vision was as practical as it was idealistic. He had made it work, after all, in the administration of Belgian relief and as food administrator during the war, when he self-consciously rejected the coercive techniques of the European belligerents and relied instead on massive educational and propaganda campaigns to spur production and limit domestic consumption of food

8. Alexis de Tocqueville, *Democracy in America* (New York: New American Library, 1956), 192–93.
9. Herbert Hoover, *American Individualism* (Garden City, N.Y.: Doubleday, Page, 1923), 28–29.

crops. He had made it work again in the sharp recession of 1921, when he had taken the unprecedented initiative of organizing the President's Conference on Unemployment. The conference publicized the plight of the nation's nearly five million unemployed workers, goading management to take corrective measures. It called for the routine collection of reliable statistical data on unemployment, so as to provide an informed basis for future federal policy. It envisioned combating future episodes of unemployment with countercyclical spending on public works. No previous administration had moved so purposefully and so creatively in the face of an economic downturn. Hoover had definitively made the point that government should not stand by idly when confronted with economic difficulty. Two years later, Hoover successfully shamed the steel industry into abandoning the man-killing twelve-hour day, again without resorting to formal legislation. Throughout the decade of the 1920s, he had promoted trade associations with the purpose of stabilizing prices, protecting employment, and rationalizing production in various industrial sectors, all through enlightened, voluntary cooperation among businessmen, with government's encouragement.

Now Hoover had the power and the pulpit of the presidency, and he meant to use the office vigorously. He had every reason to be satisfied, even exultant, over his performance in the special session of Congress that produced the Agricultural Marketing Act. He had given the country an impressive demonstration of his campaign declaration that "government must be a constructive force."[10] He intended to resurrect the reform spirit of the progressive era, buried by the war and by Harding-Coolidge conservatism. "Little had been done by the Federal government in the fields of reform or progress during the fourteen years before my time," he later reflected. "[B]y 1929 many things were already fourteen years overdue. I . . . had high hopes that I might lead in performing the task." He specified some of the reforms he had in mind: "We want to see a nation built of home owners and farm owners. We want to see their savings protected. We want to see them in steady jobs. We want to see more and more of them insured against death and accident, unemployment and old age. We want them all secure."[11]

10. Quoted in Albert U. Romasco, *The Poverty of Abundance: Hoover, the Nation, the Depression* (New York: Oxford University Press, 1965), 16.
11. Herbert Hoover, *The Memoirs of Herbert Hoover: The Cabinet and the Presidency, 1920–1933* (New York: Macmillan, 1952), 223; Arthur M. Schlesinger Jr., ed., *His-*

But Hoover's moment of exaltation was pitifully brief, and not just because of the financial crash that overtook him in the autumn of 1929. He had masterfully shepherded the Agricultural Marketing Act through Congress, but he proved far less able to control another issue that was also unleashed in the special session: revision of the tariff. The Fordney-McCumber Tariff Act of 1922 had already pegged most import levies at forbiddingly high levels, yet the Republican platform in 1928 (as well as the Democratic) called for still higher duties.[12] Hoover went along with his party's plan for tariff revision because he wanted two things: higher duties on certain agricultural imports, as part of his program to aid farmers, and a strengthened Tariff Commission, with power to adjust import duties by 50 percent. This "flexible tariff," said Hoover, would "get the tariff out of Congressional logrolling" and thus be a large step toward reducing "excessive and privileged protection." As for tariffs on manufactured goods, they should be revised upward only where "there has been a substantial slackening of activity in an industry during the past few years, and a consequent decrease of employment due to insurmountable competition."[13]

Unfortunately, this last provision, however reasonably intended, was an invitation to what progressive Republican senator George W. Norris called "protection run perfectly mad."[14] Hoover showed himself utterly unable to control the tariff legislation, and Congress proceeded to pass the Hawley-Smoot Tariff of 1930, raising import duties to their highest

tory of American Presidential Elections, 1789–1968 (New York: Chelsea House, 1971), 3:2708–9.

12. Some writers, notably Jude Wanninski, have contended that the weakening of the stock market in the fall of 1929 can be attributed to traders' fears about the prospect of higher tariffs as the legislation made its way through Congress in the summer of 1929. Other writers even blame the historically high Hawley-Smoot Tariff of 1930 for causing the Depression itself. But both these charges, especially the latter, ignore the fact that the Fordney-McCumber rates, as one historian puts it, were "already . . . high enough to cause a depression if a tariff can have such a result." Warren, *Herbert Hoover and the Great Depression,* 84. Both the Fordney-McCumber and the Hawley-Smoot tariffs are better regarded as symptoms, not causes, of economic distress in 1921 and 1929, respectively, and as continuing expressions of the protectionist pressures that were built into the very structure of congressional tariff-making. It was his desire to remedy this structural defect that led Hoover to swallow the Hawley-Smoot bill, since it provided him with a mechanism, in the form of a reinvigorated Tariff Commission, by which he might circumvent Congress in administering the tariff law and eventually lowering rates.

13. Hoover, *Memoirs: The Cabinet and the Presidency,* 292–93.

14. Warren, *Herbert Hoover,* 90.

level in American history. In the end, Hoover swallowed Hawley-Smoot because of its provisions for flexibility, but in fact the tariff bill represented both an economic and a political catastrophe.

Economically, the Hawley-Smoot Tariff signaled the world that as the depression lowered the United States was moving toward the same autarkic, beggar-thy-neighbor, protectionist policies with which other nations were already dangerously flirting. Many observers warned of the perils of this position. One thousand economists signed a petition urging Hoover to veto the bill. Thomas Lamont, a partner in J. P. Morgan and Company and usually an influential economic adviser to Hoover, recalled that "I almost went down on my knees to beg Herbert Hoover to veto the asinine Hawley-Smoot Tariff. That Act intensified nationalism all over the world."[15]

Hoover himself appreciated these arguments but possessed neither the political power to stop the congressional steamroller nor the political will to veto the final legislation. He eventually signed the tariff into law in June 1930, prompting Walter Lippmann to complain that the president had "surrendered everything for nothing. He gave up the leadership of his party. He let his personal authority be flouted. He accepted a wretched and mischievous product of stupidity and greed." In this direct confrontation with a contrary-minded Congress, Hoover had failed the first great test of his capacity for political leadership. Now even supporters like Lippmann, who had praised Hoover in 1928 as "a reformer who is probably more vividly conscious of the defects of American capitalism than any man in public life today," began to doubt him. "He has the peculiarly modern, in fact, the contemporary American, faith in the power of the human mind and will, acting through organization, to accomplish results," Lippmann wrote, but "the unreasonableness of mankind is not accounted for in Mr. Hoover's philosophy. . . . In the realm of reason he is an unusually bold man; in the realm of unreason he is, for a statesman, an exceptionally thin-skinned and easily bewildered man. . . . He can face with equanimity almost any of the difficulties of statesmanship except the open conflict of wills. . . . The political art deals with matters peculiar to politics, with a complex of material circumstances, of historic deposit, of human passion, for which the problems of business or engineering as such do not provide an analogy." Ominously, the Great Engineer was showing himself to be a peculiarly artless politician.[16]

15. David Burner, *Herbert Hoover: A Public Life* (New York: Knopf, 1979), 298.
16. Lippmann quoted in Ronald Steel, *Walter Lippmann and the American Century* (Boston: Little, Brown, 1980), 287–88. See also Lippmann, "The Peculiar Weakness of Mr. Hoover," *Harper's* 161 (June 1930):1.

LIPPMANN'S ASSESSMENT was characteristically cogent and, as events were to prove, prescient. But at this point Lippmann was almost alone in his doubts. The implications of Hoover's failure on the tariff and of what that failure suggested about the president's political ineptitude were only faintly visible in the first weeks of 1930. Most commentators were much more impressed, even dazzled, by the vigorous response that Hoover had made to the stock market crash of October 1929. No previous president, wrote Anne O'Hare McCormick, "would have been so well prepared as Hoover to deal with the emergency when the bright bubble broke. He had a concrete program ready; he gave the effect of having thoroughly anticipated the debacle and mapped out the shortest road to recovery." The liberal economists William T. Foster and Waddill Catchings declared: "For the first time in our history, a President of the United States is taking aggressive leadership in guiding private business through a crisis." The *New York Times* said: "The President's course in this troublous time has been all that could be desired. No one in his place could have done more; very few of his predecessors could have done as much."[17]

Orthodox economic theory held that business downturns were inevitable parts of the business cycle. Depressions, said Oklahoma's Democratic senator Thomas P. Gore, were "an economic disease. You might just as well try to prevent the human race from having a disease as to prevent economic grief of this sort."[18] Orthodox political theory accordingly prescribed that government should refrain from interfering with the natural course of recovery in the economic organism. Conspicuous among what Hoover called the "leave it alone liquidationists" was Treasury Secretary Andrew Mellon. "Mr. Mellon had only one formula," Hoover later wrote. "Liquidate labor, liquidate stocks, liquidate the farmers, liquidate real estate," Mellon preached to the president. "It will purge the rottenness out of the system. High costs of living and high living will come down. People will work harder, lead a more moral life."[19] Mellon was a prime exemplar of those rigidly conventional devotees of laissez-faire whom William T. Foster impishly described as the "lazy fairies." Liberal journalist Stuart Chase also made

17. McCormick, "Year of the Hoover Method"; Foster and Catchings quoted in Romasco, *Poverty of Abundance*, 36; *New York Times*, December 1, 1929, sec. 3, 4.
18. Quoted in Schlesinger 1:226.
19. Herbert Hoover, *The Memoirs of Herbert Hoover: The Great Depression, 1929–1941* (New York: Macmillan, 1952), 30.

sport of their intellectual orthodoxy: "[T]he great advantage of allowing nature to take her course," wrote Chase, "is that it obviates thought. . . . There is no need to take concrete action. Just sit and watch with folded hands."[20]

Hoover would have none of it. Despite Mellon's towering prestige and the imposing weight of the conventional wisdom that he represented, Hoover believed "that we should use the powers of government to cushion the situation. . . . [T]he prime needs were to prevent bank panics such as had marked the earlier slumps, to mitigate the privation among the unemployed and the farmers which would certainly ensue. . . . [W]e determined that the Federal government should use all of its powers."[21]

The president was not pushed into this forward position in 1929 by pressure from capital. All to the contrary, wrote Hoover, "for some time after the crash" businessmen refused to believe "that the danger was any more than that of run-of-the-mill, temporary slumps such as had occurred at three-to seven-year intervals in the past." But Hoover sensed that something far more poisonous was brewing, and though he realized that "no president before had ever believed there was a governmental responsibility in such cases," he resolved to act, swiftly and dramatically.[22] Here was the promise, at least, of innovative, imaginative leadership.

Hoover's overriding intention was to prevent the shock waves from the stock market collapse from blasting through the economy as a whole. His fundamental premises were that the basic productive facilities of the country remained healthy and intact and that government, if it moved smartly, was fully capable of insulating them from the psychological and financial explosion reverberating in the canyons of Wall Street. Offering rhetorical reassurance to bolster the confidence of nervous investors, employers, and consumers was a conspicuous part of this strategy, but it was by no means the whole of it.

"The great task of the next few months," the progressive-minded *Nation* proclaimed in November 1929, "is the restoration of confidence — confidence in the fundamental strength of the financial structure notwithstanding the strain that has been put upon it, confidence in the essential soundness of legitimate industry and trade."[23] Hoover agreed,

20. Foster quoted in Schlesinger 1:187; Chase quoted in Romasco, *Poverty of Abundance,* 25.
21. Hoover, *Memoirs: The Great Depression,* 31.
22. Hoover, *Memoirs: The Great Depression,* 29–30.
23. *Nation,* November 27, 1929, 614.

but he also knew "that words are not of any great importance in times of economic disturbance. It is action that counts."[24] Accordingly, he summoned to the White House, beginning on November 19, 1929, leaders of the nation's banking system, railroads, manufacturing industries, and public utilities. For nearly two weeks they emerged from daily sessions with the nation's chief executive emitting ritual pronouncements of confidence in the basic soundness of the economy and of their optimistic outlook for the future. These words were comforting. But as the country was about to learn, the business leaders did more than talk. They also responded to the president's call for "action."

On December 5, 1929, Hoover reviewed the results of his November meetings before an audience of some four hundred "key men" from all corners of the business world. The occasion itself was cause for remark. "The very fact that you gentlemen come together for these broad purposes represents an advance in the whole conception of the relationship of business to public welfare," Hoover told them. "This is a far cry from the arbitrary and dog-eat-dog attitude of the business world of some thirty or forty years ago. . . . A great responsibility and a great opportunity rest upon the business and economic organization of the country."[25] He was pleased to report, Hoover continued, that his conferences of the preceding fortnight had already produced tangible results in three significant areas. The Federal Reserve System, he announced, had eased credit by open-market purchases and by lowering its discount rate to member banks. The Fed was also refusing discounts to banks that made stock market call loans. Taken together, these measures ensured the availability of investment capital for legitimate business needs.

Further, the industrialists he had summoned to the White House had agreed to maintain wage rates. This was a major concession, and a novel one. The reflex of management in all previous recessions had been to slash paychecks. Now employers acceded to Hoover's request that "the first shock must fall on profits and not on wages."[26] Holding the line on wages, according to Hoover, would not only preserve the dignity and well-being of individual workers. It would also sustain purchasing power in the economy as a whole and thus arrest the downswing by bolstering consumption—a point of economic theory later credited to the Keynes-

24. Hoover quoted in Herbert Stein, *The Fiscal Revolution in America*, (Chicago: University of Chicago Press, 1969), 16.
25. Hoover, *Memoirs: The Great Depression*, 44–45.
26. Notes of Hoover's meeting with industrial leaders on November 21, 1929, quoted in Hoover, *Memoirs: The Great Depression*, 44.

ian revolution but actually quite commonplace among economic analysts in the 1920s and well understood by Hoover.

The actions of the Federal Reserve System and the agreement on wages, together with the Federal Farm Board's support of agricultural prices, were designed to brake the deflationary spiral before it could gather momentum. The final measure that Hoover announced on December 5 was potentially the most important component of his antidepression program. It looked not merely to stabilization but to revitalization of the economy by stimulating construction work. At his urging, Hoover explained, railway and public utilities executives had agreed to expand their building and maintenance programs. He had, in addition, wired the governors of each state and the mayors of major cities suggesting that "road, street, public building and other construction of this type could be speeded up and adjusted in such fashion as to further employment." Within a few months, Hoover would add the resources of the federal government to this effort by requesting from Congress a supplemental appropriation of some $140 million for new public buildings.[27]

It became fashionable in later years to dismiss these various measures as tragicomic evidence of Hoover's quaint, ideologically hidebound belief that responsibility for economic recovery lay with private business and state and local governments and that the federal government had only a modest, hortatory role to play in combating the depression. Some writers have especially mocked Hoover's conferences with business leaders in November 1929 as "no-business meetings" that had merely a ceremonial, incantatory function.[28] Their limited, do-nothing agenda, so the argument runs, confirms Hoover's fatal reluctance to depart in any significant measure from the obsolescent dogmas of laissez-faire.

To be sure, Hoover himself fastidiously gave the conventional assurances to his business audience on December 5 that his program was "not a dictation or interference by the government with business.

27. Romasco, *Poverty of Abundance*, 29. Almost every governor responded with pledges of cooperation. New York's Franklin D. Roosevelt added a cautionary note that exemplified the pervasive fiscal orthodoxy of the day: "expect to recommend to legislature ... much needed construction work program ... limited only by estimated receipts from revenues without increasing taxes." William Starr Myers and Walter H. Newton, *The Hoover Administration: A Documented Narrative* (New York: Charles Scribner's Sons, 1936), 29.

28. See John Kenneth Galbraith, *The Great Crash* (Boston: Houghton Mifflin, 1954), 145, and Schlesinger 1:165.

It is a request from the government that you co-operate in prudent measures to solve a national problem."[29] The *New Republic* observed at the time that "the historical role of Mr. Hoover is apparently to try the experiment of seeing what business can do when given the steering wheel. Mr. Hoover insists that there should be a steering wheel," the magazine conceded, "but he will also let business do the driving."[30] That indictment has echoed for decades in the history books, where Hoover has been embalmed as a specimen of the "old order" of unbridled laissez-faire capitalism. "No American," concluded Arthur M. Schlesinger Jr., "could have provided a fairer test of the capacity of the business community to govern a great and multifarious nation than Herbert Hoover."[31]

But Hoover's reliance on private business and on state and local governments for fiscal stimulus in late 1929, notes economist Herbert Stein, "is better understood if the relatively small size of the federal government at the beginning of the Depression is appreciated."[32] Federal expenditures in 1929 accounted for about 3 percent of gross national product (GNP). By the century's closing decade, by way of comparison, the federal budget represented more than 20 percent of GNP. State and local government expenditures were about five times larger than the federal budget in 1929; by century's end, those figures would be nearly equal.[33]

To that consideration it might be added that the structure, as well as the size, of the federal government severely limited the scope of its fiscal action, whatever the ideology of its chief executive. The Federal Reserve Board, for example, was legally independent of the executive branch. It could not be counted upon to help finance a large federal deficit even if the president had inexplicably chosen to profane all the canons of economic writ and request one.

When Hoover determined "that the Federal government should use all of its powers," therefore, he was professing a radical conviction, one that heralded a coming revolution in attitudes about the government's proper economic role. But he was not, by the very nature of things in the world of 1929, reaching at that historical moment for a truly powerful instrument. In the last analysis, Hoover's earliest responses to the

29. Hoover, *Memoirs: The Great Depression*, 45.
30. *New Republic*, December 11, 1929, 56.
31. Schlesinger 1:88.
32. Stein, *Fiscal Revolution in America*, 14.
33. *HSUS* 228, 230, 1104.

economic crisis revealed as much about the boundaries of available intelligence and inherited institutions in Depression-era America as they did about the alleged narrowness of his beliefs. Those boundaries were destined to circumscribe not only Hoover's struggle against the Great Depression but Franklin D. Roosevelt's as well.

Ignorance befogs all human affairs, and it enshrouded policymakers in the months after the Wall Street debacle of 1929. The future, as ever, remained veiled and inscrutable. No one — including Hoover, whose anxieties were keener than most — suspected that the country was tee-tering at the brink of an economic abyss out of whose depths it would take more than ten years to climb. As for the past, little in the lived or remembered experience of Americans provided useful analogies for un-derstanding their situation in 1929. Andrew Mellon, for example, took his chief point of reference for assessing that situation to be the depres-sion of the 1870s, which began when Mellon was eighteen years old. Mellon badgered Hoover tediously with grave lectures about that dimly remembered decade. Hoover's own memories of the depression of the 1890s could not have been powerfully instructive; he had graduated from college in the midst of it and set out almost immediately to make his fortune. Both of those downturns had in any case lasted less than five years. They were also long ago and far away. They had virtually hap-pened in another country, a country still overwhelmingly rural and ag-ricultural, many of whose inhabitants participated but marginally in the market economy and felt its distant gyrations only as faint seismic shrugs.

The more recent recession of 1921 served as the most accessible model for interpreting the events of 1929. It had been severe but brief. Unemployment was estimated to have peaked at about 11.9 percent of the work force. That was considered a historical apogee, and Commerce Secretary Hoover's decisive intervention in convening the President's Conference on Unemployment had shown that the business cycle could be shaped, and its downswing truncated, by purposeful leadership. Thus in 1929, notes Stein, "America was not prepared to visualize a decade in which unemployment never fell below 14 per cent."[34] And as the events of the gray decade that followed were to show, no politician's art, neither Hoover's nor Roosevelt's, proved capable of significantly bending upward the stubbornly bottoming curve of the economy.

Policymakers were not only unprepared to visualize the decade that lay ahead of them; they were almost equally unable to see what was

34. Stein, *Fiscal Revolution in America*, 15.

going on around them in late 1929 and through much of 1930. Despite the call of the President's Conference on Unemployment in 1921 for better information on the status of the work force, reliable data on unemployment simply did not exist. Only in April 1930 did census takers for the first time attempt a systematic measurement of unemployment. Even a year later, in mid-1931, lawmakers were still guessing, on the basis of anecdotes, impressions, and fragmentary reports, at the numbers of the unemployed.[35]

In the crucial area of construction work, long recognized as a potentially powerful countercyclical tool, the states dramatically outspent the federal government. Federal construction expenditures were scarcely $200 million in 1929. The states paid out ten times that much, nearly $2 billion, mostly for highways. Federal outlays for construction, excepting the years of World War II, would not reach that level until the 1950s. Still more dramatic was the comparison with private industry, which spent some $9 billion on construction projects in 1929.[36]

Under these circumstances, it was not simply ideological timidity but practical realism that led Hoover to search for a countercyclical instrument not in the federal budget but in the undertakings of private business and of the states. There, not in Washington, D.C., were the financial resources and the shelf of backlogged projects, their time-consuming engineering work already completed, that might be swiftly brought into play. Though Hoover was increasingly challenged by proponents of allegedly "vast" federal public works projects that envisioned spending up to $5 billion over a year or two, Stein rightly asserts that "these suggestions could not be taken seriously. The federal government could simply not raise its construction expenditures quickly by one or two billion dollars a year, for instance, and have any structures to show for it. Federal construction expenditures were only $210 million in 1930—a small base on which to erect a program of several billion dollars. . . . It is significant that the New Deal did not succeed until 1939 in raising the annual amount of public construction by $1.5 billion over the 1930 rate, in 1930 prices." Given the constraints under which he labored, in short, Hoover made impressively aggressive countercyclical use of fiscal policy. Measured against either past or future performance, his

35. See, for example, the remarks of Senator Borah in the *New York Times*, March 12, 1931, 21.
36. *HSUS*, 1123, 1127. For a general discussion of this matter, see Romasco, *Poverty of Abundance*, chap. 4; Stein, *Fiscal Revolution in America*, chap. 1; and Joan Wilson, *Herbert Hoover: Forgotten Progressive*, chap. 5.

accomplishment was remarkable. He nearly doubled federal public works expenditures in three years. Thanks to his prodding, the net stimulating effect of federal, state, and local fiscal policy was larger in 1931 than in any subsequent year of the decade.[37]

By the spring of 1930 many observers were cautiously optimistic. Hoover himself, in a statement that would later haunt him, proclaimed to the U. S. Chamber of Commerce on May 1, 1930: "I am convinced we have passed the worst and with continued effort we shall rapidly recover."[38] The following month he told a delegation from the National Catholic Welfare Conference that their pleas for further expansion of federal public works programs were "sixty days too late. The depression is over."[39]

Given available information, and given the scale against which the events of late 1929 and early 1930 could then be measured, these statements were not as outrageous as they appeared in retrospect. The wish for recovery might have been father to the thought, but circumstances lent the idea a measure of plausibility. The stock market had by April 1930 recouped about one-fifth of its slippage from the speculative peak of the preceding autumn. Some rural banks had begun to crack, but the banking system as a whole had thus far displayed surprising resilience in the immediate wake of the crash; deposits in operating Federal Reserve member banks actually increased through October of 1930.[40] The still sketchy reports on unemployment were worrisome but not unduly alarming. Major employers were apparently abiding by their pledge to maintain wage standards, and private industry as well as local and state governments had publicly acceded to Hoover's request to accelerate construction projects.

But the reality, still only obscurely visible in the meager statistical data that the government could then muster, was that the economy was continuing its mystifying downward slide. By the end of 1930 business failures had reached a record 26,355. Gross national product had slumped 12.6 percent from its 1929 level. In durable goods industries especially, production was down sharply: as much as 38 per cent in some steel mills, and

---

37. Stein, *Fiscal Revolution in America*, 23–24. The calculation of net fiscal stimulus is provided by E. Cary Brown, "Fiscal Policy in the Thirties: A Reappraisal," *American Economic Review* 46 (December, 1956) 857.

38. Hoover, *Memoirs: The Great Depression*, 58.

39. Schlesinger 1:231.

40. Milton Friedman and Anna Jacobson Schwartz, *A Monetary History of the United States, 1867–1960* (Princeton: Princeton University Press, 1963), 308–9. See also Lester Chandler, *America's Greatest Depression* (New York: Harper and Row, 1970), 80.

about the same throughout the key industry of automobile manufacturing, with its huge employment rolls. Despite public assurances, private business was in fact decreasing expenditures for construction; indeed, in the face of softening demand it had already cut back construction in 1929 from its 1928 peak, and it cut still further in 1930.[41] The exact number of laid-off workers remained conjectural; later studies estimated that some four million laborers were unemployed in 1930.

Yet most Americans in 1930 saw these developments less clearly than did later analysts and evaluated what they could see against the backdrop of their most recent experience with an economic recession in 1921. Then GNP had plummeted almost 24 percent in a single year, twice the decline of 1930. Unemployment was somewhat larger in absolute terms in 1921 than in 1930 (4.9 million versus 4.3 million) and significantly larger in percentage terms (11.9 percent versus 8.9 percent). Americans could justly feel in 1930 that they were not—yet—passing through as severe a crisis as the one they had endured less than a decade earlier. This perception of the gravity of the crisis, joined with the recurrent belief that its momentum had been arrested and the corner turned, as had happened so swiftly in 1921, inhibited Hoover from taking any more aggressive antidepression fiscal action in 1930.[42] Nor was he yet coming under any significant pressure to do more. He stood securely in mid-1930 as the leader of the fight against the depression, and he seemed to be winning—or at least not losing. Hoover, predicted the powerful Democratic financier and economic sage Bernard Baruch in May 1930, would be "fortunate enough, before the next election, to have a rising tide and then he will be pictured as the great master mind who led the country out of its economic misery."[43]

BY THE END OF 1930, however, the tide of Hoover's fortune had begun to ebb relentlessly. Congressional elections in November

---

41. See the slightly differing estimates of reductions in private construction expenditures in Stein, *Fiscal Revolution in America*, 22, and Romasco, *Poverty of Abundance*, 57–58. Both authors arrive at totals over $2 billion, or at least 20 percent below 1929 levels.

42. See Stein, *Fiscal Revolution in America*, 25–26, for further development of this idea. The events of 1930 were overshadowed in seriousness not only by those of 1921. In retrospect, neither 1930 nor even 1931 would look all that bad. All but one subsequent year (1937) of the entire decade of the 1930s saw greater unemployment than the 1931 level of eight million.

43. Schwarz, *Interregnum of Despair*, 15.

eliminated Republican majorities in both houses. Reflecting the still imperfect national focus on the severity of the economic crisis, many races turned more on the issue of Prohibition than on the depression, and though Republican losses were not overwhelming, especially by midterm election standards, they were bad enough to greatly complicate Hoover's political life. The GOP lost eight seats in the Senate, which would now be composed of forty-eight Republicans, forty-seven Democrats, and one Farmer-Labor member. This gave the Republicans a nominal plurality, but in Hoover's judgment "actually we had no more than 40 real Republicans, as Senators Borah, Norris, Cutting, and others of the left wing were against us." (The "left wing," in Hoover's view, consisted of those politicians who were calling for irresponsibly large budget deficits and direct federal aid to the unemployed.) Discouraged by the election results, a still politically innocent Hoover made the astounding suggestion that the Democrats be allowed to organize the Senate "and thereby convert their sabotage into responsibility."[44] Senate Republicans, of course, jealous of their chairmanships and other privileges of majority status, instantly rejected this proposal. The Senate remained in Republican hands, though just barely.

The situation in the House was worse. On election day in November 1930, Republicans and Democrats broke exactly even, winning 217 seats each, with the balance of power briefly held by a single Farmer-Labor congressman. Under the electoral laws then in force, the new Seventy-second Congress was at last seated only some thirteen months later, in December 1931. By that time thirteen elected representatives had died, a majority of them Republicans. Democrats thus held a slender majority, and they proceeded to organize the House for the first time in twelve years. As speaker, they elected Representative John Nance Garner of Texas.

The sixty-two-year-old Garner represented a sprawling congressional

---

44. Hoover, Memoirs: The Great Depression, 101. While it is true that Republicans lost control of the House and nearly lost the Senate in the elections of 1930, close study of the election must qualify any reading of the results as a repudiation of Hoover's—and the Republican Party's—handling of the depression. Republicans remained easily the majority party in the country as a whole, winning some 54.1 percent of the votes cast for major-party candidates in the 1930 congressional elections. They handily dominated in all regions outside the South, and in three key states—Pennsylvania, Michigan, and Massachusetts—they actually increased their 1928 share of popular votes cast for congressional candidates. See Schwarz, Interregnum of Despair, 19.

district in the parched Nueces River country in southwest Texas. He was
an ill-educated, self-made sagebrush squire who delighted in tending to
the sheep, cattle, and mohair goats that roamed his dusty estates. The
first speaker from Texas, he dreamed that he might also become the first
Texan to live in the White House. With his icy blue eyes and stubbly
white hair framing a frequently unshaven face, his stocky body draped
in a rumpled gray suit, his feet encased in big, blunt-toed shoes, he
presented a colorful figure to the amused Washington press corps, who
took to dubbing him "Mustang Jack" or "Cactus Jack." Hoover deemed
him "a man of real statesmanship when he took off his political pistols"
but also a partisan infighter of reptilian cunning. (Garner had once
proposed dividing Texas into four states—whose eight senators would
presumably all be Democrats.) First elected to the House in 1902, Garner had risen steadily through the rigid hierarchy of the congressional
seniority system. He had ingratiated himself with his colleagues, especially rural southern and western representatives, many of whom still
affected frock coats and string ties, by saying and doing little. His taci-
turnity led some to think of him as a kind of Texas Coolidge—a perception reinforced by statements like Garner's 1931 declaration that "the
great trouble today is that we have too many laws." Like Coolidge, too—
indeed, like virtually every credible public figure of the time—Garner
regarded a balanced budget as the rock on which all government financial policy rested. Garner would now be the most influential figure in
the Seventy-second Congress, the "Depression Congress" with which
Hoover would have to deal as the depression deepened drastically in
1931 and 1932. He had it in his power to save or to break Hoover's
political neck.[45]

"I thought my party had a better program for national recovery than
Mr. Hoover and his party," Garner later wrote. But if the Democratic
speaker had a program, Hoover retorted, "he never disclosed it. . . . His
main program of public welfare was to put the Republicans out." In
fact, Garner and many, perhaps most, congressional Democrats stood at
this time somewhere to Hoover's political right. This was especially true
of the Democratic leadership, overwhelmingly southern in origin and
agrarian in outlook, including Garner in the House and Joseph T. Robinson of Arkansas, the Democratic leader in the Senate. Incredibly
enough, the national chairman of the Democratic Party was a former

45. *Time*, December 7, 1931, 10; Schlesinger 1:227–29; Hoover, *Memoirs: The Great Depression*, 101–2.

Republican, the archconservative industrialist John J. Raskob, an economic reactionary and notorious wet. His paramount cause was the repeal of Prohibition, a goal to which he aspired primarily because the restoration of tax revenues from the sale of liquor would dampen the need for a progressive income tax. As for Speaker Garner, virtually his first antidepression initiative in the new Seventy-second Congress was to support a frankly regressive national sales tax as a budget-balancing measure.

As the depression thickened in 1931 and 1932, the main purpose of Garner, Robinson, and Raskob was to obstruct the president and prepare to reap the political reward in the upcoming presidential election. Democrats, said a North Carolina Democratic senator, should avoid "committing our party to a definite program. The issue in the [1932] election is Hoover. Why take any step calculated to divert attention from that issue?" Only the Democratic Party's "failure to function," said Tennessee's Cordell Hull, "can save the Republican party and its Hoover administration from overwhelming defeat in 1932." Another observer commented in 1931 that the Democrats were "more hopeful than bold[.] . . . [E]vents seemed to be going their way; they had no wish to incur premature responsibility."[46] But they did wish—and they had the ability—to make Hoover's life miserable. Raskob at the National Committee hired Charles Michelson, a seasoned publicist with a well-earned reputation for mischief, to ensure that the humiliation of Hoover would be executed with professional expertise. Michelson methodically proceeded to hang the responsibility for the gathering depression around Hoover's neck like a leper's bell. "It was Michelson's job," said Garner, "to whittle Hoover down to our size." As for himself, Garner boasted, "I fought President Hoover with everything I had, under Marquis of Queensberry, London prize ring and catch-as-catch-can rules."[47]

On Hoover's political left in the Congress stood a loose assortment of progressive and former Bull Moose Republicans like Nebraska's George Norris, New York's Fiorello La Guardia, Idaho's William Borah, Wisconsin's Robert M. La Follette Jr., and New Mexico's Bronson Cutting, along with a smattering of maverick Democrats like Montana's Burton Wheeler, Colorado's Edward Costigan, and New York's Robert Wagner. Hoover had some natural sympathies for this group's outlook. Like many of them, he had voted the Bull Moose ticket in 1912. But his measured,

46. Schwarz, *Interregnum of Despair*, 62, 180, 59.
47. Burner, *Herbert Hoover*, 314; Hoover, *Memoirs: The Great Depression*, 101n.

prudent management style and his greater degree of caution about governmental activism, especially in the area of unemployment relief, frequently set him at odds with the progressives.

Norris in particular was a perpetual thorn in Hoover's flesh. Melancholic and ascetic, clad in black suit and string tie, gray-haired and plainspoken, Norris had the air of a conscience-ridden country parson. He was approaching his fourth decade of service in Congress. First elected to the House, like Garner, in 1902 and then to the Senate in 1912, he had metamorphosed from an orthodox McKinley Republican into a ferociously independent progressive. In April 1917, for example, he had cast one of six votes in the Senate against American entry into the European War. In 1928 he refused to endorse Hoover as the Republican presidential nominee, feeding a bitter enmity between the two men.

The issue that most divided them was hydroelectric power, and their skirmish lines had been drawn long before the onset of the depression. Hoover had consistently favored conservation and reclamation projects, including the unprecedentedly ambitious Hoover Dam on the Colorado River. But he flatly and unremittingly opposed Norris's pet proposal for federal operation of the waterpower facilities constructed during World War I on the Tennessee River at Muscle Shoals, Alabama. Hoover explained this apparent contradiction by drawing a distinction between "socialist" hydroelectric plants like Muscle Shoals, which would directly compete with private power companies, and facilities that only produced power "as a by-product of dams for the multiple purpose of irrigation, flood control and improvement of navigation."[48] Norris, not without cause, railed against this reasoning as hairsplitting sophistry, another example of Hoover's maddening tendency to subordinate real human needs to his obsessive desire for ideological consistency. Norris, in contrast, remembered the inky black nights of his frugal rural childhood and saw in government hydroelectric projects the means to shed light over the darkened countryside. He dreamed of harnessing the power of all the streams in America that flowed from the mountaintops to the sea.

The rustic Nebraskan's dogged fidelity to the cause of publicly owned and operated hydroelectric plants took on the trappings of a crusade in the 1920s. Muscle Shoals became a powerfully symbolic issue. Under its banner Norris mustered a small but dedicated troop of progressives who shared his dream of an inexpensively electrified America. They also

48. Hoover, *Memoirs: The Great Depression*, 325.

shared his revulsion at the financial prestidigitation of electric utility magnates, notoriously typified by Chicago's Samuel Insull. As Insull's byzantine corporate manipulations came to light in the wake of the Crash, Insull himself was about to become a potent symbol of the shattered business idols of the 1920s.

Calvin Coolidge had vetoed a bill embodying Norris's Tennessee River plan in 1928. Nearly seventy years old in 1930, Norris morosely reflected that "the end cannot be very many years in advance. I think I have, to a great extent, run my race."[49] Before the grave closed over him, he was determined to see his crusade for Muscle Shoals succeed. Herbert Hoover was to veto another Muscle Shoals bill of Norris's in 1931. Norris grimly held on until a more friendly administration might appear.

Norris and a few of his like-minded associates in Congress called for a Progressive Conference to convene in Washington in March 1931. The date fell shortly after the adjournment of the Seventy-first Congress and some nine months before the new Seventy-second Congress was scheduled to assemble — a decidedly dead season for meeting what the conference planners called "the imperative need of formulating a constructive legislative program."[50] In two days of deliberations on March 11 and 12 at Washington's Carleton Hotel, some three dozen progressives inconclusively discussed the electrical power industry, agriculture, the tariff, representative government, and unemployment. The curious timing of the meeting, its diffuse agenda, and its meager results all served as another reminder of just how ill-focused and uncertain the perception of the depression's gravity remained, even among self-styled progressives. At this late date in March 1931, nearly a year and a half after the stock market crash, they still had no coherent analysis of what was happening and no agreed plan of action. And the sparse attendance at the Progressive Conference — New York governor Franklin D. Roosevelt declined an invitation, though he sent a sympathetic message emphasizing his agricultural and hydroelectric policies, endearing him to Norris — illustrated the continuing political weightlessness of organized alternatives to Hoover's leadership in the antidepression battle. Hoover may have lost control of the Congress, but he did not as yet face a distinct, organized opposition.

After the adjournment of the lame-duck session of the Seventy-first Congress in March 1931, Congress would not assemble again until De-

---

49. Schlesinger 1:123.
50. Quoted in Romasco, *Poverty of Abundance*, 218.

cember 1931 unless the president summoned it into special session—
something that Hoover, with his memories of the tariff debacle in the
last special session and with the prospect of a Democratic House and
an uncontrollable Senate in the new Congress, understandably declined
to do. The hugger-mugger of partisan politics continued to offend him.
He remained a manager, not a politician. Perhaps the long adjournment
of Congress even struck him as an opportunity to take charge of the
antidepression battle without being pestered by nattering, grandstanding
legislators. The virulence of Democratic antagonism, a sorely beset Hoover complained in his *Memoirs*, "no man could measure or conciliate."[51]
These anxieties over a runaway legislature reinforced Hoover's already
deep commitment to fight the economic crisis not with statutes but with
presidentially orchestrated voluntary cooperation. Nineteen thirty-one
thus marked a long season of solitary presidential combat against the
massing forces of the nation's greatest economic disaster.

IT ALSO MARKED a savage quickening of those forces. Down to
the last weeks of 1930, Americans could still plausibly assume that they
were caught up in yet another of the routine business-cycle downswings
that periodically afflicted their traditionally boom-and-bust economy.
Their situation was painful but not unfamiliar, and their president was
in any case taking unprecedentedly vigorous corrective actions. Then,
in the closing weeks of the year, an epidemic of failures flashed through
the banking system, auguring the economy's slide into dark and alien
depths.

"Our banking system was the weakest link in our whole economic
system," Hoover believed, "the element most sensitive to fear . . . the
worst part of the dismal tragedy with which I had to deal."[52] American
banks were rotten even in good times. They failed at a rate of well over
five hundred per year throughout the 1920s. Nineteen twenty-nine saw
659 bank suspensions, a figure easily within the normal range for the
decade. Nineteen thirty witnessed about the same number of collapses
through October. Then, with a sickening swiftness, six hundred banks
closed their doors in the last sixty days of the year, bringing the annual
total to 1,352.

Underlying the weakness of the American banking system was the
sheer number of banks and the muddled structure that held them to-

51. Hoover, *Memoirs: The Great Depression*, 84.
52. Hoover, *Memoirs: The Great Depression*, 21, 84.

gether—or failed to. A lingering legacy of Andrew Jackson's long-ago war on central banking, the freewheeling American financial system had grown haphazardly for a century and counted some twenty-five thousand banks in 1929, operating under fifty-two different regulatory regimes. Many institutions were pitifully undercapitalized. Carter Glass, father of the Federal Reserve System launched in 1913, denounced them as no more than "pawn shops," often run by "little corner grocery-men calling themselves bankers—and all they know is how to shave a note."[53] Branch banking, by which well-capitalized metropolitan institutions filled the banking needs of small, outlying communities, might have provided stability to the banking system. But branch banking was the historical target of populist attacks on the diabolical "Money Power" and therefore was virtually unknown in the United States, in contrast to almost all other comparably developed nations; only 751 American banks operated branches in 1930. The overwhelming majority of American banks were, for all practical purposes, solitary (in banking jargon, "unitary") institutions that could look only to their own resources in the event of a panic. About a third of all banks were members of the Federal Reserve System, which theoretically could provide some succor at a time of difficulty, but as events were to show, the Fed proved fatefully inadequate at the crucial moment.[54]

Through this ramshackle financial structure in late 1930 fear licked like fire through a house of cards. Precisely what kindled the blaze is not clear, but disaster first flared in November 1930 at Louisville's National Bank of Kentucky, then spread virulently to groups of affiliated banks in neighboring Indiana, Illinois, Missouri, and eventually Iowa, Arkansas, and North Carolina. Mobs of shouting depositors shouldered up to tellers' windows to withdraw their savings. The banks, in turn, scrambled to preserve their liquidity in the face of these accelerating withdrawals by calling in loans and selling assets. As the beleaguered banks desperately sought cash by throwing their bond and real estate portfolios onto the market—a market already depressed by the Crash of 1929—they further drove down the value of assets in otherwise sound institutions, putting the entire banking system at peril. This vicious cy-

53. Glass quoted in Schwarz, *Interregnum of Despair*, 218, and in Caroline Bird, *The Invisible Scar* (New York: McKay, 1966) 97–98.

54. Data taken from Friedman and Schwartz, *Monetary History of the United States*, chap. 7, and Susan Estabrook Kennedy, *The Banking Crisis of 1933* (Lexington: University Press of Kentucky, 1973), chap. 1. Canada, where branch banking was the norm, saw no bank failures in this period.

cle—a classic liquidity crisis magnified to monstrous scale in the inordinately plural and disorganized world of American banking—soon threatened to become a roaring tornado that would rip the financial heart out of the economy.

At first the fever of panic afflicted only the chronically anemic rural banks. But on December 11, 1930, it struck close to the central nervous system of American capitalism when New York City's Bank of United States closed its doors. The Bank of United States, known colloquially as the "Pantspressers' Bank," was owned and operated by Jews and held the deposits of thousands of Jewish immigrants, many of them employed in the garment trades. Some observers then and later attributed its downfall to the deliberate refusal of the old-line Wall Street financial houses, especially the militantly gentile House of Morgan, to heed the Federal Reserve System's call to come to its rescue.[55]

The suspension of the Bank of United States represented the largest commercial bank failure in American history up to that time. It held the savings of some four hundred thousand persons, totaling nearly $286 million, but the damage done by its closing could not be calculated in cold ciphers. The locking of its doors provided a grotesque example of the manner in which psychological perception counted as heavily as the accountants' computations in shaking confidence in the banking system. The bank's very name misled many people at home and abroad into regarding it as some kind of official institution, amplifying the fearful effects of its collapse. More important, the failure of the Federal Reserve System to organize a rescue operation, as one upstate New York banker put it, "had shaken confidence in the Federal Reserve System more than any other occurrence in recent years."[56] With that confidence broken, banks rushed still more frantically to protect themselves, with little heed to the health of the banking system overall.

The banking panic of late 1930 was frightful, but what did it portend? Was it an end or a beginning? Was it only the banking system that was sick, or were American banks merely the most visible victims of a worldwide deflationary cycle? Some observers regarded the banking panic at the end of 1930 as the last awful spasm of the economic illness that had begun a year earlier. The difficulties of the midwestern banks could be attributed to the continuing agricultural depression; the collapse of the

55. See Ron Chernow, *The House of Morgan* (New York: Atlantic Monthly Press, 1990), 323–24.

56. Quoted in Friedman and Schwartz, *Monetary History of the United States*, 357.

Bank of United States could be understood as a delayed consequence of the Crash of 1929. (Its securities affiliate had speculated in dubious stocks, and two of its owners were later jailed.) Indeed, in the first quarter of 1931 the rate of bank failures slowed dramatically, and many indices of economic activity turned upward. Industrial production rose. So did payrolls and personal income. Many Americans, including Herbert Hoover, permitted themselves the guarded hope that the financial convulsions of late 1930 might have marked the beginning of the end. Some later observers have concurred. "All in all," two leading students of the Depression conclude, "the figures for the first four or five months of 1931, if examined without reference to what actually followed, have many of the earmarks of the bottom of a cycle and the beginning of a revival."[57] But "what actually followed" showed that this apparent bottom was only a way station to still deeper depression. The banking panic of late 1930 was eventually seen to have opened the trapdoor to a still more ghastly disaster to come.

What the banks needed in this critical hour was liquidity: money with which to meet the demands of depositors. But perversely, the effort of individual banks to maintain liquidity contracted the money supply, tightened credit, and inexorably clotted the system as a whole. In Utah, banker Marriner Eccles managed to keep his institution open through an agonizing day of massive withdrawals by depositors only by instructing his tellers to work in slow motion, deliberately counting out sums in small-denomination bills to the noisy throngs of customers who crowded onto his banking floor, clamoring for their cash. Thereafter, said Eccles, "we had to adopt a rough and distasteful credit and collection policy. Living with oneself was not a pleasant experience under those circumstances."

Reflecting on his predicament, Eccles "began to wonder whether the conduct of bankers like myself in depression times was a wise one. Were we not all contributing our bit to the worsening of matters by the mere act of trying to keep liquid under the economic pressures of deflation? By forcing the liquidation of loans and securities to meet the demands of depositors, were we not helping to drive prices down and thereby making it increasingly difficult for our debtors to pay back what they had borrowed from us? By our policies of credit stringency in a time of drastic deflation, were we not throwing a double loop around the throat

57. Friedman and Schwartz, *Monetary History of the United States,* 313.

of an economy that was already gasping for breath? In a time of deflation, would not the rational policy be one of monetary ease?"[58]

That would indeed have been the rational policy. It was, in fact, the policy Hoover had promoted in the weeks immediately following the Crash. But now, in the fateful second half of 1931, a peculiar constellation of factors blocked its effective implementation. Ironically, the very existence of the Federal Reserve System seemed to relieve the big private banks like the House of Morgan from playing the liquefying role they had assumed in earlier panics, such as 1907. At the Federal Reserve System itself, a vacuum of leadership left by the death in 1928 of Benjamin Strong, governor of the New York Federal Reserve Bank and long the Fed's dominant personality, wrought near paralysis after the failed effort to prop up the Bank of United States at the end of 1930. Above all, as events were soon to demonstrate, developments beyond the confines of the United States fatally confounded the system's efforts to cope with the banking crisis.

Down to early 1931, the American depression seemed largely to be the product of American causes. A decade of stagnation in agriculture, flattening sales in the automobile and housing markets, the piratical abuses on Wall Street, the hair-raising evaporation of asset values in the Crash, the woes of the anarchic banking system—these were surely problems enough. Still, they were domestic problems, and no American better understood them than Herbert Hoover, nor was any leader better prepared to take up arms against them. But now Europe was about to add some dreadful, back-breaking weight to Hoover's already staggering burden. In short order, what was still in 1931 called the depression was about to become the unprecedented calamity know to history as the Great Depression.

58. Marriner S. Eccles, *Beckoning Frontiers* (New York: Knopf, 1951), 70–71.

3

The Ordeal of Herbert Hoover

Hoover will be known as the greatest innocent bystander in history . . .
a brave man fighting valiantly, futilely, to the end.

— William Allen White, 1932

As early as December 1930 Hoover claimed that "the major forces of the depression now lie outside of the United States." His statement may at that moment have been overly self-protective and premature, but events soon gave the president's words the chill ring of prophecy, as shock waves from the collapsing international economic system smote the United States with lethal wallop. Until early 1931, midway through his presidency, Hoover had been aggressive and self-confident, a front-line fighter taking vigorous offensive against the economic crises. Now international events remorselessly pushed him back onto the defensive. His overriding goals became damage control and even national economic self-preservation. In late 1931 he starkly announced: "We are now faced with the problem, not of saving Germany or Britain, but of saving ourselves."[1]

From the spring of 1931 onward, this became Hoover's constant theme: that the calamity's deepest sources originated beyond American shores. From this time, too, it began to be clear that this depression was not just another cyclic valley but a historic watershed, something vastly greater in scale and more portentous in its implications than anything that had gone before. An unprecedented event, it must have extraordinary causes. Hoover found them in the most momentous episode of the century. It was now that he began to elaborate the thesis with which he

1. Herbert Hoover, *The Memoirs of Herbert Hoover: The Great Depression, 1929–1941* (New York: Macmillan, 1952) 59, 90.

began his *Memoirs*: "In the large sense the primary cause of the Great Depression was the war of 1914–1918."[2]

In the spring of 1931, Hoover explained, "just as we had begun to entertain well founded hopes that we were on our way out of the depression, our latent fears of Europe were realized in a gigantic explosion which shook the foundations of the world's economic, political, and social structure. At last the malign forces arising from economic consequences of the war, the Versailles Treaty, the postwar military alliances with their double prewar armament, their frantic public works programs to meet unemployment, their unbalanced budgets and the inflations, all tore their systems asunder."[3]

History lends much credibility to this view. The war had indeed set the stage for disaster, not least by hobbling the Germany economy with reparations payments, thus weakening the European economy as a whole and, not incidentally, paving the path for Adolf Hitler's rise to power. The malign forces to which Hoover referred stalked onto this stage in September 1930, when the Nazi Party exploited festering resentments over reparations and the deeply depressed state of the German economy to score ominous gains in parliamentary elections. This sharp Nazi advance ignited a serpentine chain reaction whose detonations eventually rocked even the remotest reaches of the American heartland. Americans, Hoover later drily noted, "were to learn about the economic interdependence of nations through a poignant experience which knocked at every cottage door."[4]

Seeking to rob Hitler of his main electoral appeal by bolstering the German economy, German chancellor Heinrich Bruning proposed in March 1931 a German customs union with Austria. The French government, darkly suspicious, regarded Bruning's proposal as a first step toward the Weimar Republic's annexation of Austria — something that the defeated Germans and Austrians had wanted to accomplish in 1919

2. Hoover, *Memoirs: The Great Depression*, 2.
3. Hoover, *Memoirs: The Great Depression*, 61.
4. Hoover, *Memoirs: The Great Depression*, 80. The economic historian Peter Temin has recently lent support to Hoover's analysis of the causes of the Depression. "The origins of the Great Depression lie largely in the disruptions of the First World War," Temin writes in *Lessons from the Great Depression* (Cambridge: MIT Press, 1989), 1. Yet it remains the case that economists are if anything less confident than they once were that they have identified the precise causes of the Depression. A singular event, the Depression has thus far resisted comprehensive explanation by analysts applying supposedly universal theories of economic behavior.

but that the Versailles Treaty explicitly prohibited. The prospect that France might begin squeezing Austrian banks as a way of frustrating Bruning's design touched off a banking panic in Vienna. By May depositors were rioting outside the largest Austrian bank, Louis Rothschild's Kreditanstalt, and the bank shut its doors. The trouble then spread to Germany. Panic swelled, and many German banks closed, followed by more closures in neighboring countries.

Underlying and complicating this alarming chain of events was the tangled issue of international debts and reparations payments stemming from the war of 1914–18. One obvious way to relieve the pressure on the beleaguered Germans and Austrians was to break the chain by repudiating or suspending those obligations. The United States might lead the way by forgiving or rescheduling the $10 billion it was owed by the Allies, chiefly Britain and France, as a result of loans made from the U.S. Treasury during and immediately after the war. Morgan partner Thomas P. Lamont telephoned Hoover on June 5, 1931, to suggest just that. Hoover was already exploring the idea on his own, but he reminded Lamont of its political explosiveness. "Sitting in New York, as you do," Hoover lectured, "you have no idea what the sentiment of the country at large is on these inter-governmental debts."[5]

Lamont had rasped a knotted political nerve, its ganglia embedded in the Versailles peace settlement of 1919, and its endings raw and sensitive in the America of 1931. At Versailles the victors had forced defeated Germany to acknowledge sole guilt for the war and as a consequence to pay some $33 billion in reparations. The Germans had groaned under that debt burden through the 1920s. They had twice renegotiated its terms, securing an extended schedule of payment in the Dawes Plan of 1924 and winning further rescheduling, as well as a reduction in the overall amount owed, in the Young Plan of 1929.

Though the United States made only nominal claims for reparations from Germany, both Charles G. Dawes and Owen D. Young were Americans. They owed their eponymous roles in the debt negotiations to the fact that their country had emerged from the World War in the unaccustomed position of a leading international creditor. The U.S. Treasury had loaned money to the Allied governments in wartime, and private American bankers had loaned significant sums to Germany in the 1920s. The Germans relied on the continuing infusion of private American loans to make reparations payments to the British and the

5. Ron Chernow, *The House of Morgan* (New York: Atlantic Monthly 1990), 325.

French, who in turn applied those sums to their own bills at the American treasury.

This surreal financial merry-go-round was inherently unstable. It had been rudely shoved out of balance when the stock market crash of late 1929 dried up the well of American credit, knocking a crucial link out of the circuit of international cash flows. In this sense it could be argued that the American crash had helped to initiate the global depression, but Hoover's point still stands that the shock of the Crash fell on a global financial system already distorted and vulnerable because of the war.

For their part, the Allies had more than once offered to relax their demands on Germany, but only if their own obligations to the United States could be forgiven. The French Chamber of Deputies in 1929 made a dramatic point of this idea when it explicitly resolved to cover its payments to the United States with the proceeds of German reparations. That gesture outraged Americans.

The tightfisted Republican administrations of the 1920s had refused to admit any connection between German reparations and the debts owed by the Allied governments to the U.S. Treasury. All efforts to scale back those intergovernmental debts were widely regarded in the United States as ploys to shift the burden of the war's cost from Europeans to Americans. As disillusionment spread in the postwar decade about the futility and error of Woodrow Wilson's departure from isolationist principles in 1917, Americans were in no mood to consider absorbing a greater share of the war's cost. Popular feeling on this issue was further aroused by the attitude of Wall Street, which favored war-debt cancellation not least of all because forgiving the governmental loans would render its own private loans more secure. On Main Street, especially in the post-Crash atmosphere, this kind of thinking, so obviously willing to sacrifice taxpayers' dollars to the cause of securing the bankers', was anathema. Iron-toothed insistence on full payment of the Allied war debts thus became not only a financial issue but a political and a psychological issue as well, a totem of disgust with corrupt Europe, of regret at having intervened in the European war, and of provincial America's determination not to be suckered by silky international financiers.

THIS WAS THE SENTIMENT —penny-pinching, isolationist, anti–European, anti–Wall Street, and hotly felt—about which Hoover reminded Lamont over the telephone on June 5. To understand its depth and temperature is to appreciate the political courage of Hoover's proposal on June 20, 1931, that all nations observe a one-year moratorium on "all payments on intergovernmental debts, reparations and relief debts, both principal and interest."[6] Though Congress eventually ratified this proposal, Hoover was savagely attacked for bringing it forward. One Republican congressman denounced him as an "Oriental potentate drunk with power . . . an agent of Germany." Somewhat inconsistently, California Republican senator Hiram Johnson, already mistrustful of what he took to be Hoover's dangerous internationalism, took to calling him "the Englishman in the White House." Hoover's old nemesis George Norris expressed the anxiety of many when he said that "I cannot help but be suspicious that [the one-year moratorium] is a fore-runner for the cancellation of the balance . . . due us from foreign governments."[7] (Norris's suspicion was eventually confirmed, nourishing even more robust isolationist sentiment later in the decade.)

The moratorium on intergovernmental debt payments was intended to provide the reeling German bankers with a needed respite. Hoover followed it with a "standstill" agreement whereby private banks also pledged themselves not to present their German paper for payment. Taken together, these measures were aimed at calming the German eye of the global financial hurricane, thus sparing the American financial system from its fury. These were positive and forceful initiatives, but as Hoover later lamented, they provided "only a momentary breathing spell, for the larger forces [of the crisis] had now begun to gnaw like wolves into the financial vitals of Britain."[8] Despite his efforts, said Hoo-

---

6. Hoover, *Memoirs: The Great Depression*, 70.

7. Other voices praised Hoover and even saw political advantage for him in this forth-right, statesmanlike move. The *Nation*, usually unfriendly to the president, called the moratorium "President Hoover's Great Action . . . the most far-reaching and the most praiseworthy step taken by an American President since the treaty of peace." One newspaper opined that the moratorium rendered Hoover "a marvelously reha-bilitated candidate" for 1932. Another concluded that his action made "the picture of a cowering, dismayed and bewildered Hoover which the extremists have been so busily painting seem more or less ridiculous." Jordan Schwarz, *The Interregnum of Despair* (Urbana: University of Illinois Press, 1970), 85, 47, 82, 79.

The French balked at Hoover's proposal but eventually acquiesced, though French premier Laval, visiting Washington in October, secured Hoover's agreement that at the moratorium's expiration and before the next reparation payment fell due the twin questions of debts owed the United States and reparations due from Germany might be comprehensively discussed. These matters were now implicitly linked by the inclu-sive terms of Hoover's initiative, though the American government still officially de-nied any connection. Fatefully, the date scheduled for the first postmoratorium debt payment, and hence the target date for resolution of this vexatious issue, fell on De-cember 15, 1932 — five weeks *after* the quadrennial American presidential election.

8. Hoover, *Memoirs: The Great Depression*, 80.

ver, in a metallurgical figure of speech that befitted his mining background, "apprehension began to run like mercury through the financial world."[9]

But the metal that mattered in 1931 was not mercury. It was gold. Most countries still adhered to the gold standard, and with few exceptions most economists and statesmen reverenced gold with a mystical devotion that resembled religious faith. Gold underlay the most sacred token of national sovereignty: money. It guaranteed the value of money; more to the point, it guaranteed the value of a nation's currency beyond its own frontiers. Gold was therefore considered indispensable to the international trade and financial system. Nations issued their currencies in amounts fixed by the ratio of money in circulation to gold reserves. In theory, incoming gold was supposed to expand the monetary base, increase the amount of money in circulation, and thereby inflate prices and lower interest rates. Outflowing gold supposedly had the inverse effect: shrinking the monetary base, contracting the money supply, deflating prices, and raising interest rates. According to the rules of the gold-standard game, a country losing gold was expected to deflate its economy — to lower prices so as to stimulate exports, and to raise interest rates so as to reverse the outflow of capital. Indeed, these effects were assumed to happen virtually automatically. In actual practice, the gold-standard system was less systematic, less rule-bound, and more asymmetrical than the theory allowed. Nor did it necessarily work automatically. Countries losing gold were indeed under strong pressure to tighten credit or risk defaulting on their exchange-rate commitments. The latter option was thought to be prohibitively costly; events soon proved it was not. And creditor countries were under no like obligation to inflate when gold flowed in. They could simply "sterilize" surplus gold and carry on as before, leaving gold-losing countries to fend for themselves.

By tying the world's economy together, the gold standard theoretically ensured that economic fluctuations in one country would be transmitted to others. It was in fact that very transmission that was supposed to dampen erratic movements and keep the global system in equilibrium. In fair economic weather, the gold standard was thought to operate more or less mechanically as a kind of benign hydraulic pump that kept prices and interest rates stable, or fluctuating only within narrow bands, throughout the world trading system.

In the foul economic weather of 1931, however, huge surges emanating

9. Hoover, *Memoirs: The Great Depression*, 63.

from the national economic crises in Austria and Germany threatened to swamp other countries, and the international plumbing broke down. What Hoover called "refugee gold" and "flight capital" began to course wildly to and fro through the conduits of the gold-standard pumping system. Hoover likened the panicky and lurching movements of gold and credit, "constantly driven by fear hither and yon over the world," to "a loose cannon on the deck of the world in a tempest-tossed sea."[10]

Nations with already depressed economies proved to have little stomach for suffering further deflation through the loss of gold. To protect themselves, they raised tariff barriers and slapped controls on the export of capital. Almost all of them eventually jettisoned the gold standard itself. Frightened and battered, reefed and battened, virtually every ship of state thus set cowering and solitary course for safe haven. When the storm at last abated, it left the world forever transformed. The pre-1931 gold standard, which had been the Ark of the Covenant of the international economic order for more than a century, would never again be fully restored to the tabernacle of global commerce.

Britain took the fateful step on September 21, 1931. Drained of gold by jumpy European creditors and politically unwilling to take the deflationary steps to bid gold back to English shores, Britain defaulted on further gold payments to foreigners.[11] More than two dozen other countries quickly followed suit. John Maynard Keynes, already tinkering with heretical theories about "managed currency," rejoiced at "the breaking of our gold fetters."[12] But most observers, including Hoover, regarded the British abandonment of the gold standard as an unmitigated catastrophe. In an apt metaphor, Hoover likened the British situation to that of a failing bank, faced with depositors' demands but unable to turn its assets into cash, and thus forced to bar its doors. The difference was that Britain was not a piddling country bank but a central pillar of the global financial structure. When it suspended payments, world commerce shivered to a stop.

10. Hoover, *Memoirs: The Great Depression*, p. 67.
11. At the Royal Navy base at Invergordon, Scotland, a strike—sometimes described as a mutiny—over proposed pay cuts convinced the British government of the political impossibility of imposing the kind of austerity program that would have been required to stay on the gold standard.
12. Chernow, *House of Morgan*, 331. As early as 1923 former U.S. Treasury official and Morgan partner Russell Leffingwell had warned that "Keynes . . . is flirting with strange gods and proposing to abandon the gold standard forever and to substitute a 'managed' currency [.] . . . [I]t is better to have some standard than to turn our affairs over to the wisdom of publicist-economists for management" (271).

The moratorium, the standstill agreement, and the British departure from gold meant that a vast volume of the world's financial assets — anything that constituted a claim on Austrian, German, or British banks, or those of any of the other countries that repudiated gold — were now frozen. The United States had already helped to clog the arteries of world trade by erecting high tariff barriers and by constricting its capital outflows after the Wall Street crash. Now, as the world's financial life-blood congealed, the international economy slowed to an arctic stillness. Germany would soon declare policies of national self-sufficiency. Britain in the Ottawa Agreements of 1932 effectively created a closed trading bloc — the so-called Imperial Preference System — sealing off the British empire from the commerce of other nations. The volume of global business shrank from some $36 billion of traffic in 1929 to about $12 billion by 1932.

The blow to American foreign trade was a harmful consequence of Britain's departure from gold, but hardly a fatal one. The United States at this time simply did not depend on foreign trade to the degree that other nations did, a fact to which the high protective tariffs of 1922 and 1930 testified.

More directly hurtful was the punishment that the German panic and the British abandonment of gold inflicted on the already crippled American financial system, still shuddering from the rash of bank failures in the final weeks of 1930. American banks held on the asset side of their ledgers some $1.5 billion in German and Austrian obligations, which were for the moment effectively worthless. Worse, the psychology of fear was rapidly overflowing international frontiers, running dark and swift from central Europe to Britain. It now washed over the United States. Foreign investors began withdrawing gold and capital from the American banking system. Domestic depositors, once bitten, twice shy, renewed with a vengeance their runs on banks, precipitating a liquidity crisis that dwarfed the panic in the final weeks of 1930. That earlier crisis thus served both as rehearsal and foundation for the full-blown catastrophe that hit in 1931. Five hundred twenty-two banks failed in the single month following Britain's farewell to gold. By year's end, 2,294 American banks had suspended operations, nearly twice as many as in 1930 and an all-time American record.[13]

American banks now bled profusely from two wounds: one inflicted

13. A larger number of banks suspended in 1933, but the figures for that year are not comparable because of the peculiar circumstance of the national "banking holiday" declared in March. HSUS, 1038, n. 8.

by domestic runs on deposits and the other by foreign withdrawals of capital. Unfortunately, the rules of the gold-standard game, as Hoover and most American bankers understood them, dictated that the latter problem take precedence over the former. In theory, American central banking authorities should now undertake deflationary measures; in practice, they did. This forced deflation in the context of an already deflated economy was the perverse logic of the gold standard against which Keynes was railing. To stanch the outflow of gold, the Federal Reserve System raised its rediscount rate, as gold-standard doctrine dictated that it should. In fact, the Fed moved with unprecedented muscularity, bumping the rate by a full percentage point in just one week's time. What the banking system as a whole needed, however, was not tighter money but easier money, as Marriner Eccles and other bankers knew, so that it might meet the demands of panicky depositors.

The starkly deflationary discipline of the gold standard now stood nakedly revealed to Americans as it had to Britons just weeks earlier. Britain had slipped that discipline by breaking loose from gold, freeing it to advance down a path toward at least a modest economic recovery in 1932. Within a year and a half, Franklin Roosevelt would do the same for the United States, creating a wholly new context for the exercise of monetary and fiscal policy. For the moment, however, Hoover chose to struggle within the gold standard's severely constraining framework. Why?

The answer is to be found in a legacy of perception and understanding of economic theory that would give way only grudgingly in the generation following Hoover's presidency. The world down to his time, for a century or more, had known only brief and painful interruptions of the gold-standard regime. It was widely assumed that there was simply no other workable basis on which currencies could be rendered reliable and on which the international economy could function. Without the link to gold, the value of a nation's money was deemed to be arbitrary and unpredictable. Its currency became "soft," perhaps unconvertible, and transactions across its national frontiers were turned into risky gambling ventures. The abandonment of gold, as Hoover put it, meant that "no merchant could know what he might receive in payment by the time his goods were delivered."[14] John Maynard Keynes had been trying for nearly a decade by 1931 to develop a theory of national and international monetary management that would not depend on gold. But even Keynes's ideas at this stage were not fully developed (his great work,

14. Hoover, *Memoirs: The Great Depression*, 66.

The General Theory of Employment, Interest, and Money, would not appear until 1936), and on this point at this time he commanded the barest of audiences among both economists and statesmen.

HOOVER THUS CONFRONTED an altogether more severe and complicated crisis in late 1931 than he had just a year earlier. In the face of this new circumstance, he resorted to a new tactic: an aggressive effort to balance the federal budget by raising taxes. This policy was sharply criticized by later economists who were to learn from Keynes's *General Theory* that the cure for depressions was not fiscal balance but deliberate deficit spending. In fact, the notion that government deficits might offset downturns in the business cycle had been current in academic and policymaking circles throughout the 1920s, and Hoover himself was conversant with this line of thinking. In May of 1931, Secretary of State Henry Stimson recorded in his diary that Hoover argued strenuously against the budget balancers in his own cabinet. "The President likened it to war times," according to Stimson. "He said in war times no one dreamed of balancing the budget. Fortunately we can borrow."[15]

After the British departure from gold and renewed runs on banks in the last half of 1931, however, Hoover changed his mind and asked for a sizeable tax increase. He drafted and submitted to Congress a bill that became the Revenue Act of 1932. He faced, to be sure, prospective deficits that, like so much else in this era, went wildly beyond all known precedent. The 1932 federal budget would end up $2.7 billion in the red — by far the largest peacetime deficit in American history to that time, and a figure that represented almost 60 percent of federal expenditures. No New Deal deficit would be proportionately larger. Ironically enough, Franklin D. Roosevelt was soon to make the federal budget deficit a centerpiece of his attack on Hoover in the presidential election campaign of 1932.

But neither reflex fiscal orthodoxy nor even the staggering size of the budget numbers fully accounts for Hoover's decision in late 1931 to ask Congress for a tax increase. At least as important as those considerations were the state of Hoover's thinking at this point about the depression's causes, character, and cure and the peculiar constellation of circumstances in which he found himself. In Hoover's mind, the depression — or the Great Depression, as it might now be legitimately called — originated in the collapse of the European banking and credit structures,

15. Schwarz, *Interregnum of Despair*, 112–13.

disfigured as they were by the stresses of the World War. As Hoover saw things, the force of that collapse transmitted itself to the United States through the mechanism of the gold standard, and its impact threatened to inundate the already chaotic and floundering American banking system. Strict adherence to the gold-standard rules dictated further deflation for the United States, but outright deflation was intolerable to Hoover. His overriding goal was to pump life-giving liquidity into the American credit system, desiccated as it was by domestic runs, foreign withdrawals, and the Federal Reserve System's tight-money policies to protect the gold standard. By liquefying the system, he would make money available for business borrowing, thus promoting general economic activity and recovery. Through a complex reasoning process, one that comprehended psychological factors as well as strictly economic ones, Hoover convinced himself that a tax hike would stabilize the banking system and thus generate the desired liquidity.

Hoover's critics then and later insisted that this indirect or "trickle-down" approach was insufficient—that only a direct stimulus to the economy by large government expenditures for relief and public works would have the necessary tonic effect. An exchange between Hoover's secretary of the treasury, Ogden Mills, and New York Democratic senator Robert Wagner during hearings on an unemployment relief bill in 1932 nicely captured the differences in economic philosophies. "I want to break the ice by lending to industry so that somebody will begin to spend some money," said Mills. "I'm trying to put men to work and you won't cooperate," charged Wagner.[16]

Even Keynes at this time offered encouragement for Hoover's approach. Appearing in May 1931 at a conference on unemployment at the University of Chicago, he said: "I think the argument for public works in this country is much weaker than it is in Great Britain. . . . I think in this country . . . the means of getting back to a state of equilibrium should be concentrated on the rate of interest" — in other words, on easing credit by shoring up the banking system. Only later would Keynes develop at length the argument he briefly adumbrated in his 1930 volume, A Treatise on Money: that in some cases "it is not sufficient for the Central Authority to stand ready to lend . . . it must also stand ready to borrow. In other words, the Government must itself promote a programme of domestic investment."[17]

16. Schwarz, Interregnum of Despair, 167.
17. Herbert Stein, The Fiscal Revolution in America (Chicago: University of Chicago Press, 1969), 146, 140.

It is in this context of the state of economic knowledge and the particular circumstances in the United States and the world in late 1931 that Hoover's request for a tax increase must be understood. A government's budget was universally regarded as both symbol and substance of a nation's commitment to maintain the value of its currency. Balancing the budget, therefore, by reassuring foreign creditors, should dampen their withdrawals of gold. More concretely, raising revenues by taxation, as distinguished from borrowing, would take the government out of competition with private borrowers in the already squeezed credit markets, thus helping to keep interest rates low. Keeping interest rates low, in turn, would not only facilitate business borrowing but would preserve the value of bonds still held in the banks' badly weakened portfolios, thus easing pressures for further liquidation of bank assets. The request for higher taxes, in short, as Herbert Stein has explained, "was a kind of bond support program, to be carried out with tax receipts rather than with newly created money. It must be understood in the light of the unwillingness, or inability, of the Federal Reserve to support bonds by creating more new money in the fall of 1931. . . . The important point is that the decision to raise taxes was made in a condition of rising interest rates, falling bond prices, increasing bank suspensions, and a large gold outflow. A more relaxed attitude toward balancing the budget [such as Hoover had adopted just six months earlier] did not appear in government policy until the Roosevelt administration when all of these conditions were radically changed."[18]

The Revenue Act of 1932 made its way through Congress with only nominal opposition. A controversial proposal for a national sales tax was eventually deleted, but the final legislation raised taxes across the board and brought a half million new taxpayers (for a total of about 1.9 million) into the federal revenue net by reducing low-income exemptions. The act envisioned doubling federal tax receipts and set the essential features of the tax structure for the remainder of the decade. All subsequent efforts to revise the tax code in the 1930s, in fact, were aimed at increasing tax yields still further. On the question of the sanctity of a balanced budget, in short, Hoover stood safely within a broad consensus that endured until World War II, when, not incidentally, the federal tax system was expanded even more dramatically. Speaker Garner grudgingly withdrew his support for the sales tax feature, but he told his colleagues in the House: "I would levy any tax, sales or any other kind, in order to . . . balance the budget. . . . The country at this time is in a

18. Stein, *Fiscal Revolution in America*, 32, 35.

condition where the worst taxes you could possibly levy would be better than no taxes at all." He then histrionically requested all members who believed with him in a balanced budget to arise from their seats. Not a single representative remained seated.[19]

HOOVER'S COMMITMENT to the maintenance of the gold standard represented the purest, most conventional economic orthodoxy. But while his devotion to a balanced budget had the same appearance of orthodoxy, it actually owed more to the peculiar circumstances of the moment than to uncritical faith in the received fiscal wisdom. In his ongoing effort to liquefy the credit system Hoover would soon show himself capable of the most pragmatic, far-reaching economic heterodoxy. The effort would test all his powers of creativity and command and would in the end carry him and the country into uncharted economic and political territory. From this phase of the crisis dates the onset of a period of experimentation and institutional innovation that would continue into the New Deal.

Hoover took the first steps into that new territory on the Sunday evening of October 4, 1931, when he quietly slipped out of the White House to join a group of bankers he had summoned to meet him at Treasury Secretary Mellon's elegant home on Massachusetts Avenue. In a tense conversation that extended into the small hours of the morning, he urged that the stronger private banks create a $500 million credit pool to assist weaker institutions. Out of these talks emerged the National Credit Association. It was a private bankers' pool, and as such it testified to Hoover's continuing preference for nongovernmental, voluntaristic approaches. But the circumstances of its birth and brief life also testified to the growing recognition, even in the highest circles of capitalism long thought to be mortally opposed to governmental intrusion, and indeed in Hoover's own mind, of the irrelevance of the voluntaristic approach.

The bankers gathered under Mellon's glittering chandeliers on October 4 acceded to Hoover's request, but, he later wrote, "they constantly reverted to a proposal that the government do it. . . . I returned to the White House after midnight more depressed than ever before." After only a few weeks of activity, and after dispensing a paltry $10 million in loans, wrote Hoover, "the bankers' National Credit Association became ultraconservative, then fearful, and finally died. . . . Its members—

19. Schwarz, *Interregnum of Despair*, 124–25.

and the business world—threw up their hands and asked for governmental action."[20]

At this moment Hoover stood on the shore of a political and ideological Rubicon. He had gingerly waded into it more than two years earlier with the creation of federally funded agricultural stabilization corporations. Now he plunged in deeply. Desperate to save the banking system, disappointed at the timidity of private capital, and faced with the business community's own demand for "governmental action," he proposed a series of measures that amounted to a repudiation of his own voluntaristic principles. Sometimes lumped together as Hoover's "second program" against the Depression (to distinguish them from the voluntary wage and private construction agreements of late 1929), these measures would eventually help to revolutionize the American financial world. They would also lay the groundwork for a broader restructuring of government's role in many other sectors of American life, a restructuring known as the New Deal.

The entire national credit apparatus was under siege. The president's understanding of economic theory instructed him that what it needed was money. The Federal Reserve System, committed to protecting the nation's gold stock by lifting interest rates, was an uncooperative partner in this effort. Thus Hoover, with the grudging acquiescence of Congress, moved to reform the system and to create wholly new instrumentalities to bolster the sagging credit structure.

Among the first of his initiatives was the Glass-Steagall Act of February 1932, which markedly broadened the definition of acceptable collateral for Federal Reserve System loans and for the issuance of Federal Reserve notes. These actions allowed the system to release large amounts of gold from its reserve holdings and still significantly expand the monetary base.

Hoover also proposed in November 1931 that Congress provide for home-mortgage holders a rediscounting service similar to that which the Federal Reserve System offered to banking and commercial interests. Mortgage paper could not be presented for discounting at the Federal Reserve, but Hoover asked that it be made eligible as security for loans at up to twelve new Home Loan Banks. Like the Glass-Steagall Act, this legislation was designed to thaw millions of dollars in frozen assets. To

20. Hoover, *Memoirs: The Great Depression*, 86, 97. See also Albert U. Romasco, *The Poverty of Abundance: Hoover, the Nation, the Depression* (New York: Oxford University Press, 1965), 87–96.

Hoover's bitter regret, Congress weakened his bill by setting higher collateral requirements than he wanted and delayed final passage of the Federal Home Loan Bank Act until July 1932. In the meantime, thousands of families lost their homes. "All this seems dull economics," Hoover noted, "but the poignant American drama revolving around the loss of the old homestead had a million repetitions straight from life, not because of the designing villain but because of a fault in our financial system."[21]

By far the most radical, innovative, and ultimately consequential initiative in Hoover's "second program" was the creation in January 1932 of the Reconstruction Finance Corporation (RFC). The failure of the short-lived National Credit Association had shown the inadequacy of private measures to shore up the buckling banks. The bankers themselves wanted federal action. Swallowing his dearest principles, Hoover now gave it to them. Patterned on the War Finance Corporation that had been created to fund the construction of military plants in 1918, the RFC was an instrument for making taxpayers' dollars directly available to private financial institutions. Congress capitalized the new agency at $500 million and authorized it to borrow up to $1.5 billion more. The RFC was to use these sums to provide emergency loans to banks, building-and-loan societies, railroads, and agricultural stabilization corporations.

Business Week called the RFC "the most powerful offensive force [against the Depression] that governmental and business imagination has, so far, been able to command." Even critics of Hoover like the *New Republic* conceded that "there has been nothing quite like it." Its swift creation and sweeping mandate left Senator Norris "dazed. . . . I have been called a socialist, a bolshevik, a communist, and a lot of other terms of a similar nature," said Norris, "but in the wildest flights of my imagination I never thought of such a thing as putting the Government into business as far as this bill would put it in."[22]

However grudgingly, Hoover had now unmistakably compromised his belief in voluntarism and embraced direct government action. "Mr. Hoover," commented Columbia University economist Rexford Tugwell, "who has always described himself as one who believes 'that government is best which governs least,' is now in process of pushing the government into the banking business. At the very least his program may be de-

21. Hoover, *Memoirs: The Great Depression*, 111.
22. Romasco, *Poverty of Abundance*, 189; Schwarz, *Interregnum of Despair*, 92.

scribed as 'bank relief.' These weeks and months of depression are rapidly and inevitably weaving governmental controls into the American economy. . . . [O]ut of such a development," concluded Tugwell, who would soon become a major architect of the New Deal, "one may imagine what pictures of government in business one pleases; none of them would conform to Mr. Hoover's expressed horror of governmental interference."[23]

Tugwell astutely recognized that the creation of the RFC constituted a historical pivot. The turning was not uncontroversial. New York's Fiorello La Guardia denounced the RFC as "a millionaire's dole." But soon he and other progressives discerned, as Tugwell had, the fateful precedent that the creation of the RFC had established. If Hoover could be made to support federal relief for the banks, why not federal relief for the unemployed? By agreeing to the bankers' demands for the RFC— "bank relief," as Tugwell had called it—the president had implicitly legitimated the claims of other sectors for federal assistance. Hoover had given up the ground of high principle. He now stood ideologically shorn before a storm of demands for unemployment relief.

IT WAS NOW the third winter of the Depression. In the long-blighted countryside, unmarketable crops rotted in fields and unsellable livestock died on the hoof, as the Federal Farm Board's stabilization corporations exhausted their price-support funds. In towns and cities across the country, haggard men in shabby overcoats, collars turned up against the chill wind, newspapers plugging the holes in their shoes, lined up glumly for handouts at soup kitchens. Tens of thousands of displaced workers took to the roads, thumbs up, hitching west, huddled in boxcars, heading south, drifting north, east, wherever the highways and the railroads led, wherever there might be a job. Those who stayed put hunkered down, took in their jobless relatives, kited the grocery bills

23. Rexford G. Tugwell, "Flaws in the Hoover Economic Plan," *Current History*, January 1932, 531. Tugwell later conceded that "practically the whole New Deal was extrapolated from programs that Hoover started. . . . When it was all over I once made a list of New Deal ventures begun during Hoover's years as secretary of commerce and then as president. I had to concluded that his policies were substantially correct. The New Deal owed much to what he had begun. . . . Hoover had wanted—and had said clearly enough that he wanted—nearly all the changes now brought under the New Deal label." Tugwell quoted in Joan Hoff Wilson, *Herbert Hoover: Forgotten Progressive* (Boston, Little, Brown, 1975), 158; see also Tugwell, *Roosevelt's Revolution: The First Year, a Personal Perspective* (New York: Macmillan, 1977), xiii–xiv; and Tugwell, *The Brains Trust* (New York: Viking, 1968), xxii.

at the corner store, patched their old clothes, darned and redarned their socks, tried to shore up some fragments of hope against the ruins of their dreams.

The Depression struck with especially harsh fury in the ethnic communities so shallowly rooted in American soil. The frail institutions so painstakingly erected by the first immigrant generation simply fell apart. Banks serving immigrant neighborhoods were among the first to close their doors when the round of panics began. In Chicago, the Binga State Bank, which served the black community, folded in 1930; it was soon followed by the First Italian State Bank, the Slovak Papanek-Kovac State Bank, the Czech Novak and Stieskal State Bank, the Lithuanian Universal State Bank, the Jewish Noel State Bank, and "Smulski's Bank," where many Poles had deposited their meager savings. The mutual benefit and fraternal insurance societies and the religious welfare organizations with which immigrants had tried to defend themselves against the abundant uncertainties of everyday life collapsed under the weight of the demands now put upon them. Chicago's Jewish Charities in 1932 struggled to support some fifty thousand jobless Jews. Unemployed men skulked at home while their wives and children scrounged what work they could find. Traditional patterns of family authority and status eroded. A Polish woman told a social worker in Chicago that because she had been working for four years while her husband was jobless, "I am the boss in the family for I have full charge in running this house. You know, who make the money he is the boss." "One of the most common things," one Chicagoan later reflected about his Depression-era childhood, "was this feeling of your father's failure. That somehow he hadn't beaten the rap."[24]

No one starved, Hoover claimed, but in New York City school officials reported some twenty thousand malnourished children in 1932, while apples fell to the ground in Oregon orchards for want of buyers. This spectacle of dire want in the midst of wasting plenty bred perplexity and anger. Hillocks of unsold wheat shadowed the prairies, while in Seattle, Chicago, New York, and dozens of other cities men and women nightly scratched through dank alleys, grubbing for scraps of food in garbage cans.

No issue plagued Hoover more painfully, or caused him more political and personal hurt, than the plight of the unemployed. By early 1932

24. Lizabeth Cohen, *Making a New Deal: Industrial Workers in Chicago, 1919–1939* (Cambridge: Cambridge University Press, 1990), 248.

well over ten million persons were out of work, nearly 20 percent of the labor force. In big cities like Chicago and Detroit that were home to hard-hit capital goods industries like steelmaking and automobile manufacturing, the unemployment rate approached 50 percent. Chicago authorities counted 624,000 unemployed persons in their city at the end of 1931. In Detroit, General Motors laid off 100,000 workers out of its 1929 total of some 260,000 employees. All told, 223,000 jobless workers idled in the streets of the nation's automobile capital by the winter of 1931–32. Black workers, traditionally the last hired and the first fired, suffered especially. In Chicago blacks made up 4 percent of the population but 16 percent of the unemployed; in the Pittsburgh steel districts they were 8 percent of the population but accounted for almost 40 percent of the unemployed.[25]

Many workers who remained on the payroll went on shorter hours. Perhaps one-third of all employed persons were working part-time, so that in the aggregate almost 50 percent of the nation's human workpower was going unutilized. Those lucky enough still to hold some kind of job also found themselves working for smaller paychecks. U.S. Steel cut wages by 10 percent in September 1931, the first major employer to break the 1929 agreement with Hoover about maintaining wage rates. Its action was swiftly followed by General Motors and other major corporations employing some 1.7 million workers. Unemployment now loomed not as a transient difficulty but as a deep, intractable problem that showed no sign of abating. The feeling spread that the nation had turned a historical corner, to find itself facing an endless future of pervasive, structural unemployment. "The real problem in America," one prominent Democrat said in 1932, "is not to feed ourselves for one more winter, it is to find what we are going to do with ten or twelve million people who are permanently displaced."[26]

The country had never before known unemployment of these magnitudes or of this duration. It had in place no mechanism with which to combat mass destitution on this scale. Private unemployment insurance plans, sponsored by employers and unions, including a pioneering program at General Electric, covered fewer than two hundred thousand workers as the Depression began, less than 1 percent of the private-sector

25. Romasco, *Poverty of Abundance*, 155, 167; figures on black unemployment are from Lester Chandler, *America's Greatest Depression* (New York: Harper and Row, 1970), 40.
26. Schwarz, *Interregnum of Despair*, 160.

work force. Relief for the poor had traditionally been the responsibility of state and local governments and private charities, but their combined resources were no match for the enormous national calamity they now confronted. Many states that tried to raise more money for relief by increasing taxes faced revolts from angry and hard-pressed citizens. Almost all state and local governments had by 1932 exhausted their legal or market-dictated borrowing capacity. Pennsylvania, for example, was constitutionally prohibited from incurring a debt of more than $1 million, as well as from levying a graduated income tax.

Hoover characteristically tried to stimulate local government and charitable assistance to the unemployed with two voluntary committees, the President's Emergency Committee for Employment, chaired by Arthur Woods from its inception in October 1930 to its demise in April 1931, and its successor, the President's Organization on Unemployment Relief, headed by Walter S. Gifford, the president of American Telephone and Telegraph and chairman of the Charity Organization Society of New York City. By certain measures, these bodies achieved commendable results. Municipal government payments for relief in New York City, for example, rose from $9 million in 1930 to $58 million in 1932. New Yorkers' private charitable giving increased from $4.5 million in 1930 to $21 million in 1932. But though those figures testified to the compassion of City Hall and the perhaps surprisingly soft hearts of individual New Yorkers, they were pathetically inadequate. Combined public and private relief expenditures of $79 million in New York City for the entire year of 1932 amounted to less than one month's loss of wages for the eight hundred thousand New Yorkers out of work. In Chicago, lost wages from unemployment were estimated at $2 million per day in late 1931; relief expenditures totaled $100,000 per day.[27]

In the face of this breakdown of the traditional relief apparatus, the cry for direct federal assistance grew ever more insistent. "We can no longer depend on passing the hat, and rattling the tin cup," the famed Kansas editor William Allen White wrote to his senator in Washington. "We have gone to the bottom of the barrel." Others sounded even more alarming notes. Chicago mayor Anton Cermak gruffly informed a House committee that the federal government could either send relief to Chicago or it would have to send troops. "[I]f something is not done and starvation is going to continue," a labor leader warned a Senate com-

27. Romasco, *Poverty of Abundance*, 153–55.

mittee, "the doors of revolt in this country are going to be thrown open."[28]

These cries of impending revolution were largely empty rhetorical posturings. True, some Communists and others on the far left thought they heard the knell of capitalism and cried for action in the streets. But what struck most observers, and mystified them, was the eery docility of the American people, their stoic passivity as the depression grindstone rolled over them. There might be some nervous stirring on Capitol Hill in the winter of 1931–32, Anne O'Hare McCormick wrote, but "beyond the Potomac there is silence . . . a vacuum; no life-giving breath of popular enthusiasm or popular indignation, no current of that famous energy that propels the American dynamo. . . . Is America growing old? Have we . . . slumped into that sad maturity which submits to events?" Like Mr. Micawber, she concluded, "we are all waiting for something to turn up."[29]

The historian Gerald W. Johnson explored the popular mood at greater length in early 1932. "In the mind of the average American," he wrote, "1931 was the year of the Great Depression, for it was in the past 12 months that it really affected us who are just ordinary people, not international bankers, not financiers of any sort, not great executives, and not derelicts who are chronically on the verge of unemployment in all years." Americans were beginning to be scared, Johnson conceded, but

> we are by no means in despair. . . . [W]e do not believe for a moment that the hard times are going to continue for the next 6 years. Nineteen thirty-one was a hard year, but it saw no bayonets, heard no firing in the streets, afforded no hint of the dissolution of our institutions. . . . The revolutionists have gained no following worth mentioning in this country. There has been a great outcry against the Reds, and some persons confess to be very much frightened by them; but the sober truth is that their American campaign has fallen flatter than their campaign in any other country. To date the capitalist system seems to be as firmly entrenched in America as the Republic itself. . . . Under the most terrific strain to which it has been subjected since Gettysburg, the Republic stands unshaken.[30]

28. Schwarz, *Interregnum of Despair*, 160–61; Schlesinger 1:176.
29. Schwarz, *Interregnum of Despair*, 74.
30. Gerald W. Johnson, "The Average American and the Depression," *Current History*, February 1932, 671–75.

This odd apathy would persist and would continue to puzzle contemporaries and historians alike. Even Franklin Roosevelt found the submissiveness of the American people baffling. "There had never been a time, the Civil War alone excepted," Tugwell remembered Roosevelt saying, "when our institutions had been in such jeopardy. Repeatedly he spoke of this, saying that it was enormously puzzling to him that the ordeal of the past three years had been endured so peaceably."[31]

Then in 1932 this passivity modestly receded, giving way to a demand for federal action on at least one front—relief for the unemployed. Even this demand was qualified and halting and only gradually came to define a significant difference between the two major political parties.

The issue was older than the Depression, going back at least to Senator Robert Wagner's introduction of his "Three Bills" in 1927, calling for better statistical information on unemployment, countercyclical public works, and reforms in the United States Employment Service, a job placement bureau created during the World War. Hoover endorsed the first two of the Three Bills but rejected the third on technically niggling states'-rights grounds. When Wagner in 1930 introduced a Senate bill for federal unemployment insurance, Hoover opposed it on deeper philosophical grounds of antipathy to the bureaucratic state and fear of creating a welfare-dependent class. The president had, in fact, himself called for insurance against industrial death and accidents, as well as unemployment and old-age insurance, but he had in mind encouraging private plans, not creating new government programs.

In New York State, meanwhile, Governor Franklin Roosevelt had in 1930 publicly endorsed government-sponsored unemployment insurance and old-age pensions. In 1931 Roosevelt had secured the enactment of the New York Temporary Emergency Relief Administration, originally authorized for just seven months and funded at $20 million. Its very name and brief projected tenure bespoke the continuing anxieties in American culture, as well as in Roosevelt's own mind, about the danger of creating a permanent welfare class dependent on a government "dole." Yet Roosevelt also forthrightly declared that relief "must be extended by Government, not as a matter of charity, but as a matter of social duty; the State accepts the task cheerfully because it believes

31. Tugwell, *Brains Trust*, 295.

that it will help restore that close relationship with its people which is necessary to preserve our democratic form of government."[32]

Here was an attitude toward government—to call it a philosophy would be too much—that defined a distinct difference from Hoover, who stewed in anxieties about the dole and endlessly lashed the Congress and the country with lectures about preserving the nation's moral fiber, not to mention the integrity of the federal budget, by avoiding direct federal payments for unemployment relief. No issue more heavily burdened Hoover in the presidential election year of 1932. The Great Humanitarian who had fed the starving Belgians in 1914, the Great Engineer so hopefully elevated to the presidency in 1928, now appeared as the Great Scrooge, a corrupted ideologue who could swallow government relief for the banks but priggishly scrupled over government provisions for the unemployed. Declaiming against budget deficits and the dangers of the dole, Hoover vetoed the Garner-Wagner relief bill on July 11, though he did in the end reluctantly accede to a compromise, the Relief and Reconstruction Act, which he signed on July 21. It authorized the RFC to finance up to $1.5 billion in "self-liquidating" public works and to loan up to $300 million to the states for relief purposes. California's Senator Hiram Johnson thought Hoover's acquiescence in this legislation constituted a "remarkable somersault" from his previous opposition to all such measures.[33]

HOOVER'S SOMERSAULT came too late to bring him political credit. Cartoonists now routinely caricatured him as a dour, heartless skinflint whose rigid adherence to obsolete doctrines caused men and women to go jobless and hungry. At the Democratic National Committee, Charles Michelson's propaganda machine went into high gear, missing no chance to label the crisis the "Hoover Depression." Folk usage added its own epithets. Tarpaper-and-cardboard hobo shantytowns became "Hoovervilles." Pulled-out empty trouser pockets were "Hoover flags." Hoover grew increasingly isolated, both politically and personally. A joke circulated that when the president asked for a nickel to make a telephone call to a friend, an aide flipped him a dime and said, "Here, call them both." A newspaperman noted how the Depression trans-

---

32. Schlesinger 1:392.
33. Hiram Johnson to "My Dear Boys," May 14, 1932, in *The Diary Letters of Hiram Johnson* (New York: Garland, 1983), 5:n.p.

formed Hoover both physically and psychologically, mussing his customarily fastidious appearance, sapping his confidence, and eliciting a bitterness alien to his Quaker upbringing: "He didn't look to me like the Hoover I had been seeing. His hair was rumpled. He was almost crouching behind his desk, and he burst out at me with a volley of angry words . . . against the politicians and the foreign governments . . . in language that he must have learned in a mining camp."[34]

The expulsion of the "Bonus Army" from Washington in late July 1932 proved especially politically damaging to Hoover. Thousands of unemployed veterans of the World War American Expeditionary Force converged on Washington in the spring and summer of 1932. Styling themselves the Bonus Expeditionary Force, they lobbied Congress for early cash payment of the war service "bonus" due them in 1945. When the Senate refused to pass the bonus bill, many disappointed veterans returned to their homes, but several thousand remained, and when District of Columbia police tried on July 28 to evict them from buildings they had occupied on Pennsylvania Avenue, an ugly riot erupted. Two bonus marchers were shot dead. The district authorities thereupon appealed to Hoover for help, and he called in federal troops. Late in the afternoon, a detachment of mounted cavalrymen, sabers drawn, accompanied by six tanks and a column of infantry with fixed bayonets, cleared the buildings. The commanding officer, General Douglas MacArthur, then exceeded his orders, which were to secure the buildings and contain the marchers at their campsite on Anacostia Flats on the outskirts of the district. Instead, MacArthur's troops proceeded to Anacostia and drove the marchers out of the camp with tear gas. The soldiers then put their tumbledown shacks to the torch.

The spectacle of the United States Army routing unarmed citizens with tanks and firebrands outraged many Americans. The Bonus Army episode came to symbolize Hoover's supposed insensitivity to the plight of the unemployed. In fact the worst violence, resulting in two deaths, had come at the hands of the district police, not the federal troops, and the blame for the torching of Anacostia Flats was MacArthur's, not Hoover's. But Hoover chose to ignore MacArthur's insubordination and assumed full responsibility for the army's actions.

"The Battle of Anacostia Flats," coming just seventeen days after Hoover's unpopular veto of the Garner-Wagner relief bill, marked the lowest ebb of Hoover's political fortunes. He had been nominated for a second

34. Wilson, *Herbert Hoover*, 162.

presidential term by a dispirited Republican convention in June, but the honor was worth little. He was already a beaten man. He had grappled with the wildly swooning economy and been brought down by it. He had been broken not by "the Great Depression" but by a concatenation of crises that only cumulatively and only by sometime in 1931 deserved the perverse appellation of "Great." By the end of 1931 he had in fact taken off his ideological gloves and done bare-knuckle combat with the crisis—the "battle on a thousand fronts," he later called it. But it was too little too late, especially and woefully so in the politically crucial area of relief. He had been overwhelmed by events too large and swift even for his capacious and agile mind to grasp. He had lost. No one doubted that his defeat would be ratified by the voters in November.

Nor was the Depression the only crisis whose resolution eluded Hoover's once-vaunted genius. In faraway Asia, an explosion on the night of September 18, 1931, damaged a Japanese-controlled railroad in China's northern province of Manchuria. In a response so swift that it suggested the work of agents provocateurs, Japanese military forces overran the province. In February 1932 Japan installed a puppet government in Manchuria, which it officially recognized as the new state of Manchukuo, a prelude to an ambitious scheme to colonize the area with millions of Japanese settlers.

Those moves climaxed decades of Japanese machinations against China and foreshadowed a wider conflict to come. The incident also foretold the timid course of American diplomacy in the Depression decade and revealed the debilitating effects of American aloofness from the League of Nations. When Hoover refused to participate in an international boycott of Japan, the league could do little more than pass a resolution censuring Tokyo's action. That feeble effort to drive Japan out of Manchuria eventually resulted only in driving Japan out of the league, further weakening an already feeble instrument for maintaining international peace. Though Secretary of State Henry L. Stimson counseled a stiffer American response, a cautious Hoover stopped short of economic sanctions that might provoke Japan. Most of his countrymen had no quarrel with the president's restraint. "The American people don't give a hoot in a rain barrel who controls North China," said the *Philadelphia Record*.[35] Washington contented itself with proclaiming the ironically named Stimson Doctrine (it might more properly have been

35. Thomas A. Bailey, A *Diplomatic History of the American People*, 10th ed. (Englewood Cliffs, N.J.: Prentice-Hall, 1980), 699.

called the Hoover Doctrine), by which the United States refused to recognize Manchukuo as an independent state—but refused as well to back nonrecognition with either economic or military muscle. Faced with outright aggression, the Americans seemed capable of no more than this timid parchment protest. Japan drew the appropriate conclusions: it had little to fear either from the league or from Depression-plagued America. It could pursue its expansionist schemes with impunity. On the wind-scoured plains of Manchuria, Japan thus set the match in 1931 to the long fuse that would detonate the attack on Pearl Harbor just ten years later.

To White House visitors, the president by this time seemed prematurely aged. He kept up a punishing regimen of rising at six and working without interruption until nearly midnight. His clothes were disheveled, his hair rumpled, eyes bloodshot, complexion ashen. He grew increasingly testy and brittle. "How I wish I could cheer up the poor old President," wrote the venerable Stimson, Hoover's senior by seven years.[36] Never temperamentally suited to the pelting and abuse of the political arena, a man naturally diffident and inordinately self-protective, Hoover was painfully bruised by blows from both the left and the right. As early as 1919 he had conceded that "I do not . . . have the mental attitude or the politician's manner . . . and above all I am too sensitive to political mud."[37] By the fall of 1932 he had lost all stomach for political campaigning. He took to the hustings only in October and seemed to campaign more for vindication in the historical record than for affection in the hearts of voters. Just four years earlier he had won one of the most lopsided victories in the history of presidential elections. Now he took an even worse drubbing than he had given to Al Smith. On November 8, 1932, Hoover won just six states. The Great Engineer, so recently the most revered American, was the most loathed and scorned figure in the country. All eyes now looked to his successor, Franklin D. Roosevelt.

HOOVER BROUGHT a corporate executive's sensibility to the White House. Roosevelt brought a politician's. Hoover as president frequently dazzled visitors with his detailed knowledge and expert understanding of American business. "His was a mathematical brain," said his admiring secretary, Theodore Joslin. "Let banking officials, for instance, come into his office and he would rattle off the number of banks in the

36. Schwarz, *Interregnum of Despair*, 51n.
37. Wilson, *Herbert Hoover: Forgotten Progressive*, 77.

country, list their liabilities and assets, describe the trend of fiscal affairs, and go into the liquidity, or lack of it, of individual institutions, all from memory."[38] Roosevelt, in contrast, impressed his visitors by asking them to draw a line across a map of the United States. He would then name, in order, every county through which the line passed, adding anecdotes about each locality's political particularities.[39] Where Hoover had a Quaker's reserve about the perquisites of the presidency, Roosevelt savored them with gusto. By 1932 Hoover wore the mantle of office like a hair shirt that he could not wait to doff. Roosevelt confided to a journalist his conviction that "no man ever willingly gives up public life — no man who has ever tasted it."[40] Almost preternaturally self-confident, he had no intimidating image of the presidential office to live up to, it was said, since his untroubled conception of the presidency consisted quite simply of the thought of himself in it.

Hoover's first elected office was the presidency. Roosevelt had been a professional politician all his life. He had spent years charting his course for the White House. To a remarkable degree, he had followed the career path blazed by his cousin Theodore Roosevelt — through the New York legislature and the office of assistant secretary of the navy to the governor's chair in Albany. In 1920 he had been the vice-presidential candidate on the losing Democratic ticket.

The following year, while vacationing at his family's summer estate on Campobello Island, in the Canadian province of New Brunswick, he had been stricken with poliomyelitis. He was thirty-nine years of age. He would never again be able to stand without heavy steel braces on his legs. Through grueling effort and sheer will power, he eventually trained himself to "walk" a few steps, an odd shuffle in which, leaning on the strong arm of a companion, he threw one hip, then the other, to move his steel-cased legs forward. His disability was no secret, but he took care to conceal its extent. He never allowed himself to be photographed in his wheelchair or being carried.

Roosevelt's long struggle with illness transformed him in spirit as well as body. Athletic and slim in his youth, he was now necessarily sedentary, and his upper body thickened. He developed, in the manner of many paraplegics, a wrestler's torso and big, beefy arms. His biceps, he

38. Theodore G. Joslin, *Hoover off the Record* (Garden City, N.Y.: Doubleday, Doran, 1934), 17.
39. William Manchester, *The Glory and the Dream* (Boston: Little, Brown, 1974), 50.
40. Davis 2:64.

delighted in telling visitors, were bigger than those of the celebrated prizefighter Jack Dempsey. Like many disabled persons, too, he developed a talent for denial, a kind of forcefully willed optimism that refused to dwell on life's difficulties. Sometimes this talent abetted his penchant for duplicity, as in the continuing love affair he carried on with Lucy Mercer, even after he told his wife in 1918 that the relationship was ended. At other times it endowed him with an aura of radiant indomitability, lending conviction and authority to what in other men's mouths might have been banal platitudes, such as "all we have to fear is fear itself." Many of Roosevelt's acquaintances also believed that his grim companionship with paralysis gave to this shallow, supercilious youth the precious gift of a purposeful manhood.

Roosevelt's illness also gave him, paradoxically enough, political opportunity. By keeping him abed and convalescing for years, it made him the sole Democrat with a national reputation who was unscarred by his party's lacerating internecine battles and crushing electoral losses in the 1920s. He even turned the forced idleness of his convalescence into positive advantage. Working from a small office at the family home in Hyde Park, New York, he used the time to carry on a vast correspondence, much of it cranked out over his forged signature from what amounted to a letter-writing factory run by his shrewd and faithful operative, a crater-eyed, gnarled, wheezing homunculus named Louis McHenry Howe. Eleanor Roosevelt, meanwhile, became his public surrogate, traveling in her husband's stead and speaking on his behalf.

No less than for Franklin, his illness also proved a turning point for Eleanor. She was no stranger to grief. Her mother had died when Eleanor was barely eight years old. Within two more years, her younger brother and her father also passed away. Her surviving brother, like their father, was a chronic alcoholic, as were several of her uncles. Against the menace of their boozy, nocturnal forays the young Eleanor's bedroom door was triple-locked. After 1918 the dull ache of her husband's betrayal never left her. Her suffering deepened immeasurably in 1921 when the marriage she had agreed to preserve, despite Franklin's infidelity, was further strained by his affliction with polio. Yet despite these abundant travails, little in her life until this time had distinguished her from the smug and goosy crowd of wealthy socialites into which she was born. On her honeymoon in Europe in 1905, she had been utterly unable to answer a simple question about the structure of American government. She had taken little interest in the debate over women's suffrage that came to a climax in 1920 with the passage of the Nineteenth Amendment. She had lived complacently in an upper-crust ambience of grand houses, sumptuous entertainments, and foreign travel. Her attitudes were thoroughly conventional, her correspondence studded with examples of what a biographer calls "flip, class-bound arrogance and egregious racism."[41]

With the onset of Franklin's illness, however, Eleanor shucked off the chrysalis of the conventional society matron and emerged as an independent woman and a public figure. She got a job, as a teacher at the Todhunter School in New York. She made speeches and wrote magazine articles. She championed women's rights and spoke out against racial segregation in the South. She chaired the women's platform committee at the Democratic national convention in 1924. And all the while she worked tirelessly to keep her stricken husband's political career alive.

The Democratic Party remained badly divided in the 1920s between its urban-northeastern-wet-Catholic wing and its rural-southern-western-dry-Protestant wing. Neither faction could command a winning majority in the electorate at large, but each possessed enough power to frustrate the aspirations of the other and thus block the party from gaining a presidential victory. The denial of the nomination to William Gibbs McAdoo in 1924 demonstrated the intraparty veto power of the urban wing; the desertion of the Catholic New Yorker, Al Smith, by many southern Democrats in 1928 underscored the electoral veto power of the rural wing. The successive Democratic electoral disasters of 1920, 1924, and 1928 graphically illustrated the Democrats' weaknesses and emphasized the necessity of somehow reconciling their two wings if they were ever to win the presidency.

Roosevelt was a master reconciler. As governor, he had taken the working-class, New York City ethnic voters led by the sachems of Tammany Hall and welded them into a winning combination with the conservative, antiurban agrarian voters of upstate New York, to whom anything associated with the Tammany machine had historically been anathema. Throughout the decade of the 1920s, he had applied the same techniques on a national scale. During the years of his convalescence from polio, he had frequently sojourned at a hydrotherapy center in Warm Springs, Georgia, using it as a kind of embassy from which to conduct a diplomatic mission of reconciliation to the southern wing of his party.

41. Blanche Wiesen Cook, *Eleanor Roosevelt: A Life*, vol. 1, 1884–1933 (New York: Viking, 1992), 171.

Roosevelt believed that even a united Democratic Party could probably not win a presidential election as long as Republican prosperity lasted. He told fellow Democrats that their party's eventual success must wait "until the Republicans had led us into a serious period of depression and unemployment," a revealing indication of his sense of the relationship between economic crisis and political opportunity.[42] Through most of the 1920s, he did not foresee such an opportunity opening in the near future. His plan was to rebuild his broken body, then run for governor of New York in 1932 and perhaps the presidency in 1936. But in 1928 Al Smith persuaded him to make a bid for the New York governorship, and he won handsomely, even while Smith went down to humiliating defeat. That singular victory in a Republican year, and his massive reelection majority in 1930, positioned Roosevelt as the front-runner for the Democratic nomination in 1932. The Depression, sooner and larger than anything Roosevelt or any one else had anticipated, now made that nomination a coveted prize.

AL SMITH, STILL STINGING from his defeat in 1928 and sensing that this was surely a Democratic year, sought to be nominated a second time. John Nance Garner also commanded considerable support. But it was Roosevelt who grasped the great prize on the fourth ballot at the Democratic national convention at Chicago on the evening of July 1, 1932. The rural, southern element in the party took comfort from Garner's selection as his vice-presidential running mate. In an unprecedented gesture, Roosevelt flew to Chicago to accept the nomination in person. "Let it also be symbolic that in so doing I broke traditions," he declared to the cheering delegates. "Let it be from now on the task of our Party to break foolish traditions." There followed a familiar litany of alleged Republican misdemeanors and invocations of past Democratic heroes. The speech meandered through somewhat inconsistent proposals for cutting government spending and providing unemployment relief, for regulation of securities markets and of agricultural production, for the repeal of Prohibition, lower tariffs, and reforestation projects. And then the simple phrase that would give a name to an era: "I pledge you, I pledge myself, to a new deal for the American people."[43]

42. Frank Freidel, *Franklin Roosevelt: The Ordeal* (Boston: Little, Brown, 1954), 183.
43. See accounts of the nomination and acceptance speech in Schlesinger 1, chaps. 27 and 28; Davis 2, esp. chap. 10; and James MacGregor Burns, *Roosevelt: The Lion and the Fox* (New York: Harcourt, Brace, 1956), chaps. 7 and 8.

Conservative Democrats were aghast. Some delegates, notably those pledged to Roosevelt's old mentor and patron, Al Smith, petulantly refused to give Roosevelt the customary honor of a unanimous nomination. Smith, said H. L. Mencken, now nurtured a "fierce hatred of Roosevelt, the cuckoo who had seized his nest." Reactionary party chairman John J. Raskob regarded the Roosevelt supporters as "a crowd of radicals, whom I do not regard as Democrats." (This was strange stuff from someone who had until recently himself been a Republican.) "When one thinks of the Democratic Party being headed by such radicals as Roosevelt, Huey Long, [William Randolph] Hearst, [William Gibbs] McAdoo, and Senators [Burton] Wheeler and [Clarence] Dill," Raskob continued, "as against the fine, conservative talent in the Party as represented by such men as [Jouett Shouse], Governor Byrd, Governor Smith, Carter Glass, John W. Davis, Governor Cox, Pierre S. DuPont, Governor Ely and others too numerous to mention, it takes all one's courage and faith to not lose hope completely."[44]

What worried the Democratic old guard? In what might the "New Deal" consist? Roosevelt's prior political career offered only a few clues. He had long championed low tariffs and assistance to agriculture, but these were both familiar staples of Democratic policy. More innovative was his advocacy of public hydroelectric power projects and his passionate, even romantic, interest in conservation—positions that endeared him to many western progressives, including progressive Republicans like George Norris. Since 1930 he had embraced government-financed unemployment and old-age insurance, which brought him the warm support of urban Democrats like Robert Wagner.

Beneath these few specific policies lay a conception of government that contained elements of the patrician's condescending sense of noblesse oblige but also marked Roosevelt in the context of the 1920s and early 1930s as a progressive politician. "What is the state?" he asked in his message requesting unemployment relief from the New York legislature in August 1931. "It is the duly constituted representative of an organized society of human beings—created by them for their mutual protection and well being. The state or the government is but the machinery through which such mutual aid and protection is achieved. . . . Our government is not the master but the creature of the people. The

44. Arthur M. Schlesinger Jr., *History of American Presidential Elections, 1789–1968* (New York: Chelsea House, 1971), 3:2729; Schwarz, *Interregnum of Despair*, 191–92.

duty of the state towards the citizens is the duty of the servant to its master."[45]

This conception of government, in turn, was married to an expansive, generous, restless temperament—"a first-class temperament," in Justice Oliver Wendell Holmes's famous phrase, one that Holmes thought compensated for Roosevelt's "second-class intellect." Among the most vivid evidences of the Rooseveltian temperament was a commencement speech he gave at Milton Academy in Massachusetts in May 1926. He conspicuously did not assume the conventional commencement speaker's hectoring voice of sober authority, reminding the graduates of the end of their youthful innocence and their imminent entry into the vale of tears of adult responsibility. His theme, rather, was change—the accelerating and dizzying pace of change in the still-new century—and the need to match new conditions with new thinking, even new values. He beckoned his young listeners not to the sober stations of mature duty but to the soaring challenges of creative invention. A man born forty or fifty years earlier, said the forty-four-year-old Roosevelt, had been typically "brought up in a Victorian atmosphere of gloomy religion, of copybook sentiment, of life by precept, he had lived essentially as had his fathers before him." But then, said Roosevelt, came "sudden changes":

> [H]uman voices were carried to him over a tiny copper wire, juggernauts called trolley cars lined his peaceful roads, steam was replacing sails, sputtering arc-lights were appearing in the comfortable darkness of his streets, machine-made goods were forcing out the loving craftsmanship of the centuries. But, more dangerous, the accepted social structure was becoming demoralized. Women—think of it, Women!—were commencing to take positions in offices and industrial plants, and demanding—a very few of them—things called political rights. ... In politics, too, men were speaking of new ideals and new parties, Populist and Socialist, were making themselves heard throughout the land. ... [T]he lives of the great majority of people are more different from the lives of 1875 than were our grandfathers' lives from those of the year 1500. ... [T]here has occurred an even more rapid condition of change in the past ten years.

The problems of the world, Roosevelt concluded, were "caused as much by those who fear change as by those who seek revolution. ... In government, in science, in industry, in the arts, inaction and apathy are

45. Ernest K. Lindley, *Franklin D. Roosevelt: A Career in Progressive Democracy* (Indianapolis: Bobbs-Merrill, 1931), 325.

the most potent foes." Two obstacles, perversely complementary in their asymmetry, impeded progress. One was "the lack of cohesion on the part of the liberal thinkers themselves," who shared a common vision but disagreed on methods of realizing it. The other was "the solidarity of the opposition to a new outlook, [which] welds together the satisfied and the fearful."[46]

This handful of policies, this unapologetic embrace of the state, and this eager receptivity to change defined an attitude, not a program, and they exposed Roosevelt to the charge that he had more personality than character, more charm than substance. The *New Republic* found him "not a man of great intellectual force or supreme moral stamina." The journalist Walter Lippmann wrote to a friend in 1931 that after "many long talks in the last few years" he had concluded that Roosevelt was "a kind of amiable boy scout." In a column in January of 1932 Lippmann offered a portrait of Roosevelt that was destined to become notorious. "Franklin D. Roosevelt," wrote Lippmann, "is a highly impressionable person, without a firm grasp of public affairs and without very strong convictions. . . . [He] is an amiable man with many philanthropic impulses, but he is not the dangerous enemy of anything. He is too eager to please. . . . Franklin D. Roosevelt is no crusader. He is no tribune of the people. He is no enemy of entrenched privilege. He is a pleasant man who, without any important qualifications for the office, would very much like to be president."[47]

Roosevelt's performance in the electoral campaign of 1932 did little to dispel that kind of skepticism. He had once professed to be an internationalist, faithful to the precepts of his former chief, Woodrow Wilson, but in February 1932 he publicly repudiated the idea that the United States should join the League of Nations. That move was widely understood as naked and cynical appeasement of the powerful Democratic kingmaker, the archisolationist William Randolph Hearst. At Columbus, Ohio, in August, Roosevelt lampooned Hoover's moratorium, further evidence of his apparent apostasy from Wilsonian internationalism. He outlined his agricultural polices at Topeka, Kansas, on September 14, but the speech was in fact empty of content, designed, as one aide put it, to win the Midwest "without waking up the dogs of the East."[48]

---

46. Franklin D. Roosevelt, *Whither Bound?* (Boston: Houghton Mifflin, 1926), 4–15.
47. Schlesinger 1:291; Schwarz, *Interregnum of Despair*, 189; Walter Lippmann, *Interpretations, 1931–32* (New York: Macmillan, 1932), 260–62.
48. Raymond Moley, *After Seven Years* (New York: Harper and Brothers, 1939), 45.

Perhaps most telling, the man who had challenged Milton's graduates to welcome change and to seize the future now seemed to have embraced a different theory of history, one that emphasized stasis and closure. He cautioned the members of San Francisco's Commonwealth Club on September 23: "Our industrial plant is built; the problem just now is whether under existing conditions it is not overbuilt. Our last frontier has long since been reached." Hoover damned that sentiment as a denial of "the promise of American life . . . the counsel of despair."[49] At Oglethorpe University on May 22 Roosevelt called for "social planning" and bold experimentation; on another occasion he criticized Hoover as being "committed to the idea that we ought to center control of everything in Washington as rapidly as possible."[50] At Pittsburgh on October 19 he attacked Hoover's deficits and called for sharp reductions in government spending. Marriner Eccles opined that "given later developments, the campaign speeches often read like a giant misprint, in which Roosevelt and Hoover speak each other's lines."[51]

Even Roosevelt's own speechwriters were confused. Rexford Tugwell, one of Roosevelt's original Brain Trusters, complained that he and Roosevelt's other advisers had "started out to explain things and to deduce from the explanation what ought to be done. We were reduced now to something quite different. We were contriving ingenious accommodations to prejudice and expediency."[52] Roosevelt's mind, said another Brain Truster, Raymond Moley, "was neither exact nor orderly." On one occasion, speechwriter Moley was left "speechless" when Roosevelt, presented with two absolutely incompatible drafts of addresses on tariff policy—one calling for blanket reductions, the other for bilateral agreements—blandly instructed Moley to "weave the two together." Roosevelt, sniped Hoover, was as changeable as "a chameleon on plaid."[53]

On election day Roosevelt won by default. He held the solid South and ran strongly in the West. In a significant harbinger of the changes that were about to redefine the nature of American politics, he not only retained the support of the urban immigrant voters who had cast their ballots for Al Smith in 1928 but actually improved on Smith's margins among those crucial groups by some 12 percent. Yet Roosevelt's victory

49. PPA, (1938), 742. Hoover's remark is from his Memoirs: The Great Depression, 340.
50. Leuchtenburg, 10.
51. Marriner S. Eccles, Beckoning Frontiers (New York: Knopf, 1951), 95.
52. Tugwell, Brains Trust, 385.
53. Moley, After Seven Years, 56, 11, 48.

was less an affirmation of his policies than a repudiation of Hoover's. He remained inscrutable, his exact intentions a mystery. Tugwell, looking back years later, speculated about the purposes that might at that moment have lain deep in Roosevelt's mind. "I define these now, with the benefit of hindsight," wrote Tugwell, "as a better life for all Americans, and a better America to live it in. I think it was that general. There were items in it, but only a few he saw as fixed. One of these was security; if Europeans could have that, so could Americans. Another was a new framework for industrialism, and still another was a physically improved country. But those, as I see it, were about all."[54]

William Allen White, watching Roosevelt from a greater distance than Tugwell, also speculated on what kind of leader might emerge from the fog that surrounded the president-elect. "Your distant cousin is an X in the equation," he wrote to Theodore Roosevelt Jr. on February 1, 1933. But White sensed a momentous potential. "He may develop his stubbornness into courage, his amiability into wisdom, his sense of superiority into statesmanship. Responsibility," White prophetically concluded, "is a winepress that brings forth strange juices out of men."[55]

---

54. Tugwell, *Brains Trust*, 157–58.
55. Davis 2:392.

4

Interregnum

The country needs and, unless I mistake its temper, the country demands bold, persistent experimentation. It is common sense to take a method and try it: If it fails, admit it frankly and try another. But above all, try something.

— Franklin D. Roosevelt,
speech at Oglethorpe University, May 22, 1932

Roosevelt was now president-elect. But Herbert Hoover was still president and would remain so for four months. The ratification of the Twentieth Amendment to the Constitution in February 1933 moved the start of the presidential term to January 20 of the year following election, but the amendment would take effect only in 1937. Roosevelt's inaugural thus fell under the old rules and would not take place until March 4.[1]

History, meanwhile, refused to mark time to the antiquated cadences of the American electoral system. In the agonizing interval between Roosevelt's election in November 1932 and his inauguration in March 1933, the American banking system shut down completely. The global economy slid even deeper into the trough of the Depression. The world also became a markedly more dangerous place. Adolf Hitler was installed as chancellor of Germany, after massive unemployment had seeded despair into millions of German households and after months of bloody clashes between Communist and Nazi gangs had left scores of people dead in the streets of German cities. Japan, hell-bent on the

1. The amendment also changed the schedule for meetings of Congress, which was now mandated to begin its annual session on January 3. Theretofore, newly elected Congresses had to wait a full thirteen months, from November of election year until December of the succeeding year, to be seated. Roosevelt accelerated the seating of the new Congress elected in 1932 by calling it into special session in March 1933.

104

conquest of Manchuria, cast off all diplomatic restraint and formally announced its intention to quit the League of Nations. The vexed issue of World War I debts, temporarily allayed by Hoover's moratorium of 1931, once again stirred to troublesome life. These lowering clouds of political violence, war, and global economic turbulence cast their shadows over the rest of the decade, and beyond.

Scarcely a week after the election, as Roosevelt sifted contentedly through messages of congratulation in the governor's mansion in Albany, he received a lengthy telegram from Hoover. The British government, Hoover explained, was urgently requesting yet another review of the international debt question. To add point to their request the British proposed to suspend payment of their $95 million debt-service installment due on December 15. Congress had only reluctantly agreed to Hoover's moratorium of the preceding year, and "if there is to be any change in the attitude of the Congress," Hoover explained to Roosevelt, "it will be greatly affected by the views of those members who recognize you as their leader and who will properly desire your counsel and advice." Other questions about foreign relations were also pending, including plans for a World Economic Conference in London during the coming winter and the status of the Disarmament Conference already in progress in Geneva. Accordingly, Hoover asked for "an opportunity to confer with you personally at some convenient date in the near future."

Hoover's action in seeking the advice of his victorious opponent was unprecedented. It had all the appearance of a magnificent gesture of statesmanship. It also contained sinister political implications. The debt issue was the tar-baby of American politics. To touch it was to glue oneself to a messy, intractable problem that had defied the genius of statesmen for a decade. Most academic economists, as well as the Wall Street financial community, not to mention virtually all Europeans, favored outright cancellation of the war debts. Yet Congress and most Americans beyond the Atlantic seaboard continued to regard the debts as immutable financial and moral obligations — and as safeguards that served to remind those interminably quarrelsome Europeans that they could not expect to finance another war in the United States. Secretary of State Stimson noted in his diary: "Every Congressman is shooting his mouth off in the newspapers with fulminations against any concession of any installment, or any amount whatever."[2] Hoover had officially

---

2. Frank Freidel, *Franklin D. Roosevelt: Launching the New Deal* (Boston: Little, Brown, 1973), 28.

pledged himself against outright cancellation, and his telegram to Roosevelt had stressed that point. But as the architect of the moratorium, Hoover had also shown some flexibility, and thereby incurred the wrath of legions of isolationists. He was now suggesting that the debts might be useful bargaining levers to pry economic and military concessions out of Europe. "[W]e should be receptive," said Hoover in his telegram, "to proposals from our debtors of tangible compensation in other forms than direct payment in expansion of markets for the products of our labor and our farms." And, he added, "substantial reduction of world armament . . . has a bearing upon this question."[3] Hoover was proposing, in short, that American diplomacy should forge a strong link between the upcoming London Economic Conference and the Geneva Disarmament Conference, using the agenda of the former to shape the proceedings of the latter. This was an elaborate scheme, and an ingenious one.

But Roosevelt and his advisers quickly concluded that this apparently well-intentioned proposal concealed some explosive political dynamite. If the incoming Democratic administration agreed to let the outgoing Republicans begin negotiations along the lines Hoover was suggesting, Roosevelt's aide Rexford Tugwell wrote, "we will have to hold the bag with a hostile country and congress after they are gone."[4] From this perspective, the president's invitation to involve the president-elect in this delicate diplomacy would simply shift from Hoover's shoulders to Roosevelt's the weighty and unwelcome responsibility for the immensely unpopular policy of canceling the debts. "And if anything was clear to us," said Raymond Moley, "it was that Roosevelt must not be saddled with that responsibility."[5]

So Hoover's proposal carried with it large political risk. At the same time, according to the theory of the Depression embraced by Roosevelt and his advisers, it promised small economic reward. Hoover subscribed to a view of the Depression as stemming from international causes, especially the distortions resulting from the World War. His reverent and dogged devotion to the gold standard, the balance wheel in the international trade and financial system, owed directly to that diagnosis of the Depression's origins. His relentless and even courageous effort to resolve the international debt problem rested on the same premises.

3. *PPA* (1928–32), 873–76.
4. Freidel, *Launching*, 131n.
5. Raymond Moley, *After Seven Years* (New York: Harper and Brothers, 1939), 70.

Roosevelt, by contrast, professed to find the sources of the Depression in the United States, in structural deficiencies and institutional inadequacies that a vigorous and far-reaching reform program might remedy. This view may have owed as much to the search for a legitimating rationale for reform, or to a search for *any* policy instrument more useable than the spongy tools of international diplomacy, as it did to the rigors of economic analysis. But for whatever amalgam of reasons, international concerns were decidedly subordinate to nationalist priorities in Roosevelt's thinking at this time, and foreign relations were virtually irrelevant as a subject of economic policy. In his inaugural address Roosevelt would flatly declare that "our international trade relations, though vastly important, are in point of time and necessity secondary to the establishment of a sound national economy."[6] In June 1933 he was to remind his secretary of state, then attending the World Economic Conference in London, "that far too much importance is attached to exchange stability by banker-influenced cabinets. In our case it concerns only about 3 per cent of our total trade as measured by production."[7]

All those considerations conspired to ensure that Hoover's invitation to Roosevelt to share in the shaping of economic diplomacy had no chance of being accepted. As Moley put it, Hoover "could scarcely have chosen a field in which there was less probability of sympathetic cooperation between the two administrations." Roosevelt and his inner circle "were agreed that the heart of the recovery program was and must be domestic."[8] That was, in fact, Hoover's greatest worry about his successor: that Roosevelt's domestic priorities would encourage policies of economic nationalism, perhaps including abandonment of the gold standard, dollar devaluation, and inflation. Roosevelt and his advisers had no such clear-cut agenda in late 1932, but before another year had passed, events would confirm Hoover's fears.

In the meantime, Roosevelt could hardly ignore Hoover's invitation to consult, even if he never intended to adopt Hoover's specific suggestions. Insisting that the meeting be "wholly informal and personal," Roosevelt agreed to stop off in Washington on his way to Warm Springs, Georgia, on November 22, 1932.[9]

On the appointed day, accompanied only by his increasingly

6. *PPA* (1933), 14.
7. Freidel, *Launching*, 472.
8. Moley, *After Seven Years*, 68, 70.
9. *PPA* (1928–32), 876.

ubiquitous adviser Raymond Moley, Roosevelt was ushered into the White House Red Room, where President Hoover and Treasury Secretary Ogden Mills were waiting.[10] The air hung heavy with sullen tension. Hoover had insisted that Mills attend the meeting because he had been warned by so many people that Roosevelt would shift his words that he wanted a reliable witness present.[11] Moley thought that no two people in the country distrusted Roosevelt "as a human being and as President-elect" more than Hoover and Mills. Their manner suggested that they also regarded Moley with cold contempt. At a press conference before the meeting, Mills had publicly needled Moley as an unworldly professor inadequate to the complex demands of high statecraft. Moley now found Mills in person to be arrogant and condescending, even toward Hoover. The president, grave but jittery, stiffly addressing his treasury secretary as "Mills" and fixing his eye first on the carpet and then on Moley — but seldom on Roosevelt — smoked a fat cigar. All the others nervously lit cigarettes, and the atmosphere in the room thickened.

Roosevelt greeted Mills, his Harvard classmate and Hudson Valley neighbor, with a cheery "Hello, Ogden!" and kept up a gay and nonchalant front. But FDR, wary of his recently defeated adversary, also cupped in his hand several cards on which Moley had jotted questions that needed asking, including one about possible "secret agreements" that Hoover might have already made with British and French officials. Roosevelt may also have had in mind the sour memory of his last visit to the White House. At a presidential reception for governors the preceding April, Hoover, whether from callous design or thoughtless insensitivity, had kept Roosevelt waiting in a receiving line for nearly an hour. For a man whose bulky weight was supported entirely by the heavy hip-to-ankle steel braces that encased his useless legs, the ordeal was agonizing and humiliating. Roosevelt, for all his generous temperament, would have been less than human if the episode had not shaded his attitude toward Hoover.

In this awkward setting on November 22, Hoover spoke first, and at length. It was a typical Hoover performance, the sort that had impressed countless others in his business and political career. "Before he had finished," Moley later reflected, "it was clear that we were in the presence of the best-informed individual in the country on the question of

10. The following account of the meeting of November 22, 1932, draws heavily on Moley's description in *After Seven Years*, 67–77.
11. Stimson Diary, November 16, 1932.

the debts. His story showed a mastery of detail and a clarity of arrangement that compelled admiration."

But it did not compel agreement from Roosevelt. Nor did a second meeting on the same subject on January 20, 1933. The only concrete result of these failed attempts at cooperation was the deepened conviction of Hoover and his associates that Roosevelt was a dangerously lightweight politician. Henry Stimson thought that Hoover's mastery of the debt issue, compared with Roosevelt's display of vacuous bonhomie, made FDR "look like a peanut." Hoover deemed Roosevelt "amiable, pleasant, anxious to be of service, very badly informed and of comparatively little vision" and told Stimson that he had spent most of his time in conversation with Roosevelt "educating a very ignorant . . . well-meaning young man."[12]

Hoover was not finished with trying to educate that well-meaning young man, nor with attempting to secure his cooperation on economic policy. Late in the evening of February 18, 1933, as Roosevelt sat watching skits by New York political reporters in a banquet room of the Hotel Astor in central Manhattan, a Secret Service agent handed him a large brown-paper envelope. It contained a remarkable ten-page handwritten letter from Hoover. The banking system, said Hoover, was teetering on the brink of complete collapse. Gold was being shipped out of the country in dangerous amounts; capital was fleeing abroad, seeking safe haven; depositors were withdrawing their funds from banks and hoarding them at home; prices were falling and unemployment increasing dramatically. "The major difficulty," Hoover explained, "is the state of the public mind, for there is a steadily degenerating confidence in the future which has reached the height of general alarm." Hoover went on, provocatively, to claim that his own policies had substantially righted the foundering economy in the summer of 1932, only to see it succumb to renewed depression in the last several months. Still more provocatively, Hoover ascribed the latest crisis to Roosevelt's election and the unsettling prospect it raised of unbalanced budgets, inflation, abandonment of the gold standard, political experimentation, and even "dictatorship." "I am convinced," Hoover concluded, "that a very early statement by you upon two or three policies of your Administration would

12. Freidel, *Launching*, 34–35, 45. After several meetings of his own with Roosevelt, Stimson would change his opinion. He was deeply impressed with the "brave way" in which Roosevelt handled his disability, and found his intellectual range and analytic power "astounding" (118, 277). In 1940, at the age of seventy-two, Stimson was to join Franklin Roosevelt's administration as secretary of war.

serve greatly to restore confidence and cause a resumption of the march of recovery."[13]

The letter was astonishing in both tone and content. Roosevelt dismissed it as "cheeky" and made no reply for nearly two weeks. Its political implications were clear enough. Hoover acknowledged as much a few days later when he wrote to a Republican senator: "I realize that if these declarations be made by the President-elect, he will have ratified the whole major program of the Republican Administration; that is, it means the abandonment of 90% of the so-called new deal."[14] For their part, Roosevelt and his advisers were no less mindful of the political ramifications of the continuing banking crisis. Tugwell indiscreetly admitted to a Hoover sympathizer on February 25 that the Roosevelt camp "were fully aware of the bank situation and that it would undoubtedly collapse in a few days, which would place the responsibility in the lap of President Hoover." When this conversation was reported to Hoover, he exploded that Tugwell "breathes with infamous politics devoid of every atom of patriotism."[15]

Both sides, in fact, were stepping a dangerous political dance around the gathering economic crisis. Hoover seemed, as he had in the preceding electoral campaign, more interested in vindicating himself in the historical record than in genuinely enlisting his successor in helpful policies. On his side, as Moley later commented, Roosevelt "either did not realize how serious the situation was or . . . preferred to have conditions deteriorate and gain for himself the entire credit for the rescue operation. In any event," Moley somewhat cynically concluded, "his actions during the period from February 18th to March 3d would conform to any such motive on his part."[16]

As Hoover's last days in office slipped away, he continued to dun Roosevelt with requests for some reassuring public statement, but the president-elect kept his own counsel. The outgoing president, drained of power and nerve, was unable to lead; the incoming president, as yet, was unwilling. The country, numb and nearly broken, anxiously awaited deliverance from this deadening paralysis. As Roosevelt's entourage filtered into Washington in preparation for the inaugural ceremonies, vir-

---

13. William Starr Myers and Walter H. Newton, *The Hoover Administration: A Documented Narrative* (New York: Charles Scribner's Sons, 1936), 338–40.
14. Schlesinger 1:477; Myers and Newton, *Hoover Administration*, 341.
15. Myers and Newton, *Hoover Administration*, 356.
16. Herbert Hoover, *The Memoirs of Herbert Hoover: The Great Depression, 1929–1941* (New York: Macmillan, 1952), 215.

tually all the banks in the nation were barred shut. American capitalism seemed to be creaking to a dead halt. The thought tormented many Americans that they were witnessing the end of a historic era, an era of progress and confidence whose whimpering climax boded nothing good for the future. "When we arrived in Washington on the night of March 2," Moley wrote, "terror held the country in grip."[17] Could Roosevelt break that grip? The scale of the crisis, the completeness of Hoover's failure, and his own studious refusal to make any policy commitments during the interregnum meant that the field of political action lay before him swept of all obstructions. The power to command that field was now about to pass into his hands. What would he do?

SOME OBSERVERS, awed by Hitler's decisive march to power in Berlin, or by the enviable efficiency of Benito Mussolini's regime in Rome or Josef Stalin's in Moscow, urged that the dictators be imitated in America. Al Smith, once Roosevelt's political mentor but now an increasingly venomous critic, compared the crisis of early 1933 to the ultimate emergency of war. "What does a democracy do in a war?" Smith asked. "It becomes a tyrant, a despot, a real monarch. In the World War," he said with much exaggeration, "we took our Constitution, wrapped it up and laid it on the shelf and left it there until it was over." The Republican governor of Kansas declared that "even the iron hand of a national dictator is in preference to a paralytic stroke." The respected columnist Walter Lippmann, visiting Roosevelt at Warm Springs in late January 1933, told him with great earnestness: "The situation is critical, Franklin. You may have no alternative but to assume dictatorial power."[18]

But the affable sphinx of Hyde Park gave little clue about his reaction to such suggestions. Even his closest advisers at this time, the members of the fabled Brain Trust, marveled at Roosevelt's capacity for what Tugwell called "almost impenetrable concealment of intention."[19] Tugwell, attentively scrutinizing his chief during the electoral campaign, remarked to Moley that Roosevelt had the mobile and expressive face of an actor. His features were utterly responsive to his will, finely molding themselves to his constantly shifting purposes of persuasion, negotiation, or obfuscation, never ceasing to charm but never opening fully to reveal

17. Moley, *After Seven Years*, 143.
18. Davis 3:36; 2:3.
19. Rexford G. Tugwell, *The Brains Trust* (New York: Viking, 1968), 62.

the soul within. He could cast off one mood and assume another as easily as a mummer wiped off greasepaint. "There was another Roosevelt behind the one we saw and talked with," Tugwell later wrote; "I was baffled, unable to make out what he was like, that other man."[20]

Moley shared much of that assessment. Of course Roosevelt had an actor's manner, Moley replied to Tugwell, "and a professional actor's at that; how did I suppose he'd created and maintained the image of authority?" Moley thought that FDR had deliberately crafted his public persona in the course of a carefully constructed political career that had long aimed at the White House. "[I]t was a lifetime part that he was playing," Moley said to Tugwell, and added thoughtfully that "no one would ever see anything else."[21]

What visitors to Roosevelt did see, as they streamed by the hundreds to consult with him in Albany, Manhattan, or Warm Springs during the crowded early weeks of 1933, was a man of irrepressible vitality. He had an athlete's torso, big shoulder muscles bunched under his jacket. His vibrant good cheer was contagious. He radiated warmth and exuberance that washed over others as soon as they entered the room. He greeted visitors with easy familiarity, his upper body vigorously animated above the limp trousers and curiously unworn shoes that rested immobile below. He gestured and spoke with good-natured, head-tossing brio. His hands incessantly flourished a quill-tipped cigarette holder that flashed from his uplifted, jut-jawed face with its irregular, preorthodontic teeth to the exclamation point of a sentence — one of his endless, cascading sentences — as if he were inscribing his words upon the air.

Talk was Roosevelt's passion and his weapon. None of his associates ever knew him to read a book. It was in conversation that he gained his prodigious if disorderly store of information about the world. Drawing on that store, as Tugwell recorded, Roosevelt "could see more in an hour's drive than anyone I had ever known. He noted crops, woodlands, streams and livestock. To ride with him was to be deluged with talk, half-practical, half fanciful."[22] Moley was astonished at the amount of intellectual ransacking Roosevelt could crowd into an evening's discussion. Sitting with his advisers as a student, as a cross-examiner, as a judge, Roosevelt would listen attentively for a few minutes and then

20. Tugwell, *Brains Trust*, 27.
21. Tugwell, *Brains Trust*, 27.
22. Rexford G. Tugwell, *Roosevelt's Revolution: The First Year, a Personal Perspective* (New York: Macmillan, 1977), 160.

begin to break in with sharp, darting questions. He took in everything as a sponge absorbs water. This uncritical receptivity sometimes frightened Moley, who noted that "so far as I know he makes no effort to check up on anything that I or anyone else has told him."[23]

Herbert Hoover forged his policies in the tidy, efficient smithy of his own highly disciplined mind. Once he had cast them in final form, he could be obstinate. Especially in his last months in the White House, he had grown downright churlish with those who dared to question him. Roosevelt's mind, by contrast, was a spacious, cluttered warehouse, a teeming curiosity shop continuously restocked with randomly acquired intellectual oddments. He was open to all number and manner of impressions, facts, theories, nostrums, and personalities. He listened to everybody and anybody. Tugwell thought he especially enjoyed talking to fanatics, particularly inflation-preaching monetary heretics like Yale's Professor Irving Fisher. The countless visitors who trooped to see FDR between election and inauguration ranged from congressional barons to local farmers, from haughty industrialists to mendicant job-seekers, from silky Morgan partners to the rough-hewn old Populist Jacob Coxey, leader of "Coxey's Army," which had marched on Washington in 1894 to demand government jobs. To all of them Roosevelt gave attentive audience. As his visitors talked, FDR would nod in apparent approval, often interjecting, "Yes, yes, yes." Many who spoke with him took this to mean agreement when it merely signified that Roosevelt understood the point being made or, possibly, that he wanted to avoid the unpleasantness of open argument. Roosevelt would in time become notorious for his unwillingness to deal with disagreement face to face. From this unwillingness would come his maddening administrative habits of trying to avoid firing anyone and of putting several people of incompatible views to work on the same project, none of whom knew what the others were doing. "When I talk to him," said the volatile demagogue Huey Long of Louisiana, "he says 'Fine! Fine! Fine!' But Joe Robinson [the somewhat plodding and thoroughly conventional Democratic majority leader in the Senate, and Long's implacable antagonist] goes to see him the next day and again he says 'Fine! Fine! Fine!' Maybe he says 'Fine!' to everybody."[24]

More often, Roosevelt did the talking—all of it. His compulsive garrulity may have originated as a calculated device to divert a listener's

23. Moley, *After Seven Years*, 11, 20.
24. Schlesinger 1:452.

attention from his physical handicap. It may have been merely one more of his abundant techniques of personal and political mastery over others. But from whatever ultimate source, a Niagara of verbiage would usually fall upon a visitor even as he walked through the door to greet Roosevelt and would tumble on without stop until it was time to leave. Anecdotes, rhetorical questions that Roosevelt answered himself, gossip about other public figures, jokes, pseudo-intimate revelations about the inner workings of policymaking—all flowed from Roosevelt's mouth, flooding the room with words and utterly drowning his interlocutor, who would depart with whatever had been on his mind still unspoken, perhaps even forgotten, but with the glow of having soaked briefly in the warm bath of Roosevelt's charm. When Nevada senator Key Pittman came to Warm Springs to lobby the president-elect for a government silver-buying program, Roosevelt parried with an hour-and-a-half-long story about digging for buried silver in Nova Scotia as a boy. Through this wall of words Pittman could insert no further mention of silver into the conversation.[25]

Whether listening or talking, in public or private, Roosevelt projected a sense of utter self-confidence and calm mastery. He was "all light and no darkness," one observer wrote; a man of "slightly unnatural sunniness," said the literary critic Edmund Wilson.[26] Those traits had their origins in the unearned legacy of his privileged upbringing. Roosevelt was born in 1882 into a family of seasoned, stable wealth dwelling on their rambling estate at Hyde Park, along the Hudson River above New York City. The neighbors included scions of the old American plutocracy like Frederick Vanderbilt and Vincent Astor, toward whom the blue-blooded Roosevelts felt a kind of genteel disdain. Roosevelt's father, James, cared for his Hyde Park property with the proud solicitude of an English country squire and passed on to his son a sense of reverential responsibility for the land. James was fifty-three when Franklin was born; the boy's mother, Sara Delano Roosevelt, was just twenty-seven. The patrician father and doting mother conferred on their only son the priceless endowment of an unshakable sense of self-worth. They also nurtured in him a robust social conscience. They sent him at the age of fourteen to the Groton School in Massachusetts, an austere and demanding bastion of high Protestant earnestness. There, in this heyday of the Social

25. Freidel, *Launching*, 77.
26. Milton MacKaye, "Profiles: The Governor—II," *New Yorker*, August 22, 1931, 28; Edmond Wilson, "The Hudson River Progressive," *New Republic*, April 5, 1933, 219–20.

Gospel movement, the Reverend Endicott Peabody instilled in his young charges the lessons of Christian duty and the ethic of public service. As the new century opened, young Franklin went on to Harvard. During his freshman year, when the boy was just on the cusp of his own manhood, his father died. Franklin attended lectures by Frederick Jackson Turner, the famed historian of the frontier, and Josiah Royce, the philosopher of communitarianism. He was a middling student but distinguished himself as editor of the campus newspaper, the *Crimson*. The one disappointment of his undergraduate years was his failure to be elected to membership in Porcellian, a snooty club whose rejection stung him deeply and may have contributed something to his later animus against the American upper crust, an animus that would in time earn him a reputation in the wood-paneled clubrooms of America's self-styled aristocracy as a "traitor to his class."

In his senior year at Harvard he became engaged to Eleanor Roosevelt, the niece of his fifth cousin Theodore Roosevelt, then president of the United States. They were married in 1905. Endicott Peabody presided over the ceremony. Cousin Teddy gave the bride away. In the following decade Eleanor bore six children. After the last was born, in 1916, she withdrew to a separate bedroom and maintained one for the remainder of her married life.

Franklin's one year at Columbia Law School proved sufficient to allow him to pass the state bar examination, and he joined a prestigious New York City law firm. Politics, however, was his passion. Inspired by the example of Cousin Theodore, he won a seat in the New York state senate in 1910. He campaigned for Woodrow Wilson in 1912 and was rewarded with Teddy's old post, the assistant secretaryship of the navy. He was the Democrats' vice-presidential nominee in 1920. Then came the illness that changed his life, the long and vain struggle to rehabilitate his broken body, and election in 1928 as governor of New York.

Though Roosevelt was never a systematic thinker, the period of lonely reflection imposed by his convalescence allowed him to shape a fairly coherent social philosophy. By the time he was elected governor, the distillate of his upbringing, education, and experience had crystallized into a few simple but powerful political principles. Moley summarized them this way: "He believed that government not only could, but should, achieve the subordination of private interests to collective interests, substitute co-operation for the mad scramble of selfish individualism. He had a profound feeling for the underdog, a real sense of the critical imbalance of economic life, a very keen awareness that political

democracy could not exist side by side with economic plutocracy." As
Roosevelt himself put it:

> [O]ur civilization cannot endure unless we, as individuals, realize our
> responsibility to and dependence on the rest of the world. For it is
> literally true that the "self-supporting" man or woman has become as
> extinct as the man of the stone age. Without the help of thousands of
> others, any one of us would die, naked and starved. Consider the bread
> upon our table, the clothes upon our backs, the luxuries that make
> life pleasant; how many men worked in sunlit fields, in dark mines,
> in the fierce heat of molten metal, and among the looms and wheels
> of countless factories, in order to create them for our use and enjoy-
> ment. . . . In the final analysis, the progress of our civilization will be
> retarded if any large body of citizens falls behind.[27]

Perhaps deep within himself Roosevelt trembled occasionally with the
common human palsies of melancholy or doubt or fear, but the world
saw none of it. On February 15, 1933, he gave a memorable demonstration of his powers of self-control. Alighting in Miami from an eleven-
day cruise aboard Vincent Astor's yacht *Nourmahal*, FDR motored to
Bay Front Park, where he made a few remarks to a large crowd. At the
end of the brief speech, Mayor Anton J. Cermak of Chicago stepped
up to the side of Roosevelt's open touring car and said a few words to
the president-elect. Suddenly a pistol barked from the crowd. Cermak
doubled over. Roosevelt ordered the Secret Service agents, who were
reflexively accelerating his car away from the scene, to stop. He mo-
tioned to have Cermak, pale and pulseless, put into the seat beside him.
"Tony, keep quiet—don't move. It won't hurt you if you keep quiet,"
Roosevelt repeated as he cradled Cermak's limp body while the car sped
to the hospital.[28]

Cermak had been mortally wounded. He died within weeks, the victim of a deranged assassin who had been aiming for Roosevelt. On the
evening of February 15, after Cermak had been entrusted to the doctors,
Moley accompanied Roosevelt back to the *Nourmahal*, poured him a
stiff drink, and prepared for the letdown now that Roosevelt was alone
among his intimates. He had just been spared by inches from a killer's
bullet and had held a dying man in his arms. But there was nothing—
"not so much as the twitching of a muscle, the mopping of a brow, or
even the hint of a false gaiety—to indicate that it wasn't any other eve-

27. Moley, *After Seven Years*, 14; PPA (1928–32), 75–76, 15.
28. Freidel, *Launching*, 168–73.

ning in any other place. Roosevelt was simply himself—easy, confident, poised, to all appearances unmoved." The episode contributed to Moley's eventual conclusion "that Roosevelt had no nerves at all." He was, said Frances Perkins, "the most complicated human being I ever knew."[29]

Unflappably cool in the face of personal danger, Roosevelt was also mystifying with respect to the particular antidepression policies that his new administration would pursue. "The fact is," Moley conceded, "that I found it impossible to discover how deeply Roosevelt was impressed with the seriousness of the crisis." While Moley and Treasury Secretary–designate William Woodin fretted over the accumulating reports of gold withdrawals and bank closings, Roosevelt remained serenely unperturbed, a monument of inscrutability, exuding "nothing but the most complete confidence in his own ability to deal with any situation that might arise."[30]

Exactly what the situation might be when Roosevelt took office on March 4 was part of the mystery. Two days after the election, on November 10, 1932, his aide Adolf Berle had sketched a tentative legislative program for the new administration. Berle cautioned that "it must be remembered that by March 4 next we may have anything on our hands from a recovery to a revolution. The chance is about even either way." He added, however, "I think the economic situation may change very much for the worse during that time, so that many of the following suggestions may have to be shifted as we go along."[31] The central task of the New Deal, Berle's memorandum implied, might be either social reform in a restored economy, or political stabilization in a disintegrating society, or, most likely and most urgently, economic recovery itself. Circumstances, not human will, said Berle, would set the priorities. In fact, these three purposes—social reform, political realignment, and economic recovery—flowed and counterflowed through the entire history of the New Deal. They often undercut and intersected one another, creating riptides of turbulence and eddies of stagnation. None would be achieved to the degree desired by its particular champions. Most notably, the goal of economic recovery would remain stubbornly elusive for eight more years. But perhaps precisely *because* the economic crisis of

---

29. Moley, *After Seven Years*, 139, 191; Frances Perkins, *The Roosevelt I Knew* (New York: Viking, 1946), 3.
30. Moley, *After Seven Years*, 143.
31. Freidel, *Launching*, 73n.

the Great Depression was so severe and so durable, Roosevelt would have an unmatched opportunity to effect major social reforms and to change the very landscape of American politics.

If Roosevelt's specific policies remained ill-defined and puzzling, little mystery surrounded his general intentions. Some things were well and widely understood: that he shared his cousin Theodore's belief in the supremacy of the public interest over private interests and in the government's role as the active agent of the public interest; that he meant to preside over a government even more vigorously interventionist and directive than Hoover's; that he intended to use government power to redress what he judged to be harmful and unfair imbalances in the American economy, especially the huge income gap between the agricultural and industrial sectors; that he had long been seeking for ordinary Americans some measure of the economic security and predictability of life's material circumstances that his own patrician class took for granted; that he had a lover's passion for the cause of conservation; that he was a champion of public waterpower. It was also clear that his confessedly liberal outlook alienated many in his own party and by the same token appealed to progressive Republicans, stimulating much political gossip about the possible emergence of a new, liberal party. Beyond that, all was speculation.

If Roosevelt had a plan in early 1933 to effect economic recovery, it was difficult to distinguish from many of the measures that Hoover, even if sometimes grudgingly, had already adopted: aid for agriculture, promotion of industrial cooperation, support for the banks, and a balanced budget. Only the last item was dubious. Roosevelt had pledged himself in the electoral campaign to fiscal orthodoxy and had denounced Hoover's budget deficits, but doubts about the strength of Roosevelt's own commitment to fiscal discipline persisted. Hoover worried that FDR would unleash the hounds of inflation, inflicting on the United States the kind of monetary calamity that had befallen Germany scarcely a decade earlier. The German hyperinflation of 1923, as well as the more moderate but still unsettling doubling of American prices between 1914 and 1920, was still fresh in memory. Those examples put sound-money men on their guard. Moreover, Roosevelt was a Democrat, and the Democratic Party, since at least the time of William Jennings Bryan in the late nineteenth century, had been home to a large proinflationary constituency. Based mostly in the chronically indebted agricultural regions of the South and West, the inflationary element in the Democratic Party was a never-dormant dog roused to noisy life by the Depression crisis.

Suspicions about Roosevelt's intentions on this point ran deep within the sound-money wing of the Democratic Party and even within his own inner circle. Largely because Roosevelt refused to lay those suspicions to rest, his first choice as secretary of the treasury, Virginia senator Carter Glass, author of the Federal Reserve Act of 1914 and probably the country's leading expert on the banking system, refused to accept appointment in Roosevelt's cabinet. Even Moley, whose job it was to persuade Glass to accept, went about the task halfheartedly. While not knowing the exact nature of Roosevelt's plans, Moley knew enough about Roosevelt's "experimental, tentative, and unorthodox temperament" not to rule out monetary tinkering.[32]

FROM ALL SIDES, pressures played upon FDR to commit himself to this or that Depression remedy or structural reform. His passive, noncommittal posture in these preinaugural days, along with the ever-deepening crisis, guaranteed the wild plurality of policies that would be pressed upon him and the sometimes desperate fervor with which they would be urged.

Pressure came first of all from his own political staff, the body of economic and legal experts assembled during the campaign and known colloquially as the Brain Trust (originally styled the Brains Trust). Though much magnified in the history books, the Brain Trust was a small and decidedly transient group of advisers whose most lasting legacy lay more in the realm of literary descriptions of the early New Deal than it did in the domain of durable policy results. The founding member of the group was Raymond Moley, in 1932 a forty-six-year-old professor of government at Barnard College of Columbia University, specializing in criminal justice. Roosevelt first met him in 1928 and as governor of New York enlisted Moley's help in drafting several proposals for reform of the state prison and judicial systems. In the spring of 1932, as Roosevelt geared up for the presidential campaign, Moley responded eagerly to the candidate's request for expert professional advice on a variety of national issues. Moley began the practice of taking various academic colleagues to Albany on the late afternoon train from New York. After a meal of chronically indifferent quality, during which Roosevelt might

32. Moley, *After Seven Years*, 118ff.

murmur wistfully to his culinarily apathetic wife of dishes he wished he were eating, the group would retire to the cavernous, fusty drawing room. The discussants heaved about in the overstuffed sofa cushions, firing learned volleys across the well-worn Turkish rug, while Roosevelt listened, interrogated, opined, and absorbed. At midnight the session would end abruptly as the visitors dashed for the train back to New York.

Over the course of several weeks, Roosevelt appeared to find the counsel of three of these academic visitors particularly congenial. In addition to Moley, they were Rexford Guy Tugwell, a Columbia University economist, and Adolf A. Berle Jr., a professor at Columbia Law School. Together with longtime Roosevelt political confidante Samuel I. Rosenman, counsel to the governor, Basil "Doc" O'Connor, Roosevelt's law partner, and the financier Bernard Baruch's colorful protégé, Hugh Johnson, they constituted what Roosevelt called his "privy council" until a *New York Times* reporter coined the name "Brains Trust" in September.

The academic members of this group shared several beliefs, in addition to their personal attachment to Roosevelt. (It was Roosevelt's "vibrant aliveness, his warmth, his sympathy, his activism," that first attracted him, Moley wrote. "The rest did not precede, it followed those bare facts.")[33] Three of those beliefs were of particular significance. First, the Brain Trusters agreed that the causes as well as the cures of the Depression lay in the domestic arena. It was futile and pernicious to seek remedies, as Hoover had done, in the international realm.

Second, they all considered themselves inheritors of that tradition of progressive thought best expressed in Charles Van Hise's classic work of 1912, *Concentration and Control: A Solution of the Trust Problem in the United States*. Both Berle and Tugwell in 1932 were in the process of making important contributions to that intellectual tradition with works of their own. Berle, together with Gardiner C. Means, published *The Modern Corporation and Private Property* in 1932, a book that argued for a redefinition of property rights and more vigorous government regulation of the economy. Tugwell's *Industrial Discipline and the Governmental Arts* appeared in 1933. The thread that bound these several treatises together in a common intellectual lineage was the argument summarized in Van Hise's title: that concentration of economic power in huge industrial enterprises was a natural and beneficial feature of modern, advanced societies; and that these enormous concentrations of

33. Moley, *After Seven Years*, 9.

private power necessitated the creation of commensurately powerful public controls, or governmental regulatory bodies. Berle and Tugwell carried Van Hise's thinking a step further when they argued that it was government's right and responsibility not merely to regulate discrete economic sectors but to orchestrate the economy's various parts according to an overall plan.

Third, these ideological commitments implied hostility to what the Brain Trusters identified as "the Wilson-Brandeis philosophy" of trust-busting, or what Moley mocked as the quaint belief "that if America could once more become a nation of small proprietors, of corner grocers and smithies under spreading chestnut trees, we should have solved the problems of American life."[34]

The Brain Trusters regarded Louis Brandeis as Woodrow Wilson's "dark angel," the man whose trust-busting advice, Tugwell thought, had mischievously derailed the early twentieth-century reform movement and stalled the development of appropriate industrial policies for nearly two decades. Brandeis, appointed by Wilson to the Supreme Court in 1916, still sat on the high bench in 1932 (and would until 1939). He was consequently removed from direct influence over economic policy. But he had a faithful deputy and ideological kinsman in Felix Frankfurter, the brilliant, Vienna-born Harvard Law professor who would soon become a kind of one-man employment agency whose protégés filled many sensitive New Deal appointments. Frankfurter, too, was a frequent visitor to Albany in 1932, Tugwell ruefully noted, and "Frankfurter came from Brandeis."[35]

That the Columbia "planners" and the Harvard trust-buster were simultaneously pouring their policy potions into Roosevelt's ear was an early indication of the wide-ranging, apparently indiscriminate eclecticism that marked FDR's mental habits. In fact, despite their broad agreement on many things, the Brain Trusters themselves often disagreed about specific policies. On the most urgent issue before them, "concerning what might be done about the Depression," as Tugwell frankly conceded, "there was no agreement."[36] Berle, a Hoover supporter in 1928, applied his meticulous legal intelligence primarily to thinking about reforms in the banking system and securities markets. His basic approach closely resembled Hoover's, though he also inclined toward inflationary ideas, which neither Hoover

34. Moley, *After Seven Years*, 24.
35. Tugwell, *Brains Trust*, 59–60.
36. Tugwell, *Brains Trust*, xxv.

nor Berle's fellow Brain Trusters could countenance. Moley took another leaf from Hoover's book and promoted the idea of voluntary business-government cooperation to reduce wasteful competition.

Tugwell, whom Moley compared to a "cocktail" because "his conversation picked you up and made your brain race along," was the most politically radical of the group, as well as the most personally dashing and the most intellectually daring.[37] In the freewheeling discussions in the governor's Albany drawing room, his leaping mind frequently outpaced the others, vaulting elegantly from deep analysis to sweeping conclusions. His primary interest lay neither in reform of financial institutions nor inflation nor even industrial self-regulation but in drastic restructuring of the entire American economy under government direction. In eloquent and witty phrases, artfully deploying a master teacher's repertoire of similes and metaphors to make his points concrete and accessible, he urged upon Roosevelt an "underconsumptionist" explanation of the Depression. The owners of industry, he said, had failed to pass on a fair share of the spectacular productivity gains of the 1920s to labor in the form of higher wages or to consumers in the form of lower prices. Thus a vicious cycle had set in: workers' buying power had failed to keep pace with the productive capacity of the industrial economy, inventories had piled up, and plants eventually had to be closed and workers laid off. What was far worse, the persistent agricultural depression had denied to industrial producers a huge fraction of the consumer demand they would have enjoyed if the American economy were better balanced. "Balance" was fast becoming a buzzword in New Deal circles, and it nowhere buzzed more insistently than in Tugwell's agile, questing mind.

Deep in the substratum of Tugwell's thinking about "underconsumption" rested a largely unexcavated layer of assumptions about the historical state of development of industrial economies, particularly that of the United States. Sometimes called the "mature economy" or "stagnationist" thesis, this notion implied that the era of economic expansion had effectively ended. Technological boundaries had been reached. No great innovations of the sort that had produced the giant automobile industry were in sight. The end of immigration and declining birth rates spelled slowed or even negative population growth. Thus advanced societies need no longer concentrate on organizing themselves to produce goods more efficiently or in greater quantity. Their cardinal problem, rather, was "overproduction" — the natural reciprocal of "underconsumption."

37. Moley, *After Seven Years*, 15.

Roosevelt had given voice to that thesis in a memorable campaign speech, drafted by Adolf Berle, before the Commonwealth Club of San Francisco on September 23. "A mere builder of more industrial plants, a creator of more railroad systems, an organizer of more corporations, is as likely to be a danger as a help," said Roosevelt. "The day of the great promoter or the financial Titan, to whom we granted everything if only he would build, or develop, is over. Our task now is not discovery, or exploitation of natural resources, or necessarily producing more goods. It is the soberer, less dramatic business of administering resources and plants already in hand, of seeking to reestablish foreign markets for our surplus production, of meeting the problem of underconsumption, of adjusting production to consumption, of distributing wealth and products more equitably."[38]

Much controversy has surrounded this speech. Many historians claim that it contained more of Berle's thinking than Roosevelt's, striking, as it did, what was for Roosevelt an uncharacteristic note of entropy and pessimism. But however untypical of Roosevelt's temperament, the speech accurately reflected theories of history and economic principles that FDR had repeatedly heard discussed in his evenings with the Brain Trusters. It also fitted consistently with points he had made in other campaign speeches, notably at Oglethorpe University on May 22, when he had spoken of the "haphazardness" and "gigantic waste" in the American economy, its "superfluous duplication of productive facilities," had predicted that "our physical economic plant will not expand in the future at the same rate at which it has expanded in the past," and had called therefore for thinking "less about the producer and more about the consumer." The philosophical premises of the Commonwealth Club and Oglethorpe speeches—emphasizing consumption more than production, the economics of distribution rather than the economics of wealth creation, issues of equity over issues of growth—would be clearly discernible in much of the New Deal.[39]

Tugwell's analysis led logically to policies that would significantly redistribute income in American society. The Depression had begun in the agricultural sector, Tugwell insisted, and the agricultural sector was the place to begin the process of recovery, with some kind of program that would put more money into the hands of farmers. Tugwell would come in time to consider Roosevelt's gushy romanticism about rural life

38. *PPA* (1928–32), 751–52.
39. *PPA* (1928–32), 639–47.

one of FDR's most aggravating traits, but for now his sympathy for farmers seemed to make Roosevelt receptive to Tugwell's talk of "balance" and of the need, above all, first and foremost, to tilt the economic scales in favor of agriculture. Yet even such a persuasive mentor and such a perceptive student of Roosevelt's personality as Tugwell could not be sure that he was convincing FDR of the causal relationship between the depression in agriculture and the general depression. "We could throw out pieces of theory," Tugwell reflected; "we could suggest relations; and perhaps the inventiveness of the suggestion would attract his notice. But the tapestry of the policy he was weaving was guided by an artist's conception which was not made known to us."[40]

The Brain Trusters, especially the ever-present Moley, attracted much public notice in late 1932 and early 1933. They were a novelty in American political culture. Academic experts had played a role in the earlier progressive reform effort, but none so conspicuously or at so high a level as Moley, Tugwell, and Berle. They were newcomers to public life, amateurs, professors, refugees from the ivory tower, idea men. Those very characteristics made them objects of the public's fascination. The same facts made them objects of suspicious regard by the professional Democratic politicians who considered Roosevelt's imminent presidency their own precious personal possession, their salvation from years in the outer political darkness. "Tell the Governor that he is the boss and we will follow him to hell if we have to," vice-presidential candidate John Nance Garner instructed a messenger to Roosevelt during the campaign, "but if he goes too far with some of these wild-eyed ideas we are going to have the shit kicked out of us."[41] Moley, the nominal chairman of the Brain Trust, served for a season as Roosevelt's alter ego, his high factotum and dark familiar. He became the special focus of the party professionals' anxieties. A joke circulated to the effect that one needed to go through Roosevelt to get an appointment with Moley. Congressman Sam Rayburn of Texas accosted Moley in a railroad dining car in December 1932 and muttered menacingly, "I hope we don't have any god-damned Rasputin in this administration."[42]

RAYBURN NEEDN'T HAVE WORRIED. Neither Moley nor the Brain Trusters as a group, nor the unctuously insinuating Frankfurter, had

40. Schlesinger 1:401.
41. Schlesinger 1:416.
42. The episode is recounted both in Moley's *After Seven Years*, 83, and more colorfully in Schlesinger 1:451.

a monopoly on Roosevelt's ear. A host of other claimants also paid him court and pressed their cases. Among them was the Democratic congressional leadership, of which Rayburn, powerful chairman of the House Committee on Interstate and Foreign Commerce, was a prominent member. For the most part, the barons of Congress had been unenthusiastic, even hostile, toward Roosevelt's nomination. Preponderantly from the South, perennially reelected as beneficiaries of the Democratic Party's post-Reconstruction political monopoly on that region, many of them well advanced in years and antediluvian in their thinking, they had patiently accumulated seniority, quietly marking time against the day when their party's majority status would confer upon them the coveted committee chairmanships that were the crowning achievement of a congressional career. The Democrats had won control of the House by a slim margin in 1930. Roosevelt's landslide victory in 1932 gave them a nearly two-to-one numerical advantage in the House and a comfortable fifteen-seat majority in the Senate.[43] The old-line Democrats' hour of triumph had at last arrived. They had small desire to share it with Roosevelt.

As in the region from which they came, little had changed in the lives and outlooks of these graying southerners since the long-ago days when they had first entered politics. Many of them still clung to the political faith of their fathers, to simple Jeffersonian maxims about states' rights and the least possible federal government. They reverenced a balanced budget as the holiest of civic dogmas. After years of passivity, lack of responsibility, and the habitual naysaying typical of a minority party, they were ill suited to creative legislating. No group of legislators, Tugwell thought, "can ever have been less fitted to cope with a crisis requiring movement, adaptability, and imagination."[44] Many of Herbert Hoover's cautious innovations had unsettled them. The unpredictable, experimentally inclined Roosevelt, surrounded by his freethinking professorial claque, was downright unnerving. Their major and almost exclusive common ground with the new president lay in their shared concern for agriculture, the economic foundation of the still premodern South.

These party elders joined the procession to Roosevelt's desk in late 1932 and early 1933 to urge upon him the hoary canons of economic

---

43. With only fitful exceptions, the Democratic Party would control both houses of Congress for most of the remainder of the century, reversing decades of Republican dominance. Until the Republicans won control of both houses in 1994, they prevailed in the Senate only in 1947–48, 1953–54, and 1980–86, and Democrats lost control of the House for only two sessions in the six decades after 1933, in 1947–48 and 1952–53.

44. Tugwell, *Roosevelt's Revolution*, 71.

and political orthodoxy. In the appropriately obsolescing forum of the Republic's last lame-duck congressional session (like all its predecessors, the Congress elected in 1930 met for a final session *after* the subsequent election, in November 1932), they also staged hearings before the Senate Finance Committee, billed by the press as a "Depression clinic" to educate the new president in the proper means to deal with the crisis. For weeks, representatives of the nation's industrial, commercial, and financial elites paraded into the Senate hearing room and hymned the praises of government frugality, stiffer taxes, and the sacred balanced budget. This was the most conventional of the conventional wisdom, and it differed from Hoover's program only in its more emphatic conservatism.

Conspicuous among the conservative voices heard in these weeks was that of Bernard Baruch, head of the War Industries Board in Woodrow Wilson's government and the consummate Democratic Party insider. A fabulously wealthy Wall Street speculator, Baruch lavished money on Democrats whom he deemed sympathetic to his own big-business outlook. He was said to have contributed some $200,000 to the 1932 campaign; Roosevelt thought that he "owned" at least sixty congressmen. His advice to FDR was Spartan in its stark simplicity: "Balance budgets. Stop spending money we haven't got. Sacrifice for frugality and revenue. Cut government spending—cut it as rations are cut in a siege. Tax—tax everybody for everything."[45]

Dozens of Baruch's economic co-religionists made the same professions in these weeks, including another powerful Wall Street operator and Democratic Party financier, Joseph P. Kennedy. These men spoke with the loud and authoritative voice of money—political money, the kind that paid for campaigns and got congressmen, senators, and presidents elected. Roosevelt could not ignore them, even while he maneuvered to keep Baruch out of his cabinet and to keep the bullishly ambitious Kennedy in check. If Baruch and Kennedy were statesmen, Tugwell thought, "my definition of the public interest was all wrong. Roosevelt, however, furnished them with the public impression of intimacy, whatever his private reservations."[46]

THE CONSERVATIVE DEMOCRATIC LEADERS in Congress took some comfort from Roosevelt's necessary attendance to the likes of Ba-

45. Freidel, *Launching*, 57.
46. Tugwell, *Brains Trust*, 152.

ruch and Kennedy and from his apparently respectful attention to their own austere advice, but they were deeply agitated at his open flirtation with progressive members of the Republican Party. Several progressive Republicans had publicly repudiated Hoover and supported Roosevelt in the presidential campaign. Roosevelt found many of them, like Nebraska's George Norris, New Mexico's Bronson Cutting, and California's Hiram Johnson, much more politically congenial than he did the more conservative members of his own Democratic Party. He invited first Johnson and then Cutting to join his cabinet as secretary of the interior. After both had declined, he named to the post another progressive Republican, the rotund and crusty fifty-nine-year-old Harold Ickes of Chicago (whom he had never met, and whose name he mispronounced "Ikes" at their first encounter—the correct pronunciation rhymes with "dickies"). He appointed still another progressive Republican, Iowa's dreamy and mystical Henry A. Wallace, as secretary of agriculture.

These were key appointments in terms of both policy and politics. The secretaries of interior and agriculture would have major responsibilities for shaping conservation measures and farm relief, two matters close to Roosevelt's heart and near the top of his list of priorities on assuming office. What was more, these appointments signaled Roosevelt's intention to assemble a new political coalition, one that would transcend the regional and ideological boundaries of the historic Democratic Party and be supportive of liberal initiatives. Roosevelt was here aiming, in effect, to repeat and consolidate in 1936 Woodrow Wilson's fleeting accomplishment of 1916. In that year Wilson had won election to a second term by attracting into the fold of the Democratic Party many of the Progressive or "Bull Moose" voters who had cast their ballots for Theodore Roosevelt in 1912. But Wilson's marriage of the forward-looking, antimachine progressive reform movement of the Northeast and West to the traditional Democratic Party, with its already incongruous bases in the backwater agrarian South and the machine-oiled immigrant ghettoes of the industrial cities, had not lasted beyond his second term. Indeed, it had endured a scant two years. It buckled under wartime pressure in the election of 1918, when Republicans won both houses of Congress, and collapsed entirely in 1920, when the Democrats lost the White House as well, ushering in a decade of Republican dominance in the nation's affairs.

By 1932, however, the opportunity vividly loomed of permanently institutionalizing Wilson's transient electoral achievement. The economic debacle, and Hoover's humiliating failure to cope with it, gave to the Democratic Party the kind of political opening that FDR had long anticipated would be necessary to crack the Republican ascendancy. Roosevelt meant to seize that opportunity and to use it imaginatively. He intended not merely to expand the Democratic Party numerically but to transform it demographically and ideologically. Central to this strategy was the South. It remained safely solid for the Democrats, the political bedrock on which all durable Democratic coalitions must be erected. But the South was an anchor as well as a base, a potential drag on any effort to innovate. The iron grip of its congressional delegation on the levers of legislative power necessitated caution and deference. In time Roosevelt would try to reshape the political and economic culture of the South, to rouse it from the slumber of tradition and nudge it into the modern, industrial era. For the moment he tried simply to avoid giving it offense while he cultivated the urban industrial workers in the great immigrant cities, as well as the old Bull Moose progressives.

The steady process of urbanization had amplified the electoral power of the city-based vote, largely made up of immigrant ethnic communities sorely afflicted by the galloping unemployment in the heavy industrial sector. Their representatives, conspicuously New York's Robert Wagner, had led the drive in Congress for federal unemployment relief and public works legislation. Together with hydroelectric power, the talismanic issue for liberal Republicans like George Norris, these items were to form a large part of Roosevelt's own early New Deal legislative agenda. Their contribution to economic recovery, at least in the short run, was arguable, but they surely facilitated the kind of long-term political realignment of which Roosevelt dreamt.

Roosevelt did not dream this dream alone. To the conservative elders of the Democratic Party, shocked by Roosevelt's nomination, his vision of the party's future was an unwelcome if perhaps inescapable nightmare. Yet others cheered the prospect. In a conversation with Louis Brandeis, Roosevelt declared that "his administration must be liberal and that he expected to lose part of his Conservative supporters. I told him 'I hoped so,'" Brandeis reported to Felix Frankfurter, "that he must realign . . . part of the forces in each party." Moley, too, hailed "the opportunity we now have for a liberal party . . . what ought to be the most significant party alignment in history."[47]

Contributing to that opportunity, and complicating it, was the composition of the Seventy-third Congress elected with Roosevelt in 1932.

47. Freidel, Launching, 64, 70.

More than half of its members had been voted into office since 1930—14 new senators and 144 new representatives in 1932 and a comparable number two years earlier. Overwhelmingly they were "Depression babies," their political careers born in the crisis and their futures dependent on doing something about it, and doing it pronto. Though much of the Democratic congressional leadership remained old-guard, southern, agrarian, and conservative, the rank-and-file Democratic majorities in both houses were largely made up of fresh, northern, urban-industrial representatives of at least potentially liberal bent. At a minimum they were impatient with inaction, prodded by their constituents to take arms against the Depression, and not likely to be silenced by appeals to tradition. They were, as yet, an unformed and unreckoned force, one that Roosevelt might mold to his purposes of remaking his party—or one whose very strength and impetuosity might force the president's hand.

Inflation was one policy that might bring this disparate assemblage of congressional Democrats together. An induced rise in prices would lift the burden of debt, raise asset and commodity values, liquefy the credit system, and prompt a new economic start—or so the argument ran. New voices joined the traditional inflationary chorus in Congress, and their demands swelled to a booming crescendo by early 1933. To the Brain Trusters' dismay, Roosevelt seemed charmed by their music. He annoyed his economic advisers, Tugwell wrote, "by persistently coming back to monetary devices taken by themselves. We were at heart believers in sound money. Greenbackism was part of the populist tradition that we hoped had been left behind. We knew well enough that it hadn't; its advocates were loud and growing louder; all the old schemes for cheapening money were apparently still alive, and there were many new ones. The Governor wanted to know all about them. We shuddered and got him the information."[48]

THIS WAS THE CONFUSING ARRAY of policy advice besetting the president-elect and the unstable constellation of political forces taking shape in Washington on inauguration day. Roosevelt confronted budget-balancers and inflators, regulators and trust-busters, traditionalist southerners and restless urban liberals. To discipline the unpredictable new Congress to his will, Roosevelt calculatingly withheld the distribution of some one hundred thousand patronage jobs to deserving Democrats until after the special legislative session that he requested to convene

48. Tugwell, Brains Trust, 97–98.

on March 9, 1933, had adjourned. Consequently, well into the early months of Roosevelt's presidency, most of the government bureaus and departments were still staffed with Republican holdovers from the Hoover administration. Thus did Moley record his impression that Roosevelt and his entourage "stood in the city of Washington on March 4th like a handful of marauders in hostile territory."[49]

49. Moley, *After Seven Years*, 128.

5

The Hundred Days

Philosophy? Philosophy? I am a Christian and a Democrat—that's all.
—Franklin D. Roosevelt, responding to the question
"What is your philosophy?"

Washington in 1933 was still a spacious, unhurried city with a distinctly southern flavor. As yet unjacketed by suburbs, it slept dreamily amid the gently undulating Virginia and Maryland woodlands, its slow rhythms exemplified by the World War "temporary" buildings that were still scattered about town and by the unfinished columns of what would eventually be the Department of Labor. It was not yet an imperial city, the vibrant center of political and economic command that Roosevelt was to make it.

On the Saturday morning of inauguration day, the streets of the normally languid capital began to fill with boisterous Democrats, eager to celebrate the end of their long exile from political power. Bedecked with bunting, athrob with rollicking political junketeers, Washington tried to muster a mood to defy the gray, overcast weather, and one that would hold at bay, for a hopeful moment, the pall of gloom and anxiety enveloping the entire nation. For behind the festive trappings, Washington on March 4, 1933, was a city under siege. And in the cities and hamlets beyond the capital, millions of Americans cowered apprehensively.

The siege had begun, in the manner made sickeningly familiar in the preceding three years, with yet another banking panic. This one started in Michigan, where the governor had declared an eight-day banking "holiday" on February 14, to protect the reeling banks in his state from collapsing. This drastic action in a key industrial state set off tremors throughout the country. Public apprehension about the banking system

131

and disillusionment with bankers were amplified at this moment by revelations emanating from the Senate Banking and Currency Committee hearing room, where committee counsel Ferdinand Pecora was daily extracting scandalous admissions of malfeasance, favoritism, tax avoidance, and corruption from the princes of Wall Street. Over Hoover's strenuous objections, Congress further undermined confidence in the banks by publishing the names of institutions receiving RFC loans, a policy that amounted to broadcasting an official roster of the shakiest, most endangered banks.

After having suffered through three years of depression and witnessing more than five thousand bank failures in the last three years, Americans reacted this time with hair-trigger haste and last-ditch desperation. By the thousands, in every village and metropolis, they scurried to their banks, queued up with bags and satchels, and carted away their deposits in currency or gold. They hoarded these precious remnants of their life savings under the mattress or in coffee tins buried in the back yard. Wealthier depositors shipped gold out of the country. Stock prices plummeted again, though not from their 1929 heights.

This latest bank panic had prompted Hoover's "cheeky" appeal to Roosevelt on February 18 to make a gesture that would soothe the jittery financial world. Receiving no reply, Hoover had again beseeched Roosevelt on February 28 to make some reassuring statement. "A declaration even now on the line I suggested," Hoover pleaded, "would save losses and hardships to millions of people." He went on to suggest that Roosevelt convene a special session of Congress as soon as possible after inauguration day.[1] Again, Roosevelt demurred. Without the president-elect's concurrence, the lame-duck president would not act. From Washington came only silence.

But in bank lobbies throughout the country, there was no silence. Shouting depositors jostled and shoved up to the tellers' wickets, demanding their cash. In state after state, the banking system quivered, buckled, and was saved from final failure only by gubernatorially decreed holiday. Maryland's banks were closed for three days by executive order on February 24. Similar closings followed in Kentucky, Tennessee, California, and elsewhere. On the morning of inauguration day, the New York Stock Exchange abruptly suspended trading; so did the Chi-

---

1. Frank Freidel, *Launching the New Deal* (Boston: Little, Brown, 1973), 188; William Starr Myers and Walter H. Newton, *The Hoover Administration: A Documented Narrative* (New York: Charles Scribner's Sons, 1936), 360.

cago Board of Trade. By then governmental proclamation had shut every bank in thirty-two states. Virtually all banks in six others were closed. In the remaining states, depositors were limited to withdrawing a maximum of 5 percent of their money, in Texas no more than ten dollars in a day. Investors had ceased to invest and workers had ceased to work. Some thirteen million willing pairs of hands could find no useful employment. Many had fidgeted idly for three years. Now they wrung in anxious frustration or steepled hopefully together in prayer. History's wealthiest nation, the haughty citadel of capitalist efficiency, only four years earlier a model of apparently everlasting prosperity, land of the pilgrims' pride, of immigrant dreams and beckoning frontiers, America lay tense and still, a wasteland of economic devastation.[2]

On inaugural eve, Friday, March 3, Hoover made one last effort to secure Roosevelt's cooperation. The outgoing president's gesture was fatuous in its lateness and doomed to futility by its manner of presentation. Refusing to extend to his successor the customary invitation to a pre-inaugural White House dinner, Hoover grudgingly agreed to receive the Roosevelts for afternoon tea. He then turned this already attenuated social occasion into an awkward last-minute appeal to Roosevelt to use the doubtful authority of the World War Trading with the Enemy Act to regulate overseas gold shipments and bank withdrawals. The encounter ended badly. Hoover responded to Roosevelt's courteous suggestion that Hoover need not feel obliged to make the traditional return call on the president-elect by saying icily: "Mr. Roosevelt, when you are in Washington as long as I have been, you will learn that the President of the United States calls on nobody." A fuming Roosevelt hustled his irate family out of the room. Aside from their necessary proximity in the following day's inaugural formalities, the two men never saw each other again.[3]

ROOSEVELT BEGAN INAUGURAL DAY by attending a brief service at St. John's Episcopal Church. His old Groton School headmaster, Endicott Peabody, prayed the Lord to "bless Thy servant, Franklin, chosen to be president of the United States." After a quick stop at the Mayflower Hotel to confer urgently with his advisers on the still-worsening banking crisis, Roosevelt donned his formal attire and motored to the White House. There he joined a haggard and cheerless

2. Davis 3:26.
3. Freidel, *Launching*, 192–93.

Hoover for the ride down Pennsylvania Avenue to the inaugural platform on the east side of the Capitol.

Braced on his son's arm, Roosevelt walked his few lurching steps to the rostrum. Breaking precedent, he recited the entire oath of office, rather than merely repeating "I do" to the chief justice's interrogation. Then he began his inaugural address, speaking firmly in his rich tenor voice. Frankly acknowledging the crippled condition of the ship of state he was now to captain, he began by reassuring his countrymen that "this great nation will endure as it has endured, will revive and will prosper. . . . "The only thing we have to fear," he intoned, "is fear itself." The nation's distress, he declared, owed to "no failure of substance." Rather, "rulers of the exchange of mankind's goods have failed through their own stubbornness and their own incompetence, have admitted their failure, and have abdicated. . . . The money changers have fled from their high seats in the temple of our civilization. We may now restore that temple to the ancient truths." The greatest task, he went on, "is to put people to work," and he hinted at "direct recruiting by the Government" on public works projects as the means to do it. He then touched on the notion of "balance" as he had heard the Brain Trusters discuss it, promising "to raise the value of agricultural products and with this the power to purchase the output of our cities." He added a flourish of his own about the desirability of redistributing population from the cities to the countryside. He mentioned the need to prevent mortgage foreclosures, to regulate key industries, and especially to cut government budgets. He called for "strict supervision of all banking and credits and investments." He stressed the primacy of domestic over international concerns. He obliquely hinted at inflationary measures in a pledge to ensure "an adequate but sound currency." (One hard-money congressman complained that this meant Roosevelt was "for sound currency, but lots of it.")[4] He announced that he was calling a special session of Congress to address these issues. Then, guardedly but nevertheless ominously, he declared that if Congress should fail to act, "I shall ask the Congress for the one remaining instrument to meet the crisis—broad Executive power to wage a war against the emergency, as great as the power that would be given to me if we were in fact invaded by a foreign foe."[5]

Just weeks before his inaugural, while on his way to board the *Nour-*

4. Leuchtenburg, 42.
5. PPA, (1933), 11–16.

mahal in Florida, Roosevelt had spoken restlessly of the need for "action, action." President at last, he now proceeded to act with spectacular vigor.

The first and desperately urgent item of business was the banking crisis. Even as he left the Mayflower Hotel to deliver his inaugural condemnation of the "money changers," he approved a recommendation originating with the outgoing treasury secretary, Ogden Mills, to convene an emergency meeting of bankers from the leading financial centers. The next day, Sunday, March 5, Roosevelt issued two proclamations, one calling Congress into special session on March 9, the other invoking the Trading with the Enemy Act to halt all transactions in gold and declare a four-day national banking holiday—both of them measures that Hoover had vainly urged him to endorse in the preceding weeks. Hoover's men and Roosevelt's now began an intense eighty hours of collaboration to hammer out the details of an emergency banking measure that could be presented to the special session of Congress. Haunting the corridors of the Treasury Department day and night, private bankers and government officials both old and new toiled frantically to rescue the moribund corpse of American finance. In that hectic week, none led normal lives, Moley remembered. "Confusion, haste, the dread of making mistakes, the consciousness of responsibility for the economic well-being of millions of people, made mortal inroads on the health of some of us . . . and left the rest of us ready to snap at our own images in the mirror. . . . Only Roosevelt," Moley observed, "preserved the air of a man who'd found a happy way of life."[6]

Roosevelt's and Hoover's minions "had forgotten to be Republicans or Democrats," Moley commented. "We were just a bunch of men trying to save the banking system."[7] William Woodin, the new treasury secretary, and Ogden Mills, his predecessor, simply shifted places on either side of the secretary's desk in the Treasury Building. Otherwise, nothing changed in the room. The kind of bipartisan collaboration for which Hoover had long pleaded was now happening, but under Roosevelt's aegis, not Hoover's—and not, all these men hoped, too late. When the special session of Congress convened at noon on March 9, they had a bill ready—barely.

The bill was read to the House at 1:00 P.M., while some new representatives were still trying to locate their seats. Printed copies were not

6. Raymond Moley, *After Seven Years* (New York: Harper and Brothers, 1939), 191.
7. Moley, *After Seven Years*, 148.

ready for the members. A rolled-up newspaper symbolically served. After thirty-eight minutes of "debate," the chamber passed the bill, sight unseen, with a unanimous shout. The Senate approved the bill with only seven dissenting votes—all from agrarian states historically suspicious of Wall Street. The president signed the legislation into law at 8:36 in the evening. "Capitalism," concluded Moley, "was saved in eight days."[8]

The Emergency Banking Act furnished a startling demonstration of Roosevelt's penchant for action and of the Congress's willingness, at least for the moment, to submit to his leadership. But it did not signal any intention radically to reorder the American capitalist system. The act legitimated the actions Roosevelt had already taken under the terms of the Trading with the Enemy Act, conferred on the president broad discretionary powers over gold and foreign exchange transactions, empowered the RFC to subscribe to the preferred stock of banks, expanded the capacity of the Federal Reserve Board to issue currency, and authorized the reopening of banks under strict government supervision. It was a thoroughly conservative measure, which had been drafted largely by Hoover administration officials and private bankers. As one congressman later commented, "The President drove the money-changers out of the Capitol on March 4th—and they were all back on the 9th." Unorthodoxy at this moment, Moley explained, "would have drained the last remaining strength of the capitalist system," a result as distant from Roosevelt's mind as it was from Hoover's, not to mention that of the Congress.[9]

For technical reasons the banking holiday was extended through the following weekend, making Monday, March 13, the day scheduled for the government-supervised reopening of the banks. On the preceding Sunday evening, at 10:00 P.M. eastern time, tens of millions of Americans tuned their radio sets to listen to the first of Roosevelt's Fireside Chats. Working from a draft prepared by Hoover's undersecretary of the treasury, Arthur Ballantine, Roosevelt explained in simple terms what had been accomplished in Washington. He told his listeners "that it is safer to keep your money in a reopened bank than under the mattress."[10] In a voice at once commanding and avuncular, masterful yet intimate, he soothed the nervous nation. His Groton-Harvard accent might have been taken as snobbish or condescending, but it conveyed instead that

8. Moley, *After Seven Years*, 155.
9. Leuchtenburg, 44; Moley's remark is in *After Seven Years*, 155.
10. PPA (1933), 64.

same sense of optimism and calm reassurance that suffused his most intimate personal conversations.

On Monday the thirteenth the banks reopened, and the results of Roosevelt's magic with the Congress and the people were immediately apparent. Deposits and gold began to flow back into the banking system. The prolonged banking crisis, acute since at least 1930, with roots reaching back through the 1920s and even into the days of Andrew Jackson, was at last over. And Roosevelt, taking full credit, was a hero. William Randolph Hearst told him: "I guess at your next election we will make it unanimous." Even Henry Stimson, who so recently had thought FDR a "peanut," sent his "heartiest congratulations."[11]

The common people of the country sent their congratulations as well — and their good wishes and suggestions and special requests. Some 450,000 Americans wrote to their new president in his first week in office. Thereafter mail routinely poured in at a rate of four to seven thousand letters per day. The White House mailroom, staffed by a single employee in Hoover's day, had to hire seventy people to handle the flood of correspondence. Roosevelt had touched the hearts and imaginations of his countrymen like no predecessor in memory.

He meant to maintain that contact — and use it. Roosevelt rightly believed that the majority of the country's newspapers were in the hands of political conservatives, who could not be counted upon to support him in the court of public opinion. It was partly for that reason that he made such calculating use of the new electronic medium of the radio, through which he could speak directly to the public without editorial interference. And if publishers and editors could be expected to oppose him, he could nevertheless cultivate reporters.

Roosevelt's first press conference was a personal and political triumph. One hundred twenty-five White House reporters, sensing that the focus of power in Washington was shifting from Capitol Hill to the White House, in the process upgrading the prestige of their previously tedious assignment, crowded into the Oval Office on the morning of March 8. Roosevelt greeted them with his customary warmth. He made them feel like part of his family. He bantered and joked. Most important, he announced welcome changes in the rules governing presidential press conferences. He hoped to meet with reporters, he said, twice a week, at times convenient to both morning and evening editions. The contrast with Hoover,

11. Schlesinger 2:13.

who had held virtually no press conferences for over a year, was sharp. So too was Roosevelt's declaration that he would not require written questions to be submitted in advance, as had been the custom for more than a decade. He would not answer hypothetical questions, he said, nor permit direct quotation unless issued by his own staff in writing. His own statements would fall into three categories: news that could be attributed to a White House source; "background information" that reporters could use at their own discretion but without direct attribution; and "off-the-record" comments that were to be regarded as privileged and not for publication in any form. This last category was the master stroke. It invited the working press into an intimate, almost conspiratorial proximity to the seat of power, subtly enfolding them within the orbit of the presidential will. Flattered and exhilarated, the reporters broke spontaneously into applause. Roosevelt sat back in his chair, beaming.

On March 10, Roosevelt sent his second emergency measure to Congress, requesting authority to cut some $500 million from the federal budget. "For three long years the Federal Government has been on the road toward bankruptcy," he declared. He called for the elimination of some government agencies, reductions in the pay of both civilian and military employees of the government, including congressmen, and, even more controversial, a nearly 50 percent slash in payments to veterans, an item that then accounted for almost one-quarter of the $3.6 billion federal budget. Many congressmen balked at this attack on one of the most popular federal spending items. Noting that remnants of the Bonus Army were still encamped near Washington, and remembering Herbert Hoover's severe embarrassment at its hands, ninety-two Democrats, mostly agrarian radicals and big-city "machine" representatives, broke ranks and voted against the president. The bill carried in the House only with heavy conservative support. It moved swiftly through the Senate only because the Democratic leadership had adroitly scheduled just behind it on the legislative calendar a popular measure to legalize beer, thus forestalling extended debate.

Roosevelt signed the Economy Act on March 20 and the Beer-Wine Revenue Act two days later. The latter measure anticipated the repeal of Prohibition. The lame-duck Congress had passed a bill repealing the Twentieth Amendment on February 20, 1933. The requisite three-quarters of the states would ratify the measure by December 5, when the Twenty-first Amendment became law, ending the Prohibition experiment and signaling another setback for the mostly rural Protestant forces that had tried to make America dry.

In two breathless weeks the new administration had ended the banking crisis, drastically cut federal expenditures, and provided for new revenue with the relegalization of beer and light wines. In the process the president had taken on and vanquished two of the most powerful political lobbies in Washington: the veterans and the prohibitionists. He had also, apparently, jolted the country out of its stagnant, sour resignation and rekindled the nation's confidence in itself. Here at last was a leader who could lead, and a Congress that could be made to follow. Roosevelt continued to bend his party to his will by withholding the distribution of the patronage jobs for which Democrats thirsted. By that device, one observer noted, the president's "relations to Congress were to the very end of the session tinged with a shade of expectancy which is the best part of young love." Whether that relationship would evolve into a stable and productive marriage remained an open question.[12]

Where, exactly, was Roosevelt leading? His banking bill was essentially a product of Hoover's Treasury Department. His economy bill fulfilled the promise of his Pittsburgh campaign speech and slashed federal spending more deeply than Hoover had dared. The beer bill, opening new sources of revenue to the federal government, accomplished the dearest political objective of the archconservative Raskob forces in the Democratic Party. This hardly looked like the sort of "new deal" that had inspired progressive hope and spread conservative apprehension since the time of Roosevelt's nomination eight months earlier.

Roosevelt had little more in mind than these three emergency measures when he summoned the special session to convene. Now, sensing the unexpected pliancy of Congress, he determined to hold it in session and to forge ahead with additional proposals, proposals that would begin to fulfill liberal expectations and give meaning and substance to the New Deal. They comprised a clutch of initiatives aimed variously at recovery and reform, and not incidentally at political realignment. Pundits soon dubbed this burst of legislative activity the Hundred Days. When it ended with the adjournment of the special session on June 16, Roosevelt had sent fifteen messages to Congress and had in turn signed fifteen bills into law. Taken together, the accomplishments of the Hundred Days constituted a masterpiece of presidential leadership unexampled then and unmatched since (unless in the "second Hundred

12. James T. Patterson, *Congressional Conservatism and the New Deal: The Growth of the Conservative Coalition in Congress* (Lexington: University Press of Kentucky, 1967), 11.

Days" over which Roosevelt presided in the great reform surge of 1935). The original Hundred Days forged Roosevelt's principal weapons in the battle against the Depression and shaped much of the New Deal's historical reputation. They also have defied generations of effort to appraise their precise economic and social impact and, perhaps even more vexatiously, their collective ideological identity. Like the man who presided over them, the Hundred Days, and beyond them the New Deal itself, have puzzled historians seeking neatly encompassing definitions of this prolifically creative era.

ROOSEVELT FIRED the first salvo in his barrage of additional legislative proposals on March 16, when he sent his farm bill to Congress. "I tell you frankly that it is a new and untrod path" that his bill was breaking, said Roosevelt, "but I tell you with equal frankness that an unprecedented condition calls for the trial of new means to rescue agriculture."[13] Roosevelt here echoed Herbert Hoover's claims of innovativeness for his own farm legislation in another special session of Congress just four years earlier. That both presidents were correct testifies both to the stubbornness of the agricultural crisis and the widening circle of political possibility that the Depression was inscribing. Roosevelt's farm bill represented new thinking indeed, and lots of it. "Seldom if ever," said a writer for the *New York Herald Tribune*, "has so sweeping a piece of legislation been introduced in the American Congress." Another observer declared that the bill "sought to legalize almost anything anybody could dream up."[14]

At the core of Roosevelt's agricultural program lay the Brain Trusters' familiar idea of "balance," of increasing farmers' income as a means of bolstering demand for domestic industrial products. At this juncture, redressing the imbalance between agriculture and industry constituted the essence of Roosevelt's antidepression strategy. In notes appended to the 1938 edition of his official papers, Roosevelt explained again that he deemed "the continued lack of adequate purchasing power on the part of the farmer" to be "one of the most important reasons for the Depression."[15] This deficiency he now proposed to remedy. But how?

Agriculture was a huge and variegated sector of the American economy. It included Alabama cotton planters and Montana cattle ranchers,

13. PPA (1933), 74.
14. Schlesinger 2:40; Davis 3:69.
15. PPA (1933), 75.

Wisconsin dairymen and Dakota wheat farmers, Missouri hog raisers and New Jersey truck gardeners, California fruit growers and Wyoming sheep men, shoeless sharecroppers and lordly latifundiaries. These disparate interests spoke with no uniform voice about the nature of agriculture's grievances or what should be done about them. All that was certain was that something must be done soon. Agricultural income had plunged by almost 60 percent in the last four years alone. And the agricultural depression dated not simply from 1929. It was already nearly a decade old at the time of the Great Crash. By early 1933 banks were foreclosing on farm mortgages at a rate of some twenty thousand per month. The president of the Farm Bureau Federation, among the most conservative of agricultural organizations, warned a Senate hearing in January: "Unless something is done for the American farmer we will have revolution in the countryside within twelve months."[16]

A cacophony of farm proposals reverberated through Congress, some still echoing from the debates of the 1920s. They ranged from the old McNary-Haugen scheme of subsidized exports to Herbert Hoover's ideas about producers' cooperatives and government purchases of surplus crops, to the perennial cries for debt cancellation and inflation, and to Roosevelt's newfangled notion of "domestic allotment," which called for direct government payments to farmers who agreed *not* to produce certain crops. Domestic allotment payments were to be financed by new taxes on agricultural processors, including canners, millers, packers, and commodity brokers.

Because Hoover's Federal Farm Board had committed itself to purchase surpluses while making no effort to curtail production, it had quickly exhausted its modest financial resources. Domestic allotment sought to avoid that problem by tackling the price-depressing surpluses at their source, preventing their production in the first place. This was a drastic solution indeed. It took the logic of Roosevelt's Commonwealth Club speech about overproduction to the extreme conclusion of literally paying for nothing. The professional economist Tugwell, one of the farm bill's chief architects, conceded to his diary that "for the economic philosophy which it represents there are no defenders at all."[17]

No philosophic defenders, perhaps, but no shortage of interested advocates. Roosevelt had sketched a vague framework for his agricultural policy in his campaign speech at Topeka, Kansas, in September. There

16. Davis 3:71.
17. Leuchtenburg, 49–50.

he had unambiguously declared in favor of "national planning in agriculture." What sort of planning, and by whom, he had left unsaid. Acknowledging that "many plans have been advanced" and that no "particular plan is applicable to all crops," he had promised blandly "to compose the conflicting elements of these various plans."[18] In practice, however, Roosevelt did not compose these elements but simply aggregated them. When repeated conferences with agricultural organizations and consultations with farm leaders failed to produce consensus, Roosevelt cut the Gordian knot by proposing an omnibus bill authorizing the use of virtually *all* competing recommendations for resolving the agricultural crisis. In a hurry to enact the legislation before the spring crops were planted and before the proposed World Economic Conference took up the subject of global agricultural surpluses, the president avoided all the tough decisions about agricultural policy even as he gathered into his hands every imaginable policy instrument.

Even so, Congress balked at swallowing such a complicated and unfamiliar proposal. Roosevelt had to do some deft politicking to move the legislation along. He reassured the devotees of the McNary-Haugen scheme by indicating that he would appoint McNary-Haugenism's principal architect, Moline Plow Company president George Peek, as head of the new Agricultural Adjustment Administration (AAA). This was a recipe that guaranteed controversy and administrative confusion. Peek, a testy, combative, big-mouthed, extreme economic nationalist, loudly denounced the acreage-retirement feature of the legislation, which was the single most innovative aspect of the domestic allotment idea. He clung tenaciously to the old McNary-Haugen formula of no limits on production, a high tariff to protect the domestic agricultural market, and government assistance in dumping American surpluses abroad. These views put him on a direct collision course with domestic-allotment advocates like Secretary of Agriculture Henry Wallace and his new assistant secretary, Rexford Tugwell. They also eventually caused Peek to clash with Secretary of State Cordell Hull, who was trying to restore American foreign trade through reciprocal trade agreements that would, among other things, inhibit dumping.

For the moment the prospect of Peek's appointment mollified one important segment of the raucous and divided agricultural lobby. Others remained unsated. Roosevelt quieted another faction when he created

18. *PPA* (1928–32), 703.

the Farm Credit Administration, to be headed by his old friend and Hyde Park neighbor Henry Morgenthau Jr., and proposed adding farm mortgage relief provisions to the Agricultural Adjustment Act.

The most contentious players in the debate over agricultural policy were the inflationists. Powerful and persistent, gathering growing support from all across the usual ideological boundaries that divided the Congress, they pressed their cause with religious ardor. On April 17 the Senate nearly adopted a measure for the free coinage of silver. Other, wilder proposals for cheapening the currency were dropping into the hopper, including Senator Thomas P. Gore's facetious suggestion to license counterfeiters. The next day Roosevelt informed his advisers that for political reasons he had decided not to oppose an amendment to the Agricultural Adjustment Act proposed by the old Bryanite senator from Oklahoma, Elmer Thomas. The Thomas Amendment authorized the president to induce inflation by reducing the gold content of the dollar, by coining silver, or by issuing up to $3 billion of "greenbacks," fiat money not backed by precious metal of any kind.

"Hell broke loose" among Roosevelt's economic counselors when he told them of his decision, Moley remembered. Horrified, "they began to scold Mr. Roosevelt as though he were a perverse and particularly backward schoolboy." One adviser called the Thomas Amendment "harebrained and irresponsible" and predicted "uncontrolled inflation and complete chaos." Lewis Douglas, the respected budget director whom Roosevelt much admired, called the bill "thoroughly vicious" and almost resigned on the spot. "Well," he said to a friend later in the evening, "this is the end of western civilization."[19]

Roosevelt made a show of sharing his advisers' forebodings. He pleaded that he was only yielding to the inevitable, that his tactical retreat on the Thomas Amendment, which was merely permissive in character, would head off even worse mandatory inflationary measures. But the fact is that FDR had been fascinated with inflationary ideas for months. The Thomas Amendment, which put an array of powers in his hands and left the manner and timing of their exercise to him alone, fitted his purposes to a T. Preparatory to receiving the inflationary tools Congress was about to deliver him, Roosevelt on April 19 officially took the United States off the gold standard, prohibited most overseas shipments of gold, and let the exchange value of the dollar drift downward.

19. Freidel, *Launching*, 333–34; Moley, *After Seven Years*, 159–60; Davis 3:104–10.

On June 5 Congress took the next logical step and abrogated the gold clause in all public and private contracts. The way was now cleared for a "managed currency," its volume and value unfettered by gold.

The Thomas Amendment also unlocked the logjam blocking passage of the Agricultural Adjustment Act. On May 12 the president signed the act into law, barely in time for the World Economic Conference now scheduled for the following month in London, and too late to prevent the spring plantings that Roosevelt had hoped to forestall. To implement the key acreage-reduction feature of the legislation, therefore, the AAA could not simply pay for fallow fields to remain unseeded. The new agency now faced the far more daunting task of plowing up fully one-fourth of the acreage planted to certain crops. Doing so struck many as a crime against nature, a sentiment supported by reports that balky mules could not be made to violate all training and instinct and trample down rows of freshly sprouting crops. Before long, this mulish sabotage of the best-laid plans of men could be taken as an evil omen of the host of problems that would beset the most ambitious effort at national economic planning in American history.

MEANWHILE, THE STEADY legislative drumbeat of the Hundred Days continued. Relishing power and wielding it with gusto, Roosevelt next sent to Congress, on March 21, a request for legislation aimed at unemployment relief. Here he departed most dramatically from Hoover's pettifogging timidity, and here he harvested the greatest political rewards. He proposed a Civilian Conservation Corps (CCC) to employ a quarter of a million young men on forestry, flood control, and beautification projects. Over the next decade, the CCC became one of the most popular of all the New Deal's innovations. By the time it expired in 1942, it had put more than three million idle youngsters to work at a wage of thirty dollars a month, twenty-five of which they were required to send home to their families. CCC workers built firebreaks and lookouts in the national forests and bridges, campgrounds, trails, and museums in the national parks. Roosevelt also called for a new agency, the Federal Emergency Relief Administration (FERA), to coordinate and eventually increase direct federal unemployment assistance to the states. And he served notice, a bit halfheartedly, that he would soon be making recommendations about a "broad public works labor-creating program."[20]

20. PPA (1933), 80–81.

The first two of these measures—CCC and FERA—constituted important steps along the road to direct federal involvement in unemployment relief, something that Hoover had consistently and self-punishingly resisted. Roosevelt showed no such squeamishness, just as he had not hesitated as governor of New York to embrace relief as a "social duty" of government in the face of evident human suffering. As yet, Roosevelt did not think of relief payments or public works employment as means of significantly increasing purchasing power. He proposed them for charitable reasons, and for political purposes as well, but not principally for economic ones.

Roosevelt's New York experience taught him a lasting lesson about the political value of enlarging the federal role in relief. Since his days in the state senate before World War I, and culminating in an explosive controversy involving Jimmy Walker, the flamboyantly corrupt mayor of New York during FDR's governorship, Roosevelt's political nemesis in state politics had been Tammany Hall, the ultimate, ball-jointed, air-cushioned, precision-tooled, self-oiling, thousand-kilowatt urban political machine. Like all such machines, it was an engine of corruption, but it also delivered valuable social services to its army of faithful voters. Musing on this unholy marriage of welfare and graft during the campaign, Roosevelt ventured to Tugwell "that just possibly Tammany could be undercut by taking from it the responsibility for the unemployed. What would happen to the organization," Roosevelt wondered, "if handouts didn't have to be made . . . ? Tammany might be ruined if relief was really organized. People on relief would have no use for Tammany's services. They'd be independent."[21] Even more intriguing, perhaps their dependency could be made to shift from the local boss to the national, Democratic, administration. Like Alexander Hamilton's scheme to secure the loyalty of creditors to the new national government by federal assumption of state debts, so would Roosevelt artfully transfer the primary political allegiance of the unemployed from their local political club to Washington, D.C., in the process breaking forever the historical drive shaft of the urban political machine.

These first modest steps at a direct federal role in welfare services also carried into prominence another of Roosevelt's associates from New York, Harry Hopkins, whom Roosevelt would soon name as federal relief administrator. A chain-smoking, hollow-eyed, pauper-thin social worker, a tough-talking, big-hearted blend of the sardonic and sentimental,

21. Tugwell, *Brains Trust*, 368.

Hopkins represented an important and durable component of what might be called the emerging political culture of the New Deal. In common with Brain Truster Adolf Berle, future treasury secretary Henry Morgenthau Jr., and Labor Secretary Frances Perkins, Hopkins was steeped in the Social Gospel tradition. Earnest, high-minded, and sometimes condescending, the Social Gospelers were middle-class missionaries to America's industrial proletariat. Inspired originally by late nineteenth-century Protestant clergymen like Walter Rauschenbusch and Washington Gladden, they were committed to the moral and material uplift of the poor, and they had both the courage and the prejudices of their convictions. Berle and Morgenthau had worked for a time at Lillian Wald's Henry Street settlement house in New York, Perkins at Jane Addams's Hull House in Chicago, and Hopkins himself at New York's Christadora House. Amid the din and squalor of thronged immigrant neighborhoods, they had all learned at first hand that poverty could be an exitless way of life, that the idea of "opportunity" was often a mockery in the precarious, threadbare existence of the working class. Together with Franklin Roosevelt, they meant to do something about it. The appointment of Perkins as secretary of labor gave some clue as to how their patrician patron intended to get the job done. Perkins was not the traditional male labor leader appointed to head this most macho of government bureaus; she was a woman social worker. In common with Roosevelt, as Arthur M. Schlesinger Jr. has observed, Perkins tended "to be more interested in doing things for labor than enabling labor to do things for itself; and her emphasis as Secretary was rather on the improvement of standards of work and welfare than on the development of labor self-organization."[22]

As for public works, Roosevelt remained skeptical. Progressives in Congress still clamored for a $5 billion construction program, but Roosevelt reiterated Hoover's insistence that public works be self-liquidating. He also endorsed Hoover's conclusion that only about $900 million worth of acceptable projects were on the shelf. "Do not write stories about five or six billion dollars of public works, " he cautioned reporters on April 19. "That is wild."[23] When Perkins pressed a $5 billion list of proposed projects on him at a White House meeting on April 29, he countered by going through the New York projects item by item, pointing out in well-informed detail how unsound most of them were. In the

22. Schlesinger 2:300.
23. PPA (1933), 141.

end Roosevelt caved in to political pressure and allowed an appropriation for $3.3 billion to be made for the new Public Works Administra-
tion. But he also took steps to ensure that the PWA would be cheese-
paring and tightfisted in its disbursement of those funds.

Roosevelt further demonstrated his continuing commitment to maintain at least the appearance of fiscal orthodoxy when he established a
separate "emergency budget" for relief and employment expenditures.
The regular budget he would balance, he promised, but he did not
think it fair "to put into that part of the budget expenditures that relate
to keeping human beings from starving in this emergency. . . . You cannot let people starve, but this starvation crisis is not an annually recur-
ring charge."[24] Though mocked by Roosevelt's critics as an accounting
trick, the very idea of an emergency budget accurately registered his
persistent respect for the conventional budgetary wisdom, as well as his
belief, reminiscent of Hoover's repeatedly dashed hopes, that the crisis
might soon be over.

ROOSEVELT'S TENACIOUS FRUGALITY, especially on public works,
aggravated his progressive allies, but they found much to celebrate in
his public power policies. Here was an area to which Roosevelt, so rarely
a deep analyst of any subject, had uncharacteristically devoted painstak-
ing attention. His knowledge of the complicated accounting and valu-
ation procedures employed in the public utilities industry, thought Tugwell, "was worthy of a lifelong student."[25] His advanced views on this
subject endeared him to progressives. Accompanied by the great paladin
of public power, George Norris, Roosevelt had paid an emotional visit
to Muscle Shoals, Alabama, in January 1933. Wilson Dam at Muscle
Shoals on the Tennessee River had been built by the federal government
during World War I to facilitate nitrate production for the manufacture
of explosives; completed too late for wartime use, it had been a bone of
political contention ever since. Private utilities interests, fighting hammer and claw and with the help of Presidents Coolidge and Hoover,
had repeatedly blocked Norris's scheme for federal operation of the
dam's hydroelectric generating capacity. Roosevelt now saw the great
dam, symbol of progressive frustrations and progressive hopes, for the
first time. He was struck by the sight and sound of the foaming waters
roaring unused over its massive spillways. In the vast surrounding

24. Freidel, *Launching*, 251–52.
25. Tugwell, *Brains Trust*, 74.

valley of the Tennessee, families nightly lit their cabins with kerosene lamps and cooked on wood stoves. To Roosevelt, the contrast was intolerable.

"Is he really with you?" a reporter asked Norris on his return to Washington. "He is more than with me," the elderly senator replied, "because he plans to go even farther than I did."[26] On April 10 Roosevelt put Congress on notice just how far he intended to go. "[T]he Muscle Shoals development is but a small part of the potential public usefulness of the entire Tennessee River," Roosevelt said. He requested the creation of a Tennessee Valley Authority (TVA), a public corporation charged to generate and distribute hydroelectric power from Muscle Shoals, to build more dams for flood control and additional generating capacity, to produce fertilizers, to combat soil erosion and deforestation, to dig a 650-mile navigable waterway from Knoxville on the upper reaches of the Tennessee River system to Paducah on the Ohio, to upgrade health and educational services in the depressed valley, to promote conservation and the development of recreational facilities, and to attract new industries to the region. Roosevelt's vision of what the TVA might do was breathtaking in its imaginative reach. Even Norris was struck by its audacity. "What are you going to say when they ask you the political philosophy behind TVA?" Norris asked FDR. "I'll tell them it's neither fish nor fowl," Roosevelt answered, "but, whatever it is, it will taste awfully good to the people of the Tennessee Valley." And whatever it was, Roosevelt did not intend it to be a purely regional dish, served only within the boundaries of the Tennessee River watershed. "If we are successful here," Roosevelt told the Congress, "we can march on, step by step, in a like development of other great natural territorial units within our borders."[27]

TVA, duly created by Congress on May 18, delighted the progressives. It ratified beyond their dearest expectations the wisdom of their campaign support for Roosevelt. It also fitted perfectly with FDR's political intentions for the South. The Tennessee River cut through seven states of the impoverished, underdeveloped region. TVA would bring jobs, investment, and the promise of prosperity to a sprawling area that had stagnated since the Civil War. At a stroke, Roosevelt had thus earned the gratitude of the two most disparate elements in the unlikely political coalition he was trying to assemble: traditional southern Democrats and

26. Schlesinger 2:324.
27. PPA (1933), 122–23; Freidel, Launching, 351.

forward-looking Republican progressives. He had also taken a giant step in the direction of modernizing the South, laying the foundations for the region's federally sponsored advance into the industrial era. Surprisingly little remarked at its inception, TVA would become the forward edge of the great transforming blade of federal power that would within two generations resculpt the cotton belt into the sun belt.[28]

ON APRIL 4, 1933, Moley and Roosevelt reviewed with satisfaction the president's astonishingly successful legislative record to date. Congress had passed the banking, budget, and beer bills and had created the Civilian Conservation Corps, especially gratifying to the conservation-minded president. The farm and unemployment relief bills were making their way through the Capitol Hill machinery, as was another Roosevelt proposal for reform of the securities markets. The president was scheduled to ask for TVA within the following week and for legislation to shore up the sagging home-mortgage industry shortly thereafter. This constituted a record of considerable achievement. Roosevelt had ridden the Congress like a skilled jockey, the staccato whip-touches of his several brief, urgent messages stirring the balky House and Senate to unprecedented movement. But now, the bit firmly in its teeth, Congress theatened to buck the president and run away with its own agenda.

Virtually everything accomplished thus far consisted of emergency remedial and long-range reform measures. The banking bill, together with the pending securities and mortgage legislation, would stanch the bleeding from the nation's financial system. The budget bill aimed to restore confidence in the investing community. The beer bill modestly increased tax revenues, to the same purpose. But none of the measures thus far enacted provided positive fiscal stimulus to the economy. All to the contrary, the net effect of Roosevelt's budget cutting and tax hiking was decidedly deflationary. Even the relief bill was scaled to the prevention of human suffering, not to the revival of consumer demand. The farm program should in time furnish some economic stimulus, and so might TVA, but it would be months, maybe years, before their effects were visible. None of these measures would make any significant contribution in the short run to the urgent goal of economic recovery. With the economy prostrate and thirteen million people still unemployed, the

28. See Bruce Schulman's development of this theme in *From Cotton Belt to Sunbelt* (New York: Oxford University Press, 1991).

pressure in Congress to take swift and dramatic action was growing irresistible.

Roosevelt appreciated these facts and had been casting about for some means to stimulate industrial activity. But spokesmen for industry, supposedly a more coherent and well-organized economic sector than agriculture, were proving unable to agree on what steps should be taken or even to arrive at the kind of rough consensus on a range of possible measures that the farm leaders had managed eventually to reach. Within the government, Roosevelt's advisers were split between adherents to the Brandeisian antitrust tradition and proponents of the Van Hise philosophy of regulatory control. They too could not find common ground. Roosevelt and Moley accordingly decided at their meeting on April 4 that thinking in both the business community and in government circles on the subject of industrial recovery policy had not yet crystallized sufficiently to justify any further moves at the time. They agreed that nothing should be done yet.

In the meantime Congress, as with inflation and the Thomas Amendment, had been taking the subject of industrial policy into its own hands. Roosevelt's do-nothing decision of April 4, Moley wrote, "went out the window on April 6th."[29] On that day the Senate passed the "thirty-hour bill" sponsored by Alabama senator Hugo Black. A work-spreading device, Black's bill prohibited from interstate commerce any goods manufactured in a plant whose employees worked more than a thirty-hour week. This requirement would supposedly create some six million new jobs. Here at last, it seemed, someone was smiting the dragon of Depression with the kind of quick, clean stroke to the heart for which the long-suffering country was praying.

But Roosevelt was worried. He concurred with his attorney general's opinion that the Black bill was unconstitutional. Moreover, he deemed it unworkable in many of the rural and agricultural industries with which he was most familiar, like canneries and dairies. Black's proposal could not be adapted "to the rhythm of the cow," he told Frances Perkins, a phrase that he repeatedly invoked in his criticisms of the thirty-hour idea.[30] He also believed, correctly, that reducing the workweek without maintaining wages would simply punish workers by shrinking their paychecks. Yet to maintain wages while adding six million workers to the nation's payrolls might bankrupt already faltering businesses.

29. Moley, *After Seven Years*, 186.
30. Frances Perkins, *The Roosevelt I Knew* (New York: Viking, 1946), 194.

For all these reasons, Roosevelt felt obliged to oppose the Black bill, despite his sympathy with its goal of reducing unemployment. But he had, at first, nothing to put in its place. In what was fast becoming notorious as a standard Rooseveltian practice, he assigned several different people, none of whom had much knowledge of the others' activity, to draft proposals for an industrial recovery bill. Through the month of April they worked feverishly. In the end Roosevelt ordered the advocates for the several competing schemes that this process cast up to shut themselves together in a room and not come out until they had settled their differences.

Out of this hurried, chaotic, initially defensive and ultimately compromised endeavor came Roosevelt's message to the Congress of May 17, calling for a National Industrial Recovery Act (NIRA). The proposed legislation embodied three major elements. One, incorporated in the famous Section 7(a), was the most direct successor to the now-buried Black bill. It provided for federal regulation of maximum hours and minimum wages in various industries. Even more consequentially, and somewhat surprisingly, it stipulated the right of industrial workers "to organize and bargain collectively through representatives of their own choosing" — a historic shift away from the government's traditional refusal to guarantee labor's highest objective, the right to unionize.

A second part of the bill created the National Recovery Administration (NRA). The NRA was to be charged with overseeing a vast process of government-sanctioned cartelization. Production in whole industries would be controlled, and prices and wages would be raised, by government-sanctioned industrial compacts; the antitrust laws were largely to be suspended. The rationale, Roosevelt explained in a phrase that once again recollected his Commonwealth Club address, was "to prevent unfair competition and disastrous overproduction." To Moley he privately acknowledged that he was "taking an enormous step away from the philosophy of equalitarianism and laissez-faire. . . . If that philosophy hadn't proved to be bankrupt," Roosevelt added, "Herbert Hoover would be sitting here right now."[31]

The bill's third major component created the Public Works Administration (PWA) to undertake an ambitious public construction program. If the NRA was the chassis of the legislation, creating a framework within which American industry might be reformed and regulated, then the PWA was the engine, or at least the starting motor. Reducing hours,

31. *PPA* (1933), 202; Moley, *After Seven Years*, 189.

spreading work, and stabilizing wages would have no appreciably positive economic effect, and might even inflict additional economic damage, unless aggregate purchasing power was somehow increased. Thus
NRA and PWA were necessarily complementary. The new spending
engendered by PWA, along with the eventual boost to agricultural income envisioned in the AAA legislation, would increase the total volume
of purchases. NRA would equitably spread the benefits of rising income
between labor and capital. NRA and AAA together would ensure balance between industry and agriculture. That, at least, was the theory,
such as it was. Crucial to its successful application was the quick release
of money into the economy through a rapidly adopted public works
program. The figure finally settled on for PWA spending was $3.3 bil-
lion.

In accepting that figure, Roosevelt yielded to the will of Congress,
over his own best judgment. He remained skeptical that PWA would
prove an effective mechanism for generating employment, and he had
given up none of his objections to its budget-busting implications. Consequently, his message to Congress accompanying the NIRA bill called
for $220 million in new taxes, sufficient to service the interest payments
on the sum the government would be forced to borrow to pay for the
public works program.

The NRA would soon become the most conspicuous of all the freshly
minted New Deal agencies, and it has long stood at the center of all
efforts to explain the early New Deal's economic philosophy and antidepression strategy. Thus it is worth remembering the adventitious circumstances of the NRA's birth. Conceived as a means to block the thirty-
hour bill, NRA fused emergency relief measures with a version of the
venerable Van Hise regulatory reform program, a concept long fer-
mented in the wood of academic lecture halls but little tested in practice. The National Industrial Recovery Act, said Moley, was "a thorough
hodge-podge of provisions designed to give the country temporary economic stimulation and provisions designed to lay the groundwork for
permanent business-government partnership and planning, of provisions
calculated to satisfy the forces behind the Black bill and provisions calculated to achieve workable wage-hour agreements." Lumping all of
these provisions together in a single piece of legislation, Moley later
reflected, produced a "confused, two-headed experiment." It was, he
concluded, "a mistake."[32] This ramshackle, hastily assembled contrap-

32. Moley, *After Seven Years*, 190, 184.

tion was now rolled up to take its place alongside AAA in the battery of New Deal heavy artillery deployed in the war against the Depression.

In a final rush of legislative activity, Congress passed the National Industrial Recovery Act and adjourned on June 16. On the same day, it adopted the Glass-Steagall Banking Act, which divorced commercial from investment banking, and, over Roosevelt's objections, instituted federal insurance of bank deposits, the Farm Credit Act, and a railroad regulation bill.

So ENDED the Hundred Days Congress. As Roosevelt signed the final bills that arrived from Capitol Hill on June 16, he remarked that "more history is being made today than in [any] one day of our national life."[33] By any standard, the achievements of the Hundred Days were impressive. The New Deal had decisively halted the banking panic. It had invented wholly new institutions to restructure vast tracts of the nation's economy, from banking to agriculture to industry to labor relations. It had authorized the biggest public works program in American history. It had earmarked billions of dollars for federal relief to the unemployed. It had designated the great Tennessee watershed as the site of an unprecedented experiment in comprehensive, planned regional development. No less important, the spirit of the country, so discouraged by four years of economic devastation, had been infused with Roosevelt's own contagious optimism and hope. In the process, Roosevelt himself had dumfounded those critics who believed they had taken his measure months before and found him then so sorely wanting. Even some old acquaintances wondered if he were the same man. The oath of office, wrote one journalist, "seems suddenly to have transfigured him from a man of mere charm and buoyancy to one of dynamic aggressiveness."[34]

But for all the excitement of the Hundred Days and the rising stature of Roosevelt's reputation, the Depression still hung darkly over the land. The precise battle plan of the New Deal's attack on it remained difficult to define. Little coherent pattern could be detected in the unlikely mixture of policies that had been adopted. They ranged from orthodox budget cutting to expansive spending for relief and public works, from tough controls on Wall Street to government-supervised cartelization, from deliberate crop destruction to thoughtful conservation, from mortgage protection for the middle class to union protection for labor. "It simply has

33. Leuchtenburg, 61.
34. Leuchtenburg, 61.

to be admitted," Tugwell later wrote, "that Roosevelt was not yet certain what direction he ought to take and was, in fact, going both ways at once."[35]

Some of these measures aimed at economic recovery, but at least as many were meant to provide only palliative relief or to enact reforms long-standing on somebody's agenda but only obliquely related to combating the Depression. Some, like TVA, were Roosevelt's idea. Some, like the banking bill, were largely Hoover's. Others, like AAA and NRA, had been devised for the most part by the constituencies affected by them. Still others, like the labor provisions of the NIRA and the Thomas Amendment to the AAA legislation, had originated in Congress. About the only defensible statement that could be made about them in the aggregate was that they accurately reflected Roosevelt's penchant for action, his inclination to experiment, and his receptivity to all kinds of innovation. To look upon these policies as the result of a unified plan, Moley later wrote, "was to believe that the accumulation of stuffed snakes, baseball pictures, school flags, old tennis shoes, carpenter's tools, geometry books, and chemistry sets in a boy's bedroom could have been put there by an interior decorator."[36]

And yet, amid the chaos of the Hundred Days, and indeed through the tense stand-off of the interregnum that preceded it, one thread flashed and dove like a scarlet skein shot through brocade: inflation. Roosevelt had long flirted with inflation as a Depression remedy. In early April he called it "inevitable."[37] By June he deemed it positively desirable.

The historic check on a nation's impulse to inflate had been the gold standard, under which inflating prices attracted imports, which were paid for in gold shipments, thus contracting the monetary base, depressing prices, and nipping the inflationary cycle in the bud. It was precisely the swift power and elegant automaticity of the gold standard that had forced the decision in Britain to go off gold in September 1931. Faced with the choice of protecting the exchange value of the pound by staying on gold or protecting the domestic prices of British products, Britain had abandoned gold. Though FDR seemed slow to grasp the point, the United States faced exactly the same choice in 1933.

35. Rexford G. Tugwell, *Roosevelt's Revolution: The First Year, a Personal Perspective* (New York: Macmillan, 1977), 59.
36. Moley, *After Seven Years*, 369–70.
37. Schlesinger 2:196.

At his press conference on April 19, FDR had declared that he "absolutely" intended to return the United States to the gold standard and added that "one of the things we hope to do is to get the world as a whole back on some form of gold standard."[38] In well-publicized conferences with British prime minister Ramsay MacDonald and French premier Edouard Herriot later in the month, he further gave the impression that the United States would look to the now imminent World Economic Conference to stabilize international exchange rates and reestablish the international gold standard. In an even more lavishly publicized appeal to fifty-four heads of state on May 16, Roosevelt had eloquently called for "stabilization of currencies."[39]

The world was astonished, therefore, when shortly after the World Economic Conference convened Roosevelt scuttled it with his infamous "bombshell message" of July 3. He brusquely declared to the delegates who were waiting upon his word in London that the United States would not be a party to efforts at exchange-rate stabilization, nor would it return in the foreseeable future to gold. Without American participation, there was little the conferees could do to patch up the wounded international economic system. Roosevelt appeared not to care. He had other, exclusively nationalistic, priorities in mind. "Old fetishes of so-called international bankers," he lectured the London delegates, "are being replaced by efforts to plan national currencies."[40] Roosevelt's message not only destroyed the London conference. It also definitively killed any further prospect of international cooperation in the fight against the global depression. Among those observers of the London proceedings who drew the lesson that the United States intended to play no consequential international role was Adolf Hitler. Like Japan in Manchuria, Hitler concluded, Germany could do what it wanted in Europe without fear of American reprisal. Here, five years before the western European democracies' infamous capitulation at Munich to Hitler's demand that he be allowed to absorb part of Czechoslovakia, the Western powers had shown that they had little stomach for concerted action in the face of danger.

Vats of ink have been drained in efforts to explain Roosevelt's surprise attack on the London conference. The full story is rich in theatrics and mystery. It includes the appointment of a colorful and comically

38. *PPA* (1933), 140.
39. *PPA* (1933), 186.
40. *PPA* (1933), 265.

discordant American delegation, headed by the dignified, white-maned secretary of state, Cordell Hull, a sound-money man and fervent internationalist, and counting among its members the silver fanatic and narrow protectionist Key Pittman, Senate Foreign Relations Committee chairman and, in London, a high-living, madly carousing, knife-brandishing drunk. It contains elements of gaudy melodrama involving the dying Secretary of the Treasury Woodin, who fainted during a tense transatlantic telephone consultation. It encompasses the tragic tale of Raymond Moley, borne by navy ship and aircraft to high-seas conferences with Roosevelt, who was piloting his small sailboat along the fog-shrouded coast of New England, allegedly studying advanced treatises on monetary theory while his boat nightly swung around its anchor. Emerging from these dramatic meetings, Moley was dispatched to London, his progress across the Atlantic nervously followed in the world press. He was ostensibly sent to rescue the conference with an affirmation of Roosevelt's belief in international cooperation, but he had the ground abruptly and astoundingly cut from beneath him by Roosevelt's message, which, faithful to the protocols of tragedy, was heavily grounded in Moley's own nationalistic analysis of the Depression. In the process, Moley mortally antagonized his immediate superior, Cordell Hull, marking the beginning of the end of his meteoric political career. He was soon forced to resign his position as assistant secretary of state and drifted gradually into estrangement from the New Deal and sometimes acrid criticism of Franklin Roosevelt.

The denouement in London came with the conference's stormy adjournment, amid denunciations of FDR from all sides. Prime Minister Ramsay MacDonald expressed "the most bitter resentment" against the man who had personally assured him in Washington only weeks earlier that he favored stabilization. A British journalist called Roosevelt a "laughing stock" and damned his message as a document that "will be filed for all times as a classic example of conceit, hectoring, and ambiguity." John Maynard Keynes, the British economist busy developing his own revolutionary ideas about managed currencies, was virtually alone in his praise. The president's action, he wrote, was "magnificently right."[41]

But the histrionic pageantry of this episode should not be allowed to

41. Schlesinger 2:195–232; Davis 3:182–98; Moley, *After Seven Years*, 196–269; Herbert Feis, *1933: Characters in Crisis* (Boston: Little, Brown, 1966), 95–258.

obscure a central truth: the essential logic of Roosevelt's recovery program was inflationary and had been so from the outset. Inflation and the gold standard were incompatible. In this sense, the World Economic Conference was doomed to failure before it even convened.

Heavy majorities in Congress, especially in Roosevelt's own Democratic Party, demanded inflation. The debt-freighted agricultural sector, central to Roosevelt's antidepression strategy and sentimentally dear to him, demanded inflation. The NRA's price-fixing and wage-boosting programs demanded inflation. Inflation would make it easier to service the indebtedness required to pay for federal relief, not to mention the unwelcome debt that the PWA's public works program had forced upon Roosevelt. Inflation was necessary to virtually all parts of the president's early New Deal agenda. Roosevelt had for months displayed a persistent interest in inflationary ideas. And inflation could not be accomplished if the United States agreed to play by the rigid, anti-inflationary rules of the gold standard regime. However much Roosevelt may have believed his own statements in April about returning to gold, the inescapable anti–gold standard logic of his program must at some point have impressed itself upon him. By July 3, 1933, if not sooner, it surely had. There was by then no more chance that FDR would return to gold than there had been a chance that he would accept Hoover's invitation to cooperate on the debt question during the interregnum—and for the same reason. As FDR had proclaimed in his inaugural address, he believed America's international economic commitments to be "secondary to the establishment of a sound national economy." He sounded the same theme in his "bombshell message" on July 3: "The sound internal economic system of a Nation is a greater factor in its well-being than the price of its currency in changing terms of the currencies of other Nations."[42]

Among the consequences that flowed from that parochial belief was America's refusal to play a part in stemming the tide of economic nationalism and vicious militarism, of Nazism and Fascism and Japanese aggression, that were as much the products of the global depression as Chicago breadlines and Kansas City Hoovervilles. Keynes notwithstanding, Roosevelt was here something sadly less than "magnificently right." But in deed if not word, from his rejection of Hoover's invitation to collaborate on the international debt issue to his repudiation of

42. *PPA* (1933), 264–65.

international economic cooperation in London, Roosevelt, whatever else might be said, was with respect to American foreign policy magnificently consistent: he was for the time being a thoroughgoing isolationist.

ROOSEVELT DID NOT LACK for evidence that the world was growing more dangerous. In the month of his inaugural, Japan burned its diplomatic bridges and gave notice of its intent to quit the League of Nations in 1935. Roosevelt's ambassador in Tokyo soberly informed the president that "this step indicates the complete supremacy of the military."[43] On February 27 arsonists set fire to the German Reichstag building in Berlin. Hitler seized the occasion to demand absolute dictatorial power. The Reichstag gave it to him on March 23. Hitler proceeded to abolish the German federal system, concentrating all political power in his hands in Berlin. He dissolved the trade unions and closed the fist of Nazi control over the universities and churches. Nazi students stoked huge bonfires with books deemed offensive to *der Führer*. Nazi mobs fell upon Jews in the streets. On April 1 the Nazi Party announced a boycott of all Jewish businesses, as a preliminary to expelling Jews from government, the professions, and the arts.

Hitler, Roosevelt confided to French ambassador Paul Claudel, was "a madman." He knows some of Hitler's counselors personally, the president went on, and they "are even madder than he is."[44] Urged on by American Jewish leaders, Roosevelt expressed his dismay about Nazi anti-Semitism to Reichsbank president Hjalmar Schacht, but to no avail. Schacht, in fact, like so many visitors to Roosevelt's office, came away with the vague impression that the genial Roosevelt had no terribly serious disagreement with him or with the policies he represented.

Then, on May 16, Roosevelt had issued his "Appeal to the Nations of the World for Peace and for the End of Economic Chaos." Calling attention to the ongoing Disarmament Conference in Geneva and the upcoming World Economic Conference in London, Roosevelt declared that "if any strong Nation refuses to join with genuine sincerity in these concerted efforts for political and economic peace, the one at Geneva and the other at London, progress can be obstructed and ultimately blocked. In such event the civilized world, seeking both forms of peace, will know where the responsibility for failure lies."[45] Praising Roosevelt's

43. Freidel, *Launching*, 366–67.
44. Freidel, *Launching*, 377.
45. *PPA* (1933), 187–88.

speech, the *San Francisco Chronicle* said: "This is the end of isolation, or it is nothing."[46]

It was nothing. Within months Hitler torpedoed the disarmament talks at Geneva and began to build the fearsome Nazi *Wehrmacht*. Roosevelt, mocking his own words of May 16, sank the economic conference at London. The two forums whose agendas Hoover had urged Roosevelt to link, and that Roosevelt himself had so piously praised as the sites of efforts for international peace, stood separately silent. A thin but plausible opportunity to arrest the plunge into chaos and bloodshed, to restore international economic health and maintain political stability, had died, and the world might well have asked where the responsibility lay.

At the end of August D'Arcy Osborne, chargé d'affaires at the British embassy in Washington, summed up his impressions of the New Deal for his home office. Roosevelt's "first much advertised entry into the field of foreign politics," he observed, "was somewhat of a fiasco. . . . From President downwards immediate interest and sentiment of the country is concentrated on recovery programme and its domestic results, and this implies a nationalistic inspiration and orientation of foreign policy. . . . Situation here seems to render isolation and nationalism inevitable."

So the world slid further down the ugly helix of economic isolationism and military rearmament toward the ultimate catastrophe of global war. Roosevelt had shown no more vision than the other desperately self-protective nationalists in 1933, perhaps even somewhat less. Having bled awhile, America laid down its international commitments. Who could say if it would rise to fight again? Falsely thinking themselves safe behind their ocean moats, Americans prepared to take up arms alone in the battle against the Depression, girded now with the abundant weapons crafted in the Hundred Days, not least the inflationary powers for whose free exercise the collapse in London cleared the way. They had a resourceful if mysterious leader. He might just carry them through the crisis. "But generally speaking," D'Arcy Osborne concluded, "situation here is so incalculable and President himself so mercurial and his policies so admittedly empirical that all estimates and forecasts are dangerous."[47]

46. Freidel, *Launching*, 404.
47. Freidel, *Launching*, 498.

6

The Ordeal of the American People

*I saw old friends of mine—men I had been to school with—digging
ditches and laying sewer pipe. They were wearing their regular business
suits as they worked because they couldn't afford overalls and rubber
boots. If I ever thought, "There, but for the grace of God—" it was right
then.*

— Frank Walker, president of the
National Emergency Council, 1934

"What I want you to do," said Harry Hopkins to Lorena Hickok in July
1933, "is to go out around the country and look this thing over. I don't
want statistics from you. I don't want the social-worker angle. I just want
your own reaction, as an ordinary citizen.

"Go talk with preachers and teachers, businessmen, workers, farmers.
Go talk with the unemployed, those who are on relief and those who
aren't. And when you talk with them don't ever forget that but for the
grace of God you, I, any of our friends might be in their shoes. Tell me
what you see and hear. All of it. Don't ever pull your punches."[1]

The Depression was now in its fourth year. In the neighborhoods and
hamlets of a stricken nation millions of men and women languished in
sullen gloom and looked to Washington with guarded hope. Still they
struggled to comprehend the nature of the calamity that had engulfed
them. Across Hopkins's desk at the newly created Federal Emergency
Relief Administration flowed rivers of data that measured the Depression's impact in cool numbers. But Hopkins wanted more—to touch
the human face of the catastrophe, taste in his own mouth the metallic
smack of the fear and hunger of the unemployed, as he had when he

1. Richard Lowitt and Maurine Beasley, eds., *One Third of a Nation: Lorena Hickok
   Reports on the Great Depression* (Urbana: University of Illinois Press, 1981), ix–x.

worked among the immigrant poor at New York's Christadora settlement house in 1912. Tied to his desk in Washington, he dispatched Lorena Hickok in his stead. In her he chose a uniquely gutsy and perceptive observer who could be counted on to see without illusion and to report with candor, insight, and moxie.

Hopkins and Hickok were cast from similar molds. Both were children of the Midwest who had blossomed in New York's teeming metropolis. Both remembered their own austere childhoods on the prairie and found nothing that was romantic — and, for that matter, little that was potentially revolutionary — in the grit of hardship. Both hid soft hearts within shells of jaunty acerbity. Hopkins, forty-three years old in 1933, gaunt and chronically disheveled, was a harnessmaker's son with a lasting devotion to racehorses. Like the track touts with whom he frequently kept company, he affected a hell's-bells air that caused others to appraise him as both shrewd and faintly ominous. Yet compassion suffused his nature, tempered by a piercing intelligence that would one day lead Winston Churchill to dub him "Lord Root of the Matter."[2]

Hickok, forty in 1933, had struggled up from a painful childhood on the bleak northern plains to become, in her own unapologetic words, "just about the top gal reporter in the country." A colleague once described her as "endowed with a vast body, beautiful legs and a peaches-and-cream complexion." Five foot eight and nearly two hundred pounds, she was big, boisterous, unconventional, and irreverent. She could smoke, drink, play poker, and cuss as well as any of her male colleagues, and she could write better than most of them. After working as a feature writer in Milwaukee and Minneapolis she moved to New York, where the Associated Press assigned her in 1928 to hard-news stories, then an unusual beat for a woman journalist. In 1932 she covered the sensational Lindbergh-baby kidnaping story. Later that year she accepted the assignment that changed her life: covering Eleanor Roosevelt during the presidential campaign.[3]

Hickok did not merely report about her new subject. She grew attached to Eleanor Roosevelt in ways that eventually strained the rules of journalistic objectivity. She began clearing her stories with Eleanor herself or with Franklin's chief adviser, Louis Howe. By campaign's end

2. Robert E. Sherwood, *Roosevelt and Hopkins* (New York: Grosset and Dunlap, 1948, 1950), 1–5. See also Schlesinger 2:266.
3. Blanche Wiesen Cook, *Eleanor Roosevelt: A Life*, vol. 1, 1884–1933 (New York: Viking, 1992), 468.

Hickok had effectively ceased to be a reporter and had become Eleanor's press agent, as well as her deeply intimate companion.[4]

Hickok resigned from the Associated Press in June 1933, took a month-long motoring holiday through New England and eastern Canada with Eleanor, and started off on her new assignment from Hopkins. She set out to interview plain folk and local big shots, housewives and working stiffs, cotton lords and miners, waitresses and mill hands, tenant farmers and relief administrators. At night she holed up in spare hotel rooms and pecked out her impressions on a portable typewriter. Soon her reports started arriving in Hopkins's Washington office, from the sooty coal districts of Pennsylvania and West Virginia and Kentucky in August, from stoically suffering New England villages in September, from the wheatfields of North Dakota in October. They continued to come for nearly two more years, from the cotton belt of Georgia, the Carolinas, Alabama, and Texas, and from the ranches, mining camps, fruit orchards, and raw cities of the Far West. She saw with a seasoned reporter's eye and wrote in an earthy, no-foolin' style that managed to be at once unsentimentally cool and warmly sympathetic. "Mr. Hopkins said today," an admiring Eleanor wrote her in December 1933, "that your reports would be the best history of the Depression in future years."[5]

From the charts and tables accumulating on his desk even before Hickok's letters began to arrive, Hopkins could already sketch the grim outlines of that history.[6] Stockholders, his figures confirmed, had watched as three-quarters of the value of their assets had simply evaporated since 1929, a colossal financial meltdown that blighted not only the notoriously idle rich but struggling neighborhood banks, hard-earned retirement nest eggs, and college and university endowments as well. The more than five thousand bank failures between the Crash and the

4. By some accounts, the relationship between Eleanor Roosevelt and Lorena Hickok even transgressed conventional standards of sexual propriety, though whether their warmly intimate relationship was physically consummated remains conjectural. See Cook, *Eleanor Roosevelt*, and a rejoinder by Geoffrey Ward, "Outing Eleanor Roosevelt," *New York Review of Books*, September 24, 1992, 15.

5. Eleanor Roosevelt to Lorena Hickok, December 7, 1933, quoted in Lowitt and Beasley, *One Third of a Nation*, xxxiii.

6. Much of the discussion of the Depression's impact that follows is drawn from Lester V. Chandler, *America's Greatest Depression, 1929–1941* (New York: Harper and Row, 1970); Anthony J. Badger, *The New Deal: The Depression Years* (New York: Farrar, Straus and Giroux, 1989); and Harry L. Hopkins, *Spending to Save: The Complete Story of Relief* (New York: Norton, 1936).

New Deal's rescue operation in March 1933 wiped out some $7 billion in depositors' money. Accelerating foreclosures on defaulted home mortgages — 150,000 homeowners lost their property in 1930, 200,000 in 1931, 250,000 in 1932 — stripped millions of people of both shelter and life savings at a single stroke and menaced the balance sheets of thousands of surviving banks. Several states and some thirteen hundred municipalities, crushed by sinking real estate prices and consequently shrinking tax revenues, defaulted on their obligations to creditors, pinched their already scant social services, cut payrolls, and slashed paychecks. Chicago was reduced to paying its teachers in tax warrants and then, in the winter of 1932–33, to paying them nothing at all.

Gross national product had fallen by 1933 to half its 1929 level. Spending for new plants and equipment had ground to a virtual standstill. Businesses invested only $3 billion in 1933, compared with $24 billion in 1929. Some industries, to be sure, were effectively Depression-proof; shoe and cigarette manufacturers, for example, experienced only minor slumps. Other industries, however, dependent on discretionary spending, had all but gone out of business. Only one-third as many automobiles rolled off the assembly lines in 1933 as in 1929, a slowdown that induced commensurate shrinkage in other heavy industries. Iron and steel production declined by 60 percent from pre-Crash levels. Machine-tool makers cut their output by nearly two-thirds. Residential and industrial construction shriveled to less than one-fifth of its pre-Depression volume, a wrenching contraction that spread through lumber camps, steel mills, and appliance factories, disemploying thousands of loggers, mill hands, sheet-metal workers, engineers, architects, carpenters, plumbers, roofers, plasterers, painters, and electricians. Mute shoals of jobless men drifted through the streets of every American city in 1933.

Nowhere did the Depression strike more savagely than in the American countryside. On America's farms, income had plummeted from $6 billion in what for farmers was the already lean year of 1929 to $2 billion in 1932. The net receipts from the wheat harvest in one Oklahoma county went from $1.2 million in 1931 to just $7,000 in 1933. Mississippi's pathetic $239 per capita income in 1929 sank to $117 in 1933.

Unemployment and its close companion, reduced wages, were the most obvious and the most wounding of all the Depression's effects. The government's data showed that 25 percent of the work force, some thirteen million workers, including nearly four hundred thousand women, stood idle in 1933. The great majority of the men and many of the women were heads of households, the sole breadwinners for their families.[7] Yet if misery was widespread, its burdens were not uniformly distributed. Differences in gender, age, race, occupation, and region powerfully mediated the Depression's impact on particular individuals. To borrow from Tolstoy, every unhappy family was unhappy in its own way. Different people suffered and coped, and occasionally prevailed, according to their own peculiar circumstances.

Working women at first lost their jobs at a faster rate than men—then reentered the work force more rapidly. In the early years of the Depression, many employers, including the federal government, tried to spread what employment they had to heads of households. That meant firing any married woman identified as a family's "secondary" wage-earner. But the gender segregation in employment patterns that was already well established before the Depression also worked to women's advantage. Heavy industry suffered the worst unemployment, but relatively few women stoked blast furnaces in the steel mills or drilled rivets on assembly lines or swung hammers in the building trades. The teaching profession, however, in which women were highly concentrated and indeed constituted a hefty majority of employees, suffered pay cuts but only minimal job losses. And the underlying trends of the economy meant that what new jobs did become available in the 1930s, such as telephone switchboard operation and clerical work, were peculiarly suited to women.

Unemployment fell most heavily on the most predictably vulnerable: the very young, the elderly, the least educated, the unskilled, and especially, as Hickok was about to discover, on rural Americans. It fell with compound force on blacks, immigrants, and Mexican-Americans. Workers under twenty or over sixty were almost twice as likely as others to be out of a job. Hopkins's studies showed that one-fifth of all the people on the federal relief rolls were black, a proportion roughly double the African-American presence in the population. Most of them were in the rural South.

Some of the jobless never appeared on the relief rolls at all because they simply left the country. Thousands of immigrants forsook the fabled American land of promise and returned to their old countries. Some one hundred thousand American workers in 1931 applied for jobs in what appeared to be a newly promising land, Soviet Russia.[8] More than

---

7. Nearly four million of the nation's approximately thirty million households were headed by women in 1930. See James T. Patterson, *America's Struggle against Poverty, 1900–1980* (Cambridge: Harvard University Press, 1981), 29, and *HSUS*, 41.

8. Leuchtenburg, 28.

four hundred thousand Mexican-Americans, many of them U.S. citizens, returned to Mexico in the 1930s, some voluntarily but many against their will. Immigration officials in Santa Barbara, California, herded Mexican farm workers into the Southern Pacific depot, packed them into sealed boxcars, and unceremoniously shipped them southward.[9]

The typical unemployed urban worker on relief, Hopkins found, "was a white man, thirty-eight years of age and the head of a household. . . . [H]e had been more often than not an unskilled or semi-skilled worker in the manufacturing or mechanical industries. He had had some ten years' experience at what he considered to be his usual occupation. He had not finished elementary school. He had been out of any kind of job lasting one month or more for two years, and had not been working at his usual occupation for over two and a half years."[10] Hopkins stressed particularly the problems of the elderly, who, he concluded, "through hardship, discouragement and sickness as well as advancing years, [have] gone into an occupational oblivion from which they will never be rescued by private industry."[11] That line of thinking, driven by the specter of permanent, structural unemployment as a result of accelerating technological change, and looking toward removing supposedly obsolescent elderly workers from the wage-labor markets altogether, would in time lead to the landmark Social Security Act of 1935.

Hopkins's statistical data revealed still other aspects of the Depression's impact. Facing an uncertain future, young people were postponing or canceling plans to marry; the marriage rate had fallen since 1929 by 22 percent. The Depression's gloom seeped even into the nation's bedrooms, as married couples had fewer children — 15 percent fewer in 1933 than in 1929. Even the divorce rate declined by 25 percent, as the contracting economy sealed the exits from unhappy marriages. Unemployment could also powerfully rearrange the psychological geometry of families. "Before the depression," one jobless father told an interviewer, "I wore the pants in this family, and rightly so. During the depression, I lost something. Maybe you call it self-respect, but in losing it I also lost the respect of my children, and I am afraid that I am losing my wife." "There certainly was a change in our family," said another victim of unemployment, "and I can define it in just one word — I relinquished power in the family. I think the man should be boss in the family. . . .

9. On Mexican-Americans, see Ronald Takaki, A *Different Mirror* (Boston: Little, Brown, 1993), 333–34; and Albert Camarillo, *Chicanos in a Changing Society* (Cambridge: Harvard University Press, 1979), 163.
10. Hopkins, *Spending to Save*, 161.
11. Hopkins, *Spending to Save*, 163.

But now I don't even try to be the boss. She controls all the money. . . . The boarders pay her, the children turn in their money to her, and the relief check is cashed by her or the boy. I toned down a good deal as a result of it." Said another: "It's only natural. When a father cannot support his family, supply them with clothing and good food, the children are bound to lose respect. . . . When they see me hanging around the house all the time and know that I can't find work, it has its effect all right."[12]

When Hickok sallied forth to reconnoiter the Depression's human toll in 1933, the country was, to be sure, wallowing in the deepest trough of the unemployment crisis. But despite the New Deal's exertions and innovations, and contrary to much later mythology, in no subsequent year in the 1930s would the unemployment rate fall below 14 percent. The average for the decade as a whole was 17.1 percent. The Depression and the New Deal, in short, were Siamese twins, enduring together in a painful but symbiotic relationship that stretched to the end of the decade. The dilemmas and duration of that relationship helped to account for both the failures and the triumphs of the New Deal.

In Pennsylvania, Hickok's first destination, Governor Gifford Pinchot had reported in the summer of 1932 that some 1,150,000 persons were "totally unemployed." Many others were on "short hours." Only two-fifths of Pennsylvania's normal working population, Pinchot concluded, had full-time work. Elsewhere, the Ford Motor Company in Detroit had laid off more than two-thirds of its workers. Other giant industries followed suit. Westinghouse and General Electric in 1933 employed fewer than half as many workers as in 1929. In Birmingham, Alabama, another of Hickok's destinations, Congressman George Huddleston reported that only 8,000 of some 108,000 workers still had full-time employment in 1932; 25,000 had no work at all, and the remaining 75,000 counted themselves lucky to toil a few days per week. "Practically all," said Huddleston, "have had serious cuts in their wages and many of them do not average over $1.50 a day."[13]

Later investigators calculated that nationwide the combined effects of unemployment and involuntary part-time employment left half of America's usual work force unutilized throughout the Depression decade — a

12. Mirra Komarovsky, *The Unemployed Man and His Family: The Effect of Unemployment Upon the Status of the Man in Fifty-nine Families* (New York: Dryden, 1940), 41, 31, 98.
13. Hopkins, *Spending to Save*, 92; Chandler, *America's Greatest Depression*, 43.

loss of some 104 million person-years of labor, the most perishable and irreplaceable of all commodities. Similar calculations suggest that the "lost output" in the American economy of the 1930s, measured against what would have been produced if 1920s rates of employment had held, amounted to some $360 billion dollars — enough at 1929 prices to have built 35 million homes, 179 million automobiles, or 716,000 schools.

Like Hopkins, observers then and later have struggled to make human sense out of these numbingly abstract numbers. One thinking exercise goes as follows: imagine that on New Year's Day 1931, when the depression was not yet "Great," one hundred thousand people, all of them gainfully employed, most of them the sole means of livelihood for their families, sat beneath the beaming California sun in the Rose Bowl, filling the eight-year-old Pasadena stadium to capacity to watch Alabama's Crimson Tide play the Washington State Cougars in the sixteenth annual Rose Bowl Game.[14] When the game ended, the loudspeakers announced that every person in attendance that day had just lost his or her job. On exiting, the stunned fans were handed further notices. Sixty-two thousand were informed that they would not be employed for at least a year to follow; forty-four thousand of those were given two-year layoffs; twenty-four thousand, three years; eleven thousand received the grim news that they would be unemployed for four years or more (an approximation of the patterns in the unemployment statistics for the decade of the 1930s). Then imagine that this spectacle was repeated at the Rose Bowl, without even the consolation of a football game, the following week — and the week after that, and again after that, for 130 weeks. At the rate of a hundred thousand persons summarily laid off in successive weeks it would take two and one-half years, until July 1933, the date of Hickok's departure on her assignment for Hopkins, to reach the sum of thirteen million unemployed.

But even such mental exercises as that run up against what Hopkins called "the natural limit of personal imagination and sympathy. You can pity six men," Hopkins sagely noted, "but you can't keep stirred up over six million."[15] It was to compensate for those natural deficiencies of the

14. In fact, a less-than-capacity crowd of seventy thousand saw Alabama defeat Washington State 24–0 on January 1, 1931. On that same day, Franklin D. Roosevelt delivered his second inaugural address as governor of New York. In yet another reminder that few Americans at this date sensed the dimensions of the crisis that was developing, Roosevelt devoted most of his speech to decrying the inefficiencies of local government.

15. Hopkins, *Spending to Save*, 111.

imagination that he was sending Lorena Hickok on her mission. From her reportage he hoped to vivify real faces and voices out of the statistical dust. She did not disappoint him.

Hickok set out in quest of the human reality of the Depression. She found that and much more besides. In dingy working-class neighborhoods in Philadelphia and New York, in unpainted clapboard farmhouses in North Dakota, on the ravaged cotton farms of Georgia, on the dusty mesas of Colorado, Hickok uncovered not just the effects of the economic crisis that had begun in 1929. She found herself face to face as well with the human wreckage of a century of pell-mell, buccaneering, no-holds-barred, free-market industrial and agricultural capitalism. As her travels progressed, she gradually came to acknowledge the sobering reality that for many Americans the Great Depression brought times only a little harder than usual. She discovered, in short, what historian James Patterson has called the "old poverty" that was endemic in America well before the Depression hit. By his estimate, even in the midst of the storied prosperity of the 1920s some forty million Americans, including virtually all nonwhites, most of the elderly, and much of the rural population, were eking out unrelievedly precarious lives that were scarcely visible and practically unimaginable to their more financially secure countrymen. "The researches we have made into standards of living of the American family," Hopkins wrote, "have uncovered for the public gaze a volume of chronic poverty, unsuspected except by a few students and by those who have always experienced it." From this perspective, the Depression was not just a passing crisis but an episode that revealed deeply rooted structural inequities in American society.[16]

The "old poor" were among the Depression's most ravaged victims, but it was not the Depression that had impoverished them. They were the "one-third of a nation" that Franklin Roosevelt would describe in 1937 as chronically "ill-housed, ill-clad, ill-nourished."[17] By suddenly threatening to push millions of other Americans into their wretched condition, the Depression pried open a narrow window of political opportunity to do something at last on behalf of that long-suffering one-third, and in the process to redefine the very character of America.

DEPARTING FROM WASHINGTON in a car acquired with Eleanor's help and nicknamed "Bluette," Hickok headed first for the hills and

---

16. Patterson, *America's Struggle against Poverty*, 41; Hopkins, *Spending to Save*, 111.
17. *PPA* (1937), 5.

ravines of the Appalachian soft-coal district, a dismally hardscrabble region stretching through western Pennsylvania, West Virginia, and Kentucky. She was starting at the bottom. "In the whole range of Depression," said Gifford Pinchot, "there is nothing worse than the condition of the soft coal miners."[18] Soft, or bituminous, coal had been for nearly two centuries the basic fuel that powered the global industrial revolution, but even before World War I the coal-burning era was everywhere on the wane. Diesel engines had replaced coal-fired boilers in steamships and locomotives. Coalbins were disappearing from basements as Americans abandoned smudgy coal furnaces for clean-burning gas or oil or smokeless electric heating systems. Plagued by competition from these new energy sources, especially the recently tapped oil fields in southern California, Oklahoma, and the vast Permian Basin in West Texas, coal displayed through the 1920s all the classical symptoms of a sick industry: shrinking demand, excess supply, chaotic disorganization, cutthroat competition, and hellish punishment for workers.

The Depression exacerbated this already calamitous cycle. Operators fought more savagely than ever to stay alive by cutting prices and paychecks. At one point some of them even begged the government to buy the mines "at any price. . . . Anything so we can get out of it."[19] Coal that had fetched up to $4 a ton in the mid-1920s sold for $1.31 a ton in 1932. Miners who had earned seven dollars a day before the Crash now begged the pit-boss for the chance to squirm into thirty-inch coal seams for as little as one dollar. Men who had once loaded tons of coal per day grubbed around the base of the tipple for a few lumps of fuel to heat a meager supper—often nothing more than "bulldog gravy" made of flour, water, and lard. The miner's diet, said United Mine Workers president John L. Lewis, "is actually below domestic animal standards."[20]

Stranded without work in isolated company towns, living on the owners' sufferance in company housing, in debt to the company store, cowed by insecurity and occasional strong-arm tactics into a subdued, passive frame of mind, the miners struck Hickok as a singularly pathetic lot. "Some of them have been starving for eight years," she reported to Hopkins. "I was told there are children in West Virginia who never tasted milk! I visited one group of 45 blacklisted miners and their

---

18. Badger, *New Deal*, 19.
19. Frances Perkins, *The Roosevelt I Knew* (New York: Viking, 1946), 230.
20. James P. Johnson, *The Politics of Soft Coal: The Bituminous Industry from World War I through the New Deal* (Urbana: University of Illinois Press, 1979), 125.

families, who had been living in tents two years. . . . Most of the women you see in the camps are going without shoes or stockings. . . . It's fairly common to see children entirely naked." The ravages of tuberculosis, "black lung" disease, and asthma, as well as typhoid, diptheria, pellagra, and severe malnutrition, were everywhere apparent. Some miners' families, said Hickok, "had been living for days on green corn and string beans—and precious little of that. And some had nothing at all, actually hadn't eaten for a couple of days. At the Continental Hotel in Pineville [Kentucky] I was told that five babies up one of those creeks had died of starvation in the last ten days. . . . Dysentery is so common that nobody says much about it. 'We begin losing our babies with dysentery in September,'" one of Hickok's informants casually remarked.

Patriotic, religious, gentle, of "pure Anglo-Saxon stock," these mountain folk impressed Hickok as "curiously appealing." Yet she found both their stark destitution and their stoic resignation appalling. Here began her real education—and through her, Hopkins's and Roosevelt's—about the awful dimensions of the human damage the Depression had laid bare and about the curious apathy with which many Americans continued to submit to their fates. Sixty-two percent of the people in ten eastern Kentucky mining counties looked to federal relief for their very survival in the summer of 1933, Hickok learned. Twenty-eight thousand families, more than 150,000 souls, depended on local relief offices for grocery orders that they could present to the company store. Then, on August 12, owing to delays in the Kentucky state government's provision of funds to match the federal government's appropriations, even that minimal assistance stopped. Little groups of people, many of them illiterate, straggled to closed relief agencies, stared helplessly at written notices announcing the end of aid, and silently shuffled away. Given their desperate plight, "I cannot for the life of me understand," Hickok mused, "why they don't go down and raid the Blue Grass country."[21]

Hickok's observations about relief and its social and political impact particularly intrigued Hopkins. His Federal Emergency Relief Administration had been charged in May 1933 with dispensing some $500 million of federal relief money. Half went to the states on a matching basis, one federal for three state dollars. Hopkins had discretion to distribute the remaining $250 million on the basis of "need." Congress and various governors tried in vain to learn the "formula" by which Hopkins dispensed his discretionary moneys. Governor Martin Davey of Ohio at one point issued a warrant for Hopkins's arrest should he ever set foot

21. Lowitt and Beasley, *One Third of a Nation*, 20ff.

in the state. Later studies suggest that Hopkins indeed had a formula, and it was one that he and FDR had learned from the old urban political machines. FERA checks flowed disproportionately to certain "swing" states, outside the already secure solid South, in an effort to win votes and cultivate political loyalty.[22]

With FERA the federal government took its first steps into the business of direct relief and began, however modestly, to chart the path toward the modern American welfare state. FERA's brief history vividly exposed both the practical difficulties and the political and philosophical conflicts that beset welfare programs ever after. Its odd and unwieldy administrative architecture reflected the peculiar characteristics of the American federal system and underlined, too, the strikingly sparse administrative capacity of the federal government over which Franklin Roosevelt presided in 1933. That puny capacity was a legacy of historic Jeffersonian wariness of centralized power, among the most deeply rooted values in American political culture. Beginning with FERA and other innovative federal policies in 1933, the New Deal would change that culture, but the tortured evolution of the American welfare system, even by means artfully contrived and often sharply attenuated, would be among the most controversial of Roosevelt's legacies.

Hopkins made a conspicuous show of executive energy by allocating over $5 million during his first two hours in office in May 1933. But his very need for speed drove Hopkins into awkward and contentious relationships with state and local welfare agencies. FERA was an emergency body, hastily established and rushing without precedent or staff to cope with a vast national crisis. Its skeletal Washington office, never numbering more than a few hundred people, necessarily relied on state and county officials to screen relief applicants and distribute benefits. Though by 1933 most states had exhausted their capacity to cope with the Depression's needy, many of them nevertheless balked at participating in the federal relief program. Some, like Kentucky, pleaded that constitutional constraints blocked them from allocating the required matching funds. "Those states which took advantage of their real or alleged constitutional limitations [on borrowing for relief purposes]," Hopkins noted acerbically, "laid a crushing burden upon their local communities," whose usual source of revenue, real estate taxes, was drastically contracting.

Yet most state officials, whatever their reservations in principle about

---

22. Gavin Wright, "The Political Economy of New Deal Spending: An Econometric Analysis," *Review of Economics and Statistics* 56 (1974): 262–81.

federal intrusion into the traditionally local administration of welfare, joined hands of necessity with FERA. Some shrewdly saw political opportunity in the sudden infusion of federal dollars, to Hopkins's continuing aggravation. "Our chief trouble in Pennsylvania," Hickok reported to her chief at the very outset of her tour, "is politics. From the township to Harrisburg, the state is honeycombed with politicians all fighting for the privilege of distributing relief funds."[23] The danger of letting local pols manipulate FERA funds for their own partisan advantage compelled FERA to impose distasteful restrictions. Work relief was rare; straight cash payments, rarer still. Instead, driven by fiscal prudence and political wariness, FERA reluctantly instructed local agencies to set up commissaries to dispense food and clothing, a practice Hopkins branded the "most degrading" of all forms of relief. Scarcely less resented by recipients was the grocery order, exchangeable for designated items at the local store. Beans and rice were allowed, but no razors or tobacco or pencils or tablets. Hopkins detested these demeaning practices. "It is a matter of opinion," he drily remarked, "whether more damage is done to the human spirit by a lack of vitamins or complete surrender of choice."[24]

Beyond the realms of bureaucracy and politics, FERA encountered still more intractable difficulties in the domains of social attitudes and deeply embedded cultural values, those sometimes dark regions of the human spirit whose vitality was always Hopkins's primary concern. In the relief business, said Hopkins, "our raw material is misery."[25] Yet for all its familiarity in human annals, and despite its envelopment of millions of Americans in the Depression era, misery assuredly did not evoke universal sympathy, nor agreement about its remedy. The Depression was a wholesale social catastrophe that fell indiscriminately on vast sectors of American society. Yet the belief persisted among many Americans that the needy, new poor and old poor alike, were personally culpable for their plight, sinners against the social order, reprobates and ne'er-do-wells, spongers and bums with no legitimate claim on the public's sympathy or purse.

Local welfare administrators were sometimes among the most tenacious exponents of that view. They treated welfare applicants accordingly, especially when class, religious, or ethnic differences separated

23. Lowitt and Beasley, *One Third of a Nation*, 8.
24. Hopkins, *Spending to Save*, 105.
25. Hopkins, *Spending to Save*, 125.

applicants from administrators. In Calais, Maine, where most reliefers were out-of-work Catholic French-Canadians and most officials were Protestant Yankee blue-bloods, Hickok reported that "the people on relief in that town are subjected to treatment that is almost medieval in its stinginess and stupidity." In North Dakota, where a combination of drought, hail, grasshoppers, and collapsed markets had bankrupted nearly every farmer in the state, Hickok found the state relief committee dominated by officials who "think there is something wrong with a man who cannot make a living. . . . I find them rather like the people in Maine . . . They talk so much about 'the undeserving' and 'the bums'." A relief director in Savannah told Hickok flatly: "Any Nigger who gets over $8 a week is a spoiled Nigger, that's all. . . . The Negroes . . . regard the President as the Messiah, and they think that . . . they'll all be getting $12 a week for the rest of their lives." In Tennessee, she encountered relief workers "whose approach to the relief problem is so typical of the old line social worker, supported by private philanthropy and looking down his—only usually it was HER—nose at God's patient poor, that it made me gag a little."[26]

"Under the philosophy of this ancient practice," Hopkins lamented, the relief applicant was thought to be "in some way morally deficient. He must be made to feel his pauperism. Every help which was given him was to be given in a way to intensify his sense of shame. Usually he was forced to plead his destitution in an offensively dreary room"—the notorious "intake" facility where applicants were first screened for eligibility.[27]

"Mr. Hopkins, did you ever spend a couple of hours sitting around an intake?" Hickok asked from Texas in the spring of 1934. "[I]ntake is about the nearest thing to Hell that I know anything about. The smell alone—I'd recognize it anywhere. And take that on top of the psychological effect of having to be there at all. God!. . . . If I were applying

26. Lowitt and Beasley, *One Third of a Nation*, 37, 67, 154, 277. Even Hickok's capacious sympathies had their limits, etched by the easy racial stereotyping common to the era. As she wrote from Georgia: "More than half the population of the city is Negro—and SUCH Negroes! Even their lips are black, and the whites of their eyes! They're almost as inarticulate as animals." She worried that blacks in the South and Mexicans in the West had such low standards of living that they might choose to become a permanently dependent welfare class. She mused about a double standard of relief, with one level of support for "Mexicans and Negroes" and another for those "with white standards of living": "Two standards of relief. The idea will sound horrible in Washington, but—I'm beginning to wonder" (151–52, 238–40).

27. Hopkins, *Spending to Save*, 100.

for relief, one look at the average intake room would send me to the river."[28]

The humiliation of presenting oneself at the intake was only the beginning. Next came a "means test," entailing a detailed examination of the applicant's private life. The typical relief applicant under FERA received a home visit from a social worker who inquired about income, savings, debts, relatives, health, and diet. Then came inquiries about the applicant's circumstances "to clergymen, to school teachers, to public nurses or to whatever society might possibly assist them. . . . It is no wonder," Hopkins later commented disgustedly, "that when men knew or feared this was in store for them they kept secret from their wives and families that they had received their dismissal slips. . . . If we had not become so accustomed, and, in a sense, so hardened to the fact of poverty, we should even now be astounded at our effrontery."[29]

Hopkins saw the Depression as a social disaster, not the simple aggregation of countless individual moral failings. "Three or four million heads of families don't turn into tramps and cheats overnight," he said, "nor do they lose the habits and standards of a lifetime. . . . They don't drink any more than the rest of us, they don't lie any more, they're no lazier than the rest of us. . . . An eighth or a tenth of the earning population does not change its character which has been generations in the moulding, or, if such a change actually occurs, we can scarcely charge it up to personal sin."[30]

Still, the attitudes against which Hopkins inveighed ran stubbornly deep. Indeed, contempt for the Depression's victims, ironically enough, often lodged most deeply in the hearts and minds of the victims themselves. Social investigators in the 1930s repeatedly encountered feelings of guilt and self-recrimination among the unemployed, despite the transparent reality that their plight owed to a systemic economic breakdown, not to their own personal shortcomings. The Depression thus revealed one of the perverse implications of American society's vaunted celebration of individualism. In a culture that ascribed all success to individual striving, it seemed to follow axiomatically that failure was due to individual inadequacy.

Self-indictment was especially pronounced among many of the newly poor — the white-collar classes who had been the chief acolytes and ben-

28. Lowitt and Beasley, One Third of a Nation, 221–22.
29. Hopkins, Spending to Save, 101–2.
30. Hopkins, Spending to Save, 125, 100, 110; Badger, New Deal, 200.

eficiaries of the individualistic creed. Their sudden descent from security, self-sufficiency, and pride to uncertainty, dependency, and shame left many of them neither angry nor politically radicalized but, as Hickok said, simply "dumb with misery." "The whole white collar class," a newspaper editor told her in New Orleans, "are taking an awful beating. . . . They're whipped, that's all. And it's bad." As for seeking relief, the difficulty, said Hickok, "is in getting white collar people to register at all. God, how they hate it." An engineer told her, "I simply had to murder my pride." "We'd lived on bread and water three weeks before I could make myself do it," an insurance man confessed. "It took me a month," an Alabama lumberman explained; "I used to go down there every day or so and walk past the place again and again. I just couldn't make myself go in." A twenty-eight-year-old college-educated woman in Texas, unemployed after eight years as a teacher, spoke the thoughts of many middle-class Americans down and out in the Depression: "If . . . I can't make a living," she shrugged, "I'm just no good, I guess."[31]

"I have seen thousands of these defeated, discouraged, hopeless men and women, cringing and fawning as they come to ask for public aid," said the mayor of Toledo, Ohio. "It is a spectacle of national degeneration."[32] Hopkins agreed. By October 1933 he was sorely disillusioned with FERA's stopgap, ragtag relief effort, with its mortifying means test and niggardly, condescending local administrators. He had in any case effectively exhausted the original $500 million FERA appropriation. Yet an economic recovery that would absorb the millions of unemployed was nowhere in sight. If the nation were to make it through the oncoming winter, a new relief program was necessary.

Hopkins's answer was the Civil Works Administration (CWA), launched with Roosevelt's blessing on November 9. CWA relied for its funding on an allocation from the budget of the Public Works Administration and for its administrative apparatus on still other agencies in the pint-sized federal bureaucracy. Army warehouses supplied tools and materials for CWA projects. The Veterans Administration, one of the few federal agencies with a truly national disbursement system in place, became CWA's paymaster. With model efficiency, it issued paychecks to some eight hundred thousand workers within two weeks of the CWA's creation. By January 1934 CWA had put 4.2 million men and women to work.

31. Lowitt and Beasley, *One Third of a Nation*, 205, 220, 206–7, 223.
32. Schlesinger 2:268.

The operative word was "work." At Hopkins's insistence, CWA was not only a purely federal undertaking; it was also, more importantly, a *work*-relief program. It did not condescend to clients; it hired employees. Half were taken from the relief rolls and half from the needy unemployed, without subjection to a means test. CWA paid the prevailing minimum wage, regionally adjusted: forty cents an hour for unskilled labor in the South, forty-five cents in the central states, and sixty cents in the North. "Wages were what we were after," said Hopkins, and in its five-month existence CWA handed out paychecks totaling $833,960,000. CWA focused on light construction and maintenance projects that could be mounted swiftly. Its workers upgraded roads and bridges, laid sewer pipe, spruced up forty thousand schools, refurbished hospitals, and installed 150,000 outhouses for farm families. "Long after the workers of CWA are dead and gone and these hard times forgotten, their effort will be remembered by permanent useful works in every county of ever state," Hopkins proudly noted.[33]

"Three loud cheers for the CWA!" Hickok wrote to Hopkins from Lincoln, Nebraska, in November 1933. "[I]t's the smartest thing that has been tried since we went into the relief business. It is actually getting out some of that Public Works money," she added, in a pointed reminder that Interior Secretary Harold Ickes, whose Public Works Administration had been intended as the New Deal's premier "pump-priming" agency, had thus far proved unable to find the pump handle. Most important, Hickok and Hopkins agreed, by giving people gainful employment, CWA in federal hands removed the stigma of relief. It dignified men and women with a paycheck instead of mortifying them with a handout. "We aren't on relief any more," one woman said proudly. "My husband is working for the Government."[34]

Just that kind of reaction—not to mention the nearly $200 million monthly price tag for CWA—worried President Roosevelt. Working for the government might become a habit with the country, he brooded, just as Hoover had worried earlier. In January 1934 Roosevelt told his advisers: "We must not take the position that we are going to have permanent Depression in this country." Shortly thereafter he ordered the termination of CWA, effective on March 31. For the remainder of 1934 the federal government substantially abandoned the distasteful task

33. Hopkins, *Spending to Save*, 117, 120.
34. Hopkins, *Spending to Save*, 114.

of relief and tried to come to grips with the even more daunting task of recovery.[35]

RECOVERY REMAINED maddeningly elusive. "Balance" still seemed the key. Following the Hundred Days, Roosevelt counted primarily on two measures to effect the equilibrium between industry and agriculture thought to be essential to economic health. One was an unorthodox and controversial gold-buying scheme, aimed at depreciating the dollar and thus easing debt burdens, particularly for farmers. The other was an elaborate scheme to micromanage the farm sector through the newly created Agricultural Adjustment Administration.

For much of 1933 and 1934, however, both monetary and agricultural policy were overshadowed by the aggressively publicized endeavors of another agency: the National Recovery Administration. Though it was created virtually as an afterthought on the one hundredth day of the special congressional session that ended on June 16, 1933, the NRA almost instantly emerged as the signature New Deal creation. "In some people's minds," Frances Perkins later observed, "the New Deal and NRA were almost the same thing."[36]

The NRA owed much of its towering profile in the public mind to the extravagantly colorful personality of its chief, Hugh S. Johnson. Raised in frontier Oklahoma, Johnson was fifty-one years old in 1933, a West Point graduate who rose to the rank of brigadier general before resigning in 1919 to pursue a business career. His seamed and jowly face floridly testified to the rigors of the professional soldier's life as well as the ravages of drink. Melodramatic in his temperament, mercurial in his moods, ingeniously profane in his speech, Johnson could weep at the opera, vilify his enemies, chew out his underlings, and rhapsodize about the virtues of NRA with equal flamboyance. On accepting his appointment in June 1933 he declared: "It will be red fire at first and dead cats afterward"—one of the printable specimens of his sometimes mystifyingly inventive prose.[37]

Johnson envisioned the NRA, in Arthur M. Schlesinger Jr.'s phrase, "as a giant organ through which he could play on the economy of the country."[38] His model was the War Industries Board (WIB) of 1917–18,

35. Leuchtenburg, 122.
36. Perkins, *Roosevelt I Knew*, 210.
37. Hugh S. Johnson, *The Blue Eagle from Egg to Earth* (Garden City, N.Y.: Doubleday, Doran, 1935), 208.
38. Schlesinger 2:103.

chaired by his idol and business associate Bernard Baruch. Johnson himself had served as director of the WIB's Purchase and Supply Branch, representing the military purchasing bureaus to the various commodity sections of the WIB. Franklin Roosevelt had also conjured the World War experience in announcing the NRA's birth on June 16. "I had part in the great cooperation of 1917 and 1918," the president declared, and he called on the country to recollect the war crisis and the spirit of national unity it evoked. "Must we go on in many groping, disorganized, separate units to defeat," the president asked, extending the military metaphor, "or shall we move as one great team to victory?"[39]

But if the NRA was patterned on the War Industries Board, a crucial element was missing: the war. To be sure, a psychological sense of crisis prevailed in 1933 that was comparable to the emergency atmosphere of 1917; the difference was not mood but money. The federal government had borrowed over $21 billion dollars in just two years to fight World War I, a figure that exceeded the sum of New Deal deficits from 1933 down to the eve of World War II.[40] The National Industrial Recovery Act that established the NRA had also authorized the Public Works Administration to borrow $3.3 billion for pump-priming expenditures to infuse new purchasing power into the economy. NRA and PWA were to be like two lungs, each necessary for breathing life into the moribund industrial sector. But as Herbert Hoover had discovered, it took time, lots of it, to start up construction projects of any significant scale — time for site surveys, architectural designs, and engineering studies to be completed before actual construction could start. What was more, Roosevelt's own sense of fiscal caution, not unlike Hoover's, had led him to deprive the energetic but erratic Johnson of control over PWA and assign it instead to the irascible interior secretary, Harold Ickes. "Honest Harold," Ickes was soon dubbed, for the scrupulous care and agonizing deliberateness with which he dispensed PWA funds. Penny-pinching and cautious to a fault, Ickes was hypervigilant to forestall accusations of waste or fraud. He spent just $110 million of PWA money in 1933. "He still has to learn," said one of Ickes's exasperated assistants, "that the Administrator of a $3 billion fund hasn't time to check every typewriter acquisition." Under Ickes's obsessively prudent management, PWA contributed nothing in 1933 to economic stimulus, rendering

39. Johnson, *Blue Eagle*, 440, 443.
40. *HSUS*, 1104–5.

NRA effectively dead on arrival as a recovery measure. "Once deprived of the second lung," an NRA official wrote, "the economy had to bear too great a burden on the NRA lung—inasmuch as the PWA was scarcely palpitating for almost half a year after the NRA was organized."[41]

If Johnson, the would-be master economic organist, found himself from the outset seated at a magnificent musical instrument that lacked wind-box or bellows, he nevertheless proceeded to bang away at the keyboard of the NRA with missionary zeal and maniacal energy. There was no truer believer in the philosophy of industrial coordination that NRA was charged with implementing. "I regard NRA as a holy thing," he said. He credited his mentor, Bernard Baruch, with the best formulation of the NRA's economic creed. "The government has fostered our over-capacitated industrial combinations, and even encouraged these combinations to increase production," Baruch explained to a Brookings Institution gathering in May 1933.

> But it seems public lunacy to decree unlimited operation of a system which periodically disgorges indigestible masses of unconsummable products. In today's desperate struggle for the scant remaining business, cost and price have become such factors that, in the unstable fringes which surround each industry, a few operators have taken the last dangerous step in economic retrogression—the attainment of low costs by the degradation of labor standards. . . . Lower wages—lower costs—lower prices—and the whole vicious cycle goes on.[42]

The NRA, in Baruch's and Johnson's view, could arrest this cycle by government-sponsored agreements to curb ruinous overproduction, allocate production quotas, and stabilize wages. The last item was particularly important. If there was any defensible economic logic to NRA at all, it consisted in the idea that recovery could not come about so long as shrinking payrolls continued to leach purchasing power out of the ailing economy.

The essence of Baruch's and Johnson's thinking resided in their shared hostility to competition. "The murderous doctrine of savage and wolfish competition," Johnson called it, "looking to dog-eat-dog and devil take the hindmost," had impelled even humane and fair-minded employers to slash wages and lay off workers by the millions. In contrast, Johnson intoned, "the very heart of the New Deal is the principle of

41. Badger, *New Deal*, 83; Schlesinger 2:109.
42. Johnson, *Blue Eagle*, x.

concerted action in industry and agriculture under government supervision."[43]

These ideas may have made up the heart of the New Deal in 1933, but they were themselves scarcely new. Not only had they informed the WIB experience in the World War, but they had also found expression in Secretary of Commerce Hoover's promotion of trade associations and labor unions in the 1920s, as well as in President Hoover's meetings with business leaders in the first flush of crisis in 1929 and his highly publicized appeals for maintenance of wage rates in the first two years of the Depression. Roosevelt had embraced similar ideas in his address to San Francisco's Commonwealth Club during the 1932 campaign, when he called for "administering resources and plants already in hand . . . , adjusting production to consumption."[44] In May 1933 the new President had sounded the same note again when he complained to his advisers about the problem of "foolish overproduction."[45] That foolishness, and the cutthroat competition it engendered, NRA now sought to end.

In few industries was overproduction more problematic than in cotton textiles. Like soft coal, textile manufacturing had been sick for a long time before the Depression descended. An "old" industry, in America as elsewhere among the first to employ the factory system of production, cotton textile manufacturing had migrated in the years after Reconstruction out of its original New England home and into the South. "Bring the mills to the cotton," southern promoters had preached, seeking to raise an industrial "new South" out of the wreckage of the Civil War. By 1930 they had succeeded beyond all expectations—the South then spun two-thirds of the nation's cotton cloth—but the textile industry had become ferociously competitive, chronically beset by excess capacity, price-gouging, and the by now familiar tribulations visited upon labor.

Textile workers had long been a harshly abused lot. The greatest attraction of the South for investors had in fact not been proximity to the cotton fields but proximity to an abundance of low-wage, nonunionized labor. Keeping labor cheap and unorganized had become almost a religion among the southern mill owners. The Appalachian foothills from Alabama through the Carolinas were pocked with cheerless company mill towns where white "hillbillies," wrenched from their isolated

43. Johnson, *Blue Eagle*, 169.
44. *PPA* (1928–32), 751–52.
45. Davis 3:137.

mountain homesteads, crowded into what Lorena Hickok described as "blocks and blocks of shabby, tumbledown little houses."[46] Whole families, including children as young as seven, worked grueling hours. Sometimes they toiled through the night amid the whirling spindles and clouds of lint, earning subsistence wages, often paid in scrip good only at the company store. Like their cousins who had stayed in the hills to dig coal, the "lintheads," long oppressed by dependency, want, and fear, saw their lives go from unspeakably bad to unimaginably worse as the Depression deepened. Wages sank to as low as five dollars for a fifty-five-hour week. Thousands of mill workers were laid off altogether. Those who remained on the job submitted resentfully to the hated "stretch-out," the mill hands' term for the practice of forcing fewer and fewer workers to tend more and more of the spindles clattering in their relentless ranks on the shop floor. "They'd just add a little bit more to it," said one woman mill hand, "and you was always in a hole, trying to catch up." "There's many a times I dreamt about it," said another; "I just sweated it out in my dreams like I did when I was on the job, wanting to quit, and knew I couldn't afford to."[47] Cries for abolition of the stretch-out, along with demands for union recognition, touched off a violent confrontation between workers and management in 1929, ending in the gunshot deaths of the police chief and a woman union organizer in Gastonia, North Carolina. Now, four years later, an edgy tension shivered over the Piedmont as falling prices and deteriorating work conditions once again pushed mill owners and workers alike to the breaking point.

Not surprisingly, the textilemakers' trade association, the Cotton Textile Institute, had a draft code ready for submission to Johnson on the day the National Industrial Recovery Act was signed into law. The NRA promised to do for the cottonmakers what they had proved unable to do for themselves: end cutthroat price discounting and stabilize their destructively competitive industry by setting production quotas for individual mills. In return for government-supervised limitations on output—indeed, as the mechanism for enforcing those limitations—the manufacturers agreed to the forty-hour week as the maximum they would ask from their workers. They further agreed to set minimum wage

46. Lowitt and Beasley, *One Third of a Nation*, 176.
47. Jacquelyn Dowd Hall et al., *Like a Family: The Making of a Southern Cotton Mill World* (New York: Norton, 1987), 212.

standards. In what was hailed as a historic breakthrough, they also pledged to abolish child labor altogether. In addition, pursuant to Section 7(a) of the NIRA, the cotton producers agreed, at least in principle, to accept the principle of collective bargaining.

Thunderous applause filled the room when the textile barons announced their intention to end child labor. "The Textile Code had done in a few minutes what neither the law nor constitutional amendment had been able to do in forty years," Johnson crowed. He exulted that the textile accord "showed the way and set the tempo for the execution of the entire recovery act."[48]

Johnson later claimed that the NRA eventually put nearly three million people to work and added $3 billion to the national purchasing power, but for neither the first time nor the last, Johnson was whistling "Dixie." Much of the modest rise in production and employment in the spring of 1933 owed not to the salutary ministrations of NRA but to nervous anticipation of its impact. A wavelet of preemptive building and buying rippled through the economy between March and July, as businesses sought to build inventories and consummate purchases before government-imposed wage and price rules went into effect. And as the summer months dragged on, the Cotton Textile Code seemed less of a pathbreaking precedent and more of a singular event, as the other "Big Ten" industries—coal, petroleum, iron and steel, automobiles, lumber, the garment trades, wholesale distributors, retailers, and construction— refused to follow suit.

Johnson faced this persistent industrial recalcitrance with his trademark mix of bluster, bravado, and baloney. "Away slight men!" he railed to a group of businessmen in Atlanta. "You may have been Captains of Industry once, but you are Corporals of Disaster now." Pleading for minimum wage standards, he declaimed that "men have died and worms have eaten them but not from paying human labor thirty cents an hour." The "chiselers" who tried to shave NRA standards, he thundered, were "guilty of a practice as cheap as stealing pennies out of the cup of a blind beggar."[49]

Frustrated by his lack of accomplishment after the magnificent overture of the Cotton Textile Code, Johnson cast about for ways to make

48. Johnson, *Blue Eagle*, 233, 230, ix. In somewhat muted form, Johnson's extravagant claims for the NRA echo in many of the standard histories of the New Deal. See, for example, Schlesinger 2:174, and Leuchtenburg, 69.
49. Schlesinger 2:120; Johnson, *Blue Eagle*, 263.

more economic music. He soon encountered difficulties even graver in their implications than Roosevelt's regrettable segregation of PWA and its pump-priming money. Johnson's staff advised him that NRA would not withstand a legal challenge to its enforcement powers. The licensing provisions by which the NIRA legislation provided for government enforcement of the codes, he was told, were almost certainly unconstitutional. Johnson would never use them. Instead, he turned to the techniques of propaganda and moral suasion and once again looked to his war experience for guidance. "There have been six similar mass movements of this nation depending for support on almost unanimous popular participation," he explained, in a comparison as historically telling as it was mathematically dubious: "the Selective Draft, the Liberty Loan Campaign, the Food Administration, the War Industries Board Mobilization of Industry in 1917 and 1918, and the Blue Eagle Drive in 1933." All save the last dated from World War I. Johnson himself had a hand in two of them, the draft and the WIB. All of them, including the peculiarly administered wartime draft, embodied the reflexive American preference for voluntary rather than statutory means to social ends, for invoking mass sentiment rather than the majesty of the law, even when confronted with emergencies on the scale of war and Depression.[50]

Fired by this inspiration, Johnson launched an audacious propaganda campaign in July. He asked employers voluntarily to sign a blanket code, the President's Reemployment Agreement, pledging themselves to pay a minimum wage of forty cents per hour for a thirty-five–hour maximum week. He implored consumers to trade only with establishments that displayed the symbol of participation, the stylized Blue Eagle. Devised by Johnson himself and patterned on Native American thunderbird designs, the Blue Eagle, along with its accompanying legend, "we do our part," was destined to become a ubiquitous Depression-era logo. The president kicked off the Blue Eagle campaign with a Fireside Chat at the end of July. Once again invoking the wartime ideal of cooperation in a time of crisis, Roosevelt declared that "those who cooperate in this program must know each other at a glance. That is why we have provided a badge of honor for this purpose, a simple design with a legend, 'We do our part,' and I ask that all those who join with me shall display

50. For extended discussion of the voluntarist ethos in World War I mobilization, see David M. Kennedy, *Over Here: The First World War and American Society* (New York: Oxford University Press, 1980); and Robert D. Cuff's pioneering study, *The War Industries Board: Business-Government Relations during World War I* (Baltimore: Johns Hopkins University Press, 1973).

that badge prominently. . . . There are adequate penalties in the law," the president assured his listeners, but "opinion and conscience" were "the only instruments we shall use in this great summer offensive against unemployment." Johnson put the same matter more pungently: "May God have mercy on the man or group of men who attempt to trifle with this bird."[51]

Blue Eagle badges soon blossomed on store windows and theater marquees, on newspapers and delivery trucks. As in World War I, "four-minute men" stepped forward to preach the Blue Eagle gospel on stages and street corners. Posters proclaimed it from buses and billboards. A monster Blue Eagle parade in New York City in September drew almost two million persons into the streets. The Blue Eagle was meant to symbolize unity and mutuality, and it no doubt did for a season, but Johnson's ubiquitous "badge of honor" also clearly signaled the poverty of the New Deal's imagination and the meagerness of the methods it could bring to bear at this time against the Depression. Reduced to the kind of incantation and exhortation for which they had flayed Hoover, the New Dealers stood revealed in late 1933 as something less than the bold innovators and aggressive wielders of government power that legend later portrayed.

While the Blue Eagle ballyhoo went on, Johnson plunged ahead with his campaign to create code authorities in the major industrial sectors. By September he had largely succeeded, but with lamentably predictable results. Deprived of any formal means to compel compliance, Johnson necessarily acquiesced in codes that amounted to nothing less than the cartelization of huge sectors of American industry under the government's auspices. Various trade associations, like the Iron and Steel Institute or the National Automobile Chamber of Commerce, cloaked now with the vague mantle of governmental authority, effectively became the code authorities for their respective industries. They ignored the antitrust laws with impunity and enforced production quotas and price policies on their members. Typically, the largest producers dominated the codemaking bodies, producing squeals of complaint from smaller operators, labor, and consumers. Though the NRA contained both a Labor Board and a Consumer Advisory Board, and though in theory both those interests were supposed to be represented in code-making and code administration, in fact fewer than 10 percent of the

51. Johnson, *Blue Eagle*, 260, 263.

code authorities had labor representation and only 1 percent had consumer members.[52]

The cotton code foreshadowed many of the problems that bedeviled the NRA in later 1933 and 1934 and, more broadly, suggested some of the difficulties endemic to all government regulation of free-market economies. By stipulating that cotton spindles could not run more than two forty-hour shifts per week, the cotton code sanctioned massive layoffs in the mill towns. The mill operators effected many of those layoffs by ceasing to employ children, thus exposing the hard business logic beneath their apparently magnanimous concession to the cause of ending child labor. For those workers who remained, the owners often evaded minimum wage rules by reclassifying jobs into exempt categories such as "learners" or "cleaners." In late August a textile union representative reported that "no mills I know of are living up to the code."[53] Equally troublesome, code-sanctioned price-fixing, usually mandated with a rule prohibiting sale below the cost of production, however that might be calculated, had begun by late 1933 to raise consumer prices, in some cases pushing them 20 percent above 1929 levels.

The codes did impose a semblance of order on the chaos that beset many industries in 1933. It did so especially in those historically troubled sectors like textiles, coal, oil, and the retail trades, which were fragmented into myriad little enterprises that had been unable to cooperate sufficiently to stabilize their markets. But in other sectors, like steel and automobiles, where heavy capital requirements had long since bred oligopolistic market structures, allowing a relative handful of producers to concert their price and wage policies, the codes were largely redundant or irrelevant. And for virtually all industries, even the light hand of government authority that Johnson was able to lay upon them held deeply disturbing implications. Almost overnight, NRA mushroomed into a bureaucratic colossus. Its staff of some forty-five hundred oversaw more than seven hundred codes, many of which overlapped, sometimes inconsistently. Corkmakers, for example, faced an array of no fewer than thirty-four codes. Hardware stores operated under nineteen different codes, each with its own elaborate catalogue of regulations. In just two years NRA regulators drafted some thirteen thousand pages of codes and issued eleven thousand interpretive rulings. No

52. Bernard Bellush, *The Failure of the NRA* (New York: Norton, 1975), 47.
53. Bellush, *Failure of the NRA*, 55.

matter how constricted their formal legal power, nor how cleverly they strove to exercise what power they had, the mere appearance on the field of that unprecedented bureaucratic horde struck terror into the breasts of many businessmen. "The excessive centralization and the dictatorial spirit," wrote the journalist Walter Lippmann, "are producing a revulsion of feeling against bureaucratic control of American economic life."[54]

By early 1934 discontent with NRA prompted Johnson, in a typical grandstand stunt, to convene a "Field Day of Criticism." On February 27 more than two thousand people crowded into the Department of Commerce's cavernous auditorium, their hands clutching sheets of notes itemizing NRA's offenses. So abundant were their grievances that Johnson was obliged to extend the gripe session. For four days witnesses vented their complaints about high prices, red tape, and mistreatment of labor. A black spokesman detailed the effects of the NRA's acceptance (like CWA's) of regional wage differentials on blacks, the lowest-paid workers in the low-wage South.

Meanwhile, congressional accusations that NRA was promoting monopoly compelled Roosevelt to appoint a National Recovery Review Board, improbably chaired by Clarence Darrow, the renowned and idiosyncratic criminal lawyer. Darrow took it upon himself to champion the "little fellow," the small businessman who was allegedly oppressed by the industrial titans who sat in control of the various code authorities. Johnson retorted that the "little fellow" was often a "stingy, sleazy . . . greasy" operator whose principal complaint was that he "does not want to pay code wages for code hours." The glare of NRA's publicity, said Johnson, had revealed "black men working in a steaming lumber swamp for seven and five cents an hour. . . . Children toiling in factories for very little more. . . . Women in sweat shops and garret slums bending night and day over garments. . . . Who is the real Little Fellow," Johnson asked, "the black man in the swamp—the child in the factory—the women in the sweat shop—or is it the small enterprise that says it cannot exist in competition unless it practices those barbarisms?"[55] There was much truth in what Johnson said, but Darrow's slapdash report, the seventy-seven-year-old lawyer's last and rather embarrassing hurrah, nevertheless affirmed that the NRA did indeed sustain monopolistic practices, then inconsistently suggested both antitrust prosecutions and socialized ownership as remedies.

54. Schlesinger 2:121.
55. Johnson, *Blue Eagle*, 275–76.

No criticisms of NRA stung more sharply or more plainly revealed NRA's defects than those that focused on Johnson's policies toward labor. Business owners quickly figured out how to turn NRA codes to their advantage in setting production levels and prices, but when it came to labor regulations, management balked. Section 7(a) of the National Industrial Recovery Act obliged management to engage in good-faith collective bargaining with workers. What that requirement might mean in practice remained to be seen. Some labor leaders, notably John L. Lewis, the histrionically gifted head of the United Mine Workers, likened 7(a) to Lincoln's Emancipation Proclamation. Galvanized by the prospects that 7(a) opened up, Lewis dispatched his minions through the coal districts in the summer of 1933. "The President wants you to join a union," they urged, and within months the UMW membership quadrupled, to some four hundred thousand. But in other industries, like steel and automobiles, employers insisted that they could comply with 7(a) simply by themselves setting up a company union, a body they could tightly control. The effect of establishing a company union, Arthur M. Schlesinger Jr. aptly notes, was "to create a bargaining tableau without creating anything approaching equality of bargaining power."[56] In some steel plants, workers flaunted their contempt for company unions by throwing old washers into the barrels provided for the deposit of their union "dues."[57]

Conflicts erupted everywhere over what form of union would prevail. A season of labor unrest swept in with the warm summer weather in 1933 as other labor organizers moved to follow Lewis's energetic lead. In August Johnson set up a new body, the National Labor Board (NLB), to mediate the proliferating labor-management clashes. The NLB soon devised the so-called Reading Formula, providing for supervised elections in which workers could choose their own representatives for collective bargaining. The NLB held that a majority of workers could determine the sole bargaining agent for all the workers in a given shop. Johnson quickly undercut that ruling, however, by issuing a contrary opinion that left employers free to practice the ancient tactics of divide and conquer by recognizing any number of workers' representatives— including company unions. No mechanism existed to resolve this stand-off between the NRA chief and his own labor body. It soon became

56. Schlesinger 2:145.
57. Lizabeth Cohen, *Making a New Deal* (Cambridge: Cambridge University Press, 1990), 305.

apparent that the NLB was essentially helpless in the face of evasion or outright defiance of its rulings. "Industry generally is in revolt against NRA and is throwing down the gauntlet to the President," Hickok reported in May 1934.[58] Workers, promised so much but given so little by 7(a), grew increasingly disillusioned. "It has almost shaken their faith in the United States Government," one witness testified at Johnson's Field Day of Criticism.[59]

By late 1934, harassed by complaints from businesses big and small, as well as from workers and consumers and even from his own colleagues at the NRA, Johnson was growing more and more frenetically erratic. He disappeared for days at a time on monumental benders, reemerging wreathed in fogs of fustian to compare himself with Moses and the NRA codes with the Decalogue. Roosevelt at last secured his resignation, and he bade his staff a tearful farewell on October 1. The NRA struggled along for a few more months, rid of its egregious leader but still saddled with a host of intractable problems. It succumbed to a unanimous Supreme Court declaration of its unconstitutionality in May 1935.[60]

Johnson had failed utterly to coax out of the instrument of the NRA the mighty chords of industrial harmony that he had yearned to play. To be sure, Ickes's tightfisted control of PWA monies had hamstrung NRA from the outset as an engine of recovery, but the explanation for NRA's problems goes deeper than that. FERA and CWA, after all, did between them pump more than $1.3 billion into the economy in 1933–34, a good fraction of the original PWA appropriation and some of it, in fact, taken from the PWA budget. It was not simply want of money but the want of historical perspective, of adequate means, and of effective ideas that accounted for NRA's sorry record. Over all of NRA's history fell the shadow of the old mercantilist dream that a class of informed and disinterested mandarins could orchestrate all the parts of the economy into an efficient and harmonious whole. That dream had begun to fade with the dawn of the industrial revolution in the eighteenth century. The fantastic complexities of modern, twentieth-century economies were rendering it almost entirely chimerical. Worse, lacking proper enforcement powers, Johnson's codemakers, like their predeces-

---

58. Lowitt and Beasley, *One Third of a Nation*, 263.
59. Bellush, *Failure of the NRA*, 75.
60. The case was *Schechter Poultry Corporation v. United States* (295 U.S. 495). For further discussion, see p. 328.

sors at the War Industries Board in 1917–18, sought in vain to assert an ill-defined public interest against the quite concrete private interests, especially the interests of capital, to which they were repeatedly forced to concede. Worse still, NRA rested upon the assumption, widespread in the early New Deal years, that overproduction had caused the Depression and that in scarcity lay salvation. That premise precluded any serious search for economic growth, made stability the touchstone of policy, and underwrote the kinds of restrictionist practices traditionally associated with monopolies.

The best that could be said of NRA was that it held the line for a time against further degradation of labor standards and that it energized a much-needed and long-suppressed labor organizing drive. However fitful its progress in 1933 and 1934, that drive would soon swell to huge proportions. Within a few years it would revolutionize labor-management relations and dramatically improve the living standards of much of the American working class.

As 1934 drew to a close and the third year of the New Deal was about to open, recovery was still nowhere in sight. The curious passivity of the American people that had perplexed so many observers was waning, yielding to a mounting sense of grievance and a restless demand for answers. Especially in the ravaged countryside that had been both Hoover's and Roosevelt's first concern, things had gone from bad to worse. Up the great valley of the Mississippi and across the northern plains, as well as in the grim working-class neighborhoods of the Northeast's industrial cities, the murmur of discontent was at last threatening to swell into a cry for revolution.

7

Chasing the Phantom of Recovery

*I am a farmer. . . . Last spring I thought you really intended to do some-
thing for this country. Now I have given it all up. Henceforward I am
swearing eternal vengeance on the financial barons and will do every
single thing I can to bring about communism.*
— An Indiana farmer to Franklin D. Roosevelt,
October 16, 1933

In October 1933 Lorena Hickok steered Bluette westward into America's
agrarian heartland and back to the scenes of her own childhood.

The Depression "is 10 or 12 years old out here," she reminded Hopkins from Iowa. "These plains are beautiful," she wrote Eleanor Roosevelt from North Dakota. "But, oh, the terrible, crushing drabness of life
here. And the suffering, for both people and animals. . . . Most of the
farm buildings haven't been painted in God only knows how long . . . !
If I had to live here, I think I'd just quietly call it a day and commit
suicide. . . . The people up here . . . are in a daze. A sort of nameless
dread hangs over the place."[1]

As the NRA enclosed more and more sectors within its code agreements, prices for industrial products stabilized, then rose modestly. But
in agriculture, the sector the New Deal had identified as most in need
of revitalization and on which it pinned its chief hopes for recovery,
prices remained stuck at less than 60 percent of 1929 levels. Farmers
felt betrayed. In the farm counties of Minnesota in November, Hickok
noted "the bitterness toward NRA. . . . NRA is not at all popular, to be
sure. Well, how *could* it be?" she asked. The prices that farmers paid
"*did* go up faster than their incomes."[2] Astonishingly, the New Deal in

1. Richard Lowitt and Maurine Beasley, eds., *One Third of a Nation: Lorena Hickok
Reports on the Great Depression* (Urbana: University of Illinois Press), 73.
2. Lowitt and Beasley, *One Third of a Nation*, 74, 117.

190

1933 seemed to be exacerbating, not redressing, the problem of "balance" in the American economy. "We have been patient and long suffering," said a farm leader in October 1933. "We were promised a New Deal. . . . Instead we have the same old stacked deck."[3]

In Morton County, North Dakota, Hickok came out of a meeting in "a shabby little country church" to find several denim-clad farmers, wearing all the clothes they owned, huddled inside her car for warmth. As winter closed its grip over the northern plains, farmers were burning cow manure ("buffalo chips") and rushes cut from dried lake beds for fuel. Even the animals suffered. "The plight of the livestock," Hickok wrote, "is pitiable." Milk cows were drying up for lack of feed. Farmers eligible for relief road work did not have teams healthy enough to pull road scrapers. "Half-starved horses have dropped in the harness," Hickok related, "right on the road job. . . . They've even harvested Russian thistle to feed to their horses and cattle. Russian thistle, for your information," she explained to Hopkins, "is a thistle plant with shallow roots that dries up in the fall and is blown across the prairies like rolls of barbed wire. The effect on the digestive apparatus of an animal . . . would be, I should imagine, much the same as though it had eaten barbed wire." In neighboring South Dakota several days later, she found farm wives feeding Russian thistle soup to their children.[4]

South Dakota, she reported to Hopkins, is the " 'Siberia' of the United States. A more hopeless place I never saw. Half the people — the farmers particularly — are scared to death. . . . The rest of the people are apathetic." She poured out her feelings to Eleanor Roosevelt: "Oh, these poor, confused people, living their dreary little lives. . . . And — my God, what families! I went to see a woman today who has ten children and is about to have another. She had so many that she didn't call them by their names, but referred to them as 'this little girl' and 'that little boy.' " Far out on the wind-scoured prairie Hickok visited

> what had once been a house. No repairs have been made in years. The kitchen floor was all patched up with pieces of tin. . . . Great patches of plaster had fallen from the walls. Newspapers had been stuffed in the cracks about the windows. And in that house two small boys . . . were running about without a stitch on save some ragged overalls. No shoes or stockings. Their feet were purple with cold. . . . This, dear lady, is the stuff that farm strikes and agrarian revolutions are

3. Davis 3:89.
4. Davis 3:55–60, 91, 96.

made of. Communist agitators are in here now, working among these people.

The country west of the Missouri River, she opined, bluntly debunking the sacred tenets of frontier boosterism, "never should have been opened up."[5]

The plight of the prairie folk was even worse than Hickok had remembered from her girlhood. The gritty reality and unrelieved scale of rural poverty clearly staggered her. She may well have read *Tobacco Road*, Erskine Caldwell's best-selling 1932 tale of lust and squalor in backcountry Georgia, or while visiting Eleanor in New York she may even have seen the stage adaptation of Caldwell's novel, then playing to packed houses on Broadway. But no fiction, not even John Steinbeck's melodramatic *Grapes of Wrath* later in the Depression decade, could do full justice to the desolate facts of American rural life.

Only 16 percent of farm households earned incomes above the national median of fifteen hundred dollars per year in the mid-1930s. More than half of all farm families had annual incomes of less than a thousand dollars. In 1934 the per capita income of farm households was just $167. In that same year, even after the efforts of CWA, only one farmhouse in ten had an indoor toilet; only one in five had electricity. Frequent pregnancies, medically unattended childbirths, malnutrition, pellagra, malaria, hookworm, and other parasites exacted heavy tolls in human life and energy. More than thirteen hundred rural counties, containing some seventeen million souls, had no general hospital, and most of them lacked even a public health nurse. Illiteracy was twice as common in rural districts as in cities. Nearly one million rural children between the ages of seven and thirteen did not attend school at all. In this generally dismal picture, the southeastern states were the most dismal by far. Sharecroppers and tenants, an agrarian class peculiarly concentrated in the old South, were probably the poorest Americans. One study of *employed* sharecroppers in four southern states revealed average annual cash incomes of $350 for white families and $294 for black.[6]

Hickok found the Midwest "depressing" in the winter of 1933–34, but even the sobering scenes of want and deprivation that she confronted in the Dakotas could not prepare her for what she saw in the South in early 1934. "I just can't describe to you some of the things I've seen and

5. Davis 3:83, 90, 60–61, 83–85.
6. Anna Rochester, *Why Farmers Are Poor* (New York: International Publishers, 1940), 11–13; *HSUS*, 483.

heard down here these last few days. I shall never forget them—never as long as I live," she wrote to Hopkins from Georgia in January. Southern farm workers, "half-starved Whites and Blacks," she reported, "struggle in competition for less to eat than my dog gets at home, for the privilege of living in huts that are infinitely less comfortable than his kennel." The Depression had certainly blighted the region, Hickok acknowledged, but she was shrewd enough to note that she was also seeing the ghastly accumulation of generations of poverty, neglect, and racial oppression. "If there is a school system in the state, it simply isn't functioning," she wrote. "It can't. The children just can't go to school, hundreds of them, because they haven't the clothes. The illiterate parents of hundreds of others don't send them. As a result you've got the picture of hundreds of boys and girls in their teens down here in some of these rural areas who can't read or write. I'm not exaggerating. . . . Why, some of them can barely talk!"[7]

In the citrus groves of Florida she found seasonal farm workers living in a state of virtual "peonage," even while the nearby tourist hotels were "comfortably filled." The Florida citrus growers, she fumed, "have got the world licked . . . for being mean-spirited, selfish, and irresponsible." In North Carolina in February she gave full vent to her indignation at the historical crimes of the sharecropping system—and hinted at the kind of threat that even the modest, hesitant programs of the early New Deal were already beginning to pose to southern mores:

> The truth is that the rural South never has progressed beyond slave labor. . . . When their slaves were taken away, they proceeded to establish a system of peonage that was as close to slavery as it possibly could be and included Whites as well as Blacks. During the Depression, the paternalistic landlord was hard put to it to "furnish" his tenants [provide a credit for seed, tools, and food]. He was darned glad to have us take over the job. But now, finding that CWA has taken up some of this labor surplus . . . he is panicky, realizes that he may have to make better terms with his tenants and pay his day labor more, and is raising a terrific howl against CWA. Whatever we do down here that may take up that rural labor surplus is going to make these farmers yell.[8]

Some of those landlords, and their political protectors, yelled directly to President Roosevelt. When a farm laborer on relief wrote to Georgia governor Eugene Talmadge that "I wouldn't plow nobody's mule from

7. Lowitt and Beasley, *One Third of a Nation*, 158–59.
8. Lowitt and Beasley, *One Third of a Nation*, 164–65, 186–87.

sunrise to sunset for 50 cents a day when I could get $1.30 for pretending to work on a DITCH," Talmadge forwarded the letter to the White House. "I take it . . . that you approve of paying farm labor 40 to 50 cents per day," Roosevelt heatedly replied. "Somehow I cannot get it into my head that wages on such a scale make possible a reasonable American standard of living."[9]

Throughout the South, time and again Hickok heard the same complaints: that CWA, unlike NRA, refused to recognize historic black-white wage differentials; that the prospect of federal relief payments was sucking low-wage agricultural workers, blacks especially, into cities like Savannah, where they threatened to become a permanent welfare class; that "the Federal Government came down here and put all the bums to work at more money than labor had ever been paid down here before"; that the insistence of many federal officers on "mistering the niggers" had stirred up southern blacks and threatened to explode the region's volatile race system.[10] These criticisms exposed the depths of the region's economic backwardness, as well as the difficulties that attended any policy that might perturb the tense membrane of class and race relations in the South.

Farther west, in the region at whose center the Texas and Oklahoma panhandles touched, nature and man had conspired by the 1930s to breed an ecological and human catastrophe called the Dust Bowl. The pioneers who first ventured out onto the high southern plains had called themselves "sod-busters," and they had proceeded to break the very back of the land. By the 1920s, their tractors were clawing the skin off the earth, scratching at its fragile face to plant ever larger crops, more cotton and wheat to carry to market as prices per bale and bushel steadily fell. They seamed the land with furrows down which washed acres of topsoil when the rains came. When the rain stopped in 1930, the wounded earth cracked open and dry grass crunched under men's boots. By 1934 in some areas the tortured soil lacked any detectable moisture to a depth of three feet. The wind lifted the surface powder into the skies, creating towering eight-thousand-foot waves known as "black blizzards." Great earthen clouds rose up off the land and bore down on cities to the east. One dust storm so darkened Great Bend, Kansas, that a resident claimed, "Lady Godiva could ride thru the streets without even the

9. Schlesinger 2:274. Roosevelt dictated this reply to Talmadge but sent the letter over Harry Hopkins's signature.
10. Lowitt and Beasley, *One Third of a Nation*, 154; Leuchtenburg, 138.

horse seeing her." The Kansas newspaperman William Allen White likened it to the ashes that had buried Pompeii. In the tradition of the frontier tall tale, one joke had it that a Dust Bowl farmer fainted when a drop of water hit him in the face; he revived only when three buckets of sand were tossed over him.

The Dust Bowl coughed out thousands of "exodusters" in the Depression years. They were usually known as "Okies," but though more than three hundred thousand people were blown out of Oklahoma, more thousands came from Texas, Kansas, and Colorado. They were as much the victims of their own farming practices as they were of nature's cruelty. "Grab and greed," said the journalist Carey McWilliams, punished them as much as dust and tractors. They went to California, mostly, though to other places, too, and they soon became symbols of the decade's worst ravages. Their story had the makings of an inverted version of the epic American tale. They were refugees from the fabled heartland, outbound from the prairies that had beckoned their ancestors westward, sad testimonials to the death of the dream of America as an uncovered ore bed of inexhaustible bounty, no longer hopeful pioneers but woebegone refugees. The photographer Dorothea Lange and her husband, economist Paul Taylor, captured their gaunt faces and recorded their spare histories in *An American Exodus: A Record of Human Erosion*, published in 1938. The following year John Steinbeck bestowed literary immortality on the Okie migrants in his best-selling novel *The Grapes of Wrath*, made into a popular movie in 1940.[11]

The Midwest, besides the South the nation's other great agricultural region, meanwhile rumbled with problems of its own. Unlike the South, where a relatively small number of baronial landlords owned vast tracts of land, family farms predominated in the sprawling corn, wheat, cattle, and dairy belts that stretched across the broad midcontinent, through the Palouse country of the Pacific Northwest, and into the verdant Puget-Willamette trough in western Washington and Oregon. (In California, the state with the nation's largest agricultural output, landholding patterns more closely resembled those in the South.) Typically encumbered by debt, family farms began to go under the auctioneer's hammer as banks first foreclosed on the properties that secured defaulted

11. Donald Worster, *Dust Bowl: The Southern Plains in the 1930s* (New York: Oxford University Press, 1979); and James N. Gregory, *American Exodus: The Dust Bowl Migration and Okie Culture in California* (New York: Oxford University Press, 1989).

mortgages, then tried to recoup some value by offering the repossessed farms for sale to the highest bidder. Throughout the midwestern heartland, groups of neighbors gathered at auctions to intimidate would-be buyers from bidding. These occasionally violent tactics restored farms to their original owners, sometimes for token payments of as little as one cent. By 1933 a noisy organization, the Farmers Holiday Association, led by Milo Reno, a prairie populist and rousing orator in the William Jennings Bryan mold, clamored for an end to foreclosures and for government-sanctioned codes to control production and guarantee prices in the agricultural sector, just as NRA was doing for industry.

Rough vigilante justice often accompanied these efforts. In Le Mars, Iowa, in April 1933 a mob of farmers, their faces masked with blue kerchiefs, abducted a judge who refused to suspend foreclosure proceedings, threatened him with lynching, tore off his clothes, and left him beaten, muddy, and humiliated in a roadside ditch. The governor of Iowa soon placed half a dozen counties under martial law. Hickok reported the disruption of a foreclosure sale in South Dakota when "the Farm Holiday crowd" disarmed sheriff's deputies and "ended up by tearing the sheriff's clothes off and beating him quite badly."[12]

In October 1933 Reno called for a "farm strike" unless his demands were met: currency inflation, a moratorium on foreclosures, and, most important, price supports for farm products. For good measure, Reno threw in a slap at "the money-lords of Wall Street." At a raucous meeting in Des Moines, Iowa, on October 30, the governors of North and South Dakota, Iowa, Minnesota, and Wisconsin endorsed Reno's program. North Dakota governor William Langer had already threatened to use his state's National Guard to enforce an embargo on the shipment of any wheat out of North Dakota for a price below the "cost of production." Even as the five governors made their way as a group from Des Moines to Washington to press these demands, more violence flared across the upper Mississippi Valley. Striking farmers overturned milk vats, blocked roadways, and throttled delivery of cattle and hogs to the great stockyards in Omaha. Meanwhile, inflationists like Oklahoma's Elmer Thomas threatened a march of a million men on Washington to force the administration's hand. "The West is seething with unrest," Roosevelt acknowledged, and farmers "must have higher values to pay off their debts."[13]

12. Lowitt and Beasley, *One Third of a Nation,* 79.
13. Schlesinger 2:236–37.

The thunder rolling up out of the farm belt prompted Roosevelt to begin pursuing in earnest the inflationary policies for which his withdrawal from the London Economic Conference had prepared the way. The president embraced the highly questionable theory of Cornell professor George F. Warren that substantial government purchases of gold would spur inflation and thereby both reduce debt burdens and raise commodity prices. Orthodox bankers and mainstream economists were aghast. Roosevelt waved their objections aside. "I wish our banking and economist friends would realize the seriousness of the situation from the point of view of the debtor classes . . . and think less from the point of view of the 10 percent who constitute the creditor classes," he said to his treasury secretary. In late October Roosevelt announced in a Fireside Chat that the Reconstruction Finance Corporation would begin to purchase U.S.-mined gold at "prices to be determined from time to time after consultation with the Secretary of the Treasury and the President. . . . We are thus continuing to move toward a managed currency."[14]

There ensued one of the most bizarre episodes in the history of American finance. Each morning for the next several weeks, Roosevelt over his breakfast eggs would name the price at which the government would buy gold that day. Hard-money men quit the administration in disgust. Roosevelt personally fired one prominent dissenter, Treasury Undersecretary Dean Acheson.

When the gold-purchase program ended in January 1934, the price of gold had risen from $20.67 an ounce to $35. The dollar had lost some 40 percent of its foreign exchange value as measured in gold, a devaluation that might in theory have bolstered American exports but that in fact exported nothing but more financial turmoil to America's few remaining trading partners. Domestic commodity prices, meanwhile, actually declined slightly in late 1933. Like a cracker-barrel argument, the gold-buying scheme had proceeded from dubious premises to a sputtering conclusion. Watching from England, John Maynard Keynes sniped that Roosevelt's manipulation of the currency "looked to me more like a gold standard on the booze than the ideal managed currency of my dreams." Shortly thereafter, Keynes called on Roosevelt at the White House. "I saw your friend Keynes," the bemused president said to Labor Secretary Frances Perkins. "He left a whole rigmarole of figures. He must be a mathematician rather than a political economist." As

14. Schlesinger 2:240.

for Keynes, he somewhat undiplomatically remarked to Perkins that he had "supposed the President was more literate, economically speaking."[15]

Gold buying did satisfy Roosevelt's itch for action, even ill-founded action. The gold scheme served the president's political purposes as well. "Gentlemen," he lectured a group of skeptical government officials in late October, "if we continued a week or so longer without my having made this move on gold, we would have had an agrarian revolution in this country."[16] Roosevelt exaggerated the revolutionary proportions of whatever was astir in the American countryside in 1933. To be sure, Lorena Hickok was reporting that Communist organizers were trying to influence the Farmers Holiday movement; that Sioux City, Iowa, was "a hotbed of the 'reds' "; and that growers in California's Imperial Valley were "simply hysterical" about Communists.[17] But a few outbreaks of hooliganism and scattered milk-spillings did not a revolution make. The Farmers Holiday Association, never more than a splinter group of the National Farmers Union, itself the smallest of the farm organizations, had crested in power and influence with the Des Moines meeting of October 30, and it soon faded away. What in the end impressed Hickok more than the revolutionary potential of a host of pitchfork-wielding angry farmers was, in fact, the torpor and dispiritedness that still hung over much of the farm belt like a sultry summer haze. "I was told in Bismarck," she reported on the very day of the Des Moines meeting, "that in the country I visited this afternoon I would find a good deal of unrest—'farm holiday' spirit. I can't say that I did. They seemed almost too patient to me."[18]

Whatever else might be said about it, the gold-buying scheme kept

---

15. Keynes, "Open Letter to President Roosevelt," New York Times, December 31, 1933, sec. 8, 2; Frances Perkins, The Roosevelt I Knew (New York: Viking, 1946), 225–26. The inflationists had one more inning, when they succeeded in passing the Silver Purchase Act in June 1934. It committed the government to buy silver from domestic producers until government silver holdings reached a value of one-third of gold reserves—a considerable improvement on the whole Bryanite "16-to-1" ratio. The government only monetized a portion of its silver holdings, however, in the form of coins and small-denomination "silver certificates," which circulated for nearly thirty more years. The Silver Purchase Act in the end represented less of a triumph for the inflationists than it did a stunning victory for the silver-mining industry, which had seized the opportune political moment to guarantee government purchases of its product at wholly artificial prices.

16. Schlesinger 2:242.

17. Lowitt and Beasley, One Third of a Nation, 79, 107, 306.

18. Lowitt and Beasley, One Third of a Nation, 58.

the farm belt relatively quiescent long enough for the New Deal's major agricultural programs to begin to work their effects. By the end of 1933 Farm Credit Administration refinancing contracts began to salvage family farms threatened with foreclosure. Soon the Agricultural Adjustment Administration's benefit payments and commodity loans began flowing into the farm belt as well. Like the industrial sector under NRA, agriculture began slowly to stabilize. But full-blown recovery would long elude the nation's farmers, especially the very poorest among them.

Gold buying also reflected the spirit of beggar-thy-neighbor economic isolationism that informed the early New Deal and indeed infested virtually all the globe's chancelleries in the depths of the Depression. When pugnaciously nationalistic AAA administrator George Peek advocated dumping America's mounting agricultural surpluses abroad, the otherwise internationally minded secretary of agriculture, Henry A. Wallace, cut him off with a scarcely less nationalistic retort: "We ought to act for the moment," Wallace explained, "as if we were a self-contained agricultural economy."[19] Wallace's statement held profound implications. Economic rescue, it suggested, depended on economic isolation. Only in such isolation could American farmers come to grips with the demons of overproduction that had plagued and impoverished them for more than a decade.

The farmers' plight furnished a classical illustration of how Adam Smith's legendary invisible hand might in certain circumstances be unable to orchestrate the general welfare out of a myriad of competing self-interests. As a group, American farmers annually brought more crops to market than the market could absorb at prices farmers found acceptable. Individual farmers, logically enough, tried to sustain their income levels by compensating for lower unit prices with higher volume. They tilled more acres, laid on more fertilizer, bought more tractors and seed drills and harvesters, and carried even larger crops to market. But the sum of those individual decisions inundated markets still further and further depressed prices. Collective misery, not the common good, was the bitter fruit of free-market striving by farmers.

How to break this vicious cycle was a problem that had stumped agricultural policymakers for more than a decade before 1933. George Peek and other partisans of the McNary-Haugen legislation in the 1920s had sought to dispose of American crop surpluses abroad, moving them to foreign markets with government subsidies if necessary. President

19. Schlesinger 2:55.

Hoover had tried to induce farmers' cooperatives to create more orderly agricultural markets, and he had created the Federal Farm Board to support price levels with government purchases of surplus crops. But in the troubled international economic environment of 1933, in which all nations desperately sought refuge in policies of protectionism and autarky, Peek's search for foreign markets was doomed from the outset. So too, as the example of Hoover's swiftly bankrupted Farm Board had dismally proved, was any agricultural remedy that failed to grasp the nettle of curtailing farm output.

New Dealers believed that much more than the well-being of farmers was at stake in agricultural policy. Most of them took Secretary Wallace's idea about the "self-contained agricultural economy" one step further. Not just agriculture but the entire American economy, they believed, was a virtually self-contained entity. Its continental scale and varied physical endowment made it less dependent on foreign trade than that of virtually any other modern state. Roosevelt's policies on exchange stabilization and gold had insulated it more effectively than ever. And inside the sealed vessel of the American economy, New Dealers claimed, recovery depended above all on striking a new "balance" between productive capacity and consuming power by changing the terms of trade between industry and agriculture. No idea pulsed more vibrantly at the very heart of the New Deal in 1933 than the conviction that on the success of AAA's effort to stimulate consumer demand by raising farm incomes rode the hopes not only of the nation's farmers but of the nation itself.

Given the manifest imbalances in the American economy in the years after World War I — not to mention the national mythology about sturdy yeomen and noble sons and daughters of the soil as the backbone of the Republic — the idea that farmers held the key to recovery had an unarguable appeal. Farmers were, after all, still some 30 percent of the work force. Many Americans easily recalled the not-so-distant era when farmers made up a majority of the American population. Farm spokesmen artfully played the chords of national memory as they rehearsed the woes of the countryside in the Depression. Those woes were real enough. The "parity ratio" — the ratio between the prices that farmers received for the basket of goods they sold to the prices they paid for the basket of goods they bought — had never regained its World War I level throughout the decade of the 1920s. After 1929 it had plummeted disastrously. At the end of the 1920s the parity ratio stood at 92 percent of what it had been in the relatively prosperous baseline period of 1910–

14. By 1932 it had sunk to 58 percent. The total of farm income in 1932 was less than one-third of what it had been in the already bad year of 1929.[20]

There was no denying the destitution and squalor that lay over much of the American countryside in the 1930s. Nor was there any denying the proposition that an economically healthy agricultural sector would be good both for those who lived and worked in it as well as for their urban cousins who sold them clothing, machinery, books, and utensils. But there was more than a little that was quaintly anachronistic about the New Dealers' faith in agricultural revival as the master key to general prosperity, and there was much that was grossly opportunistic in the response of the farmers themselves to the New Deal.

The relative importance of agriculture in the American economy, and the relative size of the farm work force, had been shrinking for a long time before the Depression arrived. Global competition, mechanization, increasing agricultural productivity, and industrial growth underwrote a steady country-to-city migration that had been swelling for a century or more — not only in America but in virtually all the Western world, as the millions of displaced peasants from the valleys of the Vistula and the Danube and the hills of the Carpathians and the Apennines who had swarmed for decades into American cities extravagantly attested. In America as elsewhere in the mid-twentieth century, the long-term dynamics of increasing consumer demand and economic vitality were most prodigiously at work not in the countryside but in the industrial cities. The Populist movement at the end of the nineteenth century bore colorful if rueful witness to those developments. When William Jennings Bryan taunted urbanites in 1896 that if they were to "destroy our farms . . . the grass will grow in the streets of every city in the country," he was invoking a homely but already obsolescent economic verity. Populism had in fact been energized by the well-founded anxiety that the countryside was being steadily eclipsed, that population, power, and economic leadership were all flowing ever more rapidly into the cities.

It was to industry and the cities, to the steel-hearths and assembly lines and chemical and electronic laboratories, that a better sense of history might have guided the main efforts of policymakers seeking economic recovery in 1933. Those sectors held the potential for new technologies that promised a future of enormous economic vitality. But nostalgia, intellectual inertia, and political pressure beckoned the New

20. HSUS, 489.

Dealers backward, to the cornfields and hay-meadows and pastoral idylls of national mythology—and into the welcoming arms of a lean and hungry agricultural lobby. The Populists in the 1890s had struggled to wring from the agrarian myth some political concessions to soften the consequences of agriculture's inexorable economic diminution, and they had lost. But in the crisis of the 1930s, Bryan's avatars rose again. They rang all the changes of the same agrarian myth and won concessions beyond the Great Commoner's most sumptuous dreams. The New Deal laid the groundwork for a system of farm subsidies that in the end mocked the pieties of frontier individualism and made the agricultural sector a virtual ward of the state. Save only swaddled infants in their mothers' arms, no members of American society would emerge from the New Deal more tenderly coddled than farmers, especially those large-scale commercial growers to whom most New Deal agricultural benefits accrued.

THE PATTERN of agricultural policy that the New Deal bequeathed to later generations owed much to the peculiar conjunction in the 1930s of the history of Populist agitation, the urgent economic crisis, an aggressive agricultural constituency—and a singularly preexisting federal institutional framework. Uniquely among government entities at the Depression's onset, the Department of Agriculture in 1933 was what has been described as "an island of state strength in an ocean of weakness."[21] Both FERA and CWA in the relief field, and NRA in the industrial field, were conceived as temporary emergency measures and started out from scratch as independent agencies, but AAA immediately found a natural and comfortable home in an established cabinet department. Founded in 1889, the first cabinet-level agency created in the new American epoch that dawned after the Civil War—aptly enough in the still predominantly agricultural republic of the late nineteenth century—the Department of Agriculture represented the first halting steps in the United States toward national direction of a major economic sector. Farmers thus had a longer history than any other group of making claims on the federal government. Comparable claims emerged only much later and even more haltingly from industry and labor. Those groups received cabinet-level attention in a single Department of Commerce and Labor in 1903. Even after its separation into

21. Theda Skocpol and Kenneth Finegold, "State Capacity and Economic Intervention in the Early New Deal," *Political Science Quarterly* 97, no. 2 (Summer 1982): 271.

two distinct departments in 1913, they remained weak agencies, starved for reliable data, unsure of their mandates, thinly staffed, and lacking articulate, well-organized clienteles. Part of Herbert Hoover's notoriety in the 1920s was due to his efforts to make the Department of Commerce a modern agency, one that could bring governmental power meaningfully to bear in the industrial sector.

In the agricultural field the picture was different. By the 1930s Agriculture had an effective data-gathering arm in the Division of Crop and Livestock Estimates, a body of trained personnel in the Bureau of Agricultural Economics, a network of local institutional partners in the land-grant colleges, an in-place field administration in the Extension Service, and, not least, a vocal, experienced, and aggressive constituent pressure group, one particularly attentive to the needs of the largest commercial growers, in the American Farm Bureau Federation. These arrangements set the stage for an unusually intimate and durable relationship between the federal government and the nation's farmers.[22]

Historically, the Department of Agriculture had exercised itself to help farmers increase production. Researchers at the land-grant colleges developed more fruitful strains of wheat and corn, more bug-resistant cotton plants and grapevines, more prolific breeds of pigs and cows; the Extension Service's county agents promulgated these discoveries across the land. But in the agriculturally bountiful yet stubbornly depressed 1920s some agrarian economists, notably M. L. Wilson of Montana State College, began to rethink the wisdom of the gospel of bounty. A visit to Russia's "virgin-soil" wheat lands, where oceanic expanses of grainfields undulated from horizon to horizon, deeply impressed upon Wilson the burgeoning capacity of the planet's agricultural producers. If American farmers were to survive, he concluded, they must protect their own domestic market, then adjust production to consumption. These were the basic premises on which the idea of AAA rested.

At its core, the thinking that underlay AAA derived from the same conviction about the salutary effects of scarcity that had produced the NRA industrial codes. But willfully inducing scarcity rasped against the grain of attitudes and habits evolved since time immemorial among those who wrung their livelihood from the soil. While industrial manufacturers had slashed their output by 42 percent in the first four years

22. For further discussion of the federal government's role in fostering the American Farm Bureau Federation, see David M. Kennedy, *Over Here: The First World War and American Society* (New York: Oxford University Press, 1980), chap. 2.

of the Depression, farmers had persisted in their timeworn habit of bringing ever more food and fiber to market, thus abetting and even accelerating the downward slide of prices.

Given those millennia-old habits of the husbandman, Professor Wilson's program for agricultural revival was radical indeed. At its heart, as legislated in the Agricultural Adjustment Act, was the Domestic Allotment Plan. It proposed to levy a tax on agricultural processors and use the proceeds to pay farmers for letting acreage lie fallow or shifting it to nonsurplus crop lines. This "benefit payment" program was designed to prevent the planting of potentially surplus crops in the first place. It was soon supplemented by a "commodity loan" program that aimed to prevent storable crops that had already been harvested from reaching the market until prices had risen. The Commodity Credit Corporation, spun off from the Reconstruction Finance Corporation and funded through the RFC appropriation, offered farmers nonrecourse loans at rates above the market price of their crops. If prices rose, the farmer could repay the loan, redeem his crop, and sell it. If not, the government kept the crop, and the farmer kept his money.[23] Begun almost as an afterthought as part of the rescue operation for cotton in October 1933, the Commodity Credit Corporation essentially reinstated Hoover's old Farm Board, albeit in a context of production controls that would supposedly keep it from being swamped with limitless surpluses. Substantial surpluses accumulated nonetheless. By the eve of World War II the corporation held in its warehouses and elevators a third of a billion dollars' worth of unmarketable cotton and somewhat lesser quantities of corn and wheat.[24]

Despite Roosevelt's effort to shepherd the farm bill swiftly through Congress during the Hundred Days, it had been presented for his signature only on May 12, well after spring planting had begun. Seeds had already sprouted in thousands of cotton patches throughout the South and in the rolling wheatfields of the West. Millions of pigs had farrowed in broodsheds and barnyards across the corn belt. By an ironic and short-lived mercy, drought spared Secretary of Agriculture Henry A. Wallace

23. Some surplus foodstuffs were purchased by the Federal Surplus Relief Corporation for distribution by relief agencies, foreshadowing the Food Stamp Program established in 1939. In light of later controversy over the Food Stamp Program it is worth noting that its principal origins lay in the quest for agricultural profitability, not in concern for the undernourished urban poor.

24. *HSUS*, 488.

from resorting to drastic measures to curtail the wheat crop.[25] But to prevent cotton and hogs from glutting their respective markets, Wallace found himself in 1933 charged with the distasteful task of persuading farmers to plow up some ten million acres of sprouting cotton and to slaughter some six million squealing piglets.

Crop prevention might have been unorthodox, but outright crop destruction struck many farmers as criminal, perhaps even sacrilegious. Wallace himself conceded that the cotton plow-up and the "pig infanticide" "were not acts of idealism in any sane society. . . . To destroy a standing crop goes against the soundest instincts of human nature." Milo Reno said flatly that "for the government to destroy food and reduce crops . . . is wicked." In fact, cotton was the only crop plowed up and hogs the only livestock deliberately slaughtered, but the drama of their destruction fixed the image of the AAA in the minds of many Americans and emphatically underscored the novelty of its methods. The Department of Agriculture and the AAA, Lorena Hickok was told in Minnesota in October 1933, "are trying to do a lot of funny things." From Nebraska a few weeks later she reported that "Wallace IS unpopular out here — even among the gang that still believes in giving the Administration a chance." A prominent farm leader voiced the sentiments of many Americans when he said: "That we should have idle and hungry and ill-clad millions on the one hand, and so much food and wool and cotton upon the other that we don't know what to do with it, this is an utterly idiotic situation, and one which makes a laughing stock of our genius as a people."[26]

Wallace shrugged off these criticisms and soldiered ahead with his crusade to restore vitality to American agriculture. Rumpled and tousle-haired, plain-spoken and unpretentious, forty-five years old in 1933, Wallace then and later was a magnet for controversy. To his partisans he was an agrarian intellectual, a scientist and a visionary, like his father before him an editor of the respected farm journal *Wallace's Farmer*. Again like his father, who had been Warren G. Harding's secretary of agriculture, the younger Wallace was an agricultural statesman who moved easily between the corn cribs and feedlots of his native Iowa and

25. The wheat harvest dropped from an annual average of some 864 million bushels in 1928–32 to about 567 million bushels in 1933–35; AAA accounted for less than 7 percent of that reduction, while the weather was responsible for the rest. Schlesinger 2:70.

26. Schlesinger 2:63, 61, 65; Lowitt and Beasley, *One Third of a Nation*, 54, 106; Anthony J. Badger, *The New Deal* (New York: Farrar, Straus and Giroux, 1989), 163.

the salons and committee rooms of Washington. To his detractors he was a dreamy rustic, an awkward and swankless bumpkin, a pixilated hayseed who dabbled in fad diets, consulted Navajo shamans, and proved a sucker for the enchantments of spiritual snake-oil merchants like his confidante and guru, the emigré Russian mystic Nicholas Roerich.

Whatever his abundant personal idiosyncrasies, Wallace had an uncommonly deep and thorough understanding of American agriculture. He was at bottom a man of the soil. Yet despite his sometimes moony rhapsodizing about the virtues of the bucolic life, he never retreated from his conviction that farming was a business, nor did he apologize for his insistence that it should be a profitable business. He denounced those who bemoaned the AAA's policy of raising farm prices through planned scarcity as "standpat sentimentalists who weep that farmers should practice controlled production [but] do not suggest that clothing factories go on producing *ad infinitum*, regardless of effective demand for their merchandise, until every naked Chinaman is clad. . . . We must play with the cards that are dealt," he said. "Agriculture cannot survive in a capitalist society as a philanthropic enterprise."[27] But it could survive, as Wallace's policies ultimately demonstrated, as a thoroughly subsidized enterprise, suckled in perpetuity on the public teat.

To implement its novel policies with maximum speed, AAA turned to the network of Extension Service agents already in place in virtually every rural county in America. The county agents, in turn, arranged for the formation of local production-control committees in whom effective administrative authority over AAA programs came to reside. It pleased Henry Wallace to describe these bodies as exemplars of "economic democracy," but the reality was somewhat different. Given their history of close collaboration with the largest commercial farmers, the agents, predictably enough, tended to select the richest, most substantial growers in each locality to sit on the committees. The power of the committees was considerable. By 1934 nearly four thousand local committees set production quotas, monitored acreage-reduction contracts, and disbursed government payments.

Like the NRA, AAA was at least nominally a voluntary program. In theory, any individual farmer could elect to sign up for the acreage-reduction or crop-loan programs or to produce as much as he liked and take his chances in the open market. In practice, however, too many

27. Schlesinger 2:63.

nonsigners would undermine the whole surplus-reducing logic of AAA. Not surprisingly, the local committees therefore exerted themselves strenuously to bring their neighbors into the AAA fold. Sometimes they resorted to vigilante intimidation. In two sectors—cotton and tobacco— the effort to induce voluntary compliance gave way in 1934 to compulsory, statutory measures, requested by a majority of the producers themselves. The Bankhead Cotton Control Act and its companion measure, the Kerr-Smith Tobacco Control Act, licensed thousands of individual growers and levied a punitive tax on crops produced in excess of stipulated quotas.

These policies, helped by punishing droughts in the wheat and corn belts, achieved modest economic success. Cotton prices improved from less than seven cents a pound in 1932 to better than twelve cents a pound in 1934. Wheat went from its 1932 low of thirty-eight cents a bushel to eighty-six cents in 1934. Corn moved from thirty-two cents a bushel to eighty-two cents in the same period. Overall, net farm income rose by 50 percent between 1932 and 1936. The parity ratio, thanks partly to higher crop prices but largely to several billion dollars in processing-tax transfer payments to nonproducing farmers, improved from fifty-eight in 1932 to touch ninety-three in 1937, before slumping again to eighty-one by the eve of World War II.[28] Yet those numbers masked persistent and even worsening travails for many millions of Americans in the countryside.

Nowhere were those travails more grotesque than in the cotton South, haunted still by the racial anxieties and class antagonisms that were the malignant residue of the region's troubled history. The cotton belt was home in the 1930s to one-third of the farm population, some two million families, nearly nine million souls whose livelihoods were staked by iron necessity to the white staple. Most were tenant farmers and sharecroppers. They owned no land of their own but lived precariously from season to season by tendering the landlord a lien on their crop in return for a "furnish," usually a credit good for seed, tools, food, and clothing at a store often owned by the landlord himself. Rarely if ever did a tenant earn enough to pay off his debts and escape the system. Since the end of the Civil War this semifeudal system had swollen in the South to hold in its suffocating embrace more than a million white households and well over half a million black families. They were trapped in the system of virtual peonage that had so disturbed Lorena

28. *HSUS*, 511, 517, 483, 489.

Hickok when she first encountered it in Georgia and the Carolinas in early 1934. The croppers lived in hopeless poverty, indebtedness, and fear, fear that was especially paralyzing if they were black. Their only effective recourse against exploitative landlords was to move, as many of them did every year, wearily exchanging one master for another. It was, as Hickok said, a form of slavery in all but name.

She was not alone in the 1930s in describing the life of the southern sharecropper as something that "seemed to belong to another land than the America I knew and loved." After *Fortune* magazine sent the young poet James Agee and the photographer Walker Evans to Alabama to report on tenant farmers, the magazine found their account of the suffering they had seen too harrowing to publish—a rejection that eventually led to its release in book form as *Let Us Now Praise Famous Men*, one of the most sobering artistic achievements of the decade. The writer Erskine Caldwell, no stranger to the harsh grindstone of southern tenant life, recorded scenes of almost unimaginable degradation. Visiting a Georgia sharecropper's cabin that held three families jammed into two rooms, he saw a gaunt six-year-old boy licking the wrappings of a meat package, while "on the floor before an open fire lay two babies, neither a year old, sucking the dry teats of a mongrel bitch." An English journalist in the same year wrote that she "had traveled over most of Europe and part of Africa, but I have never seen such terrible sights as I saw yesterday among the sharecroppers of Arkansas." Henry Wallace himself in the following year declared that on a trip through the cotton states from Arkansas to the East Coast he had witnessed "a poverty so abject" that "I am tempted to say that one third of the farmers of the United States live under conditions which are so much worse than the peasantry of Europe that the city people of the United States should be thoroughly ashamed."[29]

The Depression fell with especially sharp brutality on sharecroppers. The AAA's policies, however unintentionally, cruelly exacerbated their plight. The basic mechanism by which the AAA reduced cotton surpluses was by reducing the acreage planted to cotton. It accomplished this by writing contracts with landlords, in which benefit payments ef-

29. Theodore Saloutos, *The American Farmer and the New Deal* (Ames: Iowa State University Press, 1982), 66, 187; Schlesinger 2:375–76. For a perceptive discussion of Agee and Evans's book, see Richard H. Pells, *Radical Visions, American Dreams* (New York: Harper and Row, 1973), 246ff.

fectively served as rent for land taken out of production. Since most of the withdrawn acreage was worked by tenants and croppers, AAA at a stroke deprived them of their already meager means of earning their daily bread. In theory, landlords were supposed to share their benefit payments with their tenants. In practice, few of them did. The planters pocketed 90 percent of the AAA benefit payments in 1933 and left their hapless croppers to shift for themselves. Browbeaten by generations of intimidation backed as needed by noose and fire, few tenants could find the courage or the means to make effective protest. When black and white tenants in Arkansas, where six out of ten farms were held in tenancy, organized the Southern Tenant Farmers Union (STFU) in July 1934, reprisals were swift and savage. "Riding bosses" descended on STFU meetings with whips and guns, hounded and beat organizers, and inveighed against the pernicious influence of "outside agitators," including the prominent socialist Norman Thomas. Pummeled off a speaker's platform by sheriff's deputies in the town of Birdsong, Thomas was emphatically told, "We don't need no Gawd-damned Yankee Bastard to tell us what to do with our niggers."[30]

Many displaced croppers headed for the cities, where FERA checks or CWA jobs might tide them over. Others took to the roads, joining the itinerants pathetically westering in their jalopies like human tumbleweeds, their image forever etched in American memory by Steinbeck's touching portrayal of the Joad family in *Grapes of Wrath*. But as Norman Thomas insisted, while Steinbeck's Joads had been tractored off the land in the Dust Bowl, in the cotton South "it wasn't just the tractor turning up the land that drove people out; it was the deliberate displacement of the AAA."[31] In his masterful study of race relations in America, the Swedish economist Gunnar Myrdal described the AAA as a kind of American enclosure movement:

> Landlords have been made to reduce drastically the acreage of their main labor-requiring crops. They have been given a large part of the power over the local administration of this program. They have a strong economic incentive to reduce their tenant labor force, a large part of which consists of politically and legally impotent Negroes. Yet they have been asked not to make any such reduction. It would certainly not be compatible with usual human behavior, if this request generally

30. Schlesinger 2:378.
31. Davis 3:476.

had been fulfilled. Under the circumstances, there is no reason at all to be surprised about the wholesale decline in tenancy. Indeed, it would be surprising if it had not happened.[32]

Hounded out of Arkansas, a shaken Thomas went to Washington, secured an appointment with the president, and brought with him to the White House a copy of the AAA cotton contract. Pushing it across the desk toward Roosevelt, he pointed out Section 7, which required planters to make good-faith efforts to continue to employ tenants whose land was removed from production. "That can mean anything or nothing, can't it, Norman?" the president genially responded. Thomas was outraged. He described the plight of the southern sharecroppers as "potentially the most dangerous situation I have seen in America." He demanded that the president make a stand for social justice in the South by supporting the federal antilynching bill introduced in the Senate in January 1934. Only by making lynching a federal crime could the reign of terror that brooded over the South be broken. A presumptive majority favored the bill, Thomas argued; but it could reach the floor of the Senate for a vote only if the president lent his support for a motion to invoke the cloture rule and end a threatened southern filibuster. The argument discomforted Roosevelt. Just weeks earlier he had explained to NAACP secretary Walter White that he could not support the anti-lynching bill because "Southerners, by reason of the seniority rule in Congress, are chairmen or occupy strategic positions on most of the Senate and House committees. If I come out for the anti-lynching bill now, they will block every bill I ask Congress to pass to keep America from collapsing. I just can't take that risk." Supporting the STFU would especially complicate his relationship with Arkansas's own Joseph Robinson, the Senate majority leader; crucial to Roosevelt's legislative program, he had been slandered by the STFU's newspaper as "Greasy Joe." Roosevelt shared this calculated political reasoning with Thomas. "Now come, Norman," he said, "I'm a damned sight better politician than you are. I know the South, and there is arising a new generation of leaders and we've got to be patient."[33]

The patience the president counseled did not assuage Thomas, nor did it satisfy principled reformers within the New Deal administration. The plight of the southern sharecroppers, blacks especially, became the sharpest point of contention between two factions that struggled in the

32. Gunnar Myrdal, An American Dilemma (New York: Harper and Row, 1944), 258.
33. Davis 3:483–84; Schlesinger 2:37.

Department of Agriculture for control of the New Deal's agricultural policies and, through those policies, for the power to shape the future of rural American life. On the one side were the career agricultural bureaucrats, many of them ensconced in the department since the time of the first Secretary Wallace in the Harding era. Thoroughly marinated in the commercial culture of the Farm Bureau and the Extension Service, they clung to a single-minded conception of agriculture as a business enterprise and to a no less restrictive notion of their own responsibilities as public servants. "The job's simple," said George Peek, the first director of AAA and the old guard's great champion. "It's just to put up farm prices."[34]

Arrayed against "Henry's father's gang" was a group of young New Dealers, many of them bookish intellectuals and Ivy League lawyers with no practical knowledge of agriculture nor actual experience with rural life. One of them famously betrayed his city-slicker roots when he inquired about the welfare of the macaroni growers. Peek ridiculed them as "boys with their hair ablaze," but those blazing boys were in fact dedicated, conscience-driven reformers. They aimed at nothing less than leveraging the opportunity given them by the Depression crisis not just to bring prosperity to the biggest farmers but to bring justice and decent standards of living to all rural Americans, farm workers as well as landowners, black as well as white.

The reformers were concentrated in the legal division of AAA, headed by general counsel Jerome N. Frank. He assembled an unusually talented group of young lawyers, including Abe Fortas, Adlai Stevenson, and Alger Hiss, all of whom looked to Frank and to Assistant Secretary of Agriculture Rexford Tugwell for guidance and support.[35] In January 1935 Frank sent Mary Connor Myers to Arkansas to investigate the SFTU's claims about violations of Section 7. "Have heard one long story

34. Schlesinger 2:46.
35. Some other members of Frank's staff, perhaps including Hiss but certainly not including Frank himself, were organized in 1933 into a secretive Communist group. They met clandestinely, though more for radical conversation than political conspiring, in a Washington music studio run by the sister of the chief organizer, Hal Ware. Among them were Lee Pressman, Jon Abt, and Nathan Witt. Ware, son of the redoubtable agitator Ella Reeve "Mother" Bloor, had a vaguely defined consulting relationship with the Department of Agriculture and did nurture Communist elements in the Farmers Holiday movement. Aside from that extremely marginal and inconsequential activity, none of these closet radicals exerted any significant communist influence on AAA policy. For more on this group, see Whittaker Chambers, *Witness* (New York: Random House, 1952).

of human greed," she wired back to Frank. It was apparent to her that many planters regarded payments to croppers, in the words of one land-lord, "as little more than a gracious gesture," if they bothered to make the gesture at all.[36] Frank instructed Alger Hiss to draw up a new guide-line strengthening Section 7.

Hiss, an urbane twenty-eight-year-old Harvard law graduate, by his own admission not very knowledgeable about the cotton economy, was also innocent of the explosive volatility of the race issue in the South. He had drafted the original cotton code almost immediately on his ar-rival in Washington in 1933, and soon got a rough education in the mores of the region that his directive threatened to upset. When South Carolina senator Ellison "Cotton Ed" Smith learned that Hiss's contracts provided for checks going directly to tenants, he stormed into Hiss's office. "Young fella," he blustered, "you can't do this to my niggers, paying checks to them. They don't know what to do with the money. The money should come to me. I'll take care of them. They're mine." Following confrontations like that, Hiss had few illusions about AAA's impact on southern tenant farmers. "After the first year of the cotton program," he later explained, "it was clear that, for all its idealism, it was hurting and might further hurt the tenants because if a landowner was going to reduce production by a third, he had a third too many tenants or sharecroppers. Most of them depended on the little huts that were supplied and the garden patches where they were allowed to raise vegetables for themselves." The new agreement that Hiss now drew up in early 1935 "provided that no signer of a contract, no owner of land, could get rid of his tenants. He had to retain the same number of tenants. There were clauses that indicated they should be the same individuals. . . . They had a right to live in the huts that they'd been living in and to continue to have use of work animals and garden plots." In a monumental understatement, Hiss added that "this caused real turmoil."[37]

In the absence of AAA director Chester Davis, who had replaced Peek in December 1933 but shared many of Peek's views on farm policy, Frank caused Hiss's guideline to be promulgated as an administrative directive on February 1, 1935. It was a triumphant moment for the AAA

36. Donald H. Grubbs, *Cry from the Cotton: The Southern Tenant Farmers' Union and the New Deal* (Chapel Hill: University of North Carolina Press, 1971), 48–49, 22.
37. Katie Louchheim, ed., *The Making of the New Deal: The Insiders Speak* (Cam-bridge: Harvard University Press, 1983), 238–39.

liberals, a moment when, as Hiss recollected, they felt that they "were representing Secretary Wallace's view." But their triumph was short-lived. Wallace soon let them down, and hard. Davis rushed back to Washington, canceled the directive, and demanded that Wallace allow him to fire Frank and several members of Frank's overzealous staff. Wallace acceded, Roosevelt made no objection, and the liberals were summarily purged. Friendless and powerless, the displaced sharecroppers and tenants of the cotton belt were left to their own weak devices. Curiously, Hiss was spared from Davis's ax, but "from then on," Hiss later reflected, "my interest in Triple-A lessened and the fire went out of the whole thing."[38]

Thus AAA, like NRA, proved most effective not in promoting recovery, nor in protecting what Hugh Johnson called the "little fellow," but in salvaging the bacon of the biggest commercial interests, in this case the southern cotton lords. And while NRA had galvanized leaders like John L. Lewis to invigorate a labor movement that would soon convulse entire industries and revolutionize the status of American industrial workers, no really effective champions of the farmers displaced by AAA's policies ever emerged after Frank's liberals were purged. Tractored and AAA-ed off the land, they accumulated like dried weeds in the fence-corners of the American countryside, especially in the South. They remained a dazed and almost motionless mass, saved for the while from starvation by federal relief agencies but devoid of land, work, or prospects. "By some means or other," Lorena Hickok candidly observed, "these people have to be removed from the labor market. . . . The only way out is to remove from the labor market enough poor Whites and Blacks so that members of both races who are left will have some sort of chance."[39] On the far western edge of the cotton belt, in the sere wasteland of the Oklahoma-Texas-Kansas Dust Bowl, stark necessity had already put thousands of these pioneers of misfortune into motion. For the remainder of the 1930s millions of others continued to languish hopelessly in the old Southeast. It would take a war, in the next decade, to shake them loose.

By early 1935, as the New Deal approached the beginning of its third year, the liberals purged from AAA were not alone in their disillusionment. The fire of enthusiasm for Roosevelt's Hundred Days

38. Loucheim, *Making of the New Deal,* 239–40.
39. Lowitt and Beasley, *One Third of a Nation,* 158.

policies was flickering low for many who had cheered him in 1933. Brain Truster Raymond Moley, both the agent and the victim of Roosevelt's renunciation of internationalism at the London World Economic Conference in June 1933, left his government post a few months later. The gold-buying scheme had cost the president the service of several monetary traditionalists. Hugh Johnson had departed NRA. George Peek was gone from AAA. Budget director Lewis Douglas, already rattled by the abandonment of the gold standard in 1933, grew increasingly disenchanted with Roosevelt's fiscal unorthodoxy and resigned in August 1934.

In that same month, disaffected conservatives within the president's Democratic Party formed the American Liberty League. Its members included Al Smith, former Democratic Party chairman John J. Raskob, onetime Democratic presidential nominee John W. Davis, and a raft of corporate leaders like Alfred P. Sloan of General Motors and Sewell Avery of Montgomery Ward. Growing ever more shrill in their denunciation of the New Deal, they represented what Herbert Hoover scornfully called the "Wall Street model of human liberty." (Hoover pointedly declined an invitation to join.)[40]

The birth of the Liberty League marked the beginning of organized, articulate opposition to the New Deal on the right, including the right wing of the president's own party. But the worm of doubt about the New Deal's effectiveness and even its ultimate purposes also began to gnaw at others, including liberals. As 1935 opened, some ten million persons, more than 20 percent of the work force, still remained jobless. The country seemed to flounder, without a workable remedy to the afflictions from which it had been suffering now for half a decade. Even Lorena Hickok succumbed to the mood of disaffection. As early as April 1934 she confided to Hopkins from Texas: "At no time previously, since taking this job, have I been quite so discouraged." When a Texas businessman

---

40. The Liberty Leaguers hyperbolically fulminated against state socialism and the dictatorial ambitions of Roosevelt. No doubt their anxieties would have been exacerbated had they known that one of the president's closest advisers, Adolf Berle, had adopted the joking habit of addressing all correspondence to the president "Dear Caesar" and that the guests at Roosevelt's annual birthday dinner, given by the Cuff Links Club, composed of some of FDR's oldest supporters, to whom he had given gold cuff links in thanks for support in his vice-presidential bid of 1920, came in Roman garb. FDR himself was usually attired in a royal purple toga, crowned with laurel, and played to the hilt the role of imperious master of the revels. See Davis 3:347–48.

unapologetically told her that he favored fascism for the United States, she confessed to Hopkins that "honestly, after nearly a year of traveling about this country, I'm almost forced to agree with him. If I were 20 years younger and weighed 75 pounds less, I think I'd start out to be the Joan of Arc of the Fascist movement in the United States. . . . I've been out on this trip now for a little more than two weeks. In all that time I've hardly met a single person who seemed confident and cheerful. Relief loads are mounting, They can't see any improvement. . . . Nobody seems to think any more that the thing is going to WORK."[41]

In a summary report to Hopkins on New Year's Day 1935, Hickok rehearsed her worries about a "stranded generation": men over forty with half-grown families, people who might never get their jobs back. "Through loss of skill, through mental and physical deterioration due to long enforced idleness, the relief clients, the people who have been longest without work, are gradually being forced into the class of un-employables — rusty tools, abandoned, not worth using any more. . . . And so they go on — the gaunt, ragged legion of the industrially damned. Bewildered, apathetic, many of them terrifyingly patient."[42]

But the mysterious patience of the American people in the face of adversity that had so consistently impressed Hickok and others was show-ing signs of rubbing thin. Evidence of a polarization in the electorate and of a momentous shift in the American center of political gravity was becoming increasingly apparent. The frustration born of raised hopes and stalled progress began to manifest itself ever more stridently as 1934 wore on and recovery remained beyond reach. Frustration some-times sought unconventional outlets. Louisiana's outrageous Senator Huey P. Long launched his Share Our Wealth Society in January 1934 with promises "to make every man a king" through wholesale (and wholly fantastic) redistribution of the national patrimony. In the same month, California physician Dr. Francis Townsend established Old Age Revolving Pensions, Ltd., to promote his fetching nostrum of paying two hundred dollars monthly to all Americans over sixty. Led by militant longshoremen, a general strike briefly paralyzed San Francisco in July 1934. Other strikers shut down the textile mills from New England to the Carolinas in September. The crusading novelist Upton Sinclair ran for governor in California on a utopian "production-for-use" commu-nitarian platform; he polled nearly a million votes in the November

41. Lowitt and Beasley, One Third of a Nation, 218.
42. Lowitt and Beasley, One Third of a Nation, 361–63.

election. Just days later, the Reverend Charles Coughlin, the eccentric but widely popular "radio priest" from Royal Oak, Michigan, announced the formation of the National Union for Social Justice as a vehicle to promote his own peculiar blend of inflation and anti-Semitism.

In November 1934 this bubbling discontent wrought an unprecedented political result. It had been — and remains — a truism of American politics that the presidential party loses congressional seats in off-year elections, but in the new Congress that was to be installed in January 1935, it was the Republicans who lost, going from 117 to 103 seats in the House and from 35 to 25 seats in the Senate. Democrats would now enjoy two-thirds majorities in both chambers. Roosevelt had set the stage for the sweeping Democratic victories in a June 1934 Fireside Chat, when he asked his listeners to "judge recovery" by "the plain facts of your individual situation. Are you better off than you were last year?" In fact, recovery remained out of reach, and few Americans were appreciably better off then they had been a year earlier, but Roosevelt's Democrats benefited less from what they had done than from the fact that they had done something. How long the American people would be satisfied with mere action, without measurable results, remained anybody's guess.

Enfolded in the numbers that defined the huge Democratic majorities was a development of significant political consequence: the party was growing ever more rapidly from its traditional southern base to embrace new constituencies in the great industrial cities of the North and the commercial centers of the West. Almost the only Republican gains in the 1934 congressional elections were in upstate New York, in rural Protestant districts in central and southern Ohio, Indiana, and Illinois, and on the Great Plains — all areas that were inexorably shrinking in demographic and economic importance. The fastest-growing population groups in America — Catholic and Jewish immigrants and their voting-age second-generation children — were moving en masse into the Democratic Party. So were blacks in those northern precincts where they could vote. The future of African-American political loyalties was strongly signaled in Chicago, where the black Democrat Arthur W. Mitchell defeated the black Republican Oscar De Priest to become the first black Democrat ever elected to Congress. How would these swelling constituencies, for so long made to feel like outsiders, ground down by half a decade of Depression, and now freshly and hugely enfranchised, wield their new power? That very question worried the old-guard Democratic leaders in the House, who began immediately to seek ways to control the potentially unruly majority they now commanded. When the new Congress convened in early 1935, the leadership raised from 145 to 218 the number of signatures required for a discharge petition, the motion that could compel a committee to release a bill for discussion on the House floor. Even that transparent effort to corral the new Congress's radicalism might prove insufficient—especially if the president turned radical himself.[43]

Roosevelt now stood in a position analogous to Lincoln's after the failure of the Peninsula Campaign. Had George McClellan's troops taken Richmond in the summer of 1862, the Union would in all likelihood have been restored with slavery intact, given Lincoln's stated purpose at the time that his sole war aim was to restore the Union and nothing more. By retreating from Richmond and leaving Lee and the Confederacy to fight another day, McClellan ensured that the war would escalate, that it would go on until slavery was rooted out and the social and economic order of the old South undone. As Roosevelt in the early weeks of 1935 contemplated the New Deal's disappointing economic performance, he might have reflected on what that long-ago military defeat had done for Lincoln. For had Hugh Johnson and Henry Wallace been swiftly successful in restoring prosperity by 1934, the most ambitious reform aspirations of the New Deal might never have come to pass. It was, ironically enough, the continuing economic crisis that helped elect the reform-minded Democratic majority in 1934 and gave Roosevelt his opportunity not just to revitalize the economy but to reshape the very contours of American life.

Driving with his staff to a racetrack near Washington just after the November 1934 elections, Harry Hopkins was keen with anticipation. Perhaps lacking a detailed sense of history past but sensing unerringly that much history could now be made, he burst out: "Boys—this is our hour. We've got to get everything we want—a works program, social security, wages and hours, everything—now or never. Get your minds to work on developing a complete ticket to provide security for all the folks of this country up and down and across the board."[44] As much as any statement, Hopkins's exclamation defined a charter for 1935, a year that would witness the fullest triumph of the New Deal's reform agenda.

43. See the brief but excellent summary in Michael Barone, *Our Country: The Shaping of American from Roosevelt to Reagan* (New York: Free Press, 1990), 69–78.
44. Robert E. Sherwood, *Roosevelt and Hopkins: An Intimate History* (New York: Grosset and Dunlap, 1948, 1950), 65.

8

The Rumble of Discontent

I wish there were a few million radicals.
— Louisiana senator Huey P. Long, April 1935

As 1935 opened, what history was to remember as the New Deal had not yet happened. Franklin Roosevelt had given the country an abundance of the "bold, persistent experimentation" that he had promised in the presidential campaign of 1932, as well as a stiff dose of the "action along new lines . . . action, action" that he had urged upon his advisers just before taking office in 1933. The sheer activism of the new administration no doubt helped to shore up the national spirit in a season of despair, as did Roosevelt's own carbonated optimism — "it seemed to generate from him as naturally as heat from fire," one awed presidential dinner guest wrote.[1] But nations — and their leaders — can subsist on solely spiritual nourishment little longer than they can live on bread alone. Despite the exhilaration of the Hundred Days, despite the exertions of the NRA and the AAA, despite the reopening of the banks and the efforts of federal relief agencies, despite all the ingenuity and exuberance of Roosevelt and his New Dealers, the Depression persisted. After two full years of the New Deal, one in five American workers remained jobless. The tonic effect of Roosevelt's inaugural declaration that "the only thing we have to fear is fear itself" had long since worn off. To many of those who had put their faith in Roosevelt in 1932, and especially to those who had always hoped for something more dramatic than his prudent and piecemeal reformism, the New Deal appeared, even before it reached its second anniversary, to be a spent political

1. Jerre Mangione, *The Dream and the Deal: The Federal Writers Project, 1933–1945* (Boston: Little, Brown, 1972), 11.

218

force. If the buoyant president had a coherent vision of a future that he deemed it his destiny to bring about, it remained scarcely visible to the American people.

On many sides, impatience with Roosevelt's admittedly energetic but apparently ineffective leadership deepened through 1934. On the right, conservative Republicans like Herbert Hoover and disaffected Democrats like Al Smith nattered crankily about the loss of individual liberty and the corruption of American ideals. Some of them gathered in the American Liberty League. Others worked to make the Republican Party the vessel of ultimate salvation from Roosevelt's alleged follies. For the moment they bided their time and awaited the catastrophe that they believed inevitably lay ahead.

Disillusionment with Roosevelt ran deepest and most dangerously on the left, especially among jobless workers and busted farmers, among reformers and visionaries who had been led to giddy heights of expectation by Roosevelt's aggressive presidential beginning, and among radicals who saw in the Depression the clinching proof that American capitalism was defunct, beyond all hope of salvation or melioration. The prolonged agonies and frustrations of those unquiet souls incubated countless prescriptions to lift the nation's afflictions as the Depression stubbornly lingered. Many of the nostrums that sprouted in the soil of the Depression's misery tested the limits of orthodoxy. Some tested the boundaries of credibility. Together, they tested the very fabric of American political culture — and eventually helped to stretch it.

ROOSEVELT'S DREAM of advancing liberalism by forging a new electoral union of forward-thinking Democrats and progressive Republicans threatened to degenerate into a nightmare in which the various progressive forces in the country might so fragment as to lose all capacity for common political action. The very plurality of the "different so-called progressive and liberal organizations that are cropping up all over the country," one adviser warned in early 1935, threatened the president's political viability and even the effectiveness of the liberal cause.[2] The Senate Progressive Republicans like California's Hiram Johnson, New Mexico's Bronson Cutting, and Wisconsin's Robert La Follette Jr.,

2. The remark was made by David K. Niles, a former operative in the La Follette presidential campaign of 1924, director of the liberal Ford Hall Forum in Boston, and associate of Felix Frankfurter. Niles's worries led to a meeting between Roosevelt and a group of progressive Republican senators at the White House on May 14, 1935. An account is in Davis 3:508ff.

as well as Montana's Burton Wheeler, were growing restive. Mostly from rural states, mostly in favor of inflation, and mostly isolationist in foreign policy, they increasingly chafed at Roosevelt's cautious monetary policies, at the smallness and hesitation of his steps away from fiscal orthodoxy, at his alleged mollycoddling of big business and Wall Street, and at disturbing signs of his renascent internationalism. Wheeler, a nominal Democrat who had been La Follette's father's running mate on the Progressive ticket in 1924, was openly discussing the need for a third party in 1936. In Wisconsin, the redoubtable La Follette and his brother, Philip, like their father before them, broke with the state Republican Party in May 1934 and launched a new Progressive Party, with Roosevelt's quiet support. Yet Philip La Follette soon declared: "We are not liberals! Liberalism is nothing but a sort of milk-and-water tolerance. . . . I believe in a fundamental and basic change. I think a cooperative society based on American traditions is inevitable."[3]

La Follette never explained precisely what that "cooperative society" might look like, but in neighboring Minnesota, Farmer-Labor Party leader Floyd Bjerstjerne Olson, governor since 1932, was giving extravagant definition to his own vision of a "cooperative commonwealth." Though Roosevelt had assisted his election in 1932 and tacitly backed him for reelection in 1934, Olson, like the La Follettes, loudly declaimed: "I am not a liberal. I am a radical. You bet your life I'm a radical. You might say I'm radical as hell!" Lorena Hickok reported in late 1933 that "this boy Olson is, in my opinion, about the smartest 'Red' in this country." Olson blustered to Hickok: "You go back to Washington and tell 'em that Olson is taking recruits for the Minnesota National Guard, and he isn't taking anybody who doesn't carry a Red card."[4] A former Wobbly and a child of the quasi-socialist Non-Partisan League that had swept the northern wheat belt in the World War I era, Olson was American radicalism's native son, a big, laughing, broad-shouldered, sandy-haired man with deep roots in the populist soil that covered much of the nation's agrarian heartland. Like his People's Party antecedents of the 1890s, he demanded government ownership of key industries.

Ideas like that appealed strongly to the intellectuals associated with the League for Independent Political Action, founded in 1929 by the

3. Schlesinger 3:107.
4. Leuchtenburg, 96; Schlesinger 3:99; Richard Lowitt and Maurine Beasley, eds., *One Third of a Nation: Lorena Hickok Reports on the Great Depression* (Urbana: University of Illinois Press, 1981), 136–37.

University of Chicago economist Paul H. Douglas and the dean of American philosophers, John Dewey. "Capitalism must be destroyed," the league declared. Dewey himself said of the New Deal's effort to create a "controlled and humanized capitalism" that "no such compromise with a decaying system is possible." The league advocated socialism in all but name—a controlled and humanized socialism, it might be charitably called, committed to tempering its collectivist regime with tolerance for differences and respect for individual freedoms, but dedicated nonetheless to a systemic egalitarianism under pervasive state control. Dewey and the league carried forward a thread of political thought that ran far back into the American past. Their nemesis was laissez-faire capitalism. Their Bible was Edward Bellamy's utopian tract of 1888, *Looking Backward*, which portrayed a regimented, antiseptic, but serene future society eternally prospering under a system of benevolent direction by the central state. Their forum was the magazine *Common Sense*, founded in 1932 by Yale graduate Alfred Bingham, who considered himself the chief steward of the progressive-era tradition of national economic planning and state direction of the economy. Their special hero, for a season, was Floyd Olson. In him they saw a practicing politician who seemed open to some decidedly unconventional political ideas. Olson thrilled the league's somewhat dreamy loyalists when he talked about production for use, not for profit, and declared that "American capitalism cannot be reformed." "A third party must arise," Olson wrote in *Common Sense* in 1935, "and preach the gospel of government and collective ownership of the means of production and distribution." "Whether there will be a third party in 1936," Olson told an interviewer, "depends mainly on Mr. Roosevelt." As for its leadership: maybe Bob La Follette or Burton Wheeler; "I think I'm a little too radical," Olson conceded. "How about 1940?" the interviewer persisted. "Maybe by then I won't be radical enough," Olson replied.[5] Partisans of the league loved this line of thinking. So did the handful of sincere citizens, notably the indefatigable crusader Norman Thomas, who remained in the American Socialist Party.

But for some, Olson and even the Socialists were not then radical enough, nor ever would be. Members of the Communist Party of the United States of America (CPUSA) believed that nothing less than the reconstruction of American society on the Soviet model would

5. Schlesinger 3:104. In fact, by 1940 Olson would be dead. He died in 1936, at the age of forty-four.

constitute a proper use of the opportunity the Depression presented. Now, in the moment of capitalism's unarguable collapse, was the time to catalyze the inevitable revolution that Marxist theory predicted. Party doctrine in 1933–34 dictated no compromise and no cooperation with "bourgeois democracy." The party's official organ, the *Daily Worker*, damned the NRA as a "fascist slave program." CPUSA general secretary Earl Browder said in 1934 that "Roosevelt's program is the same as that of finance capital the world over. . . . [I]t is the same," he declared with much hyperbole and no shame, "as Hitler's program."[6]

Disgruntled members of Eugene Debs's Socialist Party had broken away to form the CPUSA in 1919. Riven through the 1920s by faction-fighting between Trotskyists and Stalinists, and hobbled by endless doctrinal arguments with other leftist groups like the socialists, the party eventually united in 1932 behind presidential candidate William Z. Foster. Foster and his African-American running mate, James Ford, polled some 102,000 votes. That was an all-time electoral high for the party, but far less than the 884,000 thousand votes cast for Norman Thomas, and a number that was dwarfed by the 22.8 million ballots for Roosevelt. The Foster-Ford ticket nevertheless attracted some notable sympathizers, including the novelists John Dos Passos and Sherwood Anderson, the philosopher Sidney Hook, the literary critic Edmund Wilson, and the Harlem poet Langston Hughes, all of whom signed a manifesto declaring that "as responsible intellectual workers we have aligned ourselves with the frankly revolutionary Communist Party."[7]

The party dedicated itself in the early Depression years to staging political demonstrations (often the occasions for bloody melees pitting rock-throwing demonstrators against truncheon-wielding police), organizing Unemployment Councils to push for more generous relief payments, leading rent strikes and hunger marches, trying to unionize workers through the Trade Union Unity League, and recruiting members in the African-American community. When nine young black men were arrested and charged with gang-raping two white girls in a boxcar near Scottsboro, Alabama, in 1931, the party's legal arm, the International Labor Defense, took up their defense. The party energetically exploited its role in the case of the "Scottsboro Boys" to win support in the black community but enjoyed only modest success, especially since all nine

6. Schlesinger 3:190.
7. Harvey Klehr and John Earl Haynes, *The American Communist Movement: Storming Heaven Itself* (New York: Twayne, 1992), 67.

defendants were convicted by an all-white Alabama jury and sentenced to the electric chair.[8] The party's difficulties among African-Americans also stemmed in no small part from a 1928 Comintern resolution defining American Negroes as a subject nation and calling for black self-determination—a notion so incendiary to southern whites that most black American Communists refused to endorse it. Blacks never amounted to more than 10 percent of the party's membership.

But though they made some inroads among industrial workers, raised some hell in the streets, and fought, often courageously, for the rights of black Americans, the American Communists remained a small and isolated group. Three-fifths of them were foreign born, with especially heavy representation among Finns in the upper Midwest and Jews in the big cities. One-third of all members were New Yorkers, with other concentrations in Cleveland, Detroit, Chicago, and San Francisco. All told, the party counted fewer than thirty thousand members in 1934. After five years of depression, and with millions still unemployed, that number testified bluntly to the great distance that separated Communist doctrine and tactics from American political reality.

Yet the isolation of the Communists still left plenty of room for radicalism—a peculiarly American style of radicalism—in the churning political cauldron of the Depression decade. Whether the New Deal could contain and channel that radicalism, or whether it would be swept away by it, was a question that nagged at many New Dealers. "The country is much more radical than the Administration," Interior Secretary Harold Ickes noted in his diary on September 15, 1934. Roosevelt, he thought, "would have to move further to the left in order to hold the country. . . . If Roosevelt can't hold the country within reasonable safe limit [sic], no one else can possibly hope to do so. . . . [A] breakdown on the part of the Administration would result in an extreme radical movement, the extent of which no one could foresee."[9]

The practical difficulties that attended such a presidential move to the left soon presented themselves in California, then as later a fertile hatchery of novelties both political and social. What the visiting Englishman James Bryce wrote about California in the 1880s still held true half a century later: "It is thoroughly American, but most so in those

8. The ILD carried the case on appeal to the U.S. Supreme Court, which in 1935 reversed the original convictions and ordered a new trial. Charges against four of the defendants were eventually dropped, but the remaining five were again found guilty. None was executed, but the last defendant remained in prison until 1950.

9. Ickes Diary 1:195–96.

points wherein the Old World differs from the New..... Changes of public sentiment are sudden and violent. . . . [T]he masses are impatient, accustomed to blame everything and everybody but themselves for the slow approach of the millennium, ready to try instant, even if perilous, remedies for a present evil."[10] Among the last outposts of the American frontier, California held a disproportionate share of the frontier's usual assortment of rootless, restless souls, including sun-seekers from the Midwest, refugees from the Dust Bowl, immigrants from Mexico and the far shores of the Pacific, and drifters of every purpose and credo. As on all previous frontiers, these fluid and questing masses were ready recruits for promoters of material prosperity and merchants of spiritual solace. In the 1920s they had flocked by the tens of thousands to Los Angeles to hear the Four-Square Gospel of the melodramatic revivalist Aimee Semple McPherson.

In this California atmosphere of perpetual social and psychological ferment, the Depression summoned forth not one but two new prophets. Both were no less alluring in their assurances of earthly salvation than was McPherson in her costumed pageants evoking the heavenly reward that awaited the righteous.

The first was an obscure sixty-six-year-old physician, Dr. Francis Everett Townsend. In September 1933 he sent a letter to his local newspaper in the sun-washed community of Long Beach, where he had intermittently practiced medicine and dabbled in real estate since 1919. In a homely allusion to the tactics of the AAA, he said that "it is just as necessary to make some disposal of our surplus workers, as it is to dispose of our surplus wheat or corn."[11] (He sensitively refrained from invoking the examples of surplus cotton and pigs.) The particular surplus workers the sexagenarian Townsend had in mind were the elderly. As shortly refined, Townsend's plan called for monthly payments of two hundred to all persons over the age of sixty who agreed both to retire from active employment and to spend the money in the month they received it. A national 2 percent value-added tax, assessed at every transaction as a product made its way from raw material to final market, was to finance the scheme. The effects of his plan, Townsend claimed, were almost endlessly beneficial: it would directly aid the deserving elderly, raise wages by shrinking the labor pool, and stimulate recovery through the

10. James Bryce, *The American Commonwealth*, 3d ed. (New York: Macmillan, 1895), 2:425.
11. Schlesinger 3:31.

forced circulation of all those monthly checks. It seemed too good to be true, and it was.

Analysts then and later have agreed that Townsend's plan was as economically daft as it was politically seductive. Fully funding the recommended monthly payments to the 9 percent of the American population over the age of sixty would soak up half the national income and double the national tax burden. Simply transferring purchasing power from the taxed young to the consuming old would do little to increase aggregate consumption. And the value-added tax mechanism might well promote the growth of monopolies, as firms integrated to avoid taxable transactions with suppliers and contractors.

Despite these objections, Townsend fever spread rapidly. Within weeks after the gray-haired doctor's letter, Townsend Clubs sprouted like mushrooms after a spring rain, first in the always fertile social humus of California, then throughout the rest of the country. In meetings redolent of old-time Gospel revivalism, the Townsendites circulated and signed petitions demanding a federal law to make Dr. Townsend's dream a reality. In January 1934 Townsend formally incorporated this sprawling movement as Old Age Revolving Pensions, Ltd. A year later, he launched a newsletter, the *Townsend National Weekly*. By then the number of Townsend Clubs was approaching five thousand, with over two million members. As many as twenty-five million Americans had signed Townsend's petitions. The California congressional delegation was largely beholden to Townsendite support in the elections of 1934. One grateful recipient of that support introduced a bill containing Townsend's recommendations when the new congressional session opened in January 1935. That bill conflicted directly with the as yet unintroduced Social Security bill that the Roosevelt administration was preparing.

In the same month during which Dr. Townsend was inscribing his way to notoriety with his fateful letter to the *Long Beach Press-Telegram*, an already notorious figure was writing his own way onto the center of the California political stage. Upton Sinclair, celebrated muckraker, author of nearly four dozen books, cudgel of capitalism, lifelong member of the Socialist Party, addict of causes, romantic and eccentric champion of the underdog, a man who subsisted largely on a diet of brown rice, fruit, and celery, a conscience-driven sentimentalist whom H. L. Mencken described as believing in more things than any other man in the world, published a characteristically impassioned pamphlet entitled *I, Governor of California and How I Ended Poverty*. Like his hero

Edward Bellamy, Sinclair cast his political vision in the form of a utopian fantasy (his pamphlet's subtitle was *A True Story of the Future*). In the limpid prose that had endeared him to two generations of readers, Sinclair described his campaign and election and his swift implementation of the program he called EPIC — End Poverty in California. The genius of EPIC consisted in a proposal that Floyd Olson and the League for Independent Political Action could find congenial: the state would seize idle lands and factories and turn them over to farmers' and workers' cooperatives for production-for-use. In time, Sinclair predicted, these "public industries" would drive private industry out of business and usher in "The Cooperative Commonwealth."[12] In pursuit of that goal, Sinclair changed his party registration and declared himself a candidate for the Democratic nomination for governor.

To the astonishment of many party regulars, a groundswell of support, propelled by the desperate yearnings of Depression-plagued Californians, carried Sinclair to victory in the Democratic Party primary election in August 1934. Sinclair's candidacy created an instant dilemma for Franklin Roosevelt. Here was a bona fide gubernatorial nominee who was a Democrat, but one whose politics were wildly to the left of the president's and fantastically unsettling to most members of the president's party. Sinclair demanded a public presidential endorsement. The Roosevelt charm mollified Sinclair for a time after a personal meeting at Hyde Park in early September 1934. The president, Sinclair told reporters, was "one of the kindest and most genial and frank and open-minded and lovable men I have ever met."[13] But Roosevelt was not about to embrace what he regarded as Sinclair's lunatic proposals for confiscation of private property and the abolition of the profit system. The president kept his public silence on Sinclair's candidacy and abandoned the quixotic novelist to the ferocious assaults of California Republicans, orchestrated largely by movie magnate Louis B. Mayer. In a campaign unusually savage even by California's mud-and-circuses standards, Sinclair went down to decisive defeat. He salvaged what he could from the sorry episode by making it the subject of a new book: *I, Candidate for Governor: And How I Got Licked.*

EPIC had been endorsed by intellectuals like John Dos Passos and Theodore Dreiser, as well as by International Ladies Garment Workers Union leader David Dubinsky. They were sorely disappointed by the

12. Schlesinger 3:111–23; Davis 3:2–5, 423ff.
13. Davis 3:409.

outcome in California. Sinclair's defeat struck many on the left as emblematic of the problems with politics as usual, with the traditional political parties, and with Franklin Roosevelt himself, especially since Roosevelt's own efforts to grapple with the Depression had produced little result. "Failure is a hard word," declared the radical periodical *Common Sense* in late 1934, giving voice to the thoughts of many on the increasingly fractious and agitated left. "Yet we believe the record indicates that nothing but failure can be expected from the New Deal."[14]

As that sentiment spread, the possibility loomed that a leader might arise, someone more worldly than the moonstruck Sinclair, more broadgauged than the single-issue Townsend, more focused and disciplined than the sometimes feckless Olson, more earthy than the cerebral crowd around *Common Sense*, more in the American grain than the Socialists or the Communists — someone who could piece together a new political vessel to hold all the boiling discontents of a people increasingly confounded by the Depression. Politics, no less than nature, abhors a vacuum. Roosevelt had easily filled the space evacuated by Hoover's policy failures, but what might rush into the void created by the apparent failure of the New Deal? Perhaps this was one of those moments — rare in American history but its possibilities apparent even in other advanced democracies, as the Nazi ascendancy in Germany vividly illustrated — when a mass movement might wrest the initiative from the established political authorities and impose its own agenda on the nation.

WHO MIGHT LEAD such a movement? Extraordinary times generated extraordinary candidates, and in extraordinary profusion. Of the legions of radicals and demagogues and nostrum-mongers and just plain crackpots who flourished in the heated atmosphere of the Depression, none seemed at first a more unlikely messiah than the Reverend Charles Edward Coughlin, a Canadian-born Roman Catholic priest.

In 1926, at the age of thirty-four, Coughlin became the pastor of a tiny new parish in the Detroit suburb of Royal Oak, its church designated as a shrine to the recently canonized St. Therese of the Little Flower of Jesus. Numbering but twenty-five Catholic families, Coughlin's modest flock seemed an improbable power base from which to reach for national attention. And the bleak, gritty community of Royal Oak lay far from the hubs of national influence.

Yet Coughlin's little congregation, composed mostly of autoworkers

14. *Common Sense*, September 1934, 2, quoted in Leuchtenburg, 95.

just prosperous enough to move to suburbia from the soot and clang of Detroit's inner city, represented a rising force in American political life. These lower-middle-class Catholics, many of them scarcely a generation removed from their ancestral old countries, were grateful but wary beneficiaries of 1920s prosperity. They were not the poorest Americans, but rather those who had managed to step up just a rung or two on the ladder of social mobility. They were the kinds of people who proudly decorated their front parlors with framed photographs from the color rotogravure section of the Sunday newspaper, took an occasional vacation, bought a car on the installment plan, looked forward to one day owning their own home free and clear. The Depression had not so much impoverished them as it had swiftly checked their brave march toward realizing the American dream. In Royal Oak and in scores of other neighborhoods in and around the great industrial cities of the Northeast and upper Midwest, they huddled in their tightly knit ethnic enclaves, fretted about their precarious economic status, and fumed at what they felt was the implacable hostility of the Protestant majority. Coughlin had his own reminder of that hostility when the Ku Klux Klan welcomed him to Royal Oak by burning a cross on his church lawn. Leaders like Boston's James Michael Curley had already made careers out of quickening the anxieties and playing on the resentments of people like Coughlin's parishioners, but Curley and other Catholic mayors, like Tammany Hall's Jimmy Walker in New York and Chicago's Anton Cermak, were local figures. Coughlin aimed for national stature. The vehicle that would take him there, he believed, was a wondrous, newfangled technology scarcely a decade old: the radio.

The political and social effects of radio were only beginning to be felt in the late 1920s, let alone understood. For several years following the first commercial broadcasts on Detroit station WWJ in 1920, most radio stations operated at low power, usually under a hundred watts. Signals could be reliably transmitted only a few miles. Stations, many of them sponsored by local churches, labor unions, or ethnic organizations, served markets scarcely larger than neighborhoods. Much programming—religious services, talk shows, vaudeville entertainments, and "nationality hours" featuring news of Poland or Italy—catered to discrete ethnic communities in their native, old-world tongues. Radio thus made its debut as a technology that strengthened local institutions. But the new medium swiftly developed into an electronic floodgate through which flowed a one-way tide of mass cultural products that began to swamp the values and manners and tastes of once-isolated localities. The first five-thousand-watt transmitters appeared in 1925, and ten-thousand–watt stations were broadcasting by 1928. Networks soon provided platforms for commercially sponsored and nationally syndicated programs, beginning with *Amos 'n' Andy*, a perennially popular comedy show that first went on the air in 1928.

Radio assaulted the insularity of local communities. It also, not incidentally, catalyzed the homogenization of American popular culture. And it promised to revolutionize politics. Scholars later employed the term "disintermediation" to describe the potential political effects of radio (and eventually, of course, television). Radio provided a means to concentrate and exercise power from the top, to bypass and shrink the influence of leaders and institutions that had previously mediated between individuals and local communities on the one side and the national political parties and the national government on the other. And as in the realm of culture, in the political realm radio was for all practical purposes a one-way conduit. Powerful voices flowed out over the airwaves and washed over listeners by the millions. Few of those listeners could answer back. The radio created a political environment unimaginably distant from the give-and-take of the town meeting, which Thomas Jefferson had praised as "the best school of political liberty the world ever saw." Radio might be a medium of awesome power for good or ill. Franklin Roosevelt was among the first to sense its political possibilities. Father Charles Coughlin was another.[15]

Coughlin started modestly enough, when a microphone attached to his pulpit on October 17, 1926, carried the words of his Sunday sermon to the listening audience of Detroit station WJR. Within three years stations in Chicago and Cincinnati were also carrying his message. In 1930 he struck a deal with the Columbia Broadcasting System to transmit his sermons nationwide. By the time the Depression had fully engulfed the country, tens of millions of Americans regularly gathered around their radio receivers on Sunday afternoons to listen to the "Radio Priest." In ethnic neighborhoods in the stricken industrial belt, residents could walk for blocks on a summer Sunday and never miss a word of Father Coughlin's voice radiating out of open parlor windows.

And what a voice it was! Lightly brushed with brogue, melodic and soothing, it was a voice, the novelist Wallace Stegner said, "of such

15. Lizabeth Cohen, *Making a New Deal: Industrial Workers in Chicago, 1919–1939* (Cambridge: Cambridge University Press, 1990), 129ff., offers an excellent discussion of the earliest impact of radio.

mellow richness, such manly, heart-warming, confidential intimacy, such emotional and ingratiating charm, that anyone turning past it on the radio dial almost automatically returned to hear it again." It was, Stegner concluded, "without doubt one of the great speaking voices of the twentieth century. . . . It was a voice made for promises."[16]

It was also a voice that increasingly spoke not of religion but of politics. Coughlin's earliest broadcasts addressed such topics as the meaning of the sacraments and the evils of birth control, but he struck out in a new direction when his sermon of January 12, 1930, ferociously attacked Communism—then threatening to win converts among the swelling ranks of Detroit's unemployed autoworkers. Before long, loosely adopting the Catholic social-justice doctrines expressed in the papal encyclicals *Rerum Novarum* (1891) and *Quadragesimo Anno* (1931), Coughlin was hurling invective at Herbert Hoover, denouncing international bankers, railing at the gold standard, demanding inflation—above all, inflation through the monetization of silver—and declaiming on the virtues of nationalizing the entire American banking system. "I knew damn well," he irreverently reflected, uncloaking the megalomania that would eventually help to undo him, "that the little people, the average man, was suffering. I also knew that no one had the courage to tell the truth about why the nation was in such mortal danger. I knew that if anyone was going to inform the American citizenry, it would have to be me."[17] Millions of listeners lapped up his message. By 1932 Coughlin's fan mail, much of it stuffed with cash, required the attention of 106 clerks and four personal secretaries. Two years later, he was receiving more mail than any other person in the United States, including the president.

Little of this, especially Coughlin's readiness to rain verbal blows on an already reeling Herbert Hoover, was lost on Franklin Roosevelt. In May 1931 a relative in Detroit wrote to Roosevelt that Coughlin "has a following just about equal to that of Mr. Ghandi. . . . He would like to tender his services. . . . He would be difficult to handle and might be full of dynamite, but I think you had better prepare to say 'yes' or 'no.'"

Roosevelt hesitated at first, but no politician aspiring to the presidency

16. Alan Brinkley, *Voices of Protest: Huey Long, Father Coughlin, and the Great Depression* (New York: Knopf, 1982), 90. For much of my account of both Coughlin and Huey Long, and especially for my understanding of the ideology they represented, I am deeply indebted to Brinkley's study.

17. Michael R. Beschloss, *Kennedy and Roosevelt: An Uneasy Alliance* (New York: Norton, 1980), 114.

could afford to ignore those dazzling Coughlin numbers. More specifically, Roosevelt doubtless saw in Coughlin a bridge to the Catholic immigrant communities that he hoped to bring into his national electoral coalition. Accordingly, Roosevelt cultivated Coughlin through two dependable Irish-Catholic intermediaries: the financier Joseph P. Kennedy and the liberal Detroit mayor, Frank Murphy. At their urging, the priest—"Padre," Roosevelt intimately called him—visited candidate Roosevelt twice in 1932 and sent him a sycophantish telegram upon Roosevelt's receipt of the Democratic nomination: "I am with you to the end. Say the word and I will follow."[18]

In the ensuing campaign, Coughlin sulfurously condemned Hoover, to Roosevelt's undoubted delight and certain benefit. In the early months of the New Deal the "padre" further ingratiated himself to Roosevelt with florid endorsements of the new president's political program. "The New Deal is Christ's deal!" he intoned. The country faced the choice, said Coughlin, of "Roosevelt or ruin." Intoxicated with his apparent access to power, Coughlin took to dropping in unannounced at the White House, joking chummily with Roosevelt's staff, lacing his remarks to reporters with intimate references to "the Boss," and presumptuously suggesting lists of good Catholics who should receive ambassadorial appointments. This false familiarity got to be too much for the president. "Who the hell does he think he is?" Roosevelt asked an aide. "He should run for the Presidency himself."[19]

Given the country's religious prejudices, Coughlin's Roman collar made such a run improbable. Given the Constitution, his Canadian birth made it impossible. But neither religious scruple nor legal impediment could compromise the Radio Priest's campaign against the Money Power—that old American nemesis, ensconced in Wall Street, entwined with the dread international bankers, its machinations, Coughlin darkly hinted, cunningly orchestrated by a sinister Jewish directorate. As the Depression persisted, as Roosevelt rehabilitated rather than expropriated the banks, and especially as he failed to pursue inflationary policies with sufficient vigor, Coughlin grew increasingly critical of the New Deal. When the Treasury Department in early 1934 sought to check the silverites by publishing a list of silver speculators that included the name of Coughlin's own private secretary, Coughlin raged against the enemies

18. Charles J. Tull, *Father Coughlin and the New Deal* (Syracuse: Syracuse University Press, 1965), 15.
19. Beschloss, *Kennedy and Roosevelt*, 116.

of "gentile silver" and challenged the Democratic Party, on pain of "political death," to explain "why there is want in the midst of plenty." Now more than ever, he pointedly announced, "I am in favor of *a* New Deal."[20]

Coughlin soon went further. The old political parties, he declared late in 1934, "are all but dead" and should "relinquish the skeletons of their putrefying carcasses to the halls of a historical museum."[21] On November 11, 1934, he announced the birth of a new political body, which he christened the National Union for Social Justice. Its platform of "Sixteen Principles" encompassed pleas for monetary reforms, as well as calls for the nationalization of key industries and protection of the rights of labor. Though it had scant organizational structure and an indeterminate membership—estimates ran as high as eight million—the National Union represented a potentially formidable new political force, one that might mobilize the immigrant industrial workers who by now had been seething in unwanted idleness for five years. In all but name, it was a new political party, or certainly aspired to be. In all but its demographic base, it resurrected the Populist movement of the 1890s, complete with monetary obsessions, conspiracy theories, cranky anti-internationalism, and innuendoes of anti-Semitism. Moving ever farther away from Roosevelt, whom he shortly accused of having "out-Hoovered Hoover" and protecting "plutocrats" as well as "communists," Coughlin soon seized an opportunity to field-test this new political machine.

On January 16, 1935, Roosevelt asked for approval of a treaty providing for American affiliation with the World Court, seated at The Hague. Many members of the president's official family thought from the outset that the proposal to join the Court was a political error. "I have been surprised all along that the President should make this such an issue as he has made it," Harold Ickes wrote in his diary. "I am confident that the sentiment of the country is overwhelmingly opposed to going into the League Court. . . . [I]f this proposition were put to a vote of the people, it would be defeated two to one."[22] But to Roosevelt, the proposal represented a small gesture that might temper the isolationist image he had projected at the time of the London Economic Conference. Roosevelt was growing increasingly convinced that the international situation was deteriorating dangerously, as evidenced by Japan's recent

20. Brinkley, *Voices of Protest*, 123.
21. Schlesinger 3:24.
22. Ickes Diary 1:284.

An End and a Beginning

Armistice Day, November 11, 1918. These Philadelphians cheering the end of the Great War did not yet understand how dark a shadow the war was to cast over their future. The peace agreement that President Woodrow Wilson helped to negotiate left many questions unsettled and sowed the seeds of an even greater war scarcely a generation later. The mood of celebration in America eventually gave way to disillusionment with foreign entanglements and a reinvigorated isolationism. (NATIONAL ARCHIVES W&C 715)

American Life on the Eve of the Depression

Doing the washing, Iowa, 1922. (NATIONAL ARCHIVES RG 33SC-1241)

A *kitchen in Maryland, 1929.* Rural America was virtually another country in the 1920s, lacking amenities like indoor plumbing and electricity that were common in cities. This Iowa woman had probably pumped water from a well to do her laundry; the Maryland family whose kitchen is shown here cooked and heated their house with a wood stove and lit their spare rooms with oil lamps or candles. (NATIONAL ARCHIVES 33SC-11870)

"Little Italy," Chicago, in the pre-Depression era. Well into the 1920s and beyond, many immigrants lived in insular, parochial communities on the margins of American society. (CHICAGO HISTORICAL SOCIETY ICHI-24279)

In black America: Mississippi sharecroppers near Vicksburg, Mississippi, 1936. More than 80 percent of African-Americans dwelled in the South until the eve of World War II. Segregated, disen-
franchised, and largely confined to sharecropping, they were the poorest of the poor in the
nation's most economically backward region, and no strangers to suffering, well before the Depression descended. (LIBRARY OF CONGRESS LC-USF34T01-9575)

*Restaurant, Lancaster,
Ohio, 1938.* Racial segregation in pre–World War
II America was not con-
fined to the South, as
this Ohio restaurant
unapologetically adver-
tised. (LIBRARY OF CON-
GRESS LC-USF 3301-6392-
M4)

A Stricken People

Panic. After the great stock market crash of 1929, frightened depositors rushed to withdraw their funds before their banks failed, driving the economic spiral even more steeply downward. (FRANKLIN D. ROOSEVELT LIBRARY 7420 [1007])

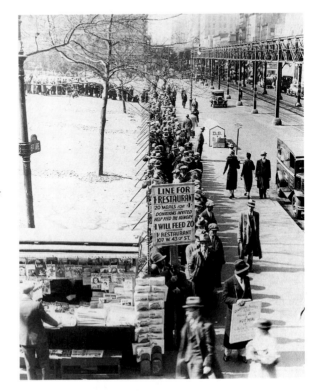

Breadline, New York City, 1932. The swelling ranks of the unemployed had overwhelmed local charities and governments by 1932, making some kind of federal relief effort all but inevitable. In the process of implementing that effort, the federal government transformed its role in American society. (FRANKLIN D. ROOSEVELT LIBRARY 97107 [1])

"Okies," California, 1935. Thousands of refugees from the drought-plagued Oklahoma-Texas-Kansas "Dust Bowl" headed west in the Depression years, with misery as their unshakeable companion. (FRANKLIN D. ROOSEVELT LIBRARY 53227 [575])

Cotton pickers, Arizona, 1940. Migrant agricultural workers lived a hand-to-mouth existence on the road, making do in crude shelters like this one, with no sanitation, no water, no electricity, and no prospects. (NATIONAL ARCHIVES 83-G-44357)

THERE IS A SANTA CLAUS!

The Great Engineer, 1929. In the early months of the Depression, President Herbert Hoover was widely regarded as a vigorous, effective battler against the economic crisis. (LIBRARY OF CONGRESS LC-USZ62-38795)

The humiliation of Hoover, 1932. After more than three years of Depression, Hoover's reputation had taken a brutal beating. (LIBRARY OF CONGRESS LC-USZ62-19646)

The changing of the guard, 1933. Hoover's and Roosevelt's faces on their way to FDR's inauguration reflected their different temperaments as well as their different political fortunes. (FRANKLIN D. ROOSEVELT LIBRARY)

The Coming of the New Deal

The blue eagle. The National Recovery Administration's symbol was ubiquitous in the early New Deal years—until the NRA was struck down by the Supreme Court in 1935. The NRA was the most ambitious federal economic program in history, but it did not bring recovery. (FRANKLIN D. ROOSEVELT LIBRARY 7163)

The Civilian Conservation Corps. The CCC was among the most popular of the New Deal's programs. It put thousands of young men to work restoring the nation's blighted forests and building outdoor recreational facilities. (FRANKLIN D. ROOSEVELT LIBRARY 7420 [273])

Work Projects Administration artists at work. WPA artists enhanced many public spaces in the Depression years. These muralists worked on "The Role of the Immigrant in the Industrial Development of America" for the dining room of the historic immigrant-receiving center on New York's Ellis Island. (NATIONAL ARCHIVES RG 69-AG-413)

The National Youth Administration. These young women at an NYA center in Phoenix, Arizona, in 1936 were being schooled for jobs as domestic servants. Taking America as it found it, the NYA dared not disturb deeply entrenched habits of racial and occupational segregation—a pattern to which many New Deal programs conformed. (FRANKLIN D. ROOSEVELT LIBRARY 5251 [107])

Social Security. Elderly Americans like this couple began to receive their first Social Security checks in 1940. Social Security laid the foundation of the modern American welfare state, and has proved among the most consequential and durable of all the New Deal's reforms. (NATIONAL ARCHIVES RG 47-GA-4-2529-2-1-C)

A Different Kind of President

The common touch. FDR chats with a North Dakota farmer in 1936. Roosevelt touched the hearts of his countrymen like no predecessor in memory. His "fireside chats" on the radio brought his voice and his warm, avuncular personality into millions of homes, revolutionizing the relationship of ordinary Americans with the presidency. (FRANKLIN D. ROOSEVELT LIBRARY)

"Come along. We're going to the Trans-Lux to hiss Roosevelt." By 1936, many well-to-do Americans condemned Roosevelt as a "class traitor" whose policies exacerbated class divisions and punished the successful. Both accusations were grossly overdrawn. (DRAWING BY PETER ARNO, © 1936, THE NEW YORKER MAGAZINE)

"Yes, You Remembered Me." Roosevelt's New Deal won the political loyalty of millions of working-class voters and helped the Democrats achieve huge electoral majorities in 1936. Yet within months of that enormous victory, Roosevelt found himself politically on the defensive. He faced a resurgent conservative bloc in Congress, a new economic crisis, and a badly deteriorating international situation. The New Deal was effectively finished even before Roosevelt began his second term in 1937. (LIBRARY OF CONGRESS LC-USZ62-34309; © NEW YORK DAILY NEWS, I.P., REPRINTED WITH PERMISSION)

The Specter of Class War

Picket line, Greensboro, Georgia, 1934. The New Deal gave a mighty impetus to union-organizing campaigns, but often proved unable to control the forces it had unleashed. These textile workers were part of an industry-wide shut-down that eventually produced scores of arrests and the deaths of fourteen strikers. It ended with an uneasy settlement that pleased neither side. (LIBRARY OF CONGRESS LC-USF33-20936-MZ)

Minneapolis, 1934. A virtual civil war rocked Minneapolis in the summer of 1934. This clash between striking truck drivers and police left more than sixty strikers wounded and two dead. (FRANKLIN D. ROOSEVELT LIBRARY 72142)

The Battle of the Overpass. Goons from the Ford Motor Company's "Service Department"—in reality a private police force dedicated to suppressing trade unions at Ford—assaulted a group of union organizers trying to distribute handbills outside Ford's River Rouge plant on May 26, 1937. Just four days later, one of the bloodiest confrontations in American labor history, the so-called Memorial Day Massacre, left ten men dead outside Republic Steel's Chicago works. (FRANKLIN D. ROOSEVELT LIBRARY 7819 [4])

Eleanor Roosevelt. The First Lady visits a WPA-sponsored Negro nursery school in Des Moines, Iowa, in 1936. She served as the New Deal's conscience and as the President's ambassador to black America. (FRANKLIN D. ROOSEVELT LIBRARY 64141)

Harry Hopkins. A former social worker, he administered the New Deal's vast relief programs and eventually became Roosevelt's most trusted adviser and confidant during World War II. (LIBRARY OF CONGRESS LC-USZ6 2-36963)

FDR, Interior Secretary Harold Ickes, and Agriculture Secretary Henry A. Wallace. Ickes and Wallace were both former Republicans. Their appointments reflected Roosevelt's strategy of trying to build a new liberal coalition that would absorb Republican progressives. Ickes served into the Truman administration, but Wallace proved too left-wing for many traditional Democrats. Sorely aggrieved when Roosevelt named Wallace as his vice-presidential running mate in 1940, they forced Wallace off the ticket in 1944, paving the way for Harry S. Truman's nomination. (LIBRARY OF CONGRESS LC-USZ6 2-98147)

Huey P. Long. The Louisiana senator seemed poised to mount a radical challenge to the New Deal, but he was cut down by an assassin's gun in September 1935. (LIBRARY OF CONGRESS LC-USZ6 2-111013)

John L. Lewis. A virtuoso of bombast and invective, Lewis galvanized the movement for industrial unionism and helped deliver the labor vote for Roosevelt in 1936. Four years later, strenuously disagreeing with FDR's pro-British foreign policies, he endorsed Wendell Willkie for the presidency. (UPI/CORBIS-BETTMANN)

Father Charles E. Coughlin. Like Roosevelt, Coughlin was a master of the new medium of radio. An early supporter of the New Deal, he later became a bitter critic. His anti-Semitic rantings eventually caused the Catholic church to silence him. (LIBRARY OF CONGRESS LC-USZ6 2-111027)

Adolf Hitler. The Nazi leader at a party rally in Nuremberg in 1928. In January 1933 he would assume the German chancellorship, just two months before Roosevelt's inauguration as president. All the New Deal was played out under the lengthening shadow of the Nazi menace. In 1939 Hitler would plunge the world—including, eventually, a reluctant United States—into history's most awful war. (NATIONAL ARCHIVES 242-HAP-1928 [46])

repudiation of the naval limitation agreements of the preceding decade and Tokyo's apparent determination to plunge ahead with the construction of a huge new battle fleet. In the face of such challenges, America could ill afford to stand by idly, Roosevelt reasoned. He hoped to send a modest signal to the world that he had not fully repudiated his own internationalist convictions, forged in the service of Woodrow Wilson, abandoned temporarily in 1932 and 1933, but awakened again in the gathering world crisis of the mid-1930s. Adherence to the Court might also serve an educational purpose at home, weaning Americans ever so slightly from the complacent parochialism they had reembraced after the debacle of the Great War. After careful polling of the huge Democratic majority in the new Senate, and with assurances that American sovereignty would be in no way imperiled by Court membership, Roosevelt went ahead, confident of success.

Coughlin had other ideas. On Sunday, January 27, he preached over the airwaves on "the menace of the World Court," denouncing Roosevelt's proposal as well as "the international bankers" who were the alleged beneficiaries of the president's nefarious ploy. He urged his listeners to send telegrams to their senators demanding a "no" vote. Prodded also by the isolationist Hearst press, Coughlin's vast audience responded with an avalanche of telegrams, wheelbarrowed by the hundreds of thousands into the Senate Office Building on the morning of Monday, January 28. The following day the Senate failed to muster the two-thirds vote necessary to ratify the Court treaty. "I do not intend to have these gentlemen whose names I cannot even pronounce, let alone spell, passing upon the rights of the American people," declared Louisiana senator Huey Long. The Court proposal, seemingly a sure thing just days earlier, died. Roosevelt was stunned. "The radio talks of people like Coughlin turned the trick against us," he gloomily wrote to a friend.[23]

The World Court fight provided a lightning demonstration of Coughlin's power and dealt a stinging blow to Roosevelt. "The legend of invulnerability fades fast," wrote the columnist Arthur Krock. Roosevelt's considerable political reputation had perceptibly shrunk, not to mention his hard political influence, especially in the increasingly urgent realm of diplomacy. If even the modest and largely symbolic act of associating

23. T. Harry Williams, *Huey Long* (New York: Knopf, 1969), 800; Elliott Roosevelt, ed., *FDR: His Personal Letters, 1928–1945* (New York: Duell, Sloan, and Pearce, 1950), 451.

with the international tribunal at The Hague could be so summarily rejected, there seemed little prospect that Roosevelt could nudge his countrymen away from their historic isolationism and toward any kind of meaningful commitment to join with the other democracies in resisting the rising menace of dictatorship and aggression. Roosevelt was especially bitter about the senators who had been swayed by Coughlin's campaign. "As to the 36 Gentlemen who voted against the principle of a World Court," he wrote to Senate Majority Leader Joseph Robinson, "I am inclined to think that if they ever get to Heaven they will be doing a great deal of apologizing for a very long time—that is if God is against war—and I think he is."[24]

No less dispiriting to FDR than the actual defeat on the World Court treaty was the manner of its accomplishment. As Coughlin moved to consolidate and wield his political influence, he exhibited a wicked genius for unsealing some of the dankest chambers of the national soul. He played guilefully on his followers' worst instincts: their suspicious provincialism, their unworldly ignorance, their yearning for simple explanations and extravagant remedies for their undeniable problems, their readiness to believe in conspiracies, their sulky resentments, and their all too human capacity for hatred. The National Union for Social Justice remained an inchoate entity in early 1935, and Coughlin's sustainable political strength was still a matter of conjecture. But if the Radio Priest could succeed in shepherding his followers into an alliance with some of the other dissident protest movements rumbling across the land, those led by Townsend and Sinclair in California, by Olson and the La Follettes in the upper Midwest, and, especially, by the mercurial senator from Louisiana, Huey Pierce Long, there was no telling what disruptive furies might be unleashed.

Of all those figures, Long was the shrewdest operator and the most thoroughly professional politician. He had brains, money, ambition, extravagant oratorical skills, a gift for political theater, and a lupine instinct for the nation's political jugular. He was the radical most likely to succeed. Long was also an extreme example of a political species native to American democracy, a species recognizable by its distinctive tongue. Long spoke a language more passionate and colorful than others of his genus, but like Coughlin he spoke nevertheless in the familiar accents of American populism. Populism was an American-made idiom. It was

24. Edgar B. Nixon, ed., *Franklin D. Roosevelt and Foreign Affairs* (Cambridge: Belknap Press of Harvard University Press, 1969), 2:381.

audible to listeners as far back as Alexis de Tocqueville in the days of Andrew Jackson. It swelled to a roar in the People's Party upheavals of the 1890s and never fully subsided. Often cast in the rough cadences of untutored, rural American speech, the populist dialect gave voice to the fears of the powerless and the animosities of the alienated. It spoke of equality and freedom, but the greater of these was equality. Equality, Tocqueville wrote, was the principal "passion" of the Americans. In pursuit of equality, the Americans were "ardent, insatiable, incessant, invincible; they call for equality in freedom; and if they cannot obtain that, they still call for equality in slavery. They will endure poverty, servitude, barbarism, but they will not endure aristocracy."[25] Populism contrasted the virtues of "the people" to the vices of shadowy elites whose greedy manipulations oppressed the poor and perverted democracy. It was always a language of resentment, of raw class antagonism, edged with envy and grudge. In the charged atmosphere of the 1930s, it could easily become a language of reprisal.[26]

Long had mastered the populist tongue to a degree that few could match, before or since. Other than Franklin Roosevelt himself, no figure flashed more incandescently across the Depression-darkened American political landscape. Fulminating against wealth and Wall Street, incanting the excellences and the tribulations of the common man, Long strutted across the national stage full of sound and fury. For a long, tense season, it seemed that the traditional political system could contain neither him nor the pent-up rancor that he threatened to release.

Long hailed from Winn Parish, a pine-covered, red-soil district in the north central Louisiana uplands. Winn was a place of one-man-and-a-mule farms, small lumber mills, and scant graces. It was peopled mainly with plain-living white Southern Baptists with little to boast of on this earth save their reputation for cussedness. For generations, they had suspicioned outsiders and writhed under the twin burdens of poverty and powerlessness, the weight of the first attributed directly to the persistence of the latter. Many of their forebears had been Unionists in secessionist Louisiana; others had spearheaded Louisiana's Populist movement in the 1890s; still others had voted heavily for Socialist presidential candidate Eugene Debs in 1912. None of these fitful gestures

25. Alexis de Tocqueville, *Democracy in America* (New York: Vintage, 1945), 2:102–3.
26. For an extended discussion of the populist strand in American political culture, see Michael Kazin, *The Populist Persuasion: An American History* (New York: Basic, 1995).

of defiance had improved their lot. Winn endured as a changeless hummock of contrariness in one of the poorest and most corrupt states of the Union. On the eve of the Depression, one-fifth of the adult white men in the state, and a much higher proportion of blacks, were illiterate. Despite Louisiana's rich natural endowments of oil and gas, an oligarchy of self-satisfied businessmen and haughty planters kept the state's per capita income lower than in all but nine other states.

Long had been born in 1893, when the Populist movement was cresting in popularity. More than the signs of the zodiac, the earthly place and historical moment of his birth marked him. He was the legatee of a rank heritage of sour resentment and frustrated radicalism. Few men more naturally came by the temperament of the aginner.

Long first ran for public office in 1918, standing successfully for the post of state railroad commissioner. Throughout the 1920s Commissioner Long made a reputation as a champion of the people and the scourge of the big corporations, especially the Standard Oil Company, that ruled the state with baronial sway. In 1928 he campaigned for governor on a slogan that distilled the essence of the old populist dream of unchained affluence and radical leveling: "Every man a king, but no one wears a crown." Capitalizing on the state's festering economic grievances, Long won handsomely. Now, Long told his followers on election night, "We'll show 'em who's boss. . . . You fellers stick by me. . . . We're just getting started."[27]

Just getting started indeed. Governor Long went to work with single-minded intensity. He jacked up taxes on oil and gas producers and used the revenue for badly needed improvements to the state's highway system, free textbooks for schoolchildren, and new hospitals and public buildings. Meanwhile he closed his grip over the state's political apparatus, making Louisiana the closest thing to a dictatorship that America has ever known.

Elected to the U.S. Senate in 1930, Long refused to vacate the governorship for nearly two more years, holding both offices simultaneously. Arriving at last to take up his Senate seat in June 1933, he called at the White House to see Franklin Roosevelt. "Frank," Long called the president, whose Harvard airs and polished manners galled the populist from Winn. In a studied gesture of brazen disrespect, Long cheekily neglected to doff his straw hat, removing it only for an occasional emphatic tap on Roosevelt's immobile knee. On this occasion and countless others,

27. Brinkley, *Voices of Protest*, 22.

Long exuded contempt for the national political establishment, for the moguls and insiders and "high hats" who looked down their noses at the likes of Winn Parish's honest rednecked yeomen. "All I care," he said, "is what the boys at the forks of the creek think of me."[28]

They loved him. Louisianans allowed Long and his lieutenants to seize unprecedented power. Through graft and coercion Long filled a bulging political war chest. Secure in his home state and robustly financed, Long strode into the national arena in the role of hillbilly hero and played it with gusto. He wore white silk suits and pink silk ties, womanized openly, swilled whiskey in the finest bars, swaggered his way around Washington, and breathed defiance into the teeth of his critics. The president's mother called him "that *awful* man." His friends called him "Kingfish," after a character on the radio program *Amos 'n' Andy*. ("*Der* Kingfish," said Long's critics, seeing parallels with another dangerous demagogue.) The *New York Times* called him "a man with a front of brass and lungs of leather." Franklin Roosevelt called him "one of the two most dangerous men in the country." (The other, said Roosevelt, was Army Chief of Staff Douglas MacArthur.)[29]

Like Father Coughlin, Long at first supported the New Deal, especially its early emphasis on inflation. But the Economy Act and especially the NRA convinced him that Roosevelt was just another contemptible high-hatter, in bed with the Money Power and the big corporations and the entrenched elites of the loathsome Eastern Establishment. Like Father Coughlin, he was soon ready openly to repudiate the Roosevelt program. And like Father Coughlin, indeed like Roosevelt himself, he relied on the radio to reach his audience and build his political base.[30]

Like Upton Sinclair, Long also relied on the written word to spread his message. In October 1933 he published an autobiography, *Every Man a King*, and in 1935, in direct imitation of Sinclair, *My First Days in the White House*. Neither book impressed the critics, one of whom sneered that Long was "unbalanced, vulgar, in many ways ignorant, and quite reckless." Long, however, cared little for the encomia of the literati. His books, says historian Alan Brinkley, were "intended for men

28. Brinkley, *Voices of Protest*, 75.
29. Schlesinger 3:61; Brinkley, *Voices of Protest*, 56–58.
30. Like Father Coughlin, too, Long found himself the object of counterattacks from the Roosevelt administration. The president blocked all federal patronage to the Long machine in Louisiana and ordered an Internal Revenue Service investigation of Long and his political associates.

and women not in the habit of reading books." Those who were in the habit could read thinly fictionalized accounts of characters based on Long in Sinclair Lewis's *It Can't Happen Here* (1935), a cautionary tale about the possibilities of a native American fascism, and later in Robert Penn Warren's *All the King's Men* (1946), a sensitive novel about the psychology of power and corruption.[31]

In 1934 Long launched the Share Our Wealth Society. He took to the airwaves to describe its simple platform: he would make "every man a king" by confiscating large fortunes, levying steeply progressive income taxes, and distributing the revenue to every American family in the form of a "household estate" of five thousand dollars — enough, he suggested, for a home, an automobile, and, significantly, a radio. In addition, each family would be guaranteed a minimum annual income of twenty-five hundred dollars per year (nearly double the median family income at the time).[32] Nor was that all: Long added promises of shorter working hours, improved veterans' benefits, educational subsidies for the young, and pensions for the elderly. ("This attracted a lot of Townsendites to us," crowed one of Long's minions.)[33] He pitched his program in terms long familiar in Winn Parish, painting a picture of an American Eden corrupted by the serpent of monopoly power:

> God invited us all to come and eat and drink all we wanted. He smiled on our land and we grew crops of plenty to eat and wear. He showed us in the earth the iron and other things to make everything we wanted. He unfolded to us the secrets of science so that our work might be easy. God called: 'Come to my feast!' [But then] Rockefeller, Morgan, and their crowd stepped up and took enough for 120,000,000 people and left only enough for 5,000,000 for all the other 125,000,000 to eat. And so many millions must go hungry and without those good things God gave us unless we call on them to put some of it back.[34]

Contemporary analysts estimated that even if all existing wealth were in liquid form and could be cashed out and distributed, confiscating all fortunes larger than a million dollars (more than Long called for) would produce not five thousand dollars per family but a mere four hundred. The heavy taxes necessary to guarantee a minimum income to all of twenty-five hundred per year would leave no individual's annual income

31. Brinkley, *Voices of Protest*, 70.
32. *HSUS*, 303, gives median family income as $1,231 in 1939.
33. Schlesinger 3:63.
34. Brinkley, *Voices of Protest*, 70.

above three thousand dollars. Long cared little for such arithmetic. He knew that though the Share Our Wealth scheme, like the Townsend Plan, might be the stuff of shoddy economic fantasy, it was shiny, twenty-four-carat political gold. "Be prepared for the slurs and snickers of some high ups," he cautioned his listeners. "Let no one tell you that it is difficult to redistribute the wealth of this land. It is simple."[35]

As 1935 opened, Long stepped up his radio appearances. On January 9 he told a national audience that he had "begged and pleaded and did everything else under the sun" to "try to get Mr. Roosevelt to keep his word that he gave us." But now he had given up. "Hope for more through Roosevelt? He has promised and promised, smiled and bowed. . . . There is no use to wait three more years. It is not Roosevelt or ruin, it is Roosevelt's ruin." Long boldly pressed the attack, indicting not just the president's policies but also his person: "When I saw him spending all his time of ease and recreation with the big partners of Mr. John D. Rockefeller, Jr., with such men as the Astors and company, maybe I ought to have had better sense than to have believed he would ever break down their big fortunes to give enough to the masses to end poverty." Before long, the Kingfish took to calling Roosevelt the "Knight of the *Nourmahal*" (Vincent Astor's yacht, on which FDR frequently vacationed).[36]

Long's broadcasts regularly elicited more than a hundred thousand letters of support. Within a year the nationally organized Share Our Wealth Society claimed five million members, perhaps an exaggeration but at least roughly suggestive of the national audience Long was awakening. Long began to reach out to other dissidents. "Father Coughlin has a damn good platform," said Long, "and I'm 100 percent for him. . . . What he thinks is right down my alley." What Coughlin and Long thought made sense to many Americans mystified by the Depression and chafing still at the persistent spectacle of want amidst plenty. In Wisconsin, the La Follettes' official organ, the *Progressive*, editorialized that it did not agree "with every conclusion reached by Father Coughlin and Senator Long, [but] when they contend . . . that the tremendous wealth of this country should be more equitably shared for a more abundant life for the masses of the people, we agree heartily with them."[37] Long made overtures to the Townsendites and the survivors of the EPIC

35. Schlesinger 3:64; Brinkley, *Voices of Protest*, 73.
36. *New York Times*, January 10, 1935, 1; Davis 3:502.
37. Schlesinger 3:249; Brinkley, *Voices of Protest*, 232.

fiasco in California. In the spring of 1935 Milo Reno introduced him to a Farmers Holiday Association convention in Des Moines. "Do you believe in the redistribution of wealth?" Long asked. The crowd of more than ten thousand roared back a unanimous "Yes!" "I could take this state like a whirlwind," Long exulted. In Philadelphia Long spoke to an enthusiastic crowd in March 1935. Surveying the scene, Philadelphia's former mayor said: "There are 250,000 Long votes."[38] "I'll tell you here and now," Long said to reporters a few months later, "that Franklin Roosevelt will not be the next President of the United States. If the Democrats nominate Roosevelt and the Republicans nominate Hoover, Huey Long will be your next President."[39]

In the Roosevelt circle, this blustering was taken seriously. On the evening of March 4, 1935, on a nationwide NBC radio broadcast marking the second anniversary of Roosevelt's inauguration, Hugh Johnson, still a Roosevelt loyalist despite being sacked from the directorship of the NRA just months earlier, loosed his intimidating powers of invective against the "great Louisiana demagogue and this political padre." Long and Coughlin spoke, Johnson complained, "with nothing of learning, knowledge nor experience to lead us through a labyrinth that has perplexed the minds of men since the beginning of time. . . . These two men are raging up and down this land preaching not construction but destruction—not reform but revolution." And, Johnson warned, they were finding a receptive audience. "You can laugh at Father Coughlin, you can snort at Huey Long—but this country was never under a greater menace."[40]

Louis Howe, Roosevelt's most trusted and loyal adviser, closely monitored the Coughlin and Long phenomena. In early 1935 he sent the president a copy of a letter from a Montana banker, "who, of all people, has been converted by Huey Long. . . . It is symptoms like this I think we should watch very carefully," Howe admonished.[41] Soon thereafter Postmaster General and Democratic Committee chairman James Farley commissioned a secret poll to "find out if Huey's sales talks for his 'share the wealth' program were attracting many customers. . . . We kept a careful eye on what Huey and his political allies . . . were attempting to do." The results surprised and dismayed Farley. The poll indicated that Long,

38. Brinkley, *Voices of Protest*, 237, 170.
39. Brinkley, *Voices of Protest*, 81.
40. Brinkley, *Voices of Protest*, 6.
41. E. Roosevelt, *FDR: His Personal Letters*, 460.

running for the presidency on a third-party ticket, could attract as many as four million votes, about 10 percent of the anticipated total in 1936. Farley's poll also demonstrated that Long was succeeding in making himself a national figure, with strength in the North as well as the South, in industrial centers as well as rural areas. "It was easy to conceive a situation," Farley concluded, "whereby Long, by polling more than 3,000,000 votes, might have the balance of power in the 1936 election. For example, the poll indicated that he would command upward of 100,000 votes in New York State, a pivotal state in any national election; and a vote of that size could easily mean the difference between victory or defeat. . . . [T]hat number of votes . . . would come mostly from our side, and the result might spell disaster." Roosevelt shared that assessment. "Long plans to be a candidate of the Hitler type for the presidency in 1936," he told William E. Dodd, his ambassador to Germany. "He thinks he will have a hundred votes in the Democratic convention. Then he will set up as an independent with Southern and mid-western Progressives. . . . Thus he hopes to defeat the Democratic party and put in a reactionary Republican. That would bring the country to such a state by 1940 that Long thinks he would be made dictator. There are in fact some Southerners looking that way, and some Progressives are drifting that way. . . . Thus it is an ominous situation."[42]

Long, said a worried Democratic senator, "is brilliant and dangerous. He is industrious and has much capacity. The depression has increased radicalism in this country—nobody knows how much. Long is making every preparation to unite it politically in 1936. . . . We are obliged to propose and accept many things in the New Deal that otherwise we would not because we must prevent a union of discontent around him. The President is the only hope of the conservatives and the liberals; if his program is restricted, the answer may be Huey Long."[43]

Comments like that have led many historians to argue that Roosevelt, who was about to propose several dramatic reform proposals in 1935, did so principally in response to pressure from Long and Coughlin. Without the demagogues, the argument implies, there might never have been a genuine New Deal, and what liberalism was in it was wrung from a reluctant, temperamentally conservative Roosevelt only under

42. James A. Farley, *Behind the Ballots: The Personal History of a Politician* (New York: Harcourt, Brace, 1938), 249–50; William E. Dodd Jr. and Martha Dodd, eds., *Ambassador Dodd's Diary, 1933–1938* (New York: Harcourt, Brace, 1941), 213–14.

43. *New York Times*, January 10, 1935, 10.

threat of his own political extinction. Even Roosevelt's son Elliott claimed that the entire epochal legislative program of 1935 — the landmark laws that constituted what is sometimes, and somewhat misleadingly, labeled the "Second New Deal," including the Emergency Relief Appropriation Act, the Banking Act, the Wagner National Labor Relations Act, the Public Utility Holding Companies Act, the Social Security Act, and the Wealth Tax Act — were "designed to cut the ground from under the demagogues."[44]

That judgment is surely exaggerated. Many of the measures that came to pass in 1935 — most notably the Social Security Act, the most consequential of New Deal achievements — had been on deck well before "the demagogue and the padre" had their innings. Roosevelt and Harry Hopkins had been seeking major revisions in relief policy since the winter of 1933–34. Banking reform had been on the New Deal's agenda since the first of the Hundred Days. Senator Robert Wagner had been pushing for years to enact policies like those embodied in the National Labor Relations Bill. Utilities reform had been among Roosevelt's highest priorities when he was governor of New York. As for Social Security, Roosevelt had endorsed the basic concept at least as early as 1930. Only the Wealth Tax Act truly answers to the description of a Roosevelt political initiative undertaken in direct response to the Coughlin and Long agitation.

YET IF COUGHLIN AND LONG did not force the Second New Deal on a resisting Roosevelt, they did threaten to hijack it. The president was obliged to dig in and defend his program against the danger that a radical groundswell might run it off the road of financial soundness and political prudence. "I am fighting Communism, Huey Longism, Coughlinism, Townsendism," Roosevelt told a journalist in early 1935, but he was not at this point battling them by stealing their thunder. He had long since stocked his own legislative arsenal with thunder enough. In his pitch for the Wealth Tax Act and in the presidential campaign of 1936, Roosevelt did in the end arguably fight fire with fire by mimicking some of the radicals' most confrontational rhetoric. But for the present he was working, he explained, "to save our system, the capitalist system," from "crackpot ideas." Steady on course, no veering leftward, or rightward either, for that matter — that was the strategy for 1935.[45]

44. E. Roosevelt, FDR: His Personal Letters, 444.
45. E. D. Coblentz, William Randolph Hearst (New York: Simon and Schuster, 1952), 178.

Roosevelt based that strategy on shrewd political calculations. Writing to his former associate from the Woodrow Wilson years, Colonel Edward M. House, Roosevelt in February 1935 offered a detailed analysis of the political opposition he faced. It embraced old-guard conservative Republicans, "more liberal Republicans," and "Progressive Republicans like La Follette, Cutting, Nye, etc., who are flirting with the idea of a third party ticket anyway with the knowledge that such a third ticket would be beaten but that it would defeat us, elect a conservative Republican and cause a complete swing far to the left before 1940. All of these Republican elements," Roosevelt continued, "are flirting with Huey Long and probably financing him. A third Progressive Republican ticket and a fourth 'Share the Wealth' ticket they believe would crush us. . . . There is no question that it is all a dangerous situation," Roosevelt conceded. But he coolly added the keen insight that "when it comes to Show-down these fellows cannot all lie in the same bed."[46]

Roosevelt may also have sensed something about the Long and Coughlin constituencies that the historian Alan Brinkley later put at the heart of his analysis of their Depression-era appeal. The men and women attracted to Long and Coughlin, Brinkley speculates, were not the most desperately poor. They seemed, rather, to be people who "had more to protect: a hard-won status as part of the working-class elite, a vaguely middle-class life-style, often a modest investment in a home. . . . They were people with something to lose. . . . What they shared was an imperiled membership in a world of modest middle-class accomplishment."[47] They were, in other words, from that petite bourgeois social stratum that Alexis de Tocqueville had long ago described as the "eager and apprehensive men of small property." They constituted the characteristic class shaped by the fluid, unstable conditions of American democracy. "They love change," Tocqueville observed, "but they dread revolutions. . . . They continually and in a thousand ways feel that they might lose by one."[48] They were never, in short, not even in the Depression, the stuff from which genuinely revolutionary movements might be forged. They might occasionally drink the demagogues' intoxicating rhetorical brew, but in the end they did their basic political business on plain water.

The real menace the demagogues posed was not that they might

46. E. Roosevelt, *FDR: His Personal Letters*, 452–53.
47. Brinkley, *Voices of Protest*, 202–3.
48. Tocqueville, *Democracy in America*, 2:265–78.

revolutionize this recalcitrant mass and use it to shove the country rudely to the left but that they might succeed for a time in so coarsening public opinion, so souring the political atmosphere, and so fracturing the traditional parties that were the usual vehicles of governance that a lengthy period of political paralysis would ensue. Not social revolution but stasis was the worst plausible outcome of the radical agitation. This was the danger Roosevelt saw in early 1935, but he was sure he could head it off. Indeed, it was a mark of Roosevelt's reflexive political genius that instead of simply bending with the pressure from his left, he capitalized on it. He could now credibly argue to conservative stand-patters that his own program, radical enough by any objective standard, was a prudent bulwark against the irresponsible radicalism of the demagogues. If others offered a politics of resentment, he would offer a politics of possibility. If Coughlin and Long appealed to the dark side of people's souls, Roosevelt would follow the example of Lincoln and speak to the better angels of their nature. "Some well-timed, common sense campaigning on my part this spring or summer will bring people to their senses," the president confidently predicted.[49]

Roosevelt had in fact been building up to that campaign for more than a year, in a remarkable series of addresses, including several Fireside Chats broadcast nationally on the radio. Despite the frequently repeated accusation that the New Deal lacked a coherent philosophy and that Roosevelt had no capacity for ordered, systematic thought, those addresses, taken together, etched at least the outlines of a structured and durable social philosophy that constituted the ideological heart of the New Deal. Roosevelt minted that philosophy from the feelings of seigneurial solicitude for his country that lay at the core of his patrician temperament. "[F]rom the bottom of his heart he wants [people] to be as happy as he is," Raymond Moley wrote. "He is outraged by hunger and unemployment, as though they were personal affronts in a world he is certain he can make far better, totally other, than it has been." Rexford Tugwell spoke in a similar vein when he described the fundamental purposes that lay deep in Roosevelt's mind when he first assumed the presidency: "a better life for all Americans, and a better America to live it in."[50]

In 1934 and 1935 Roosevelt took up the task of translating those sen-

49. E. Roosevelt, FDR: His Personal Letters, 453.
50. Rexford G. Tugwell, The Brains Trust (New York: Viking, 1968) 157–58; Raymond Moley, After Seven Years (New York: Harper and Brothers, 1939), 390.

timents and generalities into a concrete political credo. Long and the other radicals provided the occasion for Roosevelt to articulate fully and specifically just what it was that the New Deal was about. In the campaign of 1932 he had, perhaps deliberately, remained vague and inscrutable, though in retrospect the germ of his mature political thought can be found in some of his 1932 campaign addresses, especially his speech to San Francisco's Commonwealth Club. In 1933 he had pursued a bewildering array of sometimes contradictory policies and, perhaps inevitably, had little opportunity to define what architecture, if any, held them all together in his head. But as 1934 lengthened, Roosevelt at last proceeded to elaborate for his countrymen his vision of the future into which he hoped to lead them. He gave the nation a presidential civics lesson that defined nothing less than the ideology of modern liberalism. He breathed new meaning into ideas like liberty and freedom. He bestowed new legitimacy on the idea of government. He introduced new political ideas, like social security. He transformed the country's very sense of itself, and of what was politically possible, in enduring ways. Before he was finished, Franklin Roosevelt had changed the nation's political mind and its institutional structure to a degree that few leaders before him had dared to dream, let alone try, and that few leaders thereafter dared to challenge.

He began with history and with the changing role of government. As in his "Whither Bound" address to the Milton Academy graduates in 1926, change was his keynote—its inevitability and the equally inevitable obligation to adjust to it, to heal its ruptures and seize its opportunities. "[I]n the earlier days," he said in a special message to Congress on June 8, 1934, when he foreshadowed the social security program he intended to develop, "the interdependence of members of families upon each other and of the families within a small community upon each other" provided fulfillment and security. But those simple frontier conditions had now disappeared. "The complexities of great communities and of organized industry make less real these simple means of security. Therefore, we are compelled to employ the active interest of the Nation as a whole through government in order to encourage a greater security for each individual who composes it." The federal government was established under the Constitution, he recollected, "to promote the general welfare," and it was now government's "plain duty to provide for that security upon which welfare depends."

Security was the touchstone, the single word that summed up more of what Roosevelt aimed at that than any other. "Among our objectives," he declared, "I place the security of the men, women and children of the Nation first." People wanted, indeed, they had a "right"—a significant escalation of the rhetoric of political claims—to three types of security: "decent homes to live in," "productive work," and "security against the hazards and vicissitudes of life."

Figuratively nodding to his political right, in a Fireside Chat just three weeks later he explained in his reassuring, sonorous voice that some people "will try to give you new and strange names for what we are doing. Sometimes they will call it 'Fascism,' sometimes 'Communism,' sometimes 'Regimentation,' sometimes 'Socialism.' But, in so doing, they are trying to make very complex and theoretical something that is really very simple and very practical. . . . Plausible self-seekers and theoretical die-hards will tell you of the loss of individual liberty. Answer this question out of the facts of your own life. Have you lost any of your rights or liberty or constitutional freedom of action and choice?" He made no apology for his conception of government as a shaping agent in modern American life. Speaking extemporaneously at the site of Bonneville Dam on the Columbia River in the summer of 1934, he said flatly that "the power we shall develop here is going to be power which for all time is going to be controlled by Government."[51]

In a subsequent Fireside Chat in September, Roosevelt deepened his argument for positive government, quoting at length from the revered progressive-era statesman Elihu Root:

> The tremendous power of organization [Root had said] has combined great aggregations of capital in enormous industrial establishments . . . so great in the mass that each individual concerned in them is quite helpless by himself. . . . [T]he old reliance upon the free action of individual wills appears quite inadequate. . . . [T]he intervention of that organized control we call government seems necessary.

The "organized control we call government"—there was the heart of the matter. "Men may differ as to the particular form of governmental activity with respect to industry or business," Roosevelt commented, "but nearly all are agreed that private enterprise in times such as these cannot be left without assistance and without reasonable safeguards lest it destroy not only itself but also our process of civilization." Invoking another American icon, Roosevelt said: "I believe with Abraham Lincoln, that

51. PPA (1934), 287ff., 312ff., 325ff.

'The legitimate object of Government is to do for a community of people whatever they need to have done but cannot do at all or cannot do so well for themselves in their separate and individual capacities.' " In his own words, he added: "I am not for a return to that definition of liberty under which for many years a free people were being gradually regimented into the service of the privileged few. I prefer and I am sure you prefer that broader definition of liberty under which we are moving forward to greater freedom, to greater security for the average man than he has ever known before in the history of America."[52]

In his annual message to Congress on January 4, 1935, Roosevelt frankly declared that "social justice, no longer a distant ideal, has become a definite goal." He began to detail the specific proposals that would make that goal a reality. "As our measures take root in the living texture of life," he declared, "the unity of our program reveals itself to the Nation."[53]

The unifying design of that program took different forms in different sectors of the nation's life, but the overall pattern of the Second New Deal taking shape in 1935 was becoming clear. In the social realm, the dominant motif was security; in the economic realm, regulation (which was security by another name); and in the physical realm, planned development. In all those domains the common objective was stability. No other aspiration more deeply informed the Second New Deal, and no other achievement better represented the New Deal's lasting legacy. Roosevelt now sought not simply recovery, nor merely relief, nor even the perpetual economic growth that would constitute a later generation's social and political holy grail. Roosevelt sought instead a new framework for American life, something "totally other" than what had gone before, in Moley's phrase, something that would permit the steadying hand of "that organized control we call government" to sustain balance and equity and orderliness throughout American society. Roosevelt's dream was the old progressive dream of wringing order out of chaos, seeking mastery rather than accepting drift, imparting to ordinary Americans at least some measure of the kind of predictability to their lives that was the birthright of the Roosevelts and the class of patrician squires to which they belonged. It was a dream nurtured in the minds of countless reformers over a century of unbridled and unsettling industrial revolution;

52. PPA (1934), 413ff.
53. PPA (1935), 16.

a dream quickened in the progressive reform era of Roosevelt's youth, not least by his own cousin Theodore; a dream raised to insistent urgency by the catastrophe of the Depression. It was a dream now brought within reach of realization by that same Depression and by the sense of possibility and the political fluidity it induced.[54]

54. Much scholarly energy has gone into analyzing the ideology of the Second New Deal of 1935 and trying to distinguish it from the First New Deal of 1933. Arthur M. Schlesinger Jr. (Schlesinger 3, esp. 385–408) advanced the thesis that the macroeconomic planners in the New Nationalist tradition who dominated the First New Deal now gave way to the microeconomic trust busters and regulators of the Brandeisian–Woodrow Wilson persuasion, allied with proto-Keynesians increasingly convinced of the stimulatory power of deficit spending. Much of the argument over this subject has been an exercise in historiographical hairsplitting. My own view discounts the ideological coherence of the First New Deal and therefore posits no sharp conceptual break in 1935. It is also my view that not economic policy strictly defined but social security policy broadly construed — as embodied principally in the legislation of that name, as well as in the Emergency Relief Appropriation Act — constituted the heart of the Second New Deal and that the social security measures of 1935 represented no significant repudiation of previous policies. Rather, they evolved organically out of the social thought of the previous two decades as well out of the circumstances of the Depression.

9

A Season for Reform

The social objective . . . is to do what any honest government of any country would do: to try to increase the security and happiness of a larger number of people in all occupations of life and in all parts of the country . . . to give them assurance that they are not going to starve in their old age.
— Franklin D. Roosevelt, press conference of June 7, 1935, responding to the question "What would you say was the social objective of the administration?"

While Roosevelt cruised through the Bahamas on Vincent Astor's *Nourmahal* in the early spring weeks of 1935, the first part of his ambitious legislative program for the year, the Emergency Relief Appropriation Bill, sailed through the new Congress. He called it the "Big Bill," and not without reason. The bill asked for the largest peacetime appropriation to date in American history. It authorized more spending than the sum of all federal revenues in 1934. Four billion dollars in new funds, along with $880 million reallocated from previously authorized appropriations, were to be used for work relief and public works construction.

The word "emergency" in the bill's title was more than a little misleading. Roosevelt and the bill's principal architects in fact believed that they were addressing not a transient disruption in the labor markets but a long-term, perhaps permanent, deficit in the ability of the private economy to provide employment for all who sought it. In the masterwork he was then drafting, John Maynard Keynes would place that dread prospect — what Keynes called "equilibrium at less than full employment" — at the center of his analysis.[1] The social scientists who had compiled

1. John Maynard Keynes, *The General Theory of Employment, Interest, and Money* (New York: Harcourt, Brace, 1936).

249

Herbert Hoover's *Recent Social Trends* had worried half a decade earlier that long-term "technological unemployment" threatened to permanently engulf huge sectors of the work force, particularly the less skilled and the elderly. Some observers needed no sophisticated theory to suggest that deep structural changes in the economy were making what had once been almost unimaginable now seem like a distinct possibility. Lorena Hickok had opined to Harry Hopkins as early as the spring of 1934 that "it looks as though we're in this relief business for a long, long time. . . . The majority of those over 45 probably will NEVER get their jobs back."[2] Hopkins himself was soon speaking of workers who had passed into "an occupational oblivion from which they will never be rescued by private industry. . . . Until the time comes, if it ever comes," he argued, "when industry and business can absorb all able-bodied workers—and that time seems to grow more distant with improvements in management and technology—we shall have with us large numbers of the unemployed. Intelligent people have long since left behind them," Hopkins continued, "the notion that . . . the unemployed will disappear as dramatically as they made their appearance after 1929. . . . For them a security program is the only answer."[3] Roosevelt, too, had forewarned the Congress in early 1934 that government might have to become the employer of last resort and remain so into an indefinite future. "For many years to come," he said, "we shall be engaged in the task of rehabilitating many hundreds of thousands of our American families." The need for relief would continue "for a long time to come," he added in his Fireside Chat of June 28, 1934. "We may as well recognize that fact."[4]

The Big Bill met that fact head-on. Explaining the bill in his annual message to Congress on January 4, 1935, Roosevelt, instructed by Hopkins's experience with FERA and CWA, drew a sharp distinction between "relief" and "work relief." He declared emphatically: "The Federal Government must and shall quit this business of relief," by which he meant "the giving of cash, of market baskets, of a few hours of weekly work cutting grass, raking leaves or picking up papers in the public parks." In words that might have been uttered by Herbert Hoover, Roosevelt said that this sort of relief "induces a spiritual and moral disinte-

2. Richard Lowitt and Maurine Beasley, eds., *One Third of a Nation: Lorena Hickok Reports on the Great Depression* (Urbana: University of Illinois Press, 1981), 233.
3. Harry Hopkins, *Spending to Save* (New York: Norton, 1936), 180–81.
4. PPA (1934), 291, 313.

gration fundamentally destructive to the national fibre. To dole out relief in this way is to administer a narcotic, a subtle destroyer of the human spirit." *Work*, on the other hand, nurtured "self-respect . . . self-reliance and courage and determination." Therefore the federal government— "the only governmental agency with sufficient power and credit to meet this situation"—would offer employment to the approximately 3.5 million jobless but employable persons then on the relief rolls. (Another five million unemployed were not on relief and fell outside the scope of Roosevelt's proposal.) As for the estimated 1.5 million unemployable relief recipients—the ill, the aged, the physically handicapped—they had been cared for in pre-Depression days by local governments and agencies, said Roosevelt, and "it is my thought that in the future they must be cared for as they were before. . . . [C]ommon sense tells us," he added, "that the wealth necessary for this task existed and still exists in the local community." Perhaps it did, but to mobilize it local communities were levying new taxes, especially regressive sales taxes, which twenty-one states had newly imposed since 1932. This was but one of many ways in which the Depression drove the growth of government at all levels, not just at the federal center in Washington.[5]

Roosevelt laid down certain criteria to guide the expenditure of work-relief funds. Projects should be permanently useful and preferably self-liquidating; they should be labor-intensive and pay a "security wage" greater than the dole but less than private employment; they should compete "as little as possible with private enterprises."[6] Congress agreed, with one telling reservation. At the insistence of the old isolationist Senator William E. Borah of Idaho, the Senate inserted a proviso that "no part of the appropriations . . . shall be used for munitions, warships, or military and naval materiel." With that restriction, the Emergency Relief Appropriation Act became law on April 8, 1935.[7]

An omnibus measure, the act breathed new life into existing agencies like the Civilian Conservation Corps and the Public Works Administration and created new bodies besides. Though critics continued to charge

5. See James T. Patterson, *The New Deal and the States: Federalism in Transition* (Princeton: Princeton University Press, 1969), passim; and the same author's *America's Struggle against Poverty, 1900–1980* (Cambridge: Harvard University Press, 1981), 62.

6. *PPA* (1935), 19–23.

7. Robert E. Sherwood, *Roosevelt and Hopkins* (New York: Grosset and Dunlap, 1950), 67.

that the PWA under the ever-cautious Ickes was still dispensing money from a medicine dropper, Ickes in the end became, in William Leuchtenburg's phrase, "a builder to rival Cheops."[8] His PWA workers built roads and schools and courthouses and hospitals. They built the Triborough Bridge and the Lincoln Tunnel and La Guardia Airport in New York, the Skyline Drive in Virginia, and the Overseas Highway in the Florida Keys, as well as the San Francisco–Oakland Bay Bridge in California—and, using monies from the original PWA appropriation in 1933, the aircraft carriers *Yorktown* and *Enterprise* in Newport News and the light cruiser *Vincennes* in the Bethlehem Steel shipyard in Quincy, Massachusetts.

The Big Bill also spawned a prolific brood of new governmental agencies, most of them established by executive order under the unprecedentedly broad authority that the Emergency Relief Appropriation Act had conferred upon the president. The Rural Electrification Administration (REA) under Morris Llewellyn Cooke brought cheap power to the countryside, mostly by midwifing the emergence of hundreds of nonprofit, publicly owned electrical cooperatives. When REA began its work, fewer than two farms in ten had electricity; a little more than a decade later, thanks to low-cost REA loans that built generating plants and strung power lines down country lanes and across field and pasture, nine out of ten did. The National Youth Administration, under Aubrey Williams, provided part-time jobs to needy high school and college students—thus encouraging youths to stay in school and out of the regular employment markets. The Resettlement Administration, under former Brain Truster Rexford Tugwell, built three "greenbelt" suburban towns—Greenbelt, near Washington, D.C.; Greenhills, near Cincinnati; and Greendale, near Milwaukee—though its brief experiment in urban planning collapsed when it was absorbed into a new agency, the Farm Security Administration, in 1937.

The largest agency born of the Emergency Relief Appropriation Act was the Works Progress Administration (WPA; after 1939, Works Projects Administration). It was headed by the driven, savvy Harry Hopkins, a man Hugh Johnson described as having "a mind like a razor, a tongue like a skinning knife, a temper like a Tartar and a sufficient vocabulary of parlor profanity . . . to make a mule-skinner jealous."[9] WPA employed more than three million people in its first year and in the eight years

8. Leuchtenburg, 133.
9. Sherwood, *Roosevelt and Hopkins*, 80.

of its life put 8.5 million persons to work at a total cost of some $11 billion. WPA construction workers built half a million miles of highways and nearly a hundred thousand bridges and as many public buildings, erected the Dock Street Theater in Charleston and Timberline Lodge on the slopes of Oregon's Mount Hood, and laid out some eight thousand parks.

The WPA was from the outset a magnet for controversy. It was a federal program, but one that recognized the timeworn principle that "all politics is local." Roosevelt used it to build up those local bosses who would, in turn, support his national programs. Republicans complained that it was simply a gigantic federal patronage machine, operated for the sole benefit of the Democratic Party. That criticism was not unfounded, though it was not only Democrats whom Roosevelt favored with WPA patronage. In keeping with Roosevelt's larger purpose of creating a new, liberal political coalition, some progressive Republicans were also the beneficiaries of his WPA largesse. In New York City, where nearly a quarter of a million people were on the WPA rolls in 1936, the President allowed Republican mayor Fiorello La Guardia a large voice in dispensing WPA jobs. Elsewhere, however, Roosevelt often chose to work closely with the most entrenched of the old-line Democratic bosses. In Memphis, Tennessee, Democratic mayor Edward H. Crump exacted political contributions from WPA workers as the price of employment. WPA as well as PWA money flowed into the grasping hands of Missouri senator Harry S. Truman's political sponsor, the Democratic Pendergast machine in Kansas City. In Illinois, WPA workers were instructed how to vote by the Chicago Democratic boss Edward J. Kelly. Kelly repaid the favor with unstinting support for the president. "Roosevelt is my religion," he said. In New Jersey, all WPA jobholders were required to tithe 3 percent of their meager paychecks to the Democratic machine of Frank Hague. His legions of enemies dubbed Hague the "Hudson County Hitler." Roosevelt found him personally disgusting but politically useful.[10]

Still other controversies beset WPA, many of them fueled by a new militancy about the rights of the disadvantaged, others nourished by traditional skepticism about the "undeserving poor." The left-wing magazine *Nation* carped that WPA proffered help to workers in America's "crippled capitalist system" only after requiring them to toil "at

10. Lyle W. Dorsett, *Franklin D. Roosevelt and the Big City Bosses* (Port Washington, N.Y.: Kennikat, 1977), passim.

depressed wages in a federal work gang." But when WPA workers in New York, led by the Communist-inspired Workers Alliance, struck for higher wages, more fortunate New Yorkers were infuriated. Three-quarters of them told pollsters that the strikers should be summarily fired. The WPA, they said, was a "form of charity, and the workers should be glad of what they get." Other controversies reflected the great regional and racial differences in American society. To be qualified for WPA employment, a worker could not refuse private employment at pay scales prevailing in his or her community. But defining the "prevailing wage" was not easy. Nationally, the average WPA wage in 1936 was fifty-two dollars a month, but in the deepest southern states, it was as low as twenty-three dollars a month. And since the "prevailing" scale of pay for blacks in the South was lower than that for whites, Negroes refusing a three-dollar-per-week private job might be denied WPA eligibility, while whites were not. A similar differential applied to the pay scales of His-panic women in the Southwest, who were typically offered only part-time WPA jobs so they would not receive a higher wage than a full-time private employer was willing to pay. Yet Hopkins strove to keep discrimination to a minimum, and black leaders appreciated his effort. For all its timidity, the federal government was emerging as African-Americans' most reliable political ally. The NAACP resisted all proposals to place even more control in local hands. "The gover'ment is the best boss I ever had," said one black WPA worker in North Carolina.[11]

Encouraged by Eleanor Roosevelt, Hopkins also established projects that gave work to thousands of artists, musicians, actors, and writers. "Hell, they've got to eat just like other people," Hopkins replied to the inevitable critics.[12] The Federal Art Project employed painters and sculptors to teach their crafts in rural schools. It commissioned muralists to fresco post offices with depictions of ordinary American life; many of

11. *Nation*, February 13, 1935, 172; Patterson, *America's Struggle against Poverty*, 66; Donald Stevenson Howard, *The WPA and Federal Relief Policy* (New York: Russell Sage Foundation, 1943), 181–82, 291–96.
12. Jerre Mangione, *The Dream and the Deal: The Federal Writers' Project, 1935–1943* (Boston: Little, Brown, 1972), 4. Hopkins also glimpsed the employment and economic potential in the arts, entertainment, and sports industries that would grow so large in the post–World War II era. "Few things could add such a permanent volume of employment," he wrote, "as would a program of educating the public to use the services and participate in the pleasures of the culture we possess. I use the word culture as including everything from basketball to a violin performance." Hopkins, *Spending to Save*, 175.

them painted in the simple pictorial style of Breughel's portraits of Flemish peasants, enriched by the influence of the modern Mexican muralists, especially Diego Rivera. Franklin Roosevelt, in a sympathetic and sensitive appraisal of these sometimes controversial murals, thought some of them good, "some not so good, but all of it native, human, eager, and alive — all of it painted by their own kind in their own country, and painted about things that they know and look at often and have touched and loved."[13]

The Federal Music Project sponsored dozens of symphony orchestras and jazz groups. Its fifteen thousand musicians gave some 225,000 performances, including free concerts in New York's Central Park. Its researchers sought out traditional Appalachian banjo pickers and New England gut-bucket strummers and Texas fiddlers and Tennessee yodelers and Indiana jug bands, recording a unique aural archive of America's musical history.

The Federal Theater Project staged classics like Shakespeare's *Twelfth Night* and *Macbeth* (with an all-black cast). It also produced contemporary works like *It Can't Happen Here*, an adaptation of Sinclair Lewis's provocative best-selling novel of 1935, portraying the rise to power of an American fascist movement. Lewis himself played the role of his hero, Doremus Jessup, in the New York production. Taking to the road, the Theater Project brought plays and vaudeville acts and marionette shows to countless small towns. It developed an innovative production called the Living Newspaper, dramatizing headline news stories with such plays as *Triple A Ploughed Under, Power,* and *One Third of a Nation.* Federal Theater Project audiences totaled more than thirty million before the program was abolished in 1939 amid charges that it spread pro–New Deal propaganda and that it scandalously encouraged black and white mixing in its stage productions.

The Federal Writers Project, the fourth and most famous in the quartet of WPA arts programs collectively known as Federal One, put writers to work on the American Guide Series, an immensely popular set of guidebooks to each of the states, major cities, and interstate highway routes. The WPA guides, the critic Alfred Kazin wrote, "resulted in an extraordinary contemporary epic. . . . Road by road, town by town, down under the alluvia of the industrial culture of the twentieth century," the guides reflected the depression era's suddenly acute hunger to know "the whole of

13. Leuchtenburg, 128.

the American past, a need to give . . . New Deal America a foundation in the American inheritance."[14] Writers Project investigators also interviewed former slaves and chronicled their fading memories in poignant narratives that vividly preserved the human face of the peculiar institution. Federally funded folklorists recorded the bleak life histories of black sharecroppers and Appalachian lintheads and published many of them in a remarkable collection of reminiscences, *These Are Our Lives*, in 1939.

The artistic and literary outpouring of the Depression years, much of it fostered by Federal One, constituted what Kazin was soon to call "one of the most remarkable phenomena of the era of crisis. . . . Whatever form this literature took—the WPA guides to the states and roads . . . the half-sentimental, half-commercial new folklore . . . ; the endless documentation of the dispossessed in American life—it testified to an extraordinary national self-scrutiny. . . . Never before did a nation seem so hungry for news of itself."[15]

To a remarkable degree, Americans wanted that news straight, not sauced in the artifice of fiction but served plain in documentary reporting and, especially, in the unmediated images of photography and film. (*Life* magazine, devoted entirely to photographic reporting, marked the surging popularity of this medium on its first appearance in 1936.) In a stunning parade of books, in both words and photographs, Americans saw the many faces of their country as never before: not only in the WPA slave narratives and in *These Are Our Lives* but also in the portraits of tenant farmers by Walker Evans and James Agee in *Let Us Now Praise Famous Men* and by Erskine Caldwell and Margaret Bourke-White in *You Have Seen Their Faces*; in Dorothea Lange and Paul S. Taylor's Dust Bowl saga, *An American Exodus*; in the earthy social reporting of Edmund Wilson's *The American Jitters* and Louis Adamic's *My America*; in the simple place-name litany and stark images of prairie and river and forest in Pare Lorentz's films *The Plow That Broke the Plains* and *The River*.

Much of this artistic commentary was openly critical of the America it revealed. But Kazin and others noticed something else about it, too— its persistent subtext of patriotic nationalism, its "powers of affirmation," its commitment "to love what it knew."[16] It was as if the American

---

14. Alfred Kazin, *On Native Grounds* (Garden City, N.Y.: Doubleday, 1942), 393.
15. Kazin, *On Native Grounds*, 378–79.
16. Kazin, *On Native Grounds*, 378–79. See also William Stott, *Documentary Expression in Thirties America* (New York: Oxford University Press, 1973); and Richard Pells, *Radical Visions, American Dreams* (New York: Harper and Row, 1973).

people, just as they were poised to execute more social and political and economic innovation than ever before in their history, felt the need to take a long and affectionate look at their past before they bade much of it farewell, a need to inventory who they were and how they lived, to benchmark their country and their culture so as to measure the distance traveled into the future that Franklin Roosevelt was promising.

IF ROOSEVELT had had his way, the Big Bill would have been bigger still. He saw it as part of a single, integrated plan to provide present relief, future stability, and permanent security. Though Roosevelt developed his complex scheme with infinitely more financial precision than did Dr. Francis Townsend, much of the president's thinking about security—what would soon come to be called "social security"—rested on a premise little different from that of the Long Beach physician: that overcompetition in the labor markets depressed wages, spread misery rather than income, cramped the economy's aggregate purchasing power, and worked special hardship on the elderly. Like Townsend, Roosevelt was determined to find some means to "dispose of surplus workers," in particular those over the age of sixty-five. As the president saw things, the federal government would provide immediate relief to able-bodied workers by becoming the employer of last resort, even while returning traditional welfare functions to the states. Unemployment insurance would mitigate damage from future economic downturns by sustaining both the living standards of individual workers and the overall consuming power of the economy. And most important, for the lasting future, wage competition would be reduced, net purchasing power further stabilized, and the elderly made secure by removing older workers from the labor force altogether, through a system of government-guaranteed old-age pensions. "If Dr. Townsend's medicine were a good remedy," the prestigious columnist Walter Lippmann had mocked, "the more people the country could find to support in idleness the better off it would be."[17] Yet a version of that apparently outlandish idea did indeed inform Roosevelt's thinking. Warmhearted humanitarian considerations surely argued against elder labor, no less than they did against child labor. But removing both the young and the old from the work force had a cold economic logic too. Depression America had productive work only for so many, the president reasoned. Forcibly idling some was the price of securing a living wage for others.

17. Leuchtenburg, 105.

Such was the grand design in Roosevelt's mind. He regarded all three of those elements—work relief, unemployment insurance, and old-age pensions—as parts of a unitary whole, a comprehensive strategy to put the country on a pathway to sustainable economic and social stability. But on the advice of aides worried about legislative efficiency as well as constitutional challenges, he split the multipart package in two. The Emergency Relief Appropriation Act addressed only the most immediate of his goals. Most of the agencies it spawned were destined to survive less than a decade. The longer-term features of Roosevelt's grand design—unemployment insurance and old-age pensions—were incorporated in a separate piece of legislation, a landmark measure whose legacy endured and reshaped the texture of American life: the Social Security Act.

No other New Deal measure proved more lastingly consequential or more emblematic of the very meaning of the New Deal. Nor did any other better reveal the tangled skein of human needs, economic calculations, idealistic visions, political pressures, partisan maneuverings, actuarial projections, and constitutional constraints out of which Roosevelt was obliged to weave his reform program. Tortuously threading each of those filaments through the needle of the legislative process, Roosevelt began with the Social Security Act to knit the fabric of the modern welfare state. It would in the end be a peculiar garment, one that could have been fashioned only in America and perhaps only in the circumstances of the Depression era.[18]

No one knew better the singular possibilities of that place and time than Secretary of Labor Frances Perkins. To her the president in mid-1934 assigned the task of chairing a cabinet committee to prepare the social security legislation for submission to Congress. (Its other members were Treasury Secretary Henry Morgenthau, Attorney General Homer Cummings, Agriculture Secretary Henry Wallace, and Relief Administrator Harry Hopkins.) "[T]his was the time, above all times," Perkins wrote, "to be foresighted about future problems of unemployment and unprotected old age." The president shared this sense of urgency—and opportunity. Now is the time, he said to Perkins in 1934, when "we have to get it started, or it will never start."[19]

18. For a discussion of the uniqueness of the American welfare system, see Christopher Leman, "Patterns of Policy Development: Social Security in the United States and Canada," *Public Policy* 25, no. 2 (Spring 1977): 261–91.
19. Frances Perkins, *The Roosevelt I Knew* (New York: Viking 1946), 281.

Perkins brought to her task the commonsensical practicality of her New England forebears, the sometimes patronizing compassion of the social worker milieu in which she had been steeped at Jane Addams's Hull House as a young woman, and a large fund of political know-how compiled in her career as a labor lobbyist and industrial commissioner in New York. In her signature felt tricorn hat, topping an oval face punctuated by what one overawed labor chieftain called her "basilisk eyes," Perkins had evolved from a romantic Mount Holyoke graduate who tried to sell "true love" stories to pulp magazines into a mature, deadly serious battler for the underprivileged. Plain-spoken, plainly dressed, and disarmingly direct, she was thought by some to possess more earnestness than wit. Her frequently leaden garrulity in cabinet meetings irritated more than one of her male colleagues. One misogynistic wag called her "a colorless woman who talked as if she swallowed a press release." Another even more gratuitously accused her of wearing dresses "designed by the Bureau of Standards."[20]

"Madame Secretary," Perkins preferred to be called, proud of her status as the first woman cabinet member. She owed her position not only to her long comradeship-in-arms with Al Smith and Franklin Roosevelt in New York's reform battles but also to the spreading influence of an organized women's faction in the Democratic Party. Led by Mary "Molly" Dewson, head of the party's Women's Division, the group had successfully lobbied for Perkins's appointment after Roosevelt's election in 1932. In common with Dewson and other progressive reformers of her generation, especially the women among them, Perkins had been deeply affected by the 1911 fire at New York City's Triangle Shirtwaist Company, in which 146 women workers were incinerated in a burning factory whose emergency exits had been bolted shut. She directed the State Factory Commission investigation of that tragedy, which resulted in legislation mandating workplace safety and protection for workers, especially women. The Triangle Fire and its aftermath had given powerful impetus to the progressive-era movement for governmental supervision of industry, and its lessons were seared into the minds of many New Dealers. (Franklin Roosevelt alluded to it explicitly in a press conference on May 3, 1935, explaining the necessity of industrial regulation; Robert Wagner could recall minute details of the Triangle tragedy a quarter century later.) Certainly the Triangle Fire episode shaped

20. *New York Times*, May 15, 1965, 31; Lillian Holmen Mohr, *Frances Perkins* (Croton-on-Hudson, N.Y.: North River, 1979), 117.

Frances Perkins's lifelong approach to such issues. It deepened her conviction that many employers, left to their own devices, could not be counted upon to deal squarely with their employees. It also reinforced her belief that enlightened middle-class reformers could do more and better for the working classes through wise legislation than workers could do for themselves through union organization — and could do it more efficiently, without nasty industrial conflict and protracted social disruption.

A similar calculus of preemption had led Otto von Bismarck to push compulsory social insurance laws through the German Reichstag in the 1880s, and it had prompted the ruling parties in many other European countries to follow suit in the next half century. But until the 1930s no comparable movement gathered sufficient support, either from rulers or reformers, in the individualistic, laissez-faire United States. Meanwhile the American labor movement, led by the stubborn Samuel Gompers, with his deep antipathy to relying on government for anything other than protection of labor's right to organize, set its face against such schemes. Even after Gompers's death in 1924, until as late as 1932, his American Federation of Labor spurned blanket legislation to aid the toiling classes and continued to insist on bargaining for benefits piecemeal, union by union and shop by shop. The result was that the United States, virtually alone among modern industrial countries, confronted the Depression with no national system in place to compensate for the lost wages of unemployment or make provision for the old. Just a single American state, Wisconsin, had a publicly financed unemployment insurance program, and it was created only in 1932, its implementation delayed until 1934. As for pensions, more than a dozen states had old-age insurance laws on the books by the eve of the Depression, but they were so woefully underfunded that by one estimate only about twelve hundred of the nation's indigent elderly received payments from state plans in 1929, and their checks totaled a paltry $222,000 for the year, less than two hundred dollars for each recipient. Many military veterans and federal civil servants, as well as public employees like police, firefighters, and teachers, were covered by pensions, as were about 15 percent of workers in private industry. Yet the Depression badly stressed the ability of municipalities and corporations to honor pension obligations even to those lucky few. Many private plans simply folded in the years after the Crash. Others sharply curtailed benefits.[21]

21. Davis 3:442; W. Andrew Achenbaum, *Old Age in the New Land* (Baltimore: Johns Hopkins University Press, 1978), 129.

For the great majority of workers, who lacked any pension coverage whatsoever, the very thought of "retirement" was unthinkable. Most elderly laborers worked until they dropped or were fired, then threw themselves either on the mercy of their families or on the decidedly less tender mercies of a local welfare agency. Tens of thousands of elderly persons passed their final days in the 1920s in nearly thirteen hundred city- and county-supported "old-age homes." Of the 8 percent of the population who were over the age of sixty-five in 1935—a proportion that had more than doubled since the turn of the century and would rise to more than 12 percent by the century's end—nearly half were on some form of relief. As dietary and medical improvements steadily lengthened the life span and swelled the elderly cohort, that problem could only grow worse.

The problem of old-age relief had a lengthy history. The Progressive Party platform of 1912 had called for old-age pensions. A number of lobbies, including the American Association for Labor Legislation, the American Association for Old Age Security, and the Fraternal Order of Eagles, had been agitating for old-age insurance well before Dr. Townsend sent his fateful letter in 1934. Roosevelt had voiced his support for the idea at a Governors Conference in Salt Lake City in 1930. The Democratic Party platform of 1932 pledged Roosevelt's party to "unemployment and old-age insurance under State laws."

Pursuant to that goal, New York senator Robert Wagner and Maryland representative David J. Lewis cosponsored an unemployment insurance bill when the new congressional session opened in 1934. The Wagner-Lewis bill took its place alongside the Dill-Connery old-age pension bill, which had been working its way through Congress since 1932 and was now favorably reported out of committee. Together the two bills went a long way toward redeeming the Democratic platform promises of 1932. Yet to the chagrin of their sponsors the president distanced himself from both measures. Frances Perkins knew why. The president intended to seize ownership of these issues for himself. He would send a special message to Congress, appoint a presidential commission to draft the legislation, and use its deliberations to educate the public about social insurance, not least about his own commitment to it. "If possible," Perkins explained to a young aide temporarily discouraged by the president's diffidence, "it will be a campaign issue."[22]

At the outset the president entertained extravagantly far-reaching ideas

---

22. Thomas E. Eliot, *Recollections of the New Deal* (Boston: Northeastern University Press, 1992), 88.

about the welfare system he envisioned. "[T]here is no reason why every-body in the United States should not be covered," he mused to Perkins on one occasion. "I see no reason why every child, from the day he is born, shouldn't be a member of the social security system. When he begins to grow up, he should know he will have old-age benefits direct from the insurance system to which he will belong all his life. If he is out of work, he gets a benefit. If he is sick or crippled, he gets a benefit. . . . And there is no reason why just the industrial workers should get the benefit of this," Roosevelt went on. "Everybody ought to be in on it—the farmer and his wife and his family. I don't see why not," Roosevelt persisted, as Perkins shook her head at this presidential woolgathering. "I don't see why not. Cradle to the grave—from the cradle to the grave they ought to be in a social insurance system."[23]

That may have been the president's ideal outcome, but he knew as well as anyone that he would have to temper that vision in the forge of political and fiscal reality. Much of the country, not least the southern Democrats who were essential to his party's congressional majority, remained suspicious about all forms of social insurance. So Perkins, with dour Yankee prudence, went to work in a more practical vein. In the summer of 1934 she convened the Committee on Economic Security (CES), an advisory body of technical experts who would hammer out the precise terms of the social security legislation. She instructed the CES in words that spoke eloquently about her sensitivity to the novelties and difficulties of what they were about to undertake. "I recall emphasizing," she later wrote, "that the President was already in favor of a program of social insurance, but that it remained for them to make it practicable. We expected them," she recollected, in a passage that says volumes about her shrewd assessment of American political culture in the 1930s, "to remember that this was the United States in the years 1934–35. We hoped they would make recommendations based upon a practical knowledge of the needs of our country, the prejudices of our people, and our legislative habits."

The needs of the country were plain enough. But what of those prejudices and habits? What, in particular, of that phrase "under state laws" in the Democratic platform? Few items more deeply vexed the CES planners. Given the mobility of American workers and the manifest desirability of uniformity in national laws, most of the CES experts insisted that a centralized, federally administered system of social insur-

23. Perkins, *The Roosevelt I Knew*, 282–83.

ance would be the most equitable and the easiest to manage. They deemed a miscellany of state systems to be utterly impractical. Yet deeply ingrained traditions of states' rights challenged that commonsense approach, as did pervasive doubts about the federal government's constitutional power to act in this area.

Thomas Eliot, the young, Harvard-educated general counsel to the CES who played a major role in drafting the final bill, worried above all about "the omnipresent question of constitutionality." The lower federal courts, Eliot knew, had already handed down hundreds of injunctions against other New Deal measures. Constitutional tests of NRA and AAA were working their way to the Supreme Court. There, four justices — the "Battalion of Death" that included Justices McReynolds, Butler, VanDevanter, and Sutherland — were notoriously hostile to virtually any expansion of federal power over industry and commerce, not to mention the far bolder innovation of federal initiatives respecting employment and old age. Eliot brooded that "I could not honestly assure the committee that a national plan . . . would be upheld by the Supreme Court."

Political calculations in that agitated year of 1934 also played a part in driving the planners away from a purely federal welfare system. When the idea of federalizing the whole social insurance program was mentioned to the president, he quickly replied, "Oh no, we've got to leave all that we can to the states. All the power shouldn't be in the hands of the federal government. Look — just think what would happen if all the power *was* concentrated here, and *Huey Long* became president!"[24]

Against their better judgment, the CES experts therefore resigned themselves to settling for a mixed federal-state system. Perkins took what comfort she could from the reflection that if the Supreme Court should declare the federal aspects of the law to be unconstitutional, at least the state laws would remain. Though they would not be uniform, they would be better than nothing.

Under those constraints, the CES began its momentous task. Roosevelt at first charged the group to devise workable legislation not only for unemployment insurance and old-age pensions but also, reflecting the president's most unrestrained ambitions, for a national system of health care. The political obstacles in the path to that last objective doomed it virtually from the outset. Health-care provisions were to survive in the final act only as a residue, in the form of small grants-in-aid to the states

24. Eliot, *Recollections of the New Deal*, 95–98.

for rural public health programs and services for the physically handicapped.

Unemployment insurance posed a huge conundrum. The president's desire "to leave all that we can to the states," as well as the constitutional doubts that overhung any federal initiative, created a tightly confining matrix within which the CES planners were compelled to work. The Wisconsin plan, requiring individual employers to build up reserve funds for unemployment relief, was already on the books. A few other states were considering comparable laws, often with important variations such as requiring contributions from employees as well as employers or creating a single, state-managed fund rather than segregated reserves managed by individual firms. But in the absence of a national system, states that enacted any such laws put themselves at a disastrous competitive disadvantage. "Some way must be found," Eliot fretted, "to induce *all* the states to enact these laws — but what way? How?"[25]

Supreme Court Justice Louis D. Brandeis had an answer. He had a long and passionate interest in the cause of unemployment insurance. As early as 1911 he had written that "the paramount evil in the workingman's life is irregularity of employment." (This judgment was echoed in Robert and Helen Merrell Lynd's classic study *Middletown* a decade later, when they cited "irregularity of employment" as the major factor that defined the difference between the life trajectories of the working class and the middle class.) Now, as a sitting Supreme Court justice, Brandeis could not himself openly intervene in the bill-drafting process. But through the intermediary of his daughter Elizabeth, married to Paul A. Raushenbush, the director of the Wisconsin unemployment insurance plan, the seventy-seven-year-old jurist maneuvered from behind the scene to exercise a profound influence over the drafting of the Social Security Act.

In the summer of 1933 the Raushenbushes visited the Brandeis summer home on Cape Cod. Gratified by the recently enacted Wisconsin law, they wondered how it might become a model for national legislation. The shrewd old justice provocatively suggested that they read the Supreme Court's decision in a 1926 case, *Florida v. Mellon*. That case originated in a campaign to sell Florida real estate to sun-seeking wealthy northern retirees by reminding them that Florida had no inheritance tax. The frost-belt states whose revenues depended in part on taxing the estates of those potentially migratory millionaires thereupon

25. Eliot, *Recollections of the New Deal*, 75.

sought ways to check what they regarded as Florida's unfair competitive advantage. They prevailed upon Congress to enact a federal estate tax, with a proviso that the estates of decedents from a state with its own inheritance tax could deduct from their federal tax obligation the amount owed the state. Poof, went the Sunshine State's tax advantage. But Florida objected on the grounds that the federal law unconstitutionally compelled states to impose inheritance taxes, on pain of losing taxable revenues to the federal government. The Supreme Court unanimously dismissed Florida's claim and let the federal law stand.

This tax-offset device, Brandeis cleverly insinuated into the heads of his daughter and son-in-law, was the mechanism by which the states could be constitutionally coerced into enacting unemployment insurance laws. *Florida v. Mellon* thus helped to write a new chapter in the history of American federalism. In common with other New Deal–era developments, it provided yet another means by which the expansion of federal power did not come at the expense of diminished state power but worked, rather, to induce the growth of government at the state level as well.

In early January 1934 Elizabeth Brandeis Raushenbush shared her thoughts on this line of reasoning with Secretary Perkins. At Perkins's urging, an exhilarated Eliot incorporated the tax-offset feature into the unemployment insurance portion of the Social Security bill. States would face the choice of devising their own unemployment insurance schemes or watching tax revenues flow away to Washington to finance a federal unemployment program. This device removed the constitutional roadblock, but at the price of engendering a profligately disparate system that threatened to hinder labor force mobility. Forty-eight states would run forty-eight different unemployment compensation plans with minimal national standards and with benefits that were neither uniform nor portable.

If the tax-offset device displaced the constitutional obstacle to unemployment insurance, the problem of old-age insurance remained. And a huge problem it was. With that part of the bill, Perkins remembered more than a decade later, "we had an even more difficult time. . . . It is difficult now to understand fully the doubts and confusions in which we were planning this great new enterprise in 1934. The problems of constitutional law seemed almost insuperable." A special sense of urgency shadowed this part of the CES's deliberations. "One hardly realizes nowadays how strong was the sentiment in favor of the Townsend Plan and other exotic schemes," Perkins later wrote. "We must remember, those were the days of the 'share-the-wealth' schemes." Old-age insurance, Perkins concluded, was "politically almost essential."[26]

In lengthy lunchtime meetings in Perkins's office, at which Henry Wallace, then in a vegetarian phase, politely declined the proffered sandwiches, the planners wrestled through the autumn of 1934 with the old-age insurance features of the bill. They grappled mostly with the stringent conditions that the president had laid down in his special message of June 8. Any federal pension system, he had stipulated, must be based on private insurance principles. Specifically, he had said, "the funds necessary to provide this insurance should be raised by contribution rather than by an increase in general taxation." His usual fiscal conservatism led Roosevelt to that position, as did Witte's pointed warning that without a contributory system "we are in for free pensions for everybody with constant pressure for higher pensions, far exceeding anything that the veterans have ever been able to exert." Taking his own measure of "the prejudices of our people," Roosevelt clearly intended to establish his social security system not as a civil right but as a property right. That was the American way.

The contributory requirement enormously complicated the planners' task. "[W]hat in the world," Eliot asked himself, "could be devised to carry out the president's wish for a contributory old age insurance program that would pass judicial muster?" The president's insistence that workers themselves should contribute to their own individual old-age pension accounts through a payroll tax seemed to offer an open invitation to judicial nullification. "[W]ouldn't the Court say," Eliot worried, "that a law levying a payroll tax and spending the proceeds in paying old age benefits was really nothing else but a federal insurance scheme to provide annuities to the elderly, and that the Constitution gave Congress no authority to go into the insurance business?"[27]

Nor was that the only problem with the president's preferred scheme for old-age insurance. It also largely neutered the income-redistribution effects of the legislation. It meant that, virtually alone among modern nations, the United States would offer its workers an old-age maintenance system financed by a regressive tax on the workers themselves. What was more, in the short run, building a Social Security reserve fund by withdrawing money through taxation from the otherwise spend-

26. Perkins, *The Roosevelt I Knew*, 278–95.
27. Patterson, *America's Struggle against Poverty*, 73; Eliot, *Recollections of the New Deal*, 96, 97.

able incomes of workers would be sharply deflationary, hardly a welcome effect in the midst of the Depression.

Perkins explained all these objections to the president. "We can't help that," Roosevelt curtly replied. He explained his basic principle to Perkins and a soberly impressed Eliot at a meeting in August 1934: "He wanted the use of gov't [sic] funds limited as much as possible, preferring 'contributions,'" Eliot wrote. "No dole," Roosevelt emphasized, "mustn't have a dole." "No money out of the Treasury," he declared on another occasion. He understood as clearly as any the inequity and economic dysfunctionality of the contributory payroll tax, but he understood equally those "legislative habits" and "prejudices" about which Perkins had reminded the CES. "I guess you're right on the economics," Roosevelt explained to another critic some years later, "but those taxes were never a problem of economics. They are politics all the way through. We put those payroll contributions there so as to give the contributors a legal, moral, and political right to collect their pensions and their unemployment benefits. With those taxes in there, no damn politician can ever scrap my social security program."[28]

Those same "popular prejudices" cast their shadow over the CES's deliberations in other ways. What should be the size of the benefit paid to retirees? "The easiest way," Perkins wrote, "would be to pay the same amount to everyone," a way that would also imply some income redistribution. "But," she added, "that is contrary to the typical American attitude that a man who works hard, becomes highly skilled, and earns high wages 'deserves' more on retirement than one who had not become a skilled worker." Therefore, the planners again swallowed their better judgment and decided on the more complicated system of paying benefits in proportion to previous earnings, yet another borrowing from the private insurance model on which Roosevelt insisted.

A final problem remained, one whose technical complexities intersected with political considerations to work a long and vexatious effect on the Social Security program. Workers then older than forty-five years of age would have only a limited number of years to pay into the system—for the earliest retirees a maximum of three years, as it turned out, since the first payroll deductions were scheduled to begin in 1937 and the first distributions were ultimately paid in 1940. The planners therefore recommended granting those first beneficiaries retirement pay-

ments that would far exceed the value of their accumulated contributions, an arrangement that had a sizeable income-redistribution effect,
albeit an exclusively intergenerational one. According to standard accounting procedures, payments to that first generation of recipients
would create an accrued liability in the Social Security reserve fund that
would have to be covered by general revenues at some future date—
according to some estimates as early as 1965, and surely by 1980. That
anticipated shortfall flatly contradicted the private insurance guidelines
the president had laid down, including his strictures against money out
of the treasury.

But the alternatives, Perkins explained to FDR, were to levy such high
initial taxes "as to be almost confiscatory," to give this group "ridiculously
small benefits," or to postpone the start-up of payments for many years,
perhaps a dozen or more. The first alternative made no economic sense
in the depressed circumstances of 1935. Roosevelt squelched the other
two choices as politically unacceptable. "We have to have it," he told
her. "The Congress can't stand the pressure of the Townsend Plan unless
we have a real old-age insurance system, nor can I face the country."[29]
But neither would he tolerate an accrued liability. "Ah," he exclaimed,
when Perkins presented the CES's draft proposal, "but this is the same
old dole under another name. It is almost dishonest to build up an
accumulated deficit for the Congress of the United States to meet in
1980. We can't do that. We can't sell the United States short in 1980
any more than in 1935."[30]

How to break this impasse? Treasury Secretary Henry Morgenthau
had the solution. He made two proposals. First, he recommended a
modest increase in the rate of the contributory payroll tax so as to build
a large reserve fund that would permanently preclude the need for future general revenues. To avoid "confiscatory" rates, Morgenthau also
recommended a second, still more consequential, amendment to the

29. Perkins, *The Roosevelt I Knew*, 194,
30. Perkins, *The Roosevelt I Knew*, 294. The CES, in an open letter to the president
dated January 17, 1935, had noted that "Government contributions" would be necessary "after the system has been in operation for thirty years"—or 1965. *PPA* (1935),
53. Why Roosevelt sometimes thought in terms of 1980 rather than 1965 is not clear.
Further confusion about this issue is evident in Roosevelt's special Social Security
message to Congress of January 17, 1935, when he remarked that "for those who
are now too old to build up their own insurance," it would be necessary to make
payments from general funds "for perhaps 30 years to come." *PPA* (1935), 45–46.
The president heard Morgenthau's misgivings about how to finance the pensions of
the over–forty-five group only after he had delivered his January 17 message.

draft bill. He insisted on excluding from old-age coverage farm laborers, domestic servants, and workers in establishments with fewer than ten employees. "This was a blow," Perkins said. "But there were enough people afraid of the deflationary effects of this large money collection, enough people afraid of too large a system, and enough people confused about the desirability of social legislation by the Federal Government, to make it a foregone conclusion that if the Secretary of the Treasury recommended limitation, limitation there would be."[31]

So Perkins grudgingly acquiesced in Morgenthau's amendments. By this time she was grateful to accomplish anything at all. So many clashing interests and contrary ideas had contended in shaping the Social Security bill that Perkins likened her task to "driving a team of high-strung unbroken horses." Yet she could not help but regret the degree to which Roosevelt's original vision had been compromised. "The thing had been chiseled down to a conservative pattern," she rightly remarked. Health care had been dropped. Unemployment insurance fell far short of a consistent national plan. Contributory taxes for old-age insurance had been retained and even expanded beyond the planners' intentions. And 9.4 million of the least secure, most needful workers—a disproportionate number of them black farm laborers and black female domestics—had at a stroke been denied old-age coverage altogether.

All of this was lamentable to the group that crafted the legislation, but they deemed the most lamentable feature of the Social Security bill to be the virtual sacralization of the contributory principle and the consequent reinforcement of the private insurance model of social security that took root in the public mind. The "contributions" were in fact nothing more nor less than taxes by another name. But in the climate of Depression America, they could scarcely be called that in public. "The apparent analogy with private insurance," one expert wrote, made Social Security "acceptable to a society which was dominated by business ethics and which stressed individual economic responsibility." Eliot voiced the disappointment of many on the CES planning group in a statement years later:

> In 1935 ... all the members of the committee and its large staff of experts agreed on the contributory principle: the ultimate beneficiary should contribute a part of the cost of his eventual old age annuity. ... But they assumed that before long ... income taxes would supplement the employee's contributions. ... All, that is, except the Secretary

31. Perkins, *The Roosevelt I Knew*, 298.

of the Treasury, Henry Morgenthau, [who] persuaded the President that the rates of payroll and earnings taxes should be raised, to make the system forever "self-supporting." The rest of the Committee and the staff greatly regretted this, for the earnings tax, while necessary to effectuate the contributory principle, is a regressive tax and should be held at a very low rate.[32]

THE PRESIDENT at last faced the country on January 17, 1935, and unveiled his Social Security program. Though it fell far short of his grandest design, it did offer to some twenty-six million workers at least a measure of "security against the hazards and vicissitudes of life." For all its limitations, Perkins shrewdly assessed the final bill as "the only plan that could have been put through Congress."[33]

"We pay now for the dreadful consequence of economic insecurity — and dearly," the president said in his special message to Congress accompanying the draft Social Security bill. "No one can guarantee this country against the dangers of future depressions," Roosevelt conceded, "but we can reduce those dangers. We can eliminate many of the factors that cause economic depressions, and we can provide the means of mitigating their results. This plan for economic security is at once a measure of prevention and a method of alleviation." In a thinly veiled reference to the Townsend and Long schemes, he described his own proposal as proceeding from "sound caution and consideration of all of the factors concerned: the national credit, the rights and responsibilities of States, the capacity of industry to assume financial responsibilities and the fundamental necessity of proceeding in a manner that will merit the enthusiastic support of citizens of all sorts." Now was not the time,

32. Patterson, *America's Struggle against Poverty*, 74, 75; Eliot, *Recollections of the New Deal*, 103. Eliot also points out that in 1939 Congress amended the act, partly in a deliberate move to reduce the size of the accumulating "trust fund," which was then growing at a rate projected to reach $50 billion by 1980. Since that sum exceeded the federal debt outstanding in the late 1930s, the prospect loomed that the Social Security reserve might eventually have to be invested in the stocks and bonds of private corporations — creating a kind of back road to socialism that would have assuredly been an ironic result of the elaborate maneuvering in the original Social Security legislation to avoid even the appearance of socialism. The rate of growth of the reserve was slowed by lowering the payroll tax and extending coverage, principally to survivors of beneficiaries. Only in the 1950s were agricultural and domestic workers finally covered, and the system at last approached the universal coverage that Roosevelt had originally dreamed of.

33. PPA (1935), 17; Perkins, *The Roosevelt I Knew*, 284.

he warned, to jeopardize the "precious" goal of security "by attempting to apply it on too ambitious a scale."[34]

Roosevelt had prepared the ground well. His transparent allusions to less responsible schemes helped convince congressional doubters that the president's measured radicalism was far preferable to the dread Long and Townsend alternatives—or the even more dread option of a bill introduced by Minnesota representative Ernest Lundeen, which called for unemployment compensation at full wages to all jobless workers, paid for out of general tax revenues and administered by local workers' councils. After lengthy hearings through an exceptionally crowded legislative season, the Social Security Act became law on August 14, 1935.

The final act provided for unemployment insurance and old-age pensions, its principal features, and also authorized nearly $50 million in federal grants to the states for the immediate relief of the indigent elderly, another $25 million for Aid to Dependent Children, and modest sums for public health services. To finance the unemployment plan, the act levied a federal tax of 1 percent on employers of eight or more workers, rising to 2 percent in 1937 and 3 percent thereafter. States were to administer their own plans and could utilize the tax-offset feature of the law to recapture up to 90 percent of the federal levy, with most of the remaining 10 percent earmarked for administrative expenses. Old-age pension accounts were funded by employee "contributions" of 1 percent in 1937, rising in three-year stages to 3 percent in 1949, and matched by a like tax on employers. Depending on a worker's lifetime employment record and average wage, payments in retirement would range from ten to eighty-five dollars per month. Only the appropriations for the indigent elderly, seen as a transitional expense until Social Security coverage became more nearly universal, and for Aid to Dependent Children (ADC) were to come from general tax revenues. ADC—later Aid to Families with Dependent Children, or AFDC—was a "new departure," the CES report frankly acknowledged, but one that was "imperative" for "rearing fatherless families," a particular concern in a decade when so many work-seeking fathers had abandoned their families and taken to the road.[35]

With what Perkins called these "practical, flat-footed first steps," the groundwork for the modern American welfare state was laid. For all the

34. *PPA* (1935), 43–46.
35. *PPA* (1935), 55.

caution that attended its origins, Perkins said, Roosevelt always regarded the Social Security Act as the "cornerstone of his administration." On that admittedly modest foundation an imposing edifice was eventually raised.[36] In the next few years, all the states passed unemployment compensation laws of their own, to take advantage of the law's tax-offset feature and "keep the money at home." Though levels of benefits varied widely from state to state, the typical plan provided sixteen weeks of unemployment checks at half pay, up to a maximum of fifteen dollars per week, roughly equivalent to the average WPA wage. Most plans provided no further relief to an unemployed worker who still remained jobless after the initial period of coverage expired — other than to seek a WPA job. Similarly, several states expanded and upgraded their services to the indigent elderly and to dependent children, so as to receive their share of the federal grants for those purposes legislated in the 1935 act. Here, too, there was much variation among the states. Until 1939, ten states declined to join these categorical assistance plans at all. Those that did received federal moneys for old-age assistance on a one-for-one matching basis, up to a federal maximum of fifteen dollars per recipient per month. Combined federal-state payments to the indigent elderly in 1936 ranged from $3.92 in Mississippi to $31.36 in California, for a national average of $18.36 per month. Reflecting Roosevelt's notion that the "local community" had first responsibility and adequate resources to deal with "unemployable" relief recipients, the federal government contributed to ADC on a one-for-two federal-to-state basis, up to a federal maximum of twelve dollars for the first child and eight dollars for younger children. By 1939, when about seven hundred thousand children benefited from ADC, average monthly payments per family were about $32, ranging from $8.10 in Arkansas to $61.07 in Massachusetts. At the federal level, meanwhile, a vast new bureaucracy came into being. It employed over twelve thousand people in 202 regional offices and in Washington, D.C., where a central card file holding the records of some twenty-six million Social Security registrants covered an acre of floor space.[37]

On January 17, 1940, a seventy-six-year-old Vermonter, Ida M. Fuller, received the first Social Security check, for $41.30. Half a century later, forty million beneficiaries received monthly payments averaging over

36. Perkins, *The Roosevelt I Knew*, 284, 301.
37. Patterson, *America's Struggle against Poverty*, 67–77; Achenbaum, *Old Age in the New Land*, 127–41; *New York Times*, August 27, 1935, 10.

five hundred dollars. Accounting for more than $400 billion in annual expenditures by century's end, Social Security and its add-on programs, including Medicare, had become the largest item in the federal budget. With good reason does one Roosevelt biographer declare the Social Security Act "the most important single piece of social legislation in all American history, if importance be measured in terms of historical decisiveness and direct influence upon the lives of individual Americans."[38]

YET EVEN AS THE SPRAWLING Social Security administrative apparatus began to take shape, doubts were multiplying about the permanence of Roosevelt's innovative plan, and about the survivability of many other New Deal achievements as well. On May 6, 1935, the Supreme Court declared unconstitutional the Railroad Retirement Act of 1934, using language that seemed to threaten, as Eliot had feared, the old-age insurance features of the Social Security bill. Worse, on May 27 a unanimous Court nullified the National Industrial Recovery Act, in terms so sweeping as to put at risk virtually all the New Deal legislation of the preceding two years. Roosevelt called it the most troubling judicial decision since the Dred Scott case, because it brought "the country as a whole up against a very practical question. . . . Does this decision mean that the United States Government has no control over any national economic problem?" The Court's action, the president fumed, was hopelessly anachronistic. "We have been relegated to the horse-and-buggy definition of interstate commerce," he declared angrily.[39]

But rather than slowing Roosevelt's political momentum, the Supreme Court's actions seemed instead to galvanize him. On June 4 he urged the Congress to remain in extraordinary session through the sweltering summer — most government buildings, including all but a few rooms in the Capitol, still lacked air-conditioning — in order to pass four pieces of "must" legislation: in addition to the Social Security bill, they included Senator Wagner's bill to create a national labor relations board, urgently necessary for industrial peace now that the Court had voided the labor provisions of NRA; a bill to break up large public utility holding companies; and a bill to increase the power of the Federal Reserve System's Open Market Committee, making it a more effective instrument for controlling the money supply.

38. Davis 3:437.
39. PPA (1935), 200–222.

The last measure was the least controversial. When the Federal Reserve System had been created in pre–World War I days, little attention had been given to the effects of its transactions in government securities, which amounted then to a negligible sum. When the war then ballooned the national debt, the Fed set up the Open Market Committee to buy and sell government debt instruments. It soon became apparent that the committee's operations could exert a powerful influence on the money supply and the availability of credit, as well as on the interest rates at which the treasury could borrow. The committee, however, was at first an informal body. Even after being granted statutory recognition in the Banking Act of 1933, it remained under the control of the private bankers, largely based in New York, who represented the Fed's member institutions. Those institutions in any case were still free to conduct their own open-market sale and purchase of government securities. Roosevelt's banking bill proposed bringing the Open Market Committee under the direct and exclusive authority of the Federal Reserve's Board of Governors, a move aimed at enhancing central control over the nation's money markets, easing treasury funding operations, and improving the Federal Reserve's capacity to modulate swings in the business cycle. The president signed the bill on August 24, 1935. The Fed now had more of the trappings of a true central bank than any American institution had wielded since the demise of the Bank of the United States in Andrew Jackson's day. Working through the enervating humidity of a Washington summer, Congress further obliged the president and passed all of his other "must" bills substantially as he submitted them.

The record of that 1935 congressional session was remarkable by any measure, as Roosevelt acknowledged in a letter of appreciation when Congress adjourned at on August 24: "When a calm and fair review of the work of this Congress is made," he said, "it will be called a historic session," a judgment that time has ratified. Indeed, as Roosevelt said just days earlier, at the signing ceremony for the Social Security Act, "[i]f the Senate and the House of Representatives in this long and arduous session had done nothing more than pass this Bill, the session would be regarded as historic for all time."[40] The measures enacted in 1935 held the potential to transform American social and economic life. The Wagner Act, in particular, might prove second only to the Social Security Act in its power to reshape the workplace and, not incidentally,

40. PPA (1935), 325.

to determine the political future of the Democratic Party. Yet over all those prospects there still lay the shadow of constitutional challenge.[41]

There also remained the questions of Long and Coughlin. Robert La Follette and other progressives had advised the president in the spring of 1935 that "the best answer to Huey Long and Father Coughlin would be the enactment into law of the Administration bills now pending."[42] Those bills, the four on Roosevelt's June 4 "must" list, had now been enacted. Long and Coughlin supposedly had their answer. But for reasons that have long intrigued historians, the president was not content to leave matters there.

To the sharp surprise and considerable discomfort of his own mostly southern conservative legislative leaders, Roosevelt added a fifth measure to his "must" list in late June: tax reform. Just six months earlier, the president had declared the federal revenue system to be in no need of amendment. But on June 19 he told the Congress: "Our revenue laws have operated in many ways to the unfair advantage of the few, and they have done little to prevent an unjust concentration of wealth and economic power. . . . Social unrest and a deepening sense of unfairness are dangers to our national life which we must minimize by rigorous methods." Accordingly, he asked for "very high taxes" on large incomes and for stiffer inheritance taxes, since "the transmission from generation to generation of vast fortunes . . . is not consistent with the ideals and sentiments of the American people."[43] In addition, he requested a graduated corporate income tax and taxes on intercorporate dividends—a blow at the holding companies also under attack in the public utilities holding company bill. He called it a "wealth tax." Others soon dubbed it a "soak-the-rich" bill. As Roosevelt's message was read in the Senate, Huey Long strutted about the chamber, pointing to himself as the original inspiration of the president's tax proposals. Long concluded the recital with a fervent "Amen!"

But there was more rhetoric than revenue in the president's tax proposal—and some high-stakes politicking as well. Morgenthau acknowledged as much when he told a Treasury Department subordinate that the tax bill was one issue that FDR "could well afford to be defeated

---

41. For a discussion of the Wagner Act and its implications, see chap. 10. The Public Utilities Holding Company Act and other items of economic legislation are discussed in chaps. 11 and 12.
42. Ickes Diary 1:363.
43. *PPA* (1935), 270–76.

on." The president, he explained, simply had to "make his record clear." The tax proposal, Morgenthau went on, "is more or less a campaign document." As a congressman put it, "This is a hell raiser, not a revenue raiser." The president uncomplainingly acquiesced in congressional tinkering with the bill, passed in the waning hours of the session, so that it promised to generate only about $250 million in additional funds, a piddling sum. The final law imposed a tax of 79 percent on incomes over $5 million, a rate that appeared to be downright confiscatory but in fact covered precisely one individual—John D. Rockefeller. The basic rate remained at 4 percent, and in an era when three-quarters of all families earned less than two thousand dollars per year, well below the minimum taxable level for a married couple, fewer than one American household in twenty paid any federal income tax at all. A couple with an income of four thousand dollars would have been in the top tenth of all income receivers; if they had two children, they would have paid a tax of sixteen dollars. A similar family making twelve thousand dollars—placing them in the richest 1 percent of households—would pay less than six hundred dollars. As the closest student of Depression-era tax policy says, there were two tax systems in the New Deal, "one a revenue workhorse, the other a symbolic showpiece." The "wealth tax" of 1935 was decidedly more showpiece than workhorse.[44]

It was not revenue but politics that drove Roosevelt's tax strategy. Here he was indeed "stealing Huey Long's thunder," as he frankly admitted to Raymond Moley in the spring of 1935. And in the process of seeking to make Long's supporters his own, he also drew to himself the bitter enmity of Long's opponents. "It was on that day," said Moley, referring to Roosevelt's June 19 tax message, "the split in the Democratic Party began."[45] It was on that day, too, that the hatred of the rich toward Roosevelt began to congeal into icy contempt for the Hudson River squire, denounced now as "a traitor to his class." (A cartoon of the era depicted an affluent crowd on its way to the movie theater "to hiss Roosevelt.") William Randolph Hearst branded Roosevelt's tax proposal "Communism." He instructed his editors to call the tax bill the "soak-the-successful" bill and to begin substituting "Raw Deal" for "New

44. Mark H. Leff, *The Limits of Symbolic Reform: The New Deal and Taxation, 1933–1939* (Cambridge: Cambridge University Press, 1984), 91–96, 2.

45. Raymond Moley, *After Seven Years* (New York: Harper and Brothers, 1939), 312. The tax message, which Roosevelt dragooned a reluctant Moley to help draft, sealed Moley's own alienation from Roosevelt and the New Deal.

Deal" in news coverage of the administration. Privately he took to calling the president "Stalin Delano Roosevelt."

For his part, Roosevelt seemed almost to enjoy the passions he had aroused among the well-to-do. Reading aloud to Ickes from one of the barbed passages in his tax message, he looked up with a smile and said, "That is for Hearst." Some months later, FDR spoke at the Harvard University Tercentenary Celebration. Perhaps the visit awakened his long-ago rejection from Porcellian, a memory that may have inflamed his new itch to provoke the smug rich. At the university's bicentennial in 1836, he pointed out, "many of the alumni of Harvard were sorely troubled concerning the state of the Nation. Andrew Jackson was President. On the two hundred fiftieth anniversary of the founding of Harvard College, alumni again were sorely troubled. Grover Cleveland was President. Now, on the three hundredth anniversary," he concluded with relish, "I am the President."[46]

When Congress finally adjourned at the end of August, Roy Howard, head of the Scripps-Howard newspaper chain and generally friendly to the administration, wrote the president with an earnest suggestion. "I have been seeking reasons for the doubts and uncertainties of those business men who are skeptics, critics, and outright opponents of your program," Howard said. "[T]hroughout the country many business men who once gave you sincere support are now, not merely hostile, they are frightened." They had become convinced, Howard went on, "that you fathered a tax bill that aims at revenge rather than revenue — revenge on business. . . . That there can be no real recovery until the fears of business have been allayed through the granting of a breathing spell to industry." For the "orderly modernization of a system we want to preserve," Howard urged, there must be "a recess from further experimentation until the country can recover its losses."[47]

A week later the president replied, releasing both Howard's letter and his own response to the press. He rehearsed "the essential outline of what has been done," vigorously defending his measures "to seek a wise balance in American economic life, to restore our banking system to public confidence, to protect investors in the security market, to give labor freedom to organize and protection from exploitation, to safeguard and develop our national resources, to set up protection against the

46. Ickes Diary 1:384; Frank Freidel, *Franklin D. Roosevelt: A Rendezvous with Destiny* (Boston: Little, Brown, 1990), 206.
47. *PPA* (1935), 353.

vicissitudes incident to old age and unemployment, to relieve destitution and suffering and to relieve investors and consumers from the burden of unnecessary corporate machinery." It was a creditable record, Roosevelt said with much pride and not a little heat. But, he conceded, his basic program "has now reached substantial completion and the 'breathing spell' of which you speak is here — very decidedly so."[48]

With respect to substantive legislation, Roosevelt's "breathing spell" proved longer than he could have anticipated. With just a handful of exceptions, the legislative record of the New Deal was complete by August 1935. But when it came to attacks on business, the breathing spell proved much shorter than Roosevelt led Howard to expect. With his employment and security legislation, Roosevelt had apparently battened the New Deal against challengers from the left. The political threat from that quarter further dissipated in early September when Huey Long fell to an assassin's bullets in the marble corridor of the Louisiana Capitol at Baton Rouge. "I wonder why he shot me?" Long gasped, before lapsing into a coma. The question was never satisfactorily answered, as Long's bodyguards emptied their guns into the assassin's body. After lingering for nearly two days, passing in and out of consciousness, Long died on September 10. His last words were "God, don't let me die! I have so much to do!"[49]

But Roosevelt seemed to believe that neither his legislative record nor even Long's death could fully neutralize the forces of radicalism. When Ickes told him yet again, on December 10, 1935, "that I believed the general sentiment of the country to be much more radical than that of the Administration," Roosevelt readily agreed.[50] Despite his promise of a "breathing spell," Roosevelt went vigorously back on to the attack against business. From some mixture of principled conviction, personal pique, and political calculation, Roosevelt withdrew the hand of cooperation that he had extended to capital in 1933 and had proffered again in his open letter to the Scripps-Howard chief. Instead he now brandished the mailed fist of open political warfare. The undertone of truculence in his conciliatory reply to Howard swelled to a crescendo as the 1936 presidential campaign took shape.

Roosevelt effectively opened his antibusiness campaign with his annual message to Congress on January 3, 1936. Departing from prece-

48. PPA (1935), 354–57.
49. T. Harry Williams, Huey Long (New York: Knopf, 1969), 866, 876.
50. Ickes Diary 1:480.

dent, he delivered his address in the evening, to ensure the largest possible radio audience. Further breaking with tradition, he used the occasion not to describe the state of the Union but to make a blatantly political speech, pillorying his vaguely defined but nonetheless recognizable foes on the right. "We have earned the hatred of entrenched greed," the president declared. "They seek the restoration of their selfish power. . . . Give them their way and they will take the course of every autocracy of the past—power for themselves, enslavement for the public."[51] Huey Long himself could scarcely have put it more pungently. Republicans in the House chamber guffawed loudly when Roosevelt in conclusion referred to "this message on the state of the union." Even the left-leaning *Nation* was unsettled. "The President," it declared, "showed himself complete master of the grammar of vituperation." The magazine went on to condemn the president for turning "what was supposed to be a thoughtful discussion of the nation's ills and ways of treating them into a political diatribe."[52]

Diatribe was one thing. Money was another. Roosevelt soon pressed for further tax reform, reopening the wounds inflicted by his 1935 "wealth tax." On March 3, 1936, he sent Congress a supplemental budget message asking for a tax on undistributed corporate profits. This time, the government's revenue needs were real enough. The Supreme Court's elimination of the AAA had deprived the treasury of some $500 million in anticipated tax receipts. And over Roosevelt's veto, Congress had passed the long-stalled "bonus bill" in late January, calling for payments to World War I veterans of nearly $2 billion in 1936, instead of 1945. The bonus payment created a requirement for a $120 million carrying charge in each of the following nine years, to service the debt incurred to make the lump-sum distribution to the veterans. But in choosing to raise the needed revenues by taxing undistributed corporate profits, Roosevelt was threatening to shove the hand of government into the innermost workings of private businesses. Advocates of the scheme argued that a tax on retained earnings would create incentives to distribute profits in the form of higher wages or dividends, thus stimulating consumption. The tax also fitted nicely with views that Tugwell had expressed in *Industrial Discipline and the Governmental Arts* in 1933: that retained corporate earnings were one mechanism by which industrial managers loosed themselves from the discipline of the money

51. *PPA* (1936), 13–16.
52. *Nation*, January 15, 1936, 60, 65.

markets and funded bad investment decisions or built redundant industrial facilities, thus exacerbating the structural problem of excess industrial capacity. Opponents countered that the tax would crimp management's ability to save against a rainy day, would enslave businessmen to the bankers, and, most important, would make it difficult for managers to plan for the kind of expansion that fostered economic growth. Business hated the undistributed corporate profits tax. Congress in the end harkened to the critics and significantly watered down FDR's original proposal, setting the tax rate at 7 to 27 percent and largely exempting small enterprises. But the final law did establish the principle that retained earnings could be taxed. In corporate boardrooms from Wall Street to the Golden Gate, fear and loathing of Roosevelt deepened.

More was to come. On June 27, 1936, Roosevelt accepted the Democratic Party's presidential nomination in a memorable speech broadcast nationwide from Philadelphia's Franklin Field.[53] "Philadelphia is a good city in which to write American history," he began, and proceeded to compare the patriots' struggle against political autocracy in 1776 to his own struggle against "economic royalists" 160 years later. "Necessitous men are not free men," he intoned, and argued that economic inequality made political equality meaningless. Before the New Deal, he charged, "[a] small group had concentrated into their own hands an almost complete control over other people's property, other people's money, other people's labor—other people's lives. For too many of us life was no longer free; liberty was no longer real; men could no longer follow the pursuit of happiness.

"Against economic tyranny such as this," Roosevelt went on, "the American citizen could appeal only to the organized power of Government." Then, in a lyrical peroration that would long echo in American political oratory, he said:

> Governments can err, Presidents do make mistakes, but the immortal Dante tells us that divine justice weighs the sins of the cold-blooded and the sins of the warm-hearted in different scales.

53. The occasion was memorable for more than the speech. It also marked one of the few times that Roosevelt's physical handicap was publicly and humiliatingly displayed. On his way to the platform, Roosevelt reached out to shake the hand of the elderly poet Edwin Markham. The locking device on his steel leg brace sprang open, and Roosevelt fell helplessly to the ground. An aide forced the brace back into position; Roosevelt snapped, "Clean me up," and proceeded to the rostrum. Few people beyond the president's immediate entourage saw the incident. An account is in Schlesinger 3:583–84.

Better the occasional faults of a Government that lives in a spirit of charity than the consistent omissions of a Government frozen in the ice of its own indifference.

There is a mysterious cycle in human events. To some generations much is given. Of other generations much is expected. This generation of Americans has a rendezvous with destiny.[54]

This was too much for Moley. At dinner with Roosevelt in the White House family dining room three days before the Philadelphia speech, Moley's suggestion that the president strike a conciliatory tone in his upcoming address touched off a bitter exchange between the two men. Roosevelt twitted Moley about his "new, rich friends." Moley responded with heat, and Roosevelt grew snappish. "For the first and only time in my life, I saw the President forget himself as a gentleman," one of the other dinner guests recalled. "We all felt embarrassed. . . . It was an ordeal for all of us, and we were relieved when dinner finally broke up."[55]

Moley's friendship with the president effectively ended that evening. Other former allies had already parted company with Roosevelt. Al Smith told a Liberty League banquet at Washington's Mayflower Hotel in January 1936 that he would probably "take a walk" during the November elections. He compared the New Dealers to Marx and Lenin as well as to Norman Thomas. He accused Roosevelt of handing the government over to dreamy professors and bleeding-heart social workers. "Who is Ickes?" he asked. "Who is Wallace? Who is Hopkins, and, in the name of all that is good and holy, who is Tugwell, and where did he blow from?"[56]

Undeterred by this attack from his old political comrade, Roosevelt turned up the heat. When the Republicans gave their presidential nomination to the bland and genial Kansas governor, Alf Landon, touted as the "Kansas Coolidge" but in fact a mildly liberal legatee of the old Bull Moose tradition, Roosevelt largely ignored him. He especially ignored the Republican platform's pledge to "use the tax power for raising revenue and not for punitive or political purposes." He campaigned instead against "greed" and "autocracy." Business interests returned the fire. They drove Roosevelt to a cold fury late in the presidential campaign, when some employers distributed messages in paychecks charging

54. PPA (1936), 230–36.
55. Samuel I. Rosenman, *Working with Roosevelt* (New York: Harper and Brothers, 1952), 105; see Moley's own account in *After Seven Years*, 345.
56. Leuchtenburg, 178.

that the new Social Security system would require all participants to wear stainless-steel identification dogtags around their necks and that there was "no guarantee" that workers would ever see their payroll-tax deductions, scheduled to begin on January 1, 1937, returned to them as old-age pensions. Enraged, Roosevelt began to compare himself with Andrew Jackson, the president who had first demonstrated the political power of the populist style. "It is absolutely true," Roosevelt said, that Jackson's opponents "represented the same social outlook and the same element in the population that ours do."[57]

Ending his presidential campaign with a long speechmaking swing around the Northeast, especially the industrial districts of Pennsylvania, New England, and New York, Roosevelt brought his political jihad to a rousing climax in New York's Madison Square Garden on the evening of October 31, 1936. Leaning into the microphone after an uproarious thirteen–minute ovation, Roosevelt indicted his "old enemies": the sponsors and beneficiaries of "business and financial monopoly, speculation, reckless banking, class antagonism, war profiteering"—in short, "organized money." In a voice that even a sympathetic historian calls "hard, almost vengeful," Roosevelt went on: "Never before in all our history have these forces been so united against one candidate as they stand today. They are unanimous in their hate for me—and I welcome their hatred." The crowd erupted. "I should like to have it said of my first Administration," Roosevelt continued, "that in it the forces of selfishness and of lust for power met their match. I should like to have it said . . ." The crowd exploded with anticipation. "Wait a moment! I should like to have it said of my second Administration that in it these forces met their master." Bedlam broke out on the arena floor as the partisan audience roared its approval. But the spectacle at Madison Square Garden troubled other observers of the president's campaign. "Thoughtful citizens," Moley reflected, "were stunned by the violence, the bombast, the naked demagoguery of these sentences. No one who has merely read them can half know the meaning conveyed by the cadences of the voice that uttered them. . . . I began to wonder," Moley reflected, "whether he wasn't beginning to feel that the proof of a measure's merit was the extent to which it offended the business community."[58]

57. Leff, *Limits of Symbolic Reform*, 189; Schlesinger 3:637.
58. PPA (1936), 566–73; Moley, *After Seven Years*, 352. 313. Good accounts of the occasion are in Schlesinger 3:638–39; Leuchtenburg, 184; and Davis 3:644–45.

Why did Roosevelt do it? Moley asked himself. Why did the president go out of his way in 1935 and 1936 to antagonize businessmen? Why did he reject Roy Howard's counsel that "there can be no real recovery until the fears of business have been allayed" and instead insist on gratuitously provoking business and thickening its anxiety? Those questions elude easy answers if, like Moley and Howard, one assumes that economic recovery was Roosevelt's highest priority. But if one recognizes that lasting social reform and durable political realignment were at least equally important items on Roosevelt's agenda, then some of the mystery lifts. Politically, Roosevelt had little to lose by alienating the right in 1936. The reforms of 1935 had already estranged many conservatives from the New Deal. A Gallup poll in 1936 showed that while 53 percent of potential voters favored Roosevelt's reelection, only 31 percent of those listed in Who's Who did, a fair index of disaffection among the upper crust. The real danger was that Roosevelt might fail to contain and channel the restive forces swarming on his left. There, in the immigrant wards of the smokestack towns washed by the voice of the Radio Priest, and in the blighted rural districts where one-gallus farmers stirred to the dream of Every Man a King, were the makings of a permanent Democratic political majority that would safeguard the New Deal and possibly even expand it—or of endless unrest that would make it impossible for Roosevelt or anyone else to govern responsibly.[59]

Not the least of Roosevelt's worries was the Union Party, cobbled together in June 1936 by Townsendites, Father Coughlin, and the self-anointed successor to the assassinated Huey Long, a former Disciples of Christ preacher and onetime field organizer for Long's Share Our Wealth clubs, Gerald L. K. Smith. As a stump speaker, Smith outshone even the legendary Long himself. Tall, handsome, and energetic, Smith, said H. L. Mencken, was "the gutsiest and goriest, loudest and lustiest, the deadliest and damndest orator ever heard on this or any other earth . . . the champion boob-bumper of all epochs." He mesmerized audiences with his cry to "pull down these huge piles of gold until there shall be a real job, not a little old sow-belly, black-eyed pea job but real spending money, beefsteak and gravy, Chevrolet, Ford in the garage, new suit, Thomas Jefferson, Jesus Christ, red, white, and blue job for every man." He routinely closed his political rallies with a prayer: "Lift us out of this wretchedness O Lord, out of this poverty, lift us who stand here in slavery tonight. . . . Out of the

59. John M. Allswang, *The New Deal and American Politics* (New York: John Wiley and Sons, 1978), 57.

land of bondage into the land of milk and honey where every man is a king but no one wears a crown. Amen." When the Union Party nominated North Dakota congressman William Lemke for president, Coughlin declared he would produce at least nine million votes for Lemke or quit broadcasting. No one took that claim seriously, but in some states, Democratic pollsters warned, the Union Party might win up to 20 percent of Irish-Catholic votes, enough to sap the political strength of the working-class constituency on which Roosevelt's reelection depended.[60]

To bind the potentially explosive left to him and to reduce its capacity for radical mischief, rhetorical attacks on business were a cheap price to pay. To combat "crackpot ideas," Roosevelt had told a reporter during the "wealth tax" debate in 1935, "it may be necessary to throw to the wolves the forty-six men who are reported to have incomes in excess of one million dollars a year. This can be accomplished through taxation." But in fact Roosevelt's tax proposals had been more bluff than bludgeon. In reality all of Roosevelt's antibusiness "radicalism" in 1936 was a carefully staged political performance, an attack not on the capitalist system itself but on a few high-profile capitalists. This may have been class warfare, as Roosevelt's critics howled, but it was only a war of words. Roosevelt's scathing indictments of business in the 1936 campaign did not so much add insult to injury as they substituted insult *for* injury.[61]

Roosevelt's performance may have carried a low political cost, but it exacted a high price of another sort. Former Brain Truster Adolf Berle reckoned that price in psychological terms as "shattered morale" in the business community, but Berle also recognized that the state of business morale—what Hoover had called business "confidence"—had hard implications for economic recovery. "In the absence of a large Government ownership program," Berle reflected, there was no "class or group to whom we may turn for economic leadership."[62] Yet for the moment Roosevelt seemed willing to slacken his pursuit of recovery in order to consolidate his political gains.

ON NOVEMBER 3, the nation voted. The results extravagantly demonstrated the political shrewdness of Roosevelt's strategy. In the im-

60. Alan Brinkley, *Voices of Protest: Huey Long, Father Coughlin, and the Great Depression* (New York: Knopf, 1982), 173; Williams, *Huey Long*, 699–700; Leuchtenburg, 181–83.

61. Leff, *Limits of Symbolic Reform*, chap. 3, insightfully explores this theme.

62. Beatrice Bishop Berle and Travis Beal Jacobs, *Navigating the Rapids, 1918–1971: From the Papers of Adolf A. Berle* (New York: Harcourt Brace Jovanovich, 1973), 171.

migrant wards of the great industrial cities, where many people had never bothered to cast a ballot before the Depression, and where political loyalties had traditionally shifted mercurially, turnout rose nearly a third over 1932, and voters went overwhelmingly for Roosevelt and the Democrats. This was no accident. Roosevelt had assiduously wooed those voters, and his wooing took many forms. FDR's huge electoral majority of nearly twenty-eight million votes flowed from his rhetorical blasts at the right and from gratitude for unemployment relief and the prospective benefits of Social Security. He had also freely and consciously spent the oldest coin of political exchange: patronage. The New Deal had dispensed CWA and WPA jobs not only to the materially needy but to the politically needed. Roosevelt had disbursed still other favors. One out of four of his judicial appointments had gone to Catholics, more than a sixfold increase from the level of Catholic appointments to the federal bench in the decade of his Republican presidential predecessors. Where they could vote, African-Americans, too, registered their political gratitude not only for WPA jobs but for the highly publicized solicitude of Eleanor Roosevelt. Labor unions, especially the rapidly growing industrial unions robustly flexing their muscles after the passage of the Wagner Act, both contributed to Roosevelt's campaign war chest and turned out the vote for him in huge numbers. The very nature of many New Deal initiatives created political loyalty in direct, palpable ways.

As the political analyst Michael Barone later put it: "The New Deal changed American life by changing the relationship between Americans and their government. In 1930 the federal government consumed less than 4% of the gross national product; except for the Post Office, it was remote from the life of ordinary people. By 1936 the federal government consumed 9% of GNP and through WPA employed 7% of the work force; it was a living presence across the country." That presence meant votes. The four million homeowners whose property had been saved by the Home Owners Loan Corporation, for example, and the many millions more whose bank savings had been secured by the Federal Deposit Insurance Corporation also owed a weighty political debt to Franklin Roosevelt.[63]

63. Michael Barone, *Our Country: The Shaping of America from Roosevelt to Reagan* (New York: Free Press 1990) 95–96. According to Moley, Roosevelt's political adviser and Bronx Democratic boss Edward J. Flynn had laid out the basic campaign strategy at least as early as 1935, when he allegedly told Roosevelt that "there are two or three million more dedicated Republicans in the United States than there are Democrats. The population, however, is drifting into the urban areas. The election

The electoral results were unprecedented. Roosevelt, it was instantly clear, had established the basis for a new and potentially lasting political coalition. He had succeeded in drawing to himself enormous majorities in the working-class industrial cities, all but two of which went Democratic. The Union Party polled a miserable 882,000 votes—powerful testimony to the effects of Roosevelt's successful co-optation of both the program and the rhetoric of the left, as well as to the absence of Huey Long from the scene. Scarcely less pathetic was the Republican showing. Landon gathered sixteen million popular votes but won the electoral votes of only two states, prompting wags to retool the old political saw about the predictive power of Maine's presidential preference. Democrats now gloated that "as Maine goes, so goes Vermont." Among the casualties of the Roosevelt landslide was the venerable *Literary Digest* electoral poll (and soon the *Literary Digest* itself), which had fairly accurately predicted the outcomes of several preceding presidential elections and had forecast a Landon victory in 1936. But the *Digest* this time made the fatal error of polling persons whose names appeared in telephone books and automobile registration lists, unwittingly skewing its sample toward relatively well-off voters.[64]

For Roosevelt, the election was a glorious, ringing triumph. His 523–8 electoral college margin over Landon was the most lopsided result in more than a century, since James Monroe's 231–1 advantage over John Quincy Adams in 1820. In the House the Democrats took 331 seats, leaving the Republicans with but 89. Democrats would hold 76 seats in the new Senate, a crowd so large that twelve freshman Democrats would have to sit on the traditionally Republican side of the aisle. A heavy majority of governorships were now also in the hands of the Democrats. What William Allen White had said of Roosevelt after the 1934 congressional elections was now more true than ever: "He has been all but crowned by the people."[65]

---

of 1932 was not normal. To remain in power we must attract some millions, perhaps seven million, who are hostile or indifferent to both parties. They believe the Republican Party to be controlled by big business and the Democratic Party by the conservative South. These millions are mostly in the cities. They include racial and religious minorities and labor people. We must attract them by radical programs of social and economic reform." Moley, *The First New Deal* (New York: Harcourt, Brace and World, 1966), 379.

64. Peverill Squire, "Why the 1936 Literary Digest Poll Failed," *Public Opinion Quarterly* 52 (1988): 125–33.

65. Davis 3:422.

What would Roosevelt do with that clamorous mandate, and with all that political power? The nation soon had its answer. Some three-quarters of a century earlier, Abraham Lincoln had in his second inaugural address turned away from the immediate political crisis of secession that had preoccupied his first inaugural and dwelt on the stubborn moral evil of slavery. He vowed to prosecute the war "until every drop of blood drawn with the lash shall be paid by another drawn with the sword." So now did Roosevelt in his second inaugural play down the emergency of the Depression. He spoke instead of the enduring evils that he proposed in his second term to vanquish. The first president to be inaugurated in January, Roosevelt looked out over the rain-drenched crowd facing the Capitol's east facade on January 20, 1937, and laid out the manifesto for his second administration:

> In this nation I see tens of millions of citizens who at this very moment are denied the greater part of what the very lowest standards of today call the necessities of life.
> I see millions of families trying to live on incomes so meager that the pall of family disaster hangs over them day by day.
> I see millions whose daily lives in city and on farm continue under conditions labeled indecent by a so-called polite society half a century ago.
> I see millions denied education, recreation, and the opportunity to better their lot and the lot of their children.
> I see millions lacking the means to buy the products of farm and factory and by their poverty denying work and productivity to many other millions.
> I see one-third of a nation ill-housed, ill-clad, ill-nourished.
> It is not in despair that I paint you that picture [Roosevelt concluded] I paint it for you in hope—because the Nation, seeing and understanding the injustice in it, proposes to paint it out. . . . The test of our progress is not whether we add more to the abundance of those who have much; it is whether we provide enough for those who have too little.[66]

It was a noble purpose and a handsome test of progress, enunciated with clarity and passion by an American leader empowered like none before him to make his vision a reality. But as the new year of 1937 opened, Roosevelt faced a future that held perils beyond even his wizardly reckoning.

66. PPA (1937), 1–6.

10

Strike!

My boyhood was a pretty rough passage. I came through it, yes. But that was luck, luck, luck! Think of the others!
— New York senator Robert F. Wagner

Despite Roosevelt's fulminations against business, and despite the fumbling performance of the NRA and AAA, as early as 1935 the economy had begun to show at least modest signs of recovery. In the hollows of Appalachia, miners were retimbering coal shafts dank and rubbled from years of disuse. Workers oiled rusty spindles in long-shuttered textile mills from Massachusetts to the Carolinas. The clang of stamping presses and the buzz of machine tools split the stillness that had descended in 1929 over the great industrial belt between the Ohio River and the Great Lakes. Stevedores were once again winching cargoes onto the docks of Puget Sound and San Francisco Bay. Tugs taken out of mothballs nudged barge-rafts up the Mississippi from New Orleans. Along the Monongahela and the Allegheny, banked forge and foundry furnaces were coughing back to life. Haltingly, hopefully, America was going back to work.

Official figures confirmed the extent of the revival. Gross national product for 1935 stood at nearly $88 billion, well above the low point of some $73 billion in 1933, though still below the 1929 high of $104 billion. A more sensitive gauge of economic performance, measuring the volume of industrial output on a monthly basis, confirmed the steady and even accelerating pace of improvement. On a 1929 base of 100, the Federal Reserve Board's Index of Industrial Production climbed from less than 50 in 1933 to 70 in 1934 and was rising above 80 as 1935 drew to a close. These favorable trends gathered still more momentum throughout 1936 and on into early 1937. By the time of Roosevelt's tri-

288

umphal reelection in November 1936, the ranks of the unemployed had shrunk by nearly four million from the 1933 total of some thirteen million. Within weeks of his inauguration at the end of January 1937, almost two million additional workers had found jobs (though the unemployment rate in 1937 remained at 14 percent and never went lower for the remainder of the decade). Gross national product totaled almost $100 billion for 1936 and would actually exceed the 1929 figure in 1937 (though only barely and briefly).[1]

This economic revival, however tenuous, set the stage for the American labor movement's crusade to realize its most elusive goal: organizing the millions of unskilled workers in the great mass-production sectors, especially steel and automaking, into powerful industrial unions. That objective had lain beyond labor's grasp since the Knights of Labor had sputtered to an inglorious death some fifty years earlier. It had receded even further from reach as the Depression had perversely immunized firms without customers from labor's most potent weapon, the threat of work stoppage. But prosperity, especially the first prosperity after such a long interval of depression, rendered many firms vulnerable once again to the tactics of slowdown and strike.

Other elements essential to accomplishing labor's goals were also falling into place. Thanks to the Norris–La Guardia Act of 1932, which had bound the federal judiciary from issuing injunctions in labor disputes, capital could no longer look to the federal courts for help. Successful labor organizing now depended as never before on friendly, or at least neutral, state governments. Many governors in the past had proved all too willing to send in the militia to break picket lines and escort scabs into struck mills, mines, and factories. But by 1937, due largely to the active campaigning and generous funding of John L. Lewis's United Mine Workers, liberal Democrats, sympathetic to labor, held the governorships of several key industrial states. Herbert Lehman presided in New York. George Earle sat in the statehouse in steelmaking Pennsylvania, where the long-silent mills were now thundering at 90 percent of capacity and beginning to generate profits for the first time in half a decade. And on January 1, 1937, Frank L. Murphy took the oath of office as governor of Michigan, where the huge automobile plants that had lain vacant and forlorn since 1929 from Detroit to Flint and beyond were stirring back to life, gearing up for an anticipated

1. Lester V. Chandler, *America's Greatest Depression, 1929–1941* (New York: Harper and Row, 1970), 4–7, 129–32.

production run of some four million cars in the year ahead, nearly double their average annual output in the first half of the decade.

Labor also had reason to hope that as Franklin Roosevelt began his second term the federal government would not merely stand aside but would look benevolently on its purposes. Labor's Non-Partisan League, largely a John L. Lewis creation, had campaigned vigorously for Roosevelt's reelection. Lewis's United Mine Workers treasury alone had furnished the Roosevelt campaign with some $500,000 in funds in 1936. Lewis pointedly reminded the president that labor had turned out the vote for him and his party in the mining and mill districts from the Alleghenies to Chicago. Labor had helped Roosevelt to win traditionally Republican Pennsylvania, which he had lost to Hoover in 1932, and working-class votes helped to produce a 67 percent victory margin in Indiana. Lewis himself, though a lifelong Republican, had emphatically endorsed Roosevelt in 1936. For good measure he had denounced Alf Landon in front of a cheering crowd of coal miners in Pottsville, Pennsylvania, as "just as empty, as inane, and innocuous as a watermelon that had been boiled in a bathtub." For these services, political, financial, and rhetorical, Lewis believed that Roosevelt owed him one—a big one. "We must capitalize on the election," Lewis told his associates in late 1936. Labor had been "out fighting for Roosevelt and every steel town showed a smashing victory for him." Now was the time to demand that the favor be returned.[2]

Most important, the Wagner National Labor Relations Act of 1935 had put a mighty weapon at labor's disposal. The act created at least a skeletal legal framework guaranteeing workers' right to organize and requiring employers to bargain with duly recognized union representatives. It empowered the National Labor Relations Board (NLRB) to supervise elections in which workers might choose their union representatives. It prohibited such "unfair labor practices" by employers as discrimination against union members, refusal to bargain, and, most telling, management sponsorship of company unions.

But the Wagner Act was not by itself sufficient to realize labor's ends. For one thing, the act at first commanded no servile assent from employers. Invigorated by a widely bruited opinion of the American Liberty League that the act was unconstitutional and would soon be formally

2. Melvyn Dubofsky and Warren Van Tine, *John L. Lewis: A Biography* (New York: Quadrangle/New York Times, 1977), 252; Robert H. Zieger, *American Workers, American Unions, 1920–1985* (Baltimore: Johns Hopkins University Press, 1986), 46.

declared so by the Supreme Court, many employers announced that they would openly defy its provisions. For another, even should the law be constitutionally approved, workers must still take the initiative to organize themselves. And once organized, they were guaranteed no particular results by the Wagner Act, which stopped short of compelling employers to reach *agreement* with their employees. As Massachusetts senator David Walsh said during the debate on the Wagner bill:

> Let me emphasize again: When the employees have chosen their organization, when they have selected their representatives, all the bill proposes to do is to escort them to the door of their employer and say, "Here they are, the legal representatives of your employees." What happens behind those doors is not inquired into, and the bill does not seek to inquire into it. . . . The employer . . . is obliged to sign no agreement; he can say, "Gentlemen, we have heard you and considered your proposals. We cannot comply with your request," and that ends it.[3]

Yet for all its limitations, the Wagner Act opened a world of possibility to American labor. Together with the favorable political climate and the vulnerability of the steel manufacturers and automakers to any disruption of their first prospective profits in years, the act helped initiate a historic organizing drive that rearranged the balance of power between American capital and labor. Labor's awakening also secured a broad working-class constituent base that would help to make the Democrats the majority party for a long time to come. Ironically, some of the tactics that were to win labor's victories would in the end also help to hasten the closing of the New Deal era of reform.

If the stage was now set at the end of 1936, it remained for workers themselves to raise the curtain. There had already been a handful of successful, though turbulent, overtures—and many more heartbreaking false starts. The few successes had been cued, as had the several failures been miscued, by the passage of the National Industrial Recovery Act in 1933. The act's Section 7(a), by ostensibly guaranteeing labor's right to collective bargaining, had struck a spark of hope that ignited the heaps of combustibles littered across the American social and economic landscape in 1933. For the remainder of that first New Deal year and into the next, workers seized the chance to redress grievances accumulated over decades of unbridled industrialization and exacerbated by years of

3. Milton Derber and Edwin Young, eds., *Labor and the New Deal* (Madison: University of Wisconsin Press, 1957), 148.

economic collapse: poor wages, arbitrary work rules, no job security and, above all, no union. Some employers, notably General Electric president Gerard Swope, a progressive businessman who was among the architects of the NRA, welcomed and even encouraged the unionization of their employees. More employers, if they honored 7(a) at all, did so by establishing company unions, so-called Employee Representation Plans (ERPs), which were in fact the docile and housebroken creatures of management.[4] When workers persisted in their efforts to realize the promise of 7(a) and gain recognition of their own independent unions, most employers resisted, at times savagely. The federal government itself waffled in its own interpretation of 7(a), sometimes favoring workers, sometimes employers. In this fluid and volatile environment, what can only be called open class warfare, often orchestrated by bellicose radicals, erupted in scores of communities in 1933 and 1934.

In Toledo, Ohio, A. J. Muste's unapologetically radical American Workers Party forged an unusual alliance of both employed and unemployed workers to force the Electric Auto-Lite Company to recognize a new, NRA-spawned union. For several days in May 1934, knots of strikers and National Guardsmen battled through the streets of the city, repeatedly clashing in bare-knuckle brawls. On May 24 the skittish and poorly trained guardsmen botched a bayonet charge into the strikers' ranks. In desperation, they then fired a volley of rifle fire into the crowd. Two men died of gunshot wounds. Chastened, Auto-Lite's management submitted to arbitration that eventually secured the union's right to be recognized.

Elsewhere, even human life proved an insufficient price to purchase labor's goals. In southern California's lush Imperial Valley, the Communist-led Cannery and Agricultural Workers Industrial Union (CAW) set out to organize the stoop-laborers who sweated under the California sun in the Golden State's giant agribusiness "factories in the field." The California field hands, as well as the packers in the canning sheds, worked under conditions that one investigator thought "competed favorably with slavery." Given the color line that separated white growers from their mostly Mexican and Filipino workers, the Imperial Valley recollected slavery in other ways as well. In what was to become a tragically familiar pattern, the growers responded by denouncing the CAW

---

4. Company unions were the fastest-growing of all unions between 1932 and 1935, jumping from 1.25 million to 2.5 million members, who accounted for some 60 percent of all organized workers. Derber and Young, *Labor and the New Deal*, 288.

as a Communist conspiracy. They sent in toughs who strong-armed union officials and killed three unarmed strikers with rifle fire. Without consistent support from either Sacramento or Washington, the federal official sent to mediate the dispute soon resigned in disgust. The Imperial Valley, he declared on his departure in June 1934, "is governed by a small group which, in advertising a war against communism is sponsoring terrorism, intimidation and injustice. . . . It is time the Imperial Valley awakens to the fact that it is part of the United States." The CAW was licked. It withdrew from the valley and soon expired, leaving behind only a militantly antiunion growers' association, the Associated Farmers of California, Inc., and a lasting lesson in the obstacles to unionizing the farm sector. The framers of the Wagner Act acknowledged those obstacles when they specifically exempted agricultural workers from its provisions.[5]

Another explosive labor disturbance rocked California just days after the valley's tense feudal order was bloodily restored. San Francisco longshoremen, protesting shippers' control of the hated "shape-up," where mobs of men milled about at dawn near the Ferry Building and implored an imperious foreman for the favor of a day's employment, had shut down the port of San Francisco for nearly two months. The Industrial Association, a business body formed in 1921 to suppress San Francisco unions, determined to break the strike by force. The association made its move on the morning of July 5, 1934. Under heavy police escort, several red trucks threaded their way past the Ferry Building along the Embarcadero, the broad thoroughfare fronting San Francisco's docklands, to deliver their cargoes of strikebreakers to the idle wharves. The drivers proceeded in cautious convoy, nervously avoiding eye contact with the stevedores manning the picket line that straggled along the fog-laden Embarcadero. Before long the strikers' sullen anger exploded into unshirted rage. Shouting obscenities, men swarmed toward the trucks, flinging rocks and pieces of iron pipe. Police shotguns and revolvers barked; nightsticks flailed; teargas billowed through the streets; bullets shattered windows, showering the crowd with shards of glass. When the fighting finally subsided, two strikers lay dead from gunfire.

At the slain strikers' funeral several days later, thousands of

---

5. Lloyd H. Fisher, *The Harvest Labor Market in California*, quoted in Irving Bernstein, *Turbulent Years: A History of the American Worker, 1933–1941* (Boston: Houghton Mifflin, 1970), 145, 168. The federal official was General Pelham D. Glassford, who had been the Washington, D.C., chief of police at the time of the Bonus March in 1932.

sympathizers slowly shuffled for hours, eight abreast, behind the flatbed trucks bearing the coffins down Market Street. This massive display of community support inspired strike leader Harry Bridges, a wiry Australian firebrand and head of the International Longshoremen's Association (ILA). Bridges made no secret of his association with Communists. He now called for the ultimate weapon in labor's arsenal. It was a fearsome instrument that amounted to a declaration of class war: a general strike. More than 130,000 workers honored Bridges's summons. For four days beginning on July 16, San Francisco became a virtual ghost town, its streets empty, its shops closed, its freight terminals blockaded, its supplies of fuel oil and gasoline shut off. In the end faction-fighting between AFL transit and construction unions and Bridges's ILA crippled the strike, and the City by the Bay returned to its usual routines. The workers eventually secured a contract that abolished the shape-up, but San Francisco, abashed by employer brutality and bruised by the hard punch of labor's muscle, had learned a sobering lesson about the depths of class hatreds.

Other communities were soon to receive the same rough education. Along with St. Paul, its twin city on the opposite bank of the upper Mississippi, Minneapolis had long teetered on the edge of violent class confrontation. Ethnic divisions aggravated seething class antagonisms. Old-stock Yankee grandees controlled the giant flour mills that processed the northern prairie's great grain harvests. They owned the railroads that carried the flour, timber, and Mesabi Range iron ore to market. They ran the banks that financed the Twin Cities' global commodities trade. Those same pillars of the community also bankrolled the Citizens Alliance. Like San Francisco's Industrial Association, the alliance was a pugnaciously antilabor body. In 1934 it outfitted what amounted to a private army to keep the predominantly Scandinavian and Irish working class in place.

The Depression had dealt especially cruelly with the Twin Cities. The agricultural collapse shut down many mills. The slumping steel industry cut back its orders for Mesabi iron, spelling doom both for the mines and for the railroads that moved the ore. A nationwide standstill in construction slashed the demand for lumber. Unemployed lumberjacks and miners, along with foreclosed farmers, drifted into Minneapolis and St. Paul and quickly landed on the relief rolls. By the spring of 1934, a third of the people in Hennepin County depended on public support for their daily bread. The huge and growing pool of the unemployed put relentless downward pressure on the wages of those still clinging to their jobs. Truck drivers suffered particularly badly. They earned as little as twelve dollars weekly and were sometimes paid not in cash but in bruised vegetables.[6]

Led by the radical Dunne brothers, founding members of the Trotskyist Communist League of America, Teamster Local 574 demanded better wages and union recognition for its truck drivers. Like Bridges in San Francisco, the Dunnes in Minneapolis made achieving "closed shop" rules their highest priority—that is, agreement by employers to hire only union members, an arrangement that would give the union, not the bosses, control of the labor pool and hence powerful leverage over wages and work conditions. Like the Industrial Association in San Francisco, the Citizens Alliance would have none of it. When the trucking firms flatly refused to negotiate in the spring of 1934, the Dunnes vowed to stop every wheel in the city. They issued lengths of galvanized pipe and baseball bats to the striking teamsters. For its part, the Citizens Alliance organized a posse of vigilantes called the Citizens Army and armed it to the teeth.

A ragged skirmish in May left two Citizens Army soldiers dead and brought a tense truce, but neither side made meaningful concessions, despite the efforts of federal mediators. Both camps were spoiling for a fight that would break the deadlock. On Bloody Friday, July 20, they got it. A crowd of teamsters cut off a truck that was provocatively trying to move under police escort through a picket line. As if on cue, the police opened fire, pouring round after round of buckshot into the backs of the scattering teamsters. They wounded sixty-seven workers and killed two. Pandemonium convulsed Minneapolis. Governor Floyd Olson, self-described radical and a darling of the intellectual left, declared martial law. The following month, the trucking firms grudgingly accepted the teamsters' closed-shop demands. The Dunnes had won a smashing victory, though at a terrible human cost. In the process, they had laid bare the limits of Olson's vaunted "radicalism" and exposed the weakness of the civil authorities in the face of a disturbance such as the Dunnes were prepared to inflict and the Citizens Army was prepared to accept. They had also made Teamsters Local 574 into a powerful bastion of radicalism within the American labor movement.

In September 1934 even greater violence swept the textile districts from New England to the southern piedmont, as the United Textile Workers (UTW) struck to force mill operators to honor the wage, work-

6. Bernstein, *Turbulent Years*, 229–30.

sharing, and collective bargaining provisions of the Cotton Textile Code, the first and much-ballyhooed industry-wide NRA code signed in July 1933. The strike stretched through some twenty states and posed insuperable logistical problems for its organizers. It was probably doomed from the start. Poorly disciplined worker demonstrations in several New England mill towns degenerated into rioting that claimed two lives and left scores wounded. While federal officials dithered ineptly to resolve the dispute, more blood flowed. A union sympathizer and a deputy were killed in Trion, Georgia, on September 5. On the following day six strikers fell to police guns in South Carolina. Battered everywhere and badly bloodied by the murderous response in the South, the UTW called it quits in October. "We won't have our people going up against machine guns," said a union official. President Roosevelt pleaded for the reemployment of strikers without reprisals, but a reporter wrote from North Carolina in November that the workers continued to "live in terror of being penalized for joining unions." As for the employers, she said, they "live in a state of mingled rage and fear against this imported monstrosity: organized labor." Management's mood was well captured in a trade publication's brazen declaration that "a few hundred funerals will have a quieting influence."[7]

FRANKLIN ROOSEVELT was widely perceived as the patron of labor's awakening, and for a long season he was surely the political beneficiary of labor's growing assertiveness. Labor organizers knew the power of the Roosevelt magic and exploited it shamelessly. John L. Lewis shrewdly invoked the Roosevelt mystique in his organizing drive among coal miners in 1933, when he trumpeted that "the President wants you to join a union." Millions of working-class Americans came to see Roosevelt not simply as their president but as their special advocate, even their personal friend. Scrawling unschooled prose onto lined tablet paper, they reached out by the thousands to touch the presidential hem. "I am a long ways from you in distance yet my faith is in you my heart with you and I am for you sink or swim," a South Carolina textile mill hand wrote to Roosevelt. Strikers surrounding the vast Goodyear tire factory in Akron, Ohio, in 1936 named one of the strong points along their eleven-mile picket line "Camp Roosevelt." (A second was named "Camp John L. Lewis," and a third, with somewhat less ideological punctilio, "Camp Mae West.") Lewis coached his field organ-

7. Bernstein, *Turbulent Years*, 311, 315; Leuchtenburg, 113.

izers to close their speeches by leaning forward, holding high their crossed middle and index fingers, and intoning confidentially: "And I tell you, boys, John L. Lewis and President Roosevelt, why they're just like that!" One North Carolina mill worker summed up the pro-Roosevelt sentiments of many when he said that "Mr. Roosevelt is the only man we ever had in the White House who would understand that my boss is a sonofabitch."[8]

But Roosevelt was in fact a rather diffident champion of labor, and especially of organized labor unions. If he was the worker's patron, it was also true that his fundamental attitude toward labor was somewhat patronizing. Like Secretary of Labor Perkins, he was more interested in giving workers purchasing power than in granting them political power. He believed that passing pension and unemployment laws, as well as wage and hour legislation, rather than guaranteeing collective bargaining rights, was the best way to improve the workers' lot.[9] It was hardly surprising, therefore, that he had offered only episodic and inconsistent guidance to the NRA administrators charged with implementing 7(a). In March 1934 he personally broke the back of a drive to unionize the automobile industry. He imposed a settlement that disallowed the principle of majority rule in determining labor's bargaining representative and that endorsed the hated company unions, thus perpetuating management's ability to divide labor's ranks and dominate the bargaining process. Three months later, the president defied his liberal allies in Congress and supported a bill that established a decidedly weak successor to the NRA's ineffectual National Labor Board. "The New Deal," progressive Republican Senator Bronson Cutting complained, "is being strangled in the house of its friends."[10] As for the Wagner National Labor Relations Act, Roosevelt only belatedly threw his support behind it in 1935, and then largely because he saw it as a way to increase workers' consuming power, as well as a means to suppress the repeated labor

8. Jacquelyn Dowd Hall et al., *Like a Family: The Making of a Southern Cotton Mill World* (New York: Norton, 1987), 291; Robert H. Zieger, *The CIO, 1935–1955* (Chapel Hill: University of North Carolina Press, 1995), 32; Eric F. Goldman, *Rendezvous with Destiny* (New York: Knopf, 1952), 345.

9. The Walsh-Healy Government Contracts Act of 1936 well reflected Roosevelt's preferred approach. That act relied on the government's contracting power, not labor's bargaining power, to improve wages and working conditions. It provided that all government contractors should pay a minimum wage as determined by the secretary of labor and should observe the eight-hour day and the forty-hour week. It also prohibited child and convict labor on government contracts.

10. Bernstein, *Turbulent Years*, 204.

disturbances that, as the act claimed, were "burdening or obstructing commerce."[11] Small wonder, then, that the administration found itself bamboozled and irritated by the labor eruptions of Roosevelt's first term and that it moved only hesitantly and ineffectively to channel the accelerating momentum of labor militancy.

No less alarming to prolabor progressives like Cutting (and Minnesota's Floyd Olson), the house of labor was deeply divided. The self-contented craft unionists who ran the American Federation of Labor as a kind of working-class gentleman's club for skilled tradesmen were at dagger's points with the likes of radicals such as A. J. Muste, Harry Bridges, and the Dunne brothers. The desire of the traditional labor chieftains and their liberal allies to spike working-class radicalism formed no small part of the motivation behind the passage of the Wagner Act. "I am for it as a safety measure," federal mediator Lloyd Garrison testified to the Senate Labor Committee in 1935, "because I regard organized labor in this country as our chief bulwark against Communism and revolutionary movements."[12] In the alarmed eyes of men like Cutting, Olson, Garrison, and even Wagner himself, the Communists were hard, unyielding men, brined in Marxist doctrine, contemptuous of mere "reform," intoxicated with the dream of revolution, howling barbarians at the gates of American civilization. Though exaggerated, that picture was not without foundation. Many radicals, peering into the gloom of Depression America, glimpsed the approaching socialist millennium amidst the social and economic wreckage that cluttered the national landscape. They saw themselves not simply as samaritans who were comforting the working stiff but as men and women who were manipulating the very levers of history, hastening the final conflict that would kill off capitalism once and for all and usher in the promised proletarian utopia. To grasp that great prize they would pay virtually any price, come hell or armed struggle.

JOHN L. LEWIS had more modest aims, but they were ambitious enough. Asked by a reporter in 1937 what labor should have, the United Mine Workers chief quickly replied, "The right to organize," and added: "shorter hours, the prohibition of child labor, equal pay for men and women doing substantially the same kind of work," and a guarantee

---

11. *U.S. Statutes at Large* 49:449, cited in Howard Zinn, *New Deal Thought* (Indianapolis: Bobbs-Merrill, 1966), 196.
12. Bernstein, *Turbulent Years*, 332.

"that all who are able to work and willing shall have the opportunity for steady employment." The reporter pressed on: What about a living wage? "No," Lewis roared, pounding his fist on his desk. "Not a living wage! We ask more than that. We demand for the unskilled workers a wage that will enable them to maintain themselves and their families in health and modern comfort, to purchase their own homes, to enable their children to obtain at least a high-school education and to provide against sickness, disability and death."[13] Lewis, in short, dreamed a realistic, achievable dream for American labor, the dream that workers could enjoy middle-class standards of living, and he described it in terms not unlike those that defined Franklin Roosevelt's own social vision. As Lewis and Roosevelt both saw things, capitalism need not be uprooted, but its fruits must be more equitably distributed.

Dour-visaged, thickly eyebrowed, richly maned, his 230-pound bulk always impeccably tailored, Lewis was a man of ursine appearance and volcanic personality, a no-holds-barred advocate for labor and a fearsome adversary. Businessmen, as well as his own plentiful rivals in the labor movement, denounced him as a berserker and a demagogue. But like FDR, Lewis could credibly present himself in the mid-1930s as a responsible alternative to the far more disruptive radicals stirring menacingly to his left. It was both men's style, Lewis's even more than Roosevelt's, to wax rhetorically extreme but to pursue decidedly moderate policies. Both believed that if peaceful change were rendered impossible, violent revolution would be rendered inevitable. "American labor," Lewis testifed to a Senate Committee in 1933, "stand[s] between the rapacity of the robber barons of industry of America and the lustful rage of the communists, who would lay waste to our traditions and our institutions with fire and sword."[14]

Lewis had been born to Welsh immigrant parents in an Iowa coal-mining town in 1880. As a young man he had followed his father and brothers into the mines, learning firsthand what it was like to descend into the earth's bowels at first light and spend all the sunshine hours pickaxing a coal face illumined only by the wan beam of his headlamp. The young Lewis had also for a time managed the Lucas, Iowa, Opera House and occasionally acted on its stage. It was there, presumably, that he began to fashion his extravagantly thespian persona, which by the 1930s was a carefully wrought specimen of performance art. "My stock

13. *New York Times Magazine*, March 21, 1937, 3.
14. Dubofsky and Van Tine, *John L. Lewis*, 183.

in trade is being the ogre," he once said. "That's how I make my way." To Frances Perkins he estimated that his scowl was worth a million dollars.[15] His stentorian voice could shake an auditorium or bathe an outdoor crowd without help from electrical amplification. He cultivated a grandiloquent, rococo style of speech that was viscous with borrowings from the Bible and the Bard, not to mention elaborate syntactical embroideries of his own artful invention. His ego stretched as far as the undulating Iowa corn fields of his youth, and he made no apology for his incessant self-aggrandizement. "He who tooteth not his own horn," he declared in his trademark vernacular, "the same shall not be tooted."[16]

Lewis might have been the delight of the caricaturists, but he was a deadly serious, eminently practical, and extraordinarily effective labor leader—or, as he preferred to think of himself, "executive." No one inscribed his mark more deeply, or flamboyantly, into the annals of labor history in the 1930s. More keenly than any other man, Lewis understood that the peculiar constellation of political and economic conditions in the mid-1930s presented American labor with a unique opportunity. He was on fire to seize it.

Lewis had used the opening provided by NRA to triple the membership of his own United Mine Workers (UMW) in 1933. He then hoped to employ the UMW, with its bulging treasury and its cadre of seasoned organizers, as an engine to drive the process of industrial unionization in other sectors, especially steel and autos. But first he had to convince the UMW's parent organization, the AFL, to abandon its traditional practice of organizing skilled craftsmen along guild lines and to take up instead the unfamiliar task of organizing unskilled workers on an industry-wide basis. He faced formidable resistance.

Many of the complacent princelings of the AFL contemplated Lewis's plans for industrial unionism with a distaste that bordered on horror. They recollected the circumstances of the AFL's birth in the turbulent 1880s, when Samuel Gompers had led a handful of craft unionists out of the Knights of Labor. Gompers's express purpose was to protect the economic interests of the "aristocrats of American labor," like the skilled carpenters, machinists, and steamfitters, by dissociating them from the undifferentiated mass of workers that the Knights had unsuccessfully tried to weld together. The AFL had done well for its elite and exclu-

---

15. Dubofsky and Van Tine, *John L. Lewis*, 282.
16. Schlesinger 2:138.

sionary member guilds in the half century since Gompers had left the Knights, although its members never added up to more than 10 percent of American workers. Yet it was the federation's very exclusivity, according to its own canonical doctrines, that accounted for its success. The masses of unskilled factory workers whom Lewis now proposed to escort aboard labor's ark conjured visions of a return to the broadly inclusionary, ramshackle organization of the Knights, which most AFL leaders regarded as hopelessly utopian and utterly ineffectual as a guarantor of labor's interests.

More than the purely economic privileges of labor's aristocracy was at stake. With notable exceptions like the heavily Jewish garment and clothing workers, the AFL unions tended to be populated by people of English, Irish, and German stock. Their forebears were well established in the country by the late nineteenth century or earlier. The ranks of the unskilled, on the other hand, were disproportionately composed from the great waves of southern and eastern European "new" immigrants who had landed on American shores in the three decades following the AFL's founding. Teamster president Dan Tobin sneered at those latter-day immigrants as "the rubbish at labor's door." Such ethnic antagonisms, coupled with the distinct economic interests that divided skilled from unskilled workers, created yawning cultural and political chasms that badly fissured the American working class. Many of the old-line AFL chieftains would have no truck with the ethnically exotic, unwashed *Lumpen* that Lewis now hoped to mobilize. "My wife can always tell from the smell of my clothes what breed of foreigners I've been hanging out with," one AFL organizer said contemptuously.[17]

By late 1935 Lewis was fed up with the AFL's clubby disdain for the cause of industrial unionism. A year earlier, in San Francisco, the federation's annual convention had resolved to commence organizing in the industrial field, but little organizing had actually taken place. Lewis therefore arrived at the 1935 AFL convention in high dudgeon and poised for full rhetorical flight. "At San Francisco they seduced me with fair words," he proclaimed to the assembled delegates in Atlantic City when he took to the rostrum on October 16. "Now, of course, having learned that I was seduced, I am enraged and I am ready to rend my seducers limb from limb. . . . Heed this cry from Macedonia that comes from the hearts of men," he pleaded. If the AFL did not take up the

17. Dubofsky and Van Tine, *John L. Lewis*, 203; Melvyn Dubofsky, *American Labor since the New Deal* (Chicago: Quadrangle, 1971), 9.

cause of industrial unionism, he warned, a golden opportunity for labor would be lost and "high wassail will prevail at the banquet tables of the mighty."[18]

Despite Lewis's operatic oratory, the convention overwhelmingly rejected a resolution supporting industrial unionism. Lewis was infuriated. When carpenters' union president Big Bill Hutcheson called Lewis a "bastard" in the course of a haggle over parliamentary rules, Lewis's wrath exploded. With a swift jab to the jaw, he sent Hutcheson crashing over a table, blood streaking his face from forehead to chin. Then, an observer related, "Lewis casually adjusted his collar and tie, relit his cigar, and sauntered slowly through the crowded aisles to the rostrum."[19]

Given Lewis's penchant for the theatrical, the punch that decked Hutcheson may well have been a premeditated blow, an artfully staged declaration of the civil war in labor's ranks that Lewis now proposed to wage without mercy. Just three weeks later, he widened his breach with the craft unionists. Together with David Dubinsky of the International Ladies Garment Workers Union (ILGWU) and Sidney Hillman of the Amalgamated Clothing Workers (ACW), he announced on November 9, 1935, the formation of a new labor body, the Committee for Industrial Organization (CIO). Lewis pledged five thousand from the UMW treasury to get the CIO up and running. Dubinsky and Hillman contributed like amounts from their respective unions. For the moment the CIO remained within the AFL, but given its purposes and Lewis's personality, its eventual breakaway was all but inevitable. Lewis took another step in that direction on November 23, when he resigned his AFL vice-presidency.

THE CIO's FIRST OBJECTIVE was steel, a historically impregnable citadel of antiunionism. Lewis called steel the "Hindenburg Line" of American industry. Cracking that line, he believed, was the key to the success of industrial unionism everywhere. Steel posed a mountainous challenge. Because steel production was divided into many discrete stages, steelworkers were parceled out into numerous small work gangs, physically separated and often ethnically segregated, making mass organization difficult. The acrid memory of past labor defeats hung like soot over the steel districts. In 1892 a strike over recognition of the Amalgamated Association of Iron and Steel Workers had been broken

18. Bernstein, *Turbulent Years*, 392.
19. Dubofsky and Van Tine, *John L. Lewis*, 220.

in a legend-leaving clash that killed ten steelworkers at Homestead, Pennsylvania. Another huge effort to unionize steel was utterly crushed in 1919, not least by management's cynical exploitation of the ethnic and racial tensions that seamed the polyglot steel work force.[20]

A handful of enormous corporations dominated the steel industry — U.S. Steel with 222,000 employees, Bethlehem with 80,000, Republic with 49,000. U.S. Steel alone, known in the trade simply as "Big Steel," with its mammoth milling and fabricating facilities concentrated around Pittsburgh, Chicago, and Birmingham, could produce more steel than Germany, the world's second-largest steelmaking *country*. In the stark company towns that pocked the steel regions, Big Steel and the other, so-called Little Steel companies, all ruled with feudal sway. They defied labor organizers and even federal authorities with impunity. In Homestead, haunted by the specters of 1892, no union meeting had been held since 1919. In 1934 U.S. Steel's minions in Homestead had successfully prevented Labor Secretary Frances Perkins from speaking in the town's public park.

But Lewis could see that things were changing in 1936, thanks to labor's growing political clout as well as the nascent economic recovery and, not least, because the public mood was swinging in labor's favor. Since the Depression's onset, many middle-class readers had encountered poignant, sympathy-inducing accounts of working-class life in "proletarian novels" like Tom Kromer's *Waiting for Nothing* (1935) and Edward Anderson's *Hungry Men* (1935). Much art and literature reflected the leftish cultural mood of the Depression decade, when workers could plausibly be cast as heroes and capitalists as villains. Two monumental trilogies instructed large reading audiences about the stark realities of workers' culture: James T. Farrell's unsparing chronicle of an Irish immigrant family in Chicago, *Studs Lonigan* (1932–35) and John Dos Passos's phenomenally comprehensive and inventive contraption, *USA* (1930–36). Erskine Caldwell's *Tobacco Road* (1932) and John Steinbeck's *Tortilla Flat* (1935) and *In Dubious Battle* (1936) etched indelible portraits of the wretched lives of agricultural workers, still more than 20 percent of the work force. Throughout 1935 New York theatergoers were nightly brought to their feet, yelling, "Strike! Strike!" as the curtain closed on the Group Theatre's production of Clifford Odets's agitprop

20. For an account of the 1919 steel strike, see David M. Kennedy, *Over Here: The First World War and American Society* (New York: Oxford University Press, 1980), 270–79.

one-acter *Waiting for Lefty*, arguably the best work of proletarian liter-ature to come out of the 1930s. Films like King Vidor's elegaic *Our Daily Bread* further deepened a vein of sympathy for workers, especially the unemployed.

In June 1936 the U.S. Senate considerably widened the stage for prolabor propaganda. It charged a committee chaired by Wisconsin's Senator Robert M. La Follette Jr. "to make an investigation of violations of the rights of free speech and assembly and undue interference with the right of labor to organize and bargain collectively."[21] The La Follette Committee became a mighty organ of publicity, pumping out exposés of the criminal underside of corporate labor relations policies — includ-ing espionage, naked intimidation, and armed thuggery. These revela-tions further fostered a climate of opinion favorable to labor and, at least for a season, restrained management from its customary reliance on the mailed fist. And of course the Wagner Act's creation of the NLRB in-stitutionalized the government-labor partnership, a crucial political da-tum that was plain to all observers.

In a moving demonstration of labor's mounting confidence, two thousand steelworkers and coal miners gathered on a sunny July Sun-day in 1936 at the old Homestead battleground to pay homage to the martyrs of 1892. The lieutenant governor of Pennsylvania, who was also a UMW vice-president, gazed out over the picnicking crowd and de-clared the steel towns open to union organizers. On behalf of Governor George Earle, he promised public relief payments to workers and their families in the event of a strike — in effect, a taxpayers' subsidy for a la-bor action. At the graveside of the men slain in 1892, a UMW official offered a brief prayer: "We have come to renew the struggle for which you gave your lives. We pledge all our efforts to bring a better life for the steel workers. We hope you have found peace and happiness. God rest your soul."[22]

In this atmosphere the CIO's great steel organizing drive began. Hurl-ing defiance at the do-nothing AFL, in June 1936 Lewis launched the Steel Workers Organizing Committee (SWOC), with his faithful lieu-tenant, UMW vice-president Philip Murray, as its head. This was the last straw for the AFL leadership. They accused Lewis of dividing labor's ranks by organizing a rival union — the unforgivable sin of "dual union-ism" — and drubbed the CIO member unions out of the AFL, thus es-

---

21. Bernstein, *Turbulent Years*, 451.
22. Bernstein, *Turbulent Years*, 434.

calating labor's fratricidal war.[23] Lewis responded with characteristic flame and sulfur and threw in some gratuitous aspersions on his adversaries' manhood. "It is inconceivable," he wrote to AFL president William Green, "that you intend . . . to sit with the women under an awning on the hilltop, while the steel workers in the valley struggle in the dust and agony of industrial warfare."[24] The CIO, Lewis announced, would contribute up to $500,000 to finance the steel drive. That figure soon swelled to more than $2.5 million, most of it from the coffers of the UMW. In addition to Murray, the UMW also contributed twelve trained organizers to SWOC, the nucleus of a field staff that grew to 433. Dubinsky's ILGWU and Hillman's ACW seconded other experienced men to the committee. Before long SWOC organizers were motoring into steel towns from Pennsylvania to Illinois to Alabama, often accompanied by automobiles marked "Car of the United States Senate, La Follette Civil Liberties Committee Investigators."[25]

Significantly, the CIO's and SWOC's top leadership, with the conspicuous exception of Lewis himself, were themselves immigrants — as was Robert Wagner, the legislative craftsman of the epochal labor law that bore his name. They were men viscerally in touch with the fiber and rhythms of the lives of the workers they sought to organize. At the age of nine, Wagner had been the youngest of six children who migrated with their parents to New York in 1886 from the Rhineland village of Nastatten. The ILGWU's David Dubinsky had been born David Dobnievski in Brest-Litovsk in Russian Poland in the fateful year of 1892. He had traveled in steerage to New York City in 1911. Sidney Hillman was born as Simcha Hillman in the Lithuanian shtetl of Zagare in 1887 and arrived in New York twenty years later, after giving up his studies for the rabbinate. In 1936 Dubinsky and Hillman, favoring practical results over doctrinal purity, organized a mass defection from Norman Thomas's Socialist Party to Roosevelt's Democrats, effectively destroying the Socialists as a political force.

As for SWOC chairman Philip Murray, it was his special quality, a journalist wrote, "to touch the love and not the fears of men." But Murray knew their fears, too — the fears of joblessness and employer intimidation, the fears bred of being a stranger in a strange land, part

23. The CIO would formally acknowledge its departure from the AFL in October 1938, when it officially changed its name to the Congress of Industrial Organizations. The AFL and the CIO then remained separate bodies until their merger in 1955.
24. Dubofsky and Van Tine, *John L. Lewis*, 238.
25. Bernstein, *Turbulent Years*, 455.

of the flotsam torn loose by the tidal wave of industrial revolution that swept tens of millions of Europeans across the Atlantic in the years around the turn of the century. Murray's own family were immigrants twice over. His father had taken them out of Catholic Ireland to seek work in the coal mines of Scottish Blantyre. Murray was born in Glasgow in 1886 and never lost his soft Glaswegian burr. In 1902, when Phil was sixteen, the Murrays moved again, this time to the coal districts of Pennsylvania, their second uprooting in a generation. These forced removals deeply shaped Murray. In common with Wagner, Dubinski, Hillman, and Lewis, too, he was no ideologue, no bookish theorist who dealt in abstractions like "proletariat," no slave to doctrines that were unchecked by the feel of flesh and blood and the habits of fellow-feeling. Each of these men knew in his own marrow the disquiet of impermanency, the dread of tomorrow, and above all the yearning for security that daily squeezed at the hearts of the men and women in America's factories, mills, and mines. The "quest for security," Hillman declared in 1934, was "the central issue in this life of modern man."[26]

Under Murray's leadership and with the blessing of Lewis, Dubinsky, and Hillman, SWOC was determined to avoid the fate of previous attempts to unionize the steel industry, which had foundered on the rocks of ethnic and racial rivalry. History was on their side by 1936. The cessation of mass immigration in the early 1920s had given America's several immigrant communities time to stabilize. By the 1930s they contained a much larger proportion of native-born Americans who spoke English as their mother tongue than had been true in 1892 or 1919.

What was more, the pervasive influence of the new mass popular entertainments that began to flourish in the 1920s, including movies and radio, had nurtured in the immigrant neighborhoods at least the rudiments of a common culture that, for better or worse, proved powerfully corrosive to their separate old-world identities. Then the Depression had dealt a mortal blow to the fragile infrastructure of ethnic banks, neighborhood grocery stores, and nationality-based charity societies that had sustained ethnic separateness for generations. The Depression had also powerfully catalyzed a sense of common economic grievance that transcended the particular loyalties of the nation's diverse immigrant groups. For the first time since the age of mass immigration had begun some fifty years earlier, culturally variegating the American labor force

26. Steve Fraser and Gary Gerstle, eds., *The Rise and Fall of the New Deal Order, 1930–1980* (Princeton: Princeton University press, 1989), 78.

to a degree unknown in other industrial countries, the possibility hovered just over the horizon that a unified American working *class* could be forged out of America's heterogeneous ethnic enclaves.[27]

Sensing that possibility, SWOC began its organizing campaign in the fraternal and religious organizations that ministered to the various steel communities. SWOC field workers spoke reassuringly to apprehensive little groups gathered in the bare meeting halls of Lithuanian Lodges, Polish Mutual Benefit Societies, and Czech Sokols, as well as in Hungarian churches and Italian men's clubs. Black workers constituted a special case. Many blacks had found their first industrial employment as strikebreakers in the steel strike of 1919. They thereby earned the lasting resentment of the striking whites, whose proferred hand they now hesitated to grasp. They had also secured the grudging patronage of the steel companies, whose wrath they now were disinclined to provoke. SWOC consequently made little headway among blacks, though it continued to enunciate the principle, as did the CIO in general, of racial equality in union membership.[28]

In a gesture that served notice to the steelmakers that labor now meant to be recognized as an equal partner with capital, Lewis and Murray set up SWOC's headquarters in Pittsburgh's Grant Building, where several steel corporations had their home offices. Directed from Murray's thirty-sixth-floor Pittsburgh office and fueled by UMW money, SWOC organizers fanned out into the steel districts in the summer and fall of 1936. By the end of the year they had taken over the old Amalgamated Association of Iron, Steel, and Tin Workers (AA), a nearly lifeless AFL

27. For a brilliant and detailed analysis of the ways in which mass culture and the Depression forged a new class consciousness out of the ethnically divided American labor force, see Lizabeth Cohen, *Making a New Deal: Industrial Workers in Chicago, 1919–1939* (New York: Cambridge University Press, 1990).
28. Black groups like the NAACP and the Urban League had worried that the Wagner Act itself might perversely reinforce racism. To the extent that the act allowed unions to secure "closed shops," where only union members could be employed, unions could in theory bar blacks from membership and hence from employment. Senator Wagner and the act's other sponsors, however, failed to accept suggested amendments that would have defined racial discrimination by a union as an "unfair labor practice." Thus the CIO's inclusionary policy, for all its difficulties in practice, was not driven by legal requirement but by the organization's own sense of racial justice and of effective industrial unionizing strategies. Not all CIO unions consistently followed inclusionary policies; in future years, unions themselves would be major battlegrounds in the struggle for racial equality. See Bernstein, *Turbulent Years*, 189–90, 454.

affiliate, and filled its hollow organizational shell with dedicated industrial unionists. SWOC and AA organizers next systematically undertook to capture control of the various company unions, or ERPs, that management had summoned into being since 1933.

The steelmakers fought back. Invoking the American Liberty League's pronouncement on the Wagner Act's unconstitutionality, they tried to sustain the ERPs, in clear violation of the act's strictures against company unions, by offering ERP-covered workers seductively generous wage increases. SWOC organizers countered that the real issue was long-term union independence, not short-term pay. Both sides dug in for the siege of Fortress Steel. Pittsburgh's Grant Building, where Murray and the steel executives routinely rode the elevators together in stiff silence, seemed likely to become the epicenter of a titanic confrontation that would paralyze the steel industry, idle thousands of workers, snarl the economy, and perhaps touch off yet another round of violence. As winter closed over the industrial heartland at the end of 1936, a mood of nervous apprehension gripped the steel regions. The possibility loomed of a strike even more rancorous and bloody than the great upheavals of 1892 and 1919.

THE FATEFUL ERUPTION, however, came not in the steel towns around Pittsburgh but in Flint, Michigan—in autos, not in steel. It began on the evening of December 30, 1936, when a young woman at the United Auto Workers' Flint office switched on a two-hundred-watt red bulb, the signal for a meeting. The simple flick of that light switch set off a chain of events that forever altered the place of labor in American society.

Flint, some sixty-five miles north of Detroit, was a gritty monument to the transfiguring power of the industrial revolution. Just three decades earlier, Flint had been a quiet country village, devoted principally to making carriages and buggies. By the 1920s it had become a boom town, a pulsing industrial organism that pumped its myriad products through the labyrinthine arteries of the greatest of all mass-production industries, that signature creation of American consumer capitalism: automobile manufacturing. In 1936 Flint was ailing, to be sure, but it remained the solar plexus of the General Motors Corporation's colossal automaking empire.

Even bigger than Big Steel, GM was the world's largest manufacturing corporation. Its quarter million employees made nearly half of all American cars in 1936. Virtually all the rest were manufactured by just two other firms, Ford and Chrysler. GM dominated an industry even more oligopolistic than steel, and since oligopolies by their very nature impede price flexibility, the "Big Three" American carmakers traditionally sought to bolster their profit margins not by raising prices but by cutting costs, especially labor costs. Hourly wage rates for autoworkers were high, but their gross incomes were low, thanks to the industry's practice of periodically shutting down the production lines to accommodate annual model changes. The Ford Motor Company exacerbated the effects of that practice by its policy of rehiring seasonally laid-off workers, regardless of skill or seniority, at the starting rate. Autoworkers, in common with mass-production workers everywhere, also chafed at their enthrallment to the despotic tempo of the assembly line, especially the hated speed-up. They graveled, too, under the often arbitrary control of foremen who hired and fired and promoted and penalized at whim. And the Great Depression, of course, by virtually extinguishing the market for new cars, had visited upon autoworkers especially appalling rates of unemployment.

These accumulated grievances, compounded by the Depression, made the autoworkers peculiarly ripe for industrial unionism. So did the physical circumstances of auto production, where huge gangs, effectively undifferentiated by skill, worked together under one roof on enormous factory floors. At Ford's River Rouge complex alone, the world's largest integrated industrial plant, some ninety-five thousand lunch bucket–toting workers poured daily through the factory gates at peak employment. And as in steel, so too in the automotive sector did the timing seem propitious for an organizational campaign. The Big Three in late 1936 were gearing up for their largest production runs in years, rendering them especially vulnerable to the threat of work stoppage.

But labor organizers faced daunting obstacles in the auto industry. As the La Follette Committee revealed to an indignant nation, Ford Motor Company's blandly named Service Department, headed by a pint-sized ex-pugilist named Harry Bennett, ruthlessly suppressed even the faintest stirrings of union sentiment. Workers suspected of union sympathy were summarily dismissed or physically harrassed on the shop floor — "shaking 'em up in the aisles," Bennett called it. Bennett built Ford Service into a paramilitary force of some three thousand armed men who stalked and threatened "disloyal" employees and inflicted physical injuries without scruple or remorse. His minions, said Bennett, were all "tough sons-of-bitches, but every one a gentleman." At General Motors, antiunion tactics were more subtle but no less effective. In 1934 and 1935 GM spent nearly $1 million to field a force of wiretappers, infiltrators, and finks that the La Follette Committee condemned as "a far-flung industrial Cheka . . . the most colossal supersystem of spies yet devised in any American corporation."[29]

Among the consequences of the automakers' wholesale suppression of independent unions were the need for labor organizers to work under the cloak of secrecy and the need for tactics that did not depend on mass participation, as the traditional techniques of walkout and picket line required. Those stark necessities mothered a simple invention: the sit-down strike. Legend to the contrary, the great sit-down strike of 1937 in Flint did not spring from a spontaneous explosion of mass worker sentiment. It depended, rather, on the carefully laid plans and skillful execution of a cadre of highly disciplined leaders, many of them Communists. Nor was the sit-down strike, strictly speaking, an American invention. Though the tactic had been sporadically employed in strikes in the Ohio Valley's rubber industry in 1936, its efficacy was spectacularly established in 1937 in France, when a million workers took possession of scores of factories, helped bring Leon Blum to power, and wrung new social and labor legislation out of Blum's socialist government. That awesome display of the sit-down's power inspired American unionists. It also frightened many in the great property-owning American middle class.

The logic of the sit-down strike called for identifying a critical pressure point in the ganglia of the huge automaking system and pinching off production at that strategic site. Fisher Body Plant Number One in Flint was just such a point. It contained one of only two sets of body dies for GM's 1937 model Pontiacs, Oldsmobiles, Buicks, and Cadillacs (the other set of dies, for Chevrolets, was in the Fisher plant in Cleveland). If Fisher Number One could be taken off line, GM's output could be choked to a trickle. Accordingly, United Auto Workers (UAW) organizers, working nervously in an environment they knew to be honeycombed with spies and stool pigeons, were preparing in late 1936 to seize control of Fisher One, as well as Fisher Cleveland, early in the new year.

Events soon accelerated this timetable. In the fading late afternoon light of December 30, a UAW member inside Fisher One noticed that railroad cars had rolled up to the plant's loading dock, where men were

29. R. L. Tyler, *Walter Reuther* (N.p.: William B. Eerdmans, 1973), 39; Bernstein, *Turbulent Years*, 516–517.

preparing the critical dies for shipment. He phoned the information to the UAW office across the street, causing the red meeting light to go on. At 8:00 P.M., swing-shift workers on their meal break crowded into the UAW hall. Union officials instructed the men to return to the Fisher One plant, sit down, and stay put. The leaders waited anxiously when the starting whistle blew. There was no responsive throb of machinery. "She's ours!" a worker shouted from a third-story window. The dies would not move. The plant was shut down—and occupied.[30]

The Flint sit-down strike amounted to nothing less than the forcible seizure by workers of the means of production—a recognizable enactment of a core tenet of socialism, though the Flint strikers stopped well short of demanding permanent ownership of the seized plant. What they did demand, quite simply, was that the General Motors Corporation recognize the United Auto Workers as the sole legitimate bargaining agent for GM employees. There were other demands—for a grievance procedure, a shorter workweek, and a minimum wage scale—but union recognition was the essential item. The Flint sit-down, historian Robert H. Zieger has rightly concluded, "epitomized the two polar, yet complementary, tendencies within the CIO, namely the anger and resentment of large portions of the working class and the modesty of their goals."[31]

GM denounced the sit-down as an unlawful trespass. The giant automaker mounted a publicity campaign to tarnish the strike as the work of Communists and "outsider agitators" and secured an injunction ordering the strikers to evacuate Fisher One. Ignoring the court order, the UAW proceeded to seize additional, adjacent plants. Fisher Two was secured on January 11 following a clash with police that came to be known as the "Battle of the Running Bulls." After staging a clever diversion, unionists on February 1 took over Chevrolet No. 4, a huge installation capable of producing a million engines per year. Inside the plants, Reuther's UAW "captains" organized men into squads of fifteen, insisted on strict adherence to hygiene and safety rules, arranged for food to be delivered, and organized recreational activities to while away the time. Group singing was especially popular and caught the exultant mood of labor's new-found potency:

> When they tie the can to a union man,
> Sit down! Sit down!

30. This account of the automobile sit-down strike is heavily indebted to Bernstein, *Turbulent Years*, chap. 11.
31. Zieger, *CIO*, 46.

>When the speedup comes, just twiddle your thumbs,
>Sit down! Sit down!
>When the boss won't talk, don't take a walk.
>Sit down! Sit down![32]

As the sit-down spread, pressure mounted on Governor Frank Murphy to send in the National Guard. Murphy had no doubt that the strike was illegal. He also had no taste, as he exclaimed to a friend, for "going down in history as Bloody Murphy! If I send those soldiers right in on the men," he explained, "there'd be no telling how many would be killed. It would be inconsistent with everything I have stood for in my whole political life." After the Battle of the Running Bulls, Murphy did in fact mobilize the Michigan Guard, but only to keep order, not to break the strike. "The state authorities," the governor declared, "will not take sides. They are here only to protect the public peace . . . And for no other reason at all." Following the lead of Governor Earle in Pennsylvania, Murphy also authorized relief payments for the families of the strikers. For virtually the first time in the history of American industrial conflicts, state officials determined to sit on their hands, leaving labor and capital to negotiate their own way out of the impasse. Discipline and raw economic power, not legal injunction or political intervention, would determine the outcome.[33]

Discipline was no problem, thanks to the tireless and careful leadership of Walter Reuther, the president of UAW Local 174 and a key tactician of the sit-down strike. Reuther had been born to German immigrant parents in Wheeling, West Virginia, in 1907. In 1927 he went to Detroit and got his first job at the Ford Motor Company. Because he worked the swing shift, he could take classes at Detroit's municipal university (later Wayne State University), where he joined the League for Industrial Democracy and plunged into the sectarian jungle of leftist politics. In 1933 Ford laid him off. Reuther and his brother, Victor, cashed in their meager savings and set out to see the world. In Germany, Nazi guides showed them the burned Reichstag building. They worked for a time at a Soviet auto plant in Gorki, helping to make the familiar Model A from dies the Soviets had purchased from Ford. In 1936 Reuther was elected to the board of the infant UAW. He was by then a seasoned organizer and was determined to make the UAW into a powerful industrial union.

John L. Lewis, absorbed in planning for the steel strike, was caught

32. Tyler, *Walter Reuther*, 38.
33. Bernstein, *Turbulent Years*, 541, 534.

off guard by the UAW's initiative but soon scrambled to get control of events in Flint. He denounced GM's owners — singling out the duPont family, the corporation's biggest shareholders, and, not incidentally, the chief financial backers of the Liberty League — as "economic royalists." Reminding Franklin Roosevelt of his debt to labor, Lewis declared that those "economic royalists now have their fangs in labor, and the workers expect the Administration in every reasonable and legal way to support the auto workers in their fight with the same rapacious enemy." On February 3 he left Washington's Union Station to assume personal command over the UAW side of negotiations in Michigan. In a characteristically gratuitous flourish, he intoned to reporters: "Let there be no moaning at the bar when I put out to sea."[34]

Roosevelt, behind the scenes, urged the General Motors executives to reach a settlement that recognized the union. Murphy meanwhile worked on Lewis to temper the strikers' demands. The sit-down was hurting GM badly. Its output plummeted from some 50,000 cars in December 1936 to a mere 125 during the first week in February 1937. The corporation secured a second antistrike injunction in late January but was in fact edging toward agreement with the UAW's demands, especially its central demand for union recognition. Lewis, however, seemed inclined to hold out for more. How to move him the last few inches toward final accord? Murphy, citing the injunction, warned Lewis that as governor of Michigan he had no alternative but to perform his sworn duty faithfully to execute the law. He would have to send in the Guard. What, he asked, would Lewis then do? Lewis in later years gave many versions of his reply. According to one, probably embellished by time and Lewis's promiscuous imagination, he told Murphy:

> You want my answer, sir? I give it to you. Tomorrow morning, I shall personally enter General Motors plant Chevrolet No. 4. I shall order the men to disregard your order, to stand fast. I shall then walk up to the largest window in the plant, open it, divest myself of my outer raiment, remove my shirt, and bare my bosom. Then when you order your troops to fire, mine will be the first breast that those bullets will strike!
>
> And as my body falls from that window to the ground, you listen to the voice of your grandfather [executed for rebellion in nineteenth-century Ireland] as he whispers in your ear, "Frank, are you sure you are doing the right thing?"[35]

34. Dubofsky and Van Tine, *John L. Lewis*, 263–64, 267.
35. Bernstein, *Turbulent Years*, 548.

However colorful this exchange, it was almost certainly of no consequence. Murphy was bluffing. He had already made it clear that he would not send in troops. And General Motors, watching its market share shrink as rivals Chrysler and Ford boosted production to take advantage of the GM shutdown, desperately needed a resolution to the strike. On February 11, after forty-four days of dramatic stand-off, Lewis walked into the GM Building, immediately across Detroit's Grand Boulevard from the Fisher Building where Father Coughlin made his broadcasts. He signed an agreement by which GM recognized the UAW as the exclusive representative of the men in the struck factories. Other UAW demands went unmet for the moment, but the central point had been won. The men marched out of the shut plants to an uproarious celebration. Industrial unionism had established a major beachhead in a core American industry.

The lessons of Flint were not lost on the steelmakers. Given the manifest unwillingness of government to throw its weight to the side of management, the sit-down was an industrial weapon of awesome power. Accordingly, on March 2, 1937, U.S. Steel announced that it would recognize the Steel Workers Organizing Committee. That announcement was astonishing enough. No less astonishing, Big Steel added that it was also granting a pay hike, as well as an eight-hour day and a forty-hour week, with overtime clocked on a "time-and-half" basis. Incredibly, Fortress Steel, the "Hindenburg Line" of antiunionism, had surrendered without a struggle. Like GM, it had caved in to labor's economic power, not to the government's political power. The National Labor Relations Board, still intimidated by the overhanging threat of judicial nullification, had played no direct part in the breakthroughs in autos and steel. To be sure, the board's very existence signaled the changing political climate in which labor-management confrontations would now have to be resolved, but in these two landmark cases, government's most important contribution to the CIO's success had been, quite simply, to stay out of the way.

Lewis's dream of industrial unionism now became a reality at a stunning speed. UAW membership exploded, from 88,000 at the end of the sit-down to 166,000 a month later and more than 200,000 by the end of the year. SWOC signed up more than 300,000 members within two months after U.S. Steel's capitulation. By August 1937 the CIO as a whole claimed to have over 3.4 million members, more than the AFL.

The twin victories in autos and steel infused the CIO with the spirit of a folk movement, radiating camaraderie and idealism and promising to carry all before it. The feeling spread among workers that after generations of frustration, they had at last liberated themselves from legal and political repression, from the ethnic prejudices that divided them, and from the disspiriting memories of their past failures. One worker gave eloquent voice to the intoxicating mood of class solidarity that filled the air: "Once in the Ford plant," he said, "they called me 'dumb Polack,' but now with UAW they call me brother."[36] In this radiantly shining moment, almost anything seemed possible. "The CIO," a writer in the *Nation* concluded, "is changing both the structure and orientation of American labor. . . . It is gradually killing off the AFL. . . . It is profoundly affecting our two major political parties. It is transforming the relationship of government to industry."[37]

YET THE CIO's MOMENT of euphoria was brief. Its agenda remained limited, for the time being, to little more than union recognition. Its organizational structure was fragile and uncertain, hostage to the mercurial moods of John L. Lewis. Internal faction-fighting soon sapped much of the CIO's vitality, particularly in a protracted struggle over Communist influence in the UAW. American communists had long worked through the Trade Union Unity League, a rival body to the AFL, but the CPUSA officially abandoned that policy in 1934. In the following year Josef Stalin directed Communists everywhere to adopt the "Popular Front" strategy of making common cause with all parties on the left, including socialists and orthodox trade unionists, in the struggle against fascism. The asendancy to leadership in the CPUSA of Earl Browder, a Kansas-born accountant and former Socialist, signaled the shift. American Communists now abandoned their efforts to organize separate trade unions and sought cooperative relations with existing labor organizations. Scores of well-trained and dedicated Communist organizers thus became available to the CIO just as it came into being. Lewis welcomed the "red and rebellious" into the mass movement he was trying to mount and made aggressive use of their organizing talents. When the old Socialist David Dubinsky questioned the wisdom of that strategy, Lewis waved his objections away. "Who gets the bird?" Lewis asked, "the hunter or the dog?"[38]

That question was not so easily answered. Though Communists never

36. Zieger, *American Workers*, 68.
37. Dubofsky and Van Tine, *John L. Lewis*, 278.
38. Dubofsky and Van Tine, *John L. Lewis*, 289.

captured the great member-rich, core-industry prizes of the UAW or the steelworkers' union, they did acquire substantial strength in the merchant seamen's and transit workers' unions, and for a long while effectively controlled the United Electrical, Radio, and Machine Workers. The political and ideological struggles within the CIO aggravated and widened the schism with the AFL. The AFL launched a kind of "counterreformation" in 1938, presenting itself to employers—and to workers—as a safer bet than the allegedly radical-infested CIO. "Every CIO representative is looked upon as a walking strike," said one AFL official, an image that frightened both managers and the men and women on the shop floor alike.[39] When Texas congressman Martin Dies opened hearings before the House Committee for the Investigation of Un-American Activities in June 1938, among the first witnesses was the blunt-spoken AFL official John Frey, who attacked the CIO as a seminary of Communist sedition. At one point the AFL even sponsored boycotts of CIO-made goods. These tactics worked. By the end of the decade, the relatively conservative AFL had succeeded in unionizing workers outside the steel and auto industries and regained its position as the largest American labor organization.

If the aroma of radicalism clinging to the CIO repelled many, so, increasingly, did its reputation for a kind of undisciplined, wildcat unionism, permitting unauthorized work stoppages to break out repeatedly. The sit-down tactic in particular was so easily emulated that scattered groups of workers began employing it indiscriminately after the spectacular victory at Flint. GM, which had recognized the UAW in February 1937 precisely in order to end the Flint sit-down, complained to UAW officials that 170 of its other facilities were interrupted by similar actions in the next three months. As those disruptions spread, the public sympathy that had been so crucial to labor's gains began to erode. Indeed, the radical potential of the sit-down tactic had always rattled many middle-class Americans. Two-thirds of respondents in a Gallup poll in February 1937 believed that GM was right not to negotiate with the sit-downers, and strong majorities sympathized with the employers. Senator James Byrnes of South Carolina spoke the sentiments of many when he denounced the sit-down tactic in April, inducing the Senate to vote 75–3 for a nonbinding resolution declaring the sit-down illegal. Two years later, in the case of *NLRB v. Fansteel Metallurgical Corporation*, the

39. Zieger, *CIO*, 67.

Supreme Court unambiguously outlawed the sit-down as "a high-handed proceeding without shadow of a legal right."[40]

Emboldened by these shifts in the winds of public, congressional, and legal opinion, some employers reverted to the old tactics of checking unionization with unbridled force. On many fronts, the CIO was stopped in its tracks. When five UAW organizers, including Walter Reuther, tried on May 26, 1937, to distribute handbills to workers crossing an overpass to enter Ford's River Rouge complex, Bennett's goons beat them bloody. When Henry Luce's *Time* magazine opined that the publicity from the attack had inflicted more harm on Ford Motors than on Reuther, Henry Ford withdrew all advertising from Luce's publications, *Time*, *Life*, and *Fortune*, for the next year and a half. Ford held out against the UAW for four more years. So did several other major employers, including International Harvester, Westinghouse, Maytag, Allis-Chalmers, Weyerhauser, the big meatpackers, and, most notoriously, Little Steel. Only the advent of war as the next decade opened would bring gains as dramatic as those of the first half of 1937.[41]

Little Steel proved the CIO's Waterloo. The "Battle of the Overpass" was but a preview of a far bloodier encounter at Republic Steel Company's South Chicago plant just four days later, on Memorial Day 1937. Republic had been run since 1929 by Thomas Mercer Girdler, a gruff steelman as implacably dedicated to protecting the privileges of capital as Lewis was to asserting the cause of labor. Here, if ever, Lewis's near-irresistible force collided with an all but unmovable object. Girdler had earned a ruthless reputation in the 1920s as the superintendent of the Jones and Laughlin plant at Aliquippa, Pennsylvania, known to steelworkers as "Little Siberia" because of the systematic terror with which Girdler kept his workers in line and unions out. Girdler now assumed the leadership of the Little Steel group's campaign to avoid Big Steel's fate at the hands of the SWOC.

Girdler and Little Steel adopted what came to be called the "Mohawk Valley Formula," a union-busting strategy that had originated at the Remington Rand Corporation's plants in upstate New York in 1936. The Mohawk Valley Formula called for branding union organizers as

---

40. George H. Gallup, *The Gallup Poll: Public Opinion, 1935–1971* (New York: Random House, 1972), 1:41, 48–49, 52, 55; *NLRB v. Fansteel Metallurgical Corp.*, 306 U.S. 240 (1939).
41. Tyler, *Walter Reuther*, 40.

Communists, forming a Citizens Committee to deny unionists community sympathy, securing the support of local police, and fostering organizations of "loyal employees." To these items Girdler added some refinements of his own, including arming Republic Steel's private police force of nearly four hundred men with pistols, shotguns, rifles, and gas grenades. Lewis called Girdler "a heavily armed monomaniac, with murderous tendencies, who has gone berserk." Girdler did not flinch. Rather than "surrender" like U.S. Steel, he announced, he would shut his plants and "raise apples and potatoes." Girdler cannily conceded all the wage and work-condition clauses of SWOC's agreement with U.S. Steel but adamantly refused union recognition. There he drew the line. If labor wanted Little Steel, Girdler, like Grant before Richmond, was prepared to fight it out on that line if it took all summer.[42]

On the summery afternoon of Memorial Day the dreaded confrontation came. A crowd of several hundred picnicking union sympathizers, including women and children, marched toward Republic's South Chicago mill to express their support for UAW pickets pacing peacefully in front of the mill gates. A police cordon moved across the route of the march and ordered the crowd to disperse. Milling and jostling, the two groups faced off for several moments along a quavering three-hundred-foot front. A marcher some twenty feet back lobbed a stick toward the line of confrontation. Suddenly the crack of police pistol shots rent the air. The police rushed forward, firing and laying truncheons and ax handles into the fleeing and the fallen alike. A Paramount Newsreel cameraman captured the chaotic scene in a film thought to be too inflammatory for public release but privately screened for the La Follette Committee. It recorded a maniacal police riot that left ten men dead, seven of them shot in the back. Thirty others, including one woman and three children, suffered gunshot wounds. Nine were permanently disabled. "Can it be true," Lewis asked the following day, "that striking workmen may be shot down at will by the very agents of the law? Is labor to be protected or is it to be butchered?"[43]

More violence quickly followed, trying the patience even of labor's friends. Prolabor Governor Earle was forced to impose martial law on Johnstown, Pennsylvania, in June. Governor Martin Davey had to do the same in Youngstown, Ohio, following the shooting deaths of two steelworkers on June 19. On July 11 police opened fire outside a union

42. Bernstein, *Turbulent Years*, 481.
43. Zieger, *CIO*, 62.

headquarters in Masillon, Ohio, killing three. The summer of 1937 saw the deaths of eighteen workers, all, at least in the short run, in vain. Little Steel did not budge. Public opinion, meanwhile, grew increasingly disquieted at labor's mounting militancy, at the runaway spate of sit-downs, and especially at the apparently ceaseless turbulence that attended the CIO's struggle to conquer Little Steel.

Pressure mounted on Roosevelt to intervene, or at least to make his sympathies clear. He was, he knew, damned if he did and damned if he didn't. How could he take the side of labor without appearing to sanction the increasingly unpopular sit-downs, or even appearing to acquiesce in violence? But how could he condemn labor without affronting the millions of workers who had voted for him in 1936? Asked for his opinion at a press conference on June 29, 1937, he gave a reply that was couched obliquely but probably reflected accurately enough his own exasperation with labor as well as management. "The majority of the people are saying just one thing," Roosevelt declared, quoting a line from *Romeo and Juliet*: "A plague on both your houses." A radio address on the following Labor Day yielded John L. Lewis's retort, cobbled together from his own richly stocked lexical inventory: "Labor, like Israel, has many sorrows. Its women weep for their fallen, and they lament for the future of the children of the race. It ill behooves one who has supped at labor's table and who has been sheltered in labor's house to curse with equal fervor and fine impartiality both labor and its adversaries when they become locked in deadly embrace." With that, the historian Irving Bernstein concludes, "a brief and not very beautiful friendship had come to an end."[44]

THE ROOSEVELT-LEWIS ALLIANCE had lasted five years. It had brought forth a prolific brood of new unions, though many students of labor's flowering in the 1930s have charged that Roosevelt's claims to paternity were weak. As one labor historian has concluded, "one carries away a distinct impression of *inadvertency* in the role the New Deal played in the expansion of the labor movement."[45] Inadvertency, perhaps, but indispensability as well. In the agricultural and service sectors, where the NLRB's writ did not run, the union movement remained

44. *Complete Press Conferences of Franklin D. Roosevelt* (New York: Da Capo, 1972), 9:467; Dubofsky and Van Tine, *John L. Lewis*, 327; Bernstein, *Turbulent Years*, 496.
45. David Brody, *Workers in Industrial America: Essays on the Twentieth-Century Struggle* (New York: Oxford University Press, 1980), 145.

stalled before insurmountable obstacles to effective organizing. But in the industrial sectors that lay under the hand of New Deal policy, labor's gains were dramatic. The simple prospect of that hand's intervention changed the power equation between capital and labor. In fact, the CIO's largest gains in membership came in the period between 1935 and 1937, when the NLRB was hemmed in by the threat of judicial extinction. When the Wagner Act's constitutionality was at last affirmed in the *Jones and Laughlin* case (see p. 335), the NLRB's work load ballooned to thousands of cases per month. But the big organizing successes at GM and U.S. Steel were by then already well secured.

From some three million union members in 1933, the ranks of organized labor swelled to more than eight million by end of the decade — some 23 percent of the nonagricultural work force. Union membership was heavily concentrated in the mature industries of manufacturing, transportation, and mining and in the northeastern and Pacific Coast states, especially those states where prolabor governors presided. In the South, still predominantly agricultural and still wedded to the idea that cheap labor was its biggest competitive asset, only one worker in ten belonged to a union as the decade of the 1930s closed.

From a skeletal staff of 14 lawyers in 1935, the NLRB grew to employ some 226 lawyers four years later. Though criticized then and later as another example of bloated bureaucracy, the NLRB in fact provided a mechanism that quelled the raucous labor upheavals of the 1930s and served thereafter as an orderly forum where disputes between management and labor — or between competing unions — could be peaceably resolved. The kind of violence that long dogged the history of American industrialization and exploded with savage ferocity in the Depression years largely disappeared. With the passage of the Wagner Act, the locus of labor conflict shifted from the streets to the NLRB's hearing rooms — and to the courts, as labor relations became enmeshed in one of the most elaborately articulated bodies of law in the American statute books. Bloody clashes at the factory gate gave way to decorously argued points of order in front of a federal mediator or a judge. Both sides gained as well as lost. Capital gave up some of its prerogatives but won a measure of industrial peace. Labor subjected itself to the sometimes meddlesome tutelage of the regulatory state but achieved a degree of parity with management at the bargaining table and, no less important, unprecedented prosperity and security as well.

Unions made a difference. In the organized industries, wages rose after 1935 in measurably greater degree than in unorganized sectors.

Lewis's coal miners made ninety cents an hour in 1940, one-third higher than the average industrial wage of seventy-four cents. Autoworkers by 1941 earned $1.04 an hour. Union insistence on the seniority principle also rendered employment more predictable, conferring especially valuable protection on older workers, who naturally had longer terms of service. Union-negotiated grievance procedures checked the petty tyranny of foremen and supervisors. Men, who composed some three-quarters of the work force, were the principal beneficiaries of these gains. For the fourteen million women workers, mostly in the largely unorganized service sector, for the many millions of agricultural laborers, and for almost all workers of whatever description in the South, comparable benefits would be a long time coming. The heavily female garment trades paid sixty cents per hour in 1940; retail clerks made thirty-five to fifty cents; textile mill workers, forty-six cents. But for employed workers generally—always the majority, even in the 1930s, it is worth remembering—and especially for manufacturing workers, the conditions of life and work were markedly better at the decade's end than at its beginning, and the improvement was due in no small measure to the success of the union movement. In 1941 the average yearly income for a manufacturing worker was $1,449. A steelworker with a statistically typical family of 2.5 children could afford a new coat for himself and his wife every six years and could buy a new pair of shoes for each child every two years. Mother could purchase two housedresses, and father one workshirt, every year. They could afford a used car and the rent for a five-room apartment. Their household budget was well below the two thousand that experts deemed necessary for a comfortable standard of living, but it was a sum that looked almost princely to people who had scraped and fretted through the Depression decade.[46]

Whether through inadvertence or intention, Roosevelt and the Democratic Party were surely the rich beneficiaries of these changes in workers' circumstances. Before the 1930s many workers, especially if they were of immigrant stock, had rarely troubled to vote and had in any case fickle, unreliable political loyalties. To be sure, urban machines like Anton Cermak's in Chicago had begun to weld immigrant workers to the Democratic Party well before the New Deal appeared on the scene. But it was only in the 1930s, thanks largely to organized labor's achievements and Roosevelt's uncanny ability to associate himself with those achievements, that labor became a sizable and dependable

46. Zieger, CIO, 111ff.

component of the Democrats' constituency. When they next had the chance to vote for him, in the presidential election of 1940, workers went so heavily for Roosevelt that he increased his victory margin in the big industrial cities to a formidable 59 percent.[47]

In the process of becoming reliable Democrats, workers also buried once and for all the always evanescent dream of an exclusively workingpeople's party. Just as workers eschewed the overthrow of capitalism to embrace bread-and-butter unionism, so did they repudiate radical politics and attach themselves to one of the existing mainstream parties. In the process, they wrote the epitaph for American socialism and stifled American Communism in its cradle.

A heightened sense of class consciousness did indeed emerge in the United States in the Depression years, but it was of a stubbornly characteristic American type. It did not frontally challenge existing institutions but asked—demanded—a larger measure of participation in them. In the end the trade union movement, the Democratic Party, and the big corporations as well all proved sufficiently resilient to allow for that participation. As for the workers themselves, a poll in 1939 revealed that they had few illusions about their situation. Fully half of the respondents identifed themselves as belonging to the lower or lower-middle income categories. But when asked to which social class they belonged, 88 percent replied "middle." Those opinions suggested that workers realistically appraised their economic circumstance but also clung to their faith in an inclusive, egalitarian democracy and to the hope for social mobility. Even in the midst of the country's greatest depression, for millions of working-class citizens the American dream had survived. Indeed, for many it was on the way to becoming a greater reality than ever before.[48]

47. Michael Barone, *Our Country: The Shaping of America from Roosevelt to Reagan* (New York: Free Press, 1990), 144.
48. Zieger, *CIO*, 116.

11

The Ordeal of Franklin Roosevelt

Once you build a house you always have it. On the other hand, a social or an economic gain is a different matter. A social or an economic gain made by one Administration, for instance, may, and often does, evaporate into thin air under the next Administration.

— President Franklin D. Roosevelt,
radio address, November 4, 1938

Pride, the ancient wisdom proclaims, goeth before a fall. Franklin Roosevelt in early 1937 had reason to be the proudest of men. He had wrung landmark reforms from Congress in 1935. He had won reelection in 1936 by a larger margin than any president in more than a century. He had ushered new constituencies into the Democratic Party, forging an electoral coalition of formidable power and durability. And as the first year of his second term opened, the economy he had pledged to revive continued to show signs of shaking off its Depression narcosis. Roosevelt understandably took satisfaction in these political achievements and took credit, as is the politician's habit, for the country's economic reawakening as well. He boasted in his second inaugural address, not without reason or pride, that "our progress out of the depression is obvious." And yet before the year 1937 was out, both the economy and the president's political fortunes would tumble to depths not touched since Herbert Hoover's presidency.[1]

Even in the heady moments of early 1937, a quaver of foreboding crept into the president's celebration of economic recovery. His agenda had from the outset embraced more than simply restoring the economy to good health. He also aimed to enact durable reforms, to reshape the topography of American economic and social life both to prevent future

1. PPA (1937), 2.

323

depressions and permanently to improve the lot of the millions who were ill housed, ill clad, and ill nourished. Toward those goals he had made notable progress in his first term, not least with the passage of the Social Security and National Labor Relations Acts.

But those accomplishments were not yet secure, nor were his larger purposes yet fully gained. Economic recovery, he worried, though surely welcome for its own sake, might therefore be politically premature. It might dissipate the fleeting public mood that had permitted him the rare scope for presidential initiative that he had enjoyed in his first term. Future congresses might dismantle the fragile edifice of reforms thrown up hastily in the emergency atmosphere of the Depression crisis. Future presidents, even liberal presidents, might prove unable to orchestrate their party and to wield executive power as effectively as Roosevelt had between 1933 and 1936.

Most ominous, the threat of judicial nullification loomed over virtually every New Deal measure thus far enacted. The Supreme Court had already gutted many of the reform initiatives of the Hundred Days, notably NRA and AAA. Lawsuits challenging the constitutionality of all the major legislative acts of 1935 — Social Security, the National Labor Relations Act, the Public Utilities Holding Company Act — were grinding through the judicial system as 1937 opened. The president had no reason to believe that the Supreme Court would in the end give its approval to his myriad innovations, particularly if they no longer seemed necessary to effecting recovery.

And so much remained undone. There was still that "one-third of a nation" whose needs had only begun to be addressed. The achievements of his first term, Roosevelt said in his inaugural address, "were won under the pressure of more than ordinary circumstance . . . under the goad of fear and suffering." Then, he said, "the times were on the side of progress." But now, he warned, "symptoms of prosperity may become portents of disaster! Prosperity already tests the persistence of our progressive purpose."[2]

Prosperity as disaster? This was rank heresy for a politician to voice at any time. In the midst of the Great Depression it seemed to invite political anathema. Yet this was neither the first time nor the last that Roosevelt reflected on the complex relationship between economic crisis and political reform. As early as 1924, he had written to fellow Democrats that the hour of opportunity for liberalism would not arrive "until-

2. PPA (1937), 4.

the Republicans had led us into a serious period of depression and unemployment."[3] As it happened, catastrophic depression and massive unemployment, on scales Roosevelt neither anticipated nor wished, had furnished more occasion for liberal achievement than he had dared to anticipate. Now those scourges seemed to be lifting. With their disappearance the season of political reform might also be coming to a close.

Again and again in 1937, in private settings as well as public, Roosevelt returned to this theme. In his annual message to Congress in early January, he put the legislators on notice that "[y]our task and mine is not ending with the Depression," foreshadowing the even stronger warning he enunciated in his inaugural address a few weeks later.[4] In February he confided in a personal letter to Felix Frankfurter his fear that "the return of prosperity, at this moment, may blunt our senses."[5] In a Fireside Chat a few months later he declared that government could not "stop governing simply because prosperity has come back a long way."[6]

As his second term began, Roosevelt was therefore determined to strike boldly. In the waning moment before prosperity had fully returned, he must protect the New Deal and prepare the way for further reform. He struck on three fronts: at the judiciary, at Congress, and, eventually, at elements within his own party, particularly its entrenched southern wing.

FATEFULLY, HE BEGAN with the judiciary. In a singular and eventually disastrous political miscalculation, Roosevelt opened his new term by launching a surprise attack on one of the most sacred American institutions, the Supreme Court.

On February 5, 1937, Roosevelt startled Congress with a special message. He asked for a statute that would allow the president to appoint one additional justice to the Supreme Court, up to a total of six new appointments, for every sitting justice who declined to retire at age seventy. Additionally, he requested authority on a like basis to name up to forty-four new judges to the lower federal courts. These changes were necessary, Roosevelt explained, to promote judicial efficiency by clearing crowded dockets.

3. Frank Freidel, *Franklin Roosevelt: The Ordeal* (Boston: Little, Brown, 1954), 183.
4. *PPA* (1936), 642.
5. Max Freedman, ed., *Roosevelt and Frankfurter: Their Correspondence, 1928–1945* (Boston: Little, Brown, 1967), 382.
6. *PPA* (1937), 431.

There was nothing sacrosanct about the nine-justice Court that Roosevelt sought to enlarge. At various times in the Court's history Congress had specified five, six, seven, and ten justices as the high bench's statutory complement. But Roosevelt awkwardly tried to justify his proposed changes with unsupportable charges of inefficiency and with gratuitous, unpersuasive innuendoes about the senility of the current justices. "[A]ged or infirm judges—a subject of delicacy," Roosevelt conceded— were inclined "to avoid an examination of complicated and changed conditions. Little by little, new facts become blurred through old glasses fitted, as it were, for the needs of another generation; older men, assuming that the scene is the same as it was in the past, cease to explore or inquire into the present or the future."[7]

There was a wisp of truth in what Roosevelt said. The average age of the current justices was seventy-one. Louis Brandeis was the oldest at eighty. Ironically, the elderly Brandeis, along with Benjamin Cardozo (sixty-six) and Harlan Fiske Stone (sixty-four), made up the Court's most consistently liberal bloc. The notoriously conservative "Four Horsemen" were all septuagenarians: James C. McReynolds (seventy-five), George Sutherland (seventy-four), Willis Van Devanter (seventy-seven), and Pierce Butler (seventy). Chief Justice Charles Evans Hughes was seventy-five; he and Owen J. Roberts, the Court's youngster at sixty-one, made up the swing votes that held the balance of power.

But neither efficiency nor age was the real issue, and Roosevelt knew it. So did the country. The normally pro–New Deal *New York World-Telegram* condemned Roosevelt's scheme as "too clever, too damned clever." Even Roosevelt's loyal associate Samuel Rosenman later lamented "the cleverness, the too much cleverness" of Roosevelt's plan.[8] Roosevelt was proposing to fiddle with one of the most respected and immutable American institutions, one designed by the Founders and enshrined in national mythology as the ballast whose unshifting weight could be counted upon to steady the ship of state. It did the president's cause incalculable harm that he opened the national discussion about this explosive issue on a transparently disingenuous note.

Yet the causes of Roosevelt's exasperation with the Court were genuine enough. He had appointed not one of the nine sitting justices; he was at that moment the first president since Andrew Johnson not to have made a Supreme Court nomination. His Democratic predecessor and

7. *PPA* (1937), 44.
8. Davis 51, 97.

former chief, Woodrow Wilson, had appointed the liberal Brandeis and the conservative McReynolds. Republican presidents had named all the others, just as they had named a heavy majority (nearly 80 percent) of judges then sitting at all levels of the federal judiciary.[9] Though its members were not monolithic in their thinking, the "Court of Methuselahs" regularly produced majorities, with the Four Horsemen as their nucleus, for decisions that threatened everything the New Deal was trying to accomplish.

In the broadest sense, the Court's power derived from the doctrine of judicial review, a concept not defined in the Constitution but first asserted by John Marshall in *Marbury v. Madison* in 1803, when he claimed for the Supreme Court the ultimate authority to define the meaning of the Constitution and set limits to legislative action. The doctrine lay dormant for half a century thereafter, not revived again until the Dred Scott case in 1857. But in the decades following the Civil War, as both state legislatures and the federal Congress tried to assert some control over the rapidly industrializing economy, the Court was increasingly inclined to stay the legislators' hands. The specific restraint it invoked most often was one fashioned from the elusive concept of substantive due process.

Substantive due process amounted in practice to the proposition that some "substantive" rights were so inviolable — especially property and contract rights — that they lay beyond the reach of any imaginable "process," or law. Though in explaining its decisions the Court cited various specific points of the law, such as restrictions on the commerce power or freedom of contract, the environing idea that since the 1890s had shaped the Court's basic attitude toward economic legislation was the principle of laissez-faire, or noninterference in the market economy. Applying that principle made the judiciary the most powerful arm of government, though its power was wholly the power to veto. Reformers from Theodore Roosevelt onward, including on occasion jurists like Brandeis and Stone, had decried this meddlesome judicial activism, beseeching the black-robed, unelected justices to defer to the will of democratically elected legislatures. But they pleaded in vain. In the

9. Hughes and Van Devanter had been appointed by President Taft, Sutherland and Butler by Harding, Stone by Coolidge, and Cardozo and Roberts by Hoover, who had also elevated Hughes to the position of chief justice. In 1933 approximately 191 of the 266 federal judges were Republican appointees. William E. Leuchtenburg, *The Supreme Court Reborn: The Constitutional Revolution in the Age of Roosevelt* (New York: Oxford University Press, 1995), 79, n. 5.

1920s alone, no fewer than nineteen socioeconomic statutes had fallen to the judicial ax, including laws that prohibited child labor and defined minimum wages for women workers. In the 1930s the flood of New Deal legislation made a titanic duel with the judiciary all but inevitable.

The Court had already thrown down the gauntlet to the New Deal. On "Black Monday," May 27, 1935, in *Schechter Poultry Corporation v. United States*, known ever after as the "sick chicken" case, the justices had unanimously declared the National Industrial Recovery Act to be unconstitutional. Congress, said the Court, had impermissibly delegated its inalienable lawmaking authority to the National Recovery Administration—"delegation run riot," said Justice Cardozo. The opinion not only voided the NRA but jeopardized the very concept of rulemaking independent regulatory agencies like the Securities and Exchange Commission or the National Labor Relations Board. For good measure, the Court also went out of its way to define the Schechter brothers' Brooklyn kosher-poultry business as exclusively *intra*state in character. The decision thus put the Schechters' violation of NRA wage and hour codes, not to mention their sale of diseased poultry, beyond the reach of federal power, which was constitutionally confined to the regulation of *inter*state commerce.[10]

The *Schecter* decision stunned Roosevelt. What was at stake, he instantly recognized, was nothing less than what the *New Republic* called "the very foundation of national power in a modern industrial society." Could the government act in the face of the greatest economic calamity in American history, or was it to be forever hog-tied by the strictures of the Constitution? "We have been relegated to the horse-and-buggy definition of interstate commerce," Roosevelt complained. "I tell you, Mr. President," Attorney General Homer Cummings fulminated, "they mean to destroy us. . . . We will have to find a way to get rid of the present membership of the Supreme Court."[11]

Worse soon followed. In the first week of 1936 the Court took up residence in its new classic-revival temple on Capitol Hill. "It is a mag-

---

10. *Schechter Poultry Corporation v. United States*, 295 U.S. 495 (1935). On the same day as the *Schechter* decision, the Court also handed down two other decisions harmful to the New Deal. In *Louisville Bank v. Radford* (295 U.S. 555), the Court invalidated the Frazier-Lemke mortgage moratorium act. In *Humphrey's Executor v. United States* (291 U.S. 602), it sharply circumscribed the president's power to remove members of regulatory commissions.

11. Leuchtenburg, *Supreme Court Reborn*, 43, 85, 88.

nificent structure," said a *New Yorker* writer, "with fine big windows to throw the New Deal out of."[12] On January 6, in the case of *United States v. Butler*, the Court by a six-to-three vote tossed out the Agricultural Adjustment Act. The tax on processors that went to pay farmers who limited crop production, the Court declared, unconstitutionally encroached on regulatory powers reserved to the states by the Tenth Amendment. Justice Stone in dissent said that the majority's decision in the AAA case proceeded from "a tortured construction of the Constitution. . . . Courts are not the only agency of government that must be assumed to have capacity to govern," he admonished, in what was by then a familiar criticism.[13] In March 1936, again citing the Tenth Amendment as well as limitations on the commerce power, the Court struck down the Guffey Bituminous Coal Conservation Act, a "little NRA" law enacted after *Schechter* to shore up the chronically ailing coal industry.

Then came the crowning blow. Just weeks later, in *Morehead v. New York ex rel. Tipaldo*, Owen Roberts joined the Four Horsemen to form a scant five-to-four majority that invalidated a New York minimum wage law as an unconstitutional infringement on freedom of contract. The Court's other decisions in the 1936 term had circumscribed federal power, largely in the name of states' rights. Now the *Tipaldo* decision sharply curtailed the regulatory powers of the states themselves.

For the critics of substantive due process, *Tipaldo* was the final insult. Justice Stone dissented with unusual vigor. "There is grim irony," he wrote, "in speaking of the freedom of contract of those who, because of their economic necessities, give their services for less than is needful to keep body and soul together." Privately, Stone wrote to his sister that the *Tipaldo* decision climaxed "one of the most disastrous" terms in the Court's history. "[*Tipaldo*] was a holding by a divided vote that there was no power in a state to regulate minimum wages for women. Since the Court last week said that this could not be done by the national government, as the matter was local, and now it is said that it cannot be done by local governments even though it is local, we seem to have tied Uncle Sam up in a hard knot." For his part, Roosevelt trenchantly remarked that with the *Tipaldo* decision the Court had for all practical

12. *New Yorker* quoted in Irving Bernstein, *Turbulent Years: A History of the American Worker, 1933–1941* (Boston: Houghton Mifflin, 1970), 639.
13. *Butler v. United States*, 297 U.S. 1 (1936).

purposes marked off a "no man's land where no Government—State or Federal—can function."[14]

Reflecting the accumulating frustration with the Court's dogged devotion to judicial nullification, more than one hundred bills were introduced in Congress in 1936 to redefine the balance of power between the legislative and judicial branches of government. After *Tipaldo*, even Herbert Hoover called for a constitutional amendment to restore to the states "the power they thought they already had," and the Republican platform of 1936 strongly advocated such an amendment.[15]

Against this background, Franklin Roosevelt's aggravation with judicial obstruction was neither unwarranted nor singular. Nor was it precipitate. As early as November 1935, Harold Ickes had recorded in his diary: "Clearly, it is running in the President's mind that substantially all of the New Deal bills will be declared unconstitutional by the Supreme Court. This will mean that everything that this Administration has done of any moment will be nullified."[16] Throughout 1935 and 1936, at Roosevelt's urging, Justice Department lawyers had struggled to draft a constitutional amendment to curb the Court's power. But they wrestled in vain with a grotesquely cumbersome formula that would have conferred explicit powers of judicial review on the Court, while providing, after an intervening election, for legislative override of Court findings of unconstitutionality—a kind of indirect popular referendum, designed by Rube Goldberg. By early 1937 two years of effort had not yielded an acceptable draft.

The amendment process was in any case designedly difficult, requiring two-thirds approval in each house of Congress and ratification by three-fourths of the states. It was also time-consuming. The example of the amendment prohibiting child labor, first approved by Congress in 1924 but still unpassed by the requisite number of states thirteen years later, weighed heavily in the president's thinking. Time, Roosevelt knew, was of the essence. Cases testing the validity of the National Labor Relations Act, the Social Security Act, and a bundle of state minimum wage and unemployment compensation laws were already on the Court's docket by the end of 1936. Unless something were done, the new year might bring a constitutional Armageddon. The distinct possibility

14. *Morehead v. New York ex rel. Tipaldo*, 298 U.S. 587 (1936), 632; Leuchtenburg, *Supreme Court Reborn*, 159, 100.
15. Leuchtenburg, *Supreme Court Reborn*, 100–101.
16. Ickes Diary 1:495.

loomed that when the Court reconvened in January the entire New Deal might be summarily repealed by wholesale judicial annihilation—a bitterly ironic sequel to Roosevelt's smashing 1936 electoral victory. Roosevelt was understandably appalled at this prospect. "When I retire to private life on January 20, 1941," he said, dramatically revealing his own estimate of the gravity of the impending crisis, "I do not want to leave the country in the condition Buchanan left it to Lincoln."[17]

SMALL WONDER, THEN, that Roosevelt pursued Attorney General Cummings's suggestion to "get rid of the present membership of the Supreme Court." Given the decades-long agitation against "judicial supremacy," and among the array of nostrums prescribed at the time for judicial reform, the plan that Roosevelt advanced on February 5 stood out not for its boldness but for its mildness. It defined no new constitutional role for the Court and thus left the time-honored system of checks and balances unperturbed. It did not in fact propose literally to "get rid" of the Court's sitting justices but asked merely for an expansion, under stipulated conditions, of the Court's personnel, and asked for that expansion in the larger context of streamlining the entire federal judiciary. Roosevelt's Court plan was no wanton blunder. It was a calculated risk, and not an unreasonable one. He was wagering a modest challenge to the tradition of an independent judiciary against the prospect of the entire New Deal's judicial extinction.

But Roosevelt woefully underestimated the strength of popular devotion to the Court's traditional role. He also miscalculated badly in his choice of tactics and timing. From the moment of its unveiling, his Court plan stirred a nest of furies whose destructive power swiftly swelled to awesome proportions, well beyond the president's ability to control.

What the president called judicial reform a mighty host of critics throatily assailed as "Court-packing." "If the American people accept this last audacity of the President without letting out a yell to high heaven, they have ceased to be jealous of their liberties and are ripe for ruin," wrote the columnist Dorothy Thompson. A fatal elision took root in the public's mind between the Court plan, the contemporaneous sit-down strikes, and the president's role in each. Somehow, Roosevelt managed to be perceived as both the acknowledged perpetrator of one affront to traditional notions of constitutional order (by attacking the Court) and the indulgent patron of another (by remaining silent on the

17. *Time*, March 8, 1937, 13.

sit-downs). Americans overwhelmingly told pollsters that they disapproved of the sit-down strikers. Before 1937 was out, 45 percent of respondents in one Gallup poll deemed the administration "too friendly" to labor.[18]

Nor did it help matters that just weeks before his Court message, Roosevelt had asked Congress for legislation to reorganize the executive branch. The executive reorganization bill was a sensible proposal, incorporating the recommendations of independent experts to bring the federal executive into line with the principles of modern management science. But in company with the Court-reform bill, it opened Roosevelt to charges of seeking "dictatorship" by weakening other branches of government and aggrandizing the power of the presidency. Ominously, a Gallup poll in the weeks just after the bombshell Court message — when the furor over the sit-downs was at its height — showed a solid majority (53 percent) opposed to the president's Court proposal.[19]

Roosevelt seemed to have been deserted by the political muses who had guided him so surely throughout his career. He unaccountably compounded his already abundant errors by shrouding his intentions in secrecy until the last minute, robbing himself of the indispensable congressional support that might have come with the lawmakers' sense of participation in the plan's development. The first that congressional leaders heard of the Court scheme was on the morning of February 5, when Roosevelt gave them a perfunctory briefing at the White House just hours before his special message went up to Capitol Hill. Kentucky senator Alben W. Barkley, usually a staunch Roosevelt supporter, later reflected that in this case Roosevelt was a "poor quarterback. He didn't give us the signals in advance of the play." In Vice-President Garner's car headed back to the Capitol, House Judiciary Committee chairman Hatton Sumners of Texas turned to the others. "Boys," he said, "here's where I cash in." When the bill was read later that day in the Senate, Garner stood in the lobby, ostentatiously holding his nose and turning his thumb down.[20] A few weeks later, disgusted alike with Roosevelt's silence on the sit-down strikes and with the Supreme Court bill, Garner betook himself on an extended vacation to Texas. His departure deprived Roosevelt of crucial leadership in the Congress, where Garner had long

18. *Literary Digest*, February 20, 1937, 3; George H. Gallup, *The Gallup Poll: Public Opinion, 1935–1971* (New York: Random House, 1972), 1:69.
19. Gallup, *Gallup Poll*, 1:50.
20. James T. Patterson, *Congressional Conservatism and the New Deal: The Growth of the Conservative Coalition in Congress, 1933–1939* (Lexington: University of Kentucky Press, 1967), 87–92.

been a representative and now served as presiding officer of the Senate. "This is a fine time to jump ship. . . . Why in hell did Jack have to leave at this time for?" Roosevelt fumed to Jim Farley. "I don't think the President ever forgave Garner," Farley concluded.[21]

Sumners and Garner were not the only defectors. Many southern Democrats abandoned the president, fearing that a more liberal Court might open the door to a second Reconstruction that would challenge white supremacy. Roosevelt may have anticipated defections of that sort, but to his chagrin his Court-reform proposal also alienated many of his formerly reliable progressive allies like Montana's Senator Burton Wheeler. Though they shared Roosevelt's frustration with the current Court's conservatism, they objected on principle to any compromising of the judiciary's independence. In a surprising and major embarrassment to the president, many Democratic liberals also hotly denounced the Roosevelt plan. New York Democratic governor Herbert Lehman, whom FDR had once described as "my strong right arm," was among them. "Last week," a newsmagazine reported when Lehman announced his opposition to the Court plan, "the strong right arm gave [Roosevelt] a jolting blow between the eyes." As for Wheeler, he emerged as the Court plan's chief opponent in the Senate. During "the hysteria of the First World War," Wheeler claimed with some hyperbole, "I saw men strung up. Only the federal courts stood up at all, and the Supreme Court better than any of them." Republicans kept their peace, quietly savoring the Democratic fratricide.[22]

Wheeler orchestrated a brilliant series of ripostes to the president's proposal. He produced a devastatingly cogent letter from Chief Justice Hughes, a venerable, bearded figure of imperturbable dignity and the object of iconic popular veneration as the spirit of the laws incarnate. Hughes conclusively rebutted Roosevelt's specious claims about judicial inefficiency. To the president's proposal to enlarge the bench, Hughes delivered a magisterial rebuke: "More judges to hear, more judges to confer, more judges to discuss, more judges to be convinced and to decide," said Hughes, hardly constituted a formula for more expeditious litigation.[23]

By early March Roosevelt abandoned his arguments about ineffi-

21. James A. Farley, *Jim Farley's Story: The Roosevelt Years* (New York: McGraw-Hill, 1948), 84.
22. *Digest* 1, no. 3 (July 31, 1937): 5; Studs Terkel, *Hard Times: An Oral History of the Great Depression* (New York: Pantheon, 1970), 271.
23. Leuchtenburg, *Supreme Court Reborn*, 133.

ciency and senescence and began to make his case squarely on the grounds of judicial philosophy, something he would probably have been better advised to do from the outset. By this time it was too late. The president's deviousness and the responses his original message had reflexively evoked had put a framework around the Court-reform story from which it proved impossible to escape: Roosevelt was seeking dictatorial power, his critics charged, perhaps not for himself, but in ways that a future president could easily abuse. As Wheeler said in a radio address: "Create now a political Court to echo the ideas of the executive and you have created a weapon; a weapon which in the hands of another President could . . . cut down those guarantees of liberty written by the blood of your forefathers."[24]

Congress, including large elements of the president's own party, was by now in open rebellion against the Court-reform plan. The Court itself delivered the killing blows, though in laying Roosevelt's plan to rest it also opened a new constitutional era. On Easter Monday, March 29, the Court handed down an opinion in a case that at once tolled the knell for Roosevelt's proposal, even as it heralded the dawn of a judicial revolution. Like many great cases, this one had its origins in the commonest grit of everyday life. Elsie Parrish was a chambermaid who had swept rugs and cleaned toilets for nearly two years in the Cascadian Hotel in Wenatchee, Washington, a dusty farm town on the Columbia River plateau. Upon her discharge in 1935, she asked for $216.19 in back pay, which she was owed under the terms of a Washington State minimum wage law enacted in 1913. West Coast Hotel Corporation, the Cascadian's parent company, offered to settle for seventeen dollars. Elsie Parrish sued for the full amount. The corporation thereupon challenged the constitutionality of the Washington law.

Chief Justice Hughes himself delivered the majority opinion in *West Coast Hotel v. Parrish*. The Court had decided in favor of Elsie Parrish, Hughes declared, speaking with Olympian authority in language that signaled a new willingness to defer to legislatures on economic matters. Slowly, the significance of Hughes's pronouncement sank in. Astonishingly, the justices had voted by a five-to-four majority to uphold the Washington State minimum wage law—a statute effectively identical to the New York law that the same Court had invalidated by the same margin in *Tipaldo* only a year earlier!

24. Burton K. Wheeler, *Yankee from the West* (Garden City, N.Y.: Doubleday, 1962), 325.

The decision in *Parrish* amounted to "the greatest constitutional somersault in history," declared one commentator. "On Easter Sunday," said another, "state minimum wage laws were unconstitutional, but about noon on Easter Monday, these laws were constitutional." The key to this breathtaking reversal was the shift of a single vote. Justice Roberts had sided with the conservative quartet in *Tipaldo*, but now he followed Hughes and joined the liberal trio. It was later revealed that Roberts cast his critical vote in the *Parrish* case in the justices' conference of December 19, 1936—more than seven weeks *before* Roosevelt's February 5 message to Congress. But if Roberts did not change course because of the specific storm unleashed by Roosevelt's Court-packing plan, it stretches credulity to conclude that he, and Hughes, were not influenced by the high-pressure front that had been building for many months, indeed years, over the Court's obstructionist tactics. In any case, Roberts's action decisively shifted the Court's ideological center of gravity. "By nodding his head instead of shaking it," an observer noted, "Owen Roberts, one single human being, had amended the Constitution of the United States." Pundits immediately called Roberts's judicial pirouette "the switch in time that saved nine," a deft maneuver that spiked Roosevelt's Court reform while ushering in a new jurisprudential regime.[25]

Parrish dealt with a state law, not a federal one, but it proved a fateful harbinger. On April 12 the chief justice again spoke for the same five-to-four majority when he delivered the Court's opinion in the case of *NLRB v. Jones and Laughlin*, a crucial test of the Wagner National Labor Relations Act. The case stemmed from a complaint to the NLRB that ten workers had been dismissed from the Jones and Laughlin Steel Company's infamous "Little Siberia" works in Aliquippa, Pennsylvania, because they were union members—a clear violation of the Wagner Act's prohibition on unfair labor practices. Jones and Laughlin contended that the National Labor Relations Act was unconstitutional, and therefore the NLRB had no authority to receive or act upon the workers' grievance.

Once again Hughes, in all his white-bearded majesty, read the majority opinion. He spoke "magnificently," two reporters noted, with "an

25. Leuchtenburg, *Supreme Court Reborn*, 166, Roberts's action has been understandably controversial. For a summary review of the controversy, see Richard D. Freidman, "A Reaffirmation: The Authenticity of the Roberts Memorandum, or Felix the Non-Forger," *University of Pennsylvania Law Review* 142, no. 6 (June 1994): 1985.

overtone of infallibility which made the whole business sound like a rehearsal for the last judgment."[26] The Wagner Act's constitutionality depended on a broad construction of the commerce power, which the Court had been unwilling to recognize in its *Schechter* and Guffey Coal Act decisions. Now Hughes ignored those precedents, enunciated just months earlier by the same Court, and ruled that the Wagner Act fell within a constitutionally legitimate definition of the commerce power. "When I hear Wagner Bill went constitutional, I happy," said a steel-worker in Little Siberia. "I say good, now Aliquippa become part of the United States."[27] Just six weeks later, the same majority of Brandeis, Cardozo, Stone, Hughes, and Roberts voted to uphold the unemploy-ment insurance features of the Social Security Act, and the even more comfortable majority of seven to two sustained the act's old-age pension provisions.[28]

These several decisions, along with Hughes's letter and Justice Van Devanter's announcement on May 18 of his intention to retire, buried the Court-reform plan. Against all odds, Roosevelt perversely persisted for a time, but when his loyal Senate majority leader, Joseph Robinson, dropped dead from a heart attack on July 14, Roosevelt knew he was whipped. Indeed, the rage of the president's opponents was by then so great that they blamed him for the stress that killed Robinson! The bill's only statutory residue was a severely diluted Judicial Procedure Reform Act, passed in August, which tinkered with lower-court procedures but made no provision for new justices.

Father Time, not legislation, eventually allowed Roosevelt to compose a Court more congenial to his views. He named Alabama senator Hugo Black to fill Van Devanter's seat, weathering a nasty squall over Black's former membership in the Ku Klux Klan, and he made seven more appointments over the next eight years. Even the archconservative Jus-tice McReynolds, who allegedly vowed that he would "never resign as long as that crippled son of a bitch is in the White House," slipped out of his robe in 1941.[29]

Even before Roosevelt was able to staff the high bench with a majority

---

26. Joseph Alsop and Turner Catledge, *The 168 Days* (Garden City, N.Y.: Doubleday, Doran, 1938), 146–47.
27. Robert H. Zieger, *The CIO, 1935–1955* (Chapel Hill: University of North Carolina Press, 1995), 131.
28. *Steward Machine Co. v. Davis*, 301 U.S. 548 (1937), and *Helvering v. Davis*, 301 U.S. 619 (1937).
29. Leuchtenburg, *Supreme Court Reborn*, 115.

of his own appointees, he had wrought a momentous judicial transformation. He lost the battle to expand the Court but won the war for a shift in constitutional doctrine. "We obtained 98 percent of all the objectives intended by the Court plan," Roosevelt observed in late 1938.[30] The "nine old men"—or at least the youngest of them, Owen Roberts, in company with Hughes—had proved nimble enough to shift their ideological ground. In the course of countering Roosevelt's Court-packing plan, they gave birth to what has been rightly called "the Constitutional Revolution of 1937."[31] The New Deal, especially its core program enacted in 1935, was now constitutionally safe. And for at least half a century thereafter the Court did not overturn a single piece of significant state or national socioeconomic legislation. In the economic realm, at least, substantive due process was dead. As one authority concluded in 1941:

> The Court has discarded the idea that the laissez-faire, noninterventionist conception of governmental action offers a feasible approach to the problem of adapting the Constitution to the needs of the Twentieth Century. Rendered into the idiom of American constitutional law, this means that *the National Government is entitled to employ any and all of its powers to forward any and all of the objectives of good government.* This fundamental point being established . . . the principal doctrines of American constitutional theory, those which have furnished the matrix of the vastly extended judicial review which developed after 1890, have become largely otiose and superfluous.[32]

ROOSEVELT HAD WON THE WAR, but his success furnished a textbook example of a Pyrrhic victory. The resolution of the Court battle helped to secure the New Deal's achievements to date and cleared the constitutional pathway for further reforms. Ironically, however, the struggle had inflicted such grievous political wounds on the president that the New Deal's political momentum was exhausted by mid-1937. The way was open, but Roosevelt lacked the means to go forward. Most fatefully, the Court battle had exposed deep fissures in the ranks of the Democratic Party. With the president's blood on the water, Democrats who had stewed privately under Roosevelt's leadership now openly unfurled the standard of revolt. "What we have to do," North Carolina's

---

30. *PPA* (1938), 490.
31. Leuchtenburg, *Supreme Court Reborn*, 168.
32. Edwin S. Corwin, *Constitutional Revolution, Ltd.* (Claremont, Calif.: Pomona College, Scripps College, Claremont Colleges, 1941), 112–13; italics in original.

Senator Josiah Bailey wrote to his Virginia colleague Harry Byrd, "is to preserve, if we can, the Democratic Party against his efforts to make it the Roosevelt party."[33] "Who does he think he is?" Burton Wheeler remarked of Roosevelt. "He used to be just one of the barons. I was the baron of the northwest, Huey Long was the baron of the south. He's like a king trying to reduce the barons."[34] Now those Democratic barons made Capitol Hill their American Runnymede. In the chambers of the House and especially of the Senate, they gathered in 1937 not to do Roosevelt's bidding but to hurl defiance at their chief. Despite his party's command of congressional majorities far larger than those of his first term, never again would Roosevelt succeed in controlling the legislative process as he had in 1933 and again in 1935, when, it was increasingly clear, the New Deal had reached its climax. As Henry Wallace later remarked, "The whole New Deal really went up in smoke as a result of the Supreme Court fight."[35]

Yet too much can be made of the contest over the Court as the *cause* of the New Deal's attenuation in Roosevelt's second term. The opposition to Roosevelt that surfaced in 1937 may have crystallized around the Court-reform issue, but it was not Court reform that created that opposition in the first place. The Democratic Party that Roosevelt had inherited in 1933 was still in many ways the ramshackle, disarticulated assemblage of factions that had deadlocked at Madison Square Garden in 1924, unable to calm the feuds among its urban and rural, wet and dry, immigrant and old-stock, northern and southern wings. That party had always been an unlikely vehicle for the kind of reform cargo that Roosevelt had somewhat miraculously managed to make it carry, and until now he had done little to overhaul it. Since at least the time of the president's "wealth tax" proposal in 1935, that vehicle had been threatening to fall apart. The origins of its instability lay partly in the familiar conflict between the party's southern and northern wings. But that sectional tension masked a still deeper sectoral conflict between urban and rural interests. In a close analysis of congressional voting patterns in the mid-1930s, historian James Patterson found that the most powerful determinant of anti–New Deal sentiment among Democrats was "an anti-metropolitan ideology" that generated opposition to Roo-

33. John M. Allswang, *The New Deal and American Politics* (New York: John Wiley and Sons, 1978), 120.
34. Patterson, *Congressional Conservatism and the New Deal*, 115.
35. Leuchtenburg, *Supreme Court Reborn*, 464.

sevelt not only in the rural South but also in rural New England and the rural Midwest and West. As in physics, so in politics: for every action there is a reaction, perhaps not equal nor precisely opposite, but reliably contrary nonetheless. Thus as Roosevelt became ever more closely identified with urban, industrial workers, and as their representatives increasingly forced measures like Social Security and labor legislation onto the congressional agenda, a counterpressure began to build. It was, Patterson asserts, "the urban nature of the [New Deal] measures themselves" that most agitated Roosevelt's opponents. Even without the Court fight, Patterson concludes, "sizable conservative opposition to measures of this sort would have developed."[36]

It was only logical, moreover, that Congress should become the staging ground for that opposition. Because of the peculiarities of the American representational system, and given the persistently rural character of much of American society, 54 out of 96 senators and 225 of 435 representatives had been sent to Congress by predominantly rural constituencies. And virtually all representatives, urban and rural alike, chafed at Roosevelt's vigorous expansion of executive power.[37]

By 1937 that conservative coalition, an emergent alliance of congressional Democrats and Republicans, was sizeable indeed and itching to flex its muscle. Robust as it was, it had insufficient strength as yet to take the offensive, but its powers to impede by exercising a kind of legislative veto were formidable. Accordingly, when Congress in 1937 recaptured the legislative initiative from the president, it proceeded to do very little legislating. A militant minority in the Congress emulated the tactics of another militant minority in Flint and staged a legislative sit-down. Conservatives already occupied key parts of the Capitol precincts at the end of Pennsylvania Avenue. What the Fisher die plants were to GM, committee chairmanships were to Congress: strategic positions whose possession conferred command over the entire enterprise, lawmaking no less than carmaking. And thanks to seniority rules, representatives and senators from the one-party South were in possession of a disproportionate share of committee chairmanships. From those pivotal seats, they could see to it that very little legislative product left Capitol Hill in 1937. The regular congressional session in the first part of the year was almost wholly absorbed with the Court struggle and its sequellae—selecting Kentucky's Alben Barkley to replace the dead

36. Patterson, *Congressional Conservatism and the New Deal*, 160–62.
37. Patterson, *Congressional Conservatism and the New Deal*, 333.

Senate majority leader, Joseph Robinson, and confirming Hugo Black's appointment to the Court. The Wagner-Steagall National Housing Act, a weak measure passed in 1937 that only timidly encouraged the development of public housing projects, represented the sole, pallid vestige of the New Deal spirit that had pulsed so strongly through the Capitol's chambers just months earlier.

Frustrated at this unproductive result, Roosevelt summoned the Congress into special session on November 15. The president asked again for action on his executive reorganization bill, as well as a new farm bill (to replace the fallen AAA), wages-and-hours standards, and legislation to create regional bodies for the management and development of natural resources—"Seven Little TVAs." To many observers, the president seemed dispirited, discouraged, hardly the same man who had soothed the nation's fears and ringmastered the fabled Hundred Days special session in 1933. "[T]he President is showing the strain," Ickes noted in his diary. "He looks all of 15 years older since he was inaugurated in 1933. I don't see how anyone could stand the strain he has been under."[38] As events proved, the contrast with 1933 could not have been more stark. When the special session adjourned on December 21, not a single one of Roosevelt's measures had been passed.

Worse, in the special session's final days a bipartisan group, dominated by southern Democrats, issued a ten-point "Conservative Manifesto." Principally drafted by Senator Josiah Bailey, it denounced the sit-down strikes, demanded lower federal taxes and a balanced budget, defended states' rights as well as the rights of private enterprise against government encroachment, and warned of the dangers of creating a permanently dependent welfare class. For Roosevelt, this anti–New Deal blast, not more New Deal–style legislation, was the bitter fruit of the special congressional session.

The manifesto constituted a kind of founding charter for modern American conservatism. It was among the first systematic expressions of an antigovernment political philosophy that had deep roots in American political culture but only an inchoate existence before the New Deal. Then, as Calvin Coolidge famously remarked, most people would scarcely have noticed if the federal government had gone out of existence, but by the late 1930s the New Deal had begun to alter the scale of federal institutions and extend the reach of federal authority. This emergence of a large, interventionist government, accomplished in an

38. Ickes Diary 2:246.

atmosphere of crisis by a series of aggressive presidential initiatives, now began to provoke a powerful though not yet wholly coherent conservative counterattack. The crystallization of this new conservative ideology, as much as the New Deal that precipitated its articulation, was among the enduring legacies of the 1930s.

This resurgent conservatism gathered in supporters of many types: Republican partisans and others nervous about executive power; managers and middle-class property owners fearful of labor's new assertiveness and the federal government's role in nurturing it; investors worried about New Deal ambitions to wring higher wages, lower prices, and more tax revenue out of corporate profits; businesspeople resentful of proliferating federal regulations; all kinds of taxpayers anxious about shouldering relief burdens; farmers chafing under agricultural controls; and, not least, white southerners exquisitely sensitive to any possible challenge to racial segregation.

Since Reconstruction Days the solid South had been the foundational constituency of the Democratic Party. The South's peculiar racial sensitivities provided the occasion in early 1938 for a stunning demonstration of the power of that region's elected representatives to stymie the legislative process and to write finis to the New Deal chapter in American history. Southern Democrats had reluctantly agreed at their party's convention in the summer of 1936 to give up the two-thirds majority rule for selecting presidential nominees, a device that had traditionally granted the South an effective veto over any candidate judged unsafe on the race issue. (South Carolina's Senator Ellison "Cotton Ed" Smith had walked out of the convention when a black clergyman delivered an invocation. "By God, he's as black as melted midnight!" Smith exploded. "Get outa my way. This mongrel meeting ain't no place for a white man!" he announced as he departed. "I don't want any blue-gummed, slew-footed Senegambian praying for me politically." Smith exited a second time when Chicagoan Arthur Mitchell, the first black Democrat ever elected to Congress, seconded Roosevelt's nomination.)[39] Later that year Roosevelt's overwhelming victory margin dramatized the unsettling truth that a Democratic president could be elected without a single southern electoral vote. Then in 1937 many white southerners had looked on in alarm as the Supreme Court genuflected to Roosevelt's will, compromising another institution that had often served as a bulwark of the region's racial

39. Allan A. Michie and Frank Rhylick, *Dixie Demagogues* (New York: Vanguard, 1939), 266, 281.

regime. As the South's influence over the federal executive and judiciary weakened, Congress became an especially contested battleground.

A tense battle line formed in April 1937, when a hushed House listened to Michigan representative Earl Cory Michener read the press accounts of a grisly lynching in Duck Hill, Mississippi. A mob had seized two handcuffed black men from the Winona County sheriff, chained them to a tree, mutilated their bodies with blowtorches, shotgunned them, doused the corpses with gasoline, and set them afire. It was but the latest in a nauseating parade of lynchings that had claimed more than one hundred lives since 1930, all of them horrifying testimonials to the price in blood and tears of maintaining the South's segregationist order. Three days later, the House voted favorably on an antilynching bill first introduced in 1934. The bill established federal penalties for local law enforcement officers delinquent in preventing lynchings and provided for federal prosecution of lynchers if local authorities proved unwilling. For southerners, the bill unleashed all their worst fears of a revived Reconstruction Era. Reconstruction was no historical bygone so far as many white southerners were concerned. It was a living and festering memory, one whose distorted image of vindictive northern interlopers and corrupted black legislators had been reinforced in the popular mind by films like D. W. Griffith's sensational *Birth of a Nation* a generation earlier and by a steady stream of factually dubious but highly influential scholarly writing produced by the historian William A. Dunning and the students he trained at Columbia University. Inflamed at the prospect of renewed federal interference with the South's racial system, every southern representative but one, Maury Maverick of Texas, voted in the negative on the antilynching bill.

In the Senate, with its tradition of unlimited debate and thus the possibility of filibuster, the South drew up its principal line of defense. North Carolina's Bailey defined the southern position: "[T]he proposed lynching bill," he wrote, "is the forerunner of a policy studiously cultivated by agitators, not for the purpose of preventing lynching, but for the purpose of introducing the policy of Federal interference in local affairs. The lynching bill would promptly be followed by a civil rights bill, drawn upon lines of the bill which Thad Stevens tried to put upon the South. . . . I give you warning," Bailey proclaimed menacingly, figuratively nodding at the White House, "that no administration can survive without us."[40]

40. Harvard Sitkoff, *A New Deal for Blacks* (New York: Oxford University Press, 1978), 291.

Nor could any legislative business be transacted in the face of such resistance. When the bill was introduced at the opening of the congressional session in 1938, southern senators mounted a wrathful filibuster. South Carolina's James Byrnes, on most other matters one of Roosevelt's most reliable congressional lieutenants, declared that the South had "been deserted by the Democrats of the North." Mississippi's Pat Harrison, another Roosevelt ally in the early New Deal years, raised the prospect of miscegenation, the deepest pathological dread haunting the minds of segregationists. His fellow Mississippian Theodore Bilbo dusted off a nineteenth-century scheme for repatriating American blacks to Africa. Louisiana's Allen J. Ellender declared: "I believe in white supremacy, and as long as I am in the Senate I expect to fight for white supremacy." Sentiments like those, and nothing else, emanated from southerners in the Senate for six weeks, stopping the nation's lawmaking machinery cold. The legislative paralysis ended only when the antilynching bill was at last withdrawn on February 21.[41]

Despite pleas from black leaders and from his wife, Roosevelt declined to give the antilynching bill anything more than nominal support. "I did not choose the tools with which I must work," Roosevelt had earlier explained to NAACP executive secretary Walter White. "Had I been permitted to choose them I would have selected quite different ones. But I've got to get legislation passed by Congress to save America. The Southerners by reason of the seniority rule in Congress are chairmen or occupy strategic places on most of the Senate and House committees. If I come out for the antilynching bill now, they will block every bill I ask Congress to pass to keep America from collapsing. I just can't take that risk."[42]

Roosevelt's refusal to champion the antilynching bill marked the limits of his inclination to challenge the conservative southern grandees of his party. A frontal assault on the South's racial system, Roosevelt judged and the six-week filibuster confirmed, would irretrievably alienate the white southern political establishment, fracture his party beyond repair, and indefinitely deadlock the Congress.

IT WOULD BE TOO MUCH to suggest that anti–New Deal southern senators filibustered the antilynching bill merely to remind Roosevelt of the formidable powers of obstruction that remained to them. The bill, after all, had not been on the president's "must" list, and racial

41. Sitkoff, New Deal for Blacks, 292–93.
42. Walter White, A Man Called White (New York: Viking, 1948), 169–70.

anxiety assuredly trumped political signaling as the filibuster's prime motivator. But it was true nonetheless that the antilynching filibuster vividly illustrated the capacity to impede that was inherent in the American constitutional system of checks and balances, as reinforced by the rules of the Senate. The filibuster thus provided further proof, if proof were needed, of how justified were Roosevelt's fears for the future of the New Deal. It also highlighted the unique vexations that continued to enchain the South in economic backwardness and isolation.

It would also be too much to suggest that it was the antilynching filibuster that prompted Roosevelt to unsheath the sword of political retribution against southern conservatives in the 1938 electoral season. But it is true that the fate of the antilynching bill set the tone for the remainder of the legislative session of 1938, and it was surely that session's barren legislative record that convinced Roosevelt that he must try to purge his party of conservatives.

The president proved little more able in 1938 than he had in the previous year to impose his will on the Congress. Of the four presidential proposals that had been outstanding since early 1937, the farm bill passed at last in 1938, but it amounted to little more than a revival of the old AAA mechanisms, with some technical tinkering, now that the Supreme Court had registered its amenability to such legislation. In any event, farm legislation constituted no offense against the "antimetropolitan" ideology that animated the conservative coalition. On two other measures, the president lost. Congress rebuffed executive reorganization, only to resuscitate it in much weaker form in 1939. The "Seven TVAs" regional planning authority legislation was deader than a tent peg, never to be revived in any form. These defeats took their toll on Roosevelt. "It looks as if all the courage has oozed out of the President," Ickes wrote in his diary as the 1938 stalemate dragged on. "He has let things drift. . . . Ever since the Court fight, he has acted to me like a beaten man."[43]

Only a wages-and-hours bill, the fourth of Roosevelt's holdover measures from 1937, survived the legislative gauntlet as a feeble reminder of the president's once-irresistible powers. The Fair Labor Standards Act of 1938 (FLSA) was a direct lineal descendant of the NRA of 1933. It prohibited child labor and required employers in industry (but not in agriculture, domestic service, or certain other service categories) to adopt in stages a forty-cent hourly minimum wage and a forty-hour week. The

43. Ickes Diary 2:326, 339–49.

act displayed yet again Roosevelt's preferred policies toward labor, which were to confer benefits by statute rather than by collective bargaining— and in so doing, some liberals thought, to dampen incentives for form- ing unions in the first place. For just that reason, the bill troubled many labor leaders, though they hesitated to oppose it openly. One AFL spokesman remarked privately that the act was "bad medicine for us, to give those jerks something for nothing and then they won't join the cause."[44]

"That's that," Roosevelt was heard to sigh on June 25 as he put his signature to the bill—an expression to which history has attached even more finality than the president could have intended. The Fair Labor Standards Act, as it turned out, was the last New Deal reform ever to be inscribed in the statute books. With the pen that affixed his name to the bill, Roosevelt in effect drew a circle around all the New Deal that there was going to be, at least in his own lifetime.

The president's support for the Fair Labor Standards Act also widened the breach between Roosevelt and the conservative southern Democratic oligarchy and testified to Roosevelt's growing willingness to confront them directly. "Southern Senators," Attorney General Cummings noted in his diary, "actually froth at the mouth when the subject [of minimum wage legislation] is mentioned." South Carolina's Cotton Ed Smith de- clared that the law was unnecessary because a man could support a family for fifty cents a day in his home state. It was a high principle of orthodox southern thinking that low wages were the South's major— perhaps only—advantage in competition with more efficient northern industries. Not without reason did Walter Lippmann describe the Fair Labor Standards Act as "a sectional bill thinly disguised as a humani- tarian reform." Nearly 20 percent of southern industrial workers earned below the new minimum wage. Elsewhere in the country, fewer than 3 percent did. Unmistakably, the new law would lay its hand much more heavily on the South than on other regions.[45]

But as Roosevelt saw matters, it was precisely the South's miserably low wages that accounted for much of the region's economic plight. In company with a small band of southern liberals, including Alabama's

44. Joseph P. Lash, *Dealers and Dreamers: A New Look at the New Deal* (New York: Doubleday, 1988), 338.
45. Bruce J. Schulman, *From Cotton Belt to Sunbelt: Federal Policy, Economic Devel- opment, and the Transformation of the South, 1938–1980* (New York: Oxford Uni- versity Press, 1991), 54; the same source gives the figures on regional wage differ- entials at 259, n. 11.

Hugo Black and his senatorial replacement Lister Hill, Florida's Senator Claude Pepper, and Texas Congressman Lyndon Baines Johnson, Roosevelt believed that raising southern wages was a cudgel with which to bludgeon the South into the modern era. Ending the South's historic low-wage regime would force mechanization and bring greater efficiency to southern businesses. The cheap-labor textile mills that dotted the Piedmont, wheezing along with fifty-year-old spindles, were "highly, completely inefficient. That type of factory ought not to be in existence," Roosevelt unequivocally declared.[46] Moreover, Roosevelt explained, "Cheap wages mean low buying power . . . and let us remember that buying power means many other kinds of better things, better schools, better health, better hospitals, better highways."[47]

Having secured the FLSA, Roosevelt continued to press his case for uplifting the nation's poorest region. Calling the South "the Nation's number one economic problem," he commissioned *The Report on Economic Conditions of the South*, released amid great fanfare in August 1938. Disguised as an objective analysis of the southern economy, the *Report* was in fact a manifesto for the southern liberals' program for regional development. They looked to the federal government to develop the region's human and physical resources, break down the South's "colonial" thralldom to northern capital and manufacturing, and integrate the former Confederacy into the national economy. In short, they envisioned a kind of regionally targeted New Deal.

Before economic reform, however, Roosevelt and his liberal allies needed political reform. If the plan for regional development outlined in the *Report* were to have any chance of success, there had to be more pro–New Deal southern politicians like Hill, Pepper, and Johnson and fewer reactionaries like Bailey, Bilbo, and Smith. The *Report* in fact had its origins in Roosevelt's request to Clark Foreman, a liberal white Georgian who served as Harold Ickes's special assistant for Negro affairs, for advice on how to beat archconservative Georgia senator Walter George in the upcoming 1938 Democratic primary election. The *Report* was, in Foreman's words, "a part of the President's program to liberalize the Democratic Party."[48]

Emboldened by the liberal Claude Pepper's victory in the May 1938

46. PPA (1938), 196.
47. Schulman, *From Cotton Belt to Sunbelt*, 64.
48. Schulman, *From Cotton Belt to Sunbelt*, 52.

Florida senatorial primary, FDR determined to intervene in a series of primary elections. In a late June Fireside Chat he declared war on the "Copperheads" who, like their Civil War counterparts, valued peace more than justice. "An election cannot give a country a firm sense of direction," said Roosevelt, "if it has two or more national parties which merely have different names but are as alike in their principles and aims as peas in the same pod."[49] He meant to make the Democratic Party the liberal party, the party of a permanent New Deal. Now was the moment to make that goal, long fermenting in Roosevelt's mind, into a reality. It required, above all, transforming the party's historic base in the South.

Proceeding by train through sweltering Dixie in the late summer, Roosevelt recited the *Report*'s damning litany of southern deficiencies in wages, education, housing, credit facilities, and manufacturing capacity. He summoned southern voters to repudiate politicians who tolerated such conditions. In South Carolina he declared that no man or family could live on fifty cents a day—a pointed rebuke to Cotton Ed Smith. In his "second home state of Georgia" on August 11 he confronted Senator Walter George in a dramatic face-to-face encounter. Appearing on the same platform with George in the small town of Barnesville, Roosevelt taunted the senator with a candor that edged on insult. George, conceded the president, was "a gentleman and a scholar," but he "cannot possibly . . . be classified as belonging to the liberal school of thought. . . . [O]n most public questions he and I do not speak the same language." With that, Roosevelt endorsed George's primary election challenger, a reluctant young attorney named Lawrence Camp, who fidgeted uneasily in his chair while a few mixed cheers and boos floated up from the stunned crowd. George, who had sat in Tom Watson's old Senate seat since 1922, a man so haughty that his own wife addressed him as Mr. George, rose to his feet and replied stiffly: "Mr. President, I want you to know that I accept the challenge."[50]

Roosevelt went on to Maryland, where he attacked another implacably anti–New Deal Democrat, Senator Millard Tydings. The president also spoke out on behalf of his liberal allies, including Maverick in Texas and especially Murphy in Michigan and Earle in Pennsylvania, the governors who had played such pivotal roles in the great labor upheavals

49. *PPA* (1938), 395.
50. Davis 4:279.

of the preceding year. In a nationally broadcast Fireside Chat on election eve, Roosevelt summarized his case with a highly partisan recapitulation of modern American political history:

> We all remember well known examples of what an ill-advised shift from liberal to conservative leadership can do to an incompleted liberal program. Theodore Roosevelt, for example, started a march of progress during his seven years in the Presidency, but after 4 years of President Taft, little was left of the progress that had been made. Think of the great liberal achievements of Woodrow Wilson's New Freedom and how quickly they were liquidated under President Harding. We have to have reasonable continuity in liberal government in order to get permanent results.[51]

Later observers read into those remarks an adumbration of Roosevelt's intention to run for a third presidential term. Whether or not that purpose was already forming in the president's mind, he struck a note in that Fireside Chat consistent with much that he had been saying since his second inaugural address: that the achievements of the New Deal, not to mention the prospects for its extension, were endangered by conservative reaction.

Election day laid bare the depths of that reaction and the danger it held. In the South, Roosevelt failed utterly in his effort to liberalize the Democratic Party. He succeeded only in further alienating the Democratic southern leadership. George in Georgia and Smith in South Carolina were reelected decisively, as was Tydings in Maryland. All denounced Roosevelt as a meddlesome Yankee carpetbagger. George called the president's attack at Barnesville part of "a second march through Georgia." Smith stood before a statue of Confederate hero Wade Hampton and declared that "no man dares to come into South Carolina and try to dictate to the sons of those men who held high the hands of Lee and Hampton." Asked after the election if Roosevelt was not his own worst enemy, Smith snapped, "Not as long as I am alive." Surveying the wreckage of his electoral forays into the South, Roosevelt reflected glumly: "It takes a long, long time to bring the past up to the present."[52]

Elsewhere, Rooseveltian liberals fell like dead timber before the rising conservative wind. Maverick lost in Texas. So did Earle in Pennsylvania

51. PPA (1938), 585.
52. Schulman, *From Cotton Belt to Sunbelt*, 53.

and Murphy in Michigan. So, for that matter, did the Democratic congressional candidate in the district that included Flint, a bitter coda to the sit-down drama. New York's Governor Lehman barely survived a challenge from a dashing young district attorney, Thomas E. Dewey. The Republicans scored their biggest gains since 1928. They won thirteen governorships, doubled their strength in the House, and gained eight new seats in the Senate. The election was a humiliating rebuke to the president and delivered a knockout punch to the New Deal. Astonishingly, the great mountain of political capital that Roosevelt had amassed in 1936 had eroded away in the space of just two years. He had hoped to use that capital to make the Democratic Party a New Deal party and to make the United States permanently a New Deal country. But the South emerged more anti–New Deal and anti-Roosevelt than ever, and outside the South Republicans had eaten deeply into Democratic strength.

The conservative coalition in Congress now had sufficient mass and muscle to go on the offensive. Taking a leaf from the book of the La Follette Civil Liberties Committee, Texas congressman Martin Dies's House Un-American Activities Committee conducted sensational public hearings alleging Communist influence in the labor movement as well as in various New Deal projects. Dies's revelations helped kill the Federal Theater Project in 1939, the first of several New Deal agencies to be dismantled in the next half dozen years. Allegations that the WPA had been put to political use in Alben Barkeley's reelection campaign in Kentucky, as well as in other states, encouraged Congress to slash its appropriations and to pass the Hatch Act, prohibiting federal employees, including workers on federal relief projects, from participating in political campaigns. A reporter further inflamed sentiment against the WPA when he quoted WPA administrator Harry Hopkins as saying in August 1938: "We shall tax and tax, and spend and spend, and elect and elect." Hopkins almost certainly never said anything of the kind, but the phrase struck a responsive chord among those disposed to believe it and was still cited as biblical writ by anti–New Deal critics many decades later.[53]

By the end of 1938 liberal reformers were everywhere in retreat. As the next electoral season of 1940 loomed, noted an observer, the New Deal "has been reduced to a movement with no program, with no

53. The definitive account of what Hopkins did not say is in Robert E. Sherwood, *Roosevelt and Hopkins* (New York: Grosset and Dunlap, 1950), 102–4.

effective political organization, with no vast popular party strength behind it, and with no candidate."[54]

POLITICAL CHECKMATE went hand in hand with policy stalemate,
as a renewed economic crisis calamitously revealed. In May 1937 the
economic recovery building since 1933 had crested, well short of 1929
levels of employment. By August the economy was once again sliding
measurably downward; in September, rapidly downward. In October the
stock market cracked. The dread specter of 1929 once again haunted
the country. "We are headed right into another Depression," Morgenthau warned the president, and he was right.[55] Conditions deteriorated
with astonishing speed, swiftly eclipsing the rate of economic decay that
had destroyed Herbert Hoover. Within weeks, stocks gave up more than
a third of their value. Corporate profits plunged nearly 80 percent. Steel
production in the year's last quarter sank to one-fourth of its mid-1937
level, pacing a 40 percent decline in overall industrial output. In Detroit
the relief rolls in early 1938 ballooned to four times their 1937 size.
Union organizing, crimped once again by a weakening economy,
ground to a halt. By the end of the winter of 1937–38, more than two
million workers had received layoff notices. They expanded the already
crowded ranks of the unemployed to more than ten million souls, or 19
percent of the work force, numbers that evoked grim comparison with
the Hoover years.

Critics called it the "Roosevelt Recession." It was a depression within
a depression, the first economic downturn since Roosevelt had taken
office. The president paid a stiff political price for it at the polls in 1938.
What caused it? Equally important, what did Roosevelt, with the example of Hoover before him, and with more than four years of his own
Depression-fighting experience behind him, do about it?

The recession touched off an acrimonious, prolonged, and in the end
maddeningly inconsequential policy debate within the Roosevelt administration. Seldom has so much intellectual and political energy been
expended with such slender result. Yet the peculiar array of explanations
and nostrums that contended in this episode, and the particular equilibrium in which they finally came to rest, reveal much about the character and the historical significance of the New Deal.

54. James MacGregor Burns, Roosevelt: The Lion and The Fox (New York: Harcourt,
    Brace, 1956), 375.
55. Alan Brinkley, The End of Reform: New Deal Liberalism in Depression and War
    (New York: Knopf, 1995), 17.

The downturn was perhaps due in part to nothing more than the familiar rhythms of the business cycle, which dictated some inevitable measure of contraction after four years of expansion. But in the newly politicized economic atmosphere of 1937, when government as never before was claiming responsibility for economic performance, such explanations got short shrift.

One school of thought laid the blame for the recession on the administration's antibusiness policies or, somewhat more benignly, on the inevitable uncertainties brewed by the New Deal's "regime change" in the rules of the economic game. Repeated budget deficits, escalating regulatory burdens, threats of higher taxes, mounting labor costs, and, most important, persistent anxiety about what further provocations to business the New Deal had in store, so the argument ran, sapped the confidence of investors and inhibited the commitment of capital to new enterprises. The proof of this thesis seemed to be in the numbers: net new private investment in the mid-1930s was running at only about one-third of its rate a decade earlier. Capital, in short, was hibernating. Lammot du Pont explained why in 1937:

> Uncertainty rules the tax situation, the labor situation, the monetary situation, and practically every legal condition under which industry must operate. Are taxes to go higher, lower or stay where they are? We don't know. Is labor to be union or non-union? . . . Are we to have inflation or deflation, more government spending or less? . . . Are new restrictions to be placed on capital, new limits on profits? . . . It is impossible to even guess at the answers.[56]

These views were not simply the property of conservative business interests. They also found support within the administration. "You could not have a government," former Brain Truster Adolf Berle wrote, "perpetually at war with its economic machinery." Business was demoralized, said Berle, and for obvious reasons: "[p]ractically no business group in the country has escaped investigation or other attack in the last five years . . . [T]he result has been shattered morale. . . . It is, therefore, necessary to make that group pull itself together."[57] At a cabinet meeting

56. Quoted in Robert Higgs, "Regime Uncertainty: Why the Great Depression Lasted So Long and Why Prosperity Resumed after the War," *Independent Review* 1, no. 4 (Spring 1997): 576.

57. Brinkley, *End of Reform*, 20; Beatrice Bishop Berle and Travis Beal Jacobs, *Navigating the Rapids, 1918–1971: From the Papers of Adolf A. Berle* (New York: Harcourt Brace Jovanovich, 1973), 171.

in early November 1937, Treasury Secretary Morgenthau and Postmaster General Farley both urged this diagnosis on the president and begged him to apply the appropriate remedy: a balanced budget, along with a general detente in the administration's relationship with business. "Oh, for God's sake, Henry," said Roosevelt exasperatedly to Morgenthau, "do you want me to read the record again?" The public utilities companies, Farley argued, were especially critical. They were hugely capital-intensive enterprises, capable of generating enormous new jobmaking investments in dams, power plants, and transmission lines, but they had been knocked off balance by the Public Utilities Holding Company Act of 1935, aimed at drastic restructuring of the industry. Uncertain of their future, the utilities companies had choked their new investment to a trickle. They "would spend a lot of money," Farley said, "if they knew where they are heading." Roosevelt replied petulantly that in his view the utilities were overcapitalized, greedy for returns on bloated evaluations of their stock. "Every time you do anything for them, they want something else," Roosevelt said. "You can't get anywhere with any of them."[58]

Roosevelt went on in later weeks to speculate that the slowdown in investment was not economically explicable but was, rather, part of a political conspiracy against him, a "capital strike" designed to dislodge him from office and destroy the New Deal by inducing another economic breakdown that would subject him to Hoover's fate. In a reprise of his tactics in the "wealth tax" battle of 1935 and the electoral campaign of 1936, Roosevelt loosed Assistant Attorney General Robert Jackson, along with Ickes, to give a series of blistering speeches in December 1937. Ickes inveighed against Henry Ford, Tom Girdler, and the "Sixty Families" (a phrase borrowed from the title of Ferdinand Lundberg's muckraking exposé) who, he charged, made up "the living center of the modern industrial oligarchy which dominates the United States." Left unchecked, Ickes thundered, they would create "big-business Fascist America — an enslaved America." For his part, Jackson decried the slump in private investment as "a general strike — the first general strike in America — a strike against the government — a strike to coerce political action." Roosevelt even ordered an FBI investigation of possible criminal conspiracy in the alleged capitalist strike, but it revealed nothing of substance.[59]

58. Farley, *Jim Farley's Story*, 105.
59. Brinkley, *End of Reform*, 45–46; Brinkley, "The New Deal and the Idea of the State," in Steve Fraser and Gary Gerstle, *The Rise and Fall of the New Deal Order* (Princeton: Princeton University Press, 1989), 113, n. 8.

The theory of a conspiratorial capital strike had little basis in fact, but it nevertheless fell on receptive ears among a group coming to be known simply as the "New Dealers." The New Dealers were a kind of party within a party, or, more precisely, a faction within the administration. They were mostly young men, and mostly protégés of Harvard Law professor Felix Frankfurter, though from time to time they also enjoyed the patronage of Harold Ickes, Henry Wallace, and Frances Perkins in the cabinet and occasionally Harry Hopkins at the WPA and Marriner Eccles at the Federal Reserve. With exceptions like William O. Douglas, who chaired the Securities and Exchange Commission, they were scattered through the middle ranks of the federal bureaucracy, in obscure posts that belied the influence they wielded: Thomas G. Corcoran at the Reconstruction Finance Corporation; Benjamin V. Cohen at the National Power Committee in the Interior Department; Isador Lubin at the Bureau of Labor Statistics; Lauchlin Currie at the Federal Reserve; Mordecai Ezekiel in the Agriculture Department; Leon Henderson at the WPA; Jerome Frank at the SEC. They numbered perhaps two to three hundred people, mostly young lawyers and economists. Corcoran, a gifted speechwriter and legislative draftsman and a canny political tactician, was a wily operator who gave definition to the emerging political type of the "Washington insider." As much as anyone, he served as the leader of this informal group. He was also their chief recruiting officer, consulting closely with his mentor, Frankfurter, to identify and place new talent. To his home in Georgetown, dubbed the "Little Red House" by conservative pundits, the New Dealers came to eat and drink and hone their wits in argument.

Many of the New Dealers had arrived in Washington in the earliest days of the Roosevelt administration. They were talented and hungry youngsters for whom government employment in those lean times was the best, or perhaps the only, job opportunity available. But it was not just the accident of employment that bound the New Dealers together. Though they represented a broad range of opinions and sometimes clashed over specific policies, they shared certain core beliefs: a deep suspicion of businessmen and a fierce faith in government as the agency of justice and progress. Some of them blamed the 1937 recession, and indeed all the ills of the Depression decade, on the insidious influence of "monopolies," for which evil the appropriate remedy was vigorous enforcement of the antitrust laws. For others, the NRA had embodied the dream of a vast governmental superagency that could wring order out of the vast, seething, wasteful chaos of American capitalism.

An aura of youthful glamour and political idealism emanated from the New Dealers, but the strong scent of mandarinism clung to them as well. None held elected office — ever. They took their inspiration from books like James Landis's *The Administrative Process* (1938) and Thurman Arnold's *Symbols of Government* (1935) and *The Folklore of Capitalism* (1937), all of which argued for more plentiful and more powerful government agencies, administered by technicians with wide discretionary authority, who would be charged with overseeing and fine-tuning the increasingly complex industrial economy. What America needed, Arnold declared in *The Folklore of Capitalism*, was "a religion of government."[60]

Above all, many of the New Dealers were especially enthusiastic about the novel economic doctrines of John Maynard Keynes, published in 1936 as *The General Theory of Employment, Interest, and Money*. They found particularly congenial Keynes's claim that government's role in promoting consumption, rather than directly stimulating investment, was the key to economic health. Governments, Keynes argued, must be willing to sustain purchasing power with "compensatory" fiscal policies, including heavy government borrowing, to offset downward swings in the business cycle. In this view, government deficits were necessary and powerful tools of economic recovery, not signs of fiscal malfeasance. Accordingly, deficits should be embraced boldly, without stint or apology, as the occasion demanded. This advice, of course, was the most outrageous heresy among orthodox economists and was still anathema, at least in theory, to most statesmen — including, as it turned out, to Franklin Roosevelt. But the renewed economic crisis of 1937–38, coming after almost a decade of the Great Depression, opened the field to heresies of all kinds, and the New Dealers were nothing if not heterodox.

To their defenders, the New Dealers were selfless civil servants, paladins of the public interest, the inheritors of the progressive tradition that placed its faith in disinterested expertise as the surest safeguard of democracy in the modern world. To their detractors, like former AAA administrator George Peek, they were a "plague of young lawyers" who had "crossed the border line of sanity," arrogant manipulators of the increasingly elaborate and arcane New Deal–spawned governmental apparatus whose mysteries only this new class of secular priests could penetrate.[61] Even Harry Hopkins, their sometime champion, said of them

---

60. Thurman Arnold, *The Folklore of Capitalism* (New Haven: Yale University Press, 1937), 389.

61. George N. Peek, *Why Quit Our Own?* (New York: D. Van Nostrand, 1936), 12, 20. Many of the New Dealers went on to lucrative private careers, often in Washington

in 1939 that "there are people in this town who don't want recovery. . . . There are a lot of the younger fellows sitting around who talk things over who don't want recovery, because they want the government to stay on the top deck."[62]

Not surprisingly, the New Dealers sought the principal cause of the recession in government policy and the cure in the same place. In a memorandum that was destined to assume the status of a kind of New Dealers' Nicene Creed, Currie, with the help of Henderson and Lubin, drafted an analysis of the recession and a program for coping with it. Together, they presented it to the president in early November.

As the three New Dealers saw things, the government had committed several economic crimes in late 1936 and early 1937. First the Federal Reserve, inexplicably worried about inflation even in the midst of high unemployment, contracted the money supply by sterilizing gold imports and raising member bank reserve requirements. Then came a sharp reversal in the federal government's fiscal policy. In 1936, thanks largely to the payment of the veterans' bonus that had passed over Roosevelt's veto, as well as to continuing WPA and PWA expenditures, the New Deal had poured nearly $4 billion in excess of tax receipts into the economy. These deficits, virtually equivalent to the entire federal budget in 1933, had stimulated consumption and spurred economic recovery. But in 1937 the one-time bonus payment had disappeared, and the new, regressive Social Security taxes bit some $2 billion out of the national income without yet returning anything as benefits (the first of which would be paid only in 1940). Worst of all, Roosevelt worried as ever about balancing the budget. Eager to make the political statement that with the end of the Depression in sight relief could be cut back, he ordered deep reductions in both WPA and PWA expenditures in the summer of 1937. For the first nine months of 1937, the federal budget was actually in the black, by some $66 million. So: government deficits had underwritten the 1933–37 recovery; the reduction of the deficits had caused the recession; ergo, the New Dealers argued, the antidote was obvious. The federal government must resume large-scale spending: Q.E.D.

---

law firms, selling to corporate clients their special expertise in the workings of the very government agencies they had helped to build. Corcoran's career served as the prototype for this new type of legal practice, which virtually required some sort of apprenticeship in government service. See Peter H. Irons, *The New Deal Lawyers* (Princeton: Princeton University Press, 1982).

62. John Morton Blum, *From the Morgenthau Diaries: Years of Urgency, 1938–1941* (Boston: Houghton-Mifflin, 1965), 26.

Marriner Eccles, Currie's boss and a vociferous champion of spending, later chronicled the fate of that tidy syllogistic analysis. At a meeting at the White House on November 8, 1937, he recalled, "the pattern of discussion was provided by a now famous memorandum prepared by Isador Lubin, Leon Henderson, and Lauchlin Currie, indicating how a reduction in government spending had helped to precipitate the recession. There were indications that Roosevelt was impressed by the argument advanced to him." At a subsequent meeting on the afternoon of November 10, Roosevelt again agreed that what was needed was "a resumption of government spending and not a curb on it."

But then, to Eccles's astonishment, on the evening of that same November 10, Treasury Secretary Morgenthau, with Roosevelt's evident blessing, addressed an audience of business leaders in New York and pledged a balanced budget—a statement that elicited honks of laughter from some of his auditors. But what bothered Eccles was not the incredulity of businessmen about the promise of a balanced budget. It was the fact that the president on the exact same day had "assented to two contradictory policies"—deficit spending in the afternoon and a balanced budget in the evening. This legerdemain led Eccles to what he conceded was an "ungenerous" conclusion. "The contradictions between the afternoon and evening positions made me wonder," Eccles recalled, "whether the New Deal was merely a political slogan or if Roosevelt really knew what the New Deal was."[63]

What the New Deal was—the question has echoed down the years and at no time sounded more urgently than in this crisis within a crisis in 1937–38. Yet to Eccles's continuing dismay, Roosevelt moved with glacial slowness toward resolving the contradictions that beset his administration's policies. In his message to the special session of Congress that convened on November 15, the president scarcely mentioned the recession. For nearly five more months the debate within the administration churned on, pitting budget-balancers against spenders, business conciliators and confidence-builders against regulators and trust-busters. It was, says historian Alan Brinkley, "an intense ideological struggle—a struggle among different conceptions of the economy, among different views of the state, and among different . . . political traditions. . . . It was a struggle to define the soul of the New Deal."[64]

Ironically enough, victory in the struggle for the New Deal's soul

63. Marriner S. Eccles, *Beckoning Frontiers* (New York: Knopf, 1951), 304.
64. Brinkley, *End of Reform*, 18.

would not in the end be worth much, since the New Deal, bleeding from the Court battle and jacketed by newly militant conservatives, was in the process of giving up the ghost. That very prospect, exacerbated by the prolonged paralysis of the Roosevelt administration as 1937 passed into 1938, excited anxieties well beyond the United States.

In a widely publicized open letter to Roosevelt in 1933, the British economist John Maynard Keynes had praised the American president as "the trustee for those in every country who seek to mend the evils of our condition by reasoned experiment within the framework of the existing social system. If you fail, rational change will be gravely prejudiced throughout the world, leaving orthodoxy and revolution to fight it out."[65] Now, four years later, as the American economy slid toward the lip of a catastrophe potentially even greater than that of 1929, Keynes wrote the president again, this time privately. "I am terrified," he confided, "lest progressive causes in all the democratic countries should suffer injury, because you have taken too lightly the risk to their prestige which would result from a failure measured in terms of immediate prosperity." He praised Roosevelt's reforms, citing the New Deal's agricultural policies, the SEC, the promotion of collective bargaining, and the wages-and-hours bill. But without economic recovery, Keynes feared, all those gains and more would be lost.

The president had to decide, Keynes insisted, on the balance of private and public means that might be mobilized to stimulate the economy. New investment in housing, public utilities, and the railroads would create jobs, generate income, and restore economic vitality by increasing aggregate demand. But where was the money for that new investment to come from? Keynes made no secret of his own preferences: "[D]urable investment must come increasingly under state direction." He favored public ownership of the utilities, nationalization of the railroads, and direct subsidies for "working class houses," as in Britain. Housing, above all, said Keynes, was "by far the best aid to recovery" because of the large and geographically dispersed potential demand. "I should advise putting most of your eggs in this basket," Keynes urged. But in the case of the railroads and utilities, and by implication other industries, Keynes acknowledged that in America "public opinion is not yet ripe" for public ownership. Therefore, he asked sharply, "what is the object of chasing the utilities round the lot every other week?" Businessmen, Keynes concluded, "have a different set of delusions from

65. *New York Times*, December 31, 1933, sec. 8, 2.

politicians; and need, therefore, different handling. . . . It is a mistake to think that they are more immoral than politicians. If you work them into [a] surly, obstinate, terrified mood . . . , the nation's burdens will not get carried to market; and in the end public opinion will veer their way."[66]

This was stern stuff, delivered with a note of professorial hauteur that could not have charmed Franklin Roosevelt. But it was also useable stuff, even commonsensical stuff, despite Roosevelt's belief that Keynes was good for little except arcane, abstract theorizing. The British economist's advice pointed clearly to a two-pronged policy of mollifying business and thereby reinvigorating private investment, while in the meantime "priming the pump" with substantial government outlays, especially in the field of housing. This combination of government stimulus to consumption and resumed private capital formation seemed a sensible formula for effecting a recovery that could be durable and self-sustaining. Its logic would, in time, constitute the operational heart of "Keynesian economics." It was not a conceptually difficult formula to grasp. Indeed, many American policymakers like Eccles, and even, in a limited way, Herbert Hoover, had intuited the essence of these ideas well before Keynes famously put them to paper. To reverse Keynes's notorious dictum to the effect that practical men are but the unwitting slaves of some defunct economist, it may be equally true that many economists in the last analysis simply wrap the mantle of academic theory around the practical dictates of instinct and necessity. Surely what the world eventually came to know as "Keynesianism" grew as much from the jumble of circumstance, politics, and adaptation as it did from the pages of the textbooks. So what, in the end, did Roosevelt, supposedly a keen student of circumstance, a master of politics, and a genius of adaptation, do?

The answer is that he did a little of everything and a lot of mischief. In April 1938 he acceded to the importunings of the spenders and requested an emergency appropriation of some $3 billion. Many historians have hailed that decision as establishing the first deficit deliberately embraced for purposes of economic stimulus. But in a $100 billion economy, with more than ten million persons unemployed, $3 billion was a decidedly modest sum, not appreciably larger than most earlier New Deal deficits, considerably less than the unintended deficit of 1936, and far short of the kind of economic boost that Keynes envisioned as nec-

---

66. Keynes's letter to Roosevelt of February 1, 1938, is reprinted in Howard Zinn, *New Deal Thought* (Indianapolis: Bobbs-Merrill, 1966), 403–9.

essary to overcome the Depression once and for all. Moreover, Roosevelt chose virtually the same moment to renew his perturbations of the business climate by launching the so-called Temporary National Economic Committee (TNEC, with Leon Henderson as its executive secretary), charged with conducting, amid glaring publicity, a joint congressional-executive probe of "monopolies." For good measure, he appointed Thurman Arnold head of the Justice Department's Anti-Trust Division. Arnold proceeded to expand the division's staff from a few dozen lawyers to nearly three hundred. They brought a flurry of antitrust suits, designed less to eradicate monopoly, as Arnold later explained, than to remind businessmen, as Theodore Roosevelt had done at the century's opening, that not they but the government held ultimate power. As for the TNEC, said *Time*, after three years of investigation, "a terrific broadside might have been expected. Instead, the committee rolled a rusty BB gun into place [and] pinged at the nation's economic problems."[67]

These decisions spelled a messy conclusion to the protracted policy debate of 1937–38. They also signaled what some critics have identified as a defining historical moment, a quiet revolution that fundamentally transformed the assumptions, aspirations, and techniques of modern American liberalism. In this view, Roosevelt's deliberate embrace of deficit spending—and, more generally, the New Dealers' enthusiasm for the Keynesian economic theory that informed and ratified that policy—tolled the knell for an older reform tradition. The progressives of an earlier day, and even the liberals of Franklin Roosevelt's own generation, so this argument runs, had been preoccupied with effecting structural economic reform, achieving distributive justice, and guaranteeing full citizenship to all Americans. The new generation of liberals coming of age in the late 1930s supposedly repudiated that reforming heritage in order to reach an accommodation with their traditional nemesis, capitalism. In the process they abandoned the strategy of direct governmental interventions to secure equality and protect the disadvantaged, and instead established a new political religion devoted to the god of economic growth. "With reasonably full employment, adequate purchasing power, and near capacity production," one of them explained in 1938, "many problems now appearing to call for government intervention or control might solve themselves."[68] If earlier liberals conceived of the economy as a mechanism that needed fixing, the Keynesians

---

67. Fraser and Gerstle, *Rise and Fall of the New Deal Order*, 92.
68. Beardsley Ruml quoted in Dean L. May, *From New Deal to New Economics: The American Liberal Response to the Recession of 1937* (New York: Garland, 1981), 160.

thought of the economy as an organism that needed feeding but that should otherwise be left to its own devices. The political theorist Michael Sandel has spelled out the alleged deficiencies of this new ideology:

> Keynesian fiscal policy is neutral . . . in its assumption that government should not form or revise, or for that matter even judge, the interests and ends its citizens espouse; rather, it should enable them to pursue those interests and ends, whatever they may be, consistent with a similar liberty for others. It is this assumption above all that distinguishes the political economy of growth from the political economy of citizenship, and links Keynesian economics to contemporary liberalism.[69]

Yet so far as the economy was concerned in 1938, Roosevelt's actions looked for the moment to be something considerably less than revolutionary. The president may have planted the seeds of the "Keynesian Revolution" in American fiscal policy, but it would be some time before they would fully flower. In the meantime, Roosevelt seemed to have wrought the worst of all worlds: insufficient government spending to effect recovery, but sufficient government sword-rattling to keep private capital cowed. "The President won't spend any money," an exasperated Jerome Frank exclaimed. "Nobody on the outside will believe the trouble we have with him. Yet they call him a big spender. It makes me laugh."[70] As for private businessmen, they still hesitated to make new investments. Why, the president mused one night at dinner, did they lack confidence in the economy? Because, Eleanor replied tellingly, "They are afraid of you."[71] Deprived of adequate public or private means of revival, the economy sputtered on, not reaching the output levels of 1937 until the fateful year of 1941, when the threat of war, not enlightened New Deal policies, compelled government expenditures at levels previously unimaginable.

Various explanations have been offered for Roosevelt's belated choice in 1938 of these weak and contradictory instruments of economic policy. In part, he may have simply succumbed to the politician's natural urge to do a little something for everybody. Probably he also felt, as his political capital melted away under the heat from the Court fight in 1937

69. Michael J. Sandel, *Democracy's Discontent: America in Search of a Public Philosophy* (Cambridge: Belknap Press of Harvard University Press, 1996), 267.
70. Lash, *Dealers and Dreamers*, 322.
71. Frank Freidel, *Franklin D. Roosevelt: A Rendezvous with Destiny* (Boston: Little, Brown, 1990), 257.

and the worsening economic crisis in 1938, that a *little* something was all he could do in the face of waning presidential influence and waxing congressional autonomy. Despite the lamentations of later critics, the fact was that further structural reform was for the moment a political impossibility. Deficit spending was about the only policy on which the fractious Congress, liberals and conservatives alike, could unite, and even then Congress didn't want too much of it. Neither, apparently, did Roosevelt. He was a decidedly reluctant and an exceedingly moderate Keynesian. He was still hemmed in by intellectual limitations, scarcely more able than Herbert Hoover had been to think his way out of the box of orthodoxy and boldly repudiate the dogma of the balanced budget. And perhaps at some level deep within Roosevelt's mind he may have shared a version of the perversely inhibiting sentiment that Harry Hopkins ascribed to the band of New Dealers who now seemed to have the president's ear: the feeling that with full recovery the government would no longer be on the top deck, and the door would shut forever against the possibility of further reform.

WHAT WAS THE NEW DEAL? Marriner Eccles had wondered. Whatever it was, Roosevelt conclusively demonstrated in 1938 that it was not a recovery program, at any rate not an effective one. There was a paradox here, and no little danger. Serious structural reform seemed possible only in the context of economic crisis, but the prolongation of that crisis, as Keynes warned, would in the end jeopardize all that Roosevelt had achieved, and thereby jeopardize the cause of liberalism everywhere.

Liberal democracy was everywhere in peril in 1938. Mussolini and Hitler had long since closed the fist of dictatorship over Italy and Germany. In Spain a civil war pitting fascists against republicans had been raging for two years. Italy had conquered Ethiopia in 1936. Japan had invaded China in the summer of 1937. In March 1938, even as Roosevelt groped for policies to right the economy and save the New Deal, Hitler annexed Austria to the German *Reich*. Reports arrived almost immediately of Nazi reprisals against Viennese Jews. Before the year was out, Hitler absorbed the Czechoslovakian Sudetenland as well, then forced the European democracies at Munich to legitimate his grab. In November 1938 he loosed his Nazi thugs against Germany's Jews in an orgy of violence known as *Kristallnacht*, the night of the broken glass.

It was against this backdrop of gathering global menace that Roosevelt spoke to the nation in a Fireside Chat on April 14, 1938, to announce at last the request for increased spending that constituted part of his hesitant and contradictory response to the deepening American economic crisis. "Security is our greatest need," the president intoned into the microphones on his White House desk. Then he alluded to the Nazi ingestion of Austria just a month earlier: "Democracy has disappeared in several other great nations," he said, "not because the people of those nations disliked democracy, but because they had grown tired of unemployment and insecurity, of seeing their children hungry while they sat helpless in the face of government confusion and government weakness through lack of leadership in government." Some listeners might have wondered if he was not talking about his own government and his own leadership. "History proves," Roosevelt concluded, "that dictatorships do not grow out of strong and successful governments, but out of weak and helpless ones."[72]

Yet Roosevelt himself stood before the world in 1938 as a badly weakened leader, unable to summon the imagination or to secure the political strength to cure his own country's apparently endless economic crisis. In the ninth year of the Great Depression and the sixth year of Roosevelt's New Deal, with more than ten million workers still unemployed, America had still not found a formula for economic recovery. From such a leader, what could the democracies hope? From such a troubled nation, what did the dictators have to fear?

72. PPA (1938), 242.

12

What the New Deal Did

At the heart of the New Deal there was not a philosophy but a temperament.
　　　　　—Richard Hofstadter, *The American Political Tradition*, 1948

Not with a bang, but a whimper, the New Deal petered out in 1938. Roosevelt's annual message to Congress in January 1939 was his first in which he did not propose new social and economic programs. "We have now passed the period of internal conflict in the launching of our program of social reform," he announced. "Our full energies may now be released to invigorate the processes of recovery in order to preserve our reforms."[1] As it happened, recovery awaited not the release of more New Deal energies but the unleashing of the dogs of war. Yet the end of reform scarcely meant the end of social and economic change, nor even the end of pursuing those goals the New Deal had championed, especially the goal of security. When the war brought recovery at last, a recovery that inaugurated the most prosperous quarter century America has ever known, it brought it to an economy and a country that the New Deal had fundamentally altered. Indeed, the achievements of the New Deal years surely played a role in determining the degree and the duration of postwar prosperity.

The era of reform might have ended in 1938, but it is worth remembering just how much reform had already taken place by that date. Into the five years of the New Deal was crowded more social and institutional change than into virtually any comparable compass of time in the nation's past. Change is always controversial. Change on the scale the New Deal wrought has proved interminably controversial. Debate about the

1. *PPA* (1939), 7.

New Deal's historical significance, its ideological identity, and its political, social, and economic consequences has ground on for more than half a century. Roosevelt's reforms have become an unavoidable touchstone of American political argument, a talisman invoked by all parties to legitimate or condemn as the occasion requires, an emblem and barometer of American attitudes toward government itself. So just what, exactly, *did* the New Deal do?

It might be well to begin by recognizing what the New Deal did not do, in addition to its conspicuous failure to produce economic recovery. Much mythology and New Deal rhetoric notwithstanding, it did not substantially redistribute the national income. America's income profile in 1940 closely resembled that of 1930, and for that matter 1920.[2] The falling economic tide of the Depression lowered all boats, but by and large they held their relative positions; what little income leveling there was resulted more from Depression-diminished returns to investments, not to redistributive tax policies. Nor, with essentially minor exceptions like the TVA's electric-power business, did the New Deal challenge the fundamental tenet of capitalism: private ownership of the means of production. In contrast with the pattern in virtually all other industrial societies, whether Communist, socialist, or capitalist, no significant state-owned enterprises emerged in New Deal America.

It is also frequently said that the New Deal conformed to no preexisting ideological agenda and that it never produced a spokesman, not even Franklin Roosevelt, who was able systematically to lay out the New Deal's social and economic philosophy. Then and later, critics have charged that so many inconsistent impulses contended under the tent of Roosevelt's New Deal that to seek for system and coherence was to pursue a fool's errand. That accusation has echoed repeatedly in assessments that stress the New Deal's mongrel intellectual pedigree, its improbably plural constituent base, its political pragmatism, its abundant

2. See, for example, Mark H. Leff, *The Limits of Symbolic Reform: The New Deal and Taxation, 1933–1939* (Cambridge: Cambridge University Press, 1984); U.S. Bureau of the Census, *Income Distribution in the United States* (Washington: US GPO, 1966); Simon Kuznets, "Long Term Changes in the National Income of the United States of America since 1870," in Kuznets, ed., *Income and Wealth Series II* (Cambridge: Bowes and Bowes, 1952); Jeffrey G. Williamson and Peter H. Lindert, *American Inequality: A Macroeconomic History* (New York: Academic, 1980); Robert Lampman, *The Share of Top Wealth-Holders in National Wealth* (Princeton: Princeton University Press, 1962).

promiscuities, inconsistencies, contradictions, inconstancies, and fail-ures.[3] What unity of plan or purpose, one might ask, was to be found in an administration that at various times tinkered with inflation and with price controls, with deficit spending and budget-balancing, cartel-ization and trust-busting, the promotion of consumption and the intim-idation of investment, farm-acreage reduction and land reclamation, public employment projects and forced removals from the labor pool? "Economically," one historian concludes with some justice, "the New Deal had been opportunistic in the grand manner."[4]

And yet, illumined by the stern-lantern of history, the New Deal can be seen to have left in place a set of institutional arrangements that constituted a more coherent pattern than is dreamt of in many philos-ophies. That pattern can be summarized in a single word: security — security for vulnerable individuals, to be sure, as Roosevelt famously urged in his campaign for the Social Security Act of 1935, but security for capitalists and consumers, for workers and employers, for corpora-tions and farms and homeowners and bankers and builders as well. Job security, life-cycle security, financial security, market security — however it might be defined, achieving security was the leitmotif of virtually everything the New Deal attempted. Unarguably, Roosevelt sought to enlarge the national state as the principal instrument of the security and stability that he hoped to impart to American life. But legend to the contrary, much of the security that the New Deal threaded into the fabric of American society was often stitched with a remarkably delicate hand, not simply imposed by the fist of the imperious state. And with the notable exceptions of agricultural subsidies and old-age pensions, it was not usually purchased with the taxpayers' dollars. Nowhere was the artful design of the New Deal's security program more evident than in the financial sector.

At the tip of Manhattan Island, south of the street laid out along the line where the first Dutch settlers built their wall to defend against ma-rauding Indians, beats the very heart of American capitalism. Deep in the urban canyons of the old Dutch city sits the New York Stock Exchange,

3. The classic study of the New Deal's tangled intellectual genealogy in the realm of economic policy is Ellis W. Hawley, *The New Deal and the Problem of Monopoly* (Princeton: Princeton University Press, 1966).
4. James MacGregor Burns, *Roosevelt: The Lion and the Fox* (New York: Harcourt, Brace, 1956), 322.

whence had come the first herald of the Depression's onset. As the Great Crash of 1929 reverberated through the financial system, annihilating billions of dollars in asset values and forcing bank closures, it raised a mighty cry for the reform of "Wall Street," a site that early and late has been beleaguered by threatening hordes incensed at its supposedly inordinate power. The New Deal heeded that cry. Among its first initiatives was the reform of the American financial sector, including the banks and the securities markets. What did it accomplish?

Faced with effectively complete collapse of the banking system in 1933, the New Deal confronted a choice. On the one hand, it could try to nationalize the system, or perhaps create a new government bank that would threaten eventually to drive all private banks out of business. On the other hand, it could accede to the long-standing requests of the major money-center banks—especially those headquartered around Wall Street—to relax restrictions on branch and interstate banking, allow mergers and consolidations, and thereby facilitate the emergence of a highly concentrated private banking industry, with just a few dozen powerful institutions to carry on the nation's banking business. That, in fact, was the pattern in most other industrialized countries. But the New Deal did neither. Instead, it left the astonishingly plural and localized American banking system in place, while inducing one important structural change and introducing one key new institution.

The structural change, mandated by the Glass-Steagall Banking Act of 1933, was to separate investment banks from commercial banks, thus securing depositors' savings against the risks of being used for highly speculative purposes. The same Act created a new entity, the Federal Bank Deposit Insurance Corporation (FBDIC, later simply FDIC). Guaranteeing individual bank deposits up to five thousand dollars (later raised) and funded by minimal subscriptions from Federal Reserve member institutions, the FDIC forever liberated banks and depositors from the fearful psychology of bank "runs," or panics. These two simple measures did not impose an oppressively elaborate new regulatory apparatus on American banking, nor did they levy appreciable costs on either taxpayers or member banks. But they did inject unprecedented stability into the American banking system. Bank failures, which had occurred at the rate of hundreds per year even before the Depression's descent, numbered fewer than ten per year in the decades after 1933.

If speculation and lack of depositor confidence had been the major problems of the banking system, the cardinal affliction of the closely related securities industry had been ignorance. Pervasive, systemic ignorance blanketed Wall Street like a perpetual North Atlantic fog before the New Deal, badly impeding the efficient operation of the securities markets and leaving them vulnerable to all kinds of abuses. Wall Street before the 1930s was a strikingly information-starved environment. Many firms whose securities were publicly traded published no regular reports or issued reports whose data were so arbitrarily selected and capriciously audited as to be worse than useless. It was this circumstance that had conferred such awesome power on a handful of investment bankers like J. P. Morgan, because they commanded a virtual monopoly of the information necessary to making sound financial decisions.[5] Especially in the secondary markets, where reliable information was all but impossible for the average investor to come by, opportunities abounded for insider manipulation and wildcat speculation. "It's easy to make money in this market," the canny speculator Joseph P. Kennedy had confided to a partner in the palmy days of the 1920s. "We'd better get in before they pass a law against it."[6]

The New Deal did pass a law against it, then assigned Joseph P. Kennedy to implement that law, a choice often compared to putting the fox in the henhouse or setting a thief to catch a thief. In 1934 Kennedy became the first chairman of the new Securities Exchange Commission (SEC), one of just four new regulatory bodies established by the New Deal.[7] The SEC's powers derived from statutes so patently needed but so intricately technical that Texas congressman Sam Rayburn admitted he did not know whether the legislation "passed so readily because it was so damned good or so damned incomprehensible." Yet some years later, Rayburn acknowledged that the SEC, thanks in part to the start it got from Kennedy, was "the strongest Commission in the government."A study of the federal bureaucracy overseen by Herbert Hoover called the SEC "an outstanding example of the independent commission at its best."[8]

5. For a vivid description of the workings of the pre–New Deal financial marketplace, see Ron Chernow, *The House of Morgan* (New York: Atlantic Monthly, 1990).
6. Kennedy quoted in Michael R. Beschloss, *Kennedy and Roosevelt: An Uneasy Alliance* (New York: Norton, 1980), 60.
7. The others were the National Labor Relations Board, the Civil Aeronautics Authority, and the Federal Communications Commission. Some existing agencies were also considerably strengthened, notably the Federal Power Commission, the Federal Trade Commission, the Interstate Commerce Commission, and the Federal Reserve Board.
8. Congressman Sam Rayburn and the Hoover Commission Report quoted in Thomas K. McCraw, *Prophets of Regulation* (Cambridge: Belknap Press of Harvard University Press, 1984), 175, 153–54.

For all the complexity of its enabling legislation, the power of the SEC resided principally in just two provisions, both of them ingeniously simple. The first mandated disclosure of detailed information, such as balance sheets, profit and loss statements, and the names and compensation of corporate officers, about firms whose securities were publicly traded. The second required verification of that information by independent auditors using standardized accounting procedures. At a stroke, those measures ended the monopoly of the Morgans and their like on investment information. Wall Street was now saturated with data that were relevant, accessible, and comparable across firms and transactions. The SEC's regulations unarguably imposed new reporting requirements on businesses. They also gave a huge boost to the status of the accounting profession. But they hardly constituted a wholesale assault on the theory or practice of free-market capitalism. All to the contrary, the SEC's regulations dramatically improved the economic efficiency of the financial markets by making buy and sell decisions well-informed decisions, provided that the contracting parties consulted the data now so copiously available. This was less the reform than it was the rationalization of capitalism, along the lines of capitalism's own claims about how free markets were supposed to work.

The New Deal's housing policies provide perhaps the best example of its techniques for stabilizing a major economic sector by introducing new elements of information and reliability. By its very nature, the potential demand for housing was large, widespread, and capable of generating significant employment in countless localities. John Maynard Keynes was not alone in recognizing that housing was a sector with enormous promise for invigorating the economy. Well before Keynes urged Roosevelt to put his eggs in the housing basket, Herbert Hoover had patronized the Better Homes for America Movement in the 1920s. In 1931, as new home construction plunged by 95 percent from its pre-1929 levels, he had convened a national presidential conference on Home Building and Home Ownership. Its very title, especially the latter phrase, advertised Hoover's preferred approach to the housing issue.[9]

As in the banking sector, the New Deal faced a choice in the housing field. It could take Keynes's advice and get behind proposals from congressional liberals like Robert Wagner for large-scale, European-style public

9. For a study of Hoover's policies, see Karen Dunn-Haley, *The House That Uncle Sam Built: The Political Culture of Federal Housing Policy, 1919–1932*, Ph.D. dissertation, Stanford University, 1995.

housing programs, or it could follow Hoover's lead and seek measures to stimulate private home building and individual home ownership. Despite its experimentation with government-built model communities like the so-called Greenbelt Towns (of which only three were built) and its occasional obeisance to public housing programs (as in the modestly funded Wagner-Steagall National Housing Act of 1937), the New Deal essentially adopted — and significantly advanced — Hoover's approach. Two new agencies, the Home Owners Loan Corporation (HOLC) and the Federal Housing Administration (FHA), supplemented by the Veterans Administration's housing program after World War II and the creation of the Federal National Mortgage Association (Fannie Mae) under the auspices of the RFC in 1938, implemented the New Deal's housing program.[10]

The HOLC began in 1933 as an emergency agency with two objectives: to protect defaulting homeowners against foreclosure and to improve lending institutions' balance sheets by refinancing shaky mortgages. With much publicity, the HOLC stopped the avalanche of defaults in 1933, but its lasting legacy was a quieter affair. Just as the SEC introduced standardized accounting practices into the securities industry, the HOLC, to facilitate its nationwide lending operations, encouraged uniform national appraisal methods throughout the real estate industry. The FHA, created in 1934 to insure long-term mortgages in much the manner that the FDIC insured bank deposits, took the next logical step and defined national standards of home construction. The creation of Fannie Mae completed the New Deal's housing program apparatus. Fannie Mae furnished lending institutions with a mechanism for reselling their mortgages, thus increasing the lenders' liquidity and making more money available for subsequent rounds of construction. Taken together, the standardization of appraisal methods and construction criteria, along with the mortgage insurance and resale facilities the New Deal put in place, removed much of the risk from home-lending.

The FHA and Fannie Mae themselves neither built houses nor loaned money, nor did they manage to stimulate much new construction in the 1930s. However, they arranged an institutional landscape in which unprecedented amounts of private capital could flow into the home construction industry in the post–World War II years. The New Deal's hous-

10. The discussion of housing here is much indebted to Kenneth T. Jackson's pioneering work, *Crabgrass Frontier: The Suburbanization of the United States* (New York: Oxford University Press, 1985). Parallel programs, legislated by the Farm Mortgage Refinancing Act of 1934 and the Frazier-Lemke Federal Farm Bankruptcy Acts of 1934 and 1935, gave similar relief to farm owners.

ing policies, cleverly commingling public and private institutions, demonstrated that political economy need not be a zero-sum game, in which the expansion of state power automatically spelled the shrinkage of private prerogatives. Once the war was over, this New Deal "reform" proved not to have checked or intimidated capital so much as to have liberated it. And eventually it revolutionized the way Americans lived.

Before the New Deal, only about four Americans in ten lived in their own homes. Homeowners in the 1920s typically paid full cash or very large down payments for their houses, usually not less than 30 percent. The standard mortgage was offered by a local institution with a highly limited service area, had only a five-to-ten-year maturity, bore interest as high as 8 percent, and required a large "balloon" payment, or refinancing, at its termination. Not surprisingly, under such conditions a majority of Americans were renters.

The New Deal changed all that. Uniform appraisal procedures made lenders much more confident in the underlying value of mortgaged properties. FHA insurance made them less nervous about loans going sour. Consequently, lenders began to accept down payments of 10 percent and to offer thirty-year fully amortized mortgages with level monthly payments. Interest rates on mortgages also came down as the element of risk diminished. Finally, nationally standardized appraisal and construction standards, along with Fannie Mae's national market for mortgage paper, allowed funds to flow out of regions of historic capital surplus to regions of historic capital deficit—that is, from city to suburbs and from the Northeast to the South and West.

The New Deal, in short, put in place an apparatus of financial security that allowed private money to build postwar suburbia and the sun belt. Private money built private homes. Four decades after the New Deal, nearly two-thirds of Americans lived in owner-occupied houses. Only 1 percent, usually the poorest of the poor, lived in public housing. By contrast, in John Maynard Keynes's England, nearly half the population lived in public housing in the early postwar years, as did more than a third of the population of France.[11]

IN THE FINANCIAL AND HOUSING SECTORS, the New Deal built structures of stability by the inventively simple devices of standardizing

11. Jackson, *Crabgrass Frontier*, 224. Jackson also demonstrates that both the private and public housing programs encouraged by the New Deal frequently reinforced and even exacerbated racial segregation in housing. It is also worth noting that by the 1990s Britain had substantially abandoned the public housing model, and a majority of Britons had become homeowners.

and promulgating relevant information and by introducing industry-wide self-insurance schemes that calmed jittery markets and offered dependable safeguards to capital. In many other sectors, the New Deal's technique was somewhat less artful; it was, simply, to suppress competition, or at least to modulate its destructive effects. But everywhere the objective was the same: to create a uniquely American system of relatively riskless capitalism.

The New Deal applied its crudest version of the anticompetitive approach to the chronically volatile agricultural sector. There it contained destabilizing competition with the ham-handed device of simply paying producers not to produce, keeping price-depressing surpluses off the market altogether. Some of the same logic of mandatory and even subsidized reduction of competition was also apparent in the New Deal's treatment of labor markets. Franklin Roosevelt declaimed about social justice in his campaigns for the Social Security Act and the Fair Labor Standards Act, and he achieved much justice, too. But those acts also shaped a manpower policy that had nearly as much to do with stability, plain and simple, as it did with social justice. Prohibitions on child labor, combined with virtually obligatory retirement by age sixty-five, statutorily shrank the size of the labor pool and therefore reduced wage competition. Retirees were, in effect, paid not to work, just as farmers were paid not to produce (though all but the first generation of Social Security pensioners were ostensibly paid from their own forced-savings accounts, while farmers unapologetically drew their subsidies from general treasury revenues). The Fair Labor Standards Act, as well as the industry-wide bargaining power of the new CIO unions, also built broad floors under wages and thereby further reduced the ability of employers and employees alike to compete by lowering labor costs.

In some sectors, new regulatory commissions provided orderly forums where the rules of competition could be agreed on and the clash of interests accommodated in a peaceful manner. The National Labor Relations Board provided a compelling example of that technique. Elsewhere, as in large infrastructural industries like transportation, communications, and energy, as well as in the wholesale distribution and retail marketing sectors, the New Deal sought stability by directly curtailing price and cost competition, often by limiting new entrants. The Civil Aeronautics Board, created in 1938, performed those functions for the infant airline industry; the Interstate Commerce Commission for the older railroad industry, and, after the passage of the Motor Carrier Act of 1935, for truckers as well. The Federal Communications Commission, born in 1934, did the same for telephones, radio, and, later, television; the Federal Power Commission, though with more difficulty, for oil and gas production. The Federal Trade Commission, newly empowered by two New Deal "fair trade" laws, was charged with limiting price competition in the retail and wholesale trades. (The Robinson-Patman Act of 1936 prohibited chain stores from discounting below certain stipulated levels, a way of insulating "mom-and-pop" corner stores against aggressive price pressure from the high-volume giants. The Miller-Tydings Act of 1937 legalized price-maintenance contracts between wholesalers and their distributors, a way of stabilizing the prices of nationally marketed name-brand goods.)

The creation of this array of anticompetitive and regulatory instruments has often been criticized as an inappropriate response to the Great Depression. The economic historian Peter Temin, for example, writes that "the New Deal represented an attempt to solve macroeconomic problems with microeconomic tools."[12] That judgment rests on the assumption that solving the macroeconomic problem of insufficient demand and high unemployment by inducing economic recovery was the New Deal's highest priority. Certainly Roosevelt said on countless occasions that such was his goal. But if actions speak louder than words, then it may be fair to conclude that perhaps not in stated purpose, but surely in actual practice, the New Deal's premier objective, at least until 1938, and in Roosevelt's mind probably for a long time thereafter, was not economic recovery but structural reform. In the last analysis, reform was the New Deal's lasting legacy.

The pattern of economic reforms that the New Deal wove arose out of concrete historical circumstances. It also had a more coherent intellectual underpinning than is customarily recognized. Its cardinal aim was not to destroy capitalism but to devolatilize it, and at the same time to distribute its benefits more evenly. New Deal regulatory initiatives were precipitated from decades of anxiety about overcapacity and cutthroat competition, the very issues that had so disrupted the first great national industry, the railroads, in the nineteenth century and led to the creation of the country's first regulatory commission, the Interstate Commerce Commission (ICC), in 1887. Against that background, the Depression appeared to signal the final, inevitable collapse of an economy that had been beset for at least fifty years by overproduction and an excess of competition. The regulatory regime that the New Deal put in

12. Temin's remark is in Gary M. Walton, ed., *Regulatory Change in an Atmosphere of Crisis: Current Implications of the Roosevelt Years* (New York: Academic, 1979), 58.

place seemed, therefore, but a logical extension of the kind of competition-controlling remedies that the ICC had first applied to the railroads half a century earlier and a fitting climax to five decades of sometimes wild economic turbulence.

Those views found their most systematic formulation in Franklin Roosevelt's 1932 campaign address at San Francisco's Commonwealth Club. As much as any single document can, that speech served as a charter for the New Deal's economic program:

> The history of the last half century is in large measure a history of a group of financial Titans. . . .
>
> As long as we had free land; as long as population was growing by leaps and bounds; as long as our industrial plants were insufficient to supply our own needs, society chose to give the ambitious man free play and unlimited reward provided only that he produced the economic plant so much desired. During this period of expansion, there was equal opportunity for all and the business of government was not to interfere but to assist in the development of industry.
>
> [But now] our industrial plant is built; the problem just now is whether under existing conditions it is not overbuilt. Our last frontier has long since been reached, and there is practically no more free land. . . . We are now providing a drab living for our own people. . . .
>
> Clearly, all this calls for a re-appraisal of values. A mere builder of more industrial plants, a creator of more railroad systems, an organizer of more corporations, is as likely to be a danger as a help. The day of the great promoter or the financial Titan, to whom we granted everything if only he would build, or develop, is over. Our task now is not discovery, or exploitation of natural resources, or necessarily producing more goods. It is the soberer, less dramatic business of administering resources and plants already in hand, of seeking to reestablish foreign markets for our surplus production, of meeting the problem of underconsumption, of adjusting production to consumption, of distributing wealth and products more equitably, of adapting existing economic organizations to the service of the people. The day of enlightened administration has come. . . . As I see it, the task of government in its relation to business is to assist the development of . . . an economic constitutional order."[13]

The National Recovery Administration, of course, with its measures to stabilize production and limit price and wage competition, was the classic institutional expression of that philosophy. But even after the

13. *PPA* (1928–32), 742–56.

NRA's demise in 1935, the thinking that had shaped it continued to inform New Deal efforts to erect a new "economic constitutional order."

That thinking rested on three premises, two of them explicit, the other usually implicit. The first was the notion, so vividly and repeatedly evident in Roosevelt's Commonwealth Club Address, that the era of economic growth had ended. With his references to the closing of the frontier, Roosevelt, echoing Frederick Jackson Turner's celebrated thesis about the 1890s, suggested that the Depression did not mark a transient crisis but heralded instead the death of an era and the birth of a new historical epoch. Many other New Dealers, from Rexford Tugwell to the young Keynesians who rose to prominence in the second Roosevelt administration, shared this view. It deeply colored their thought right down to the end of the Depression decade. "The economic crisis facing America is not a temporary one," the economist Lauchlin Currie wrote to his boss, Marriner Eccles, in 1939. "The violence of the depression following 1929," Currie continued, "obscured for some time the fact that a profound change of a chronic or secular nature had occurred."[14] That change, Currie concluded, was the emergence of a "mature" economy, one whose capacity for growth was largely exhausted. The best that could be hoped for, therefore, was to restore the gross levels of production of the late 1920s and to effect a more equitable distribution of consuming power so as to sustain those levels indefinitely. Roosevelt himself said consistently that his "goal" was to raise national income to "ninety or one hundred" billion dollars. "When, the Lord only knows," he remarked to reporters as late as October 1937, "but that is a perfectly sound goal."[15] Measured against a national income of nearly $87 billion in 1929, it was also a perfectly modest goal, a goal inspired by visions of economic restoration, not economic expansion.

The second premise that informed New Deal policy was closely related to the first and was also evident in Roosevelt's Commonwealth Club address. It was the idea that the private sector, left to its own devices, would never again be capable of generating sufficient investment and employment to sustain even a 1920s-level economy. That premise was the starting point for Harry Hopkins's Works Progress Administration. Both he and Roosevelt presumed that WPA would be a

14. Currie quoted in Alan Brinkley, *The End of Reform: New Deal Liberalism in Recession and War* (New York: Knopf, 1995), 122.
15. *PPA* (1937), 476; see also Roosevelt's annual message to Congress of January 3, 1938, *PPA* (1938), 3.

permanently necessary government employment program. ("The time
. . . when industry and business can absorb all able-bodied workers," said
Hopkins in 1936, "seems to grow more distant with improvements in
management and technology.")[16] The same assumption about the long-
term structural inadequacies of the private sector in "mature" economies
formed much of the intellectual core of Keynesian analysis. Even before
Keynes gave the idea full articulation, this motif ran like a bright thread
through the writings of the professional practitioners of the dismal science in the 1930s. Alvin Hansen, a Harvard economist destined to become America's leading Keynesian, gave forceful expression to this notion in 1938 in *Full Employment or Stagnation?*, a book that helped to
popularize the concept of "secular stagnation" while also arguing that
government spending was indispensable to make up for the permanent
deficiencies of private capital.[17]

The third premise that molded the economic thinking and policies
of the New Deal was the assumption, less consciously held than the
other two but powerfully determinative nonetheless, that the United
States was an economically self-sufficient nation. That concept of economic isolationism had underlain Roosevelt's frank declaration in his
first inaugural address that "our international trade relations . . . are in
point of time and necessity secondary only to the establishment of a
sound national economy." It had formed the basis of his inflationary
schemes of 1933 and 1934. It formed the filament on which a series of
New Deal measures, from crop supports to minimum wage and price-
fixing legislation, was strung. When Roosevelt spoke of "balance" between American industry and agriculture, or when he posited the requirement "that the income of our working population actually expands
sufficiently to create markets to absorb that increased production," he
was clearly envisioning an America for which foreign markets, not to
mention foreign competitors, did not exist.[18]

FROM THOSE INTELLECTUAL BUILDING BLOCKS, composed of a
theory of history, a conception of the nature of modern economies, and
an appraisal of America's unique position in the world, the New

16. Harry Hopkins, *Spending to Save* (New York: Norton, 1936), 180–81.
17. Alvin H. Hansen, *Full Employment or Stagnation?* (New York: Norton, 1938). Wit-
    nessing the economic impact of World War II, Hansen later revised his views on
    secular stagnation. "All of us had our sights too low," he wrote in 1944. See Alvin
    H. Hansen, "Planning Full Employment," *Nation*, October 21, 1944, 492.
18. PPA (1933), 14, (1937), 496.

Deal erected an institutional scaffolding designed to provide unprecedented stability and predictability for the American economy. In time, that edifice would serve as the latticework on which the postwar economy grew like kudzu, the "mile-a-minute vine" that carpets much of the South. To be sure, the unparalleled economic vitality of the post-1940 decades was attributable to many factors, not least the gusher of deficit spending triggered by World War II, as well as the long exemption from foreign competition that the results of the war conferred on the United States. But the elements of financial reliability, modulated competition in commodity, transportation, communication, retail, and labor markets, well-ordered relations between management and labor, and government support of at least minimal levels of aggregate demand — developments that owed much to the New Deal — must surely figure largely in any comprehensive explanation of the performance of the American economy in the postwar quarter century.

Yet economic growth as a later generation would know it formed little part of the New Deal's ambition, even after FDR's timid, attenuated acceptance of Keynesian deficits in 1938. Roosevelt remained reluctant to the end of the 1930s to engage in the scale of compensatory spending adequate to restore the economy to pre-Depression levels, let alone expand it. Nor would he relax his attacks on business sufficiently to encourage capital to take full advantage of the stabilizing elements his own government was putting in place. Ironically, he succeeded in building structures of stability while maintaining throughout the 1930s, so far as businessmen were concerned, an atmosphere of uncertainty. Capital can live with restrictions, but it is terrorized by insecurity. "Business is now hesitant about making long term plans," the head of the New York Federal Reserve Board wrote to Marriner Eccles in 1937, "partly because it feels it does not know what the rules of the game are going to be."[19] That sentiment was widely shared in the business community. It was not so much the regulations that the New Deal imposed that intimidated businessmen in the 1930s; it was the fear of what new and unknown provocations Roosevelt might yet unleash. When at last Roosevelt declared the New Deal's reform phase at an end, and when the war compelled government spending on an unexampled scale, capital was

19. Quoted in Richard Polenberg, "The Decline of the New Deal, 1937–1940," in John Braeman et al., eds., *The New Deal: The National Level* (Columbus: Ohio State University Press, 1975), 255.

unshackled, and the economy energized, to a degree that he and other New Dealers could scarcely have imagined in the Depression decade. And ever after, Americans assumed that the federal government had not merely a role, but a major responsibility, in ensuring the health of the economy and the welfare of citizens. That simple but momentous shift in perception was the newest thing in all the New Deal, and the most consequential too.

HUMANKIND, OF COURSE, does not live by bread alone. Any assessment of what the New Deal did would be incomplete if it rested with an appraisal of New Deal economic policies and failed to acknowledge the remarkable array of social innovations nourished by Roosevelt's expansive temperament.

The world is not a finished place, the philosopher William James once said, nor ever will be. Neither was the New Deal a finished thing, though in later years some scholars lamented its incompleteness, its alleged political timidity, and its supposedly premature demise.[20] But what needs emphasis, in the final accounting, is not what the New Deal failed to do but how it managed to do so much in the uniquely malleable moment of the mid-1930s. That brief span of years, it is now clear, constituted one of only a handful of episodes in American history when substantial and lasting social change has occurred—when the country was, in measurable degree, remade. The American political system, after all, was purpose-built in the eighteenth century to prevent its easy manipulation from the national capital, to bind governments down from mischief, as Jefferson said, by the chains of the Constitution, especially by the notoriously constraining system of checks and balances. It is hardly surprising, therefore, that political stasis defines the "normal" American condition. Against that backdrop, what stands out about the New Deal are not its limitations and its timidity but the boldness of its vision and the consequent sweep of its ultimate achievement.

For all his alleged inscrutability, Franklin Roosevelt's social vision was

20. Works that generally share a critical posture toward the New Deal include Barton J. Bernstein, "The Conservative Achievements of Liberal Reform," in Bernstein, ed., *Towards a New Past* (New York: Pantheon, 1968); Howard Zinn, *New Deal Thought* (Indianapolis: Bobbs-Merrill 1966); Paul Conkin, *The New Deal*, 3d ed. (Arlington Heights, Ill.: Harlan Davidson, 1992); Brinkley, *End of Reform*; and Michael Sandel, *Democracy's Discontent: America in Search of a Public Philosophy* (Cambridge: Belknap Press of Harvard University Press, 1996).

clear enough. "We are going to make a country," he once said to Frances Perkins, "in which no one is left out."[21] In that unadorned sentence Roosevelt spoke volumes about the New Deal's lasting historical meaning. Like his rambling, comfortable, and unpretentious old home on the bluff above the Hudson River, Roosevelt's New Deal was a welcoming mansion of many rooms, a place where millions of his fellow citizens could find at last a measure of the security that the patrician Roosevelts enjoyed as their birthright.

Perhaps the New Deal's greatest achievement was its accommodation of the maturing immigrant communities that had milled uneasily on the margins of American society for a generation and more before the 1930s. In bringing them into the Democratic Party and closer to the mainstream of national life, the New Deal, even without fully intending to do so, also made room for an almost wholly new institution, the industrial union. To tens of millions of rural Americans, the New Deal offered the modern comforts of electricity, schools, and roads, as well as unaccustomed financial stability. To the elderly and the unemployed it extended the promise of income security, and the salvaged dignity that went with it.

To black Americans the New Deal offered jobs with the CCC, WPA, and PWA and, perhaps as important, the compliment of respect from at least some federal officials. The time had not come for direct federal action to challenge Jim Crow and put right at last the crimes of slavery and discrimination, but more than a few New Dealers made clear where their sympathies lay and quietly prepared for a better future. Urged on by Eleanor Roosevelt, the president brought African-Americans into the government in small but unprecedented numbers. By the mid-1930s they gathered periodically as an informal "black cabinet," guided often by the redoubtable Mary McLeod Bethune. Roosevelt also appointed the first black federal judge, William Hastie. Several New Deal Departments and agencies, including especially Ickes's Interior Department and Aubrey Williams's National Youth Administration, placed advisers for "Negro affairs" on their staffs.

In the yeasty atmosphere of Roosevelt's New Deal, scores of social experiments flourished. Not all of them were successful, not all of them destined to last, but all shared the common purpose of building a country from whose basic benefits and privileges no one was excluded. The

21. Frances Perkins, *The Roosevelt I Knew* (New York: Viking, 1946), 113.

Resettlement Administration laid out model communities for displaced farmers and refugees from the shattered industrial cities, though only a handful of those social experiments survived, and they soon lost their distinctive, utopian character. The Farm Security Administration maintained migrant labor camps that sheltered thousands of families like John Steinbeck's Joads. The Tennessee Valley Authority brought electricity, and with it industry, to the chronically depressed upper South. The Bonneville Power Authority made a start on doing the same for the Columbia River Basin in the long-isolated Pacific Northwest. The New Deal also extended the hand of recognition to Native Americans. The Indian Reorganization Act of 1934—the so-called Indian New Deal— ended the half-century-old policy of forced assimilation and alienation of tribal lands and encouraged tribes to establish their own self-governing bodies and to preserve their ancestral traditions. Though some Indians denounced this policy as a "back-to-the-blanket" measure that sought to make museum pieces out of Native Americans, the act accurately reflected the New Deal's consistently inclusionary ethos.

The New Deal also succored the indigent and patronized the arts. It built roads and bridges and hospitals. It even sought a kind of security for the land itself, adding some twelve million acres of national parklands, including Olympic National Park in Washington State, Isle Royal in Lake Superior, the Everglades in Florida, and King's Canyon in California. It planted trees and fought erosion. It erected mammoth dams— Grand Coulee and Bonneville on the Columbia, Shasta on the Sacramento, Fort Peck on the Missouri—that were river-tamers and naturebusters, to be sure, but jobmakers and region-builders, too.

Above all, the New Deal gave to countless Americans who had never had much of it a sense of security, and with it a sense of having a stake in their country. And it did it all without shredding the American Constitution or sundering the American people. At a time when despair and alienation were prostrating other peoples under the heel of dictatorship, that was no small accomplishment.

The columnist Dorothy Thompson summed up Franklin Roosevelt's achievements at the end of the Depression decade, in 1940:

> We have behind us eight terrible years of a crisis we have shared with all countries. Here we are, and our basic institutions are still intact, our people relatively prosperous, and most important of all, our society relatively affectionate. No rift has made an unbridgeable schism between us. The working classes are not clamoring for [Communist Party

boss] Mr. Browder and the industrialists are not demanding a Man on Horseback. No country in the world is so well off.[22]

In the last analysis, Franklin Roosevelt faithfully discharged his duties, in John Maynard Keynes's words of 1933, as "the trustee for those in every country" who believed in social peace and in democracy. He did mend the evils of the Depression by reasoned experiment within the framework of the existing social system. He did prevent a naked confrontation between orthodoxy and revolution. The priceless value of that achievement, surely as much as the columns of ciphers that recorded national income and production, must be reckoned in any final accounting of what the New Deal did.

22. *New York Herald Tribune*, October 9, 1940, rpt. in Arthur M. Schlesinger Jr., *The History of American Presidential Elections, 1789–1968* (New York: Chelsea House, 1971), 4:2981–93.

13

The Gathering Storm

To hell with Europe and the rest of those nations!
— Minnesota senator Thomas Schall, 1935

For all its agony of carnage and destruction, the Great War of 1914–18 settled little. In time, it would come to be seen as but the opening chapter in the twentieth century's own Thirty-Year War, a conflict that endured thirty-one years, to be exact, from 1914 to 1945, and at the price of some sixty million lives forever transformed the world. To be sure, the First World War had shattered the Austro-Hungarian empire and left Germany defeated. But the treaty signed in the Hall of Mirrors at Versailles on June 28, 1919, neither extinguished the ambitions that had ignited the war nor quieted the anxieties it had spawned. Victors and vanquished agreed only that the conflict had been a dreadful catastrophe, a blood-spilling, man-killing, nation-eating nightmare of unprecedented horror. All were determined to avoid its reoccurrence. More precisely, each nation was determined to avoid the repetition of its own role in it.

For two countries, Italy and Japan, it was not so much the war itself as its disappointing outcome that rankled. The Italians and the Japanese alike felt cheated at Versailles out of their victors' just desserts and eventually fell under rulers dedicated to redressing that grievance, by force of arms if necessary. Italy's Fascist leader Benito Mussolini came to power in 1922. *Il Duce* dreamed of a new Roman empire in Africa and the eastern Mediterranean. Militarists in Japan cast covetous eyes on China, especially the rich northern region of Manchuria, and ultimately on Southeast Asia and the Dutch East Indies as well.

Russia, revolutionized by the Bolsheviks in 1917, had made its own peace with Germany at Brest-Litovsk in March 1918 and then found itself shut out entirely from the negotiations at Paris that shaped the Versailles Treaty. The chief lesson the new Soviet regime took from the war was the usefulness, indeed the necessity, of a wily neutrality. Feared and isolated by the Western democracies, the Soviets under Josef Stalin dedicated themselves to building "socialism in one country" while waiting for the reeruption of the capitalist fratricide that Marxist-Leninist theory confidently predicted.

France, able to repel the German invaders of 1914 only with the help of British and, at the eleventh hour, American allies, drew two conclusions from its war experience: that the French frontier with Germany must be massively fortified, so that any future war would not be fought on French soil; and that France could not successfully grapple alone against German power. Neither of those prescriptions proved very useful in practice. French war minister André Maginot ordered the construction along the French-German frontier of the supposedly impregnable network of forts that bore his name. But the Maginot Line came in time to symbolize the futility of static tactics in the dawning era of mobile warfare and, more broadly, the stolid vacuity and rigidly defensive logic of interwar French military thinking — a classic instance of military planners fighting the last war. As for allies, the French suffered bitter disappointment when the Americans failed to honor Woodrow Wilson's promise at Versailles that they would sign a treaty pledging the United States to guarantee France's security. Britain, France's other former comrade-in-arms against the kaiser's Germany, proved scarcely more dependable. Anxious and adrift, France played an uncertain, negligible international role in the postwar decades.

Bled to the point of exhaustion by four years of trench warfare, Britain after 1918 resolved not to allow a local irritation in Europe, like the clash between Austria-Hungary and Serbia that had touched off the Great War, to metastasize into another great-power bloodbath. In a single battle on the Somme River in 1916, 420,000 Britons had perished; at Passchendaele a year later, another 245,000 died. After such horrendous losses Britain vowed never again to hurl a large ground force against an enemy's main strength on the European continent. In any future conflict, Britain would rely principally on sea power and air power and leave most of the ground fighting to others. But public sentiment in Britain, as in France, was above all staunchly committed to avoiding another war altogether. "This house will in no circumstance fight for its King and its Country," the students of the Oxford Union notoriously voted in February 1933. Two years later, thousands of young, pacifistic Britons joined the Peace Pledge Union to oppose their government's then-modest rearmament measures.

In defeated Germany, Adolf Hitler distilled the war's lessons for his country into a prescription for victory next time. Virtually alone among the Great War's survivors, ex-corporal Hitler ravened for more war still. He calculated that the very inconceivability of another war in the eyes of most statesmen—particularly in France and Britain, not to mention the faraway United States—would for a long time blind them to his own intentions and rob them of the will and the means to resist him.

Those intentions were as simple as they were grotesque: to secure living space (*Lebensraum*), into which a racially purified German people could expand indefinitely. Purged of what Hitler identified as the Jewish incubus in their midst, the "master race" would sweep aside the "inferior" Slavic peoples and the many millions of additional Jews who dwelled to Germany's east, claim new sod for the German plow, and create a greater *Reich* that would last a thousand years. That grand racialist geopolitical vision, Hitler reckoned, could be realized only by war—but not by employing the tactics of the Great War of 1914–18. Hitler, too, learned from history. The defeat of 1918 confirmed that in a protracted war of Germany against all, Germany could not win. Hitler therefore determined to fight his war in stages, one foe at a time, with swift, overpowering blows delivered serially against isolated enemies. He would seek allies where he could and maneuver when possible behind the cloak of diplomacy. He would take full advantage of modern technology, especially rapid means of transporting troops and firepower, and the fearsome striking power of armored divisions. Hitler's strategy cunningly exploited the greatest weaknesses of his adversaries: their morbid fear of renewed fighting, their inability to make common cause, their reluctance to rearm, their slavish devotion to outmoded doctrines of warfare.

Hitler moved first to consolidate his power within Germany itself. Within months of his installation as chancellor in January 1933, he contrived to eliminate all opposition and turn Germany into a totalitarian regime, with himself as its supreme and sole leader: *der Führer*. In the charged atmosphere following the burning of the Reichstag building on the night of February 27, 1933, his government issued emergency decrees effectively suppressing freedom of speech and assembly. The following week, just as Franklin Roosevelt was being inaugurated in Washington, D.C., the German people gave his Nazi Party nearly 44 percent of the votes in the last parliamentary election in which they would be allowed to participate for the next dozen years. Emboldened, Hitler invoked the emergency decrees and stepped up the arrests of those Communist deputies who were his principal parliamentary opposition. Now a majority in the Reichstag, on March 23 the Nazis passed an Enabling Law that invested all legislative power in Hitler's hands. While Franklin Roosevelt was coaxing the Hundred Days' legislation out of the American Congress in the spring of 1933, Hitler was dissolving the trade unions, putting his Nazi cronies in control of the various federal states, and Nazifying the press and the universities. On July 14 the government declared the Nazis the only legal political party in Germany. Hitler now ruled without opposition. A reign of terror descended over Germany, enforced with remorseless efficiency by the Geheime Staatspolizei, or Gestapo. A year later, while Roosevelt was contending with conservative dissidents like those in the Liberty League, Hitler dispatched his main Nazi rival, SA leader Ernst Röhm, by having him summarily executed. The following year, the year of Social Security and the Wagner Act, Hitler codified his policies against the Jews in the Nuremberg Decrees, which stripped German Jews of their citizenship, excluded them from the professions and military service, and prohibited marriage between Jews and "Aryans."

Hitler matched the pace of his drive toward dictatorship at home with the accelerating tempo of his foreign provocations. In October 1933 he withdrew Germany from the League of Nations and from the Disarmament Conference in Geneva. On March 16, 1935, speaking at the magnificently ornate Berlin Opera House, the last surviving field marshal of the Imperial German Army at his side, he renounced the disarmament clauses of the Versailles Treaty, revealed the existence of a clandestinely built German air force, and ordered a vast program of rearmament, including the raising of a half-million-man conscript army.

One year later, on March 7, 1936, Hitler marched thirty-five thousand German troops into the Rhineland, in flagrant violation of treaty promises that the strategic Rhine buffer zone that lay between France and the German industrial heartland of the Ruhr would remain forever demilitarized. The remilitarization of the Rhineland was Hitler's most brazen gamble to date. He later acknowledged that he would have been compelled to withdraw had he met armed resistance.[1] But Italy was

1. "The forty-eight hours after the march into the Rhineland were the most nerve-racking in my life," Hitler later admitted. "If the French had then marched into the

otherwise engaged, Britain had no stomach for standing firm, and France, left to its own devices, could only acquiesce. The Ruhr now lay safely insulated from French attack. Hitler was well on his way toward assuming a commanding military position in Europe.

Hitler proceeded to cement an alliance with Fascist Italy in the so-called Rome-Berlin Axis agreement and to join hands with Japan in the Anti-Comintern Pact, both consummated in November 1936. Like a drunken reveler calling for madder music and stronger wine, *der Führer* grew ever bolder. When civil war erupted in Spain in July 1936, Hitler and Mussolini both sent aircraft to bolster General Francisco Franco's rebels. Two years later, Hitler annexed Austria, incorporating it into the *Reich* as the German province of Ostmark. On March 14, 1938, Hitler motored triumphantly through Vienna, the city where he had lived in lonely poverty as a youth. Cowering before Hitler's bullying, the other European powers swallowed this latest violation of the Versailles Treaty as meekly as they had the others.

As THE SPECTACLE of swelling Nazi power unfolded in Europe, most Americans looked on with an air of detached indifference. In the war of 1914–18 that had set the stage on which Hitler now strutted, no people had been more reluctant combatants, and few more disappointed with the result, than the Americans. The United States had abandoned its historic policy of isolationism and entered the European conflict only when the war was already two and one-half years old, in April 1917. By the time an American army could be raised, trained, transported, and deployed, the fighting in Europe had already slaughtered millions. American troops fought only two major battles under American command, at St. Mihiel and the Meuse-Argonne, both in the closing weeks of the war. Though the latter in particular exacted a heavy toll in American lives, neither contributed significantly to Germany's defeat. Even as a co-belligerent alongside England and France, Woodrow Wilson stopped short of becoming their formal "ally." The official name of the anti-German coalition after the United States had joined it in April 1917 was "the Allied *and Associated* Powers," nomenclature that testified

---

Rhineland, we would have had to withdraw with our tails between our legs, for the military resources at our disposal would have been wholly inadequate for even a moderate resistance." William L. Shirer, *The Rise and Fall of the Third Reich* (New York: Simon and Schuster, 1960), 293.

awkwardly but unmistakably to the Americans' continuing desire to keep their distance from the conflicts of Europe. And as in war, so in peace. No nation had more definitively repudiated the settlement inked at Versailles, despite the fact that an American president had been among its principal draftsmen. In the postwar decade, Americans said no to Woodrow Wilson's League of Nations, no to the French security treaty, no to freer trade policies, no to pleas from France and Britain to forgive their wartime loans from the U.S. Treasury, and no to further unlimited immigration from Europe, when Congress passed the highly restrictive immigration quota laws of 1921 and 1924.

No people came to believe more emphatically than the Americans that the Great War was an unalloyed tragedy, an unpardonably costly mistake never to be repeated. More than fifty thousand American doughboys had perished fighting on the western front, and to what avail? So far from being redeemed by American intervention, Europe swiftly slid back into its historic vices of authoritarianism and armed rivalry, while America slid back into its historic attitude of isolationism. Isolationism may have been most pronounced in the landlocked Midwest, but Americans of both sexes, of all ages, religions, and political persuasions, from all ethnic groups and all regions, shared in the postwar years a feeling of apathy toward Europe, not to mention the rest of the wretchedly quarrelsome world, that bordered on disgust. "Let us turn our eyes inward," declared Pennsylvania's liberal Democratic governor George Earle in 1935. "If the world is to become a wilderness of waste, hatred, and bitterness, let us all the more earnestly protect and preserve our own oasis of liberty."[2]

Both the accident of geography and old habits of mind underlay that attitude. America had grown to national maturity on a remote continent in the absence of threats from abroad, a luxury history has afforded to few nations. That peculiar circumstance bred in Americans the dangerous illusion that they could choose whether and when to participate in the world. The idea of isolation was as old as America itself. From John Winthrop's declaration that Americans dwelt in a "city upon a hill" through George Washington's admonition to beware "the insidious wiles of foreign influence," Thomas Jefferson's repudiation of "entangling alliances," Mark Twain's satirical anti-European diatribes in *The Innocents Abroad* and *A Connecticut Yankee in King Arthur's Court*, and Henry James's sensitive "transatlantic novels," down even to F. Scott's Fitzger-

2. Leuchtenburg, 197n.

ald's poetic conclusion to his 1925 novel *The Great Gatsby*, with its lyrical invocation of the "fresh green breast of the New World," Americans had thought of themselves as not simply distant from the Old World but different from it as well. That difference, indeed, defined for many the essence — and the superiority — of the American national identity. International involvement was therefore worse than useless. It risked contaminating the very character of the nation. "Rejection of Europe," the novelist John Dos Passos once wrote, "is what America is all about."

In the Great War — what Americans often tellingly called "the European War" — the United States had haltingly abandoned that centuries-old cultural wisdom, only to reembrace it with deepened conviction in the war's aftermath. Popular writers like Dos Passos and e. e. cummings fed the public's sense of disillusion with the war in books like *Three Soldiers* (1921) and *The Enormous Room* (1922). Antiwar fiction reached a crescendo in 1929 with the publication of Ernest Hemingway's *A Farewell to Arms* and Erich Maria Remarque's international best-seller, *All Quiet on the Western Front*. A spate of revisionist histories of American involvement in the war also drove the isolationist moral home to a broad reading audience. Taken together, books like Harry Elmer Barnes's *Genesis of the World War* (1926), C. Hartley Grattan's *Why We Fought* (1929), Walter Millis's *Road to War* (1935), and Charles C. Tansill's *America Goes to War* (1938) composed a formidable brief that indicted the folly of America's departure in 1917 from its historic policy of isolation. The war had been fought, those authors argued, not to make the world safe for democracy but to make it safe for Wall Street bankers and grasping arms manufacturers. The American public had been duped by British propaganda, and Woodrow Wilson had been trapped by his stubborn Presbyterian moralism and slavish, unrealistic devotion to the principle of "neutral rights." The only winners were the "merchants of death" — the financiers and munitions-makers who harvested obscene profits from the war. Ordinary Americans had no appreciable interests at stake in 1917, so the argument ran, and the country should have stayed out of the fray.

The indictment was grossly overdrawn, but it fell on receptive ears, especially in the antibusiness atmosphere of the Great Depression. The isolationist implications of that message drew powerful reinforcement in the mid-1930s from the accusations emanating from the Senate's Special Committee Investigating the Munitions Industry. Chaired by progressive Republican North Dakota senator Gerald Nye, the committee owed its existence to a growing American peace movement that through petitions, pamphlets, and demonstrations had become a force to be reckoned with. Spurred especially by a sensational exposé that appeared in *Fortune* magazine in March 1934 entitled "Arms and the Men," by publication soon thereafter of H. C. Engelbrecht's and F. C. Hanighen's *Merchants of Death*, a Book-of-the-Month Club selection, and by the indefatigable lobbying of the Women's International League for Peace and Freedom, the Nye Committee served for two years after its formation in April 1934 as the country's principal platform for isolationist preachments. It served, too, as a pulpit for indignant condemnations of the crimes of big business, which had somehow, the committee insinuated (though never proved), covertly forced the Wilson administration into war.

President Roosevelt at first encouraged the Nye Committee, not least because its revelations discredited the corporate titans and the bankers, the Du Ponts and the Wall Street investment houses, that were then among his fiercest political adversaries. In time the president would have reason to regret the strengthened sentiment of inward-looking nationalism that the Nye Committee helped to foster. But when the Nye group began its labors, Roosevelt himself showed every sign of swimming with the same isolationist tide that had swept up his countrymen in the years after the Great War.

In the 1932 presidential campaign, Roosevelt had disavowed his earlier support for American membership in the League of Nations. In his inaugural address he had declared that "our international trade relations, though vastly important, are in point of time and necessity secondary to the establishment of a sound national economy." He gave concrete meaning to that principle when he scuttled the London Economic Conference in June 1933 and embarked thereafter on the highly nationalistic monetary policy of abandoning the gold standard and devaluing the dollar. Many New Deal measures, such as the NRA's wage-pegging and price-setting and the AAA's efforts to raise agricultural prices, depended on keeping the American economy insulated from foreign competition. In keeping with the temper of the times and with his own budget-cutting agenda, Roosevelt also moved swiftly after his inauguration to shrink the already skeletal 140,000-man army. Army Chief of Staff Douglas MacArthur remonstrated vehemently. Meeting with Roosevelt at the White House, MacArthur later recalled, "I spoke recklessly and said something to the effect that when we lost the next war, and an American boy, lying in the mud with an enemy bayonet through his belly and an enemy foot on his dying throat, spat out his last curse, I wanted the name not to be MacArthur, but Roosevelt." A livid president shouted that MacArthur could not talk that way to the commander-in-chief. MacArthur, choked with emotion, hurried outside and vomited on the White House steps. The army's budget stayed cut.[3]

To be sure, Roosevelt also made internationalist gestures in the early New Deal years, suggesting that he had not entirely lost touch with the ideals that he had espoused as Woodrow Wilson's assistant secretary of the navy. Few presidents, indeed, brought to their conduct of foreign affairs a more sophisticated internationalist background. Roosevelt had been reared in that cosmopolitan, Anglophilic social class that took for granted the organic unity of the Atlantic world, a cultural affinity that rasped against the grain of popular American attitudes. His education on two continents had given him a working knowledge of the German and French languages, as well as an intuitive understanding of foreign affairs rivaled among modern presidents only by his cousin Theodore. Like Theodore, he favored the navy as his instrument for projecting American power, though his naval enthusiasm was attenuated after 1933 by financial and legal constraints. Unable to secure large shipbuilding appropriations directly from the Congress, Roosevelt did direct some money from public works appropriations toward constructing a modern fleet, but only up to the rather modest strength allowed by the naval-limitation treaties signed at Washington in 1922 and London in 1930. Though Franklin Roosevelt's White House had no national security adviser or formal foreign policy decision-making apparatus, the president relished interrogating foreign visitors and was a keen consumer of information from several American diplomats. They included especially William C. Bullitt, his ambassador to Russia and later to France, and the president's fellow Grotonian, Sumner Welles, who served as assistant secretary of state for Latin America and, after 1937, undersecretary of state. The brash Bullitt and the silky Welles cordially detested one another, but they agreed that the United States must take a more active role in the world and encouraged the same attitude in their chief. Roosevelt also anointed Cordell Hull, a relentless advocate of free trade, as his secretary of state. He supported Hull's campaign for the Reciprocal Trade Agreements Act in 1934, as well as Hull's subsequent efforts to negotiate reciprocity treaties incorporating the trade-expanding unconditional most-favored-nation principle. Defying the venomous invective of conservatives—and the scolding of his own mother—Roosevelt

3. Douglas MacArthur, *Reminiscences* (New York: McGraw-Hill, 1964), 101.

extended the hand of diplomatic recognition to Soviet Russia in November 1933, a move designed both to broaden American trade opportunities and to strengthen Soviet resistance to possible future Japanese expansionism in China (in both of which hopes Roosevelt was ultimately disappointed). He made partial amends for his destructive role in helping to sink the 1933 London Economic Conference when he concluded an exchange stabilization agreement with Britain and France in 1936.

But for a long season, Roosevelt seemed more committed to a kind of abstract, prospective internationalism than to anything concrete in the here and now. As a Wilsonian, he no doubt hoped that a world of liberalized trade and international cooperation would one day emerge from the sorry mess that war and depression had inflicted on the planet. But during his first term, the mood of the country, as well as Roosevelt's personal priorities and the practical realities of New Deal politics, dictated that he promote no serious American effort to bring that better world about. No politician as sensitively attuned to the popular temper as Roosevelt was could have failed to register the isolationist spirit that pervaded Depression-era America. Moreover, domestic reform, along with economic recovery, was Roosevelt's own most urgent preoccupation. All other political desiderata shriveled to trivial proportions in comparison. And indispensable to the success of the New Deal, and to Roosevelt's longer-range goal of creating a durable liberal political coalition, was the support of a band of progressive Republican senators, including Gerald Nye and his North Dakota colleague Lynn Frazier, George Norris of Nebraska, Robert La Follette Jr. of Wisconsin, William Borah of Idaho, Hiram Johnson of California, and Bronson Cutting of New Mexico. These men were implacable isolationists. Norris, along with La Follette's father, was among the half-dozen senators who had voted against American entry into the First World War in 1917. Borah and Johnson had constituted themselves as a "truth squad" that shadowed Woodrow Wilson around the country in 1919 to undermine his appeals for ratification of the Versailles Treaty. As the historian Robert Dallek has succinctly said of Roosevelt at this time, "a struggle with his progressive Republican friends for minor foreign policy goals at the likely expense of domestic advance was something he would not do."[4] Indeed, to curry favor with this group Roosevelt acquiesced in legislation sponsored by Hiram Johnson in 1934 that prohibited loans to governments that were in default on their existing obligations to the U.S. Treasury—a

4. Dallek, 71.

measure that would in time threaten to stifle Roosevelt's efforts to get American aid into the hands of Hitler's foes.[5]

Even the modest foreign policy initiatives that Roosevelt undertook in his first term suggested that he had only a limited internationalist agenda. He persisted in Herbert Hoover's "Good Neighbor" policy toward Latin America, honoring Hoover's agreement to withdraw the U.S. occupation force from Haiti. When the marine buglers sounded their final notes at Port-au-Prince in 1934, the last Yankee garrison in the Caribbean folded its tents, ending (for a while) more than three decades of armed American intervention south of the border.[6] Roosevelt instructed Hull to vote in favor of a resolution at the Pan-American Conference in Montevideo, Uruguay, in December 1933, proclaiming that "no state has the right to intervene in the internal or external affairs of another." That statement explicitly repudiated the bellicose "corollary" that cousin Theodore had attached to the Monroe Doctrine in 1904, when TR had claimed the right for the United States to exercise international police power in the Western Hemisphere. Roosevelt followed up in 1934 by releasing Cuba from the terms of the Platt Amendment of 1901, whereby the Cuban constitution had conceded the right of intervention to the United States. Mexico put this good neighborliness to a stiff test in 1938 when it nationalized its oil industry, expropriating the property of several American firms. But Roosevelt, faithful to the Good Neighbor creed, rejected demands that he intervene and successfully negotiated acceptable compensation for the confiscated American holdings.

All this assuredly pleased the Latin Americans. They cheered Roosevelt warmly when he toured the Caribbean in 1934 and sailed to South America in 1936, the first American president to travel to the

5. The attorney general interpreted the Johnson Act to mean that token payments would be insufficient to prevent a declaration of default. The long-suffering European debtors, save only Finland, thereupon defaulted outright on June 15, 1934, thus cutting themselves off from any future American credits. This situation vastly complicated Roosevelt's efforts at the beginning of the next decade to provide Britain with the means to purchase arms in the United States.

6. Since the Spanish-American War of 1898, the United States had repeatedly dispatched troops to Nicaragua and Cuba, as well as to the Dominican Republic from 1916 to 1924, and to Haiti, where they had been stationed since 1914. After the withdrawal from Haiti, American forces remained in the Caribbean at the Guantánamo naval base in Cuba and in the Panama Canal Zone, though strictly speaking, in neither of those places did they constitute an occupational force that dictated to the governments of Cuba and Panama respectively.

southern continent. But in Rome and Paris and London and Moscow, and especially in Berlin and Tokyo, the Good Neighbor policy could be seen simply as another calculated American abandonment of unwanted foreign burdens. In company with the torpedoing of the London Economic Conference, the farewell to the gold standard, and the passage of the Johnson Act, Roosevelt's overtures to the Latin Americans seemed to be part of a systematic American retreat from the world, one that would leave the United States with some enhanced moral influence in the Western Hemisphere, perhaps, but few formal obligations there and none elsewhere. Roosevelt strengthened that impression in March 1934 when he signed the Tydings-McDuffie Act, promising independence to the Philippines at the end of a ten-year transitional period—a strong signal that the United States intended to terminate its four-decade-old imperial fling in Asia.

Watching these events from Berlin, Adolf Hitler feared nothing from the United States as he began methodically to unspool his expansionist schemes. In Hitler's reading of history, America had been an irrelevant latecomer in the Great War. Its presence on the battlefield formed no part of his explanation for Germany's defeat, which he attributed to a "stab in the back" by effete politicians in Berlin. Neither then nor later, he thought, did Germany need to worry about American military power. At some distant date, Hitler occasionally imagined, he might have to confront the United States, and he dabbled with contingency plans for a blue-water navy and a long-range air arm that could carry the eventual battle to North America. But for the foreseeable future the Americans simply did not figure in his calculations. They were, he concluded in his own peculiar reading of the American people and past, a mongrel race, doomed to the trash heap of history when the timid shopkeepers of the North had defeated the race-proud lords of the plantation in the Civil War and proceeded to open the national bloodstream to indiscriminate immigrant inflows and, worse, black contamination. Even Aryan peoples could be corrupted by infection with the bacillus of American mediocrity. "Transport a German to Kiev," Hitler said, "and he remains a perfect German. But transplant him to Miami, and you make a degenerate out of him—in other words, an American." As time went on, der Führer found confirming proof of these views in Roosevelt's continuing inability to overcome the Depression, a demonstration of political helplessness that Hitler scornfully contrasted with his own unarguable economic success in Germany. He bizarrely seized on the panic set off by Orson Welles's elaborate radio-show hoax in 1938, which led millions of Americans to believe that Martians had invaded the country, as further ratification of his low estimate of American intelligence. When he later watched the film *The Grapes of Wrath*, he concluded that its portrait of a destitute and conflicted country accurately depicted America as it ever was and ever would be. "America," he sneered in 1939, "is not dangerous to us."[7] Though forged in the overheated smithy of Hitler's lurid brain, that conclusion was for the time being not without foundation in fact.

AFTER THE SENATE had refused Roosevelt's request for American participation in the World Court in January 1935, the president lamented to a friend that "we face a large misinformed public opinion." Because that opinion seemed so entrenched, he predicted to his ambassador to Germany, "we shall go through a period of non-cooperation in everything, I fear, for the next year or two." To another correspondent he said glumly that "today, quite frankly, the wind everywhere blows against us."[8] As it happened, much more than "a year or two" had to pass before that isolationist wind abated. Beginning in early 1935, American isolationism hardened from mere indifference to the outside world into studied, active repudiation of anything that smacked of international political or military engagement—or even, under some circumstances, economic engagement. From about the same time may be dated the origins of Roosevelt's own growing conviction that the weight of the United States must somehow be put into the scales to counterbalance the aggressive designs of the dictators and the militarists. Ironically, just as the president's internationalist convictions began to deepen, the isolationist mood of his countrymen started to congeal all the more stubbornly. What emerged was a stalemate in foreign policy no less intractable than the stalemate that paralyzed the movement for domestic reform after 1936. Indeed, at many points it seemed that Roosevelt himself was less the principled opponent of the isolationists than their willing captive.

Before the year 1935 was out, Congress codified isolationist sentiment into the first of five formal neutrality laws that aimed to insulate the United States from the war-storms then brewing across the globe from

7. Gerhard Weinberg, "Hitler's Image of the United States," *American Historical Review* 69 (July 1964): 1006–21.

8. Edgar B. Nixon, ed., *Franklin D. Roosevelt and Foreign Affairs* (Cambridge: Belknap Press of Harvard University Press, 1969), 2:386–87; Elliott Roosevelt, ed., *FDR: His Personal Letters, 1928–1945* (New York: Duell, Sloan and Pearce, 1950), 1:450–51.

Europe to Asia. A long-simmering dispute between Italy and Ethiopia provided the occasion for the first of the neutrality statutes enacted between 1935 and 1939. As Mussolini blustered against the Ethiopians and prepared to avenge the humiliating Italian defeat at Adowa four decades earlier, Europe seemed to teeter in early 1935 on the brink of a general war. These were "hair-trigger times," Roosevelt wrote in March, worse even than the fateful summer of 1914, "because at that time there was economic and social stability."[9] While Europeans trembled at the prospect of imminent war, Americans demonstrated for perpetual peace. On April 6, the eighteenth anniversary of American entry into the Great War, fifty thousand veterans staged a "march for peace" in Washington, D.C. They laid commemorative wreaths on the graves of three of the fifty representatives who had voted against the declaration of war in 1917. Three days later some 175,000 college students mounted a one-hour "strike for peace" on campuses across the country. They demanded the abolition of Reserve Officer Training Corps (ROTC) programs and called for "schools, not battleships." One student leader warned that the strike was "a dress rehearsal of what students intended to do should war be declared."[10] On Capitol Hill, the House chamber reverberated with pacifist oratory. Representatives vied with one another to toughen the neutrality bill then making its way through the legislative mill. Roosevelt himself, to the surprise of Senator Nye, had endorsed neutrality legislation in a meeting with the Munitions Committee on March 19, just three days after Hitler's dramatic rearmament announcement at the Berlin Opera House.

The bill that finally emerged required the president, after proclaiming that a state of war existed between foreign states, to impose an embargo on the shipment of arms to *all* the belligerents. It also empowered the president to declare that American citizens traveled on belligerent vessels at their own risk. The statute was clearly precipitated out of the political atmosphere created by what one senator called "that fool munitions committee."[11] It sought to avoid the perceived mistakes of Woodrow Wilson by removing the possibility that either the economic or the emotional provocations of 1914–17 could be repeated—a clear case of fighting, or trying not to fight, the last war. In effect, the statute formally

---

9. Nixon, *Franklin D. Roosevelt and Foreign Affairs*, 2:437.
10. Dallek, 101.
11. Pittman used the term in a telephone conversation with presidential assistant Stephen T. Early on August 19. Nixon, *Franklin D. Roosevelt and Foreign Affairs*, 2: 608.

renounced certain "neutral rights," even with their rather substantial attendant economic benefits, as the price the United States was willing to pay for peace.

Roosevelt would have preferred a slightly different bill, one that would have given him the discretionary authority to impose an arms embargo selectively, against an aggressor nation, rather than automatically and indiscriminately applying it to all belligerents. But Senate Foreign Relations Committee chairman Key Pittman of Nevada warned him that he would be "licked as sure as hell" if he insisted on the right to designate the aggressor. With his epochal domestic reform program at risk of being filibustered to death by a showdown over neutrality legislation in that momentous summer of 1935, Roosevelt took Pittman's advice. He agreed to be shackled by the mandatory features of the law. "[T]he inflexible provisions might drag us into war instead of keeping us out," he warned while signing the bill on August 31, but signed it nonetheless, while telling reporters that it was "entirely satisfactory" and would in any event expire in six months, when Congress reconvened in February 1936.[12]

On October 3, 1935, just weeks after Roosevelt signed the Neutrality Act, Mussolini's troops at last crossed from Italian Somalia in the Horn of Africa into the parched mountains of Ethiopia. The infantry were preceded by bombers that blasted mud-hut villages and strafed defenseless horsemen. The widely publicized boast of Mussolini's son that he exulted in the "magnificent sport" of watching his victims blow up like "a budding rose unfolding" helped to clinch American sympathy for the hapless Ethiopians and their diminutive emperor, Haile Selassie. But moral sympathy did not mean material support. The League of Nations voted on October 10 to take collective action against Italian aggression. When the league appeared ready to embargo oil shipments to Italy, a move that would have stopped Mussolini's war machine in its tracks, the league's Coordination Committee inquired if nonmember states would cooperate in the embargo. The United States, then the producer of more than half the world's oil, was the key to this strategy. But Roosevelt demurred. Oil was not among the "arms, ammunition or implements of war" enumerated in the Neutrality Act's list of goods to be embargoed. Putting it on the list, and applying the embargo to only one of the belligerents, would require a presidential initiative that would have violated the letter as well as the spirit of the statute that Roosevelt

12. Nixon, *Franklin D. Roosevelt and Foreign Affairs*, 2:632–33, 623.

had just signed. Moreover, Roosevelt appreciated that any semblance of cooperation with the diplomats in Geneva would expose him to attack by isolationists as the pliant creature of the league. In the current American political climate, that charge was anathema. "I'm walking a tight rope," Roosevelt confided to Democratic Party chairman Jim Farley; "I realize the seriousness of this from an international as well as a domestic point of view."[13] Alignment with the league might help to halt Mussolini, but it would almost certainly defeat Roosevelt's hope of wringing more discretionary authority out of the Congress when the Neutrality Act came up for revision in February 1936. What was more, such action might hand the isolationists a sword with which they could slash at Roosevelt in the next year's presidential election. Under the circumstances, Roosevelt contented himself with announcing a "moral embargo" on the shipment of oil and other raw materials to Italy. The moral embargo, not surprisingly, proved to be a thinner-than-paper barrier. American shipments of oil to Italy, as well as of copper, scrap iron, and other critical raw materials, nearly tripled in the following months.

The United States thus posed no significant obstacle to *Il Duce's* imperial ambitions in Africa. But whether American cooperation would have sufficiently braced the league and stopped the Italian invasion is dubious. In any apportionment of responsibility for the subjugation of Ethiopia, the Europeans must shoulder most of the blame. London and Paris, still traumatized by the memories of the Great War and inordinately fearful of "losing" Mussolini to Hitler, muffled their protests. They never did impose the oil embargo. They also conspicuously refrained from closing the Suez Canal, which at a stroke would have marooned Mussolini's troops in Ethiopia and doomed his military adventure to failure. In December 1935 the British and French governments even briefly endorsed an agreement between Sir Samuel Hoare and Pierre Laval, their respective foreign ministers, that handed over most of Ethiopia to Mussolini. The public outcry in Britain against this cynical ploy forced its retraction, as well as Hoare's resignation. But in Rome and Berlin, the fact that the Hoare-Laval deal had been advanced at all confirmed the weakness of the democracies. In the United States, the deal deepened the contempt that many Americans, including Roosevelt, felt for European diplomats. "I am not profoundly impressed with European ideology," Roosevelt's ambassador to Turkey wrote archly. "I

13. James Farley, *Jim Farley's Story: The Roosevelt Years* (New York: Whittlesey House, 1948), 55–56.

feel just the way you do," Roosevelt replied. "What a commentary on world ethics these past weeks have shown." At tea in the White House with the visiting archbishop of York, Roosevelt went out of his way to say that his disgust with the "attempt on the part of Great Britain and France to dismember Ethiopia" had snuffed out any inclination on his part to cooperate with the league. The Hoare-Laval scheme, Roosevelt told the clergyman, was simply "outrageous."[14] The Italians completed their conquest of Ethiopia in May, without significant further remonstrance from the league or its member states. Soon thereafter Mussolini withdrew from the impotent league. On November 1, 1936, the Rome-Berlin Axis agreement was announced. Three weeks later, Germany and Japan signed the Anti-Comintern Pact.

The crisis in barren and remote Ethiopia was a turning point. The inability of the powers to stop Mussolini's war of aggression, Winston Churchill later reflected, "played a part in leading to an infinitely more terrible war. Mussolini's bluff succeeded, and an important spectator drew far-reaching conclusions from the fact. Hitler had long resolved on war for German aggrandizement. He now formed a view of Great Britain's degeneracy which was only to be changed too late for peace and too late for him. In Japan, also, there were pensive spectators. . . . [I]t was a grievous deed to recoil. . . . Unless [the British] were prepared to back words and gestures by action, it might have been better to keep out of it all, like the United States, and let things rip and see what happened."[15]

Letting things rip and seeing what happened served as a fair description of American foreign policy for much of the rest of the 1930s. Congress extended the Neutrality Act for fourteen additional months in February 1936, without acceding to Roosevelt's requested revision allowing greater presidential discretion. The new law even added prohibitions on loans or credits to nations at war, a largely redundant feature given the strictures of the 1934 Johnson Act, but a provision that reminded the world of America's determination to wash its hands of whatever mischief the dictators might be plotting.

THE ETHIOPIAN EPISODE had exposed for all who cared to notice both the dithering of the European democracies and the studied irrelevance of the United States in the face of an international crisis.

14. Nixon, *Franklin D. Roosevelt and Foreign Affairs*, 3:112, 130; Ickes Diary 1:484.
15. Churchill 1:177, 183.

The road now lay wide open to further aggressions. In January 1936 Japan walked out of the London Naval Conference that was trying to sustain the British-American-Japanese ship-tonnage ratios of 5:5:3 that had been agreed in the naval limitation treaties of 1922 and 1930. The Imperial Japanese Navy began laying keels for a modern battle fleet designed to turn the western Pacific into a Japanese lake. Hitler proceeded with his own rearmament program and militarized the Rhineland in March.

On July 17, 1936, the European scene grew still more ominous. General Francisco Franco raised a Spanish army revolt in Morocco, crossed to Cadiz, and inflamed Spain in a bloody civil war that was to endure for three years. Franco sought by force of arms to reverse the electoral victory of the left-leaning republican government that had come to power in Madrid just months earlier, following riotous clashes between Spanish fascists and leftists. Both sides soon appealed for aid to their ideological sympathizers abroad: the republicans to Stalin in Moscow and to the newly elected Popular Front government of Léon Blum in Paris; Franco and the fascists to Berlin and Rome. Hitler and Mussolini responded readily, sending airplanes and pilots and, later, tens of thousands of infantrymen. Stalin sent tanks and aircraft and military "advisers," though Russia's distance from the Iberian peninsula seriously hampered his ability to supply the republicans. But Blum's government in Paris, though well positioned to help and drawn by political affinity toward the republicans, succumbed to pressure from the ever-cautious British and in the end declined to send any aid at all. Instead, Blum joined with London in a Nonintervention Committee that sought to "localize" the Spanish conflict by embargoing arms shipments to both sides. International law recognized that in the event of internal rebellion neutral states had a right to supply a legitimate government such as the republican regime in Madrid, but London and Paris were clearly willing to give up that right. They would sacrifice a sister republic rather than risk a wider war. While the democracies stood fastidiously aside, the conflict in Spain developed into what the American ambassador to Madrid, Claude Bowers, correctly called "a foreign war of the Fascist Powers against the Government of Spain."[16]

Most Americans could not have cared less. A Gallup poll in January 1937 found that two-thirds of the American public had no opinion about

16. Dallek, 140.

the events in Spain.[17] With only one dissenting vote, on January 6 Congress passed the third of the neutrality laws. It took the form of a joint resolution explicitly extending the arms embargo, originally drafted with international conflicts in mind, to the civil war in Spain. Roosevelt offered no objection. Poised to launch his campaign for Supreme Court reform, he was in no mood to borrow additional trouble over a distant squabble about which the American public cared little. As with the nonintervention formula embraced by London and Paris, the resolution's practical effect was to deny the republicans the means to defend themselves, while the dictators in Rome and Berlin continued to send supplies to Franco.

Not all Americans shared in the general apathy about Spain. The republican government's aggressively anticlerical policies had badly upset the Roman Catholic hierarchy, which therefore generally favored Roosevelt's course of action—or inaction. On the political left, some impassioned idealists saw Spain as the arena in which the great moral confrontation between fascism and democracy was being fought. Several thousand young Americans traveled to France with passports stamped "not valid for travel in Spain," then slipped over the Pyrenees and shouldered arms alongside their republican comrades. In February 1937 the Abraham Lincoln Battalion, an ill-trained and ill-used force of some 450 American volunteers, was recklessly thrown into battle in the Jarama Valley near Madrid, where 120 died and another 175 were wounded. For many on the left, the Spanish Civil War was the unhealing wound in the heart, the occasion when the cause of justice was betrayed not only by the cowardice of the democracies but also by the cynical callousness of the Communists who controlled much of the republican military effort. The spirit of despair and the sense of looming disaster that the war bred among many were later well captured in Ernest Hemingway's novel about the conflict, For Whom the Bell Tolls (1940).

With substantial German and Italian help, Franco overcame the last of the republican opposition in early 1939. Britain and France quickly recognized his government. So did Roosevelt, though with evident distaste. His government's Spanish policy had been "a grave mistake," he conceded to his cabinet, a recognition that came too late to do any good. Republican Spain, he said, should have been allowed to buy arms to "fight for her life against Franco—to fight for her life and for the

17. George H. Gallup, The Gallup Poll: Public Opinion, 1935–1971 (New York: Random House, 1972), 1:49.

lives of some of the rest of us well," Roosevelt added, "as events will very likely prove."[18]

THE NEUTRALITY LAW OF 1935, renewed for fourteen months in February 1936, was due to expire on May 1, 1937. Given the increasingly unsettled state of the world, Congress in 1937 resolved to enact "permanent" neutrality legislation. Roosevelt still preferred to have a degree of flexibility, but in the midst of his bitter confrontation with the Congress over Court reform and with the country convulsed by controversy over the sit-down strikes, he was in no position to impose his will. Nor was the Congress, where the charge of "dictatorship" was being leveled at Roosevelt's Court proposal and at his executive reorganization bill, in any mood to expand the scope of presidential authority. The Neutrality Act of 1937, the fourth of the neutrality laws, reaffirmed the mandatory ban on arms and loans to countries at war, as well as to disputants in civil wars (with an exception for Latin America, where the United States clearly wished to persist in its traditional policy of upholding legitimate regimes). It toughened the sanctions against American passengers on belligerent vessels by making such travel illegal. The question of selling "nonmilitary" commodities like oil and copper to belligerent states, even when they were clearly the aggressors, remained vexed. As they had demonstrated during the Ethiopian crisis, American businesses were reluctant to give up such lucrative commercial opportunities. On the other hand, isolationists were determined not to walk again down the path that had led to war in 1917, when German U-boat attacks on American ships, and the alleged desire to protect American loans, had apparently made war inevitable. The result was a compromise, known as "cash-and-carry." It stipulated that shipments to belligerents of raw materials and other items not explicitly military in nature might be permitted, but only if the buyers paid in cash and carried the goods away from American ports in their own ships. This provision was limited to two years.

The new statute accurately reflected the anti-internationalist American mood. It also dictated the formal, statutory framework within which Franklin Roosevelt would be compelled to conduct American foreign

18. Dallek, 180. Roosevelt did for a time conspire in covert shipments of materials through France to the Madrid regime, acting through his brother-in-law G. Hall Roosevelt. The scheme collapsed when the French government definitively sealed the French-Spanish border in mid-1938. See Frank Freidel, *Franklin D. Roosevelt: A Rendezvous with Destiny* (Boston: Little, Brown, 1990), 271–72.

policy for the remainder of the decade. With stout legal thread, Congress had spun a straitjacket that rendered the United States effectively powerless in the face of the global conflagration that was about to explode.

With Mussolini now in possession of Ethiopia, Hitler entrenched in the Rhineland, Franco advancing in Spain, and the Americans formally proclaiming their "permanent" neutrality, Japan lit the next match. A minor clash between Chinese and Japanese troops at the Marco Polo Bridge near Peking (Beijing) touched off full-scale war between Japan and China in July 1937. Japan was by then spoiling for the fight. Japanese units soon landed at Shanghai, entered the teeming valley of the Yangtze, and headed for the Nationalist Chinese capital at Nanking (Nanjing), which fell on December 12. For the next several weeks, Japanese troops rampaged through the city and its surroundings. In an orgy of rape, bayoneting, beheading, and machine-gunning, they murdered as many as two hundred thousand Chinese, providing a harrowing preview of the atrocities that modern warfare could visit upon civilians. What came to be known as the Rape of Nanking left Americans agape at its cruel ferocity but little inclined to do anything meaningful to halt the Japanese juggernaut.[19]

As in Ethiopia, American sympathies instinctively went out to the victims of aggression. A Gallup poll in late 1937 found 59 percent of respondents favored China, while only 1 percent backed Japan.[20] Thanks to generations of American missionaries in China and to the editorial interest of Henry Luce, the son of one of those missionary couples and the publisher of *Time* magazine, China had long enjoyed an emotional hold on American hearts. That grip was tightened in the 1930s by the runaway popularity of Pearl Buck's sentimental novel *The Good Earth*. By uncanny coincidence, Buck's book was first published in 1931, just as the Japanese were seizing Manchuria. Some two million Americans had read it by 1937, when the film version appeared at virtually the same time the Sino-Japanese war broke out. The film was seen by more than twenty million Americans. "In a way that never could have been accomplished by event or propaganda," Harold Isaacs later wrote, Buck's touching portrayal of a Chinese peasant and his wife "humanized the people who became Japan's principal victims. . . . Although it did not

19. See Iris Chang, *The Rape of Nanking: The Forgotten Holocaust of World War II* (New York: Basic, 1997).
20. Cantril, 1081–82.

deal with the war itself, it gave the quality of individual recognition to the figure of the heroic Chinese peasant or peasant-soldier who offered battle to the Japanese against such great odds."[21]

But as in Ethiopia and Spain, moral sympathy did not easily translate into material support. Even when Japanese pilots sank the United States gunboat *Panay* during the assault on Nanking on December 12, the American response was muted. In an earlier era, the sinking of the *Panay* would have raised an unshirted outcry for retaliation. Japanese warplanes bombed the *Panay* in broad daylight as it lay at anchor in the confined waters of the Yangtze channel. Two eighteen-by-fourteen-foot American flags were conspicuously laid out on its top deck. Film shot by a Universal Newsreel cameraman who happened to be aboard clearly belied the Japanese claim that the pilots had been flying too high to discern the ship's markings. The film also showed Japanese planes repeatedly strafing escaping survivors. By the time the *Panay* settled to the bottom of the turbid Yangtze, two people aboard had been killed and some thirty wounded. But the *Panay* was not to be a modern *Maine*, nor even a *Lusitania*. Its sinking produced a cry for withdrawal, not for war. "We should learn that it is about time for us to mind our own business," Texas Democrat Maury Maverick declared in the House.[22] A few months later, a *Fortune* magazine poll showed that a majority of Americans favored getting the United States out of China altogether.[23] When Japan tendered an official apology for the *Panay* incident and paid some $2 million in reparations, the crisis swiftly blew over.

The principal residue of the *Panay* affair in Congress was not more bellicosity but more pacifism. The incident boosted Indiana Democratic representative Louis Ludlow's three-year-old campaign for a constitutional amendment requiring a national referendum for a declaration of war (except in case of invasion). A transparently silly idea, accurately likened by critics to convening a town meeting before authorizing the fire department to put out a blaze, Ludlow's amendment enjoyed strong

21. Harold R. Isaacs, *Scratches on Our Minds: American Images of China and India* (New York: John Day, 1958), 157.

22. An explosion aboard the U.S. battleship *Maine* in Havana harbor led to war with Spain in 1898. The German sinking of the British liner *Lusitania*, with heavy loss of American lives, produced a loud clamor for war against Germany in 1915. Maverick quoted in Manny T. Koginos, *The* Panay *Incident: Prelude to War* (Lafayette, Ind.: Purdue University Studies, 1967), 46.

23. *Fortune* 17 (April 1938): 109.

public support. A Gallup poll in October 1937 registered 73 percent approval.[24] In the wake of the *Panay*, Ludlow's proposal now also found remarkable favor in the House. Its supporters, many of them Democrats, overrode the House leadership and forced the Ludlow bill out of committee on a discharge petition. After strenuous administration lobbying against it, when it came to a vote on January 10, 1938, the Ludlow Amendment was defeated only by the narrow margin of 209 to 188. The episode provided a dramatic demonstration of the formidable strength of the isolationist bloc on Capitol Hill, even in the wake of an inflammatory act such as the wanton sinking of a U.S. Navy vessel.

At the other end of Pennsylvania Avenue, Franklin Roosevelt took what consolation he could from the final Ludlow vote, but an effective policy to cope with the situation in Asia—not to mention Europe—continued to elude him. Strictly speaking, the recently passed Neutrality Act of 1937 did not apply to the Asian crisis, since neither China nor Japan bothered to issue a formal declaration of war. Roosevelt came under isolationist pressure to invoke the act by declaring that a state of war existed, but he refrained. He knew that applying the neutrality legislation's arms embargo would preclude any possibility of American military aid to China, while the cash-and-carry provisions would still allow Japan to provision itself from American sources. In the event, both sides sought supplies in the United States, though Japan, as a relatively wealthy sea power, was by far the larger purchaser of American goods— especially scrap iron and petroleum products. AMERICAN SCRAP IRON PLAYS GRIM ROLE IN FAR EASTERN WAR, the *Washington Post* headlined on August 29, 1937. JAPANESE RAIN DEATH WITH ONE-TIME JUNK. GUNS, BOMBS, AND BATTLESHIPS, ALL MADE FROM OLD METAL, SHIPPED ACROSS PACIFIC IN GROWING AMOUNTS.[25] Neutrality Act or not, pro-Chinese sympathies or not, the effect of American policy in practice was to provide assistance for Japan's war of aggression against China.

For more than four years, the Sino-Japanese "incident" dragged on, while Roosevelt struggled to find ways to aid China and restrain Japan without antagonizing the isolationists at home or further provoking what Secretary Hull called the "wild, runaway, half-insane men" in Tokyo.[26] "Minds were ransacked," the historian Herbert Feis later wrote, "in a

---

24. Gallup, *Gallup Poll* 1:71.
25. Herbert Feis, *The Road to Pearl Harbor* (New York: Atheneum, 1963), 11.
26. Dallek, 154.

search for effective ways of causing Japan to desist, while staying unin-volved. Unhappily none was found."[27]

When Neville Chamberlain, who some six months earlier had suc-ceeded Stanley Baldwin as British prime minister, raised the question in December 1937 of impressing Japan with a joint U.S.-British dem-onstration of naval force at Britain's great Asian base of Singapore, Roo-sevelt squelched the idea outright. "[T]hough the President and the Secretary of State . . . had been doing their best to bring American pub-lic opinion to realize the situation," the British ambassador in Washing-ton informed his government, "they were not yet in a position to adopt any measures of the kind now contemplated." The opportunity for show-ing a united Anglo-American naval front in the Pacific was lost. Cham-berlain expressed his disappointment to his sister: "[I]t is always best and safest," he said, "to count on *nothing* from the Americans but words."[28]

The Americans offered ample confirmation for Chamberlain's lack of confidence in them. On October 5, 1937, Roosevelt spoke what sounded like some big words indeed. The occasion took on added drama because the president chose to speak them in Chicago, a city fed a daily diet of Roosevelt-be-damned invective by Robert R. McCormick's militantly anti–New Deal and obstreperously isolationist *Chicago Tribune*, on whose masthead McCormick emblazoned the motto THE WORLD'S GREATEST NEWSPAPER. McCormick himself, at six feet four inches, with a fifty-two-inch chest and thirty-six-inch arms, was a bullying giant of a man and a towering colossus of provincialism. He routinely pronounced upon the world in steely aphorisms that left no room for nuance or argument. The *Tribune*, with its million daily readers, and its sister radio station, whose call letters, of course, were WGN, provided McCormick with incomparable pulpits from which he trumpeted his trademark prej-udices across what he called "Chicagoland"—the five-state region that stretched from Iowa to Ohio, the very heartland of American isolation-ism. Little escaped the copious arc of McCormick's rage. Wisconsin he declared "the nuttiest state in the Union, next to California." The north-eastern United States swarmed with the "dodging, obligation-shifting idle rich . . . diluted in their Americanism by other hordes of immi-grants." Foreign service officers were "he-debutantes, dead from the

---

27. Feis, *Road to Pearl Harbor*, 10.
28. William R. Rock, *Chamberlain and Roosevelt: British Foreign Policy and the United States, 1937–1940* (Columbus: Ohio State University Press, 1988), 54, 48.

neck up." Herbert Hoover was "the greatest state socialist in history." Franklin Roosevelt was "a Communist." McCormick, said the British ambassador to Washington, was "stubborn, slow-thinking, and bellicose." He was also enormously influential. By speaking in Chicago, Roosevelt was apparently bearding the isolationist lion in his den.[29]

"The epidemic of world lawlessness is spreading," the president declared, in what seemed to be a stout-hearted challenge to the insular prejudices of his hostile Chicagoland listeners. "When an epidemic of physical disease starts to spread, the community approves and joins in a quarantine of the patients in order to protect the health of the community against the spread of the disease. . . . War is a contagion, whether it be declared or undeclared," he said, in obvious reference to the Sino-Japanese conflict. "There is no escape," he warned his presumably skeptical audience, "through mere isolation or neutrality. . . . There must be positive endeavors to preserve peace."[30]

The "Quarantine Speech" seemed to throw down the gauntlet to the isolationists and to herald a presidential crusade to educate the American public about the necessity for international engagement. What could Roosevelt's words mean, other than a pledge of American support for a concerted plan of action against Japan? British foreign secretary Anthony Eden, who, like Winston Churchill later, made Anglo-American cooperation the supreme goal of British policy, pressed Washington for an "exact interpretation" of Roosevelt's remarks. What "positive endeavors" did the president have in mind? What, Eden wanted particularly to know, would be the American position at the nine-power meeting soon to convene in Brussels to discuss the Asian crisis? Eden advised that only a policy of active assistance to China combined with economic pressure on Japan would be effective. Was this what Roosevelt intended?

Roosevelt gave his answer through his emissary to the Brussels talks, Norman Davis. Tell the British "that there is such a thing as public opinion in the United States," the president instructed Davis. He could not afford, Roosevelt continued, "to be made, in popular opinion at home, a tail to the British kite." In London, the *Times* opined that in the last analysis "Mr. Roosevelt was defining an attitude and not a program." That description proved prophetic. The Brussels conference

29. Richard Norton Smith, *The Colonel: The Life and Legend of Robert R. McCormick* (Boston: Houghton Mifflin, 1997), passim.
30. *PPA* (1937), 406–11.

convened and adjourned in November without consequence. The last reasonable chance to settle the Sino-Japanese war by joint international action was lost. The Americans, Neville Chamberlain's sister acidly remarked, were "hardly a people to go tiger shooting with."[31]

"It's a terrible thing," Roosevelt allegedly said about the failure of his Chicago speech to make a dent in isolationist opinion, "to look over your shoulder when you are trying to lead—and find no one there." But Roosevelt's leadership in this case was neither valiant nor consistent. Though he had chosen to challenge McCormick and the isolationists in their midwestern heartland, he had shown no stomach for the kind of prolonged confrontation with them that might change the course of American foreign policy. Indeed, he scarcely waited to gauge the reaction to his Chicago address before he started backpedaling. Just one day after the Quarantine Speech, reporters asked Roosevelt if he cared to amplify his remarks. No, Roosevelt blandly replied. The reporters pressed on: Was there any conflict between what he was suggesting and the Neutrality Act? No, said Roosevelt. Did his speech imply economic sanctions against Japan? they persisted. No, insisted Roosevelt. "Look," he said, " 'sanctions' is a terrible word to use. They are out of the window." If not sanctions, then what program might the administration follow? "We are looking for a program," Roosevelt explained to the astonished journalists. "It might be a stronger neutrality."[32]

European leaders, particularly in Britain, were meanwhile looking over their own shoulders and wondering where Roosevelt was. The American president's failure to follow up on the Quarantine Speech made an especially deep imprint on Neville Chamberlain, desperately searching for his own program to cope with the dictators. Britain needed partners if it were to make an effective stand against the aggressors. No reliable partnership seemed likely with the Americans. "The main lesson to be drawn" from the failed Brussels Conference, Chamberlain told his cabinet on the day the conference adjourned, "was the difficulty of securing effective cooperation from the United States of America."

Those events at the end of 1937 formed the backdrop for the reception that Chamberlain gave in January 1938 to Roosevelt's plan for an international peace conference, an episode that excited hot argument at

31. Dallek, 152; Davis 4:133–36; Rock, *Chamberlain and Roosevelt*, 43.
32. Samuel I. Rosenman, *Working with Roosevelt* (New York: Harper and Brothers, 1952), 167; PPA (1937), 414ff.

the time and has remained controversial ever since. The president proposed to invite to Washington representatives from a number of small states — Sweden, the Netherlands, Belgium, Switzerland, Hungary, Yugoslavia, Turkey, and three Latin American countries to be designated — to discuss rules of international behavior, arms reduction, access to raw materials, and the rights and obligations of neutrals. After coming to such agreement as they could, these states would then promulgate their conclusions to other nations. What, the president inquired, did the British government think of this proposal?

Chamberlain, not without cause, instinctively judged the plan to be "rather preposterous . . . fantastic & likely to excite the derision of Germany and Italy." It scarcely helped that Roosevelt accompanied his inquiry with a reminder that the United States still held fast to its "traditional policy of freedom from political involvement."

Despite Chamberlain's skepticism, the British cabinet met in several urgent sessions in mid-January to consider Roosevelt's idea. The atmosphere at Whitehall was tense, because the American proposal exacerbated a tortuous policy debate already in progress. Chamberlain in December had received from his chiefs of staff a secret report emphasizing that in light of Britain's military unpreparedness, it was imperative to pursue "any political or international action that can be taken to reduce the numbers of our potential enemies and to gain the support of potential allies." But in Chamberlain's eyes, what the chiefs described as a two-pronged strategy — splitting the German-Italian-Japanese alliance *and* finding new allies — boiled down in practice to a painful choice: detaching one of the adversaries from the others by judicious concessions *or* securing a dependable ally, namely, the United States. This choice became a bitter point of contention between Prime Minister Chamberlain and Foreign Secretary Eden. Chamberlain believed in the first strategy, one that fitted the usual definitions of diplomacy as the search for workable concessions and compromises to avoid open conflict, but a strategy that was soon to be called and forever to be damned as appeasement. Eden believed in the latter, emphasizing the crucial importance of the United States. Roosevelt's overture, Eden argued, might provide the opportunity at last to clasp hands with the Americans and begin to knit a thick cable of opposition to Hitler's ambitions. Chamberlain countered that while the potential strength of the United States was undeniable, "he would be a rash man who based his calculations on help from that quarter." The "isolationists" were "so strong

& so vocal," Chamberlain noted in his diary, that the United States could not be "depended upon for help if [Britain] should get into trouble."[33]

Chamberlain's eventual reply to Roosevelt's inquiry, said Sumner Welles, was "like a douche of cold water."[34] He showed no enthusiasm whatsoever for Roosevelt's proposal. What was more, the British prime minister revealed that he was about to embark on a policy designed to wean Mussolini away from his attachment to Hitler by extending de jure recognition to the Italian occupation of Ethiopia. By feeding Mussolini at least some of what he wanted, Italy might be sated, and Britain would have one less adversary to worry about. Appeasing Mussolini, Chamberlain calculated, would pacify the Mediterranean, guarantee the Suez gateway to India and beyond, and give Britain a freer hand to deal with the Germans in Europe and the Japanese in the Pacific. Chamberlain extended recognition on April 16. Roosevelt, cautioned even by his trusted adviser Bullitt that his plan for a Washington conference would strike the rest of the world as "an escape from reality," allowed the idea to die.[35]

Chamberlain's rejection of Roosevelt's initiative and his embarkation on the road of appeasement thereafter have earned him almost universal condemnation in the history books. Eden, who had earlier proclaimed his willingness to trek from Australia to Alaska to secure American cooperation, resigned as foreign secretary in protest against Chamberlain's decision. Winston Churchill, who would in time stake his entire strategy for British survival on American aid, later wrote of these weeks that "no event could have been more likely to stave off, or even prevent, war than the arrival of the United States in the circle of European hates and fears. To Britain it was almost a matter of life and death. . . . We must regard its rejection . . . as the loss of the last frail chance to save the world from tyranny otherwise than by war. That Mr Chamberlain . . .

33. Rock, *Chamberlain and Roosevelt*, 45–70.
34. Sumner Welles, *Seven Decisions That Shaped History* (New York: Harper and Brothers, 1951), 27.
35. Bullitt to Roosevelt, January 20, 1938. Bullitt thought little more of the scheme than did Chamberlain: "It would be as if in the palmiest days of Al Capone you had summoned a national conference of psychoanalysts to Washington to discuss the psychological causes of crime." Orville H. Bullitt, ed., *For the President: Personal and Secret, Correspondence between Franklin D. Roosevelt and William C. Bullitt* (Boston: Houghton Mifflin, 1972), 252.

wave[d] away the proffered hand stretched out across the Atlantic leaves one, even at this date, breathless with amazement."[36]

But had Roosevelt's proffered hand held anything useful? The thinking behind his conference scheme was unorthodox to the point of being fanciful. How could a proclamation of principles by a gaggle of small and peripheral states realistically be expected to rein in Hitler's headlong plunge toward war? Even with American endorsement, would such a statement have meaningfully signaled "the arrival of the United States in the circle of European hates and fears"? And if one remembers how often the American hand had been proffered, only to be withdrawn, as at London in June of 1933, or Chicago in October of 1937—or how often it had not been extended at all, as in Ethiopia in 1935, or in Spain in 1936, or in the Pacific in late 1937—one's breath returns, and with it a measure of sympathy for Chamberlain's predicament. Judging Roosevelt to be "a dangerous and unreliable horse in any team," keenly aware of how inadequately armed and politically isolated Britain was, Chamberlain concluded, not altogether unreasonably, that he had little choice but to seek some kind of accommodation with the dictators. Appeasement had begun.[37]

But Hitler was unappeasable. Unknown to Chamberlain, *der Führer* had already announced to his senior political and military officials that "Germany's problems could be solved only by means of force."[38] In a systematic four-hour-long exposition on November 5, 1937, in the *Reichkanzlei* in Berlin, Hitler flabbergasted his subordinates with the boldness of his war plans and his detailed analysis of the probable reactions of the other powers. With methodical confidence, he predicted the responses of Britain, France, Russia, Italy, Japan, Czechoslovakia, Belgium, Holland, and Spain. Significantly, the United States figured not at all in his thinking. War must come within the next few years, he declared, perhaps as early as 1938, and no later than 1945, after which Germany would no longer enjoy uncontested superiority in armaments. First steps would be the annexation of Austria and the elimination of Czechoslovakia. Officers who questioned the wisdom of these policies were dismissed. In March 1938 Hitler executed the first part of this plan, absorbing Austria into the *Reich*.

---

36. Churchill 1:254–55.
37. Freidel, *Rendezvous with Destiny*, 260.
38. Shirer, *Rise and Fall of the Third Reich*, 306

WITHIN DAYS of the German takeover of Austria, reports came out of Vienna about atrocities inflicted on Jews. The reports made for grim news, but by this date they were hardly surprising. Nazi racial policies were no secret by 1938. Hitler's manic tract of 1924, *Mein Kampf*, had conjured the fantastic web connecting "international Jewry" and the "Bolshevik conspiracy" that became a central tenet of Nazi ideology. Immediately on taking power in 1933, the Nazis had begun to persecute Germany's half-million Jews. They organized boycotts of Jewish enterprises, and Nazi toughs openly abused Jews in the streets. The Nuremberg Laws in 1935 tightened the noose further, barring Jews from broad categories of employment and severely limiting their civil rights. When the Germans swallowed Austria, they imposed all those restrictions on an additional 190,000 Jews. Faced with pauperization and worse, thousands of Jews tried to flee from the spreading Nazi menace. As German troops fanned out through Vienna, three thousand Jews per day applied for visas to enter the United States. By then the American consulate in Stuttgart, Germany, authorized to issue 850 visas per month, had a backlog of some 110,000 visa applications.

The American press had long reported on Nazi mistreatment of the Jews. Dorothy Thompson's many articles and two books, *Refugees: Anarchy or Organization* (1938) and *Let the Record Speak* (1940), constituted an especially searing indictment of both Nazi misanthropy and American apathy. The virulence of Nazi anti-Semitism had no comparably malignant American analogue, not even the septic rantings of Father Coughlin against the "Jew Deal" or the scattered outpourings of a handful of other hatemongers. American society in the 1930s was not free of the stain of anti-Semitism, but most Americans, Jews and gentiles alike, generally condemned Nazi racialism. Yet while both private organizations and government officials in the United States expressed dismay over the plight of the Jews in German Europe, few understood as yet the genocidal implications of Nazi racial ideology, and fewer still found the means to make effective protest. As happened so often in this melancholy decade, sympathy stopped short of concrete support.

Sometimes sympathy stopped short even of symbolic gestures. When Hitler ruled that no German Jews would be allowed to compete in the 1936 Berlin Olympic Games, several American athletic organizations proposed to boycott the event. For nearly a year, debate over participation in the Berlin Games raged through the American sporting community, in the process educating broad sectors of the public about the depths of Nazi brutality. But in a formal vote in December 1935, the Amateur Athletic Union, America's credentialing sport bureaucracy, narrowly rejected a boycott resolution. The American Olympic Committee, headed by Avery Brundage, encouraged American athletes to participate, lending some aura of legitimacy to the Hitler regime and wasting an opportunity, as the *Washington Post* commented, "to let the Germans see what the outside world thinks of their present rulers."[39]

Divisions among America's nearly five million Jews also impeded the search for useful tools to mitigate Hitler's racial policies. Both the degree of the impending danger and the method for dealing with it were questions that excited sharp disagreement and exacerbated old tensions among American Jews. The American Jewish Congress, led by Rabbi Stephen Wise, represented the masses of East European Jews who had flooded into the United States beginning in the 1890s. Often socialist in politics, orthodox in religion, and Zionist in aspiration, they organized drives in the 1930s to boycott German goods, staged mock trials of Hitler in several American cities, and pressed for relaxation of the American immigration laws so that more Jewish refugees could enter the United States. But the American Jewish Committee, an older and more moderate body, displayed the measured caution typical of its mostly German-Jewish constituents. Their American roots reached well back into the nineteenth century. Conservative in politics, adherents of reform Judaism if they practiced their faith at all, and generally well assimilated, they opposed both the boycotts of German goods and the mock trials. They were also temperate in their advocacy of policies that would bring large numbers of additional Jews to the United States—particularly

39. Deborah E. Lipstadt, *Beyond Belief: The American Press and the Coming of the Holocaust, 1933–1945* (New York: Free Press, 1986), 78. See also Arthur D. Morse, *While Six Million Died: A Chronicle of American Apathy* (New York: Random House, 1968), 172ff. As it happened, the African-American athlete Jesse Owens spectacularly discredited Hitler's theories of Aryan superiority at the Games when he won four gold medals in the track and field events: for the 100-and 200-meter dashes, the broad jump, and as a member of the 400-meter relay team. Hitler conspicuously refused to shake Owens's hand, or the hands of the three other black American athletes who won gold medals: Archie Williams, John Woodruff, and Cornelius Johnson. In another highly controversial episode, the American track coach changed the lineup of the 400-meter relay team, preventing two athletes from running—Sam Stoller and Marty Glickman, the only two members of the American Olympic track team who did not get a chance to compete, and the only two Jews. See Marty Glickman, *The Fastest Kid on the Block* (Syracuse: Syracuse University Press, 1996).

more East European Jews of the sort whose recent arrival had already proved unsettling to the old German-Jewish establishment. Walter Lippmann, perhaps America's foremost political commentator of the time, exemplified German-Jewish sentiments when he wrote that "the rich and vulgar and pretentious Jews of our big American cities are . . . the real fountain of anti-Semitism." The American Jewish Committee was even wary of proposals to unify the American Jewish community in a single organization, for fear of validating anti-Semitic propaganda about the Jewish "state within a state" and touching off a barrage of reprisals. Most important, few Jews of any persuasion, in America or elsewhere, including Germany, and few gentiles either, for that matter, as yet fully comprehended the force of the systematic onslaught against Jewry that Hitler would soon unleash. How, indeed, could it be comprehended? Generations later, the moral enormity of what came to be known as the Holocaust still quivered painfully in the world's conscience, a ghastly icon of humankind's capacity for fiendishness. In the meantime, as one Jewish commentator said in 1933, "What else can we do but scream? Jewish power lies in screaming . . . we are powerless."[40]

Bounded by ignorance as much as by apathy and anti-Semitism, Roosevelt's government felt itself to be legally powerless as well. "The German authorities are treating the Jews shamefully," Roosevelt remarked as early as 1933 when he sent William E. Dodd off as his ambassador to Germany. "[W]hatever we can do to moderate the general persecution by unofficial and personal influence ought to be done," the president instructed Dodd. "But this is also not a governmental affair," Roosevelt cautioned. "We can do nothing except for American citizens."[41]

But if the United States could do little for the Jews inside Germany, could it not open its doors to those trying to leave? After the announcement of the Nuremberg Laws in September 1935, New York governor Herbert Lehman, a prominent Jewish leader and usually a close political ally of Roosevelt's, proposed doubling the number of German Jews annually admitted to the United States, from twenty-five hundred to five thousand — "almost a negligible number," Lehman noted. Roosevelt responded sympathetically that consular officials had been instructed to

40. Ronald Steel, *Walter Lippmann and the American Century* (Boston: Atlantic–Little, Brown, 1980), 192; A. Ginsburg, "Our Protest," *Forwards*, April 1, 1933, 8, quoted in Henry L. Feingold, *The Politics of Rescue: The Roosevelt Administration and the Holocaust, 1938–1945* (New York: Holocaust Library, 1970), 13.
41. William E. Dodd Jr. and Martha Dodd, eds., *Ambassador Dodd's Diary, 1933–1938* (New York: Harcourt, Brace), 1941, 5.

offer "the most considerate attention and the most generous and favorable treatment possible under the laws of the country."[42] The numbers of German-Jewish immigrants grew modestly but nevertheless stayed "negligible." Immigrants of whatever faith from Germany totaled some six thousand in 1936 and eleven thousand in 1937.[43]

Why did the potential refugee flood remain such a trickle? The explanation lay partly in the intersection of Nazi policy with those "laws of the country" about which Roosevelt reminded Lehman. Nazi regulations severely restricted the sum of money that a departing Jew could take out of Germany. As early as 1934 the amount had been reduced to the equivalent of four dollars, essentially pauperizing any Jew trying to leave the country. In the United States, immigration statutes forbade issuing visas to persons "likely to become a public charge." Herbert Hoover in 1930 had ordered consular officials to apply that clause strictly, as the American unemployment crisis worsened. Under the circumstances, few systematically impoverished German Jews could qualify for visas.

Congressman Emmanuel Celler, who represented a heavily Jewish Brooklyn district, criticized the State Department's consular service for having "a heart beat muffled in protocol," but even after the Roosevelt administration liberalized visa application rules in 1935, the problem remained.[44] Its deeper roots lay not in the technical minutiae of consular procedures but in pervasive anti-immigration attitudes and especially in the very nature of the 1924 National Origins Act that governed all American immigration policy. That law constrained Roosevelt's refugee policy as tightly as the Neutrality Acts constrained his diplomacy. It imposed a ceiling of 150,000 immigrants per year, with quotas allocated by country on the basis of a given nationality's proportional presence in the census of 1920. Quotas were not fungible among countries—that is, an unfilled quota from Britain could not be assigned to Germany. Moreover, the 1924 law took no official cognizance of "refugees" and thus made no provision for offering asylum to the victims of religious or political persecution. No American contribution to solving the looming catastrophe of European Jewry was possible without revising those

---

42. Lehman to FDR, November 1, 1935, in Nixon, *Franklin D. Roosevelt and Foreign Affairs*, 3:51, 65.

43. *HSUS*, 105. By one estimate, 102,000 Jews made their way into the United States between 1933 and 1938. See I.C.B. Dear, ed., *The Oxford Companion to the Second World War* (New York: Oxford University Press, 1995), 366.

44. *New York Times*, February 4, 1938, 12.

numerical restrictions or, at a minimum, amending the law to exempt from the quota system persons who were designated as refugees. Neither development seemed likely. The country had effectively barred its doors to further mass immigration in 1924. It was in no mood now, in the midst of the Great Depression, to change its mind and take the barriers down. Persistent unemployment, which had sharply worsened in the "Roosevelt Recession" of 1937–38, posed an iron obstacle to opening the gates to more immigrants of whatever description. And in the world of 1938, advertising asylum for refugees might invite a massive Jewish exodus — or expulsion — from countries like Poland and Romania, which were all too eager to declare their many millions of Jews "surplus" and be rid of them forever. Polish officials even hinted that they would happily arrange pogroms to demonstrate the urgency of their own Jewish "problem."

Shortly after the Austrian *Anschluss*, Roosevelt stretched the limits of presidential authority when he ordered the merging of the German and Austrian quotas and the special expediting of Jewish visa applications, measures that permitted some fifty thousand Jews to escape Nazi hands in the next two years. He was under no illusions about the political risks. "[T]he narrow isolationists," he confided to Governor Lehman's brother, might "use this move of ours for purely partisan objectives." At the same time, the president also called for an international conference to discuss the impending refugee crisis, while carefully noting in his invitation that "no country would be expected to receive greater number of emigrants than is permitted by its existing legislation." Lehman wired Roosevelt a single word: "Splendid!" Roosevelt answered: "I only wish I could do more." In the event, his initiative amounted to pathetically little indeed.[45]

The refugee conference convened in the French resort town of Evian-les-Bains on the shores of Lake Geneva on July 6, 1938. Even before the delegates gathered, the prospects for helpful action seemed dim. Switzerland, wary of provoking its powerful German neighbor, had asked not to be the host country. Britain agreed to attend only on condition that Palestine, the historic Jewish homeland and long the object of Zionist agitation, not be discussed. Delegates from several Latin American states, regarded by many as possible sites for Jewish resettlement, rejected all such ideas outright. "[E]lements that might endanger the solid basis of our Ibero-American personality [and] our Catholic

45. Feingold, *Politics of Rescue*, 3, 23, 24.

tradition," declared a Peruvian newspaper, would find no welcome in Latin America. Nazi propaganda chief Josef Goebbels announced that "if there is any country that believes it has not enough Jews, I shall gladly turn over to it all our Jews." Hitler declared himself "ready to put all these criminals at the disposal of these countries, for all I care, even on luxury ships." The conference ended with a whimper. Its only tangible outcome was the creation of an Intergovernmental Committee on Political Refugees (IGC). Based in London and headed by an American, Roosevelt's fellow Grotonian George Rublee, the IGC spent the next several months floundering through byzantine negotiations with the Nazis to ransom German Jews for badly-needed foreign exchange.[46]

The problem of where to relocate Germany's Jews proved an insuperable obstacle. A Nazi newspaper commented: "We are saying openly that we do not want the Jews while the democracies keep on claiming that they are willing to receive them—and then leave the guests out in the cold! Aren't we savages better men after all?" The *Richmond* (Virginia) *News Leader* was a lonely voice criticizing the Roosevelt administration for resting "content with friendly gestures and kind words. . . . [S]ome of us," the paper concluded, "are a bit ashamed of our country." But a *Fortune* survey in 1938 showed that fewer than 5 percent of Americans were willing to raise immigration quotas to accommodate refugees. More than two-thirds agreed that "with conditions as they are we should try to keep them out." The Depression had helped to reinforce an isolationism of the spirit, a kind of moral numbness, that checked American humanitarianism as tightly as political isolationism straitjacketed American diplomacy.[47]

A new eruption of Nazi ferocity soon highlighted the tragic futility of Evian. On November 7, 1938, a seventeen-year-old German Jewish refugee shot and killed a German diplomat in Paris. Reprisals followed swiftly. Hitler's government organized a pogrom that exploded all over Germany on the night of November 9–10. Nazi thugs looted Jewish homes, burned synagogues, smashed Jewish shops, killed dozens of Jews, and arrested some twenty thousand Jewish "criminals." Known as *Kristallnacht* (Crystal Night) for the pools of broken glass that littered German streets on the morning of November 10, this officially sanctioned orgy of pillage and arson and murder had not yet drained the

---

46. Morse, *While Six Million Died*, 344, 228, 204.
47. Morse, *While Six Million Died*, 288; *Richmond News Leader* quoted in Lipstadt, *Beyond Belief*, 96.

vials of Nazi wrath. Two days later, with lunatic cruelty, the German government announced that the property damage incurred during *Kristallnacht* would be repaired by levying a huge "atonement fine" on the Jews. At the same time, it ordered all Jewish retail establishments closed. A few weeks later, the government announced the confiscation of all Jewish assets.

These barbarities outraged many Americans. Protesters threatened to bomb the German consulate in New York City, to which Mayor Fiorello La Guardia responded by assigning an all-Jewish police detail to guard duty. Herbert Hoover, Al Smith, Alf Landon, Harold Ickes, and other prominent figures went on the radio to denounce Germany's night of horror. The German ambassador in Washington cabled Berlin that *Kristallnacht* had raised a hurricane of condemnation in the American press, which "is without exception incensed against Germany[.] . . . [E]ven the respectable patriotic circles which were thoroughly . . . anti-Semitic in their outlook also begin to turn away from us."

Roosevelt took what action he could. He recalled American ambassador Hugh Wilson from Berlin, for "consultation," and Wilson never returned to his post. (The Germans reciprocated by withdrawing their ambassador from Washington.) Again pushing the limits of presidential authority, Roosevelt by executive order extended the visas of some fifteen thousand German and Austrian nationals already resident in the United States, including the great emigré physicist Albert Einstein. Speaking to reporters five days after *Kristallnacht*, the president pointedly declared that he "could scarcely believe that such things could occur in a twentieth-century civilization." Yet the familiar political restraints stayed Roosevelt's hand from more forceful measures. "Would you recommend a relaxation of our immigration restrictions so that the Jewish refugees could be received in the this country?" a reporter asked. "That is not in contemplation," Roosevelt shot back. "We have the quota system."[48]

Kristallnacht prompted several attempts to modify the quota system. Congressman Samuel Dickstein sponsored legislation that would "mortgage" future quotas, accelerating Jewish immigration by allowing refugees in 1938 and 1939 to anticipate the quotas for 1940 and 1941. New York's Senator Robert Wagner and Representative Edith Nourse Rogers of Massachusetts introduced a bill to allow twenty thousand German children under fourteen years of age to enter outside the quota limits. Emmanuel Celler tried to secure an exemption from quota restrictions

48. *PPA* (1938), 597–98.

for racial or religious refugees. All these proposals were in vain. Two-thirds of respondents told pollsters in January 1939 that they opposed the Wagner-Rogers bill to admit young children. (When the question was modified to specify admitting Jewish children, opposition dropped slightly, to 61 percent). In mid-1939, the *Fortune* poll asked: "If you were a member of Congress, would you vote yes or no on a bill to open the doors . . . to a larger number of European refugees?" Eighty-five percent of Protestants, 84 percent of Catholics, and an astonishing 25.8 percent of Jews answered no. Americans might extend their hearts to Hitler's victims, but not their hands.[49]

Events in mid-1939 starkly demonstrated the potentially lethal implications of the quota system. As Europe's Jews scrambled for the rapidly closing exits from Hitler's *Reich*, a cynical business developed in the sale of visas, especially by grasping Latin American officials, with the connivance of the Gestapo. Hundreds of desperate refugees clutching visas of dubious legality crammed aboard ships, seeking safe haven in the New World. Many of the destination countries simply refused to honor the visas. Mexico, Paraguay, Argentina, and Costa Rica all denied entry to arriving Jews bearing documents sold by corrupt officials at their European consulates.

One such ship, the Hamburg-American line's SS *St. Louis*, steamed into Havana harbor on May 27 with 930 Jewish refugees. The Cuban government refused to allow the passengers to disembark and was deaf to arguments that most of the exiles had no intention of remaining permanently in Cuba. More than seven hundred of them were on waiting lists for future admission to the United States. They planned to stay in Cuba only until their quota-allocation numbers came up—a date that might have come sooner rather than later had Samuel Dickstein's legislation passed.

American Jewish philanthropies offered to post a bond guaranteeing eventual transit to the United States, but the Cuban government was not interested. Aboard ship, two passengers committed suicide. Captain Gustav Schroeder reprovisioned his vessel and sailed away from Havana. He made half speed up the eastern seaboard of the United States while negotiators begged the State Department to allow the refugees to disembark at an American port. For days Schroeder steamed within sight of Miami and other American cities, shadowed by a Coast Guard cutter with orders to pick up and return to the *St. Louis* any passengers who

49. Cantril, 1081, 1150.

went overboard. On June 6 Schroeder finally set his return course east-ward, bearing his doomed cargo back to Europe. He managed to dis-tribute his passengers among Britain, France, Holland, and Belgium—all but Britain destined to fall under German rule within two years, exposing the Jews once more to Nazi reprisals. The bright lights of Miami remained a sorrowing memory of how tantalizingly close they had come to sanctuary—and salvation.

HAVING SHOWN THEMSELVES incapable of finding a solution to the refugee crisis, the Western powers proved equally unable to resist Hitler's next provocation. Even while he was ingesting Austria in the spring and summer of 1938, Hitler was preparing to chew up Czecho-slovakia. The feeble response of the democracies to his intensifying war against the Jews only deepened his contempt for his adversaries. Now was the time to strike. In Czechoslovakia in 1938 he meant to have the war he had described to his senior officials in November 1937. "It is my unalterable decision," he declared in a directive dated May 30, 1938, "to smash Czechoslovakia by military action in the near future."[50] The pretext would be the alleged desire of the more than three million eth-nic Germans in Czechoslovakia's Sudeten region to join their kinsmen in the *Reich*. Hitler, proclaiming loftily the Versailles principle of self-determination, demanded the annexation of the Sudetenland to Ger-many.

The Western powers proved willing to sacrifice the Sudetenland on the altar of appeasement. The Czech crisis, said Britain's Chamberlain, was "a quarrel in a faraway country between people of whom we know nothing."[51] In two meetings in southern Germany with Hitler in mid-September 1938, the first at Berchtesgaden and the second at Bad Go-desberg, Chamberlain agreed to a gradual, orderly transfer of the Su-detenland to German control. But Hitler greeted every concession with a fresh escalation of his demands. He meant to have war, not simply the Sudetenland. With each passing September day, the war he wanted seemed more imminent. France called up half a million reservists. The British began digging air-raid shelters in London parks. Then, in a last, fateful concession, Chamberlain agreed to attend a third conference on September 29 in Munich, where the fate of Czechoslovakia was to be infamously sealed. Franklin Roosevelt sent Chamberlain a two-word ca-

50. Shirer, *Rise and Fall of the Third Reich*, 365.
51. Rock, *Chamberlain and Roosevelt*, 122.

ble: "Good man." Meanwhile the American president assured Hitler: "The Government of the United States has no political involvements in Europe, and will assume no obligations in the conduct of the present negotiations."[52]

Like a thunderclap, the settlement agreed at Munich, providing for the immediate incorporation of the Sudetenland into Germany, reverberated around the world. In the streets of London, huge crowds cheered Chamberlain's announcement that the Munich agreement meant "peace in our time." On the floor of the Mother of Parliaments, in contrast, Winston Churchill called the Munich accord "a total and unmitigated defeat. . . . This is only the beginning of the reckoning," Churchill warned. "This is only the first sip, the first foretaste of a bitter cup which will be proffered to us year by year unless . . . we arise again and take our stand for freedom as in the olden time."[53] In Prague, the stunned Czechs stared at the maps of their shrunken state, shorn by a few pen-strokes of its rich Sudeten province. They had looked on as helpless witnesses at their own national evisceration. In Berlin, Hitler felt cheated. He had sought war, but had to settle for the Sudetenland. The next time, he would not be so easily bought off.

In Washington, Roosevelt likened the British and French diplomats who had signed the Munich agreement to Judas Iscariot. As the Czech crisis unfolded, Roosevelt had dunned the Europeans with private and public appeals for peace, and he had given the British ambassador vague assurances about American participation in a possible blockade of Germany. But in fact the American president was a powerless spectator at Munich, a weak and resourceless leader of an unarmed, economically wounded, and diplomatically isolated country. He, and America, had counted for nothing in the scales of diplomacy — or worse than nothing if one agrees with the thinking of Eden and Churchill that some greater American presence would have stiffened the spines of the European democracies. For all Roosevelt's moral dudgeon at Chamberlain's supposedly craven behavior, the sobering truth was, in the words of the historian Robert Divine, that "American isolation had become the handmaiden of European appeasement."[54]

Yet the Munich crisis marked a turning point of sorts in American

---

52. *FRUS* (1938) 1:688, 685.
53. Roosevelt quoted in Ickes Diary 2:469. Churchill remarks from Churchill 326–28.
54. Robert A. Divine, *The Reluctant Belligerent: American Entry into World War II* (New York: John Wiley and Sons, 1965), 55.

foreign policy, or at least in Franklin Roosevelt's sense of urgency about America's role in the world. "We had to [overhaul] our entire preparedness [program] in the light of Munich," Roosevelt later reflected. Three items commanded the highest priority. "First, place more emphasis on the North-South American axis; Second, Revise the neutrality act; Third, use our diplomatic influence to hamper the aggressors."[55]

Some of these objectives proved more easily achievable than others. A United States delegation to the Conference of American States in December 1938 persuaded the other American republics to sign the Declaration of Lima, pledging consultation in case war threatened anywhere in the hemisphere. The Declaration represented one of the first tangible diplomatic rewards of the vaunted Good Neighbor policy and constituted a halting, tentative step toward hemispheric solidarity.

Revising the Neutrality Act proved to be a tougher proposition. Roosevelt at this moment, following the disastrous 1938 elections, had less influence on Capitol Hill than he had in the conference hall at Lima. Nevertheless, in his State of the Union message of January 4, 1939, Roosevelt opened the campaign for revision of the neutrality law. He now took up the task he had so long postponed: seriously educating the American people about the international menace that was looming. In a thinly veiled reference to Nazi persecution of the Jews, Roosevelt began his address with a warning that "storms from abroad directly challenge . . . religion. . . . There comes a time in the affairs of men when they must prepare to defend not their homes alone but the tenets of faith and humanity on which their churches, their governments and their very civilization are founded. The defense of religion, of democracy, and of good faith among nations is all the same fight. To save one we must now make up our minds to save all." The world had grown small, Roosevelt said, "and weapons of attack so swift that no nation can be safe." There were "many methods short of war," the president declared, that might protect America and allow the United States to use its influence for good. First among those methods was revision of the neutrality statutes. "We have learned that when we deliberately try to legislate neutrality, our neutrality laws may operate unevenly and unfairly—may actually give aid to an aggressor and deny it to the victim," the president said. "[W]e ought not to let that happen anymore."[56] But before he could begin to specify just how he proposed to prevent that

---

55. Freidel, *Rendezvous with Destiny*, 306.
56. PPA (1939), 1–4.

from happening, the movement for neutrality revision was badly derailed.

Less than three weeks after Roosevelt's address, an experimental American military aircraft crashed in southern California. A badly injured French officer was hauled from the wreckage, igniting a furor about alleged secret presidential agreements to sell arms in violation of the neutrality law. Roosevelt met with members of the Senate Military Affairs Committee on January 31 to quell the uproar. Yes, he said, the French were negotiating to buy American military aircraft, and they were prepared to pay in cash. This was good for American business and workers, perfectly legal, and a boost for the cause of democracy into the bargain. Then Roosevelt went on, taking the senators into his confidence. He spoke candidly about his growing conviction that America must become engaged in Europe. "So soon as one nation dominates Europe, that nation will be able to turn to the world sphere," he explained. The nations on Germany's periphery, France not least of all, were in imminent danger of subjugation, as the examples of Austria and Czechoslovakia attested. "That is why the safety of the Rhine frontier does necessarily interest us," Roosevelt said.

Despite assurances of confidentiality, a source Roosevelt identified as "some boob" leaked to the press that the president had said that "America's frontier is on the Rhine." A storm of imprecations against Roosevelt's dangerous internationalism forced him to back away from neutrality revision. The country's "foreign policy has not changed and it is not going to change," Roosevelt declared to reporters a few days later, in flat contradiction of his State of the Union remarks. An American diplomat reported to Roosevelt the mounting feeling in Europe that the president's swift and unseemly retreat from neutrality revision after the "frontier-on-the-Rhine" flap gave Hitler and Mussolini "reason to believe now that American public opinion will not tolerate any other than an attitude of the most rigid neutrality. . . . [Y]our disavowal has cleared the atmosphere concerning America as far as the dictators are concerned."[57]

At 6:00 A.M. on March 15, 1939, Hitler completed his conquest of Czechoslovakia. Armed columns poured over the Czech border and swiftly overran the rump state that was the sad and short-lived legacy of

57. Eamon de Valera quoted by John Cudahy in Cudahy to Roosevelt, February 9, 1939, in Donald B. Schewe, ed., *Franklin D. Roosevelt and Foreign Affairs* (New York: Clearwater, 1969), 13:273. Roosevelt's remark to reporters is in the same volume, 243.

Munich. By nightfall Hitler motored triumphantly through Prague, just as he had through Vienna almost a year to the day earlier.

The extinction of what was left of Czechoslovakia also extinguished Chamberlain's policy of appeasement. Within weeks his government reversed the course to which it had hewed for nearly two years and announced that Britain was now committed to the defense of Poland, Hitler's next presumptive target. That British pledge armed the mechanism that at Hitler's next probe would pitch the world into war.

Czechoslovakia's death throes also revived Roosevelt's campaign to overhaul the neutrality laws. "If Germany invades a country and declares war," Roosevelt remarked on the day following the Czech invasion, "we'll be on the side of Hitler by invoking the act." Repeal of the arms embargo was desperately needed, said Roosevelt, though he was willing to leave in place the cash-and-carry provisions of the 1937 statute, which expired just a few weeks hence, in May 1939. Roosevelt appreciated that cash-and-carry worked all wrong in the Pacific, where it favored Japan, but it worked just fine in the Atlantic, where the wealthy sea powers, Britain and France, would be its chief beneficiaries.

The administration exerted itself vigorously for repeal of the arms embargo. Secretary of State Hull lobbied indefatigably for the change. The coming clash in Europe, Hull warned, would not be just "another goddam piddling dispute over a boundary line." It would be a global struggle against barbarism. The existing legislation, Hull said, amounted to "a wretched little bobtailed, sawed-off domestic statute" that cut across the grain of international law and diplomatic practice. It "conferred a gratuitous benefit on the probable aggressors." To leave it in place, said Hull, was "just plain chuckle-headed."[58]

Even Hull's impassioned pleading proved inadequate to the task. By a narrow margin, the House voted to retain the arms embargo on June 29. In the Senate, Roosevelt faced a special problem. On the Foreign Relations Committee sat two senators, Walter F. George of Georgia and Guy M. Gillette of Iowa, whose unquenchable enmity Roosevelt had earned when he campaigned against them in the Democratic primary elections in 1938. Added to the already considerable weight of the isolationists, George's and Gillette's disinclination to do Roosevelt's bidding doomed his request to defeat. At a bitterly argumentative meeting at the

58. Joseph Alsop and Robert Kintner, *American White Paper: The Story of American Diplomacy and the Second World War* (New York: Simon and Schuster, 1940), 41–42.

White House on the evening of July 18, 1939, Roosevelt and Hull pleaded with Senate leaders to let neutrality revision move through the upper chamber. "Our decision may well affect not only the people of our own country, but also the peoples of the world," said Roosevelt. Rehearsing his failed efforts to make American influence felt, he told the senators: "I've fired my last shot. I think I ought to have another round in my belt." His listeners were unmoved. Archisolationist Senator Borah so adamantly and arrogantly dismissed Hull's warnings of imminent war that the courtly secretary of state was struck dumb with indignation. Vice-President Garner polled the participants as to whether the Senate would approve the administration's proposal. All answered no. "Well Captain," Garner said summarily to Roosevelt, "[y]ou haven't got the votes, and that's all there is to it."[59]

ROOSEVELT FARED no better with the third of his initiatives in early 1939, his effort to "use our diplomatic influence to hamper the aggressors." On April 15, 1939, he sent a widely publicized message to Hitler and Mussolini. He listed thirty-one countries by name and asked for an assurance that neither Italy nor Germany would attack them for at least ten years. Mussolini saw no reason to respond to the leader of a government restricted to "its customary role of distant spectator, " and he scoffed at the message as attributable to Roosevelt's "infantile paralysis." Nazi Air Marshal Hermann Goering sneered that "Roosevelt was suffering from an incipient mental disease." Hitler, too, at first refused to reply to "so contemptible a creature" as Roosevelt.[60]

Soon, however, *der Führer* saw in Roosevelt's appeal an opportunity to make political hay. The German Foreign Office on April 17 put two questions to all the states enumerated by Roosevelt, with the conspicuous exceptions of Poland, Russia, Britain, and France: Did they feel threatened by Germany? Had they authorized Roosevelt to make his proposal? Armed with their replies, Hitler rose before the Reichstag on April 28 to make what the American journalist William Shirer later described as "the most brilliant oration he ever gave, certainly the greatest this writer ever heard from him. For sheer eloquence, craftiness, irony, sarcasm and hypocrisy, it reached a new level that he was never to approach again." For more than two hours, Hitler heaped scorn on the American president. He also rehearsed many of the arguments of

59. Alsop and Kintner, *American White Paper*, 44–46.
60. Shirer, *Rise and Fall of the Third Reich*, 470; L & G, *Challenge*, 87.

the American isolationists: that Germany aimed only to redress the grievances of the Versailles Treaty, that it was the British who could not be
trusted, that Western propaganda organs painted an unfair picture of
Germany, that he alone was ever ready to come to the negotiating table.

Hitler then turned to Roosevelt's specific questions. As Shirer remembered it:

> The paunchy deputies rocked with raucous laughter as the Fuehrer
> uttered with increasing effect his seemingly endless ridicule of the
> American President. One by one he took up the points of Roosevelt's
> telegram, paused, almost smiled, and then, like a schoolmaster, uttered
> in a low voice one word, "Answer"—and gave it.

Who had scuttled the League of Nations by refusing to join? Hitler
asked. America. And how had the United States come to dominate
North America in the first place? Not at the conference table, said Hitler. Any who doubted it should look to the history of the Sioux tribes.
Gratuitously, Hitler added that he had no intention of invading the
United States. Then came the peroration, at once a sharp personal jab
at Roosevelt and a reinforcing stroke for the American isolationists:

> Mr. Roosevelt! I once took over a State which was faced by complete
> ruin. . . . I have conquered chaos in Germany, re-established order and
> enormously increased production [the implied contrast with America's
> continuing Depression stung], developed traffic, caused mighty roads
> to be built and canals to be dug, called into being gigantic new fac-
> tories. . . . I have succeeded in finding useful work once more for the
> whole of the seven million unemployed. . . .
>
>   You, Mr. Roosevelt, have a much easier task in comparison. You
> became President of the United States in 1933 when I became Chan-
> cellor of the Reich. From the very outset you stepped to the head of
> one of the largest and wealthiest States in the world. . . . Conditions
> prevailing in your country are on such a large scale that you can find
> time and leisure to give your attention to universal problems. . . . [M]y
> world, Mr. Roosevelt . . . , is unfortunately much smaller.

For sheer gall, guile, and hoodwinking, the speech was a black masterpiece. American isolationists crowed that this was Roosevelt's reward
for his gratuitous meddling. "Roosevelt put his chin out, and he got a
resounding whack on it," said California's Republican senator Hiram
Johnson, to which Senator Nye laconically added: "He asked for it."
The speech also vividly demonstrated Hitler's utter contempt for the

United States. A few weeks later he declared: "Because of its neutrality laws, America is not dangerous to us."[61]

The drums of war now quickened their tempo. Mussolini invaded Albania on April 9. Britain introduced conscription a few days later. Hitler made menacing gestures toward Poland. Britain and France sent diplomatic missions to Moscow, seeking to enlist Russia in the anti-Nazi front. That effort yielded no result. Stalin had viewed the Munich agreement as a betrayal of Russian security interests, and especially at this late date he had no confidence in British or French determination to stand firm against Hitler.

The breakdown of Soviet-Western talks gave Hitler one more opportunity to exploit the divisions among his potential foes. In an announcement that stunned the world, not least the antifascist left in the Western countries, Berlin and Moscow revealed on August 23 that they had signed a nonaggression pact. Secret protocols provided for the partition of Poland and for Soviet absorption of the Baltic states, as well as territory in Finland and Bessarabia. The die was now all but cast.

The death watch for Europe began. In Washington, one State Department official likened the atmosphere to "the feeling of sitting in a house where somebody is dying upstairs." Adolf Berle noted in his diary: "I have a horrible feeling of seeing the breaking of a civilization dying even before its actual death." The last days of August, Berle wrote, "produced almost exactly the sensation you might have waiting for a jury to bring in a verdict on the life or death of about ten million people."[62]

At 3:00 A.M. on September 1, 1939, the telephone rang at Franklin Roosevelt's bedside in the White House. It was Ambassador Bullitt calling from Paris. "Mr. President," Bullitt said, "several German divisions are deep in Polish territory. . . . There are reports of bombers over the city of Warsaw."

"Well, Bill," Roosevelt replied, "it has come at last. God help us all!"[63]

---

61. Johnson to Hiram W. Johnson Jr., April 29, 1939, in Robert E. Burke, ed., *The Diary Letters of Hiram Johnson* (New York: Garland, 1983), 7:n.p. Nye quoted in L & G, *Challenge*, 89. Hitler quoted in Weinberg, "Hitler's Image of the United States," 1013.

62. Dallek, 197; Beatrice Bishop Berle and Travis Beal Jacobs, *Navigating the Rapids: From the Papers of Adolf A. Berle* (New York: Harcourt Brace Jovanovich, 1973), 244, 245.

63. Alsop and Kintner, *American White Paper*, 1.

Bibliographical Essay

The literature concerning the major subjects of this book—the Great Depression and the New Deal—is enormous. What follows is not an exhaustive bibliography, but a highly selective one, intended as a guide for further reading.

World War I and its immediate aftermath are the subjects of David M. Kennedy, *Over Here: The First World War and American Society* (New York: Oxford University Press, 1980); Thomas A. Bailey, *Woodrow Wilson and the Lost Peace* (New York: Macmillan, 1944), and the same author's *Woodrow Wilson and the Great Betrayal* (New York: Macmillan, 1945). Indispensable to an understanding of the war's economic sequelae are John Maynard Keynes, *The Economic Consequences of the Peace* (New York: Harcourt, Brace and Howe, 1920); Charles Kindleberger, *The World in Depression* (Berkeley: University of California Press, 1973); and Peter Temin, *Lessons from the Great Depression* (Cambridge: MIT Press, 1989).

Frederick Lewis Allen's *Only Yesterday* (New York: Harper and Brothers, 1931) fixed the historical image of the 1920s in the minds of several generations of readers. Its many deficiencies can be offset by reading Preston Slosson, *The Great Crusade and After* (New York: Macmillan, 1930); William E. Leuchtenburg, *The Perils of Prosperity* (Chicago: University of Chicago Press, 1958); Lizabeth Cohen, *Making a New Deal* (New York: Cambridge University Press, 1990); Thomas J. Archdeacon, *Becoming American* (New York: Free Press, 1983); Harvey Green, *The Uncertainty of Everyday Life* (New York: HarperCollins, 1992); Oscar Handlin, *Al Smith and His America* (Boston: Little, Brown, 1958); David Burner, *The Politics of Provincialism* (New York: Knopf: 1968); Allan J. Lichtman, *Prejudice and the Old Politics* (Chapel Hill: University of North Carolina Press, 1979); and Samuel Lubell, *The Future of American Politics* (New York: Harper and Row, 1952). Two exceptionally rich contemporary sources are Robert and Helen Merrell Lynd, *Middletown: A Study in Modern American Culture* (New York: Harcourt, Brace and World, 1929), a classic of sociological investigation; and The President's

427

Research Committee on Recent Social Trends, *Recent Social Trends in the United States* (Westport, Conn.: Greenwood, 1970; originally published 1933).

John Kenneth Galbraith, *The Great Crash* (Boston: Houghton Mifflin, 1955) is a popular history of the stock market debacle of 1929. Like Allen's *Only Yesterday*, it is more charming than analytical, and should be supplemented by Robert Sobel, *The Great Bull Market* (New York: Norton, 1968), and the same author's *Panic on Wall Street* (New York: Macmillan, 1968). See also the relevant portions of Milton Friedman and Anna Jacobson Schwartz, *A Monetary History of the United States* (Princeton: Princeton University Press, 1963), which in turn should be supplemented by Peter Temin, *Did Monetary Forces Cause the Great Depression?* (New York: Norton, 1976). Herbert Stein, *The Fiscal Revolution in America* (Chicago: University of Chicago Press, 1969) does an especially good job of putting Herbert Hoover's anti-Depression policies in historical perspective.

On Hoover and his calamitous presidency, see the highly critical discussion in Arthur M. Schlesinger Jr., *The Crisis of the Old Order* (Boston: Houghton Mifflin, 1956), and the somewhat more sympathetic accounts in Joan Hoff Wilson, *Herbert Hoover: Forgotten Progressive* (Boston: Little, Brown, 1975); David Burner, *Herbert Hoover: A Public Life* (New York: Knopf, 1979); Harris Gaylord Warren, *Herbert Hoover and the Great Depression* (New York: Oxford University Press, 1959); Albert U. Romasco, *The Poverty of Abundance: Hoover, the Nation, the Depression* (New York: Oxford University Press, 1965); Jordan A. Schwarz, *The Interregnum of Despair: Hoover, Congress, and the Depression* (Urbana: University of Illinois Press, 1970); William Starr Meyers and Walter H. Newton, *The Hoover Administration: A Documented Narrative* (New York: Charles Scribner's Sons, 1936); and the relevant volumes of Hoover's own *Memoirs: The Cabinet and the Presidency* and *The Great Depression* (New York: Macmillan, 1952).

A sizable scholarly industry has been devoted to trying to explain the causes of the Great Depression, without conclusive results. A good summary source of data is Lester Chandler, *America's Greatest Depression* (New York: Harper and Row, 1970). A more recent comprehensive survey is Michael D. Bordo, Claudia Goldin, and Eugene N. White, eds., *The Defining Moment: The Great Depression and the American Economy in the Twentieth Century* (Chicago: University of Chicago Press, 1998). See also Michael Bernstein, *The Great Depression: Delayed Recovery and Economic Change in America, 1929–1939* (New York: Cambridge University Press, 1987); and Barry Eichengreen, *Golden Fetters: The Gold Standard and the Great Depression, 1919–1939* (New York: Oxford University Press, 1992).

The human toll of the Depression is captured especially well in Richard Lowitt and Maurine Beasley, eds., *One Third of a Nation: Lorena Hickok Reports on the Great Depression* (Urbana: University of Illinois Press, 1981); see also Studs Terkel, *Hard Times: An Oral History of the Great Depression* (New York: Pantheon, 1970); Caroline Bird, *The Invisible Scar* (New York: McKay, 1966); Ann Banks, *First-Person America* (New York: Knopf, 1980); Mirra Komarovsky, *The Unemployed Man and His Family* (New York: Dryden, 1940); and Lois Scharf, *To Work and to Wed: Female Employment, Feminism, and the Great Depression* (Westport, Conn.: Greenwood, 1980).

Of the several biographies of Franklin Delano Roosevelt, I have found the following to be most useful: James MacGregor Burns's two volumes: *Roosevelt: The Lion and the Fox* (New York: Harcourt Brace, 1956), and *Roosevelt: The Soldier of Freedom* (New York: Harcourt Brace Jovanovich, 1970); Kenneth S. Davis, *FDR* (New York: Random

House, 4 vols., 1985–1993); Frank Freidel, *Franklin D. Roosevelt* (Boston: Little, Brown, 4 vols., 1952–1976), and his one-volume *Franklin D. Roosevelt: A Rendezvous with Destiny* (Boston: Little, Brown, 1990); Patrick Maney, *The Roosevelt Presence* (New York: Twayne, 1992); and, for Roosevelt's last year of life, Robert H. Ferrell, *The Dying President: FDR, 1944–1945* (Columbia: University of Missouri Press, 1998). The *Public Papers and Addresses of Franklin D. Roosevelt* (New York: Random House and Harper and Brothers, 13 vols., 1938–1950) is an indispensable source on Roosevelt's presidency, as is *The Complete Presidential Press Conferences of Franklin Delano Roosevelt* (New York: DaCapo, 1972); and Russell D. Buhite and David W. Levy, eds., *FDR's Fireside Chats* (Norman: University of Oklahoma Press, 1992). Also useful is Elliott Roosevelt, ed., *FDR: His Personal Correspondence, 1928–1945* (New York: Duell, Sloan and Pearce, 2 vols., 1950).

Various New Dealers produced notable memoirs, including Raymond Moley, *After Seven Years* (New York: Harper and Brothers, 1939); Rexford Tugwell, *The Brains Trust* (New York: Viking, 1968), the same author's *Roosevelt's Revolution* (New York: Macmillan, 1979), and his *The Democratic Roosevelt* (Garden City, N.Y.: Doubleday, 1957); Frances Perkins, *The Roosevelt I Knew* (New York: Viking, 1946); Samuel I. Rosenman, *Working with Roosevelt* (New York: Harper and Brothers, 1952); Edward J. Flynn, *You're the Boss* (New York: Viking, 1947); George Peek, *Why Quit Our Own?* (New York: Van Nostrand, 1936); and Harold L. Ickes, *The Secret Diary of Harold L. Ickes* (New York: Simon and Schuster, 3 vols., 1953–1954). See also John Morton Blum, *From the Morgenthau Diaries* (Boston: Houghton Mifflin, 3 vols., 1959–1967), condensed into a one-volume edition as *Roosevelt and Morgenthau* (Boston: Houghton Mifflin, 1972); Hugh S. Johnson, *The New Deal from Egg to Earth* (Garden City, N.Y.: Doubleday, Doran, 1935); Harry Hopkins, *Spending to Save* (New York: Norton, 1936); Marriner Eccles, *Beckoning Frontiers* (New York: Knopf, 1951); James A. Farley, *Behind the Ballots* (New York: Harcourt, Brace, 1938), and the same author's *Jim Farley's Story* (New York: McGraw-Hill, 1948); David E. Lilienthal, *The Journals of David E. Lilienthal* (New York: Harper and Row, 7 vols., 1964–1983); Jesse H. Jones, *Fifty Billion Dollars* (New York: Macmillan, 1951); Thomas E. Eliot, *Recollections of the New Deal* (Boston: Northeastern University Press, 1992); and Eleanor Roosevelt, *This I Remember* (New York: Harper and Brothers, 1949).

Biographies of significant figures from the New Deal era include: Blanche Wiesen Cook, *Eleanor Roosevelt: A Life* (New York: Viking, 1992); Lois Scharf, *Eleanor Roosevelt: First Lady of American Liberalism* (Boston: Twayne, 1987); Joseph T. Lash, *Eleanor and Franklin* (New York: New American Library, 1973); T. H. Watkins, *Righteous Pilgrim: The Life and Times of Harold L. Ickes, 1874–1952* (New York: Holt, 1990); Graham J. White and John Maze, *Harold Ickes of the New Deal* (Cambridge, Harvard University Press, 1985); and T. Harry Williams, *Huey Long* (New York: Knopf, 1969), which should be supplemented by Alan Brinkley's insightful *Voices of Protest: Huey Long, Father Coughlin, and the Great Depression* (New York: Knopf, 1982). On Coughlin, see also Charles J. Tull, *Father Coughlin and the New Deal* (Syracuse: Syracuse University Press, 1965). For Felix Frankfurter, see Michael E. Parrish, *Felix Frankfurter and His Time* (New York: Free Press, 1982), and Max Freedman, ed., *Roosevelt and Frankfurter: Their Correspondence, 1928–1945* (Boston: Little, Brown, 1967). Other biographies are J. Joseph Huthmacher, *Senator Robert F. Wagner and the Rise of Urban Liberalism* (New York, Atheneum, 1968); Ellsworth Barnard, *Wendell Willkie, Fighter for Freedom* (Marquette: Northern Michigan University Press, 1966); Richard Norton Smith, *Thomas E. Dewey and His Times* (New York: Simon and Schuster, 1982); and David McCullough, *Truman* (New York: Simon and Schuster, 1992).

General histories of the New Deal include Arthur M. Schlesinger Jr., *The Age of Roosevelt* (Boston: Houghton Mifflin, 3 vols., 1956–1960); William E. Leuchtenburg, *Franklin D. Roosevelt and the New Deal, 1932–1940* (New York: Harper and Row, 1963); Anthony J. Badger, *The New Deal* (New York: Farrar, Straus and Giroux, 1989); Paul Conkin, *The New Deal* (Arlington Heights, Il.: Harlan Davidson, 3d edition, 1992); and Robert McElwaine, *The Great Depression* (New York: Times Books, 1984). Harvard Sitkoff, ed., *Fifty Years Later: The New Deal Evaluated* (Philadelphia: Temple University Press, 1985) summarizes several generations of scholarship.

The New Deal's economic programs are analyzed in Ellis W. Hawley, *The New Deal and the Problem of Monopoly* (Princeton: Princeton University Press, 1966); Albert U. Romasco, *The Politics of Recovery* (New York: Oxford University Press, 1983); Bernard Bellush, *The Failure of the NRA* (New York: Norton, 1975); Bruce J. Schulman, *From Cotton Belt to Sunbelt* (New York: Oxford University Press, 1991); Kenneth Jackson, *Crabgrass Frontier* (New York: Oxford University Press, 1985); Richard K. Vietor, *Contrived Competition: Regulation and Deregulation in America* (Cambridge: Belknap Press of Harvard University Press, 1994); Mark H. Leff, *The Limits of Symbolic Reform: The New Deal and Taxation* (New York: Cambridge University Press, 1984); Gary M. Walton., ed., *Regulatory Change in an Atmosphere of Crisis* (New York: Academic Press, 1979); and the pertinent chapters of Thomas K. McCraw, *Prophets of Regulation* (Cambridge: Belknap Press of Harvard University Press, 1984).

Agriculture is the focus of Theodore Saloutos, *The American Farmer and the New Deal* (Ames: Iowa State University Press, 1982); Donald H. Grubbs, *Cry from the Cotton: The Southern Tenant Farmers' Union and the New Deal* (Chapel Hill: University of North Carolina Press, 1971); Anthony J. Badger, *Prosperity Road: The New Deal, Tobacco, and North Carolina* (Chapel Hill: University of North Carolina Press, 1979); and Donald Worster, *Dust Bowl* (New York: Oxford University Press, 1979), to which James Gregory, *American Exodus: The Dust Bowl Migration and Okie Culture in California* (New York: Oxford University Press, 1989) serves as an intriguing sequel.

Specialized studies of various New Deal initiatives include: Donald Stevenson Howard, *The WPA and Federal Relief Policy* (New York: Russell Sage Foundation, 1943); Jerre Mangione, *The Dream and the Deal: The Federal Writers' Project, 1935–1943* (Boston: Little, Brown, 1972); the chapters dealing with the Social Security Act in Andrew Achenbaum, *Old Age in the New Land* (Baltimore: The Johns Hopkins University Press, 1978), and the same author's *Social Security: Visions and Revisions* (New York: Cambridge University Press, 1986); Thomas K. McGraw, *TVA and the Power Fight* (Philadelphia, Lippincott, 1971); James T. Patterson, *The New Deal and the States* (Princeton: Princeton University Press, 1969), and the relevant chapters of the same author's *America's Struggle against Poverty, 1900–1980* (Cambridge: Harvard University Press, 1981); William E. Leuchtenburg, *The Supreme Court Reborn: The Constitutional Revolution in the Age of Roosevelt* (New York: Oxford University Press, 1995); and, also on the "Court-Packing" episode of 1937, Joseph Alsop and Turner Catledge, *The 168 Days* (Garden City, N.Y.: Doubleday, Doran, 1938). See also Peter Irons, *The New Deal Lawyers* (Princeton: Princeton University Press, 1982); Betty Houchin Winfield, *FDR and the News Media* (Urbana: University of Illinois Press, 1990); Nancy Weiss, *Farewell* to the Party of Lincoln: Black Politics in the Age of FDR (Princeton: Princeton University Press, 1983); Harvard Sitkoff, A New Deal for Blacks (New York: Oxford University Press, 1978); Graham D. Taylor, The New Deal and American Indian Tribalism (Lincoln: University of Nebraska Press, 1977); Kenneth R. Philp, John Collier's Crusade for Indian Reform (Tucson: University of Arizona Press, 1977); Susan Ware, Beyond Suffrage: Women and the New Deal (Harvard University Press, 1981), the same author's Holding the Line: American Women in the 1930s (Boston: Twayne, 1982), and her Partner and I: Molly Dewson, Feminism, and New Deal Politics (New Haven: Yale University Press, 1987). See also Elizabeth Israels Perry, Belle Moskowitz (New York: Oxford University Press, 1987).

Several books examine the dramatic changes in working-class life and in the status of organized labor during the New Deal era. The standard work is Irving Bernstein's masterful Turbulent Years: A History of the American Worker, 1933–1941 (Boston: Houghton Mifflin, 1970). Also valuable are Robert Zieger, American Workers, American Unions (Baltimore: The Johns Hopkins University Press, 1986), and the same author's The CIO: 1935–1955 (Chapel Hill: University of North Carolina Press, 1995); Melvyn Dubofsky, American Labor Since the New Deal (Chicago: Quadrangle, 1971); Melvyn Dubofsky and Warren Van Tine, John L. Lewis (New York: Quadrangle/New York Times, 1977); and James Gross's two volumes, The Making of the National Labor Relations Board and The Reshaping of the National Labor Relations Board (Albany: State University of New York Press: 1974 and 1981, respectively). Jacquelyn Dowd Hall, et al., focus on southern textile workers in Like a Family: The Making of a Southern Cotton Mill World (New York: Norton, 1987); Lizabeth Cohen examines Chicago industrial workers in Making a New Deal (cited above).

Politics is covered in John Allswang, The New Deal and American Politics (New York: Wiley, 1978); Lyle W. Dorsett, Franklin D. Roosevelt and the Big City Bosses (Port Washington, N.Y.: Kennikat, 1977); Charles Trout, Boston, the Great Depression and the New Deal (New York: Oxford University Press, 1977); Bruce Stave, The New Deal and the Last Hurrah: Pittsburgh Machine Politics (Pittsburgh: University of Pittsburgh Press, 1970); James T. Patterson, Congressional Conservatism and the New Deal (Lexington: University Press of Kentucky, 1967); Clyde P. Weed, The Nemesis of Reform: The Republican Party During the New Deal (New York: Columbia University Press, 1994); Alan Brinkley, The End of Reform: New Deal Liberalism in Depression and War (New York: Knopf, 1995); and in the relevant sections of Michael Barone, Our Country (New York: Free Press, 1990), and of Steve Fraser and Gary Gerstle, The Rise and Fall of the New Deal Order, 1930–1980 (Princeton: Princeton University Press, 1989). For the activities of the radical left, see Irving Howe and Louis Coser's exhaustive account The American Communist Party (New York: Praeger, 1962); and Harvey Klehr and John Earl Haynes, The American Communist Movement: Storming Heaven Itself (New York: Twayne, 1992).

On specific regions, see Richard Lowitt, The New Deal and the West (Bloomington: Indiana University Press, 1984); Gavin Wright, Old South, New South: Revolutions in the Southern Economy Since the Civil War (New York: Basic Books, 1986); James Hodges, New Deal Labor Policy and the Southern Cotton Textile Industry, 1933–1941 (Knoxville: University of Tennessee Press, 1986); and James Cobb and Michael Namaroto, eds., The New Deal and the South (Jackson: University Press of Mississippi, 1984).

The cultural history of the Depression decade is treated in Edmond Wilson, *The American Earthquake: A Document of the 1920s and 1930s* (Garden City, N.Y.: Doubleday, 1958); Alfred Kazin, *On Native Grounds* (Garden City, N.Y.: Doubleday, 1942); Richard Pells, *Radical Visions, American Dreams: Culture and Social Thought in the Depression Years* (New York: Harper and Row, 1973); William Stott, *Documentary Expression in Thirties America* (New York: Oxford University Press, 1973); and Karol Ann Marling, *Wall-to-Wall America: A Cultural History of Post Office Murals in the Great Depression* (Minneapolis: University of Minnesota Press, 1982).

Two excellent compendia on public opinion in the Depression and World War II years are Hadley Cantril, ed., *Public Opinion, 1935–1946* (Princeton: Princeton University Press, 1951); and George H. Gallup, *The Gallup Poll: Public Opinion, 1935–1971* (New York: Random House, 1972).

Of the many studies of the rise of Nazism and Japanese expansionism, I have found the following most useful: Joachim Fest, *Hitler* (New York: Harcourt Brace Jovanovich, 1974); Alan Bullock, *Hitler: A Study in Tyranny* (New York: Harper and Row, 1962); William Shirer, *The Rise and Fall of the Third Reich* (New York: Simon and Schuster, 1960); A. J. P. Taylor, *The Origins of the Second World War* (London, Hamilton, 1961); Winston S. Churchill, *The Second World War* (Boston: Houghton Mifflin, 6 vols., 1948–1953); Donald Cameron Watt, *How War Came: The Immediate Origins of the Second World War, 1938–1939* (New York: Pantheon, 1989); Dorothy Borg, *The United States and the Far Eastern Crisis of 1933–1938* (Cambridge: Harvard University Press, 1964); Robert J. C. Butow, *Tojo and the Coming of the War* (Princeton: Princeton University Press, 1961); Herbert Feis, *The Road to Pearl Harbor* (Princeton: Princeton University Press, 1950); and Paul W. Schroeder's especially provocative *The Axis Alliance and Japanese-American Relations, 1941* (Ithaca: Cornell University Press, 1958).

On American isolationism, see Manfred Jonas, *Isolationism in America* (Ithaca: Cornell University Press, 1966); Wayne S. Cole, *Roosevelt and the Isolationists* (Lincoln: University of Nebraska Press, 1983), and the same author's *Charles A. Lindbergh and the Battle against American Intervention in World War II* (New York: Harcourt Brace Jovanovich, 1974); Mathew Coulter, *The Senate Munitions Inquiry of the 1930s* (Westport, Conn.: Greenwood, 1997); and Richard Norton Smith's biography, *The Colonel: The Life and Legend of Robert R. McCormick* (Boston: Houghton Mifflin, 1997), about the publisher of the *Chicago Tribune* and arguably the nation's most influential isolationist.

Essential to any study of the diplomacy of this period are the several relevant volumes of *Foreign Relations of the United States*. Two special collections are also highly valuable: Edgar B. Nixon, ed., *Franklin D. Roosevelt and Foreign Affairs* (Cambridge: Belknap Press of Harvard University Press, 3 vols., 1969), which covers from January 1933 to January 1937; and the eleven volumes of the same title edited by Donald Schewe, covering January 1937 to August 1939 (New York: Clearwater, 1969). A pair of volumes based on early access to official documents are so meticulous and comprehensive that they are virtually primary sources: William L. Langer and S. Everett Gleason, *The Challenge to Isolation, 1937–1940* and *The Undeclared War: 1940–1941* (New York: Harper, 1952 and 1953, respectively). Other useful collections of contemporary materials are Orville H. Bullitt, ed., *For the President: Personal and Secret, Correspondence between Franklin D. Roosevelt and William C. Bullitt* (Boston: Houghton Mifflin, 1972); William E. Dodd, Jr., and Martha Dodd, eds., *Ambassador Dodd's Diary, 1933–1938* (New York:

Harcourt, Brace, 1941); and Beatrice Bishop Berle and Travis Beal Jacobs, *Navigating the Rapids: From the Papers of Adolf A. Berle* (New York: Harcourt Brace Jovanovich, 1973).

Memoirs that shed light on the diplomacy of the prewar and wartime years include: Cordell Hull, *Memoirs* (New York: Macmillan, 2 vols., 1948); Henry L. Stimson and McGeorge Bundy, *On Active Service in Peace and War* (New York: Harper, 1948), easily supplemented by Stimson's diary, which is available on microfilm; Joseph C. Grew, *Turbulent Era* (Boston: Houghton Mifflin, 1952); Charles E. Bohlen, *Witness to History* (New York: Norton, 1973); William Leahy, *I Was There* (New York: Whittlesley House, 1950); James F. Byrnes, *Speaking Frankly* (New York: Harper, 1947); Robert Murphy, *Diplomat Among Warriors* (Garden City, N.Y.: Doubleday, 1964); Dean Acheson, *Present at the Creation: My Years in the State Department* (New York: Norton, 1969); W. Averell Harriman and Elie Abel, *Special Envoy to Churchill and Stalin, 1941–1946* (New York: Random House, 1975); two titles by Sumner Welles: *The Time for Decision* (New York: Harper, 1944), and *Seven Decisions That Shaped History* (New York: Harper, 1951); and Harry S. Truman, *Memoirs* (Garden City, N.Y.: Doubleday, 2 vols., 1955, 1956). See also Robert H. Ferrell, ed., *Off the Record: The Private Papers of Harry S. Truman* (New York: Harper and Row, 1980).

Biographies of leading diplomatic figures are Robert E. Sherwood, *Roosevelt and Hopkins* (New York: Grosset and Dunlap, 1950); Waldo Heinrichs Jr., *American Ambassador: Joseph C. Grew and the Development of the United States Diplomatic Tradition* (New York: Oxford University Press, 1996); David Robertson, *Sly and Able: A Political Biography of James F. Byrnes* (New York: Norton, 1994); and Irwin F. Gellman, *Secret Affairs: Franklin Roosevelt, Cordell Hull, and Sumner Welles* (Baltimore: The Johns Hopkins University Press, 1995).

The foreign policies of the four Roosevelt administrations are ably presented in Robert Dallek's encyclopedic *Franklin D. Roosevelt and American Foreign Policy, 1932–1945* (New York: Oxford University Press, 1979). See also Robert A. Divine, *The Reluctant Belligerent* (New York: Wiley, 1965), and the same author's *The Illusion of Neutrality* (Chicago: University of Chicago Press, 1962); Waldo Heinrichs Jr., *Threshold of War* (New York: Oxford University Press, 1988); Lloyd Gardner, *Economic Aspects of New Deal Diplomacy* (Madison: University of Wisconsin Press, 1964); Warren F. Kimball, *The Juggler* (Princeton: Princeton University Press, 1991); and Frederick W. Marks, *Wind Over Sand: The Diplomacy of Franklin Roosevelt* (Athens: University of Georgia Press, 1988).

Relations with Britain are documented in William R. Rock, *Chamberlain and Roosevelt* (Columbus: Ohio State University Press, 1988); Warren F. Kimball, ed., *Churchill and Roosevelt: The Complete Correspondence* (Princeton: Princeton University Press, 3 vols., 1984), an indispensable source, and in the same author's *The Most Unsordid Act: Lend-Lease, 1939–1941* (Baltimore: The Johns Hopkins University Press, 1969), as well as his *Forged in War: Roosevelt, Churchill, and the Second World War* (New York: Morrow, 1997). See also Joseph P. Lash, *Roosevelt and Churchill: The Partnership that Saved the West* (New York: Norton, 1976).

Many scholars have examined American policy concerning refugees, predominantly Jewish, from Hitler's Reich: Arthur Morse, *While Six Million Died* (New York: Random House, 1968); Henry L. Feingold, *The Politics of Rescue: The Roosevelt Administration and the Holocaust, 1938–1945* (New York: Holocaust Library, 1970); Deborah E.

Lipstadt, *Beyond Belief: The American Press and the Coming of the Holocaust, 1933–1945* (New York: Free Press, 1986); and two titles by David Wyman: *Paper Walls: America and the Refugee Crisis, 1938–1941* (Amherst: University of Massachusetts Press, 1968), and *The Abandonment of the Jews: America and the Holocaust, 1941–1945* (New York: Pantheon, 1984).

For various other specific diplomatic episodes in the pre-war years, see Bryce Wood, *The Making of the Good Neighbor Policy* (New York: Columbia University Press, 1961); Irwin F. Gellman, *Good Neighbor Diplomacy* (Baltimore: The Johns Hopkins University Press, 1979); Allen Guttmann, *The Wound in the Heart: America and the Spanish Civil War* (New York: Free Press, 1962); Douglas Little, *Malevolent Neutrality: The United States, Great Britain, and the Origins of the Spanish Civil War* (Ithaca: Cornell University Press, 1985); and William L. Langer, *Our Vichy Gamble* (New York: Knopf, 1947).

Index

Note: FDR is the abbreviation for Franklin Delano Roosevelt.

Blacks: in cities, 194; and communism, 222–23; in Congress, 18, 216; and Democratic Party, 216; and Eleanor Roosevelt, 285, 343, 378; and elections of 1936, 285; Hitler's views about, 392; impact of New Deal on, 378; in judiciary, 378; and Ku Klux Klan, 15; and labor, 26, 307, 307n; migration of, 18, 194; in 1920s, 15, 18–19; in 1930s, 164, 173, 173n, 186; profiles about, 41; relief for, 164, 173, 173n, 194; in rural areas, 193, 194, 208, 210–11; as sharecroppers, 208, 210–11; and social security, 269; unemployment of, 87, 164; voting rights for, 19; wages for, 186, 194, 254; and WPA, 254. See also Race issues; Race riots; specific person
Bloody Friday (July 20, 1934), 295
Bloor, Ella Reeve "Mother," 211n
Blue Eagle campaign, 183–84
Blum, Léon, 310, 398
Bolsheviks, 381
Bonneville Dam: FDR speech at, 246
Bonneville Power Authority, 379
"Bonus Army"/bonus bill, 92, 138, 279, 355
Borah, William E., 60, 62, 251, 390, 423
Borrowing, 36, 36n, 80, 81, 178, 274, 354
"Bourbon" Democrats, 31
Bourke-White, Margaret, 256
Bowers, Claude, 398
Brain Trust: on cures for Great Depression, 121–22; disagreements among, 121–22; and FDR style, 111; Hoover's influence on, 121–22; legacy of, 119; Moley as nominal chairman of, 124; as novelty, 124; as progressives, 120–21, 124; role of, 119–24; views about Great Depression of, 120. See also specific person
Brandeis, Elizabeth, 264–65
Brandeis, Louis D., 46, 121, 128, 264–65, 326, 327, 336
Brest-Litovsk Treaty (1918), 381
Bridges, Harry, 294, 295, 298
Brinkley, Alan, 237–38, 243, 356
Britain. See Great Britain
British chiefs of staff, 407
Browder, Earl, 222, 315, 380
Brundage, Avery, 411
Bruning, Heinrich, 71–72
Brussels (Belgium), 405–6
Bryan, Charles W., 31
Bryan, William Jennings, 20, 31, 118, 196, 201, 202

Bryce, James, 223–24
Buck, Pearl, 401–2
Budget, federal: balanced, 29, 79–82, 109, 118, 125, 126, 147, 340, 352, 355, 356, 361; and "Conservative Manifesto," 340; conservatives' advice to FDR about, 125, 126; deficits in, 79, 91, 102, 118, 248n, 351, 354, 355, 356, 358–59, 361–62, 376; and Democratic Party, 125, 126; and elections of 1932, 79; and FDR's first hundred days, 138, 147, 149; FDR's views about, 118, 134, 147, 279; and Hoover, 79–82, 91, 102, 109; in New Deal, 79; in 1920s, 29; in 1936, 279; and recession of 1937–38, 351, 352, 356, 358–59, 361–62; size of, 55; and southern Democrats, 125; and taxes, 79–82, 279
Bull Moose Republicans, 32, 62, 127, 128, 281
Bullitt, William C., 389, 408, 408n, 425
Bureau of Agricultural Economics, U.S., 203
Bureau of Labor Statistics, U.S., 353
Bureaucracy: Hoover's study of federal, 367
Burke-Wadsworth Selective Service Act (1940). See Selective Service Act
Business: as anti-FDR, 276–77, 280, 281–83, 351–52, 359, 360, 376–77; as anti-New Deal, 376–77; data about, 163; and economic recovery, 283, 284; and elections of 1936, 278–79, 281–82; failures in, 58; FDR's attack on, 278–79; FDR's meetings with leaders of, 356; and FDR's political strategy, 284; FDR's views about, 376; and Hoover, 11, 53, 54–55, 180; impact of New Deal on, 376–77; and isolationism, 387–88; Keynes' views about, 357–58; Long's views about, 279; morale of, 284, 351; in 1930, 53, 54–55, 58; psychology of fear in, 376–77; and recession of 1937–38, 351–52, 356, 359, 360; taxes on, 275–77, 279–80. See also Big business; Corporations; Crash of 1929; Stock market
Butler, Pierce, 263, 326, 327n
Byrd, Harry, 338
Byrnes, James F., 316, 343

Cabinet, FDR, 260
Caldwell, Erskine, 192, 208, 256, 303
California: agriculture in, 292–93; French pilot crash in, 421; labor in, 292–94; poverty in, 226–27, 239–40; radicalism